THE
gap year
BOOK

Charlotte Hindle, Joe Bindloss, Matt
Fletcher, Abigail Hole, Andrew
Humphreys, Joshua White

OVERLAND TRAVEL ROUTES

Trans-Siberian Railway	——————	Route 66
Silk Road	——————	West Coast Trail
Karakoram Highway	——————	Trans-Canada Highway
Trans-Mongolian Highway	——————	NY to San Francisco
London to Cape Town	——————	Gringo Trail

See Part II for more information on all routes shown on this map

Contents

The Authors

CHARLOTTE HINDLE   **Coordinating Author**

After university Charlotte worked in a coat-hanger factory to earn money for her gap year. She then worked as a waitress in a Swiss ski resort, which was followed by six months of travel through central and Eastern Europe, Turkey, Egypt and India to Australia. There she got a job temping as a foot courier before landing a job with Lonely Planet (LP) in Melbourne. She worked at LP's Head Office for three years. In 1991, she returned to England to set up LP's UK office, which she ran until June 2002. She then decided to change career and become a freelance travel writer, photographer and mum. Over the years Charlotte has written for the following LP guides: *Australia*, *Mediterranean Europe*, *Walking in Britain*, *England* and *Britain*.

JOE BINDLOSS

Joe was born in Cyprus, grew up in England and has since lived and worked in the USA, the Philippines and Australia, though he currently calls London home. He first developed an incurable case of wanderlust on family trips through Europe in an old VW Kombi. A degree in biology eliminated science from his future choice of careers and Joe moved through a string of occupations, including painting and sculpting, before finally settling on journalism. Joe has previously written for Lonely Planet's *Australia*, the *Philippines*, *Kenya*, *India*, *Mauritius, Réunion & Seychelles* and *London*. During his gap year, Joe went to work in Chicago as a mural painter and bookshop manager and taught children how to rock climb in a converted Baptist church. He also drove right across America and twice made the pilgrimage to Graceland, Memphis, to visit the grave of The King.

MATT FLETCHER

Duped into not taking a gap year after school, Matt had to put up with an under-funded beer-and-train-station tour of Europe and summers in Spain and Morocco until, emerging from art college with a 'sportsman's' degree, he left for east and southern Africa. This year-long trip kick-started a writing career and enabled him to embark upon a gap life during which he has so far contributed to Lonely Planet's *Walking in Spain*, *Walking in Australia*, *Morocco*, *Kenya*, *West Africa* and *Tonga* guides. In order to contribute to the company's *Unpacked* and *Unpacked Again* titles, he got stranded in a Madagascan swamp and had a dingo steal his breakfast.

ABIGAIL HOLE

Abigail spent her gap year studying in France, working in London and going to Graceland, Memphis, and has been trying to attain a similar state of purposeful idleness ever since. She worked for a literary agency and mental-health charity before moving to Hong Kong in 1997. Three years in Asian publishing later, she came back to London and edited Lonely Planet guides for two years. Her travels have taken her from China to the Channel Islands, and she's written for Lonely Planet's *Out to Eat - London*, *Britain*, *England*, *India* and *Africa on a Shoestring*.

ANDREW HUMPHREYS

Andrew took off abroad on a whim after university and took 11 years to come back home again. In that time he worked as a teacher (variously of English, maths, physics and general decorum), a movie extra, a private tutor, a cartographer, an ad salesman, a radio presenter, an editor, a journalist and a publisher. He failed to find his fortune but wound up with a passable career as a guidebook writer. His numerous Lonely Planet author and co-author credits include guidebooks to *Central Asia*, the *Middle East*, *Israel & the Palestinian Territories*, *Jerusalem*, *Egypt*, *Cairo* and *Syria*.

JOSHUA WHITE

Joshua spent his gap year making tea for an Australian film agent and slouching around Bondi Beach. He learnt to drive in Sydney's eastern suburbs before taking a tricky Ford Valiant into the outback. Despite two flat tyres and running out of money in Alice Springs, he found his way home to study Modern History. After graduation he went looking for adventure in New York City where he read scripts and became a reviewer for Metrobeat, the city's first online guide. More recently, he has produced the BBC's homepage, written *Taking A Career Break*, co-authored *Live and Work in the USA* and been a guest on Radio 4's *Excess Baggage*. He is a freelance writer and journalist in London.

Foreword

A gap year is a life-changing experience. For a growing number of people, the chance to take some time off from studies or work is just too good to resist – and who can blame them? Given the choice between more work or more stamps in your passport, what would you choose?

At STA Travel we send more than six million young people round the world every year and the Year Out section on our website is extremely popular, as it includes comprehensive information to offer travellers a helping hand for that big trip. The majority of our consultants have taken gap years themselves and loved it so much we now employ them to pass on their knowledge to you. Universities encourage gap years, employers value them and you will learn a whole new set of life skills along the way.

With such a lot of time to yourself, it's the perfect time to try something new. Build schools in Africa, teach English in Japan, lasso cattle in Montana, work on an outback farm in Australia or drive travellers and tour-guide across the Serengeti. Seize the opportunity to give something back to the community with voluntary work or a conservation project. Set yourself a challenge like trekking the Himalaya – whatever you do, revel in your personal achievement.

A gap year may seem slightly daunting but this excellent *Gap Year Book* from Lonely Planet has all the advice and information you need to get on the road. Your questions are answered: will my university mind if I take a year out? Will I be left behind if I take time off? Parents' concerns are also addressed. The pre-trip planning advice is invaluable: how to budget for your trip and how to raise or save the cash; who to travel with or whether to explore alone; what to pack and where to buy it; how to keep in touch while you're away; how to stay safe and healthy on the road; what visas to get and which tickets to buy; and finally advice on coming home (because you're bound to…eventually).

Preparation is essential, so use all the tools at your fingertips. Read this guidebook, visit our website at **W** www.statravel.co.uk and talk to our experienced staff to ensure you get the most out of your trip.

Take *The Gap Year Book* with you – it's the essential travel companion.

Have fun planning and happy travels!

Litsa Constantinou
Managing Director – STA Travel

Part I

Introduction: Why Take a Gap Year?

You are about to finish school or university. Big decisions are looming like belligerent gate-crashers at your end-of-term party. Now is the best opportunity you will ever get to chase a dream, do something outrageous, extraordinary, fulfilling, and explore the world. Of the pre-university gappers (people taking gap years), around 50,000 students (about one in five) are out there at the moment doing something different before getting back on the educational treadmill, and this number is predicted to rise to 90,000 in the next five years. And a forlorn 85% of students who didn't take a gap year wish that they had. It's not just the preserve of the Prince Williams of the world; 60% of gappers come from state schools. Don't think just because the closest thing you have to a healthy bank account is a pig-shaped china object that you need give up hope – raising money is much easier than you might think and this book will advise you on ways to do it.

It's the perfect time to go out and meet some people outside your postcode. Leaping into a gap you will learn about different cultures, be it Namibian nomads or Osterley office politics. It'd be such a shame to look back and wish that you had done something while you had the opportunity. Edith Piaf was able to sing *Je Ne Regrette Rien* with such feeling because she did a season as an Alpine chalet cleaner. Well perhaps not, but you get the idea. Zabrina Shield went to South America, and says:

I gained so much more from having travelled than I could've ever gained in that first year at university. The experiences aren't comparable. The people that I met were so diverse and refreshing that it was inspiring. It made you feel that there was so much to do in life and so much to learn.

People who take a gap year usually emerge more mature, self-confident and focussed, or at least with a bit more to talk about. Louise Treves spent part of her gap in Costa Rica with Raleigh:

On our last morning, we had a two-hour journey by traditional canoe at dawn. We were all incredibly sleepy and sad, but it was the most magical boat trip, utterly silent, except for the river and the birds, and with no civilisation in sight. I kept expecting dinosaurs to wander out of the jungle – it looked so prehistoric.

Maybe your intended career or course, from Arabic to zoology, would benefit from a stint abroad. A gap year is an ideal time to learn a language properly. Voluntary work may be very rewarding: you can help people, learn about a culture, learn skills and feel invested with an air of nobility. Or you can learn a new skill, such as skiing, salsa or sailing, like Finola Collins, who worked on a tall ship – a huge traditional sailing boat:

My experience was completely inspirational. I saw some amazing things – whales, sharks – and swam with dolphins! Even sitting alone at night on watch was completely magical. My gap year gave me a huge amount of confidence.

Then again, you may want to get a job during your gap year – either to save for your student days or, if you've just finished university, to pay off debts you accrued during them.

Or perhaps you're just unsure what to do next. Away from the rigours of formal education you might discover what actually interests you. Mark Morris, a freelance journalist, went to Italy, where he: *'...learnt Italian, learnt to type, wrote an unpublishable novel and watched dubbed episodes of Hunter'.*

Many people change their mind about what they want to do. Tony Lewis, an economics graduate:

...was all prepared, in a kicking and screaming kind of way, to go into the City, but did a job in a music distribution company over the summer. I had a great time and I've been in the music business ever since, so my year off changed my future entirely.

Perhaps you have missed your grades or need to save up before you can go on to higher education. Your enforced gap might throw you at first, but you'll soon find out that there are thousands of ways to fill your time.

Having taken the decision to do it, you are faced with a fantastic but bewildering number of choices. Do you want to work abroad, or travel around? Your friend's going to Honduras but you want to go to Australia, and your boy/girlfriend doesn't want to take a year off but will it affect your relationship? And the course you want to do will cost £2985 more than you possess. And is crewing on the Côte d'Azur (France) better than basking in Brazil?

With so many of your mates going off on gap years it's tempting to trump people with your destination – working with orphans in India might sound more exotic and worthy than au pairing in France, but if it's not what you want to do, don't do it. If you put together and work towards your own plan – and it's something you are excited about – you'll get a lot more out of it.

The definitive gap-year satire is the very funny, acerbically observant *Are You Experienced?*, by William Sutcliffe, based on his own experiences travelling in India. He says:

This may seem hypocritical, since a large chunk of my living these last few years has been from a book that takes the piss out of backpackers, but I am all in favour of gap years in general and gap-year travellers in particular. My defence is that while young backpackers are a great topic for satire, and do many ridiculous things, I learnt an enormous amount from my gap year, and feel that it really did open my eyes and mind to a huge range of new ideas and experiences. I probably behaved as stupidly and pretentiously as many of the characters in my book, but I don't regret a second of it.

The best things to do in a year off are to earn some money, read widely and pursue your interests. If your interests lie close to home, that doesn't make you a less imaginative or interesting person. Remember that the education system, which can seem like the whole world when you are 18, for most people comes to a sudden end after a degree. After that, there is no system – there are no rules. No one will ever tell you what career you must pursue. The range of choices is infinite.

Use your year to think about what you value in life – if what you need to be happy is financial security, or fresh air, or a fast car, or time to travel, or time at home or contact with strangers, or isolation, or a big city, or artistic fulfilment, or the thrill of deadlines, or a slow pace of life, or the feeling that you are making the world a better place. If you can get some sense of what it is you want from life, you will, I think, stand a much better chance of being a contented and fulfilled 30-year-old than the guy standing next to you in the matriculation photograph who's only just finished his A levels.

With the information in this book, you can find out what is out there. Part I contains essential predeparture reading, Part II gives you a continental lowdown and Part III details all the different things you can do.

Do You Mind the Gap?

You might worry that it'll be a gaping gap – a setback, getting to higher education or on the job market a year later. But a year is a very short time (ask anyone aged over 30 about this). You are likely to spend a lot of your life working, so to take some time out can only be good. Dave Strachan travelled around India independently:

I got a sense of the world for the first time, a tremendous drive to travel more, and an appreciation that there was more than the European way of life...and that these alternative options were in many ways better.

A concern is that you will lose your will to work. How will you settle into an everyday routine after a year spent climbing volcanoes and bungee jumping? However, university students are less likely to drop out if they have taken a gap year. Tony Higgins, the Chief Executive of the Universities & Colleges Admissions Service (UCAS), says:

UCAS believes that students who take a well-planned, structured year out are more likely to be satisfied with and complete their chosen course. The benefits of a well-structured year out are now widely recognised by universities and colleges and cannot fail to stand you in good stead later in life. Planning is the key.

A gap year gives employers some way of differentiating you from hoards of indistinguishable graduates. Sophia Haque taught in Pakistan:

I haven't met anyone who has not been interested or full of admiration on hearing about my gap year. It is definitely something prospective employers like to talk about in an interview, which is great, as I love talking about it!

Concerns

You might not have been away from home for an extended period before and this may be enough to keep you from deciding to go away. You will undoubtedly miss people and you may feel gripped with fear at the thought of being alone and lonely in an unfamiliar place. But there are ways to make the prospect a lot less intimidating – read on to find out about organisations, activities and approaches that will make the idea of a gap less like peering into a scary void. Bear in mind that keeping in good contact with your friends and family is an excellent way to combat homesickness (see the Keeping in Touch chapter later), and that people tend to cement strong friendships while living an intense existence abroad – most gappers point to this as one of the chief benefits they took away from their experience.

One of the most frightening things to face is the unknown – this is always the case, however old you are. Once you get to a place, you will find that it's easy to adjust – this is a great confidence booster, as your jitters disappear and you start to feel both at home and exhilarated by the sense of difference.

Another worry might be: what if you expend all this time and effort, and then don't like it? Or it doesn't live up to your expectations? A good way to get around this one is to think about what you want to get out of it and take the time to plan. If you research what you're going to do, you're less likely to have unrealistic expectations of what you're going to do, and so are less prone to disappointment.

And what if you run out of money when you're there? This is another nightmare scenario that may easily be avoided or addressed – see the Money & Costs chapter later for some solutions to keep you solvent.

A daunting thought is what will you return to (apart from a bank account bleaker than Scarborough in February)? Try to plan so that you won't be starting university or looking for work with debts weighing you down. Avoid crashing down to earth on your homecoming by thinking ahead (see Timing & Planning and the Coming Home chapter later).

The prospect of launching off into the unknown with your mate Kevin, who up till now has found negotiating supermarket aisles pretty challenging, can be enough to make you think you'd better just carry on down the well-worn trail to working life. But first, don't underestimate your own abilities, and second, there are plenty of companies who arrange gap-year activities, from building schools in Nepal to studying Art History in Florence (Italy).

Leaving someone behind can make you waver too. If you have a steady boy/girlfriend, you might feel bad about leaving them. Isabel Young had a serious boyfriend whom she left for a year:

The internet helped us keep in touch, and I loved my time away despite the separation. I was so relieved as it was a real concern – I almost went for a shorter time because of it, but if I had I would've regretted it.

Timing & Planning

Before or after university is when you have fewest ties – you won't have to leave a secure job, are unlikely to have dependants and rarely – unless you are a middle-aged kid – will you have mortgage payments to consider. You might worry that you will fall behind your peers as they will be a year ahead on the education-work ladder. But you won't have been earning much, if at all, and so won't be facing a big pay cut on your return. You won't have lost a year but gained incredible experience and memories, which will stand out in the future as other years merge into one. Nick Wheeler, having been backpacking, says:

If you've had a year off already, you're less likely to want a sabbatical later. I've lost count of the amount of people who hadn't taken a gap year getting itchy feet later when they are working.

If you want to get onto something run by a gap-year organisation, then you might need to apply as early as Easter in the Lower Sixth. If you give yourself a year to raise the money, it'll make it easier. If you are travelling or working independently, you may want to avoid planning your time too much – one of the beauties of taking a gap year is breaking away from the strictures of structure. And after all that education, perhaps the last thing you need is more training and another timetable. Goal-led gap-year thinking might frown on such frivolity, but a year spent exploring may be just as rewarding and adventurous as something more structured. But, you footloose types, just remember it can be financially beneficial, if not exactly thrilling, to plan a bit to avoid blowing all your cash after two hedonistic months in Thailand and to help you get the most out of your time. Clare Barlow did some voluntary work in the UK, worked on a project in South America, and various jobs:

I don't think I spent enough time planning. I had a great three months abroad, but the rest of my time was spent trying things out and deciding I didn't like them.

Sorting out college applications or having an idea of what you might do when you get back will only add to your free-and-easy feeling. But before or after higher education, that is the question.

BEFORE HIGHER EDUCATION

Having been at school since the age of five, you might feel that you'd quite like to do something different. A gap year is welcomed by most universities. You'll be less likely to drop out

Persuading Your Parents

If your parents did something similar when they were younger, they might feel easier about waving you off into the unknown, but however cool they try to be, they are going to worry. And the global climate since September 11, 2001 has made foreign travel seem more threatening. But it's the rare horror stories that make the news – around half a million pre-university gappers are travelling or working abroad with no mishaps. The world has shrunk over the last 30 years – far-flung places seem to have got nearer – and many routes are well worn. Driving to your local shopping centre could pose greater dangers. The far-reaching tentacles of the internet make it both easy and cheap to keep in touch. If your parents are not on email, now is the time for them to get connected – this way communication will be immediate and easy.

It's important that young travellers take care, but even living at home you will have developed your common sense. And when in a strange place, you are far more likely to be on your guard. If travelling around, give your family a rough idea of your itinerary (nothing precise, you don't want them to be unduly worried when you're not somewhere on a certain day), and talk about how regularly you should keep in touch. Get all your immunisations, take malaria medication if necessary, and if you are going to do a challenging activity, such as trekking, read up on it first, go well prepared, and tell your parents about your preparations – this should help to ease their minds. (See the Courses chapter in Part III for details of survival courses.)

Many gappers raise their own money to go abroad. Working or thinking up imaginative ways of fundraising will convince your parents of your belief in what you want to do.

If you work, you'll have gained valuable experience. Travelling and exploring the world you'll learn to be independent and gain knowledge about other cultures. Catherine Bruzzone's daughter spent a year in China with Project Trust:

She was able to break away and assert herself much more successfully and be more relaxed about life. She was obviously able to cope in the most incredible situations and get on with all sorts of diverse people. We were all in awe!

The best insurance for a trip is preparation, and...good insurance. Explain to your parents how your cover includes an emergency flight home, insurance for extreme sports, etc. If you are venturing on a trip run by a gap organisation, this will provide back up (see Part III for details on gap organisations).

What if you like it so much you never come home? Wishful thinking: gappers who settle down to run a beach bar with a bunch of international nomads are few and far between. It's most likely that your parents will welcome home an individual who has learned more about other places and about his or herself.

Note to parents: however much you are fretting about your son or daughter heading off, it's unwise to let them have a credit card on your account.

and will be more mature, and have had a chance to work and satisfy a bit of wanderlust. It means that you don't have to rush into a decision about your choice of university and course, but can take time to think about what you want to do. Dave Strachan says his travels to Asia:

…gave me a chance to see some of the world for the first time, and made me grow up a little before heading to college.

You'll also have 15 months to play with, as you'll leave school in early July and start university in early October. Taking a gap year before college also means that you have something very specific to return to, solving the pesky problem of what to do next.

It might be the ideal time for some R&R. Tony Lewis found it easier to relax pre-college:

Post-uni you have the whole world ahead of you and you can't help feeling guilty having fun.

If your friends are going on to university straightaway, you may feel worried that you will slip behind them, or that everyone will be a year younger than you when you get there. Banish those feelings – you'll soon find age difference doesn't matter. Or, if you can't, take a gap year after you leave university instead.

You might think that after a year out, the prospect of becoming an impoverished student will be as appealing as a prawn-and-chocolate sandwich. But it's more likely that your time will impress on you the joys of further education, rather than the reverse. William Sutcliffe, author of *Are You Experienced*:

The most basic benefit of a year off is that you are a year older when you start university. This, I found, is of enormous help in doing university academic work with an adult approach, thinking of it as a privilege to be studying rather than out in the world earning a wage. Without the year out, a school-like mentality can prevail, which is completely wrong for enjoying and succeeding in a degree.

This change in attitude is won not just by the year out, but by having a job. Working and earning money is the most important aspect of any year off – far more important than any travelling you may do. Going out to work each day and getting paid at the end of the week is a great novelty after years in the school system, and gives you a vital sense of how the world works. However menial your jobs, they will give you a new perspective on the world, and will give you a better sense of what you want to do after university.

You can make your UCAS application before you get your A-level results, but ask for deferred entry. This means that you should explain on your form what you are going to do with the time and be prepared to discuss at interview what you are going to do. Once you have submitted your UCAS forms you will have six to eight months to plan your year.

Or you can defer after your results – people often do this if they did better than expected. In this case you will have to contact the college directly. They are usually quite flexible, but if not, the other option is to refuse the place and reapply the following year.

If your results were worse than expected, you will have probably failed to get on a course. You'll need to contact your preferred university to see if they'll take you the following year, and if not, go through clearing or retake.

On the UCAS Case

UCAS (☎ 01242-227788; e enquiries@ucas.ac.uk; W www.ucas.com) Some key dates:

15 October	closing date for applications to Oxbridge, medicine, dentistry and veterinary medicine or science.
15 January	closing date for other applications.
30 June	last date for amendments and closing date for applications from outside the UK or EU.
mid-July	clearing begins.
20 September	closing date for clearing.

If you already have gap-year plans but uni entrance has not gone as hoped, sorting what you're going to do before heading off will give you peace of mind. That's what Lizz Harrison did:

I didn't do as well as expected in my A levels so during September to January I retook. I then went to Costa Rica on a three-month project, taking a loan to pay for it and working to pay it off afterwards.

AFTER HIGHER EDUCATION

After leaving higher education, you'll feel less constrained, as you will be older and inordinately wiser. You might feel that it's delaying your launch into the job market. However, employers will look at a gap year well spent favourably – it will give you something to offer them other than a degree. You'll have more time to plan what to do and where to go, and could do something directly related to the career you want to pursue, from a film course in New York to teaching in Japan.

It might be financially frightening, as most students have built up hefty debts – around £12,000 on average. If the proposed introduction of top-up fees in 2006 goes ahead these debts could rise to a chilling £21,000, depending on the university. However, you don't have to pay off your student loan until you earn above £10,000 a year, and the amount you repay is then directly linked to your income, so don't let your debt get you down – if you do take a gap year you'll be in a better situation, as you'll have more experience. If you can't save or fundraise to pay for your gap year, you can always work abroad. Some rare creatures even manage to save their student loans.

During your final year, there will be numerous graduate job fairs set up by various universities and colleges (the main season is from October to March, but some take place in the summer too). Go to these and ask companies that tickle your fancy about how they view a gap year. Find out when you need to apply to them for graduate jobs – there's no need to miss out because you're taking a year out. As you can apply online for most jobs, it doesn't matter if you're in Australia when you do it. But if you are intending to do this, you must take everything you need with you: electronic files of your CV and references. And you'll need to be available for interview too. If you are a rare bird, you may be able to apply before you go, and defer your starting date – but companies who'll accept this are uncommon, though not unknown. You get free careers advice at the end of your final year – don't skip this, as you won't be able to access it a year later. The best thing you can do if considering a gap year post-college is to talk to your careers advisors who'll tell you the best course of action.

Won't employers assume you'll have itchy feet? Not at all – your experiences will mark you as an interesting candidate with get-up-and-go (as long as it's not so much get-up-and-go that you drool at planes going overhead).

You may be unsure about what you want to do now. Taking a year out will give you time to think, while doing something exciting and constructive. Richard Satchell studied maths and so was advised not to take off pre-university. He managed to defer a job offer after finishing college and go away, and was mighty pleased about it:

At times I felt like I'd slipped behind my friends. However, in the grand scheme of life, one year is nothing. When else will I get such a golden opportunity to do everything that I did?

Ask Yourself

Having addressed your doubts and thought about timing, now ask yourself what you want to do. Ask yourself what are the three most important things you want to achieve or experience, and use these as a starting point. Why do you want to take a gap year? What do you hope to get out of it? You can use this book to help you think about these questions and plan your adventure.

Who to Go With

Often people are put off travelling because they don't have anyone to tag along. Or they're worried they'll fall out with the people they're going with. Or they suddenly decide they can't come. Don't let this put you off – looking back and thinking 'if only I'd been a bit bolder' is no fun: go alone, with a travel mate or with a gap-year organisation.

When you're thinking about going away with someone, consider how you get along with that person. What are the pros and cons of company? Will you feel safe? How much will it cost?

Solo

Going it alone is a rewarding way of getting about. You never have to ask anyone what they want to do, your plan is always the most popular and you never have to take anyone else's feelings into account. Travelling alone gives you a wonderful feeling of freedom, chance and possibility that can be lost when you're in a pair or a group. Jess Huard travelled through Europe and went to Ghana and Costa Rica:

I was never really alone for long. I liked travelling by myself – it was refreshing to be away from people I had known my whole life and it also encouraged me to make new friends.

And you can choose exactly the gap-year activity that you want. No-one shared your passion for bagging the world's underground railways?

Travelling with a companion is more insular. You are probably most concerned about loneliness but the lone life forces you to meet many more new people. You are more approachable and you often bond much more readily with local people without the buffer of hangers on, as they are far more likely to take pity on you and start to chat. You also tend to be more receptive to your surroundings with no-one else to distract you from your soulful contemplation. You don't even have to be naturally outgoing to travel on your own; frequently other people will make life easy for you by starting up conversation.

You don't have to worry about falling out with yourself (if you do, you may have hit a problem and should head back home). The feeling of having achieved something impressive will be even more intense as you haven't got to share the glory with anyone else. You'll also get a lot of people telling you how brave they think you are, so practise your self-deprecatory it-was-nothing-but-I-am-very-brave look. However, you are bound to feel lonely at times . On your own you don't have anyone else to consult about what to do next. It's worrying and depressing to be ill when you're by yourself. You will have to take decisions about how you feel, which can be difficult: are you too ill to travel? Should you see a doctor? These are questions that are much easier with someone else to help you judge the situation. But you'll find local people are usually extremely helpful when you're ill. If you are staying in a hotel and get sick, if you ask the staff they will get you to a doctor, or get someone to come to see you. It's important to take care and not soldier on just because you have no-one around to tell you not to. Tanika Perera experienced being ill alone in Senegal:

I lay in bed for days, paranoid that I had one of the exotic diseases listed in my guidebook. The staff at my hostel were really nice and arranged a taxi to take me to hospital. I asked the doctor if he thought it might be typhoid and he thought this very funny!

Eating alone can be a dispiriting experience but if you take a book or occupy yourself inventing lives for your fellow diners, it's much more entertaining – and remember: you're not having to talk to anyone boring either.

Just because you leave home alone doesn't mean that you have to stay alone. There are so many opportunities for hooking up with other people once you get out on the road. Starting off alone gives you the chance to meet like-minded travellers along the way, to travel together for a while, and then take off on your own again whenever you want to.

If, after all this persuasion, travelling alone is as inviting as dinner with cannibals, join a gap organisation or arrange to do a course or a job so you stay in one place. This will give you a greater opportunity to form relationships and is a sure-fire way of meeting people.

There's a travelling-alone discussion board at **W** www.etravel.org.

FEMALE SOLO

Establishing the status and position of the local women in a society is important – how they behave and are expected to behave. In many cultures, drinking alcohol, smoking and wearing make-up – as well as inappropriate clothes – may all be indications to the men of 'availability'. While it may appear unfair to change your dress according to the perceptions of others, a little sensitivity can not only protect you from harassment but will show respect to the people of the country you are visiting.

You'll find that people are more likely to offer you hospitality – you are so much less threatening than a man alone. You are also perceived as much more vulnerable and people will fall over themselves to offer you assistance. In some countries you can take advantage of separate carriages, waiting rooms and even queues for women.

Sexist sound effects might form a soundtrack to your visit; ignoring these is usually the best policy. Walk confidently and try not to let it get to you. Be assertive but not antagonistic. In some places foreign women (and men) do get stared at, so unless you get used to it, you are going to have an aggravating time. It's amazing how quickly you can learn to ignore it. If it's getting to you, try thinking of yourself as a visiting celebrity – this changed point of view can at least make you smile.

Invasive behaviour is another story. If you get groped in a crowded place, you'll have to assess what response will work best given the situation and the culture. You can try to move

---

And Where Is Your Husband?

I was asked this question about hourly while travelling in India. Despite feeling uneasy about claiming to be married, I managed to come up with varied stories about this phantom character when the occasion seemed to warrant it. The interesting thing was the reaction of local people to the sight of a lone woman – from sympathy to shock and from admiration to pity. Whatever the reaction, I certainly received an enormous number of random kindnesses.

In places such as India and North Africa, it may be a good idea to claim you're married even if you're not (even sporting a wedding ring), as it can prevent an unwelcome turn in conversation. In India, after being offered more than a tour by a guide, my imaginary family grew still larger: 'I am married and have a two-year-old son!' I said – whereupon the ground opened and swallowed up the forward young man (well that's what he wished).

Sometimes it doesn't work though, and you'll just have to start fielding questions about how you're coping during this sexual hiatus. Try to keep calm and not to take the routine harassment that occurs in many places too seriously – it's not dangerous, just annoying.

Abigail Hole

away but if this is not practical, make a bit of a scene. Public embarrassment is very effective if spoken in the local language but people will get the picture even if you say it in your own, or you can try a stern bit of pointing and wagging a finger.

Don't encourage overtures you have no intention of entertaining, or hang out till the wee hours getting drunk. You should also take extra care not to find yourself alone on empty beaches, alone in dark streets or in any other situation where help might not be available. Keep some cash on you at all times, in case you want to take a taxi back to your hotel or guesthouse.

For the most part, travelling or living abroad by yourself is a rewarding and usually safe experience. As a woman you face subtle discrimination in your everyday life anyway, and you'll likely to be perfectly familiar with the behaviour you encounter in a foreign place. This won't necessarily make it any easier to deal with, especially if you're feeling lonely or homesick.

Above all, try to stick to your own moral code. Some people may feel that it's OK to touch or bully you. Don't allow yourself to be pushed around or made to feel like a victim. If you are clear about your rules, others will soon get the message. Remember, you've gone abroad to see and experience new cultures, and you can't do that if you're entirely protected and afraid to meet people's eyes.

There's lots of solo female travel advice on the net if you run a search. You can ask fellow travellers about your destination on Lonely Planet's Thorntree at W thorntree.lonelyplanet .com, or there's a useful dedicated forum at W www.eurotrip.com/forum.

With a Friend/Friends

It's often the greatest thing to go away with a good friend. You're with someone who shares your sense of humour, someone who has the same frame of reference. Tony Lewis backpacked around the world, sometimes alone, sometimes with friends:

It was good to have the contrast. My experience is that you will meet more people and be more outgoing if you travel alone. Having said that, it's good to have someone to share and relive those memories with – otherwise they're just your memories.

However, if it doesn't work, it could be the worst thing: is there anything that has always annoyed you about your friend? Their endless pedantry? The way they can never make a decision? Their tuneless whistling? Their penchant for Progressive Rock? Their intolerance? (If it's yes to all these, it might be time to cut them loose.) Foibles can seem quite charming when you don't have to suffer them 24 hours a day but can take a whole new aspect when you do. Even if you can put up with the strange gargling noise they make when brushing their teeth, you really get to know someone when travelling or living abroad with them in a way you didn't have a chance to while at school or university. This can work out really well but you will come up against times of difficulty. Laura Wade travelled around North Africa with her closest friend:

Most of the time it was fantastic but at one point we were getting so wound up by each other that we were sitting in icy silence. We kept falling out over how we should respond to the hassle we got and where we should go next. We decided to part company for a while, and when we met up again we just made sure we had the occasional breather from each other.

Going with a friend might mean you have a great time but you don't quite get everything done that you'd hoped. Rachel Harrison stayed with an English friend in the South of France:

We both did French courses. It wasn't the greatest idea from the language angle (supposedly the main purpose of the trip) but we had a really memorable time.

Sharing a trip with a friend or a group can mean saving money. If you are travelling, it's cheaper to share a room rather than get singles, and sharing a flat abroad works out less expensive. It's best if you're quite evenly matched financially. If you've got a lot more to play with, it'll feel weird as you tuck into your king prawns while they chew on their porridge, and you'll both feel agitated at the imbalance.

Going in a group is a lot of fun, and not as intense as the one-on-one scenario. You're bound to come back with brilliant memories of funny times but it does make it more difficult to make decisions, and can be more restrictive than going with just one other person or on your own. You can always get around this by breaking away from the group as well – getting the best of both worlds. Dave Strachan travelled in India with a group of five friends, then left them to travel on his lonesome:

I enjoyed the laughs and security of the group but loved travelling alone and felt a real freedom.

With a Boy/Girlfriend

Karen Vost taught and travelled in India with her man, and says:

A gap year makes it clear whether your partner is a dear.

If you've got it going on, going away together is fantastic. You're with the person you're closest to, sharing excellent experiences and you don't have to leave them behind. As for the economics, two people can't travel as cheaply as one but depending on the destination they can travel as cheaply as one-and-a-half.

But you could end up storming off into the sunset. When you're travelling together, you probably spend more time in each other's company than any couple ever should. Some of this time will be spent in difficult circumstances – on long, uncomfortable bus trips, or in cramped and sweaty hotel rooms – sometimes tired and tetchy.

And how will you cope with all the shared decisions? Is it worth £10 to stay in the concrete boxes called Paradise Bungalows? Do we trust a guy selling Rolex watches on the street? Will we get cholera eating this stuff? The couples who have it together agree on most things, whether it's trying street-stall noodles or a seven-day trek. The feuding couples bicker over a 10-rupee trinket, and spend the evening sniping at each other as the sun sets superbly behind the snow-capped Himalayas.

Being in a couple, your relationship does appear more self-contained. If you are working abroad, there's not the same drive to go out and meet people, and other people don't find you so approachable. But if you're open and friendly, you'll meet loads of people despite your loved-up status.

And the security of a relationship really means something when you're in a crowded, chaotic bus station, and one person can sit on the luggage while the other buys the tickets. Sophie Gorell Barnes hitchhiked through France and Spain and has the last word:

Travelling with a boyfriend is good as you have someone to fend off creeps and carry your bags, and they're better fun to sleep with than mosquitoes.

Travel Mates

If you're going somewhere no-one you know wants to go, there are various ways you can advertise or search for a like-minded travel partner or group. Of course, this is a bit of a risky business: what will this random character be like? But it's quite an adventure, and you're starting off with a major interest in common. If it doesn't work out, you'll have someone to accompany you in those difficult first few weeks, and you can always ditch each other once you find your feet.

To meet potential travel companions, you could advertise in the Connections page of *Wanderlust* magazine, or try travel clubs such as Globetrotters – you can advertise in their magazine or use the website at **W** www.globetrotters.co.uk. The website **W** www.gapyear .com has a messageboard section, with the specific strands: 'Find a travel mate' and 'Meet up with people overseas'. On the Lonely Planet website **W** www.lonelyplanet.com, people often use the Thorntree (the travellers' notice board) to find people going the same way. Or you could try the notice board at **W** www.payaway.co.uk.

Another great way to bump into travellers is at travel-slide nights or talks in bookshops. You can also advertise at the spring travel fairs – there are notice boards for people wanting to meet other travellers, or you might find details of a trip in the classifieds. Jenny Heyward travelled through Africa in a truck with 23 people after answering a notice wedged between kissagram ads:

I loved it but it had more to do with Africa and the way we travelled than the people, although I liked the kind of family atmosphere.

With so many people, you have a lot of choice of who to spend your time with, and a bit more of a party atmosphere than if you're travelling alone or in a couple. There were a few weird people though! But I felt very secure – it felt like safety in numbers.

Meeting Other Travellers

Common spots where this multicoloured, multifaceted species gather are cafés, bars, beaches, internet cafés, hostels, guesthouses and centres for adventure activities. Sometimes they are spotted in self-contained, less-approachable packs, sometimes in more serene gatherings of two or three, and sometimes solo, concentrating furiously on a book, their demeanour shouting – I'm *loving* my book and don't need anyone to talk to.

Most travellers are interested in chatting to other travellers – you all have something in common. You can make some great friends while on the road and meet some really interesting people. You will find out good places to go and get ideas about what you might want to do.

It's not always the case, though. You'll be amazed how often you'll meet some other travellers and all they want to do is complain about the locals. Or you meet someone that you think is very nice, amusing and laidback and then later find yourself in a bad-tempered argument with them about their obsessive and irrational intolerance of Slovakians. So how do you get away from people if they begin to irritate you? Well people generally get the message if you refuse to answer to your name, wear a disguise and affect amazement when they approach.

There are simpler ways though, if you're travelling. It's usually very easy – all you need to do is change your plans – decide to leave a place, or stay on a bit longer if they're heading off. Travelling is usually so flexible that you will have no problem escaping if that's what you want to do. Travellers are usually quite relaxed about arrangements as it's not feasible or appealing to stick to a very tight schedule when you're trying to get around. Avoid getting stuck in situations unless you've really hit it off, for example, going on a 10-day, or even a four-day, trek or safari with someone you've only just met, as they may start to irritate you after a couple of hours... it could prove one of life's longer journeys.

Hell Is Other Travellers

Sometimes it's not the mosquitoes that get yo
just the darn people. Maybe it's the one who tra
Guatemala/Colombia (delete as appropriate) horseridin
living off rats, or the one who misses the supermarkets at h
it? And the people! Or the one who can't believe you paid th
here, she got them down to 25p after a two-day stakeout, or the
moon parties aren't what they were, he's heading to Central America t
or the one who won't stop juggling fire and murdering the drums, or the
meditating over there for the last three hours, and has an alarmingly serene e
the one who wants to give something back to this country, because travel for tra
is so shallow.

Before you cash in your ticket in horror, many gap-year travellers are funny, interestin
and interested in the place they've got to without being annoying about it, just like
yourself: as you prepare to tell the story about when you travelled with nomads across an
uncharted desert for two weeks and it was horribly hot and camels are so smelly and
nomads so humourless but you did get them down to £2, and since then you've done the
party scene to death, learnt to juggle, got a sense of rhythm and found internal peace –
shanti – and now you're volunteering in a leprosy colony because you just want to give
something back...

Organised Tours

If the idea of heading off unguided is as appealing as a mussel-topped meringue, an organised tour may be the way to go. This is a halfway house between true independent travel and a package tour. You will still feel much like an independent traveller but all those tricky arrangements, organising where to stay, buying bus tickets, negotiating a midnight bungee jump in Outer Mongolia, will be conveniently taken out of your hands.

Of course this all comes at a price, and not being able to set your own budget means that you'll spend more than you would as an independent traveller. Trips range from £500 for a week to £10,000 for 10 months and this doesn't usually include flights, activities, entrance fees or spending money. So what on earth does it include? Well, accommodation, travel once you get there, food and the pleasure of not having to worry about the nitty gritty.

The one disadvantage of this is that it's often the nitty gritty that provides those 'you'll never guess what happened when I...' stories and countless opportunities to meet the locals. However, most companies take you in small groups of around 15 and many trips involve camping off the beaten track so you do still get away from the tourist trail to meet some 'real' people.

The types of trip available range from two weeks travelling down the Yangtze River to seven months on the road from Alaska to the southern tip of South America. Different companies specialise in different areas, and tours usually have a set itinerary, so shop around to find the one that suits you best.

There are hundreds of good companies out there, see Part III for a selection (with a view to working rather than holidaying with them) and the Global Tour Companies Appendix for an extensive list.

our main means of identification
al right to be in a country. Always
r to anyone for any length of time
desk at a hostel or hotel.

your nationality and you'll need it
back pages and all pages with pre-
ese separately from your passport.

. If it's going to peter out within six
on your itinerary, then get it replaced
port is valid for some time after you
leave their coun...   e date of departure), so the longer the
validity of your passport the bett...   are valid for 10 years.

How many blank pages do you have left? You ...ght need quite a few for visas and entry
and exit stamps, and many officials will refuse to issue a visa or stamp your passport unless
it's on a clean page. It would be a real drag to run out of spare pages when you've just spent
three days getting to the Mongolian border.

If you don't have a passport – get one. It can take anything from one week to a month.
You will also have to hand over your passport for some visa applications (these can take
from five minutes to one month each).

The Home Office agency responsible for issuing passports is the UK Passport Service
(UKPS; ☎ 0870 521 0410; W www.ukpa.gov.uk).

You'll require the following, together with the application form:

- **Payment** – A passport will set you back around £33 for a standard adult one of the minimum
  number of pages, issued within the usual processing time.
- **Proof of identity** – You need someone to verify that it's your scary likeness in your passport
  snaps, as well as vouch for you on the application form. This can be either the holder of a
  current passport from your country who has known you for two years (but is unrelated to
  you) or a citizen of (you'd hope) good standing such as a justice of the peace, lawyer, employer,
  doctor or teacher.
- **Photographs** – Two recent head-and-shoulder shots of you taken against a white background
  (you'll look like a criminal, it's inescapable), signed and identified on the back by the same
  person who vouches for you on your application form.
- **Proof of any name change** – Such as a marriage or deed-poll certificate.
- **Proof of citizenship** – Such as a birth, naturalisation or registration certificate.

Issuing Period & Rush Jobs

Applications made at the Post Office or Worldchoice normally take two weeks, while those
made by post directly to the UK Passport Service take around three weeks. However, if you've
left your application until the last moment or – oh no! – lost your passport, then you might need
to get a new or replacement passport in a hurry. You can do this by upgrading to the Premium
(for same-day results) or Fast Track (if you've got a week's grace) service. Of course you have to
pay extra for this – £63 for the Premium service or £78 for the Fast Track service and this only
works if your application is properly completed and you've provided everything they need.

LOST OR STOLEN PASSPORTS

Losing your passport while you're in a foreign country will catapult you into a Kafkaesque realm of bureaucratic hassles. But, hey, it's not the end of the world.

If you lose your passport, contact the consulate immediately. If your home country does not have diplomatic representation where you are, then contact the consulate in the nearest neighbouring country. Ask the consular staff whether you need to notify the local government of the loss, and how to handle it if you do. If your passport is stolen, inform the local police and get a police report before heading to your consulate.

You'll need some form of identification (a driver's licence, student card, an old passport, your birth certificate etc – preferably something with your photo on it) to satisfy the consular staff before they'll issue a replacement. This is your passport photocopy's (see earlier) big moment.

Your consulate should be able to issue an emergency passport within a couple of days but you may pay extra for the privilege. If you had visas in the passport that need replacing, you'll have to go to the nearest consulate of that country and reapply – and pay the visa fee again.

DUAL CITIZENSHIP

If you've got two passports they can come in very handy. You can pick the passport that will get you the better visa – perhaps cheaper or providing a longer stay – and the one the country likes best. John Hayes has an American and a British passport:

I wanted to get a visa for China, and found that Americans can get one at the border, while British citizens have to apply in advance, so that day I was American.

Check out your own situation, and if you decide to travel under two passports, be wary: it's wise not to let on to immigration officials that you have dual citizenship. You should also try to stick to the same passport when travelling between neighbouring countries – if you've entered Thailand on your British passport then try to enter Malaysia on your Australian passport, officials might wonder how you got into the region.

Tickets

Unless your year off involves swimming, a unicycle and a shed load of sponsorship, or you're not going outside your local bus network, you'll probably be travelling by plane at some point. It may be your biggest expense (see the Money & Costs chapter for more information about planning your budget). There's a bewildering mass of tickets and places to buy them but with a bit of research and shopping around, you can bag a bargain.

It's worth thinking about buying your ticket as soon as possible, as the best deals tend to be available well in advance of your departure date. You can get cheap tickets at the very last moment but this is a big risk unless you're serenely flexible. If you do manage to find such a ticket, arranging visas in time might be tricky. If you can't find a good deal, you'll either have to pay more than you bargained for or delay your departure. Possible sources of these elusive bargains include W www.lastminute.com and W www.cheapflights.co.uk.

TYPES OF TICKET

Tickets and deals are governed by some pesky rules and restrictions. Common ones include:

- **Cancellation or change penalties.** Cancelling your ticket or changing your route once it's booked may mean you lose the entire value of the ticket (most travel insurance policies will protect against unavoidable cancellations).

- **Directional limits.** Most round-the-world (RTW) tickets only allow you to travel in one direction.
- **Minimum or maximum limits.** For example, you may have to be away at least 14 days, or for 12 months at the most.
- **Refund policy.** Some refunds can only be made through the travel agency where the ticket was purchased – not much good to you when you're in Timbuktu.
- **Seasonal limits.** A ticket may only be available in off-peak or shoulder (February to March and October to November) periods.
- **Stopover limits.** You might only be allowed to stop over a certain number of times.

Your basic ticket is a plain old full-price one-way or return between two cities. London–Ljubljana in June is £150 return with Adria Airways and London–Lima in June is £600 with KLM. Conditions multiply as the price drops. Here are some of the common deals.

Discount Return Tickets
If you're just heading to one area, then a no-nonsense return ticket is probably your best bet. Michelle Hudson managed to get around Asia very cheaply:

I got a ticket for £300 to Delhi, and then used a combination of local flights, boats, trains and buses to get to the other Asian countries on my itinerary.

Or you could fly to a European city and then travel around using an Inter-Rail pass. This assumes you have time on your side and that you're not planning to travel massive distances, as you'll have to return to your entry point to fly home. For more flexibility, you may be able to include one or more stop-offs at cities en route to your destination. Stop-offs can last several weeks, allowing you to explore one region before you resume your journey. For example, a London–Sydney ticket with a stop-off in Singapore would allow you to travel through Southeast Asia for a bore-your-friends-about-what-a-bargain fare.

Open-Jaw Tickets
These snappy little numbers are return tickets that allow you to fly to one destination but return home from another, saving you a lot of backtracking and time. Open-jaw tickets are generally more expensive than standard return fares but can allow you to see a lot more of a region, especially if the distance between the two cities on your ticket is great. The UK's no-frills airlines always sell single tickets, often jaw-droppingly cheap, so it's easy to put together an open-jaw arrangement.

One-Way Tickets
Often pricier than return tickets but you may want one of these if you are unsure of your itinerary or return date. Having no commitments or definite places to be, and complete freedom to follow your whims, can give you a weird but nice floaty feeling, completely drug free. The drawback is that many countries require an onward ticket before they'll issue you a visa (see later in this chapter). But if you know which way you're going to exit the country (be it by rail, bus or air) and you can prove you have the cash reserves to keep you solvent during your stay, it should be fine. Also, there's absolutely no reason why you can't buy a return ticket and then not return. If you've got a good deal on a return on a charter flight to Sharm-el-Sheikh (Egypt) and you're going down through Africa then it's cool to ditch the second part – they certainly won't come looking for no-shows.

Round-the-World Tickets

If you plan to travel to more than one continent, you're probably best off getting yourself a round-the-world (RTW) ticket. This fare gives you a limited period (usually 12 months) to get around the globe, and you can only go in one direction (so no backtracking). There'll be a predetermined number of stop-offs but you can often buy extra stops. The biggest constraint is that you're limited to the flight paths of the airline and its partners but these fares tend to be such bargains (just add up how much all the individual flights would cost for that smug, I-got-it-in-the-sales vibe) that paying an extra flight to another destination during one of your stop-offs doesn't seem any hardship. The other great advantage is the air mileage you accumulate for your frequent-flyer programme, even though RTW fares collect very low-rent points. (See the Round the World chapter in Part II for more details on RTW tickets.)

Circle Fares

These are tickets that allow you to make a number of stops within a region. The main example is the Circle Pacific Fare, which allows you to travel to all the exciting and intriguing countries around the Pacific Ocean. However, there are some restrictions: you have to travel within a six-month period, you have to start and finish in set cities, and there is usually a limited mileage allowed. Having said that, you are free to make up your own itinerary and you can generally change your flights without penalty as long as your route remains the same. Prices depend on your itinerary and mileage. These fares are offered by Star Alliance (W www.staralliance.com) and oneworld (W www.oneworldalliance.com), two groups of major airlines, who also do RTW tickets. The main disadvantage of the Circle Pacific Fare if you're travelling from Britain is that we're not on the Pacific Ocean so you'll have to add that journey into your costs.

Student & Youth Fares

Your student or youth card will get you a discount of up to 30% with some airlines (see Discount Cards in the Money & Costs chapter), usually on ordinary economy-class fares. You wouldn't get one, for instance, on a RTW ticket since these are already as low as they'll go.

Courier Flights

Courier flights can be truly a bargain. You either carry documents for the company, in which case you get a baggage allowance, or an air-freight company takes over your baggage allowance and you may only bring along a carry-on bag. In return, you get a steeply discounted ticket, this can be as much as 75%.

There are other restrictions – courier tickets are sold for a fixed date and schedule, so changes are pretty much impossible. Tickets are usually return, although one-way tickets can sometimes be negotiated. The length of stay depends somewhat on the destination. It is generally two weeks, unless extended by special arrangement, although trips to South America and Asia tend to be longer.

If you decide to take this route you need to register with a courier organisation such as the International Association of Air Travel Couriers (W www.aircourier.co.uk), which costs £32. You are then free to check the website for a flight that suits you. Although they are based in the US there are lots of flights available out of London.

e-tickets

Some companies issue e-tickets as an alternative to paper tickets on certain routes. This just means that instead of worrying about losing your ticket you can worry about losing your credit card, as this is all you need to prove your booking. You will also be issued with a paper receipt/itinerary, which you can use to show immigration officials that you have onward travel booked.

No-frills Tickets
No-frills airlines, such as easyJet or Ryanair, prefer to issue their tickets online as there are fewer administration costs. These savings are then passed on to you; their online fares are usually around £5 cheaper than those booked over the phone.

TICKETS TO AVOID
Second-hand Tickets
You'll occasionally see adverts on youth hostel message boards and sometimes in newspapers for 'second-hand tickets', meaning that somebody is trying to offload their unused return ticket like a worn-out jumper.

It's a nice idea and the prices can look tempting. Unfortunately, these tickets are usually worthless, as the name on the ticket must match the name on the passport of the person checking in. Some say that the seller of the ticket can check you in with their passport, and then give you the boarding pass. Usually, however, immigration officials will check that the boarding pass matches the name in your passport, and you won't go anywhere.

WHERE TO BUY THEM
Buying Your Ticket
Airlines range from snazzy outfits such as Singapore Airlines, with a modern fleet where you get personal movie-and-game screens even in the lowliest class, to cut-rate fleets of old bangers with shoestring services featuring meals of rancid butter on polystyrene bread. Rather more importantly, cheaper operators have older fleets, which tend to have greater safety risks and a lower level of reliability, making cancellations and delays more frequent.

Cheaper long-haul operators have a lot more stops on their routes, so you really feel you've understood the meaning of 'long haul'. However, there are many good options in the middle ground, particularly within the European and American carrier markets.

Before you get caught up in the finer details of your route, pick up information on several airlines from a travel agency. Check out frequent-flyer programmes, the age of the fleet, options for booking, payment and alteration of prebooked tickets, and the cancellation policies of each airline.

Most airlines have a website providing information on the routes they fly, their schedules and their frequent-flyer programmes. A few to try include:

Aeroflot (Russian Airlines)	W www.aeroflot.com
Air France	W www.airfrance.com
Air New Zealand	W www.airnez.com
Alitalia	W www.alitalia.com/
American Airlines	W www.americanair.com
British Airways	W www.british-airways.com
Canadian Airlines	W www.cdnair.ca
Cathay Pacific	W www.cathaypacific.com
Continental Airlines	W www.flycontinental.com
KLM	W www.klm.com
Lufthansa	W www.lufthansa.com

Qantas	W www.qantas.com
Singapore Airlines	W www.singaporeair.com
TAP Air Portugal	W www.tap.pt
United Airlines	W www.ual.com
Virgin	W www.fly.virgin.com

Buying from Airlines

Buying your ticket directly from an airline is like heading to Harvey Nichols to stock up on frozen peas: you won't get a bargain. Airlines use travel agencies to sell any discounted tickets. These tickets are generally sold in blocks to the travel agent and part of these savings is passed on to you. So, unless you're trying to organise your ticket at the last minute, it's almost inconceivable that you won't get a better deal by going through a travel agent. The exception to this golden rule is the no-frills airlines, which sell tickets direct to customers on the net.

Buying from Travel Agents

Years ago, the travel industry included some very dodgy agencies that could sell you tickets for flights that didn't exist, or simply scarper with your cash. These days, thankfully, the industry has cleaned up its act. So long as you book your plane ticket through an agent that has an ATOL (Air Travel Organiser's Licence), your money should be safe. If you want to be doubly sure, then look for the ABTA (Association of British Travel Agents) logo as well. These difficult days, though, you run some risk that the airline you book with will not exist by the time you begin your journey – or, possibly worse, it will go out of business while you are out on the road. When Ansett, the big Australian airline, went bust within hours of the September 11 attack, thousands of gappers found their plans thrown into expensive turmoil. So you will probably have no choice but to fork out an extra fiver for scheduled airline failure insurance.

Two favourite agents with gappers – because they offer some under-26 and student-only deals that no ordinary agency can match – are:

| STA Travel | (☎ 0870 160 0599; W www.sta-travel.co.uk) |
| Student Flights | (☎ 0870 890 0092; W www.studentflight.co.uk) |

Other good, reputable bonded travel agencies include:

Airline Network	(☎ 0870 241 0011; W www.airline-network.co.uk)
ebookers	(☎ 0870 010 7000; W www.ebookers.com)
Flight Centre	(☎ 0870 890 8099; W www.flightcentre.co.uk)
North South	(☎ 01245-608291; W www.northsouthtravel.co.uk)
Quest Travel	(☎ 0870 442 3542; W www.questtravel.com)
Trailfinders	(☎ 020-7938 3366; W www.trailfinder.com)

Buying Online

You can find astonishing bargains on the web if you spend (what feels like) a few days of your life online – the really amazing deals do not last long. A good way to do things is to research fares online, and then approach a real live travel agent to see what you can get. Try looking at:

| ebookers | W www.ebookers.com |
| Expedia | W www.expedia.co.uk |

Opodo	W www.opodo.co.uk
Travelocity	W www.travelocity.com

Or, for travel within Europe, check out the no-frills airlines, which offer some amazing deals:

bmibaby	W www.bmibaby.com
easyJet	W www.easyJet.com
Jet2	W www.jet2.com
MyTravelLite	W www.mytravellite.com
Ryanair	W www.ryanair.com
Virgin Express	W www.virgin-express.com

Round-the-World Tickets

STA Travel has a special department to help you circumnavigate the globe, and Trailfinders' long-haul agents will advise you on this too. The very cheapest fares involve some overland bits where you make your own way. Under-26 fares are often available. (See Part II for more details.)

Boat, Train & Coach

Flying is not the only way to travel, although it's the quickest and generally most convenient method. If you're hopping across the channel you might want to consider the ferry W www .ferrybooker.com is just one of many booking agents. Or, for longer trips, cargo ships are a unique, sedate but expensive means of travel. To increase revenue, some shipping lines carry up to about 12 passengers. It's not banana boat stuff, cabins are quite luxurious. A journey from Southampton to Buenos Aires (Argentina) would take about three weeks and cost £1410. The main agent in the UK is Strand Voyages (W www.strandtravel.co.uk). Other useful sites are W www.freighter-cruises.com and W www.atwtraveler.com/frei-faq.htm, which answers frequently asked questions.

If you want to see more of the country, train travel is definitely the way to go. Inter-Rail (W www.interrail.com) does a month's pass, which gives you nearly unlimited travel in Europe, with a few restrictions, for £265. The most famous train journey in the world, the Trans-Siberian (W www.trans-siberian.co.uk), is an amazing way to see Russia. Or you could cross Canada (W www.train-canada.net).

A not-so-comfy alternative to rail travel, going by coach is nevertheless a lot cheaper. A return from London to Krakow (Poland) is only £73 with Eurolines (W www.eurolines .com). This is because it takes 27 hours and you won't be able to feel your legs when you get there.

Visas

Visas are stamps or documents in your passport that say you may enter a country and stay there for a specific time. You usually have to pay and they can be pricey. Your first step is to find out whether you need one or not. Check with the Foreign & Commonwealth Office (☎ 020-7008 0232; W www.fco.gov.uk) for information, contact the country's embassy or consulate, or try Thames Consular Services (☎ 020-8996 2912; W www.thamesconsular .com), a visa agency. Trailfinders (☎ 0845 050 5905; W www.trailfinder.com) also has a visa and passport service at its offices in Kensington and the City. In some cases, you won't be able to apply for a visa until you have a plane ticket, so if you need to sort out your visa here, don't wait to book your flight until the day before you leave.

You can get visas before you go, from the country's local diplomatic mission, or upon entry to the country – it all depends on your destination. Different types of visas may be available when entering the country via different means of transport. For example, you can get a visa on arrival if you fly into Oman but if you arrive by land you must have organised your visa in advance.

For those who do require visas, it's important to remember that, like yogurts, these have 'use-by' dates, and you'll be refused entry after the set closing date. Some visas start from the day you get the stamp in your passport, some from when you enter the country. Isabel Neil says:

I thought I was being really organised getting my visa early but then for various reasons I had to change the date I was flying there. My visa started from the day they stamped my passport, and by the time I got to Mali I only had two weeks left to run on it and had to pay for an extension.

An Israeli stamp in your passport can cause problems when trying to enter certain countries. You will be refused entry to Iran and most other Arab states (apart from Jordan and Egypt). Ask the Israeli officials to stamp your separate entry permit or even a loose sheet of paper instead and always check visa and passport regulations with the relevant embassies prior to departure. A Northern Cyprus stamp in your passport will not affect your visit to Greece, nor will it prevent you entering the Republic of Cyprus but customs officials will delete your stamp upon arrival. Again, play safe and get the officials to stamp a piece of paper instead of your passport.

There are essentially five types of visas (but each can have varying categories such as length of stay, or single or multiple entry). They are transit, tourist, business, student and working-holiday visas.

Transit visas are valid for only one or two days: you need these if you're just passing overland through a particular visa-hungry country but you don't intend to stay there.

You're most likely to be getting tourist visas – these allow you to stay for a restricted period, usually between 30 and 90 days – but don't panic, they can often be extended once you're in the country. A business visa is required if…you're visiting to do business.

If you are an EU national, you can work in any other member state for up to three months. After that, you need to apply for a residence permit (for which you need to show your passport and contract). It's best to check with the relevant embassy before travelling as countries differ.

If you plan to study overseas you will usually need a student visa. Conditions and application procedures vary from country to country. Check with the relevant embassy.

If you are under 31 and you want to work in Australia, you can apply for a Working Holiday Maker Visa. This allows a 12-month stay, although you can only work for any one employer for a maximum of three months. You can apply for this through the embassy, or online. To apply online, first get your passport and credit card, then log on to [W] www.immi.gov.au and

---

Home or Away?

Whether to get your visa while at home or when you arrive really depends on where you are going and your itinerary. It can be much less hassle to get a visa at home but then this might not be practical, or it might be just as easy to get one on the border. You have to check out the regulations for each country. If you wait until reaching the region, it can be time-consuming but also useful, as you can find out from other travellers about the current best way to get a visa.

go to Online Services (e-visas). The fee is AUD$160 fee (approx £60), £10 cheaper than the conventional method. Applications are processed in two days and there's no need for a bank statement or proof of funds. However, you won't have a paper visa in your passport and you have to go into the local DIMIA (Department of Immigration and Multicultural & Indigenous Affairs) office on your arrival in Australia to get your passport stamped.

British nationals travelling to the United States are eligible for the Visa Waiver Program which allows you to visit the US for business, pleasure or transit for up to 90 days, visa free. However, if you wish to stay longer, study or work you'll need to apply for a visa. The US does not usually issue work visas unless a specific offer of employment has been made. Contact the US embassy (**W** www.usembassy.org.uk) for application details.

PLANNING YOUR VISAS

Visa arrangements seem almost wilfully complex, and every country differs in the price, length of stay and extension requirements it offers. For example, a tourist visa for India costs £30 for British passport holders, is valid from the day of issue but for no longer than six months, and is not extendible. On the other hand, British passport holders do not need a visa for Canada provided you are not planning to stay more than six months, and you have sufficient funds for your stay and medical insurance.

Here's some stuff to check, mull over and provide smashing conversational gambits for people at parties:

- Can you get a visa at the border you are planning to cross?
- If so, how long is it valid? Will you get a longer stay and/or save money if you buy the visa before you go? Romania, for example, will give you a great six-month porker if you apply in your home country but only 30 days at the border.
- Do you get a different type of visa if you enter by different means of transport? Is it for a shorter stay and/or more expensive if you enter by train than plane?
- Will getting a visa at home fit in with your itinerary? Will you have to stick to a rigid plan to fit in with your pre-arranged visas?
- Is there diplomatic representation in your country? (If not, you may have to go to a visa or travel agent, or wait till you arrive in the region to apply for a visa.)
- Does the country demand the exact days and towns through which you plan to enter and leave the country? (If so it's probably best to arrange from a neighbouring country.)
- Is your visa activated on entry or on issue? In some countries visas are activated as soon as the stamp appears in your passport, so if you wait too long before you enter the country, you might be left with just a long weekend to explore the place.
- Can you extend your visa once you're in the country? If this is pretty straightforward, you might opt for a cheaper, shorter-stay visa at the border. If it's going to be difficult, consider a longer-term visa arranged outside the country.
- Are you going to want to enter the country several times? If so, a multiple-entry visa is the one for you. Depending on the country, it may be best to apply for these while at home.

Applying

No matter where you apply for your visa, you're likely to face short opening hours, long queues (especially in London) and stony-faced staff. To make this experience as close to a great day out as possible, consider the following:

- Phone in advance to find out the embassy's opening hours and requirements for costs, photographs, identification and documents. Leave yourself plenty of time – your visa may not be processed on your first attempt.

- Arrive early and be prepared to queue. Bring a book to help pass the time.
- Have all your documentation in order and ready to present to the clerk, including your planned entry and departure dates. Make sure you have the correct fee in the appropriate currency – those granite-featured staff sometimes can't or won't provide change.
- When you pick up your visa, make sure that the dates, length of stay and other details are all correct before you leave the embassy.
- Often you can apply for your visa online or by post. If you're in no hurry then these options can save you lots of time.

PHOTOS

Bring passport-size photographs with you. Many countries will require two to four photos to process a visa, and you may not be able to find a cheap, instant-photo booth in which to do your criminal imitation when you need one. Some countries also need these photos endorsed on the back. See the Documents section in the Packing chapter for more information on useful bits of paper to bring along.

Travel Insurance

Besides being another great conversational icebreaker for social occasions, travel insurance seems an annoying cost to factor in to your expenses, as, if all goes well, you shouldn't have to use it. But you mustn't miss this off your list of things to do. If you fall ill, have an accident or even get your camera stolen, you will be *really* sorry if you're not insured. It costs the equivalent of £30,000 to be airlifted in Thailand – now, just take a quiet moment to imagine covering this expense without insurance. Sam Flynn got his insurance as an afterthought at the airport:

Two weeks later I was so relieved I had taken that last-minute decision to get insurance as I had a car accident that meant a really expensive week in an American hospital.

You must have a policy that will at least partially stump up the costs of emergency medical evacuation (flight home), as well as treatment in the country you will be visiting. Some policies only cover evacuation to the nearest regional medical facility, rather than back to your home country. You also want to be covered for cancellation penalties on advance-purchase flights, theft or loss of your possessions, and the cost of extra plane tickets if you need to arrange an earlier flight because of emergency or illness.

Before arranging a travel insurance policy, check to see whether any personal medical insurance you already have (either private or government funded) applies internationally. If you are an EU national and you are suddenly taken ill or have an accident during a visit to any EU country plus Iceland, Liechtenstein and Norway, you can get free or reduced-cost emergency treatment. All you need is an E111 form. Pick one up from the Post Office. Check your home-contents insurance policy too, as it might cover your possessions. Then you can save a bit of cash by buying a policy without the possessions cover component.

Louise Treves suggests insuring credit/debit cards with a company such as Card Protection Plan (W www.cpp.co.uk), as she had in Mexico:

If you lose any of your cards, they will contact your banks and order new ones immediately. I thought I had lost one of my cards, so rang up CPP, who cancelled the card and arranged for a new one to be sent home. What was so reassuring was that after I had told CPP, they asked me if I was OK for money – they will help you out if you are in trouble.

BUYING YOUR INSURANCE

Once you have sorted out whether you are covered for anything already, you can begin to investigate policies. These are offered by travel agencies and student travel organisations, as well as by general insurance companies. And don't forget to scour the fine print before handing over your hard-earned cash.

If you're planning an extended trip, for work or study, consider whether you want full cover for the whole trip, or only while you're actually travelling. Remember that the longer your period of cover, the cheaper it becomes per month.

Here are some top insurance-buying tips:

- Ask your credit-card company what they cover – they may provide limited insurance if you pay for your airline ticket with their card. If the operator/travel agency doesn't deliver, you should be able to reclaim the payment.
- See whether you can extend your policy if you decide to stay away for longer than you anticipated, and whether you can get a cheaper family policy if you're travelling with a friend.
- Tot up the value of the possessions you're taking with you and then measure it up against the amount allowed on the policy. Most will have a stingy ceiling on the value of possessions to be insured, especially in the case of hi-tech items such as still cameras, and video equipment. A cunning notion is to leave details of such items (purchase receipts or valuations, serial numbers, make and model, and date of purchase) at home.
- Find out the 'excess' (an agreed amount of money you must cough up for each claim) that is imposed by almost all policies. Sometimes it may be cheaper and quicker for you to bite the bullet and pay all expenses out of your own pocket rather than making a claim.
- Check whether your policy obliges you to pay on the spot and redeem the money later, or whether the company will pay the providers direct. If you have to claim later, make sure you keep all documentation. If you have a medical problem, some policies will ask you to call back (reverse charges) to a centre in your home country where an immediate assessment of your problem will be made.
- Tell the insurance company about any pre-existing medical condition you may have. If you gloss over a problem in the quest for a cheaper deal, the company will have grounds not to honour your claims.
- Are you going to do any 'dangerous activities'? These, in the wonderful world of insurance, can include scuba diving, motorcycling, skiing, mountain climbing and even trekking. A locally acquired motorcycle licence may not be valid under some policies. Make sure you will be covered if your plans involve any such dicing with danger. This is where most travellers get caught out.

There are hundreds of insurance companies out there. Here are a few with packages aimed at backpackers and gappers:

- **Columbus Direct** (☎ 020-7375 0011; W www.columbusdirect.com). Offers 'The Backpacker', with several options, for example, it's cheaper if you are going to spend less than 10 days in the USA, and spend 75% of your time in Australia and New Zealand with only 25% or less in Asia. This costs £251 or £282 with sports cover. Worldwide cover costs £364, or £409 with sports cover. Columbus has a 10% discount for YHA members, and often has discount offers in the press so keep an eye out for these.
- **Endsleigh** (☎ 0800 028 3571; W www.endsleigh.co.uk). Has a range of different packages including 'Backpacker' (£251 for a year), 'Gap Year' (£339) and 'Extreme Activity' (£371).
- **STA** (☎ 0870 160 0599; W www.sta-travel.co.uk). Has various different covers depending on the area you are travelling to: 'Backpack' costs £180 and is aimed at those on a budget, 'Standard' costs £248, 'Premier', which covers a range of adventure activities and hazardous sports, costs £314 and Premier Inc USA, which does the same and includes the US, costs £341.

Know Before You Go

Around eight million of us leave home without travel insurance and around a quarter of us will have a serious problem when we're overseas. The Know Before You Go campaign, run by the Foreign & Commonwealth Office (FCO) provides information to help you prepare before you go overseas. It's fairly simple but basically they are calling on all travellers to:

- Get comprehensive travel insurance
- Check out the FCO travel advice before going away
- Be properly prepared for your trip

You can visit their website at **W** www.fco.gov.uk/knowbeforeyougo for more information. Also, they list the five locations where you're most likely to come to grief. They are: on the roads; at the beach; at hotels (falling off balconies or diving into the wrong end of the swimming pool); in remote locations; and on ski slopes.

Don't become one of their statistics!

Money & Costs

Planning Your Budget

You need to work out how much money you need. You might have already got a figure from the gap organisation that you are using, or you might have to do this all by yourself.

First you should work out the money you'll have to lay out on pre-departure costs such as flights, visas, immunisations, insurance and kit.

Next, look at the cost of living in the place you are headed. Lonely Planet provides an idea of daily costs in its guidebooks. Check these out and work out how much you might be able to afford to spend each day. You need also to allow for the occasional freak occurrence, and for some emergency or leeway money. It can affect how long you go away for, and what level of comfort you can aim at when you're there. That way, you can avoid splurging uncontrollably in the first three weeks and living off rice and peas for the last 10. You should also allow some money so that you can treat yourself from time to time. You'll need some comforts, and being able to have the odd fantastic meal or a big night out will make all the difference to your trip.

Then, get some weird organisational kicks. Use a computer to set up spreadsheets – this can help you divide up your money and work out exactly how much you can afford to spend on what, for example, accommodation, food and entertainment. Colour-code them, if you like.

PLANE TICKETS

Start your research by browsing the advertisements in travel magazines and major newspapers and contacting a few of the major airlines to see which routes they fly. Together with the websites listed in the previous chapter, you will get a good idea of the bargains available (always check the conditions and restrictions).

Buy your ticket as early as possible, preferably more than three months before you plan to depart. Most of the really good deals will be quickly snapped up, while others may require full payment well in advance of your departure date. You will also have plenty of time to arrange visas and immunisations (see the Passports, Tickets, Visas & Insurance and Health chapters for more details).

Check out a few travel agencies – a well-travelled, enthusiastic agent will be a big help. Sara Robertson says that:

I planned my itinerary on the net and then took it to a travel agent to see how it would work. It was a big help as I had some idea of the options available.

Here are a few tips on beating down those prices:

- Take a roundabout journey to reach your destination. Talented travel agents may get you a dirt-cheap fare which is made up of several flights (rather than one direct flight), transiting in different countries over a few days. This is a pretty exhausting way to travel, and you'll spend many empty hours in transit lounges but if you want to keep your costs down whatever the cost, this could have your name on it.
- Be flexible about your departure date. If you were hoping to head off in the peak season, have a rethink. Could you instead leave in the shoulder (February to March or October to November) or low season? Fares will be cheaper and special deals will be available.

- Be prepared to alter your itinerary to nab a particularly good deal. If you're set on visiting a place that doesn't come into your deal of the century, you can treat yourself to a separate sector air fare, or an even cheaper train, boat or bus ride.
- Once you've decided on a fare type, get a quote from your travel agent and take it to several other agencies to see if they can beat it. Some airlines have preferred agents and send their best deals through them, so different agencies don't necessarily have access to the same flights and deals. Also check out the payment options – most fares only require full payment around six weeks before departure, so many travel agents will request a small, non-refundable deposit to ensure that you're a serious buyer.

COURIER FLIGHTS

You can save cash by getting yourself on a courier flight (see the Passports, Tickets, Visas & Insurance chapter earlier). It can take some effort. They are limited in availability and you won't find them on rarefied routes like London–Bamako: main drags such as London-Hong Kong or -New York offer the best possibilities.

AIRPORT DEPARTURE TAX

Be aware that this pesky little number might not be included in your ticket, and that you might be required to pay it in cash at the airport. It's not usually a lot of money, around £15, but if you don't have the cash you won't be allowed to leave (not always a bad thing). To avoid this, check exactly which taxes are included in your ticket and keep a spare bit of local currency on you just in case.

VISAS

Don't miss these out when working out your expenses. They're sometimes free but if you've got a few hefty charges, they might mount up and take an unexpected bite out of your budget. For example, a tourist visa for Cuba costs £15, for Tanzania £38 and British nationals don't need one at all for Peru.

INSURANCE

Risking a bit of stuck-record syndrome, this is a necessity. Don't skimp on it – and this includes buying cheaper packages. Your cover should include health, emergency flights home, possessions and cancellation insurance. You can frequently get cheaper insurance if you are a student, or have a discount card (see Discount Cards later in this chapter). You might be able to save money if you are already covered by a policy at home, for example, if your possessions are covered by your home-contents policy, you can knock off the payment for that part (see the Passports, Tickets, Visas & Insurance chapter for costs).

IMMUNISATIONS

Most of these are free on the NHS in the UK but some are not. For example, yellow fever will set you back £40. Check with your GP or health centre for current fees.

KIT

For complete kit stuff, rummage through the recesses of the Packing chapter. Kit is another place you might be able to scrimp, for example, by borrowing it. Or you can cleverly use kit to save you money – for example, if you take a tent, you'll save on accommodation costs. A lightweight, two-man tent will set you back £200 but if you're using it for six months you'll be more than grateful that you spent the money.

If you're going to Asia or the US, you can save money by buying clothes there, where they are usually cheaper (not if you buy loads of them, mind).

Another cash-saving kit tip is, if travelling with a friend, share some items to save on space, money and weight (but make sure you're sharing these out fairly...).

Some bits of kit, however, are worth splashing out on, for example, you'll be really thankful for a good rucksack. For one that'll last expect to pay between £75 and £140, and a sturdy, comfortable pair of boots will cost you between £80 and £120. Believe me, it'll be worth the expense.

COST OF LIVING

It's going to be higher if you're hot-tailing it to Tokyo or making it in New York than if you're in Bangladesh. To check out the cost of living destination by destination, see the continent chapters in Part II. There are lots of ways you can keep a lid on your spending while away – the list below sheds some light on ways to be tight. And add up your daily spending to avoid any nasty surprises, especially if you're battering the plastic.

Accommodation

As previously pointed out, kipping under canvas can save you cash. It's also cheaper to rent accommodation if more of you are travelling or sharing rent. At many hotels and hostels, quads (four-person rooms) are cheaper than triples, which are cheaper than doubles. In some countries a triple room is cheaper than three dormitory beds. In many places it's always worth asking for a discount – you'll be surprised how hotels will reduce room rates if you ask.

Jenny Long travelled in Central America and Asia and says:

I would always take an overnight train or bus if I could – it saved time and the cost of a night's accommodation.

Food & Drink

Buy food from open-air markets and supermarkets. Most hostels and many camping grounds have kitchen facilities so you can cook your own meals. This works out even cheaper if shared between a group. If you don't like cooking, try to eat out on the cheap – student and self-serve cafés are a good bet. Avoid restaurants catering to tourists (they're always overpriced) and instead seek out the places where locals eat. If you do eat at a restaurant, ask to see a menu with prices and find out if there are surcharges (for example, for sitting at a table – it's often cheaper sitting at the bar, or at outdoor seating). Take a picnic lunch, particularly if you're going sightseeing – touristy areas will mean pricier places to eat.

Going veggie will also work out cheaper. If you're drinking a lot of bottled water, purifying your own will save money, as well as being kinder to the embattled environment (see the Safe Drinking Water section in the Health chapter).

Sightseeing

In lots of places, museums and galleries are free or cheaper on certain days or at certain times of day. Where there is an admission fee, your student or discount card will almost always get you a discount.

Entertainment

Look out for specials at bars or nightclubs, or for places with no cover charge...don't overdo it though. Clubs and bars are cheaper midweek, and many cities have cheap days for cinemas too. Concerts and cultural events are often free; ask at the tourist office and check around town for fliers and posters.

Shopping

Some things cost less if you buy them abroad – it depends where you're going. If you're travelling almost anywhere (except perhaps Japan and Hong Kong) outside Europe, toiletries, clothes and shoes are usually cheaper. So you could, in principle, save by buying on arrival – particularly items such as sandals. What's more *likely* to happen is that you'll take what you need, then buy more stuff when you're there. Joanne Hollingsworth worked and travelled in West Africa:

Check out the price of something in a few shops before you buy, or ask a few local people what the cost should be to get a rough idea of what to aim for before you start to bargain.

Laundry

Handwash your clothes – to save laundry costs get busy in the sink.

Transport

Deign to take the bus – even though the prospect can be daunting, you'll save crisp notes by avoiding taxis. Or you can always walk – it's cheap! It's fun! It's one of the best ways to appreciate a place!

Countryside

Prices are always lower in the sticks.

Communication

If you can use them, phonecards often work out cheaper. Also make international calls during off-peak times (usually evenings and weekends). Better still, use email. If you only want to check your email, look for a cybercafé that charges by the minute or in 15-minute blocks.

ACTIVITIES

If you want to take part in an expensive activity such as diving or skiing, probably the best way to do this on a budget is to look for some work in that kind of area. You might want to apply to do a season as chalet or hotel staff or as an au pair, which'll give you a free lift pass and a few hours skiing a day. Adam Cameron worked as a ticket validator:

I got about four hours skiing a day, and enough money to cover my living costs.

Or if you want to get some more serious skiing in, take a ski-instructor's course – it might be more expensive but you'll have a qualification that will mean many more years of fun in the white stuff.

In big diving centres in Australia, Egypt, Malaysia, Thailand etc there are jobs in the industry, and you might get free diving lessons thrown in. Or you can train as a dive instructor on a programme that will offer you work once you have finished. A way to get work in parts of Asia is to get your dive master qualification and then work in a dive shop in one of the diving hotspots. It's highly competitive though; see the PADI website at **W** www .padi.com for more information.

Another way to save money on diving lessons is to do your PADI course before you go – searching for old plasters in your local swimming pool can prove a lot cheaper than taking the test in more exotic locations. And when you get there you won't have to be stuck in a classroom learning your PADI theory while yearning to be out in the sun. See the Courses and Casual/Seasonal Work chapters for more ideas on earning while you travel.

Discount Cards

You can save packets of money by getting a discount card or two. A student card allows you reduced entry to many tourist sites, for example, half-price entry to the Pyramids at Giza (Egypt), as well as commission-free exchange in some places. It's always worth asking if you'll get a discount.

The Youth Hostel Association (YHA) issues cards that get you hostel discounts. Hostelling International (W www.iyhf.org) has information on cards, or you can contact the YHA for more information.

UK

HI (☎ 028-903 15435, fax 028-904 39699; e info@hini.org.uk; W www.hini.org.uk; 22 Donegall Rd, Belfast BT12 5JN) £10

YHA of England & Wales (☎ 0870 770 8868, fax 0870 770 6127; e customerservices @yha.org.uk; W www.yha.org.uk; Trevelyan House, Dimple Rd, Matlock, Derbyshire DE4 3YH) £13.50

Scottish YHA (☎ 01786-891400, fax 01786-891333; e info@syha.org.u; W www.syha .org.uk; 7 Glebe Crescent, Stirling FK8 2JA) £6

Ireland

An Óige (Irish YHA; ☎ 01-830 4555; e anoige@iol.ie; W www.irelandyha.org; 61 Mountjoy St, Dublin 7) £25

The International Student Identity Card (ISIC) is the Elvis of student cards. It qualifies the holder for discounts on airline tickets, rail passes, accommodation, shopping and entrance to museums and cultural events. Although the availability and level of discounts varies from country to country, it can save you a small fortune in Europe. The ISIC is available only to full-time students (there is no age limit) and is issued by accredited travel agencies (such as STA) through the International Student Travel Confederation (ISTC; W www .isic.org/index.htm). You'll need to prove you're a full-time student, and it costs £7 from STA.

Because of the proliferation of fakes (like the King, the ISIC has lots of imitators) that can be picked up in Asia and the Middle East, it's wise to carry your home student card as supplementary proof. If you want to get a student discount from an airline, you may need a letter of proof from your home school or university, so get one and make photocopies before you go.

The International Youth Travel Card (IYTC) is more of a Barry White, not as widely recognised but still pretty good. Non-students under the age of 25 can take advantage of this one. It is also issued by ISTC, costs £7 from STA, and has similar benefits.

The Euro<26 Card is accepted in 31 European countries and is available to travellers aged under 26. Wherever the card is issued, it carries the Euro<26 logo, which marks the places offering advantages and discounts. Check W www.euro26.org, or order it in the UK via W www.youthinformation.com.

Getting Your Cash

Now you've worked out roughly how much your gap year is going to cost, all you need to do next is find the money (top tip: it doesn't grow on trees).

SAVING UP

The first option is to work. Jobs such as waiting tables or bar work, working in shops or factories are usually pretty easy to get. And the more hours you work, the less time you have to squander the money. Night shifts can be good in this way too – not only do you earn a higher wage in the small hours but also usually the only shops open when you're awake are all-night garages – so unless you develop a voracious passion for soggy pasties, your savings are safe. Justin Everett worked as a chauffeur during his summer holiday:

The long hours, seven days a week meant I never got a chance to spend any money, and I got a big tip at the end.

You can get a kick out of having a proper job and doing the adult thing: especially if you know it's not for good.

And if your mind is getting thoroughly numbed, you can get through it by reminding yourself of your aim and dreaming of your plans laid out for the more-exciting portion of your gap year. Isobel Franks saved money to do a building project in Argentina:

I had a rubbish job. I packed football kits into boxes. I was also given some money by my church and I wrote to some Grant Awarding Trusts. I don't think money issues should put anyone off because there are so many ways you can raise it.

Join a few temping agencies – it's often easy to pick up clerical or reception work. If you're a graduate, you may be able to get a more skilled job that will bring in more money. If you can get something relevant to your degree – so much the better. Even if you can't, the office administration jobs you'll get will be better quality (you'll make the tea *and* answer the phone).

You'll need to cut out extravagances – the quickest way to spend your money is by going out drinking, eating out and shopping. This doesn't mean you have to stay in all the time but be very careful how much you spend if you do venture into a social situation. Allow yourself a certain amount of money and then go home when it's spent. Find things to do in the evening that don't involve spending money – use your imagination. If you have a weakness for shopping – avoid shops. Keeping your goal in mind and building up that inviting glittering pile will help you deal with being broke. Quite a few of your friends should be in the same boat, so why not all pitch in and rent a video to watch rather than go to the cinema, or take turns to cook each other meals rather than go out to eat. Babysitting and bar work are ideal ways of keeping you from spending money in the evenings.

A good ruse is to open a bank account especially for your going-away fund, and set up standing orders so that you feel restricted about your saving.

FUNDRAISING

Think about what you like doing and whether there's a way you can raise money doing it. This way, you'll get more of a kick out of it. If you like drinking and dancing – how about a sponsored clubnight? If you like clothes – why not design and sell T-shirts?

Other things you could do include washing cars, walking dogs, selling home-made cakes and biscuits, or doing gardening.

Collect all the junk you can from friends and relatives and sell it at a car-boot sale – you'll not only raise money but also be amazed at the tat people will buy. You could also auction stuff on eBay at **W** www.ebay.co.uk – you can sell almost anything on here – John Freyer, an American artist, auctioned everything he owned on the site as an experiment, from half-full packets of tacos to his sideburns.

If you are doing a project or a placement, or some kind of voluntary work, you can use many more methods than those who are simply going to backpack. Often people do a job alongside a bit of fundraising to get their pot of money together.

Gap-year organisations such as Raleigh International, GAP Activity Projects or Project Trust will give you lots of fundraising ideas, and arrange large-scale sponsored events to raise money. Louise Treves went away with Raleigh, as well as on projects in Italy and travelling in Mexico, and raised the money in a variety of ways:

It's easier once you get going. I worked in a clothes shop for six months. Living at home was brilliant for my finances (though not so good for my parents). Raleigh also organised a massive sponsored walk around Richmond Park. I wrote to everyone I could think of, businesses, friends, relatives and so on, and made sure I sent round an update letter afterwards. A friend of mine buys jewellery in India, so she sold me some at trade prices and I sold it on at profit at school – timing is important for something like that – people tend to be a bit more generous at Christmas, especially if you're giving them present ideas.

Any event you do, make sure it's well publicised: put up posters and give out leaflets. Clearly set out why you want the money, giving details of your project.

From parachute jumps to trampolining to pie-eating in a bath of jelly, the sponsored world is your oyster. If you do something original, you will attract more attention.

You could auction your time – offering a few hours for a fee. Organise a concert, hold a fashion show or set up a cinema night. If you can think of an original way to pitch your mission, this'll capture people's imagination and attract attention. Sian Robertson hired a cinema for a private screening of *Romancing the Stone* to raise money for her trip with Raleigh to Costa Rica and Nicaragua, positioning herself as a young Kathleen Turner type!

A good way to raise money is a party – get a venue for free (many places will do this as they'll make lots of money on the bar – they might even give you a cut if they feel it's for a good cause), charge a fee to get in, and once you have your guests trapped in an alcoholic, generous-spirited haze, hit them with a raffle.

Get your friends and relatives to help. Catherine Bruzzone has been through the fundraising process with two daughters:

It was pretty exhausting for all of us, especially as it was the A-Level year but now (looking back!) it was enjoyable and represented the last year our daughters were fully part of the family. So it was good that we could all work together and have happy memories of the parties, sponsored cycle rides, car boot sales etc.

If you ask for money from relatives or businesses, offer to give something in return, for example, supplying regular reports about the project, working for the company for a week for a donation, or setting up an exhibition about it when you get back. It's also worth approaching your old school and local organisations. Finola Collins worked to raise some of the money she needed:

I also got sponsorship from various local companies, and the local council. When I got back I gave a talk about my experience to the council to say thanks for their support.

You could also ask shops and businesses to donate equipment, either to use on the road, or to auction or raffle.

Most large companies have philanthropic funds – swilling around with money for worthy causes – and they may pay out if you approach them with the right sort of project. Try looking up a company's website and searching for key words such as 'community' to find out what kind of projects they might sponsor. You could also consult the *Directory of Grantmaking Trusts*, which lists companies that give out funds for projects, and write to any appropriate ones (your local library should hold a copy or will help you track one down – at £80 it's rather expensive to buy). Or look up **W** www.charitiesdirect.com or **W** www .caritasdata.co.uk. But be warned that these rarely sponsor individuals, so you might not hit gold. From such letters you might expect about a one in 20 success rate. When sending them off, avoid the mass-mailout look, it won't do you any favours.

Four French ex-students set out to travel to every continent recording world music for their post-university gap-year 'L'Odyssée de Musiques'. The project was sponsored by various companies with cash and equipment to the value of €100,000. You can check out how it was spent at **W** www.2001-odyssee.net. Cedric Robion says:

You need to present a project that will reflect well on the company by their association. The hardest part is getting the first sponsor – once you have the first, others tend to follow suit. Ask your first sponsor for their address book: they will suggest who else to approach, as it's in their interest that you succeed.

Some schools and universities have funds set aside for sponsoring appropriate projects – for example, if you are going to study or research something that is related to your degree. Some organisations will help fund study or voluntary work abroad (see Part III for information). Francesca Gowing found that she was able to take advantage of a charitable donations system:

Because Raleigh International is a registered charity my dad was able to match every pound I raised with the equivalent value via the pound for a pound scheme for donations to charity at his work. This effectively halved the total amount I had to raise, £3200.

Various gap-year organisations have bursary schemes to help out candidates without funds. For example, Gap Activity Projects (GAP) has such a scheme: for details contact Hatty Masser (**☎** 0118-956 2921; **e** hmasser@gap.org.uk).

LOANS

A loan may seem like the easiest solution to your cash conundrum. But think carefully about it. Do you want to start college with a loan hanging over your head from a gap year? Especially if you'll probably have to get a student loan to fund your college years anyway. And if you're leaving college, do you want to take out yet another loan? An additional consideration is that, however precise your planning, you might find yourself skint at some point and have to apply for a loan – not good if you've raised all your money via a loan in the first place.

If you want to do some vocational education at home or abroad, you can apply for a career-development loan – but you must be a UK citizen. This will pay a large proportion of your course fees, and your living expenses if you're studying full time. Call ☎ 0800 585505, or check the fine print at Ⓦ www.lifelonglearning.co.uk.

Richard Satchell used loans to fund his post-university gap year:

One advantage of being a graduate is that you can get credit easier than as an 18-year-old. With my graduate job in place, I was both more willing and able to take loans to fund a year off.

The best place to find a loan is through your bank or building society. Don't go to private moneylenders – they often charge thumbscrew rates of interest. Some schools and universities have loan schemes too – check these out. When choosing your loan, think about how large your repayments will be, how long you will have to pay them, and how you will manage your repayments.

You could also approach your parents for a loan: you'll need to do this professionally though, to be fair on both parties and avoid it proving problematic. Draw up an agreement of the amount you need, when you'll pay it back, and what interest you'll give them.

WORKING ON THE ROAD
If you don't save before you go, then you can work while you're there. If you have a good balance of spending and earning, you should end up breaking even, or even coming out richer. See Work your Route in Part III for information and inspiration about what you might do, as well as the Proper Jobs and Casual/Seasonal Work chapters.

Carrying Money
TRAVELLERS CHEQUES
Travellers cheques are still tops when it comes to carrying your money while abroad. If they get lost or stolen, they'll be replaced by the issuing bank within a few days. In many places, you'll get better exchange rates for travellers cheques than for cash.

To help with replacement if your cheques go astray, always keep the purchase agreement of the cheques with you and record the serial numbers of the cheques as you cash them, so you can tell the bank which ones are missing. Keep your receipt, list of cashed cheques and the company's emergency contact number in a separate place, so that they are not lost or stolen along with the cheques.

In most places, US dollar travellers cheques issued by American Express (AmEx) or Thomas Cook are the most commonly accepted. Other major banks and credit card companies issue travellers cheques but you may have trouble changing these in the back of beyond. It's a good idea to carry large-denomination cheques (say US$100 or US$50) since some places charge a per-cheque cashing fee and this can really add up if you're constantly cashing smaller cheques (though a few smaller cheques are handy for the last few days of your trip). However, anything greater than US$100 is likely to leave you with a nerve-racking amount of cash bulking out your money belt.

CREDIT CARDS
Credit cards are useful, although how useful depends on your destination – check this out before you go. Many budget travellers use them to get cash advances from local banks. However, in lots of places you can't get cash advances or it'll take ages to do so. Your best bet is to use an unstoppable combination of credit cards and travellers cheques. Credit cards are also invaluable in an emergency, so it's definitely worth having one: but just be aware of the pitfalls.

The credit card catch is that by using them you end up in debt. On most cards, including Visa and MasterCard, if you don't pay the account in full each month, you'll be charged interest and the rates are usually exorbitant. You can arrange a standing order with your bank and credit-card company to avoid this.

You can also use credit cards to pay for more expensive items such as plane tickets, and the occasional splurge. However, take care, plastic money can zoom through your fingers much quicker than the paper stuff as it doesn't seem quite as real. Daisy Poppy ran into trouble in India:

My dad made me take an MX card with me so that I could use it to get out of trouble. In fact, it ended up landing me in trouble because I fell for one of those carpet scams. If I hadn't had a credit card, I couldn't have afforded to buy the carpets but because I did I signed over all my money and lost out big time.

MasterCard and Visa are most commonly accepted and handy for cash advances. Get both cards if possible.

With your PIN number, you can withdraw cash from ATMs (automatic teller machines) in many countries. Check the back of your card to see if it matches any of the network stickers displayed on the ATM in question. You can search for ATMs that accept Visa or MasterCard on W www.mastercard.com/cardholderservices/atm or W www.visa.com/globalgateway.

Finally, always check the invoice and the receipt when you buy something with a credit card, and carefully check your account statement when you get home. Credit-card fraud is on the increase.

DEBIT CARDS

With a debit card, the money you spend or withdraw comes straight from your account. If you don't have enough money, you can't make the transaction. Debit cards can be used to withdraw cash from ATMs and to make purchases at some stores – depending on the country. If you have a MasterCard or Visa debit card, you can search for ATMs using the websites included in the Credit Cards section earlier.

CASH

Obviously, you don't want to carry a big wad around – if it's stolen or lost you'll never see it again. But it's a good idea to keep some cash on you. You will inevitably find places that only exchange cash; you can change a small denomination of cash when you don't want to cash a big travellers cheque, and some countries use foreign notes as their main source of exchange.

Many travellers carry a few hundred dollars in cash. Keep your notes in a very safe place, perhaps carrying some in your money belt and stashing some away as emergency money (for example, inside a backpack frame). If you are planning to spend a long time in countries that use US cash as their main currency, you probably won't need to bring as much cash from home but can change travellers cheques after you arrive.

INTERNATIONAL MONEY TRANSFERS

If you're going to be on the road for a while and don't want to carry too much money at the start of your trip, or if you run out of money while on the road, you can have money sent by wire from your home country to a local bank.

If you arrange a transfer, you will have to wait a few days for it to clear. You'll usually be given your money in local currency, either as cash or travellers cheques. Bring with you the details of your home bank account (account number, branch number, address and telephone number) to speed up the process. Most banks charge a relatively hefty fee for wiring money, so don't do it unless you really have to.

If you intend to spend a lot of time in a particular country, enquire with your bank about having money transferred directly into an account in a bank of that country. Alternatively, you can open an account when you arrive (you'll need to provide a local address and have appropriate ID) and have the money wired over.

Running Out of Money

This is something none of us likes to think about but it is a real possibility, so it helps to be prepared. If you realise you are getting skint, do something before you go flat broke, or you'll have no money to make arrangements for more. If the worst comes to the worst, you may be able to borrow money from a fellow traveller. Daniel Stevens was rescued by a kind hotelier:

I had run out of money and just needed to get to a big city so that I could make arrangements to get home or be wired some more. I told the hotel owner about my problem and he lent me the money for my ticket.

You could also sell a few possessions to boost your funds – from jewellery to guidebooks. Talented broke gappers could try busking or selling artwork to get by. Other things to consider are babysitting, washing up, hair braiding or renting out your equipment (such as your tent, bike or sleeping bag). If you take some hair clippers with you, you can offer handy homestyle hair cuts. Writing letters or emails for local people may be worth a try, or offering computer training or English lessons. Fiona Lewis ran out of cash in Hong Kong:

Treat Yourself

Perhaps you've just been on a bus for the last 24 hours and you're so tired you want to cry. Maybe you've got a high fever and a dire case of diarrhoea. Or maybe you're just sick of grotty guesthouses and grim food. Whatever the case, there are times when you should forget about the money and give yourself a treat. Splurging on nights out, comfy hotel rooms or cross-town taxi rides can make the difference between losing it or having a great trip. If you need a break, heed the call, even if it means shocking your pocket. It's better to spend the money and stay well than to save your way to becoming a shadow of your former self.

But you don't have to limit treats to those times when you're feeling tired or sick. If you're not prepared to spend the money, how will you enjoy the experience? Emily Simms dithered between taking a boat along the Niger to Timbuktu or the cheaper bus option and was so pleased to spend the extra money:

It was an extraordinary journey – the river is edged by sand dunes and we kept seeing hippos. I would have really missed out if I had taken the bus, and saved about £5.

Don't choke the life out of your trip. You need to preserve your sanity and health as much as your money, and you will probably have a far more enjoyable time if you're not too hard on yourself. Budget travel shouldn't be an endurance contest – there's no moral superiority in surviving on the least money, so plan your budget with the occasional treat in mind.

I was sleeping on the floor of an acquaintance and had almost run out of cash. I borrowed a pager, put up notices and set myself up as a private English tutor. I saved enough to get to Japan, where I'm now a full-time teacher.

Some travellers work in exchange for food and accommodation, like Jay Reynolds who ran low on funds in Malaysia:

I'd stayed on this island for a few weeks and got friendly with the guesthouse owner. His wife was expecting a baby, so he wanted to spend some time on the mainland, so we arranged that I would spend a couple of months looking after his business – cleaning and cooking for the guests in return for my keep.

If none of your entrepreneurial ventures pan out, there are two ways to have money sent from home. The first is an international money transfer (see earlier). The second is through a service like Western Union, which specialises in sending cash to all parts of the world. To receive cash this way, you'll have to arrange for someone in your home country to take cash to one of their offices. This is a convenient service, though the rates are significantly higher than those charged by banks for international money transfers. For more information, call Western Union (☎ 0800 833833; Ⓦ www.westernunion.com). Another option if you're running out of money is to find work. For inspiration, see Part III.

Changing Money

Sorting your cash out is one of those little chores that you'll have to attend to every few days or weeks.

Before you change money, check in your guidebook or ask locals or other travellers where the best place is to go. In some countries, banks are the best or only places to change money, while in others you'd be a crazy son-of-a-gun not to use a moneychanger. The latter is usually quicker. Hotels usually offer poor exchange rates and high commissions but can be a godsend when all the good places are closed. Check a local newspaper for the official exchange rate, and compare the exchange rates and commission fees of several places before deciding where to change. You may have to do some calculations here, as the rate, and the commission, will vary from place to place. Be sure to ask when cashing travellers cheques if the commission is per cheque or per transaction.

Save the foreign-exchange certificates every time you change money to prove you've exchanged your money legally. Though you will rarely be asked to produce receipts for this purpose, some countries may request the foreign-exchange certificates to reconvert leftover local currency.

In some countries, it's possible to change money on the black market, though this is illegal and may leave you vulnerable to arrest or bribery attempts. If you're ripped off, you'll have no legal recourse, and all sorts of scams exist designed specifically to short-change you. Ask other travellers for advice about a trustworthy person to change money with, and keep your wits about you.

You'll usually get the best exchange rates in large cities, so change your money before heading to the outback.

Try not to change at border crossings, where exchange rates are often very low, or change just enough to get you to a major city. In some countries, airports offer poor exchange rates, though moneychangers at some airports will offer the same rates as those in the city centre.

Each time you change money at a moneychanger or bank, you will be given a slip with the details of the transaction to sign. Inspect it carefully. If anything is amiss, you can stop the transaction immediately.

Before you sign a travellers cheque, make completely sure that the changer will accept it, as you'll find the signed cheque difficult to change elsewhere.

If you're using a credit card for a cash advance, shop around for the best rates and commission fees. Also, check that the figures are correct on the credit card slip before you sign it.

Always count the bills carefully after you change your money, cash a travellers cheque or get a cash advance to ensure you haven't been short-changed – it pays to be particularly vigilant when you are changing money the first few times and are unfamiliar with currency notes.

Be super cautious when changing money. This is one of the few times when you'll get your money belt out in public; you'll be particularly vulnerable at street-side money-changers. Keep everything together and where you can see it, and check that you've got everything before walking away from the counter. Keep in mind, too, that most people are robbed on the day they change money. This is no unhappy coincidence – thieves hang around banks, bureaux de change, ATMs and so on, tail doshed-up travellers and look for the opportunity to relieve them of said dosh.

Don't change a large-denomination bill or travellers cheque just before leaving a country as you'll lose on commissions and exchange rates when you reconvert unspent money. Some currencies are not convertible outside the country, so you'll have the hassle of reconverting just before you leave.

Bargaining

If you've grown up in the UK, you might've only had to haggle down a late-night taxi fare, not the best preparation for going up against people who have been at it their whole lives. You'll save yourself a lot of anguish by accepting that you'll pay more than the locals. The best you can hope for is a price reasonably close to that. There's nothing more pathetic than those

---

Obsessed with Haggling

Haggling is not a vicious contest. Stop to think as you try to beat someone down and walk away in disgust as you couldn't knock off that final...10p? It's small change to you but a significant sum of money to the vendor.

Many countries across the world lack government-funded social-security systems and charity-run support services and it's every person for themselves – especially in the cities where they might be separated from the family or village-based networks that would normally look after them during difficult times.

Compared with this, even the poorest foreign visitor is loaded. Your clothes, backpack, watch, personal stereo and spending on food, accommodation and souvenirs mark you as a person of wealth. The fact that you have done time at the local pork-pie factory to get here is not going to register with the locals. The mere fact that you can afford to go abroad or take any time off means you are in a different league.

The envy this can produce is often aggravated by the never-ending flow of tourists (who are often demanding, rude and heedless of local customs) and the changes that the travel industry works on local cultures, from inappropriate redevelopment to the breakdown of family and social values. Your gap year might be doing wonders for your confidence and self-esteem but take time to think about what you are doing for your destination.

Being 'ripped off' can leave you feeling a noodle, especially if the amount is significant, but beware of adopting a siege mentality. There is, as yet, no awards system for the traveller who got by on the least money. Keep it in perspective and empathise with the other person's circumstances. They'll be happier and you'll maintain a steadier blood pressure.

travellers who are obsessed by paying only the 'local price', whose trip has been reduced to a series of bitter and humourless head-to-heads. You should check out where it's appropriate to bargain – don't try it at a US gas station or the Louvre ticket office, for example – this will be clear in your guidebook. There are also lots of implicit bargaining rules.

Most important is to conduct the procedure in a friendly, polite, good-natured way – getting angry won't make it any cheaper, is offensive and will usually simply bring the negotiations to a halt. Also, never offer a price unless you're willing to go through with the transaction if that price is accepted – bargaining for sport is cruel (the vendors are trying to earn a living) and can even lead to violence.

And never lose a sense of how much money you're haggling over. You should pay what's fair: don't take advantage of poor and desperate traders by forcing them to sell too low.

Tipping

To tip or not to tip varies from country to country, so you'll have to read up on and adjust how you splash out your 10%, according to your destination. In many countries a discretionary service charge will be added to your bill (check to see whether it has), and porters and guides often expect a tip wherever you are. In most circumstances tipping is up to you. If you feel that someone has done you a good service, then leave them some cash. If service has been lousy then skip the tip.

Packing

That's Not My Bag

If you're going to be a backpacker, you'll need a backpack. Snails aren't stupid: it's the most practical way to carry stuff, even if you're not going to be constantly on the move. It's worth buying a good one. You'll be eternally grateful that it's comfortable, that it doesn't fall apart and that you can manage it on your back, rather than dragging it, cursing, along the street. And you'll use it over and over now you've developed these itchy feet.

HOW TO CHOOSE IT

You have two main choices – toploaders and travel packs.

Toploaders

Toploaders tend to be more comfortable, hardwearing and watertight than travel packs (fewer seams) but less convenient. It's a secret backpack law that anything you need will be at the bottom. If you plan to do a lot of mountain climbing or rafting, the comfort and waterproofing qualities will win you over. If, however, you're going to stay mostly in hostels or homestays, then your dream date will be the travel pack.

Travel Packs

The travel pack's not-so-secret weapon is the zip that runs all the way around the edge and top, allowing you to open up the main compartment completely and your belongings to explode colourfully all over your room. Easy to pack, easy to unpack. The time and frustration it will save you is almost enough to have you digging out your credit card, and listen to this: it has other advantages too. A zippered flap (which is stowed at the base of the back) can be used to hide and protect the harness when necessary. A travel pack also has side handles and a detachable shoulder strap, making it easy to carry in cramped spaces. It also looks more respectable if you have to deal with officialdom, and is easier to lock up.

Having decided which type to go for, now ask yourself:

- **How big is it?** Resist the temptation to buy the biggest pack in the shop – it will probably be an equally big pain, and you won't ever use all that space. Have a good idea of what you plan to take with you, and then buy the smallest pack possible. You can always post things home. A peanut-sized pack will make you travel light. A 60L pack will fit enough equipment, clothes and obligatory souvenir wallhangings for a three-month trip; if you're carrying a tent you might want to go for a slightly more voluminous version.
- **How strong is it?** Look for durable material and double stitching at weight-bearing places. Also ensure the zippers are strong. If the pack looks lightweight or flimsy, surge upmarket.
- **How comfy do I feel?** Good packs will be amply padded at the shoulders and hips, as well as lightly padded down the back. The hip pads are the most important as the bulk of the weight is carried there, not on the shoulders.
- **Does my back look big in this?** Always try on your pack before buying it. Put something heavy in it to see how it feels. Most decent packs have an adjustable internal frame that you can fit to the length of your back. Also keep an eye on the shape of the back. If it's too tall, you might stagger about; too wide and you'll be whacking people left and right. Most companies now have male- and female-specific models too.

- **Does it have lots of handy bits?** We're talking compartments. A bottom section is ideal for your sleeping bag or laundry and will also protect more fragile items in the main compartment, while front and side pockets are good for things you need regularly such as toiletries, water-proof gear and torch. Many packs include a zip-off daypack (see Daypacks later). Loops are useful as tie-down straps for carrying a sleeping bag, sweater or tent outside your pack.

Prices start at around £80 and disappear into the stratosphere for a super-duper pack – so expensive you wouldn't want to take it anywhere, just build it a shrine. You'll need to factor your pack price into your budget (see Money & Costs chapter).

DAYPACKS
During the day, you'll want a little bag to carry all those things you need: camera, guide-book, map, water bottle, sunscreen etc. Assuming you're taking the daypack route, when assessing candidates for this challenging, yet rewarding role, make sure the shoulder straps and back section are padded and that the fabric is strong and durable. Let's talk pockets again: they make smaller items easier to store and find; a side pocket for your water bottle is particularly useful.

Some backpacks have detachable daypacks. However, these are often too small, so make sure it will take more than your toothbrush. An overstuffed daypack is a pain to carry, as it lacks a solid frame, and will end up tiring your shoulders and back.

One more thing: if you plan to reconnect your daypack to your main pack when travelling long distances, use padlocks and remember to remove fragile or valuable items.

A daypack will set you back from around £15 and is another cost to add to your list (see Money & Costs chapter).

Where to Buy It
Recognised brands Karrimor (W www.karrimor.co.uk), Berghaus (W www.berghaus.com), Lowe Alpine (W www.lowealpine.com) and Fairydown (W www.fairydown.co.uk) all have ergonomic designs and are made from futuristic fabrics, which will protect your stuff from showers (if not a downpour) and allow your skin to breathe during long-distance walks.

In the UK you can immerse yourself in equipment at W www.yhaadventure.com, W www .gearzone.co.uk, W www.outdoorgear.co.uk, W www.travelwithcare.co.uk or W www.inter hike.com. The best thing to do when actually buying is to visit a store and have a 'fitting'. YHA Adventure have stores in 19 locations throughout England and Wales, Itchy Feet have stores in Bath and London (Wardour St), and Blacks (W www.blacks.co.uk) have 68 stores in Britain. Pop onto their website to find the one nearest you.

You can buy most of the 'Useful Kit' items listed below from these places too, as well as loads of other stuff you didn't know you needed.

Useful Kit
- **Money belt** A money belt is vital – it's the safest way to carry your cash, travellers cheques, credit/debit cards, passport, ticket and other important items. You want one that can be worn unobtrusively beneath whatever you're wearing. Keeping your stuff in a bumbag or other-wise exposed outside your clothes is like wearing a sign saying 'Here are my valuables, please rob me.'

  The most common types are worn either around the waist or the neck. Neither design is particularly easy to access, so don't keep your ready cash in it or you'll be delving under your clothes every five minutes and attracting attention. Think about the fabric too. Plastic sweats, while leather is heavy and will get stinky. Cotton is the best bet as it's washable and most comfortable. If you use a cotton money belt, put your ticket, passport and other documents in a plastic bag so they don't get damaged by sweat.

Check out the belt's clasp or attachment. You'll want to keep your money belt secure at all times. Finally, consider taking a waterproof container for your documents and money that you can wear when swimming, diving or snorkelling.

- **Address book** To keep in touch with friends and family, plus all the people you'll meet.
- **Alarm clock** OK, it may be your year off but you don't want to miss your flight/bus/train. Travel alarm clocks are tough, light and cheap. Be warned, they're also very popular with light-fingered hostel-dwelling travellers.
- **Batteries** Bring spares for all your equipment (camera, personal stereo, alarm clock, torch etc) and put new batteries in each before you depart.
- **Contraception** Condoms can be found in most countries but the quality can be variable depending on where you are (always check the use-by date). It's easier to bring a supply with you. If you use the pill, then bring enough to cover your whole trip as it is difficult to get in many countries.
- **Eye wear** Sunglasses are indispensable for both comfort and protection. If you wear prescription glasses or contact lenses, take the prescription with you, along with extras such as a case and contact-lens solution. Contact-lens wearers should also take a supply of dailies – really useful in an emergency.
- **Guidebooks, maps and phrasebooks** Fran Neames suggests:

  It was brilliant having a world map with me on my round-the-world trip. If ever in doubt or for want of anything else to chat about, I'd get the map out and local people would pore over it for ages.

- **Padlocks and a chain** Apart from securing your backpack, you can use a padlock to fasten the door of your hotel room and give your belongings extra security. Chains are useful for attaching your backpack to the roof rack of a bus or the luggage rack on trains.
- **Pocketknife** A Swiss army knife (or good-quality equivalent) has loads of useful tools: scissors, bottle opener, can opener, straight blade and all those strange ones that you're not sure what they do (remember not to keep this in your inflight luggage, as it'll be confiscated).
- **Sunscreen** You may be going to spend long hours in the sun and, apart from the long-term risk of melanoma, sunburn is painful and shameful. A moisturiser with sunscreen included will save some doubling up.
- **Tampons or pads** Depending on your destination, these might be hard to find.
- **Toilet paper** Never leave home without it! Always keep a stash in your daypack.
- **Toiletries** Most items are widely available – and often may be cheaper – but take any speciality products with you.
- **Torch** Most helpful to find stuff late at night in a dorm or in your hotel room, to avoid mishaps in outside toilets in the dead of night, or if the electricity packs it in. It's also handy for exploring caves and ruins. The Penlite range is almost indestructible. Consider a miner-style lamp that straps to your forehead and frees up both your hands (and is vaguely less comic than light-up slippers).
- **Towel** For swimming, as well as for showers in budget places (not all will supply one, or at least one you'd want to use). A beach towel will take ages to dry, take up lots of space, weigh a tonne and get whiffy. A quick-drying travel towel (made from a chamois-like material or one of the new microfibres) is OK. Tom Grieves travelled around Central America and suggests taking a sarong:

I used mine as a towel, a beach mat, bed sheet and a curtain. Although not all at once.

Medical Kit

You can buy prepared kits (conventional or homeopathic) from many travel health clinics, mail-order companies and homeopathic practitioners, or you can make your own. Use a container that's waterproof, rattleproof and squashproof – a see-through plastic box or a zip-up, pocketed plastic case is good.

The following is a list of items you should consider including in your medical kit – consult your pharmacist for brands available.

If you're allergic to any drugs (such as penicillin), it's a good idea to carry this information on you at all times. Jim Bell travelled in Tanzania as part of his year off and suggests:

Take health leaflets about how to treat yourself if you get ill. A phrasebook with a good medical section is helpful too.

LOTIONS, POTIONS & PILLS

How much medication you take with you depends on your destination – a lot of this stuff may be available there. Check your guidebook. But if you don't use it all, you can always open a pharmaceutical outlet on your return:

- Any prescription medicines, including malaria prevention drugs.
- Antibiotics or any other regular medication. Antibiotics are useful if you're travelling well off the beaten track but they must be prescribed and you should carry the prescription of these (and any other regular medication you use) with you.
- Paracetamol (acetaminophen) or aspirin for pain and fever; consider also taking a stronger painkiller like co-codamol or an anti-inflammatory like ibuprofen.
- Antidiarrhoeals – loperamide (probably the most useful and effective) or the preventative, bismuth subsalicylate (Pepto-Bismol).
- 'Indigestion' remedies such as antacid tablets or liquids.
- Oral rehydration sachets and measuring spoon for making up your own solution.
- Antihistamine tablets for hay fever and other allergies, and for itching.
- Sting-relief spray or hydrocortisone cream for insect bites.
- Emergency bee-sting kit containing adrenaline (epinephrine) if you are severely allergic to stings.
- Sunscreen and lip salve with sunblock.
- Insect repellent (DEET or plant-based) and permethrin (for treating mosquito nets and clothes).
- Anti-motion-sickness remedies (such as promethazine or ginger – if you suffer from this).
- Water-purifying tablets or water filter/purifier (see the Safe Drinking Water section in the Health chapter).
- Over-the-counter cystitis treatment (if you're prone to this).
- Calamine cream or aloe vera for sunburn and other skin rashes.
- Antifungal cream. Francesca Gowing worked on a project in a tropical rainforest, and advises:

Although it was the dry season we still encountered a lot of rain and the damp conditions meant athlete's foot and fungal infections were inevitable. Mycil powder or equivalent athlete's foot treatment is a must. If the conditions are so boggy that you are reduced to living in welly boots, as we were, then zinc-oxide tape is useful in preventing welly rub and blisters! Finally, plenty of spare socks are a good idea as it is almost impossible to handwash the mud out of sodden ones.

In addition, you could consider taking:

- Cough and cold remedies, and sore-throat lozenges (be aware that decongestants are banned

in certain countries, for example China).
- Eye drops for tired or dusty eyes.
- Multivitamins (if your diet is likely to be poor).
- Laxatives (in an area where there is little fibre in the diet, for example Mongolia).

FIRST-AID EQUIPMENT

You'll want to have at least some of these items with you for most destinations, and probably all of them for off the beaten track. Remember you mustn't pack anything sharp in your in-flight luggage as it'll be confiscated:

- Thermometer.
- Scissors.
- Tweezers to remove splinters, cactus needles and ticks.
- Sticking plasters (such as Band-Aids) of various sizes.
- Gauze swabs and adhesive tape.
- Bandages and safety pins to fasten them.
- Non-adhesive dressings.
- Antiseptic powder or solution (eg, povidone-iodine), antiseptic wipes.
- Wound closure strips or butterfly closures (can sometimes be used instead of stitches).
- Syringes and needles. In case you need injections in remote places that may have medical hygiene problems. Ask your doctor for a note explaining why you have them.

Wilderness Activities & Remote Areas

If you are planning on trekking or travelling in remote areas you should think about lugging along:

- Antibiotic eye and ear drops.
- Antibiotic cream or powder.
- Emergency inflatable splints.
- Blister kit.
- Elasticated support bandage.
- Triangular bandage for making an arm sling.
- Dental first-aid kit (either a commercial kit, or make up your own – ask your dentist to advise you).

Natural Remedies

Some alternatives to conventional medicine that you might want to consider are:

- Lactobacillus to aid recovery following diarrhoea.
- Tea tree oil for use as an antiseptic and antifungal ointment.
- Ginger for travel sickness.
- Tiger Balm for relief from insect bites, headaches and muscle ache.

Cameras/Video Cameras

You could just forget taking a camera. Apart from being another expense, it can be a pain if you keep worrying whether it will be stolen, lost or damaged. And it might become a barrier between you and places. If you're constantly taking shots, or thinking you should, or fumbling to get your camera out of your pack, you won't be able to enjoy the sights yourself.

If you think a camera will only drag you down, there are alternatives to taking your own pictures: postcards, photo books or getting copies from other people. Susie Clements and

Maria Ducannan shared a camera on their travels:

We thought it a good way of saving space, especially as we were likely to be taking photos of the same scenes. We often had different ideas on what makes a good photo and who was going to take the shot but a little diplomacy, violence and a lot of film eased the way.

If you decide to take a camera, the one you choose will depend on the type of photos you want. If you just want to take high-quality, creative shots, you'll need a single-lens reflex (SLR) camera. But if you just want to take shots to show your friends and remember your trip by, you'll do fine with a point-and-shoot beaut. If you're torn between quality and convenience, you could get a digital camera, or a classy compact with a built-in zoom.

Weight is another consideration. SLRs and their lenses are heavy – usually several times the weight of point-and-shoot cameras – and take up a lot of room.

As well as the following information, check out Lonely Planet's *Travel Photography*, by Richard I'Anson, or Photo.net (**W** www.photo.net) for information on all aspects of photography.

SLR CAMERAS

The main advantage of an SLR camera is that it allows you to get all creative by shooting with the camera on its manual setting (perhaps using the built-in light meter as a guide) and using different lenses. Many SLRs also have automatic settings, which are handy for when you want to take a quick snap. You can buy SLRs with lightweight plastic bodies but these are significantly more fragile than those with metal bodies or frames.

With an SLR, you'll also need the following:

- A couple of lenses: a 24-100mm and an 80-200mm zoom should be sufficient for most situations.
- Skylight (UV) filters for each of your lenses. These protect your lenses and screen out excess ultraviolet light (which makes pictures look dull).

POINT-AND-SHOOT CAMERAS

These snappy little cameras take the stress out of photography. As they focus almost instantaneously, you can take those spur-of-the-moment and natural people shots really easily. They range from cheap disposables to mighty fine models with precision lenses and a foolish number of features. Ask at a trustworthy camera shop for a recommendation.

With both types of camera, it's good to bring:

- A camera case will protect your camera and it can be used to keep it handily outside your backpack.
- A couple of spare camera batteries.
- Lint-free lens paper.
- Silica gel packets to keep the moisture out of your film and equipment.

FILM

Good-quality film can be hard to find in some places. Even if you do find what you're looking for, it may've been stored in a heap of old mould. So you may want to bring film from home. If you buy it on the road, shop in big cities before heading into the countryside.

Film comes as slide or print; colour or black-and-white; and fast or slow. If you have professional aspirations, take slide film. Otherwise consider print film, as it's easier to look at your shots and costs less. You will achieve sharper results with slower films (around 100 ASA) but you may not be able to use these films in dark conditions. If you're going somewhere sunny, this is the speed to pick. For darker situations, bring 400 ASA film. If you want every kind of potential scenario covered, stock up on several speeds or go for 200 ASA.

Heat can damage film – a day in a car's hot glove compartment is usually enough to toast a roll. Store your film in as cool a place as possible, and always out of direct sunlight.

When flying, carry your film on with you to protect it from the high-energy X-ray machines used in some airports to inspect baggage. The metal detectors used to check your carry-on baggage are usually film-safe. If you're concerned, simply take out your film and ask that it be hand-checked. To make this easier for the airport staff, you may want to store your film in a small bag or plastic container.

Developing Film

To prevent your pictures indicating you spent your gap year in a spotted cloud, have film developed as soon as possible after exposing it. You can send process-paid slide film off to your home country for developing and get slides sent to your home address. If you want to have film developed on the road, results will vary widely, so ask other travellers for recommendations. Once you have done the deed, consider sending the slides or prints back home, as they will get mashed up in your pack.

DIGITAL CAMERAS

These are getting more affordable and their results better quality. They're small and convenient and less immediately obvious to people with designs on your possessions. Sam Caulfield took a digital camera when working in Africa and says:

It's easy to email pictures around the world, so friends and family can get a really good idea of what you're doing. The best thing is that the viewing facility means that you can get rid of crap shots immediately, and also show your subjects their picture straight away, which, like Polaroids, people love. If you're interested in taking portraits, it's ideal.

Batteries do wear out quickly, so you have to carry a charger and plug adapters, and if you can't recharge the batteries, then the number of shots is quite limited. Another issue to consider is the size of your memory card: a 128 mega octets memory card enables you to take about 1000 reasonable-quality photos (1cm) but will only take 100 better-quality photos. If your memory card gets full, you can either download your pictures and store them on an internet account or write them to a CD – if such facilities are available. You'll need a cable to link it to a computer and a driver to install the necessary software. However, technology is improving very fast, so by the time you read this, large memory cards may be available which will make this storage problem a distant archaism.

VIDEO

Video cameras are increasingly lightweight and simple, though expensive. Film is not always available, and you'll need a range of plug converters, plus a transformer, to recharge the batteries. Here are a few handy tips:

- As well as filming the obvious – sunsets, sights and spectacular views – remember to record some everyday details. Often the most interesting things happen when you're actually intent on filming something else.

- Unlike still photography, video 'flows'. This means you can shoot scenes of a winding road from the front window of a vehicle to give an overall sense of a place.
- Try to film in long takes, and don't move the camera around too much. If your camera has a stabiliser, you can use it to obtain good footage while travelling on bumpy roads.
- Video cameras have amazingly sensitive microphones, and you might be surprised by how much sound is picked up. This can be a problem if there is a lot of ambient noise – filming by the side of a busy road might seem OK when you do it but makes viewing it back home like sitting under a flyover.
- Remember to follow the same rules regarding people's sensitivities as you would when taking photographs – having a video camera shoved in your face is probably even more annoying and offensive than a still camera. Always ask permission first.

Non-essential Items

These items may make your trip that bit more pleasant:

- **Binoculars** Kind of a luxury item really but handy for wildlife spotting and spying on your neighbours.
- **Books** Take a couple of decent-sized books. You can swap them later on and they'll help pass endless hours waiting for trains or planes.
- **Calculator** Good for currency conversions and other exciting sums. Forget gimmicky electronic converters, a calculator is better (you could just use the one on your mobile).
- **Camping gear** Only lug this around if you're really going to do the tent thing properly. It's bulky, heavy stuff.
- **Candles** Can lend a nice atmosphere to an otherwise dull room, and are also useful if the electricity packs up.
- **Earplugs** You'll never regret these if you spend a lot of time in cities or take a 10-hour ride in a bus with a blaring stereo.
- **Food** It's nice to have a small stash of your favourite food from home, as long as it's not smelly cheese or kippers. Gillian Hindmarsh was amazed at the kind of things she missed:

    I began to crave food that I probably wouldn't have had in the three months had I been at home. The main things were tea with real milk and butterscotch Angel Delight.

    Finola Collins suggests chocolate for its therapeutic properties:

    There are moments where you do feel a bit lonely or down, and a chocolate bar is just the thing!

    But note that if you're travelling somewhere hot, it might just melt all over your clothes.

- **Games** Chess, backgammon, scrabble, dominoes, snakes & ladders...whatever's your favourite, it's likely there's a travel edition (maybe not Twister). Often magnetic, with monstrously small pieces, these are excellent for alleviating boredom and a good way to meet people. Also consider dice, cards and hand-held computer games (Game boy etc).
- **Gifts** If you are going to stay with a family, you'll want to take a few of these.
- **Glue stick** The glue on stamps and envelopes can be remarkably unsticky. It's also useful to stick scraps into your journal.
- **Inflatable pillow** This will allow you to sleep like a baby on long, bumpy bus trips (you hope).
- **Lighter/matches** For campfires, mosquito coils, candles and fags.
- **Mosquito net** Malaria is no joke. In risky places, many cheap hotels provide mosquito nets but it's good to have your own.
- **Personal stereo/radio** Good for whiling away idle hours and, if you have a record function, you can send tapes home. Short-wave radios can keep you in touch with news from home.

- **Photos** You might want to take some photos of your nearest and dearest. Louise Treves suggests that these are great to cheer you up (perhaps to remind you why you went away...) and:

  ...to show other people. And take something that will make you feel good at any time such as nice-smelling bath bubbles.

- **Plug** A rare commodity in some cheaper accommodation. Double-sided rubber or plastic plugs will fit most bath and basin plugholes.
- **Sewing kit** Needle, thread, a few buttons and safety pins to mend clothing, mosquito net, tent or sunglasses.
- **Sleeping bag/sleeping sheet** Only take a sleeping bag if you plan to camp a lot, as they're heavy. If you're going to need a bag in only one of the countries on your itinerary, then think about hiring one there. A sleeping sheet is a much better bet. Two sheets sewn together, it will give you some protection from over-friendly bedbugs and dodgy beds, and it's light and easily cleaned. Stick to natural fibres (cotton or silk).
- **Travel journal and pens** This will contain your great travelogue.
- **Washing detergent** For handwashing your clothes.
- **Washing line** A piece of string, or even dental floss, will do the job but there are relatively cheap lines on the market with suckers, hooks or both on each end which makes them much more versatile.
- **Water bottle** You can just refill a standard plastic bottle but a more sturdy model will last a lot longer and be more suitable for purifying water on a regular basis.

Clothes

What will you wear? Choosing your clothes can leave you in a quandary. You want to bring a versatile range, particularly if you're flitting from climate to climate but too many items will weigh you down. Sara Smith, who went Inter-Railing during her gap, suggests:

Roll your clothes up – they'll be less creased and take up less space.

Research what people wear at your destination before you go and pack accordingly. Travellers who flaunt their flesh when in conventional and religious societies are showing flagrant disregard for local sensibilities and will make a bad impression.

Don't bring precious items – humid climates and the rigours of the road will wreck anything fragile. It's best to view the things you take as expendable. Remember you can always deck yourself out in climatically suitable stuff once you arrive.

DAY TO DAY
Here are some hot and cold options. No matter where you're headed, it's a good idea to have something presentable to wear when out on the town, for job interviews or when dealing with police, clearing customs or other officials.

Keeping Cool
If you're travelling in hot climates then look for lightweight, loose-fitting clothes. Light colours will keep you cooler than dark ones but will look grubbier. Jeans are heavy, bulky and take ages to dry; cotton trousers, sarongs or long skirts are much lighter and will keep you cooler. Take a couple of short-sleeved shirts if you want but long-sleeved shirts are more useful, as they will keep the sun off and be more appropriate at religious sites. The same applies to shorts. Don't forget a wide-brimmed hat – a cap won't protect your neck or ears.

Does my bum look big in this?

There's not a huge scope for style when you're out on the road or doing a gap-year project. You'll want to wear the most practical and appropriate clothes. On long journeys you might find that you wear the same clothes day after day, and emerge at your destination looking like a scary monster. Not to worry, as you won't find many fashionistas in the jungle or ice-climbing – for one thing, rainforests and glaciers are so last season. So when you're doing your packing, you may have to leave behind your vanity, in the interests of your personal comfort. It's one less thing to carry.

Keeping Warm

Several layers of natural fibres, topped by a good-quality jacket, will give you the versatility you need. A good combination starts with thermal underwear (or a lightweight, cycling-style, thin silk T-shirt); then add a cotton T-shirt, long-sleeved cotton shirt, sweater and jacket. Also consider two pairs of socks – cotton under wool. If you get too hot you can ditch the woollies, while the cotton will absorb your sweat and prevent itchiness from damp wool on bare skin. Also bring waterproofs (a good-quality jacket might be adequate), gloves and a woolly hat. Don't forget a brimmed hat and sunscreen, as you can burn quickly in the thin air at high altitudes.

SPECIALISED CLOTHES

If you're doing activities such as trekking or cycling, this is the moment you've been waiting for...where synthetics come into their own. Hi-tech fabrics such as Gore-Tex are light, pretty waterproof and have a one-way design to their knit so your sweat can escape, while keeping you protected from external water. This makes them ideal cold-weather gear. Trousers of the same fabric will be useful if the weather turns really nasty but mostly you can do without them. Fleecy jackets don't have the waterproofing abilities of Gore-Tex but are lighter and smaller to pack and are more suitable for use in lower altitudes.

FOOTWEAR

Those fetching rubber-soled sandals are the standard issue for many travellers. A good-quality pair will be comfortable, airy and hard-wearing. However, they do not have either the strength or support required for long-distance trekking, and let in far too much mud, water – and twigs – during forest or jungle treks. If you plan to do any trekking, get a decent pair of leather hiking boots and wear them in properly before you start any serious walking. A compromise option is a pair of lightweight boots made from a synthetic material. These won't be as waterproof or hard-wearing as leather but they'll be much more comfortable.

Shoes are quite heavy, so try to limit yourself to two pairs – preferably something sturdy enough for day-to-day use, plus a pair of flip-flops for relaxing, showering in dodgy hostel bathrooms or hanging out on the beach.

Specialist Equipment

Diving, snorkelling, surfing, windsurfing, rafting, climbing, skiing or cycling equipment can be hired at recognised sites. If you prefer your own equipment, or will be heading off the beaten track, then bring everything with you. If you're into more esoteric activities such as caving, you'll have to bring the lot.

Documents

All important documents (passport data and visa page, credit cards, travel insurance policy, driving licence, International Driving Permit, air/train/bus tickets, vaccination certificates, etc) should be photocopied before you leave home. Leave copies with someone at home and take one set with you (keeping it separate from the originals). You can also scan them and keep them electronically, either on your email account, or in an online travel vault.

If you're planning to look for work abroad, you'll need copies of an up-to-date CV, primed for the type of thing you're after. Some references will be essential in some places too, so sort these out before you go.

What to Leave Behind

You probably won't need a hairdryer and three different types of hair gel. Aftershave and perfume often change their scent in a hot climate, and, wherever you're headed, are just cluttering up your bag. Your favourite high heels might not be ideal for the high seas. A whole suitcase of CDs is probably overdoing it. And perhaps your 'I Love NY' T-shirt and bikini are not the best attire for North Africa or Pakistan.

You might have only included seemingly essential items but paring stuff down to the barest minimum will make you much more content lugging it about. Ben Barnes went on a round-the-world trip and says: ·

Pack what you need. Then take it all out and leave half behind. Pack attitude, not socks.

Health

Sources of Information & Advice

Ideally you should go to your doctor or a travel clinic to discuss your travel health preparations such as immunisations and antimalaria medication, six to eight weeks before going away.
Once you've done this, your health concerns are not over. You must keep aware of health
issues on the road. The Department of Health publishes an invaluable leaflet called Health
Advice for Travellers. You can get a copy by calling ☎ 0800 555777, or online at Ⓦ www
.doh.gov.uk/traveladvice. It includes information for EU nationals about the E111, a certificate that allows you to get treatment anywhere in the EU. If you are a student staying in
another area of the EU as part of your studies, you'll get Form 128. *Travellers' Health – How
to stay healthy abroad*, by Dr Richard Dawood, is the travel health 'bible'. It has practical
advice on how to stay healthy abroad with input from over 80 travel medicine experts and
chapters on everything from deep vein thrombosis (DVT) to venomous bites. It's published
by Oxford University Press and the fourth edition is in the shops priced at £14.99. Read
this and reassure your parents that you're thoroughly prepared. You don't want to succumb
to Japanese encephalitis in Southeast Asia or bilharziasis while swimming in Africa.

DIGITAL RESOURCES

African Medical & Research Foundation Ⓦ www.amref.org
Altitude Sickness Ⓦ www.princeton.edu/~oa/altitude.html
BBC Health Ⓦ www.bbc.co.uk/health/travel
British Airways Travel Clinic Ⓦ www.britishairways.com/travel/healthclinintro/public/
en_us
CDC (US Centers for Disease Control & Prevention) Ⓦ www.cdc.gov/travel/index.htm
International Society of Travel Medicine Ⓦ www.istm.org
London Hospital for Tropical Diseases Ⓦ www.uclh.org/services/htd/index.shtml
Marie Stopes Ⓦ www.mariestopes.org.uk
MASTA (Medical Advisory Services for Travellers) Ⓦ www.masta.org
Mefloquine Ⓦ www.geocities.com/TheTropics/6913/lariam.htm
Nomad Travel Ⓦ www.nomadtravel.co.uk
Shorelands Ⓦ www.tripprep.com
Travellers' Health Ⓦ www.travellers-health.co.uk
Travellers Medical and Vaccination Centre Ⓦ www.tmvc.com.au/info.html
WHO (World Health Organization) Ⓦ www.who.int/en/

Immunisations

You are young and will live forever but you can assist your longevity by getting an armload
of jabs.

You'll need to get individual advice on which immunisations to have, as this depends on
various factors. Some shots are not suitable for everyone, especially if you have a medical
condition that weakens your immune system, and some shots can provoke allergic reactions
in susceptible people.

VACCINATION CERTIFICATE

A top tip is to make sure your immunisations are recorded on an official certificate. This is
useful for your own information and, if necessary, you will be able to show it to any doctor
treating you.

TIMING

We've all been there – that I've-forgotten-to-get-my-shots panic. You usually need to wait one to two weeks after a booster or the last dose of a course before you're fully protected, and some courses may need to be given over a period of several weeks. For example, a full course of rabies vaccine takes a month.

If you have left it to the last minute, immunisation schedules can be rushed if necessary and squeezed into a couple of weeks. This is likely to mean that you have less cover, particularly in the first week or two of your trip.

WHICH ONES

Working out which jabs you need depends not only on where you're going but on how long for and whether you're planning to work or just holiday. Other factors that need to be considered are what immunisations you've had in the past, any medical conditions you have and medications you're taking, and any allergies you have.

All vaccines can cause side effects, usually minor (sore arm, fever for half a day) but very occasionally serious allergic reactions can occur. There is no evidence that immunisations damage your immune system in any way. Recommendations change, so you'll need to discuss these with your doctor or travel health clinic.

Cholera

Immunisation against this diarrhoeal disease is not available in the UK at this time.

Hepatitis A

All travellers to Latin America, Africa, Asia (apart from Japan), the Pacific Islands and off the beaten track in Eastern, Central or Southern Europe and Turkey should be protected against this common viral infection of the liver. Protection is either with hepatitis A vaccine or immunoglobulin. Although it may be more expensive, the vaccine is recommended as it gives good protection for at least a year (longer if you have a booster). Immunoglobulin needs to be given as close as possible to your departure date.

A combined hepatitis A and typhoid vaccine has recently become available – good news if you're not keen on needles.

Hepatitis B

Protection against this serious liver infection is recommended for long-term travellers to Latin America, Asia, Africa, Eastern Europe and Turkey. It is also recommended if you're going to be working as a medic or nurse, or if needle sharing or sexual contact with a local person is a possibility. If you need both hepatitis A and B immunisations, a combined vaccine is available.

Japanese Encephalitis

This vaccination may be something you'll need to consider if you're planning a long stay in some rural areas of Papua New Guinea, the far north of Australia (mainly Torres Strait islands and Cape York) or rural, rice-growing areas of Asia. Discuss this with your doctor if you think this could be relevant.

Meningococcal Meningitis

There are occasional outbreaks of this serious brain infection in some areas of Latin America (eg, around São Paulo in Brazil) but immunisation for travellers is not generally recommended. If Asia-bound, you might need it for Nepal, northern Pakistan, parts of India, Mongolia and, in certain circumstances, Vietnam. In Africa, epidemics occur periodically, mainly in the Sahel area in the dry season, although the so-called 'meningitis belt' extends as far south as Zambia and Malawi. Immunisation is usually recommended if you are travelling in risk areas in the dry season. There have been reports of travellers needing to be immunised at borders into Burkina Faso and possibly other countries in the region – check this out before you go.

Rabies

With rabies, you have the choice of either having the immunisation before you go, or after you've been bitten by a rabid-seeming beast. If you have a pre-trip immunisation, you will need to have a course of three injections over a month, which gives you some (but not complete) protection against the disease. Whether you have been immunised or not, you need to have booster injections as soon as possible after a suspect bite – you will need more if you haven't been immunised.

This vaccine doesn't prevent rabies totally but it does give you more time to get medical help. It's recommended for travel off the beaten track or for handling wild animals in high-risk areas. Rabies hotspots include Africa, the Indian subcontinent, Thailand and the Philippines, Latin America and, although rare, it does exist in many European countries, with the exception of the UK, Ireland, Portugal, Monaco and Malta.

Tick-Borne Encephalitis

Tick-borne encephalitis (TBE) can occur in most forest and rural areas of Europe, especially in eastern Austria, Germany, Hungary and the Czech Republic. Consider a vaccination against this tick-transmitted disease if you plan to do extensive hiking between May and September.

The vaccine is available as a series of two or three injections and can be administered quickly; it takes about 28 days to get the three shots.

Tuberculosis

You may already have had this immunisation as a child. Although tuberculosis (TB) is common worldwide, short-term travellers are at very low risk of the disease.

Typhoid

You'll need a vaccination against typhoid if you're travelling in Latin America, Africa, the Pacific Islands or most parts of Asia, except Japan, for longer than two weeks, or you intend to really rough it in remote areas of Turkey and Eastern European countries, including Albania, Croatia and Romania, or if you're at risk from the disease. Typhoid vaccination is available as an injection or as tablets (oral form), although you may find availability of the oral form limited. The old injectable typhoid vaccine can produce some pretty unpleasant reactions (eg, fever, chills, headache) but the new injection causes few side effects. However, the oral form can sometimes give you an intestinal upset.

Yellow Fever

Proof of immunisation against yellow fever is a statutory requirement for entry into all Latin American and African countries if you are coming from a yellow-fever infected country in South America or the African continent.

The yellow fever vaccine occasionally causes low-grade fever and a sore arm. It's not recommended if you have a severe egg allergy or your immunity is lowered for some reason (for example, you are HIV-positive).

ROUTINE IMMUNISATIONS

Everyone should make sure they are up to date with these, which include:

- Tetanus, usually given together with diphtheria.
- Polio.
- Childhood illnesses.

Malaria

If you're going to a malarial area, you need to get expert advice on how to prevent catching this potentially fatal mosquito-borne disease – a travel health clinic is the best place to go.

If you're headed to a malarial area:

- Get the latest information on risks and drug resistance from a reliable information source.
- Take suitable malaria preventive drugs and carry malaria treatment with you if appropriate, and discuss this with your doctor or a travel health clinic before you go.
- Avoid insect bites. This is even more important now that malarial parasites have become resistant to many commonly used antimalarial drugs.

You need to know a little bit about the symptoms and signs of malaria and what to do if you think you have it.

Remember, if you need to take malaria pills, they generally need to be started at least one week before you leave (see Doses & Timing later in this section). Minor side effects are common with all the drugs but if you get major side effects that make you unsure about continuing the drug, seek advice about changing to a medication that suits you better. Some malaria pills are not suitable for everyone, so check this with your doctor.

MALARIA INFORMATION SOURCES

Malaria risks and antimalarial drug resistance patterns change constantly, so it's important to get the most up-to-date information before you go. You've got no excuse not to – information on all aspects of malaria prevention is readily available from travel health clinics and specialist centres via phone, fax or the internet. In particular, you can get reliable information from the following sources:

CDC W www.cdc.gov/travel
Malaria Foundation W www.malaria.org – a good source of general information on all aspects of the disease
Travellers Medical and Vaccination Centre W www.tmvc.com.au
WHO W www.who.int

Because malaria prevention is such a complex and changing issue, it's best not to rely completely on advice from friends or other travellers, however well intentioned or knowledgeable they are.

ANTIMALARIALS – THE GREAT DEBATE

Mefloquine (Lariam) is one of the most effective antimalarials available but it's also one of the most controversial. Side effects range from common ones such as sleep disturbance (especially vivid dreams) to uncommon but more serious ones such as panic attacks, hallucinations and fits. Most people who take mefloquine do not, however, have any problems.

Malaria – Did You Know...

The majority of travellers diagnosed with malaria on their return home acquired the infection in sub-Saharan Africa. Some more facts to ponder:

- Malaria is spread by mosquitoes.
- Malaria is a potentially fatal disease.
- Malaria is becoming more common and more difficult to treat (because of drug resistance).
- Most cases of malaria in travellers occur in people who didn't take antimalarials or who didn't take them as recommended.
- Most malaria deaths in travellers occur because the diagnosis is delayed or missed.
- Malaria can be transmitted by transfusion of blood and other blood products, by needle sharing among intravenous drug users and from mother to foetus.

Because of the risk of dizziness and fits, mefloquine is best avoided if you're going to be doing precision tasks like scuba diving or flying a plane. If you are going to high altitude, it could mask signs of altitude sickness although this is very unlikely.

For more specific information about the mefloquine issue, you could check out the excellent 'Lariam or not to Lariam' on **W** www.geocities.com/thetropics/6913/lariam.htm, which has a comprehensive list of links, including one to Roche, the manufacturer of Lariam.

If you cannot, or would prefer not to take mefloquine, there are other options, for example, doxycycline. Side effects to this one include heartburn, diarrhoea, hypersensitivity of your skin to sunlight, and vaginal thrush. It may make the oral contraceptive pill less effective, so if this is relevant to you, get advice from your doctor before you go. Doxycycline can cause irritation to your stomach, so you should always swallow it with plenty of water, either in the middle of or straight after a meal.

Malarone is a very effective antimalarial with very few side effects (nausea and possible mouth ulcers). The downside is that it is very expensive – over £100 for a month's course. Currently it is only licensed for 28 days in a malarial area but evidence suggests that it is safe to take for up to three months.

Alternatively you could take chloroquine plus proguanil but because of high levels of resistance in some areas, chloroquine (or chloroquine plus proguanil/Paludrine) may not be an option. Minor side effects are common and include headaches, nausea, diarrhoea, indigestion, blurred vision (temporary) and itching (especially if you're of African or Afro-Caribbean descent). It isn't suitable for everyone: you shouldn't take it if you have epilepsy or are taking medication for epilepsy or psoriasis, although evidence suggests it is OK to use for up to three months. Proguanil (Paludrine) has few side effects but can cause mouth ulcers and nausea.

Antimalarials work by killing off the malarial parasites at a stage of their development before they can cause the disease; they don't prevent malarial parasites from entering your body. In recent years, there has been an inexorable rise in resistance of the malarial parasite to many of the antimalarial drugs, including chloroquine, making prevention and treatment of malaria a whole lot more tricky.

There are hopes of a malarial vaccine but there's still a long way to go.

DOSES & TIMING

You need to start taking malaria pills before you leave, so that they have a chance to reach maximum protective levels in your body before you arrive at your destination. It also gives any side effects a chance to show themselves so you can change medication before you go if necessary.

Malaria in the Area (and You're There for over Six Months)

If you're hanging out in malarial areas for six months or more, you may be wondering what to do about malaria prevention. You've got two options: continue to take your usual malaria preventive pills or give up on them. Taking malaria pills for more than six months can work out quite expensive. If you do decide to stop them, and this is not recommended, discuss this with your doctor before you go, be aware that you need to be extremely vigilant about avoiding mosquito bites, be very clear about where your nearest doctor is and when to take emergency stand-by treatment, and don't underestimate the risks to your health and your life. Note that you don't build up immunity to malaria with time, so you're still at risk of getting it, even if you've been in a risk area for ages.

See Insect Bites later in the chapter for prevention techniques.

It's best to start mefloquine two to three weeks before you go, doxycycline needs to be started one week before you leave, and chloroquine (with or without proguanil) needs to be started at least one week in advance. Malarone only needs to be started one or two days before you go.

Make sure you are clear on what dose to take before you leave – some drugs need to be taken weekly, and some need to be taken daily, and you don't want to get it wrong.

- Chloroquine   500mg once weekly
- Proguanil   200mg once daily
- Mefloquine   250mg once weekly
- Doxycycline   100mg once daily
- Malarone   1 tablet daily

For the best protection, you need to take antimalarials regularly – try to get into a routine before you leave. Take them after food, as this makes side effects less likely.

Don't be tempted to stop taking your malaria pills as soon as you leave a malarial area, or you may get malaria from parasites you picked up in the last few days of your trip. All malaria pills need to be continued for four weeks after returning home or leaving the area, except Malarone, which only needs to be taken for one week.

Whatever you decide, remember that malaria is a potentially fatal disease and it's vital you take precautions against it in risk areas.

Travel Health Insurance

However lucky (or poor) you're feeling, it's vital you have adequate health insurance to cover your whole trip, usually as part of a general travel insurance covering loss of belongings, flight cancellations etc. For more details, see the Passports, Tickets, Visas & Insurance chapter earlier.

Many insurance providers have a 24-hour hotline you can ring for assistance in an emergency, and they can usually provide you with names of English-speaking doctors (if necessary), arrange referral to a hospital and guarantee payment if you need to pay upfront.

You will often have to pay cash for medical treatment and be reimbursed later, so it's a good idea to have an emergency stash just in case (your insurance provider may be able to provide a guarantee of payment that will be accepted instead but don't count on it). Always keep any receipts in case you need to present them later to be reimbursed.

Pre-travel Checkups & Other Preparations

It may be worth making an appointment with your doctor to discuss the following issues:

- If you suffer from any ongoing conditions like asthma, hay fever or dermatitis, try to clarify any specific problems travelling may cause and what to do about them.
- To get supplies of prescription medicines you might need and to discuss taking emergency treatment for diarrhoea or chest infections, especially if you will be travelling in remote areas.
- To discuss problems that travel may pose to any contraceptives you are using, or to discuss options if you want to start contraception.
- If you're going on a long trip and planning to spend time in remote areas, especially if you're going trekking, you might want to consider doing a first-aid course before you leave.
- If you're planning on doing any diving while you are away, remember to get a specific diving medical checkup before you go as, in theory at least, you'll need a certificate of fitness before any dive centre will let you dive.

DENTAL
It's time to stop putting off going to your favourite place. You don't want to find you need a filling when you're in a remote area far from the nearest pain-killing injection. Your teeth can take quite a battering when you're abroad because you often end up drinking gallons of sweet drinks, and inadequate water supplies may mean you can't keep up your usual highly vigilant dental health routine.

OPTICAL
If you wear contact lenses, your optometrist can advise you about hygiene on the road; you'll want to take a plentiful supply of any cleaning solutions you use. If you wear glasses, consider taking a replacement pair or take your prescription with you. In many countries you can have prescription lenses made up quite cheaply.

Health-related Documents
When you're travelling, it's a good idea to keep the following information on you at all times, in case of emergency:

- Travel insurance hotline number.
- Serial number of your travel insurance policy.
- Contact details of the nearest embassy.
- Summary of any important medical condition you have.
- Contact details of your doctor back home (if necessary).
- Copy of prescription for any medication you take regularly.
- Details of any serious allergies.
- Blood group.
- Prescription for glasses or contact lenses.
- If you are a diabetic, a letter from your doctor explaining why you need to carry syringes etc for customs.

First-Aid Training
If you're not accident prone, you're bound to bump into someone who is. It's good to know some basic first aid, and knowing some techniques is even more important if you are going to places without emergency services around the corner. Consider doing at least a basic course before you leave. Contact your local first-aid organisation for details of courses. Training in appropriate survival skills is usually offered by organisations that run activities such as mountaineering and trekking. The BBC has a 'course finder' at **W** www.bbc.co.uk/health/first_aid_action/ that does exactly what it says on the tin, and the British Red Cross (**W** www.redcross.org.uk) runs courses all over the country.

Staying Healthy

Guess what – avoiding illness and injury can help make your trip a lot better. Staying healthy becomes even more important if you're planning to spend some time in a remote location, where medical help is a couple of days away. It's also vital if you're doing outdoor activities such as trekking that rely on your physical – and mental – fitness. If you're aware of potential health hazards and take some basic steps to avoid them, you shouldn't find it too tricky to stay safe and healthy. Zabrina Shield spent six months travelling through Costa Rica, Nicaragua, Guatemala, Belize and Honduras, and advises:

Find out where the nearest medical centre is when you arrive in a place, so that you know what to do if a situation arises.

MEDICAL KIT

You'll want to take some basic medical supplies. See the Packing chapter to check out what this should include.

ACCLIMATISATION: HEAT, SUN, COLD, ALTITUDE

Allow yourself time to adjust physically and mentally to your new place. You'll probably need time to recover from jet lag, catch up on sleep and perhaps missed meals, and settle into your new venue slowly.

Feeling Hot Hot Hot

If you've gone from a cool climate to a baking one, make sure you give yourself a chance to get used to the heat. Your body has an amazing capacity to adjust to temperature changes but it doesn't happen overnight. Jake Fowler found it difficult to do everything he'd planned in his first few weeks in Ghana:

I felt exhausted. I had intended to start travelling straight away but soon realised I had to allow myself time to adapt so changed my plans.

It takes about a week for your body to make initial adjustments to deal with the temperature change. After this, you'll probably find you can cope with the heat much better, and your capacity for activity gets back to normal.

If you want to avoid serious problems such as heat exhaustion and heatstroke, it's vital to drink like a fish (not booze though) to replace the amount you're sweating out. Cool water is best. Don't wait until you feel thirsty before drinking; thirst is a very bad indicator of your fluid needs, and if you're thirsty, you're already dehydrated. You should keep a supply of water with you and drink it regularly. Remember that tea, coffee and alcohol all have a diuretic effect (ie, they make you lose fluid), so it's best to go easy on these. If you sweat a lot, you may need to intake extra salt to avoid cramps.

Physical activity generates heat, which means that your body has to work even harder to stay cool if you're exercising. If you're getting busy in a tropical climate, plan to take it easy during the first week, building up slowly as you acclimatise.

Avoid overexerting yourself (and this includes eating loads of food) during the hottest part of the day; it's the perfect time for a siesta. As far as clothing is concerned, you need to choose clothes that will protect your skin from the sun (and insects) but that won't make you too darn hot. Sunburn makes your body less able to cope with the heat. So, sorry to disappoint but skin-tight lycra outfits are probably out, at least off the beach; loose, light-coloured clothing made of natural fibres like cotton are in. (Dark colours will absorb the heat more.) You'll need to consider any local cultural considerations when deciding what to wear – see your travel guidebook for more details.

If you're so white that people don shades as you pass, it can be hard to resist the temptation to stretch out in the sun. If you're determined to tan, then at least take some damage-control measures. Make sure you allow your skin to tan slowly without burning, starting with 15 or 20 minutes exposure a day. As soon as your skin starts to feel sore or look red, and preferably long beforehand, head for the shade. Remember that freckles may be cute but they're also a sign of skin damage.

Sunlight or solar energy is made up of radiation of many different wavelengths, including ultraviolet (UV) rays, the bad guys. UVA rays used to be thought to be less harmful than UVB but there's plenty of evidence that they are just as bad, so you need to look for sunscreen products that protect against both types. In the short term, UV radiation causes redness, blisters and soreness – sunburn. If you've ever frazzled yourself, you'll know how painful this can be but the long-term effects are even scarier. Many of the skin changes that were thought just to be part of the ageing process, including wrinkling, broken veins and pigmented patches ('liver spots'), are now known to be due to sun damage. Worst of all, UV rays can damage the metabolism of skin cells, leading to skin cancer.

Skin damage doesn't just start with sunburn; any time you spend in the sun contributes in the long term. And sun overexposure is thought to result in suppression of the immune system, and may make you more vulnerable to infectious diseases.

A suntan is a layer of skin pigment (melanin) that forms in response to sunlight falling on your skin. It can protect against sunburn but not against the ageing or cancer-inducing effects of UV radiation. In any case, it takes two to three weeks before a suntan can provide good protection against sunburn.

If you're somewhere where the sun is almost always shining and you're spending a lot of your time outdoors; it can be hard to be on your guard all the time. It takes a bit of effort but protection against the sun will just become part of your daily routine. Sun intensity is greatly increased at altitude and by reflection off water and snow, so you need to take particular care in these situations. The state of the protective ozone layer is another good reason to take care, especially in Australia and New Zealand. Unless you're a mad dog (in which case, why are you reading this), keep out of the sun in the middle of the day.

Do the slip, slop, slap thing:

- Slip on a shirt – covering up with clothing of a reasonable thickness provides by far the best protection from harmful rays; special protective sunsuits are available for wearing on the beach, and are ideal if you're doing watersports; sun does just as much damage to your eyes, so slip on some shades too.
- Slop on sunscreen – use liberal amounts of high-protection factor (SPF 60 is currently the highest available), broad-spectrum sunscreen on any exposed bits of skin; apply 30 minutes before going into the sun and splash it on frequently, especially after swimming.
- Slap on a hat – a wide-brimmed hat or a cap with a neck protector will help to keep damaging rays off your face, ears and back of the neck.

Remember:

- You can get sunburnt through water (snorkelling can leave you smouldering), so take care to cover up with a T-shirt and use plenty of water-resistant sunscreen.
- The ambient temperature doesn't make any difference to the burning power of the sun – you can still get burnt on a cold day if the sun is shining.

- You can also fry on a cloudy day (because clouds let through some UV radiation) and in the shade (from reflected light, often off water).

Cold Comfort

You may be exposed to the opposite extreme, especially if you are trekking or just travelling through highland areas. In the desert, it can get nippy at night as there is nothing to retain the heat. Clare Hall got chilly in Australia:

I've never been so cold as when I was sleeping out in the desert near Ayers Rock in Australia. The days were boiling but the nights freezing. In the morning we'd all find frost on our sleeping bags and it didn't matter how close we tried to get to the camp fire, my friends and I shivered all night.

Your body is fairly limited in what it can do to stay warm – saying 'brrr' and shivering are just about the only things in the short term – so it's up to you to minimise the dangers by wearing lots of the right clothes and avoiding temperature extremes (unless you're well prepared). Food equals heat – make sure you eat regularly and get sufficient calories in cold climates.

Other chilling problems are dehydration (cold makes you urinate more, you might not feel thirsty and cold air is very dry), constipation and sunburn (especially at altitude). Worse problems are general body cooling (hypothermia) or localised cooling, usually affecting hands and feet, called frostnip or frostbite.

Getting High

The lack of oxygen at altitude (usually over 2500m) affects most people to varying degrees, especially if you fly straight there.

You can get advice on preventing AMS (Acute Mountain Sickness) from a travel health clinic or expedition organiser, or read up about it in your guidebook. An authoritative website with information about AMS and other altitude-related problems is **W** www.princeton.edu/~oa/altitude.html.

Before you leave, it's a good idea to check that your insurance covers altitude sickness. If you have any ongoing illnesses like asthma or diabetes, or you're taking the oral contraceptive pill, discuss with your doctor the possible effects altitude may have.

Symptoms of mild altitude sickness are common when you first arrive at altitude and include headache, nausea and loss of appetite, difficulty sleeping and lack of energy. They usually respond to rest and simple painkillers. More serious forms of altitude sickness are less common but can be fatal.

The best way to prevent AMS is to ascend slowly. Try to sleep at a lower altitude than the greatest height you reached during the day, and make sure you allow extra time in your schedule for rest days. Drugs such as acetazolamide (trade name Diamox) are sometimes used to prevent AMS, although this is controversial. Taking drugs is no substitute for proper acclimatisation.

The best treatment for AMS is descent; never continue to ascend if you have any symptoms of AMS.

SAFE FOOD & DRINK

Food, rather than water, is the most common source of gastro problems. Unfriendly fauna can contaminate your snack at many stages of the production chain, including during harvesting, transportation, handling, washing and preparation. Many forms of diarrhoea and dysentery (bloody diarrhoea) are transmitted in this way, as well as other diseases such as hepatitis A (common in travellers) and typhoid (uncommon).

You can get sick from dodgy food anywhere but it's more likely when you're living in a less-developed country or travelling, for a variety of reasons. Sewage-disposal systems may be inadequate, and this, together with higher levels of disease in some parts of the population, means there's more chance that food will have a not-so-tantalising topping of disease-causing microorganisms. It sounds simple but do remember to wash your hands before you eat. Theresa Holt suggests not sharing food with ill-looking travellers:

I shared a juice with an exceedingly sickly Israeli, and regretted it later when I lost my voice, about a stone in weight, and spent a few weeks in Nepal, not trekking but puking.

In foreign countries you may eat out a lot more and have to rely on other people to prepare your food safely. This is always a risk, and even in countries with supposedly high food-safety standards such as Australia, outbreaks of food poisoning still occur with alarming regularity.

Eating safely is about taking simple precautions to minimise your risk of getting something nasty – you don't need to live in a germ-free bubble. Some common sense and background knowledge are the ideal accompaniments to your meal.

Microorganisms love to multiply in food sitting around in hot, humid climates. Heating kills germs, so food that's served piping hot, or you see cooked in front of you, is likely to be safer than lukewarm or cold food, especially if it's been sitting around in the open. Emma Tang ate a lot of street food and didn't get ill:

The good thing is that it's cooked in front of you and is fresh and hot. Street stalls might not look so clean but I have friends who got really sick after meals at expensive hotels.

Fruit and vegetables can be difficult to clean (and may be contaminated where they are grown) but they should be safe if they're peeled or cooked. Well-cooked meat and seafood is usually OK; but raw or lightly cooked meat and seafood can be a disease danger zone.

Dry food such as bread, biscuits and plain cakes are safe on the whole, although it's best to avoid cream-filled goodies, as microorganisms such as salmonella (a cause of food poisoning) have a bit of a cream fetish.

Your belly's natural defences (mainly acid) can cope with small amounts of contaminated foods – if you're not sure about something, don't eat a stack of it.

What to Avoid

Here are some food-and-drink guidelines:

- The more food has been handled (for example, through peeling, slicing and arranging), the more chance it has of being contaminated by unwashed hands.
- Food can be contaminated by dirty dishes, cutlery or utensils; blenders or pulpers used for fruit juices are often suspect.
- You can't necessarily tell if food is contaminated by looking at it; food that is seething with disease-causing microorganisms may still look and smell delicious.
- Hot spices don't make food safe, just more tasty.
- Salads, like other vegetables, are hard to clean and may be contaminated where they are grown – if you've any hygiene doubts, it's best to say no to salads.

- Avoid ice cubes in drinks, they might be made from contaminated water.
- Fruit juices and other drinks may be diluted with unsafe water, or tainted by contaminated ice cubes.
- Freezing doesn't kill disease-causing microorganisms; and be wary of frozen food (including ice cream) if refrigeration is questionable (because of power cuts or lack of availability).
- Unpasteurised milk may be offered to you in rural areas but is best avoided as it can be a source of illnesses such as TB in less-developed nations. Boiling milk will make it safe if you're unsure. Sally Schama found that her standards began to change while away:

I got more and more blasé about what I ate and drank – you do develop more tolerance. But I'd say be careful: don't let your standards slip too much, or you might end up coming home with a few bacterial souvenirs!

SAFE DRINKING WATER

Water, water everywhere but not a drop to drink…You need to drink lots of water to stay in sparkling health, especially in hot climates. Although contaminated food is probably the most common source of bad belly when you're travelling, water can also bring illness on, including diarrhoea, dysentery, hepatitis and typhoid.

In countries with good infrastructure and resources, communal water supplies are generally safe from contamination but you can't rely on this in nations with fewer resources. Contamination of the water supply can occur at some point, usually by human or animal sewage. Your travel guidebook or a reliable local source will be able to give you specific information on water safety.

Unless you are sure that the water is safe from contamination, it's best to err on the side of caution.

Ice is the cause of many a downfall. It's only as safe as the water it's made from, so it's best avoided if you're unsure. Paul Benson says:

One of the first phrases I learned in Hindi was 'no ice please'. Sometimes I felt like I was being rude if I were offered a drink and refused it but I weighed it up: a minute's awkwardness versus four days of hell.

Drinking bottled water is an obvious answer to the water question. As a general rule, it's best to stick to major brands of bottled water, and make sure the seal on the lid is not broken (this means the bottle can't have been refilled with any old dodgy water). If you're in any doubt, choose carbonated water (for example plain soda water), as the acidity from carbonation kills off any microorganisms.

The cost of bottled water can add up over a long trip, especially if you're travelling in hot climates, and the millions of discarded and unrecycled plastic bottles are having a severe environmental impact in many countries. If you're trekking or travelling off the beaten track, bottled water is just not practical and may not be available in remote areas. In these situations, you'll have to have some means with you of making water safe to drink. Options are boiling, using chemical disinfectants or using a water-purification device. Make sure you have more than one means of purifying water in case one method fails (for example, take some iodine as well as a pump-action purifier).

The simplest and most effective way of making water safe to drink is to boil it, which kills all disease-causing critters. You just need to bring it to a rolling boil for a minute or two and then let it cool – prolonged boiling is not necessary. If it's not practical, it's relatively easy to disinfect clear water with chemicals. Chlorine and iodine are the chemicals most widely used, and at optimal concentrations both kill bacteria, viruses and most parasites (one exception is cryptosporidium). Iodine and chlorine are both available as tablets or liquids ('tincture' of iodine), and iodine is also available as crystals. You can usually buy them from good pharmacies, travel health clinics or outdoor-equipment suppliers.

Factors that affect the ability of these chemicals to disinfect water include concentration, how long you leave the water to stand after adding the chemical, water temperature (the colder the water, the longer it needs to be left to stand before use) and any particulate matter in the water.

Make sure you follow the manufacturer's dosage and contact time if you're using tablets but as a rule, you'll need to leave the water for at least 20 minutes before drinking it. If the water is really cold, you will need to leave it for longer, sometimes an hour or two; alternatively, you could add the chemicals the night before and leave it to stand overnight. With 2% tincture of iodine you need to add five drops to every litre of water to be purified.

Chlorine is considered less reliable in general than iodine, as it is more likely to be affected by factors such as water alkalinity. Silver tablets are also available but they are not effective against parasite cysts, so they shouldn't be used without filtering the water first.

Iodine should not be used continuously to purify water over a long period of time (more than six weeks) as it can cause thyroid problems. Unsurprisingly enough, it should be avoided if you already have thyroid problems.

Chemically treated water – mmm how nice. But there are ways of neutralising its grim taste. Charcoal resins or a carbon filter can remove the taste and smell of chemicals, or you can add ascorbic acid (vitamin C) or flavouring. These need to be added after the treated water has been allowed to stand for the required length of time.

If the water is cloudy, chemicals won't be effective because organic matter tends to neutralise the chemical – you'll need to filter the water first.

Simple filters are just sieves or strainers, and their effectiveness depends on how fine they are. Generally, they don't make water safe to drink without further treatment (boiling or chemicals), as they don't remove the smallest disease-causing organisms (viruses and some bacteria), although fine-pore ceramic filters are exceptions. Purifiers are dual action: they filter water and disinfect it (for example with an iodine resin) to remove viruses; often they include a final step to remove the taste of the chemical disinfectant and any other chemicals such as pesticides.

Filters and purifiers can be gravity or pump action. Pump action is probably the more realistic option unless you have plenty of time on your hands but can be hard work. Water purifiers often contain a carbon filter to remove traces of chemicals used to disinfect the water but note that using a carbon filter on its own does not make water safe to drink.

It's worth having an idea beforehand of what you're looking for; here's a suggested pre-purchase checklist for purifiers:

- What does it claim to remove? Does it make water totally safe to drink?
- What do you want to use it for? Some devices are suitable for occasional or emergency use, whereas others are good for continuous use over a long period of time.
- What's the flow rate like? You don't want to pump for two hours per sip.
- How portable/breakable is it? Ceramic filters are very effective but need a bit of care, as they can crack.
- How often does the filter need to be replaced? Filters can get clogged and there's a risk of bacterial growth occurring in them, so they usually need to be cleaned or replaced after a while.
- How easy is it to take apart and clean if it becomes clogged?
- Is it endorsed by an independent organisation?

There are some curious convolutions available such as a filter that fits onto a tap and a straw (for reaching those inaccessible puddles...), so it's worth shopping around. Water filters and purifiers are available from most major travel health clinics and from outdoor equipment suppliers, often by mail order. Alternatively, you could search on the internet.

DIGESTIVE PROBLEMS (DIARRHOEA)

Many globetrotters will get the trots at some point. Just in case you've led a sheltered life: diarrhoea means passing loose, frequent faeces, often associated with vomiting.

Although there are many causes of travellers' diarrhoea, your risk of getting ill mainly depends on how likely it is that the food and drink you are consuming is contaminated with disease-causing nasties. The risks vary with your destination but diarrhoea affects about 50% of travellers to developing countries. Even if it's relatively mild, you're probably going to feel sorry for yourself for a day or so as it passes through your system, so it's worth building a few rest days into your travel schedule to allow for this. Taking basic precautions with food and drink and paying attention to your personal hygiene (washing your hands before eating) are the most important preventive strategies.

If you get it, diarrhoea usually strikes about the third day after you arrive and lasts about three to five days. It's caused by many factors, including jet lag, new food, a new lifestyle and new bugs. It can come back again in the second week, although you do build up immunity to some of the causes. Symptoms are diarrhoea without blood, mild fever, some nausea and stomach cramps.

The most important aspect of treatment is to prevent dehydration by replacing lost fluid – and to rest. You can drink most liquids, except alcohol, very sugary drinks or dairy products. Oral rehydration sachets can be useful but aren't essential if you're usually healthy. Starchy foods like potatoes, plain rice or bread are thought to help fluid replacement, and you need to stick to a bland diet as you start to feel better.

Antidiarrhoea tablets are of limited use as they prevent your system from clearing out the toxin and can make certain types of diarrhoea worse, though they can be useful as a temporary stopping measure, for example if you have to go on a long bus journey. Antibiotic treatment for simple travellers' diarrhoea may shorten the illness but side effects are possible, so you might want to discuss this with your doctor before you leave.

Sometimes diarrhoea can be more serious, with blood, a high fever and cramps (bacterial dysentery), or it can be persistent and bloody (amoebic dysentery) or persistent, explosive and gassy (Giardia). All need treatment with specific antibiotics.

If you're going to a remote area far from medical help, you may want to consider taking antibiotics with you for self-treating diarrhoea. However, it's generally better to seek medical advice to diagnose which type of diarrhoea you have and decide which antibiotics you should be taking.

INSECT BITES

Insect bites can be brain-scramblingly itchy as well as a health hazard.

Currently the main way to minimise your risk of diseases caused by the little blighters is to avoid getting bitten. Even if you're taking antimalarials the rise in resistance of the malarial parasite makes bite avoidance a vital prevention measure.

Like protecting yourself against the sun, insect-bite prevention should become part of your daily routine. Biting insects are attracted by many variables, not many of which you can directly affect: body heat, body odour, chemicals in your sweat, perfumes, soap and types of clothing. Most mosquitoes are night-biters but the dengue mosquito bites mainly during the day.

Mock those mozzies:

- Cover up with long-sleeved tops and long trousers; light-coloured clothing is thought to be less attractive to mosquitoes than dark colours.
- Use insect repellents on any exposed skin.
- Sleep in a screened room or under a mosquito net and always cover children's beds or cots with mosquito nets; air-conditioned rooms are usually insect-free zones.
- Remember day-biting mosquitoes, and avoid shady conditions in the late afternoon or taking an afternoon siesta without the protection of a mosquito net.
- Spray your room, tent or campervan with a knock-down insect spray before you bed down for the night.
- Consider using electric insecticide vaporisers (you'll need a power socket for this) or mosquito coils – both are less effective if you have a fan going.

Insect Repellents

There are many repellent products out there but the most effective are those containing the compound DEET (diethyltoluamide) – check the label or ask your pharmacist to tell you which brands contain DEET. Some major brands include Autan, Doom, Jungle Formula, the strikingly named Off!, Repel and Rid.

DEET is very effective against mosquitoes, midges, ticks, bedbugs and leeches, and slightly less effective against flies. One application should last up to four hours, although if it's very humid or you're very sweaty it may not last as long. Different formulations have different concentrations of DEET. The higher the concentration, the longer it will last, with around 50% being the optimal concentration, although there are some longer-acting formulations with lower strengths of DEET. It's a good idea to try a test dose before you leave to check for allergy or skin irritation.

You may prefer to use one of the new lemon eucalyptus-based natural products, which have been shown to be an effective alternative to DEET, with similar action times (although DEET is probably still your best bet in high-risk areas). Other natural repellents include citronella but these tend to be less effective and to have a short action (up to an hour), making them less practical.

Cotton bands soaked well in insect repellent can be useful to wear around your wrists and ankles – a prime target for mosquitoes – and the repellent will not rub off quite as easily.

If you're using sunscreen or other lotions, apply insect repellent last, and reapply after swimming if necessary; insect repellent may reduce the protection of a sunscreen. Don't apply insect repellents before going to bed as this can cause irritation.

This has been said many times before but the best way to avoid getting bitten is to use a mosquito net and cover up as much skin as possible during the evening.

Insecticides

Permethrin is a pyrethrum-like compound that can be applied to clothes and mosquito nets (but not on your skin). It repels mosquitoes, fleas, ticks, mites, bedbugs, cockroaches and flies. If you're planning on trekking through potentially tick-infested areas, it's probably worth treating your clothes, particularly your trousers and socks, with permethrin before you go.

You get the best protection against insect bites if you apply a DEET-based product on your skin and use permethrin-treated clothes and nets.

Mosquito Nets

Consider tucking a mosquito net into your pack. They don't weigh much and don't take up much room. Get one that has been soaked in permethrin, or you can treat your own net if necessary.

Travel health clinics and travel-equipment or specialist outdoor-equipment suppliers generally have all sorts of mosquito nets. Freestanding nets are a great option and widely available but quite costly.

ACCIDENTS & INJURY

Although travellers tend to worry about getting a tropical illness that will make their heads shrivel up, you're actually at far greater risk from accident and injury than from any exotic infection. Accidents are the most common cause of death in young travellers, and (especially road accidents) are the main reason for travellers to need emergency medical treatment, including the possibility of a blood transfusion – risky in less-developed countries.

When you're in a foreign place, you tend to take all sorts of risks you probably wouldn't dream of taking at home. It's part of what makes getting away so good but you do need to use a bit of common sense, especially if you are in a remote location. You're not immune. Most of you don't have an invisible protective cloak. If you're riding a bicycle, moped or motorbike, a helmet and sensible clothing are wise even if they aren't the local norm.

While we don't want to rain on your beach party, just be aware that alcohol and other mind-altering substances are major factors in accidents of all types in travellers, from dignity-challenging falls to life-threatening road-traffic accidents.

Obviously, the risk of having an accident increases if you're doing potentially risky outdoor activities such as white-water rafting or mountaineering. This is something to take into account when you're planning your trip.

Accidents are preventable to a great extent. Awareness of potential risks, together with good planning for outdoor activities and a few sensible precautions, especially if you are driving or swimming, should see you relatively safe. And don't sit under a coconut tree...

DRUGS & ALCOHOL

Be wary of local brews, especially distilled spirits, as they may contain undesirable additives or methanol, a highly toxic form of alcohol that can cause permanent blindness.

Other mind-altering substances are readily available throughout much of the world, and in tourist haunts especially you may be offered drugs at every opportunity. If you decide to use drugs, be aware that there's no guarantee of quality, and locally available drugs can be unexpectedly strong or mixed with other harmful substances. Acute anxiety and panic attacks are common with many drugs, especially if you're taking them for the first time under stressful conditions. Acute paranoia can occur with cocaine, amphetamines, ecstasy, LSD and mushrooms and is very frightening. Drugs can accentuate or trigger a mentally fragile state. If you take drugs intravenously, remember that needle-sharing carries the risk of HIV or hepatitis B or C infection. Because unexpected reactions can occur, never take drugs when you are on your tod.

SAFE SEX

While it's true that sexually transmitted infections (STIs) are a risk anywhere if you're having casual sex, it seems that you're more likely to meet casual partners and be careless when you are away from home, and are therefore more at risk. Added to this, levels of STIs in the countries you are visiting may be higher. Of course, abstaining from shagging strangers is the safest option; otherwise, remember to use condoms. They will protect you against HIV, hepatitis B and C, gonorrhoea, chlamydia and syphilis but won't stop you getting any of the charming trio: genital herpes, genital warts or pubic lice. Take a familiar, reliable brand with you. Rubber condoms disintegrate in the heat, so take care to store them deep in your pack and to check them carefully before use.

Women Travellers

PERIOD PROBLEMS

Most women have few period problems when on the road. You might find that it is affected by time changes and the stress of travelling but in most cases it will soon settle down. You may find that your periods stop altogether when you're away – affected by you changing your routine and having different stresses (but have a pregnancy test done if you think you may be pregnant). You're just as likely to find, however, that travelling makes your periods heavier. If you suffer from PMT, be prepared for it to be worse while you are away and take plentiful supplies of any painkiller or other remedy you find helpful.

If you think you may need contraception, you could consider starting the pill before you leave – it can reduce PMT and gives lighter and regular periods.

VAGINAL INFECTIONS

Hot weather and limited washing facilities make thrush (yeast infection) more likely when you're travelling. If you know you are prone to thrush, it's worth taking a supply of medication with you.

A new partner could mean you acquire an STI. Get any symptoms like an abnormal vaginal discharge or genital sores checked out as soon as possible. Some STIs don't cause any symptoms, even though they can cause infertility and other problems, so if you have unprotected intercourse while you're away, be sure to have a check-up when you return home.

THE PILL

If you think you'll need this while you are away, see your doctor, a family planning clinic or your local women's health organisation before you leave. The Marie Stopes website at W www.mariestopes.org.uk has useful information on your options.

The timing of pill-taking can be tricky if you're crossing time zones, and diarrhoea, vomiting and antibiotics used to treat common infections can all reduce its effectiveness. Take a plentiful supply of your medication with you, as it may be difficult to get your brand. In some countries, oral contraceptives may not be readily available.

Diabetic Travellers

This section was written by Michelle Sobel, a Type 1 diabetic who has never let her condition get in the way of her travels.

Preventative self-care is your aim, travel is your game. Prepared and in good diabetic control, you're in the best position to enjoy your experiences abroad. Before you go, discuss with your doctor or specialist what to do if you get sick, as well as dosage adjustments, immunisations and other travel-related health issues.

The level and type of care offered to diabetics varies from country to country. Find out before you go what to expect in your destinations. National diabetic associations are usually the best source of information on local diabetic care:

American Diabetes Association (☎ 1800 342 2383; **W** www.diabetes.org; National Call Center, 1701 North Beauregard St, Alexandria, VA 22311, USA).

British Diabetic Association (BDA Careline; ☎ 020-7636 6112; **W** www.diabetes.org.uk; 10 Queen Anne St, London W1M 0BD) Produces a useful leaflet on travel with diabetes, as well as a number of specific country guides for diabetics.

Diabetes Australia (☎ 61-8-82226821; **W** www.diabetes.org.au; Queen Elizabeth Hospital, Woodville, South Australia).

International Diabetes Federation (☎ 32-2-5385511; **W** www.idf.org; Av Emile de Mot 19, B-1000 Brussels, Belgium) Maintains a listing of diabetic associations in different countries around the world, as well as other information on diabetes.

Alternatively, check out **W** www.diabeticresource.com (click on 'Travel'). A useful publication you could consider getting is the *Diabetic Traveller's Companion*, by Nerida Nichols.

Insulin & Other Diabetic Supplies

Carrying syringes and meters can sometimes prompt questions from customs and other officials, so make sure you have a letter from your doctor as well.

Before you leave, call the relevant manufacturer to get information on the availability abroad of diabetic supplies like test strips, medication (oral and insulin) and glucose meters. Consumer-friendly meter and pump manufacturers will advise you on repair, replacement and delivery policies if your equipment malfunctions or is lost abroad.

Note that most nations measure blood glucose in mmol/L; the US, however, primarily uses mg/dL. Different meters report glucose readings using either or both of these standards. To convert mmol/L to mg/dL, multiply the glucose reading by 18 (ie, 4mmol/L = 72 mg/dL). To convert mg/dL, divide the glucose by 18.

Take two to three times the medical supplies you expect to use (in carry-on, waterproof packs), to protect against loss or damage. On day trips, I carry two half bottles (instead of one or two full bottles) of insulin, so there's backup in case of breakage.

To reduce bulk, try insulin pens over syringes. However, note that manufacturers state that at room temperature some insulin pen cartridges (particularly some slow-acting and premixed insulin) may have shorter lives (as short as seven or 14 days) than vials (which last about a month).

Some diabetic care providers suggest reusing sharps, at your own risk. Consult your physician about reusing, and ask for advice on sterilising syringes and needles if necessary. Always discard needles and lancets appropriately when dull, and never share sharps or meters.

You should be aware that insulin may be sold in different concentrations from country to country. If you have to replenish abroad, use the appropriate syringe with the appropriate concentration. If you mix and match syringes and concentrations (for example, if you use U-40 insulin in a syringe marked 'for U-100 insulin only'), you'll be at greater risk of over- or under-injecting insulin. Also, it's a good idea to retain generic-name prescriptions (even if invalid abroad) and medication inserts, as medications may have different brand names in different countries.

If you find you are running out of supplies in a place with limited resources, be prepared (financially and time-wise) to flee to a better-stocked country. For extended travel and for emergencies, consider making preparations before you go for medical supplies to be mailed to you. Packaging is available to insulate insulin from heat and physical damage in the mail.

On the Move

Crossing time zones can be problematic, especially for insulin-dependent diabetics. Before you leave, take a copy of your itinerary to your diabetic care provider and ask for guidance on adjusting your individual protocol en route and as you acclimatise. As a rule, though, keep your watch on home time until the morning after you land.

It's always important to check blood sugars frequently to modify dosages, mealtimes and food choices, and flying presents its own issues. If you make adjustments based on how you feel – a very unreliable indicator whether you're travelling or not – hyper and hypoglycaemic reactions are almost inevitable. Remember that jet lag can further impair your ability to recognise highs and lows.

Staying Healthy

Unaccustomed physical activity, erratic sleep and meal times, unfamiliar foods, climate change, altitude sickness and stress are just some of the many variables that can aggravate control while you are away. All the potential effects of unstable blood glucose (like disorientation, headaches and lethargy) are especially unwelcome when you're away from home.

When you're travelling, insulin-dependent diabetics need to take particular care to prevent hyper and hypoglycaemic reactions. Ideally, monitor at least six times daily; if possible, bring two meters as well as visual blood glucose strips as backup. Carry emergency food, foil-wrapped ketone strips and glucagon. In the event of a reaction, wearing a medical bracelet showing that you are a diabetic can help prevent misdiagnosis (symptoms are often otherwise presumed to be induced by alcohol or illegal substances).

All diabetics should follow basic guidelines to prevent food-borne illness. If you do (or don't) take extra risks and end up ill, know what you need to do to prevent highs and lows related to illness.

Wounds in hot, humid climates get infected easier and faster – always keep your feet dry, clean and comfortable. Never walk barefoot, even on the beach. In hot or remote regions, take special care to stay hydrated. Pack extra supplies of medication, food and water. Protect your skin from the sun (severe sunburn can elevate blood sugars).

Keep insulin chilled in thermoses or insulated cool packs. Gels that freeze when shaken can protect insulin for a few hours. Make sure you don't freeze insulin, and don't place it directly against ice. Keep insulin out of direct sunlight. And ask hostels, friends etc to refrigerate your supplies when they have the opportunity.

And finally, keep in touch: a mobile phone is handy, and if you're travelling solo, check in with contacts.

Safety

Safe travel is about being sensible. You might want to do a self-defence course before you go to increase your confidence and teach you how to watch out for and deal with certain situations. Read up on your destination before you go – your guidebook will warn you of any potential dangers.

Theft/Mugging

Now, here's an idea: you want to avoid being robbed. And you pretty much can, as long as you're not careless. Try to keep your wits about you all the time. If your money belt is stolen, it may spell the end of your trip, or at least several days wasted replacing your passport and travellers cheques, and cancelling your credit cards. The following should help you avoid donating your belongings to a crafty thief:

- Always keep your passport, plane tickets, travellers cheques, most of your cash and important travel documents in your money belt. The only time you shouldn't be wearing your money belt is when it's in a secure safety-deposit box at the place you're staying or when you're sleeping (in which case it should be under your pillow).
- Keep photocopies of all your important travel documents in a separate place from your money belt.
- When swimming, diving or snorkelling, bring your important documents and money with you in a waterproof container, or leave them in a safety-deposit box (if you're confident it's safe).
- When you're in a restaurant or bar, secure your pack with a lock or strap or lean it against you so that you'll know if someone is trying to take it.
- Have a small padlock to secure your room door, and to lock your luggage to overhead racks on long-distance buses or trains.
- Keep an eye on your backpack when on long bus trips. If it is on the roof or in a luggage compartment, make sure it's secure (add your own lock if possible). During rest stops, make sure no-one tries to walk off with it.
- Don't flash your cash, valuables or camera around. If possible, do not let people see that you are wearing a money belt.
- Never accept drinks or food from strangers. In some countries, thieves have been known to put drugs in drinks or food and then rob the unconscious victim. Be careful with your water bottle, as thieves may try to inject drugs into it!
- Don't close the door of a taxi or pay the driver until your baggage has been unloaded.
- Don't give the name of your hotel or room number to strangers, as they might follow you back and try to rob you.
- Pickpockets usually work in teams. If you feel that people are jostling or crowding you for no reason, stand back and check discreetly to see that your valuables are still on you.
- It's difficult to keep your wits about you when you're drinking. If you know you're going on a bender, try to store your valuables and most of your cash in a secure safety-deposit box at your accommodation.
- Be careful of your valuables while you're taking a shower. If you're not sure that your room is safe, bring them into the bathroom with you.
- Don't walk alone at night or in unfamiliar areas. If you find yourself in an unsavoury spot, flag down a taxi or tuk-tuk.
- Be careful of unregistered taxis and never fall asleep in the back of a taxi.
- Be especially careful when boarding and riding buses and trains. You're at your most vulnerable

to pickpockets at these times. If the bus or train is really crowded, try to keep your hands unobtrusively over your wallet and money belt.

- Remember that it's not just locals who may steal your belongings – there are quite a few unscrupulous travellers around who pay for their trips by ripping off other travellers.
- If you are mugged, just give them what they want. There's no point putting yourself at risk for the sake of some things – they can be replaced, you can't.

Scams

Scams are concocted to prey on gullible or careless travellers.

You will quickly come to recognise the type of person who will try to win you over – usually a charming man (rarely a woman) who speaks good English, is very friendly, and goes out of his way to be helpful. There are lots of scams, varying from country to country, but they frequently share a common feature – lulling you into a false sense of trust. At some point your new friend will gently suggest something that, under normal circumstances, you would not do. Many scams take the form of an offer from a businessperson or local who befriends you. Perpetrators can be enormously charming and convincing, with testimonials from previous happy business partners. Scams can take on myriad forms, but if you're offered any kind of too-good-to-be-true deal, it really is just that. Scams change all the time, and your guidebook will point out the most common and up-to-date tricks tried at your destination. But, as a general rule of thumb, a few things to sprint a mile from are:

- **Gem or carpet deals** Someone might suggest you carry valuables home for them, or buy some items to sell at enormous profits back home – these are most commonly spotted in India and Morocco.
- **Transporting packages** Don't take anything for anyone across a border, even if they are a good chap. You might be offered money to take something (drugs, gold, electronic items) – watch out in Thailand, Central and South America.
- **Card games for money with friendly locals** They'll be a lot better at them than you.
- **Blackmarket moneychangers** Common in many African and Asian countries, if you change money on the black market you're risking robbery or blackmail.
- **Offers of food and drink from friendly strangers** Be particularly on your guard on trains and buses in India, Europe and the Americas. The typical ploy involves someone you've just met offering to buy or share a drink or snack. This happened to Charlie Flynn in Italy:

The bloke seemed very nice. He bought me a drink and I didn't want to offend him by turning it down, it seemed unnecessarily suspicious. The next thing I knew, it was 10 hours later. I had a throbbing headache and a missing backpack.

- **Letting your credit card out of your sight** Carefully watch what is done with it. If you are trekking be wary of leaving your valuables in a guesthouse safe. If you find charges on your card that don't belong there, call the credit-card company to have them removed.
- **Fake police or immigration officials** In Africa, India and Central and South America, men in official-looking outfits might demand to see your passport and then order you to pay a fee for some fabricated reason, or even to come to the police station. Never hand over your passport, and always demand to see their ID. If they won't leave you alone, insist on walking to the police station or phoning their buddies ahead.
- **Buying drugs** You are taking the risk that the dealer may rip you off or may be about to call their mate in the police. If you're unwise enough to buy from a stranger, don't be surprised if the local authorities soon pay you a visit. This is particularly common in some African countries, such as Morocco or Mali, India, South and Central America.

- **Shady tour guides** Women in particular should only sign up with reputable tour agencies that employ licensed guides. Each country has different requirements for accrediting guides, but if you ask to see a guide's licence and he/she doesn't show it to you, move on; do not be swayed by whatever story is offered as to why the licence can't be produced. Travelling to very remote areas is best done with a larger tour group. Get recommendations from other travellers.

Don't be paranoid, and don't cut yourself off from the people you meet, 99% of whom are interested in striking up a friendship. Yet it pays to be suspicious of overly friendly people, especially on long-distance trains and buses. Don't let a sense of obligation make you go along with things when you have a bad feeling about them. If you feel uncomfortable – trust your instincts – it's time to do a runner.

Natural Disasters & Wild Animals

Natural disasters, political unrest and marauding wild beasts are far less a risk than you might suppose (especially in Kent). Doing a bit of research before you travel will alert you in most cases to any potential problem areas. A good guidebook will have a detailed section on the dangers and how to avoid them. Update your information through newspapers, magazines and the internet just before visiting a country.

Drugs

Many countries, such as Thailand, Singapore, Malaysia and India, have exceedingly strict laws on drugs, ranging from long sentences to the death penalty, and worldwide, grim jails have their share of travellers frittering away their time inside. Just because other people are openly taking drugs doesn't mean that it's OK to do so, and you might find your time away turns into time inside if you get caught. And it's not just your own safety you should think about before building a bong or popping a pill, but the effect you are having on your surroundings; travellers' drug use can have a detrimental impact on the local economy and society as people get caught up in this lucrative industry.

In certain countries, particularly where the drug trade is a powerful force, such as in parts of South and Central America, Thailand and Jamaica, other travellers or locals may try to use you as a 'mule' to carry drugs or other illegal items across international borders. If you agree, you really are a bit of a mule. People may approach you with an opportunity or they may just hide parcels of drugs in your pack. Do not accept packages from anyone and check your bag carefully before boarding planes or crossing borders in countries where this might be a risk.

The dangers involved in attempting to buy any drugs are that the dealer may be the police or a police informer, or may simply rip you off. Being under the influence of drugs can also make you a target for thieves.

Hitchhiking

Hitchhiking is not usually recommended and a woman should never hitchhike alone. However, in certain parts of the world hitching is more of a norm than others. Simon Calder, Travel Editor of the *Independent* says one rule has helped him to stay safe in more than 30 years of hitchhiking:

If in any doubt, turn down a lift. If the driver screeches to a halt across three lanes of traffic, or you can smell alcohol on their breath or you don't like the look of the occupants, don't get in. That applies even if you have been standing in the rain for seven hours and night is falling. There are enough good people around that you will get a ride…eventually.

If You Do Get into Trouble

If the worst happens and you're the victim of a crime or some other disaster, try to take decisive steps to set things right as quickly as possible. As long as you are physically in one piece, the simple fact that you are taking action will go a long way towards making you feel better. You can always enlist the assistance of another traveller or trustworthy local, and you may be surprised how helpful others can be when you're in need.

If something has been stolen or you've been the victim of any other crime, immediately report it to the police. Even if you've lost your passport, you will need a police report so you can get a new one. A report will also be necessary for replacing travellers cheques or claiming on insurance. Someone in the police station should be able to speak English. If not, an interpreter should be organised or your embassy may be able to write a report to give to the police.

In the case of lost or stolen passports, you should go to your embassy or consulate, which can issue you a new passport, advise you about local laws, put you in touch with English-speaking lawyers or doctors, and contact friends or relatives back home in the case of an emergency. They will not, however, lend you money, get you out of jail or pay to fly you home.

Tips for Women Travellers
Women can be particularly vulnerable when travelling on their own. Here are a few tips to keep you safe:

- Only use registered or government-run taxis. If you don't know which they are, go to one of the upmarket hotel chains and get the staff to call one (ask them how much you should expect to pay while you're at it).
- Don't forget that when you're wearing sunglasses you tend to make less eye contact and so you'll get fewer approaches.
- If you're travelling in a sleeping compartment on a train sleep on the top bunk; this makes you less visible and therefore less vulnerable.
- Don't say you'll meet men later to try to get rid of them as they'll turn up and if it's a small town, you'll never get rid of them. Say 'no' politely and firmly.
- Wear a wedding ring and say you've got seven kids if anyone asks. Yes, you shouldn't have to but sometimes it's just a waste of time and energy having that argument.
- Think about how your clothing will fit in with local customs and attitudes. Wearing skimpy clothes or sunbathing nude will draw unwelcome attention to you in most cultures.
- Avoid flights that arrive late at night, especially if you are a first-time visitor to that country. These are often cheaper but safety is not worth saving money on.
- Thoroughly explore the area where you are staying during the day: it's important to have your bearings and know the dodgy parts to avoid.
- Spend a bit extra on a hotel in a decent area: the streets will be safer at night, there will be more security in the hotel and single women will get less hassle.
- If you want a big drink, stick to the hotel bar. You won't have to negotiate unfamiliar streets whilst tipsy.
- Never leave your key where someone can note your room number.
- Try to look confident about where you are going; stride out, you will be less of a target.

Travelling Hotspots

Find out where's hot and where's not on travel-advisory sections of websites. Up-to-date information is posted on the UK Foreign & Commonwealth Office website at **W** www .fco.gov.uk.

Lonely Planet provides a Travel Advisory service on its website at **W** www.lonelyplanet .com/travel_ticker/travel_advisories.htm, which provides information on international situations, from civil unrest to public holidays. Another useful Lonely Planet service is the monthly Comet email newsletter – you can sign up to get regular news on travel issues.

Keeping in Touch

While you're on the other side of the world having rip-roaring adventures, it's all too easy to forget about keeping in touch. Home is a distant, hazy place, and there may be a temptation to put that call off or send that postcard...er, from the airport while waiting for your flight back. Meanwhile, the folks back home are wondering about you all the time.

It's only fair to ease the minds of those at home with the occasional phone call or postcard, and to let your friends know you're still thinking about them (lie through your teeth). And hearing familiar voices can cheer you up no end when you're in an unfamiliar place. There's no better way of appreciating the experiences you're having than relating them to someone at home. If something goes wrong, the best way to pick yourself up is to listen to a few comforting words from the people who care.

It costs some cash to keep in touch with home, particularly by phone, so do some budgeting for it. Some top staying-in-touch tips include:

- If on the road, give those at home a rough itinerary.
- If heading out on long treks or trips into remote areas where you may be out of touch for a while, let your family and friends know (and call again to let them know you're OK when you get back).
- Ask someone at home to save the letters or emails you send them. This is almost as good as keeping a diary and they make great reading when you get home.
- Work out ideal times to call family and friends to minimise the chance of calling when they're out. Don't make definite calling times or schedules in case you forget to make that call and people start to worry.
- If you get bored of writing the same news to everyone, write up one good, detailed letter or email and send copies to everyone, masterfully adapted so that they're personalised.
- If your personal stereo has a record function, you can warble away and send a tape home – these are particularly fun if you're giving a running commentary while out and about, and again, a great reminder when you're back home again.
- Include a few photos that you've had developed to illustrate what you're describing and give people a feel for the place.

Email/www

It's electronic, easy, cheap, and faster than the nippiest postal worker. A country's internet (and email) access will only be as good as its phone lines and internet is still not available everywhere. Access to the net in some countries, such as Morocco or Nepal, may be limited to the big cities and often the fewer internet resources there are, the more expensive and slower access will be. The main places to access email worldwide are internet cafés and some hotels.

The easiest email addresses to access worldwide are through internet providers, such as Yahoo! and Hotmail (be warned the latter's so subscribed it can be life-sappingly slow to access in some places such as India). If you travel with a laptop, hooking up to the internet with your machine may be a challenge, depending on your destination – check your guidebook.

Some gappers even set up their own websites: this is a superb way to keep friends, family and random websurfers up to date on your progress. If you are doing charitable or voluntary work, you could try to get a company to sponsor you to set up a site.

FREE EMAIL

It's a breeze to set up and it's free! If you don't have a computer, you can do it at an internet café. If for some reason you've managed to float through life not knowing about computers, the staff at these outfits get paid to help people and they'll give you more advice than you could ever possibly want.

With a free email service, you register an email address and you're given a password. The address is your 'mailbox' where you receive email. You can retrieve email from this mailbox on any computer in the world that has internet access. Internet cafés will often have the usual suspects Yahoo! and Hotmail in the Bookmarks or Favourite menu of internet programmes. You just have to click on that menu, pull down your provider, enter your password and you're in your mailbox. Here you can read, write, send and save email messages and build up your electronic address book as you gather friends along the way. Be warned that space is limited on many free mail options, and you often get inundated with junk mail, which you will keep having to clear out, otherwise mail won't get through because your mail box is full.

INTERNET CAFÉS

These handy concerns are getting more and more prevalent all over the world, ranging from glitzy giants to joints the size of a jellybean. For a list in individual countries go to The Internet Café Guide (**W** www.netcafeguide.com). These cafés charge by the hour – there's usually a minimum charge, which is often the rate for half an hour, so check this out before logging on. Some charge by the minute, which is handy if you just want to skim through your mail.

Telephone

Should you take your mobile? Check with your service provider about whether your phone will work where you're going, and beware of calls being routed internationally (very expensive for a 'local' call). Texting internationally is a relatively cheap way to keep in contact and a good way of arranging when to call as you can text someone to arrange a good time for a telephone call.

One way of making cheaper mobile calls is to buy a local SIM card and use it in your handset. However, check that this will operate in your phone – handsets may not work with a different SIM card, or may be locked by your home network. A sales assistant at a mobile-phone store will advise you. Another solution is to buy a pay-as-you-go phone, if this option is available.

WHERE TO CALL FROM

Being in the depths of the jungle, in a remote rural area, or perched on a peak will make phoning home tricky but you should be able to place international calls in most towns in Asia, Africa and Central and South America, and from phone booths all over the place in Western countries and places such as Singapore and Hong Kong. If you're calling within a region or country, remember that the rings and busy signals will vary from the ones at home.

Telephone systems are wildly different in individual countries. However, you can usually place international calls from a pay phone in countries such as France, Spain and America. Phones may accept credit cards or phonecards. Prices can be very expensive or, where competition flourishes, very cheap. Try to call during off-peak hours for discounts.

In countries such as Mexico, Costa Rica and Thailand you sometimes have to go to a centralised telephone office to place calls. Often you go to a counter where an operator takes your number and places the call. You'll be pointed to a booth where you take the call. In many countries there is a three-minute minimum for international calls, though if you get an answering machine or a busy signal you may be allowed to pay just a nominal fee. Always check the rate per unit before you call. Sylvie Cox failed to do this in a private telephone office in Mali:

I hadn't called home for ages and in my rush to do so didn't think to check the rate before calling. I was on the phone for around 20 minutes – the bill came to about £50. The shop hiked up the charge and I couldn't really argue as I hadn't confirmed the rate first.

Reverse-charge calls are only possible between specific countries. This changes frequently and you'll have to check with the telephone office.

Some internet cafés such as those in Bangkok, now offer nifty Net Phone technology, which allows you to place calls over the internet via a headset. These calls are super cheap (about one-fifth of what you'll pay at a phone office) and efficient. The connection won't always be the best and there can be lengthy delays between when the person talks and you hear them but the price can't be beaten.

INTERNATIONAL PHONECARDS

International phonecards can save you lots of cash and mean you don't have to have pockets swilling with coins to make a call.

Plastic phonecards with a magnetic strip (variously known as *teletarges*, *telekartes*, *cartela telefonica* etc) are a good way to make phone calls in places such as Europe and Morocco. Where they are available the cards are sold at post offices, newsagents, tobacconists or general stores.

The cards come in various denominations of local currency; a card purchased in one country often cannot be used in another country, so it pays to use up the credit before moving on.

Apart from the official phonecards, in some places such as the US and Australia you can get special prepaid phonecards that can offer international calls up to 10 times cheaper than the national company. You dial a freephone number and then an account number before dialling the number you want, and the cost is deducted from what's on your card. If you're buying abroad, make sure it'll definitely work where you're going.

TYPES OF CALLS

There are different types of international calls and separate price structures for each kind. Your options dwindle the farther off the beaten track you roam:

- **Direct (person-to-person)** This is the easiest way to make a call: you pick up the phone and dial. This requires the International Direct Dialling (IDD) system. To place an international call you dial the IDD number, the country code, the area code and finally the number of the party you're calling. Phone or credit cards can be used for these calls.
- **Operator assisted** Anytime you go to a centralised telephone office, you're placing an operator-assisted call. These are usually pricey and have a minimum charge.
- **Reverse charge (collect)** An operator places this type of call for you and the party you're phoning agrees to pay. These are usually very expensive and in certain countries prohibitively

so. In this case it's better to have the person call you back than pay the reverse charge. Some operators or telephone services will also charge you a small fee for placing this type of call. It's very dificult to place reverse-charge calls from some places such as West or North Africa.

- **Home Country Direct** By calling an access number, Home Country Direct bypasses local operators and connects you directly with an operator in the country you're calling. Once connected, you can place credit-card or collect calls. Call your telephone company for more information.
- **Credit card** Public phones where you can swipe your credit card and have the call billed to it are becoming more common in places such as European countries, the US, Hong Kong and Singapore. These calls may be charged at a higher rate so beware. Often the phones accept both credit cards and phonecards.

FAX

In most countries, from Mauritania to Peru, you can send and receive faxes. Many businesses and hotels offer fax services but they will charge an arm and a leg to send them, though not too much to receive. Consider giving friends your hotel's fax number if you'll be in one place for a while. Even better are internet cafés, most of which send and receive faxes, in addition to offering email services. Fax machines can be useful for making bookings or receiving confirmations but generally email wins the communication contest hands down.

Post

Navigating post offices is part of being in a foreign country. Services are about as varied as facilities. Some Central American countries are so notorious for bad postal services that even the locals don't use them. Surface mail from Guatemala or India can take months to arrive, if it ever does. Generally it's wise to convey important news by telephone, fax or email and important documents should be sent through a private courier service or an international shipper such as DHL or Federal Express.

Have an idea of what it should cost to send a letter or postcard and buy a bunch of stamps at once (but keep in mind that in hot countries they might just all stick together and be useless) so you can write and send letters spontaneously to avoid carrying around soggy, unstamped postcards for months at the bottom of your daypack. Mail sent from rural offices usually takes much longer to reach its destination than letters posted from a city.

Each country has its own postal quirks, which you can find out from your guidebook.

There are several ways to receive mail while you're on the road, and what a joy it is to have a letter waiting for you in a strange city.

The three basic ways to receive mail are by poste restante (general delivery) at post offices, at American Express (AmEx) offices if you're a card member, or at your accommodation. The first is the most common. The AmEx mail service is efficient and conscientious. If you're on the road, having mail sent to your guesthouse or hotel can work but it's far more practical if it's addressed care of someone specific at the hotel and they've agreed to be responsible for your incoming mail.

SHIPPING ITEMS

Post offices are particular about sending packages and there may be weight and size limits and packaging requirements. Plus, everything has to be inspected by customs. Still, sending things home is a superb way to lighten your pack.

In some countries you will have the choice of sending your package by air or surface mail. Airmail is always more expensive but it's also more reliable and faster. Sea mail may be your very cheapest option. Packages may arrive up to four to six months later. Skip all these options if you're sending anything valuable, and instead go with a reliable courier or shipping service.

If you have lots of stuff to ship or a few heavy items, you may save some money by using a shipping agent. These companies charge by space rather than weight. One cubic metre is usually the minimum amount and maybe you can team up with friends to maximise your savings. Shipping agents offer door-to-door service, though it's likely you'll have to pick up your goods at the port nearest your destination address. The goods must pass through customs and you may have to pay an import tax before you can collect them.

POSTE RESTANTE

Poste restante is a good way to receive letters while on the road, provided you give those back home a rough idea of your itinerary. You simply ask people to send their letters to the general post office of a city along your route, with your name (surname in block letters and underlined) and the words 'poste restante' written clearly on the envelope. For example, if your name were Sancho Panza, a letter addressed to you in Nairobi would look like this:

PANZA, Sancho
Poste Restante
General Post Office (GPO)
Nairobi
Kenya

Normally, poste-restante letters are filed under your surname. However, confusion can arise and letters are sometimes filed under your given name. If a letter you're expecting can't be found by searching under the first letter of your last name, try looking under the first letter of your given name.

In most countries you will need to show your passport when picking up a letter at poste restante. Most post offices also charge a small fee. In some post offices there's a separate room or counter for poste restante; in others, just ask for it at the main desk. Poste restante facilities are only offered by certain post offices – usually the main office in a large city – smaller rural offices don't have the staff to offer this service.

Many post offices will only hold mail for a month or so before either discarding it or returning it to the sender, though there are some that will hold it for up to four months. Thus, you'll need to give people a fairly accurate itinerary if you want to receive their letters. If you're not sure of your plans, a good solution is to ask people to send copies of the same letter to two or three different post offices along your route, although the postage for this can add up.

It's possible to receive packages by poste restante but this is unreliable in most places. In some countries, when you receive a package it will have to be inspected before being turned over to you. You'll usually be notified of a package via a slip of paper in the letter-box corresponding to your surname. You'll probably have to fill out some forms when receiving a package this way and you may have to pay some import duties. Of course, any prohibited items will be confiscated and you could land in trouble. As with letters, if you want something important sent or you're in a hurry, you should probably have the item shipped by an international courier service like Federal Express or DHL.

Because some poste-restante offices are poorly supervised and other travellers can search through the mail by themselves, it's possible that things will get stolen. So it's a good idea never to have anything of value sent poste restante.

Media

You'll get more out of your visit if you take an interest in local news, and keeping an eye on international events will help keep you feeling part of the real world. It might help you avoid dangerous situations as well, unlike the Japanese backpackers who in April 2002 turned up at the Church of the Nativity in Bethlehem, and were surprised to learn that it was the 16th day of an Israeli siege upon the Palestinian gunmen inside.

INTERNET

The internet is a fabulous way to catch up, as the level of international news varies in the press from country to country (and might not be available in English). You can probably read about what's happening in your home town as almost every newspaper has a web page.

PRESS

Many countries have either an English-language daily or weekly. In cities, you will often find the *International Herald Tribune*, and you can buy copies of the *New York Times* and *USA Today*. International copies of *Time* and *Newsweek* may be available too. Airports are the best places to find international newspapers and magazines, though top-end hotels and some bookshops may have them.

RADIO & TV

The two most accessible English-language stations worldwide are the soothing tones of the BBC World Service and the Voice of America; you could also try Australia's Radio National. For scheduling and frequency information, visit their websites: **W** www.bbc.co.uk/world service, **W** www.voa.gov and **W** www.abc.net.au/ra. These services often also broadcast features and music.

Hotels and guesthouses often have TV sets, and many hostels have TV rooms. These will invariably have cable or satellite connections, otherwise you'll have to get familiar with the local stations. CNN and BBC World are the stations most commonly picked up globally. Bars worldwide often screen major sporting events, which can be unforgettable to watch if there's a good crowd.

Being a Good Traveller

Respect Local Cultures

Even the most grizzled travellers suffer culture shock. This is the disoriented feeling you get from all the strange and perhaps offensive behaviour and customs you experience in a new country. It might be pollution, dangerously crowded buses or exotic foods that get your goat, and there will be something new at every turn challenging your perceptions. If you look at culture shock as an inevitable part of travelling to which you have to adjust slowly but surely, you'll be able to handle the peculiarity of it all with aplomb and humour.

The extent to which you feel culture shock will depend on your previous travel experience, language skills and what you learned to expect before you left home. Culture shock and homesickness often go hand in hand because the confusion you feel over a foreign culture evokes a desire for the familiar. Just ease into it; there's no good reason to tuck into fried guinea pig on your first day. Being well rested will help you appreciate your new surroundings. To help you avoid being stunned by culture shock, do some research before you leave home. Read travelogues and history books, cruise the web and talk to other travellers who have been where you're going. Eleanor Jacobs found the treatment she received in China very off-putting at first:

People would stare at me relentlessly for hours of entertainment and some even went as far as poking me or touching my hair. It was really unsettling. If I'd been warned about what to expect I might have found it easier those first few weeks.

Research before you go will help you gain an understanding of and respect for local culture and, most importantly, avoid shocking people yourself. Tourists can have a detrimental impact on the places they visit if they are careless about behaving appropriately.

AVOIDING OFFENCE

One culture's horror is another's norm. Behavioural taboos are usually related to clothing, religion, expressions of affection, and rudeness. For more information on specific countries, consult your guidebook:

- Places of worship have codes of conduct. Always remember to show respect – don't kid around or smoke.
- You should dress respectfully when visiting any religious place such as a church, mosque or temple – long trousers for men and long skirts or trousers for women. You may be required to remove your hat at some temples, while at mosques you should cover your head. At both temples and mosques, remove your shoes.
- Do not point at Buddha images, especially with your feet. If you sit in front of a Buddha image, sit with your feet pointing away.
- Women are not usually allowed in the main prayer hall of a mosque, and non-Muslims of either sex may not be permitted to enter some mosques, especially during prayer times. Before taking pictures, make sure photography is permitted. Don't take photos when people are praying. You cannot take photos of holy images in many temples.
- At Hindu temples, you will sometimes have to remove leather objects, such as belts, before entering.

No Knees Please

Your guidebook will also advise you on how to dress appropriately and looking at the locals is a good way to gauge what to wear. In some countries – particularly Muslim ones, and in the Indian subcontinent – it's offensive to flash your flesh, particularly for women – you'll be confirming suspect ideas about Western women if you do, as well as attracting unwanted attention. In Latin America, where even the poorest people strive to look neat and clean, grubby, torn clothing is considered disrespectful.

In some places, there is an unspoken understanding about appropriating indigenous clothing while you're still in that country. In Guatemala, for example, it is considered in poor taste to wear the beautifully woven *huipiles* (blouses) for which the country is known.

Taking Photos

Don't let the temptation to get that shot get the better of you. Treat locals with respect when taking pictures. The following are some basic tips to make sure that both you and your subject come away happy:

- If you are taking a picture of a person, ask their permission. Do not treat people like zoo animals. Some people enjoy having their picture taken and some do not – just as in the West. Obviously, you lose some spontaneity by asking permission. There are ways around this however: for example, take two pictures – the first posed and the second when your subject has relaxed; or use humour to relax your subject.
- Do not take photos of private or sacred events unless you are absolutely sure it is OK to do so (by asking permission). Just imagine if a stranger burst in on a wake in your home country and started taking pictures. Crazy as it sounds, this is pretty much what lots of foreign travellers do at the ritual cremations performed on the banks of the Ganges in Varanasi, India.
- If you are photographing a religious ceremony or similar event, take care not to bother the participants and onlookers with the sound of your camera or the light of your flash.
- Do not take photographs inside religious structures such as temples or shrines, unless you are sure it is OK to do so.
- People whose pictures you take may sometimes ask you to send them copies; do not promise to do so unless you really intend to follow through.
- Some people might charge money to have their photo taken. There is no need to regard this as a detrimental effect of tourism: it is a way of supplementing what is often a meagre existence, and when people allow themselves to be used as subjects for your photography they are providing you with a service.

Ecotourism

While tourism can be an enormous boon, it can also have negative effects that result in destruction of both natural and social environments. Ecotourism is travel that conserves the natural environment and helps local people in a sustainable way. The concept was born as a backlash against destructive travel practices, particularly in more remote regions of the world. Unfortunately, the term has rapidly become meaningless, particularly in popular trekking and hiking areas, with companies hitching a ride on the eco-bandwagon without having any substance behind their claims.

As a foreign visitor, you should ensure that you are helping to protect and support the environment and communities of the areas you visit. In the case of tour operators, this means you'll need to take a bit of extra time to look beyond glossy brochures and vague 'eco-friendly' claims and ask what they are really doing to support the environment (which includes local people, as well as animals and plants). Then, patronise only those companies that make these issues a priority. Remember that just because an activity is outdoors, it is not necessarily 'eco-friendly'. Depending on how they are carried out, camping, white-water rafting trips, game viewing (especially by car or balloon) or sightseeing excursions to remote or fragile areas can be more environmentally or culturally harmful than a conventional hotel holiday in a specifically developed resort.

You can do your bit to preserve the environment in developing countries by conserving water, filtering or purifying water yourself to avoid adding to the masses of plastic mineralwater bottles cluttering up some countries, and recycling wherever possible. If you use small-scale businesses you will be more likely to be contributing to the pockets of local people.

Ecologically sound tourism encompasses people as well as the natural environment, and focuses on your own actions, as well as those of organisations. Behaving in a culturally sensitive way – learning some words of the local language, dressing appropriately, not haggling aggressively, not giving out sweets and pens to children and showing respect for the place you are visiting are ways to ensure that when you visit somewhere, you only leave behind a footprint. To learn more about some of the issues, the resources listed below will provide further information.

Ecotourism Resources

Climate Care (☎ 01865-777770; Ⓦ www.co2.org) This organisation works to encourage people to become 'carbon neutral' by planting trees to counter the effects of CO_2 emissions from planes etc.

Responsible Travel (Ⓦ www.responsibletravel.com) Based in Brighton this company has a comprehensive database of responsible tourism trips, links to other sites and information on how to be a good traveller and more.

Tourism Concern (☎ 020-7753 3330; Ⓦ www.tourismconcern.org.uk; Stapleton House, 277–281 Holloway Rd, London N7 8HN) This is a membership organisation. If you would like to support its work, it costs £24 per year to join.

World Tourism Organisation (Ⓦ www.world-tourism.org) This is an international organisation with information on the Sustainable Development of Tourism.

Coming Home

Culture Shock

Weirdly, it can be shocking coming back home, particularly if you have been experiencing a different culture, your own is cast into relief. It's so quiet, so clean and so...boring. Buses are understuffed, there are no animals in the street, food seems tasteless; it all seems colourless. Catherine Bruzzone's daughter found it troublesome returning from China:

For the first week she only wanted to use chopsticks to eat her meals! She found it strange to be surrounded by westerners and also very irritating that we hadn't changed at all whereas she felt so different. She was longing to start afresh at university, which has proved to be a great success.

You've experienced so much and been so independent and now your parents are asking you what time you'll be home. Zabrina Shield saw England differently:

It felt surreal – everything suddenly felt very English, the country roads, the pubs, the village greens. I felt as though I was in a large dolls house. However I soon began to feel at home and it was nice to have a hot shower and sleep in my own bed.

Factors that contribute to the blues are the difficulty of reconciling the realities of life in the place you've been to those at home, and the need to adjust to a daily routine after facing so many varied challenges. Sophia Haque found returning from Pakistan problematic:

It was difficult as everything seemed dull. I'd recommend that people have a clear date when they will return home, which makes it easier to work towards. I also think it is a great idea to become involved in a job or some sort of activity soon after you return so you feel a sense of belonging.

The best way to fight feeling forlorn is to plunge back into life at home. Whether you've already completed higher education or are about to launch into it, you're heading for something new. And at the same time, don't let your trip evaporate. It already seems like a dream: just pin it down – it won't ever float away entirely. Make a photo album, keep reading about the places you've visited, study the language, and re-read your journal. Eleanor Romaine says keeping in contact with the people she had met made her feel better:

You have to come home. It was really, really hard. Keep in touch with everyone. It's only now, really, that I appreciate what I had when I was there.

If you promised to send people photos, do it now. Write thank-you letters and emails. You'll find continuity of contact will help keep your memories vivid.

What Am I Going to Do Now?

Confronted with the mundanities of everyday life, it's enough to make you want to turn around and get on the next plane out of town. But it doesn't have to be like that. If you've already sorted out going to college, then you'll have that to prepare for and look forward to. Get on the university website and plan what societies you're going to join and what sports you're going to take up – you know you've always wanted to be a synchronised swimmer. Perhaps you've had a rethink about what you want to do. If you've left making a decision about a course till you get back, then make sure you time your homecoming right so you can sort out an application. UCAS (**W** www.ucas.ac.uk) and your school will help you with the application procedure.

If you've already finished college, you can set about applying for jobs as soon as you get back. Check out your local newspaper for vacancies or if you're thinking of moving further afield the *Guardian* has excellent listings (**W** www.guardian.co.uk). There are many, many recruitment agencies; **W** www.agencycentral.co.uk and **W** www.jobs1.co.uk are two websites where you can find out more. If this doesn't work or you want to pay off your debts before you start college you might want to temp for a while. Again, there are literally hundreds of agencies.

If your financial position isn't causing you too many headaches then some voluntary work might be just the thing to keep you occupied (see the Volunteering, Conservation & Expeditions chapter in Part III for more information). Or do some work experience to enhance your CV. If you're not sure which direction you want to go in, call a number of different companies and ask to do some work experience for a couple of weeks. This will help you make an informed decision about your career. Go back to your school or university for contact numbers and advice. The other alternative is to do a short course (see the Courses chapter in Part III for details).

To ease yourself into life back home, it helps to give the end of your trip some serious thought while you're still on the road. You'll have had a lot of time to think about what you want to do when you get back. Ideally, your time will have recharged your batteries, given you a new perspective on the world and realigned your priorities. If you simply avoid thoughts of home while you're on the road, you'll be in for a big shock when you arrive back at the airport.

Lizz Harrison had planned to relax for a few weeks but decided against it:

I felt quite lonely because I'd been used to having lots of people all around me and being really busy all the time. In the end I started work after a week of getting back! One piece of advice is to keep in touch with the people you travelled with as they know how you feel.

When you do arrive home, you may find that you are suffering from post-holiday blues or that you are infused with a kind of manic energy. Either way, you'll want to get started on your new life as quickly as possible and implement the changes you've decided to make.

Itchy Feet

When you come back, you usually have a brief excited phase when it's thrilling to have returned. The familiar looks strange, everyone wants to hear about your trip, and you can indulge in some deliciously novel home comforts. This phase lasts three-quarters of a day max. By the next day, people aren't so interested to hear about it, the hot shower's lost its beguiling quality, and you sit in your room and the four walls close in, like that scene from *Star Wars*. Your feet are so goddamn itchy you can't wear socks. You want to go back to experiencing things intensely. Life at home seems half-hearted after all the colour, thrills and bellyaches of your time away. Richard Satchell got through it by reminding himself of his amazing trip:

Things I had done and experienced that nobody else at home would have a true sense of. That's special and something I can remember forever...And there's always the next trip to plan!

You'll gradually settle back into your home life, and you'll be going on to something different: perhaps higher education or setting about finding yourself a job. Having developed a taste for travel will drive you to create more opportunities to do it. Coming back doesn't mean: game over, you've used up all your travel points for this lifetime. Your itchy feet will stand you in good stead.

Talk about It (but Not Too Much)

One of the hardest aspects of returning home is that your friends and family may not be particularly interested in hearing about your experiences. So what if you've trekked the Everest Base Camp? You try to relate your incredible experience, and notice their eyes glaze over as they cut you off with the latest gossip about your friends or what's been on TV. Try not to let this lack of appreciation get you down, and don't ditch all your friends as a bunch of small-minded bores.

The reality is that the world you experienced is so far removed from their daily lives that it's difficult for them to get engaged hearing your stories. What is so vivid to you doesn't have the same resonance for them. There may be an element of jealousy floating around about the good times you've had, and it's unpleasant for your friends to feel you're looking down on them for not having experienced them. Maybe you need to exercise some restraint and not wave your experiences in the faces of those who stayed at home doing the humdrum ho-hum thing. And refusing to answer to anything but your Tibetan name IS annoying. You'll soon learn who really wants to hear your stories. But do avoid starting every sentence with 'When I was in Tanzania...'

A way to keep your memories alive is to write them down: write articles for your university or local newspapers and magazines. You'll often find it's a better way to express what you saw and discovered than trying to explain it to people. And write to Lonely Planet – we want to hear about your experiences and views for the next Gap Year Book.

Part II

Round the World

Many round-the-world (RTW) tickets are designed to transport young masses to the land of boomerangs and decent cricket players, Australia. For the airlines' part, they are a rather good way of using up spare capacity but they are food and drink for the breed of gapper who wants to see a lot of the world in a relatively short time.

Travelling around the whole world is quite an achievement (imagine the diversity, the sights to see!) but not all RTW tickets concern themselves with getting to Australia or even going around the world (although they are a little more expensive). In any case, the airlines can rest easy in the knowledge that once you've had your first taste of long-haul travel, well, you're going to want to do it again and again, and that's good business.

Given the history between Britain and Australia/New Zealand and the high volume of both transpacific and transatlantic traffic, RTW deals from the UK are just about the cheapest and sweetest in the world. We are blessed and it would be rude not to take advantage.

Pros & Cons

RTW tickets are an excellent way to see a huge amount of the world for not that much cash. You can also travel assured that no matter how many crazy nights you have or how much of your budget gets blown on an impulse, with a good RTW ticket you won't be stuck in Australia desperately trying to earn cash for a ticket home.

The world's tourist highlights are all there for the taking with a RTW; the most amazing cultures of the world can be explored; the world's greatest trekking destinations or surf breaks could be compiled into one glorious trip; you could witness some of the greatest wildlife spectacles on earth; or simply go on a quest for the planet's top-10 palm-fringed beaches. One of the great benefits of travelling like this is that everything is fresh; every experience can be mentally boxed up and sent home with your photos before you move on to the next country or experience. And, of course, if a place gets you down or disagrees with you, you can just change your itinerary and split to greener pastures. With some tickets you get unlimited stops which, travelling quickly, will enable you to see just how varied and wacky the world really is and ensures that you'll experience some wonderful contrasts – there's nothing like arriving in Delhi after visiting Singapore. Finally, a RTW ticket will be far more flexible than a multi-stop return or one-way fare.

But there is a downside. Most RTW tickets are valid for a year but if you've had to work in order to fund your trip you may be left with only six or nine months to travel. This means you'll have limited time in each country that you've added to your ticket, which means you may gravitate towards famous cities and the most popular tourist attractions. Many tickets require you to move in a fixed direction, to a fixed itinerary with a set allowance of miles allowed, and this means you can't necessarily blow like the wind – extra miles and changes in itinerary will cost you. Moving fast and not really getting under the skin of anything can make you feel like you're on some global air-bound package tour. Travel quickly through a bunch of countries and you may see too much of the bad side of travel (too many bus stations and border hassles can get you down) and you may miss the 'real' country. There's nothing better than taking a little time to get off the beaten track, kicking back in some obscure town and letting the country wash over you. The cheapest and most popular RTW tickets can be prescriptive (none really allow exploration of Eastern Europe, Russia or Central Asia), which can also be frustrating. It's ironic that RTW tickets offer so many tasters and glimpses of intriguing travel experiences that some gappers are left wishing they could break off their RTW route and head off at a giant tangent.

Classic Routes

The cheapest classic RTW ticket goes something like London–Bangkok (Thailand)–Sydney (Australia)–Los Angeles (USA)–London. You can get these beauties for under £700 if you can spend a little time sniffing out the bargains. These tickets don't really come from any one source. What usually happens is an agent talks to a few airlines and puts together a cheap deal with a very fixed itinerary (for something more tailor-made you'll pay much more).

More expansive (and expensive) RTW deals are essentially based on five or six products that act like wrappers within which RTW tickets are constructed. These are put out by cooperation between airlines and popular airline alliances. Asia–Australasia–North America is a common routing but more tickets now offer some variation and the more you spend the more weird and wonderful destinations you can include. All the fares given in the following ticket descriptions exclude tax (usually between £80 and £125 depending on each unique routing) and are valid for the low season at the time of writing.

World Discovery

A popular RTW ticket offered by British Airways (BA), Qantas, Cathay Pacific and Air Pacific. This ticket gives you an allowance of 29,000 miles to make it to Australasia and back allowing for a maximum of seven stopovers (four of which can be in Australia and/or New Zealand). The student/normal fare is £829/891 (student fares don't allow routes into South America). These tickets are good for simple trips to Australia and New Zealand but do not include India or the Middle East. Routes do not have to circumnavigate the globe. The Outback ticket is a cheaper, simpler version, the World Voyager fare more expensive with some smoother routings and good access to Central/South America.

A possible routing is: London–Lima (Peru) overland to São Paulo (Brazil)–Buenos Aires (Argentina)–Santiago (Chile)–Auckland (New Zealand)–Sydney–Brisbane (Australia)–Singapore–London.

Global Explorer

A ticket that's offered by BA, Qantas, Cathay Pacific, American Airlines, Iberia, Gulf Air, LanChile, LanPeru, Air Pacific and others. This ticket can take you everywhere, really opens up South America and includes Easter Island. Tickets are organised on a mileage basis – 29,000 miles (10 stopovers permitted) costs £1299 and 34,000 miles (15 stopovers) is £1699. You must circumnavigate the globe and backtracking between regions is not permitted. This is a good option for RTW trips that include South America or link Africa and Asia.

One possible routing is: London–Tehrān (Iran)–Bahrain–Trivandrum (India) overland to Colombo (Sri Lanka)–Bangkok overland to Ho Chi Minh City (Vietnam)–Sydney–Port Vila (Vanuatu)–Nadi (Fiji)–Honolulu (Hawaii) –Los Angeles–Denver (USA)–London.

oneworld Explorer

This ticket springs from the airlines of the oneworld alliance (see Airlines Appendix) and routings are determined by continent. Three-, four-, five- and six-continent schemes are available and cost £1149, £1299, £1699 and £1899 respectively. Each continent is divided into four flight sectors (six in the case of North America, two in Europe) and a flight is permitted within each sector. Travel must be in one direction and backtracking is only permitted within continents. This ticket is great if you want to make loads of stops and get to some more unusual destinations – it's particularly good for South America and Africa.

A five-continent itinerary could be: London–Los Angeles–Hong Kong–Bangkok–Singapore–Sydney–Cairns (Australia)–Darwin (Australia)–Perth (Australia)–Harare (Zimbabwe)–Johannesburg (South Africa)–Victoria Falls (Zambia)–London.

The Great Escapade

This is one of the best RTW packages; Virgin, Air New Zealand, Singapore Airlines and SilkAir are the main movers. You've 29,000 miles to play with and unlimited stopovers are permitted (limited to three in New Zealand) plus extra blocks of 1500 miles can be bought to extend your possibilities. This ticket is a little limited in some areas but includes loads of South Pacific destinations, though none in South America. Fares start at £825 for 29,000 miles and the maximum of 33,500 miles costs £1040. You must circumnavigate the globe with this ticket, which is good if you want lots of stops in Southeast Asia, Australia or the Pacific.

One possible itinerary is: London–Delhi (India) overland to Mumbai (Bombay, India)–Singapore–Perth overland to Sydney–Christchurch (New Zealand)–Queenstown (New Zealand)–Auckland–Nadi (Fiji)–Rarotonga (Cook Islands)–Tahiti (French Polynesia)–Los Angeles overland to Miami (USA)–London.

The Star Alliance

This major RTW scheme is run by the 15 partners of the Star Alliance (see Airlines Appendix). Fifteen stopovers are allowed within set mileage allowances, so is backtracking. This ticket is non-seasonal (29,000 miles costs £1249, 34,000 miles £1549 and 39,000 miles £1749) and fabulous for almost all RTW routes and ideal for those who don't care about visiting Australia or New Zealand.

A good itinerary could be: London–Cairo (Egypt)–Singapore–Ho Chi Minh City–Bangkok–Kunming (China) overland to Hong Kong–Tokyo (Japan)–Honolulu–San Francisco (USA)–Los Angeles–Mexico City–Bogota (Colombia) overland to Caracas (Venezuela)–London.

KLM (along with Northwest and other alliance partners) and Air France (plus their SkyTeam partners) both run RTW schemes that offer excellent coverage of the northern hemisphere, plus some rather offbeat destinations, and don't go through Australia. However, both schemes are not widely patronised by UK travel agents and going to the airlines can be very costly. Expect to pay well over £1000.

Feeling Maverick

If these packages don't seem like your cup of tea or are too downright expensive for you, don't fear, there are a few little tricks and options that may help. First off, talk to your travel agent – a good one well used to dealing with RTW tickets may be able to put together a custom job that gets you to Australia while still including Alaska (USA) and Tonga or the Maldives and Cairo or whatever you're after. The second thing to do is put aside the notion that actually going around the world is the be all and end all. After all, many gappers use the stops en route to Australia and New Zealand as little holidays on the way to the main event and there are a few ways you can explore many continents in one hit.

Standard Return Tickets

Don't discount the humble return fare. For the big boys and their global alliances all may be sweet on the RTW scene but some cunning carriers have developed partnerships, alliances and systems of 'on-line stopovers' (which allow you to get off at any airport your carrier uses that happens to lie roughly in between your starting and finishing points). This means you can put together a natty little trip on the back of a return ticket to Australia or New Zealand.

Examples of this airline behaviour include (prices are for the low season and exclude tax):

Emirates & Sri Lankan Airlines – thanks to a groovy policy of on-line stopovers this nice little alliance allows a routing of London–Dubai (United Arab Emirates)–Maldives–Colombo–Singapore–Melbourne (Australia) for £675. You can take some of these stops on the way back and there are other stopover options in the Middle East.

Royal Air Brunei – allows a return flight to Darwin with a London–Dubai–Kolkata (Calcutta, India)–Brunei–Darwin routing (£610). On the way back you can leave from Perth and include other stopovers.

United Airlines – this big US carrier allows three stops in North America en route to Sydney (£596). These could include Vancouver (Canada) and Mexico City.

Aerolineas Argentinas – on a ticket to Sydney a London–Madrid (Spain)–Buenos Aires–Sydney routing is possible (£900) and cheap deals sometimes come up.

Malaysia Airlines – buy a flight to Auckland with these boys (£594) and you can stop in Brisbane as well as Kuala Lumpur (from where additional free side trips within Malaysia are possible). In addition, Malaysia Airlines' flights to Melbourne stop in Sydney first thus allowing what's essentially an Australian internal flight.

Thai Airways – this carrier stops in Sydney, as well as Bangkok, en route to Auckland (£800), which could be handy as they sometimes have cheap deals.

If you're keen on getting a return ticket somewhere check with your travel agent to see if any cheap and useful regional 'sector' flights are available. For example, a £120 flight from Belize to Miami coupled with a cheap United Airlines fare to Los Angeles (on which many stops are allowed within North America) creates a great loop through North and Central America.

One-way Tickets

If you've got a working visa for Australia they'll let you in with a one-way ticket. This can be amazingly handy if you, wisely, intend to turn your gap year into a couple of gap years and spend a whole year in Australia and New Zealand working out your visa in between two long trips.

One-way tickets can be built in the same way and along the same routes as conventional RTW fares, with overland and open-jaw sections as and when. They can also be pretty cheap (less than half the price of a World Discovery fare).

If this seems a little too loose, some travel agents will be able to put together two one-way tickets in a tailor-made RTW package, which with a little cunning can allow a huge number of stopovers. This mix-and-match type of ticket also enables pre-booked trips of well over a year.

Buying Tickets

If you're considering a RTW ticket then the first thing you should do is read through the rest of Part II and see where takes your fancy – the regions you would really like to explore might not be possible or desirable to visit with a RTW ticket. A standard return or open-jaw ticket may be more appropriate. The next step is to get an atlas and try plotting your dream trip into some semblance of a loop around the globe – most RTW tickets (with the notable exception of the oneworld ticket that is based on routes within continents) keep you moving in a continuous direction. Once you've fixed a budget, the best way of getting a feel for what's out there is to visit one of the many RTW route generators on the internet. The simplest one to use is that of STA Travel ([W] www.statravel.co.uk). It uses pretty broad brushstrokes but you'll quickly get the idea of possibilities, costs and restrictions. Also try TravelBag at [W] www.travelbag.co.uk, and [W] www.roundtheworldflights.com. Also check out the networks of the major airlines offering popular RTW tickets (see Classic Routes previously). This insight should enable you to choose more unusual destinations, should you want to. When you're prepped and have a better idea of what you want, talk to a travel agent because despite the advances of online fare generators, there's nothing better than talking through your travel plans with a human who knows the business inside out. The following pointers should be considered in your discussions:

- Budget is likely to play as much of a part of your decision as possible routings.
- Flying between South America and Africa can add to costs big style as does having Africa, India and Asia on your ticket. Australia is often the only option as a next stop after Africa. In fact, sticking to three continents will keep costs down.
- Money is going to buy you more flexibility and more offbeat destinations. Many cheap tickets don't go between North and South America, and RTW tickets that don't include Australia and New Zealand are more expensive.
- If you're leaving in October head somewhere hot first and arrive in Australia for Christmas and the summer.
- The most expensive time to leave Blighty is roughly mid-June to mid-August, or during the Christmas period. The cheapest times to travel are March, April and May. Mid-September to November is not bad either.
- You must set all your travel dates before departure. After you hit the road, date changes are often free but some airline offices 'reserve the right' to charge a small administration fee. Basically you may pay, sometimes you may not.
- When booking onward travel dates bear in mind that your next onward ticket should not exceed the maximum stay on the tourist visa you've been/will be issued with – ie, rocking up in Thailand with a 60-day visa but with a ticket that says you'll be flying out in four months causes trouble and tears – rely on the flexibility of your RTW ticket, not the generosity of immigration officials.
- Re-routing tickets is perfectly possible on many RTW packages but a charge of at least £50 is levied.
- On restricted-mileage tickets you can usually pay a reasonable surcharge to increase your permitted total.
- Backtracking can be included on some RTW tickets but you can't return to any city on the route (ie, a side trip out to India from Bangkok before returning to Singapore and heading on to Sydney is OK).
- Be flexible in your travel plans and don't be afraid to try something new or unusual; the Maldives, Easter Island, Sri Lanka, Tonga, Tahiti, Windhoek (Namibia), Mexico City, Bermuda, Moscow (Russia), Kathmandu (Nepal) and Shanghai (China) are all possible destinations.
- Try to include a few overland sections in your trip. This means travelling to a new city to pick up your next flight and in some cases these journeys will be the highlight of your trip (see Going Overland later).

See Passports, Tickets, Visas & Insurance in Part I for more information on travel agents and how to get the best, most flexible deal.

Do-It-Yourself

There's no doubt that flying around the world on an ad hoc basis, picking up a ticket when you feel like moving on, is going to cost you a darn sight more than the cheapest RTW ticket. It's just not worth entertaining the idea. What's more, many countries don't permit entry to travellers on one-way tickets. However, there's a lot to be said for flying into some far-flung destination and just seeing how you get on. After all, the difference between a cheap return ticket into Bangkok and a cheap RTW ticket is about enough to secure five weeks' beach time on some sunny Thai island. If you like the place, you may want to stay the whole year or be content to move slowly overland throughout a region you can really enjoy in depth. You can always move continents if the urge takes you and you've money left (remember to keep £500 aside for that all important ticket home!).

Going Overland

Travelling overland is a great option for tough travelling DIY round the worlders, although all those bus tickets could easily add up to the price of a RTW ticket. However, the wild and wonderful Hippie Trail from London to Kathmandu and the remarkable Trans-Siberian Railway between Moscow and Beijing get you within easy reach of Southeast Asia from where a well-worn trail leads to Bali or Timor, a short flight from Australia. If you've a working visa you can save for the ticket home or fly (unless you hitch a lift on a yacht) across to Santiago (Chile) and head up the Gringo Trail along the west coast of the Americas. Once in the USA, a road trip through the delights of the Southwest and on to New York (where cheap one-ways to the UK are bountiful) beckons. That's if you don't want to make another great overland journey up to Alaska…

Overland journeys need not supplant all air travel. Some wonderful overland trips (often referred to as 'surface' on itineraries) can be built into your RTW ticket, although these still count as part of your total mileage on most tickets:

Los Angeles to New York is a classic American road trip.
Vancouver to Toronto is a huge, beautiful trip across Canada best done by rail.
Mexico City to San José (Costa Rica) takes in many of Central America's glories.
Río de Janeiro or Buenos Aires to Santiago leads across the pampas and into legendary Patagonia.
Nairobi to Cape Town will take you through the best of Africa.
Melbourne to Cairns is the classic East Coast trail.
Bangkok to Singapore includes many Asian delights and wonders.
Bangkok to Bali (via Indonesia) leads through a remarkable archipelago.
Tokyo to Kyoto offers some fantastic Shinto and Zen Buddhist culture.
Beijing to Hong Kong is a window on the incredible development of China.
Mumbai (Bombay) to Kolkata (Calcutta) leads through some mind-blowing cultural sites.
Islamabad (Pakistan) to Beijing (China) starts on the stunning Karakoram Highway and ends on the ancient Silk Road.

Many of these are detailed in the continent sections that make up the rest of Part II.

Europe

Introduction

Europe is our backyard. We need no visas in advance, borders are easy to cross, our cashpoint cards work in the ATMs, there's an efficient public-transport network, much of the continent now uses the euro (which is also handy currency in Eastern Europe) and you can fly 'no-frills' into the heart of the continent for the price of a big night out in London. Within the Europe you think you know, there are a million things you don't. The continent is unique, with an incredible depth and diversity of geography, history and culture crammed into a relatively small area. There's so much to discover and no time like the present to start exploring.

Why Europe?

One of the great things about Europe is that it's so much like here but a little bit different. This may not appeal to folks wanting to leave Western culture and consumerism behind but it does mean that Europe is a great place to travel with a specific purpose or interest in mind – many people will have similar interests and whatever you're into there'll be organisations and some sort of infrastructure already set up. It's relatively easy to spend a year skiing and then surfing, undertaking forest conservation, walking the mountains of central Europe or immersing yourself in the alternative and underground art, culture and music scenes of Paris (France), Berlin (Germany), Barcelona (Spain) and London, which are among the most vibrant in the world. Alternatively you can dive into the staggering European history and culture, much of which is laid bare in architectural relics that range from the Neolithic tombs of Sweden to the Byzantine monasteries of Macedonia. The region also has some of the most amazing museums and art galleries on the planet.

Europe can be costly but travellers here have one undeniable advantage. Should you blow half your travel money in one crazy weekend there's bound to be seasonal work somewhere on the continent that will stave off a premature journey home. Which is handy as there are some great places to blow your stack. In the summer, few party havens rival Ibiza but the Greek Islands of Mykonos, Ios and Santorini do their best. Lisbon (Portugal), Madrid (Spain) and Barcelona are established all-night, buzzing cities but Valencia (Spain) is underrated. Dublin (Ireland) has some of the best pubs, Prague (Czech Republic) offers endless good times, Copenhagen (Denmark) is cosmopolitan, Reykjavík (Iceland) hedonistic, chic, trendy and expensive, while the clubs of London and Berlin are among the best in the world. True, your parents may not like the idea of you working from one party to another, or spending a year in a squat in Berlin, but it doesn't have to be that way, and if you're going to spend nine months in Ibiza at least you'll learn Spanish.

The region is full of surprises, especially in the east. Why fly halfway around the globe for beautiful beaches and strange, majestic peaks almost unknown in the UK when they are just two hours flying time away? How much do you know about the Vysoké Tatry (High Tatras) in Slovakia (which have some of the most spectacular trekking trails in Europe) or the coastal hotspots of Croatia? Then there are opportunities in the parts you think you know well. The slow pace of life still pootles on in much of inland Spain, Portugal and Italy, areas rarely touched by tourists until recently. Headline-grabbing attractions may be few but small rural communities, hearty long lunches, wine, fiestas, olive groves, stunning arid mountain scenery and ancient trails more than compensate.

Europe is a place for all seasons. The summer offers the opportunity to visit the Arctic Circle, stunning glaciers, the fjords of Norway and the high mountains of central Europe in relative comfort, while the winter offers some stunning landscapes, and fantastic sports and adventure experiences. Whenever you want to go and whatever you want to do, don't discount Europe. It has a staggering capacity to amaze, entertain and enthral just like India, Central America or China.

What to Do?

There are loads of things to do and languages to learn in Europe. Happily Brits can work in any other EU member state, there's loads of seasonal work and a pre-arranged job or the intention to work in a specific place forms the focus of many gap years. The prospect of overseas employment could allow you to skip toil in the UK and hit the road early into your year off but investigate work opportunities carefully beforehand.

Many a European gap year has been based around a job or single activity (eg, skiing, surfing, climbing) but this can tie you into a specific region or place at the expense of wider travels. For some, work is a fallback proposition, to be considered only in emergencies. Certainly it's possible to stretch your funds by camping, living on pasta and spending a lot of time in Eastern Europe.

If you've a desire to do some voluntary work in a specific field (eg, conservation) then Europe could be your bag. See Part III for more information on overseas jobs, volunteer work and courses.

GET ACTIVE

In Europe you'll find world-class locations for just about any activity you care to mention. There are also training courses on every activity, from ice climbing and snow shoeing to surfing and diving.

Top 10 Must-Sees

Grand Place (Brussels, Belgium) – the magnificent square at the heart of Brussels; cafés, guildhouses and gothic masterpieces.

Uffizi Gallery & Ponte Vecchio (Florence, Italy) – famous art collection and stunning 14th-century bridge at the heart of Italy's Renaissance city.

Alpujarras (Spain) – charming foothills of the Sierra Nevada.

Santorini (Greece) – the sheer walls of its volcanic caldera are magical.

Camargue (Provence, France) – desolate, beautiful delta famed for its birdlife and cowboys.

Sognefjord (Norway) – near the cultured city of Bergen this is Norway's longest (200km) and deepest (1300m) fjord.

Białowieża National Park (Poland) – ancient forest packed with wildlife such as bears and European bison.

Istanbul (Turkey) – stroll around Ottoman mosques in the heart of the old city.

Painted Churches of Bucovina (Romania) – 16th-century frescoes ensured UNESCO World Heritage status.

Dubrovnik & Dalmatian Coast (Croatia) – fabulous 1300-year-old city and one of Europe's loveliest coastlines.

Fishermen's Bastion (Budapest, Hungary) – wonderful viewing platform giving commanding views of the magnificent city.

Cycling & Mountain Biking

On Europe's smaller islands a bike is a great way to get around. Recognised cycling regions (with huge cycle-path networks) include the Netherlands, Belgian Ardennes, Scandinavia, the west of Ireland, the upper reaches of the Danube in southern Germany and southern France. The Dordogne and Provence (France) and Tuscany (Italy) provide leisurely, picturesque cycling. Fitter cyclists and mountain bikers have mountain ranges across Europe to choose from (see the following Skiing & Snowboarding section) and hire bikes are widely available.

Skiing & Snowboarding

The ski season runs from December to April and the Alps are the best and most popular ski destination in Europe but the Pyrénées (France/Spain) are not far behind (and cheaper). The Sierra Nevada (Spain), a handful of Eastern European countries (Romania, Slovakia, Czech Republic and Poland) and Norway and Sweden (very cold) all have limited ski facilities.

Cross-country skiing is very popular in Scandinavia and the Alps, while snow shoeing (a great alternative to winter walking) is possible – these activities are more popular from February to April.

Trekking & Mountaineering

There are thousands of trekking and mountaineering opportunities in Europe, not just alongside the region's ski resorts but in low-land and coastal areas too where cheap village accommodation provides an alternative to mountain refuges, huts and campsites, thus allowing a year-round walking season.

The Alps offer the greatest variety to mountaineers. The Dolomites (Italy) offer some cracking trekking, while Slovakia, Romania (especially the Bucegi Mountains) and Bulgaria all offer well-developed trekking trails. In Scandinavia trails lead into the Arctic Circle and on Corsica up some taxing wild mountains. For serious walkers there are some marked transcontinental routes (known as GR – *Gran Recorrido* – routes in Spain and France).

Via Ferrata (W www.viaferrata.org) is quite a new thing in southern France. Basically it's assisted climbing and mountaineering. Routes are made using steel rope bridges and huge steel loops and steps in the rock. You attempt these routes roped up.

Watersports

There are some good surf breaks on the Atlantic coasts of southern France, Portugal, Spain and the Canary Islands. Southern Spain (Tarifa in particular) is one of the best windsurfing locations in Europe.

Canoeing is possible on rivers and lakes across Europe and sea kayaking around the Greek Islands and the fractured Scandinavian coast is popular.

White-water rafting and kayaking in the Alps, Greece, Norway, Pyrénées, Slovenia, Slovakia and Turkey is possible. Turkey and Slovenia are arguably the best locations.

Great sailing locations include the Greek and Balearic Islands, Croatia, southern France, Ireland and Turkey. Look out for crewing along the Côte d'Azur (France) and Europe's wealthier sailing centres. (See the Work your Route chapter in Part III.)

Other Activities

There are dive centres all around the Mediterranean. Croatia, Malta, Ibiza and the Azores (off the coast of Portugal) can be particularly recommended and you can dive among antiquities in Turkey and Greece.

Guided caving and excellent horse trekking, paragliding and hang-gliding are available in many hilly and alpine areas.

WORK A LITTLE

Although the paperwork can be a hassle and jobs are scarce in some countries (ie, Eastern Europe), employment avenues for gappers include seasonal agricultural work (fruit-picking mostly), the tourist industry (flipping burgers in ski resorts, teaching windsurfing on the Mediterranean etc) and au pairing. You'll need excellent language skills to pick up a 'proper' job (ie, office work) and British expat communities can sometimes provide more diverse employment. Wherever you work, wages will usually be lower than back home.

TRAVEL AROUND

British nationals heading into Europe don't have to worry about getting visas in advance. Following the Schengen Agreement that abolished border controls between many EU states, getting around the continent is very easy. With some exceptions (Britain and parts of Eastern Europe) Europe has a vast and well-funded public-transport network. Cities (and Switzerland) are particularly blessed.

Rail passes (for 12-/22-/30-day Inter-Rail passes contact Rail Europe; ☎ 0870 584 8848; [W] www.raileurope.co.uk) and cheaper coach passes (city to city passes for up to 60 days from Eurolines; ☎ 0870 580 8080; [W] www.gobycoach.com) are good for starting your travels and blasting through numerous European capitals (The *Thomas Cook European Rail Timetable* and The *Thomas Cook Rail Map of Europe* are invaluable to serious rail travellers) but not so good for getting off the beaten track, when you'll need local buses. Busabout ([W] www.busabout.com) and the Stray Travel Network ([W] www.straytravel .com) offer hop-on, hop-off tours of Europe, and similar local services are sometimes available. So are country-specific rail and bus passes and discount cards.

Having a vehicle (and knowing how to fix it) allows total freedom and flexibility. A camper van is ideal but security can be a headache and your metal bubble can put more 'distance' between you and the places you're travelling through. The Van Market in Market Rd (off Caledonian Rd) in London is a long-running institution useful to buyers and sellers.

Hitching around Europe is feasible but never 100% safe and can't be recommended. Happily there are lift-sharing organisations in France (Allostop Provoya and Auto-Partage) and Germany (Mitfahrzentrale). These organisations remove the hassle and inevitable, despondent road-side waits to provide one of the cheapest ways to get around Europe.

No-frills airlines are great for starting/ending your travels but more limited within Europe itself (see No Frills Please, We're British under Getting There later in this chapter). If you have the cash to chuck at regular airlines then a vast, complex air network opens up to you.

Classic Routes

There aren't really any classic European routes as such but with so many things to see and do there's no point trying to see the whole continent in one hit. Concentrate your efforts.

Many travellers head south from northern Europe, hopping from major city to major city until reaching the Mediterranean's warm shores. The Greek Islands are the final destination of many, Andalucía (Spain) of others but southern France, Italy and Portugal are all popular destinations. Another great possibility would be a trip skirting the northern shores of the Mediterranean from Gibraltar to Istanbul. Maybe pick up a lift on yachts moving east across the Mediterranean. Or you could spend the whole summer in the Greek Islands.

Alternatively start in Denmark and take in all of Scandinavia then catch the ferry over to Iceland (via the Faroe Islands) before returning to the UK, again by ferry, via the Shetland Islands. The Baltic States could be included in this trip or you could loop through Eastern Europe.

If this seems a little predictable you could give a theme to all or part of your travels; an exploration of the great food or wine centres of Europe; a wildly optimistic search for endangered wildlife (brown bear and Iberian lynx in Spain, for example); a 'Grand Tour' of classical art, architecture and antiquities concentrating on the Renaissance cities of Italy; or the route of the Orient Express (which now terminates in Vienna but you can still take local trains to Istanbul), a task easily accomplished by train. Save a little time for the clubs of Ibiza, fiestas of Italian towns too numerous to mention or the fantastic monasteries of Eastern Europe.

When to Go?

Anytime is the right time for Europe, there's always somewhere worth visiting. The Arctic Circle and the region's high mountains are amazing places to visit during winter, while alpine flowers carpet high valleys in spring. The great forests of central and Eastern Europe are beautiful in autumn, and at the height of summer when tourists overwhelm many popular tourist destinations, Eastern Europe and Scandinavia can be pleasant and quiet. If you don't want quiet, the clubbing season in Ibiza and the Greek Islands of Mykonos, Ios and Santorini is between June and September.

France, Italy and Germany are essentially on holiday during August, the time to avoid Mediterranean beaches that are blisteringly hot in any case. Conversely, from October to May some coastal resorts can be desolate places.

If you can, travel in the south between April and June, move to Scandinavia for the height of summer (the midnight sun on June 21 is a fantastic experience) and then back to the Mediterranean for September and October before going skiing between December and April (you'll need to be there by November if you're looking for work).

CLIMATE

The seasons of Europe are similar to Britain. Winters in southern Europe are mild, with Andalucía, the Greek Islands, Malta, the Canary Islands and Cyprus the warmest places to visit (temperatures rise to the mid-teens). In central and northern Europe (and central Spain) temperatures in winter are low (below freezing at night) and snowfalls common (although snow doesn't linger long in the west). Scandinavian winters are extremely harsh but the aurora borealis, or northern lights, are some compensation between December and March.

Generally speaking, spring and autumn are wetter and windier across the continent. Spring occurs first in the south. Winter lingers longer in Eastern and northern Europe and arrives earlier in upland and mountainous areas, which tend to experience extremes of climate. Autumn may bring the occasional 'Indian summer' (mild, sunny and warm weather) in the south. The temperate Atlantic Coast is steadily wet throughout the year.

You could spend the whole year in Spain and Portugal (which have temperate northern coasts and semi-deserts in the south) and experience a whole range of climates.

FESTIVALS

Europe holds so many annual festivals that you'd be most unlucky not to attend at least one. They range from small-scale traditional village festivals to manic, sometimes riotous, week-long festivals in Spain, Portugal and Italy. Many of these events have their basis in the celebration of various Christian saints and other religious events. A few major festivals are listed below:

Venice Carnevale (Italy) is held in the 10 days leading up to Ash Wednesday (January/ February). Venetians don masks and costumes for a continuous street party. The carnival season in Germany also leads up to Ash Wednesday with colourful events in Cologne, Munich, Dusseldorf and Mainz, among others.

Sumardagurinn Fyrsti (Iceland) celebrates the first day of summer in Reykjavík on the third Thursday in April. There is much merriment.

Las Fallas (Spain) is a week-long party in Valencia held in mid-March. All-night drinking, dancing and fireworks feature heavily.

Athens Festival (Greece) is a feast of opera, ballet and classical music lasting from mid-June to November. Other Greek festivals take place at Easter (March/April).

Bastille Day (France) on July 14 is a national holiday and celebrations take place across the country but the biggest celebration is in Paris (check out the fireworks at the Eiffel Tower).

Fiesta de Sanfermines (Spain) is a non-stop eight-day party and bull-fighting celebration in early July that begins each day with the famous Running of the Bulls through the streets of Pamplona.

Festival of Avignon (France) is held between early July and early August and features some 300 shows of music, drama and dance. There's also a fringe festival.

Il Palio (Italy) is an extraordinary horse race held in the main piazza of Siena on July 2 and August 16. Get to it if you can.

Baltica International Folk Festival (Estonia, Latvia & Lithuania) is a week-long celebration of Baltic music, dance and parades, held in mid-July.

Oktoberfest (Germany), Munich's legendary beer-drinking festival, starts in late September and lasts two weeks.

What to Expect?

TRAVELLERS

Travellers from a huge number of countries are found wandering around Europe. It's very difficult to generalise but Eastern Europe is not as widely visited by Brits as it is by Germans, Austrians and Scandinavians. British travellers still seem to prefer the traditional package-tour destinations of France, Greece, Italy and Spain but, together with German travellers, are exploring Turkey in large numbers. Travellers in Albania and Yugoslavia are a little harder to find (see the Issues section later in this chapter) but some people tip Albania to become increasingly popular thanks to its beautiful coastline.

It's difficult to tie down specific places where travellers congregate. Certainly backpacker-orientated hostels, overnight trains and festivals attract travellers like bees to a honey pot but for the most part travellers are scattered across the continent. The Greek Islands, Provence and Andalucía are perhaps the most popular destinations.

LOCALS

There are a huge variety of traditions across Europe but common traits are a little more respect for elders, politeness and a less hurried attitude than back home. In the east a sprinkling of Islam becomes a blanket of belief in Turkey, while in much of southern, Western and Eastern Europe Christian traditions still dominate cultural life. Attitudes and practices also vary within countries. The industrial north of Italy and Spain show all the outward signs of chic western capitalism but in remote rural southern areas farmers still ride donkeys (they may well have mobile phones though). These rural areas are more conservative and often considerably poorer than cities, and you are more likely to experience traditional practices.

In northern Europe dressing just like you would at home and wearing shorts or a bikini on the beach is not a problem. A little more sensitivity should be taken in rural southern

Spain, southern Italy (especially Sicily) and Greece, where for a few men male chauvinism and sexist behaviour are a sport and a lifestyle. Marriage is well respected, however, and a wedding ring can deter some unwanted attention.

Looking like Stig of the Dump doesn't do you any favours when dealing with officialdom, so try and keep a clean appearance. Extra care with dress (long sleeves, and trousers or skirts below the knee) needs to be taken when visiting churches, monasteries and mosques.

By and large Europe is a friendly place and shaking hands and kissing when greeting someone is very common. A greeting to a proprietor of a quiet shop or bar goes a long way in many countries.

LANGUAGE

English is the most widely understood second language on the continent but speaking it loudly and slowly isn't going to cut it. You are going to need a little of a variety of languages to get by, especially in rural areas and Eastern Europe.

See Courses in Part III for information on language courses. Reading Material later in this chapter gives information on Lonely Planet's useful phrasebooks.

HEALTH RISKS

Europe is, on the whole, a pretty healthy place. A change of diet may give you the squits but other than getting sunburned or heatstroke, being bitten by insects or giving yourself the devil's own hangover, there's little to worry about. That said, it's worth bearing in mind that instances of AIDs and sexually transmitted infections are on the rise in Europe and a typhoid vaccination is recommended for some southeastern countries. Tuberculosis is becoming more common, especially in the east, and there is the odd case of rabies.

Consult the Health section in Part I and seek professional medical advice for more travel health information. Remember to take along your E111 form to EU nations.

TIME & FLIGHT TIME

Three time zones cover the continent, starting with Greenwich Mean Time (GMT) in the UK, Portugal and Iceland. The vast majority of the continent is one hour ahead while Sweden, Eastern Europe, Greece and Turkey are two hours ahead. Between the end of March and end of October many European countries push their clocks forward one hour for summer daylight savings.

From London, Paris is just a 1¼-hour flight away, while Madrid is 2½ hours away and Istanbul 3¾ hours.

ISSUES

The only possible tricky border crossings surround Yugoslavia, where some border posts are not recognised by the central Yugoslav government, who have in the past required travellers to get visas in advance. Visitors not staying at hotels in Yugoslavia must register with the police within three days of arrival but visa and registration and regulations are prone to change.

Kosovo, although fascinating, is not now a great holiday destination and northeastern Albania is a definite no-go area thanks to banditry. In Croatia, Bosnia, Kosovo and Yugoslavia, unexploded ordnance and landmines remain a problem. Keep an eye on political events if you're considering visiting the Balkans including Macedonia and Turkey where the long-running conflict between the government and Kurdish separatists (especially the PPK) in the East could reignite despite the current peace.

Border guards, police, train conductors and other low-level bureaucrats in Eastern Europe *may* ask you for a bribe to oil their creaking bureaucratic machines but more common are rip-offs, scams and petty thefts in more popular tourist destinations – you need to keep your wits about you on overnight trains and at bus stations.

For further information on travel hotspots, general safety issues and governmental travel advice see Safety in Part I.

INTERNET & COMMUNICATIONS

There are internet cafés in major towns and cities, from Seville to Sofia, and usually they're very reasonably priced.

Affordable pay-as-you-go mobile services are available across Europe and worth considering if you're spending a considerable amount of time in one country. Your UK mobile will cost you a fortune to use unless you are just accepting text messages.

Daily Spend

Eastern Europe, Greece, Portugal, southern Spain and Turkey are cheapest, Iceland (followed closely by Scandinavia where a night on the pop can cost twice your daily budget) the most expensive. Northern Europe is going to drain your finances pretty quickly too, while Switzerland is not the place to save money.

Long-time travellers wanting to keep costs below £20 per day will have to stay in cheap (and sometimes free) campsites, self-cater and not move around too quickly. Fun for a while, especially when 'free' camping out in the wilds but the novelty soon wears off, particularly when you realise that a night out drinking is going to mean two nights sleeping under a hedge to balance the books. Bread and cheese/chocolate spread for tea every night gets a little wearing.

A little more cash (say £25–35) allows for a more varied diet, the odd good meal out, a bed to sleep in (usually in a dormitory or cheap guesthouse – £6–10 a night) and less tramp-like behaviour. This isn't five-star travel though, and in Europe's most expensive countries you'll struggle to get by on this. Forty or fifty quid will enable you to use nicer guesthouses, have a room to yourself and not think twice before ordering a dessert/round of tequila.

It's still possible to get a good three-course meal for under £5 in Mediterranean Europe and much, much less in the East. In northern Europe you're looking at £5 a course.

Visa or MasterCard credit cards are widely accepted and European ATMs accept a huge variety of debit cards.

Getting There

Getting to Europe can be as easy as jumping on a coach in your local town but a lot depends on where and how you want to travel. Getting to Scandinavia is easy by ferry and if you want to start and finish in France then you may as well take the coach or train. For elsewhere a cheap flight into the heart of Europe might be just the ticket.

AIR

No-frills airlines concentrate on Western and southern Europe but do service a handful of destinations in Eastern Europe and Scandinavia (see No Frills Please, We're British later). If you want to wait and see where your travels take you before booking a return flight you can either pick up a standby ticket on a UK charter flight leaving southern Europe, or book online with a no-frills airline once you know where you're going to end up.

All the major European carriers offer flights to a bewildering number of destinations across the continent. While British Airways (BA) and respective national carriers will offer the most comprehensive and convenient services to Europe, they are not necessarily the cheapest.

Consult the Airlines Appendix at the back of the book for more information on airlines and routes.

Ticket Costs

The best available student/under-26 fares are quoted here. See Passports, Tickets, Visas & Insurance in Part I for more information on how to get the best, most flexible deal.

Flights into Scandinavia, Western and southern Europe tend to be cheapest, those into Eastern Europe the most expensive. *Really* cheap fares with no-frills carriers must be booked months in advance. If you want to change the date you'll have to pay a charge plus the difference between the price of your ticket when you bought it and the price on the day you now want to travel (hey presto, a £15 ticket transforms into a £150 ticket). The cheapest no-frills deals come as part of brief online promotions and an average no-frills ticket costs around £45 one way and is almost always the cheapest option for one-way flights. One-way standby tickets on charter flights coming back from southern Europe cost around £85.

Many established carriers such as BA, BMI and british european ([W] www.flybe.com) were offering rock-bottom prices (for example, Budapest, Hungary £70) on fixed-date return tickets to numerous destinations at the time of writing. BMI and flybe also offer some great one-way deals (£30–50). In some instances the cheapest deals are only available through the airline itself and are cheaper online. This is certainly not the case for long-haul fares.

Nearer the time of departure, and often giving more flexibility, are under-26 return tickets on established airlines such as Air France (via Paris), KLM (via Amsterdam), Lufthansa (via Munich and Frankfurt) and Swiss (via Zurich). You must book through a youth/student travel agent but £150–200 for a return ticket is easily achievable. Flexible 'open-jaw' tickets (flying into one city and out of another) are available for the same sort of money and most are valid for a year.

As a rule of thumb, when booking flights into Europe remember to shop around, check the flexibility and validity of your ticket (one-, two- or three-month fixed returns are common) and book well in advance.

No Frills Please, We're British

Flying has never been cheaper and the network of routes into northern, southern and Western Europe never so great. By taking advantage of cheap (and reasonably cheerful) no-frills airlines you can drastically reduce your initial and final expenditure.

Flying no-frills is not without its pitfalls. To get the well-advertised, dirt-cheap fares you need to book two to three months in advance and sometimes pick anti-social flight times. Even then, getting to and from airports at either end of your journey can eat up the price difference between your cheapo deal and a more convenient discounted flight out of Heathrow or a regional airport closer to home.

Here is a list of no-frills airlines:

Basiq Air ([W] www.basiqair.com) flies from Amsterdam and Rotterdam to destinations in France and Spain.

bmibaby (☎ 0870 264 2229; [W] www.bmibaby.com) operates a wide network from East Midlands, Manchester and Cardiff airports.

easyJet (☎ 0870 600 0000; W www.easyjet.com) has a huge network, including some services between Geneva, Barcelona, Nice, Paris and Amsterdam.

Germanwings (☎ 020-8321 7255; W www.germanwings.com) flies out of Cologne and with a little cunning you can get from Stansted to Istanbul for under £50.

Globespan (☎ 0870 556 1522; W www.flyglobespan.com) flies out of Edinburgh and Glasgow to Spain and France.

Hapag-Lloyd Express (☎ 0870 606 0519; W www.hl-express.com) flies into Luton and Manchester from Cologne and operates a few European flights from its other German hub in Hanover.

Iceland Express (W www.icelandexpress.com) flies from Stansted to Reykjavík from £56 one way. It also flies between Copenhagen and Reykjavík.

Jet2 (☎ 0870 737 8282; W www.jet2.com) operates out of Leeds-Bradford airport servicing mostly southern European destinations.

Monarch Airlines (☎ 0870 040 5040; W www.monarchairlines.co.uk) charters from package-tour companies are its bread and butter, scheduled flights to southern Spain from Manchester and Luton an extra service.

MyTravelLite (☎ 0870 156 4564; W www.mytravellite.com), part of a bigger travel company, flies to limited destinations from Birmingham.

Ryanair (☎ 0870 156 9569; W www.ryanair.co.uk) is Europe's second-biggest budget carrier (with over 100 routes) and many continental destinations are serviced from Brussels Charleroi, Dublin, Frankfurt Hahn, Milan Bergamo, Stansted and Stockholm Stavsta.

Virgin Express (☎ 020-7744 0004; W www.virgin-express.com) serves a wide range of European destinations (including London City) from Brussels.

SEA & OVERLAND

There are numerous options for crossing the channel into France and Belgium. Calais is the main gateway to Europe and there are a dozen more channel crossings further west but they tend to be a little more expensive. The Eurostar train is offering serious competition to these services, especially for travellers who wish to head directly into the heart of Paris (from £40 one way for those aged under 26). There are ferries to Scandinavia, Germany, the Netherlands and Belgium from Harwich and Newcastle plus services to Ireland from Fishguard, Pembroke, Holyhead, Liverpool, Stranraer, Troon and Port Douglas (the Isle of Man). There's also a ferry to Iceland (via the Faroe Islands) from the Shetland Islands and a ferry from Portsmouth to Santander in northern Spain.

Holders of Inter-Rail passes get reduced fares on some ferries.

SPECIALIST TOUR OPERATORS

There are hundreds of tour operators running specialist activity and sight-seeing tours in Europe (see the Global Tour Companies Appendix at the back of the book). Contiki and Top Deck Travel are very popular for bus tours across the continent.

Europe & Beyond

Classic overland routes from Europe include journeys across Russia on the Trans-Siberian Railway, through the Middle East and on to the Indian subcontinent or down through Africa via Morocco, Tunisia or Egypt. Some of these routes can be travelled as part of an overland tour package.

Further Information

READING MATERIAL

Lonely Planet publishes a massive range of guidebooks covering Europe. *Read This First: Europe* gives the complete low-down on European travel, *Europe on a Shoestring* provides a complete overview of the continent, and there are dozens of separate country, cycling and walking guides, books on European food, maps of European cities and 14 pocket phrasebooks for Europe's major languages.

Every aspect of Europe is covered in print. There are specialist books on everything from travelling down Europe's great rivers to the best of Scandinavian cuisine. On top of that there are hundreds of specialist guides to the far-flung corners of the continent, weighty tomes of the entire European rail timetable and many others covering all kinds of specialist activities, especially walking.

Bill Bryson's humorous take on Europe, *Neither Here Nor There*, is a great read, while Mark Twain's *A Tramp Abroad* is a classic. Paul Theroux wrote *The Pillars of Hercules* about his contemporary 'Grand Tour', while *On the Shores of the Mediterranean*, by Eric Newby, is a fantastic book about southern Europe.

George Orwell's *Down and Out in Paris and London* and *Homage to Catalonia* give a tramp's view of travel and war in Europe. *Through the Embers of Chaos: Balkan Journeys*, by Dervla Murphy, details a sober cycle ride through the Balkans, while *Driving Over Lemons* and *A Parrot in the Pepper Tree*, by Chris Stewart, provide an optimist's view of expat life.

USEFUL INFORMATION SOURCES

The weekend papers are a great source of information about travel in Europe and almost every European country has a tourist office in the UK. Needless to say, there are hundreds of thousands of websites covering many places and activities on the continent.

Been There, Done That

In 1997 crazy Dave Weir and myself embarked on a chronically under-funded tour of Europe. Sardinia had swallowed up the majority of our meagre finances, drunk in the various bars of Santa Marie. It had been the best of times but the hangover was going to last all the way back to Dover – we were on the sleeping rough and eating pasta tour of Europe.

We were not proud and our financial priorities ensured that we slept everywhere and anywhere – outside Verona train station with the smack heads and pimps, under the jetties of the super-rich in Beaulieu-Sur-Mer, in the first-class toilets of the Istanbul Express and on popular coastal paths where we were woken by tourists stepping over us. We lived on an Austrian mountainside for a week, camped beside a fire watchtower, which was perfect for drinking whisky and watching the sun go down behind the snow-capped mountains.

We lived on Nutella chocolate spread, bread, pasta, cheese spread and cigarettes. As self-caterers, we could eat and cook anywhere, and did so, on train platforms and ferry decks (not a good idea). When the money was about to totally run out I met up with my girlfriend, who was an au pair for a German family. It was going to be one of the highlights of my trip but she had waited most of the summer to tell me to my face that it was over. So I split, hid in the toilet on one of those fast and expensive German express trains and hightailed it back to the UK where I discovered that I'd been overpaid by my last employer. Bingo. I hitched a lift with some roadies from Sonic Youth and made for the Reading Festival, finishing the summer on a very wild and high note.   Jon Cummins

Africa

Introduction

Africa is a place of majestic landscapes, stunning wildlife and diverse cultures. English may be widely spoken but Africa challenges you like no other place; getting around is not always easy, the continent is home to the poorest people on earth and its cities can be ugly, hot and frantic. At the same time, from the ancient cities of the Arabian north to the South African townships of Soweto, the honesty and vitality of African people is second to none. Despite the occasional hardship or logistical disaster, Africa is always enlightening, surprising and intriguing. The rewards to the gapper are as huge as the continent itself and many people find themselves returning over and over again.

Why Africa?

Africa is a travel destination known to strike fear into the hearts of parents everywhere. It's widely perceived as a corrupt basket case, full of civil war, plague, famine and lawlessness. Not so. The vast majority of this 30-million-sq-km continent is trouble-free, relaxed and safe. People are, by and large, hospitable, ceaselessly cheerful and gregarious. These traits are certainly not dependent on material wealth and seem to increase the further you venture into remote and isolated territory.

Africa is not cheap compared with Asia or India (accommodation can be particularly poor value in some places) and perhaps it doesn't have the scale and depth of tourist sites found elsewhere but Africa is the continent of adventure. It's a place where an eight-hour bus ride can turn into a two-day epic and travel in Africa isn't so much about the places you see as the journey itself. It's about bus rides through splendid landscapes on rarely used (and probably terrible) roads, spending time in isolated communities and being out in a stunningly different environment. People play a great part in this. Of all the gappers who head to the continent in search of an 'Out of Africa' animal experience, many end up exploring the continent's cultures far more deeply. Although ruins and other physical evidence tell the tale of ancient Africa, for the most part history doesn't often manifest itself in worthy texts and ancient buildings but in evolving traditions and cultures. West Africa, home to over half the continent's people, is particularly rich culturally and music-ally (the capitals of Senegal and Mali seem to be constantly jumping to some African beat) but first-time British travellers who speak little French often overlook West Africa.

Africa hosts many geographical marvels. Fantastic beaches are found along its coasts, and herds of tourists congregate in and around the Great Rift Valley, the birthplace of humanity that stretches from Ethiopia to Mozambique. Not a valley in the typical sense, geological fault lines have formed lakes, escarpments and volcanoes. The geography of the place is stunning and provides one of *the* great wildlife habitats of the world. Elsewhere, the Victoria Falls, the Nile and Niger rivers, the Okavango Delta, the Aïr Mountains and Ténéré Desert in Niger (connected by charter flights from France), the Skeleton Coast (lined with shipwrecks) in Namibia and the general wondrous weirdness of Madagascar's wildlife draw travellers to the continent.

As you'll soon find out, things are done differently in Africa. The simplest task can take an age to complete and travel is beset by organisational chaos, random mechanical failure and comedy infrastructure. Dictatorship hangovers and uncertain regimes mean that road-blocks are a feature of overland travel, although these are the least of many local people's worries whose leaders have looted billions of dollars and helped further impoverish the continent. You'll be confronted by utter poverty and crushing hardship and sadly there's a list of countries that travellers really shouldn't travel (see Issues later in this chapter). But in Africa there are signs of hope and while some options close, others open up. Mozambique, a war zone 10 years ago, is now a fantastic traveller destination, one among dozens of potential adventure playgrounds. The shores of Lake Malawi are a great place to party and let your hair down while Uganda is building a reputation as a backpacker destination. Certainly Africa is the sort of place where opportunities and surprises wait around every corner.

What to Do?

Many gappers undertake a little pre-planned voluntary work and then travel. Others just concentrate on travelling (it's a huge continent after all) and often set themselves great overland challenges. You have, alas, little chance of finding paid work to subsidise your travel.

See Part III for more information on overseas jobs, volunteer work and courses.

GET ACTIVE

There are loads of possibilities for the active gapper in Africa; all can be arranged by local companies and guides.

Trekking & Climbing

From the Drakensberg and Transkei in South Africa to the Atlas Mountains in Morocco there are mountain ranges and upland areas that offer fabulous trekking. Some places like the Fouta Djalon plateau in Guinea, Dogon Country in Mali or Fish River Canyon and the Namib-Naukluft national parks in Namibia are quite easy going and as much about experiencing the environment and/or local culture as anything. On the other hand, the high peaks of East Africa (Mt Kilimanjaro at 5892m is Africa's tallest peak) and Morocco all offer strenuous summit treks, climbing and mountaineering. Trekking with camels on the fringes of the Sahara, as well as in arid regions of Kenya and Namibia, is also possible.

Top 10 Must-Sees

Victoria Falls (Zambia & Zimbabwe) – stunning scenery and some seriously adventurous white-water rafting.
Table Mountain (South Africa) – a magnificent site above a magnificent city.
Aïr Massif & Ténéré Desert (Niger) – rock art, camel trains and fabulous Saharan land-scapes.
Tsingy de Bemaraha National Park (Madagascar) – an amazing wildlife park in a country of incredible wildlife.
Fès (Morocco) – one of the most incredible and complex North African cities.
Okavango Delta (Botswana) – one of the most stunning wetland wildlife habitats in the world.
Dogon Country (Mali) – a stunning escarpment forms the backdrop for a unique, animist culture.
Cape Coast (Ghana) – the famed colonial fort in this lively town is just one of many along the West African coast.
Sinai (Egypt) – great trekking, desert adventures and fantastic coral reefs.
Lake Turkana (Kenya) – the stunning, arid and inhospitable cradle of mankind.

Desert trekking in the Sinai (Egypt) can also be highly recommended.

Rock climbers should check out South Africa, East Africa and Mali (which has some truly world-class climbing).

Wildlife Watching

Going on safari (from the Swahili for 'journey') is undoubtedly the highlight for many travellers. The savanna, showcased in a series of parks in East and southern Africa, is home to the 'Big Five' (buffalo, elephant, lion, leopard and rhinoceros). In July, August and October the wildebeest migration between the Serengeti and Masai Mara reserves on the Tanzanian-Kenyan border provides one the world's great wildlife spectacles. Safaris are possible year round.

Away from East Africa's wildly popular parks are many opportunities to mix it with other creatures. There are Madagascar's unique ecosystems for a start, or you could visit mountain gorillas in Uganda and Rwanda; track desert elephants in Burkina Faso and Mali; look for chimpanzees in Senegal, Guinea and Tanzania; dive with great white sharks in South Africa; or just sit back and enjoy the blooming deserts of Botswana and Namibia after the year's first rains.

Budget camping safaris are easily arranged for £50 a day but the cheapest safaris often deliver far fewer smiles per mile. Spend some serious time in Africa and you may become more interested in birds than mammals. Great birding spots are to be found in Nigeria, Senegal, The Gambia, Ethiopia, Kenya and South Africa.

Other Activities

The Red Sea offers truly world-class diving, and there are a string of affordable diving resorts in the Sinai. Cheap diving is available through charter packages from the UK. The whole east coast of Africa is peppered with great dive resorts. Africa's cheapest dive centres are on the shores of Lake Malawi.

White-water rafting below the Victoria Falls (Zambia-Zimbabwe) is simply incredible (it's the hardest commercially run rapid in the world); rafting or kayaking trips can also be arranged in Ethiopia, Kenya, Namibia, Swaziland and Uganda. The Okavango Delta in Botswana and Zambezi in Zimbabwe are the ultimate locations for paddling kayak safaris.

Between April and July there's world-class surfing in South Africa (notably Jeffrey's Bay) and there are also good breaks in Mozambique, Senegal and Namibia. The Cape Verde Islands and Morocco are emerging as strong windsurfing (and surfing) destinations.

You can ski in Morocco (January–March) and South Africa (mid-May–September), ride horses in Lesotho and Swaziland, as well as Malawi, South Africa, Zambia and Zimbabwe, while deep-sea game fishing is possible all over the continent.

You don't need an endorsement from the Royal Geographic Society to travel adventurously. You can join traditional camel trains heading into the Sahara in Timbuktu (Mali) or Agadez (Niger), reach the source of the Niger River in Guinea and the Nile in Uganda, or retrace the footsteps of European explorers into the heart of Africa.

WORK A LITTLE

For those without specialist skills and training there's little chance of getting paid work in Africa. A tiny number of travellers get lucky and find jobs in the tour business or bar work in major Western-orientated backpacker destinations (especially in East and southern Africa) but don't expect great (if any) wages. Travellers with a degree can sometimes get teaching work without formal teaching qualifications, most commonly in private schools.

Most voluntary work in Africa focuses on teaching English, health education and social developmental projects. Many of these projects are organised through Christian organisations. Placements are usually prepaid and sorted out in advance, although there's no shortage of local voluntary organisations that may consider taking on self-supporting volunteers (but again try to arrange something in advance). Major humanitarian disasters do attract more adventurous volunteers but paid work is rare.

TRAVEL AROUND

Travelling around much of Africa is simply a matter of catching a bus between towns, cities and tourist resorts. In more remote country, transport is more circumspect and unreliable but there are few interesting places that you cannot reach, even if you have to wait for a few days for transport.

Time, patience and stamina are qualities you'll need in abundance for travel in Africa. Roads (many of which are dirt or returning to dirt) can be truly terrible, especially during the rainy season. Vehicles are unreliable and uncomfortable, although transport *sometimes* leaves/arrives roughly on time.

Buses, minibuses, pick-up trucks and shared taxis (often Peugeot 505s that follow fixed routes but to no set timetable) all serve as road transport. In rough, remote areas flatbed trucks converted to carry passengers are used, although you may find yourself at the roadside effectively hitchhiking. Apart from the most expensive buses, transport is completely packed with people, goods and livestock, and bus stations can be chaotic and taxing places.

Train travel is a wonderful way to get around Africa but outside of South and North Africa journeys are slow and possibly uncomfortable. Security is often poor but some rail trips within Africa are simply stunning (see Classic Routes following).

Africa's internal air network is pretty comprehensive, and can save you considerable time and hardship. Some airlines (like South African, Ethiopian and Air Kenya) are first-class operations; others are about as reliable as a chocolate fireguard. Check flight details carefully but be prepared for delays, cancellations and bureaucratic pantomimes.

Classic Routes

If you dream of travelling from Cap Blanc, Tunisia, all the way down to Cape Agulhas in South Africa (the northernmost and southernmost points on the continent), do not despair, it can be done despite conflicts in northern Algeria, southern Sudan and the Congo (RDC; formerly Zaïre) and pockets of occasional unrest/banditry elsewhere (see Issues later for details). Pioneering overland travellers (with their own vehicles) travel through Tunisia, Libya and Egypt before cutting down through Sudan and Ethiopia onto the easier roads of East and southern Africa. A new alternative route cuts into southern Algeria from Libya and through the Hoggar mountains to Niger, before crossing Nigeria to Cameroon. From Cameroon it's possible (but difficult) to cross through Chad and Sudan to Ethiopia before heading south. A more established trans-African route, and one that's possible by public transport plus a little hitching, starts in Morocco, drops through Mauritania and then cuts east through West Africa to Chad. Getting across Chad and Sudan to Ethiopia is not easy without a vehicle but it can be done.

Cairo (Egypt) to Cape Town (South Africa), via Botswana and Namibia, is a classic overland trail but Nairobi (Kenya) is a more popular starting point. A circuit of Kenya, Uganda and Tanzania is also popular, while farther south travellers regularly tour South Africa, Botswana and Namibia in one trip.

Africa also has its fair share of classic train, river and lake journeys. Think about travelling by train between Dakar (Senegal) and Bamako (Mali), Cairo to Aswan (Egypt), Nairobi to Mombasa (Kenya), Harare (Zimbabwe) to Pretoria (South Africa) via Victoria Falls or Johannesburg (South Africa) to Maputo (Mozambique). Alternatively head down the Niger (Mali) and Nile (Egypt) rivers or catch a ferry across lakes Tanganyika, Malawi, Volta or Nasser. Few of these vessels or trains would pass a safety inspection in Europe but there you go.

When to Go?

The equator cuts through the middle of this vast continent, which enjoys a huge variety of climate so there's never a bad time to visit Africa. The weather is always perfect somewhere. The British winter is a great time to visit the fringes of the Sahara or enjoy the warm summer days of southern Africa. Spring is ideal for North Africa when the usually arid lands are green and fresh. Winter and early spring are ideal for coastal West Africa, and late winter perfect for East Africa when wildlife is concentrated around water sources. Trans-continental trips should begin in November.

CLIMATE

The rains in West Africa begin between March and June, and finish between September and October, their exact timing influenced by distance from the coast. Temperatures are generally higher just before the torrential downpours begin.

North Africa has climatic seasons similar to southern Europe but summer is terribly hot, even in the High Atlas. Winters can be cold and nasty.

In East Africa the 'long rains' occur between March and May, while the 'short rains' are between October and December. June and July are the coolest months and temperatures and rainfall vary less along the coast. Between June and October is the best time to visit. The western side of Madagascar is wetter and more exposed to cyclones than the eastern side. Visit between April and October.

In southern African summers (that's November to March) are hot and wet while winters can be surprisingly cold. Not all areas experience spring and the four-season pattern is most pronounced in South Africa.

FESTIVALS

Festivals take place across the continent and almost every nation holds a handful of religious and cultural events. Here are some of the highlights:

Mbapira/Enjando Street Festival, in Windhoek, Namibia, takes place in March. It's an extravaganza of music, dance and ethnic dress.

Festival Pan-Africain du Cinema (Fespaco or Pan-African Film Festival; W www.fespaco .bf) is of international renown and held over nine days in Ougadougou, Burkina Faso, during late February/early March in odd-numbered years. Fespaco's Oscar equivalent is the Étalon de Yennenga.

Dogon festivals Agguet, Ondonfile and Boulo (the rain-welcoming festival) include complex masked dances and take place in April and May in Mali. The *Sigui* takes place roughly every 60 years in Dogon Country depending on the position of the star, Sirius.

Grahamstown Festival is a 10-day South African celebration of arts and crafts with an associated fringe festival beginning at the end of June.

Cure Salée, held in Niger during late September, is famed for the Gerewol festival, which includes a male beauty contest of the Woodaabé people (fula cattle herders). Bachelors paint their faces and bear amazing facial expressions for inspection by eligible single women.

Fête de l'Abissa in Côte d'Ivoire celebrates the dead and exorcising of evil spirits for a week in late October or early November.

Fula festivals, held annually during November and December, celebrate cattle crossings (to better grazing lands) on the Niger River (Mali). The most famous one is at Diafarabé.

Igue/Ewere Festival is a colourful seven-day event of traditional dancing, mock battles and processions to the Oba's Royal Palace in Benin City, Nigeria, in early December.

Islamic festivals are widely celebrated in the north, west and coastal regions of East Africa (See the Middle East chapter for details). Christian festivals are common elsewhere in Africa.

What to Expect?
TRAVELLERS
Africa attracts a huge cross section of nationalities, although French-speaking nationals are more prevalent in West and northwest Africa (where French is an official language). East and southern Africa's huge tourist profile ensures the widest variety (and number) of nationalities, including the most English-speakers.

There are a number of classic traveller hangouts in Africa. Morocco gives many gappers their first taste of Africa (if you can survive getting off the ferry in Tangier you can survive anything) and Chefchaouen in the Rif Mountains and Essaouira on the southwest coast are hotspots. The beaches of West Africa (the Casamance in Senegal, for example) are very popular, as are Dahab (a resort on the Red Sea coast of Egypt), Lamu Archipelago and Tiwi Beach (Kenya), Zanzibar, the shore of Lake Malawi and Vilankulo (formerly Vilanculos, Mozambique). Cape Town (South Africa), Dakar (Senegal) and Maputo (Mozambique) have party-town reputations.

LOCALS
By and large Africans are easygoing and polite. Good manners are respected and many people will think you most rude if you do not say hello and inquire after their health before asking them when the bus is going to leave. In some African societies greetings can go on for minutes.

Hospitality to travellers is common but in a few tourist destinations hospitality comes with a catch (travellers are often asked for money by people who they believed were their friends – Egypt and Morocco are among the worst places) and travellers are exploited for income but this is an exception rather than the rule.

It's hard to generalise about appropriate behaviour given the diversity of cultures. Certainly cultural values remain strong and vibrant across the continent, even when they are masked with a veneer of westernisation. It's common in Kenya to see a Masai *moran* (warrior) dressed in trousers and shirt in town and then in traditional Masai garb once he's home.

Africans are generally conservative in their outlook. It's inappropriate to wear revealing clothes and display affection in public. There are few queues in Africa, just scrums, and people (many of whom are used to sleeping eight to a room) have a different perception of personal space. Travellers in some remote areas are treated pretty much as curiosities and their habits and dress are often a source of considerable amusement.

LANGUAGE

Africa is a place of quite literally thousands of languages but happily for gappers English is widely spoken except in large swaths of West and northwest Africa where French is the most common second language. Portuguese is good for Angola, Mozambique and São Tomé, while Swahili is the trading language of East Africa, just as Hausa is in West Africa and Arabic in North Africa. Creole (a mixture of West African and European languages) is spoken on the coast of West Africa.

See Courses in Part III for information on language courses. Reading Material, later in this chapter, gives information on Lonely Planet's phrasebooks.

HEALTH RISKS

All the great world diseases are found in Africa. Malaria is a problem from the southern fringes of the Sahara down as far as the South African border. Yellow fever is similarly spread but not endemic south of Namibia and Zambia. It's impossible to overstate the disaster wrought by HIV/Aids in sub-Saharan Africa. Infection rates of over 20% of the adult population aren't uncommon in some regions and there are an estimated 8000 new infections per day, the huge majority from heterosexual intercourse (see **W** www.unaids .org for more information).

Schistosomiasis (bilharzias) is sadly present in many beautiful (and inviting) lakes and waterways, including the ever-popular Lake Malawi. The risk to tourists is pretty low, but if you do get wet, dry off quickly and dry your clothes as well. The greatest danger is in areas of standing water with little circulation and reedy shorelines.

Consult the Health chapter in Part I and seek professional medical advice for more travel health information.

TIME & FLIGHT TIME

Four time zones cover Africa, starting with London time (GMT) in the far west of the continent. Egypt and Libya are the only countries to have summer time variations.

Casablanca is just a short hop away from London (3½ hours flying time). Cairo is a little farther (five hours), and Nairobi (eight hours) and Cape Town (11½ hours) are long haul.

ISSUES

Crossing between countries in East and southern Africa is relatively easy and usually straightforward. West African borders are generally OK but requests for petty bribes aren't uncommon. At remote border posts and in rarely visited countries, all kinds of obstacles and terrible hassle can be put in your path, along with demands for 'fines'. At other remote frontiers you'll receive nothing but welcome and interest.

Dangerous and tricky African regions include many areas on the fringes of the Sahara, central Sierra Leone, Côte d'Ivoire, Liberia, parts of Nigeria, northern Algeria, northern Chad, southern Sudan, Central African Republic, Congo, Democratic Republic of Congo (Zaïre), Somalia and Angola. In addition, rebel activity continues in parts of Burundi, Rwanda and Uganda, and there are pockets of banditry and general looseness in northern Kenya and southern Ethiopia.

Zimbabwe is a fantastic travel destination but beset by political unrest, famine and lawlessness. Many travellers are avoiding the place but some parts are still attracting tourists. Check the situation carefully before making any decision. Also keep an eye on Namibia and Eritrea and the improving situation in Angola.

For further information on travel hotspots, general safety issues and governmental travel advice see Safety in Part I.

INTERNET & COMMUNICATIONS

It may come as a surprise to many readers that cheap internet cafés are available in major towns and cities from Cape Town to Timbuktu. Connections vary in speed and quality but the majority allow you to access web-based email servers such as Yahoo! and Hotmail.

Mobile-phone technology is changing communications in many parts of Africa. Unreliable state-run telephone systems are being usurped by affordable pay-as-you-go mobile services in countries from Morocco to Uganda. These phones can be ideal if you're spending a long time in one country as using your UK mobile will cost a fortune.

Daily Spend

Compared with most of the developing world Africa is expensive. Budget travellers can scrape around for £10 per day but for a degree of luxury, like a toilet in your room (although this can be a mixed blessing), you're looking at £20. Cities are obviously more expensive than out in the sticks and some countries (like Zambia) have a policy of low-impact, high-cost tourism. Accommodation in national parks commonly costs over £80 per person per night. The actual cost of living (food, transport etc) varies only a little around the continent (North, East and southern Africa are the most expensive) but some sectors of countries are better value than others – for example, accommodation in Mozambique and Mali is poor value.

Travellers commonly blow big chunks of their wedge on car/4WD hire (£60 per day on average), internal flights and partying. Try to save some cash for going on safari; a course in Swahili, Hausa or other useful African languages; camel trekking; doing a PADI open-water dive course; climbing a big impressive mountain; and perhaps quad-biking, a 4WD desert trip or learning to surf.

Getting There

You could hitch there or even get the train via Spain. Driving down the continent via Morocco, Tunisia or Egypt would be fantastic but most travellers pick up a cheap airfare and head straight into the heart of Africa.

AIR

The UK has air connections with almost all African countries, some directly, others via a European hub. The main gateway into East Africa is Nairobi, although Dar es Salaam (Tanzania) is also busy. Flights into Zimbabwe have decreased in recent years. Johannesburg is by far the busiest hub in southern Africa but there's plenty of traffic into Cape Town (South Africa). In West Africa, Accra (Ghana) and Lagos (Nigeria) are the busiest gateways but considerable traffic heads into Dakar (Senegal). Casablanca (Morocco) and Cairo are the busiest gateways in North Africa.

Many major European airlines offer open-jaw tickets that allow you to fly into, say, Cairo and out of Nairobi, Harare or Cape Town. Air France even allows gappers attempting one the world's great overland journeys to fly into Dakar and out of Cape Town! Shorter overland routes include flying into Dakar and out of Ouagadougou (Burkina Faso) or Accra and into Nairobi and out of Harare, Cape Town or Johannesburg.

Africa features on a few round-the-world (RTW) tickets. Nairobi and Johannesburg are the usual options. Sadly, putting Africa onto your ticket can cut down options elsewhere (Australia is often the next available destination).

Air France has some of the best connections to French-speaking West and Central Africa but SN Brussels Airlines provides stiff competition. British Airways (BA) has good connections across Africa and offers some flexibility, although not always the cheapest fares. KLM has a huge African network and cheap fares. Lufthansa, Ethiopian Airlines, South African Airways and Kenya Airways are all good bets for flights to Africa.

Consult the Airlines Appendix at the back of the book for more information on airlines and routes.

Ticket Costs

The best available student/under-26 fares are quoted here. See Passports, Tickets, Visas & Insurance in Part I for more information on how to get the best, most flexible deal.

For around £200 you can get a return flight to Cairo or Casablanca, while flights into Dakar, Cape Town and Nairobi should cost around £400. Return flights into places such as Douala (Cameroon) cost between £600 and £800.

A standard open-jaw ticket into Nairobi and out of Johannesburg should cost around £500 while anything using Cairo is often around £100 cheaper. Into Dakar and out of Cape Town costs around £600.

It's sometimes possible to pick up cheap charter flights into Morocco, The Gambia, Kenya and airports across Egypt. If you can get to Paris first, cheap charter flights into Saharan West Africa are possible during winter.

SEA & OVERLAND

The days of working your way to Africa aboard a cargo ship are, alas, over but ferries link Spain and France with Morocco, France with Algeria and Tunisia, Italy with Tunisia, Malta with Libya, and Egypt with Jordan and Saudi Arabia (which also has a ferry to Sudan and Eritrea).

The only land access is across the Sinai from Israel to Egypt (cross at the Taba/Eilat boarder post and not at Rafah in the troubled Gaza Strip).

SPECIALIST TOUR OPERATORS

Dozens of British tour operators operate trips in Africa (see the Global Tour Companies Appendix at the back of the book). Other region-specific operators include:

African Trails (☎ 01772-330907, fax 01772-628281; e sales@africantrails.co.uk; W www .africantrails.co.uk; 3 Conway Ave, Preston PR 9TR) offers truck tours through East Africa plus a trans-African route.

Truck Africa (e sales@truckafrica.com; W www.truckafrica.com), an internet-based company, runs overland-truck safaris from London to Cape Town and shorter tours around East Africa.

Africa & Beyond

From Cape Town at the bottom of the continent, flying is your only option and there are occasionally good deals to Oz, India and South America. If you're doing it the other way around then it's easy to continue (by bus) into the Middle East before heading east into Asia, northeast towards Russia, or to rail links through China or northwest through Europe. Cheap flights to India are often also found in Nairobi and Dar es Salaam.

Further Information
READING MATERIAL
Useful Lonely Planet guides include *Africa on a shoestring*, *Healthy Travel Africa* and regional guides to southern, eastern and western Africa. There are also over a dozen individual country guides, *Trekking in East Africa*, *Watching Wildlife: East Africa* and phrasebooks to Egyptian and Moroccan Arabic, Swahili and the complex Ethiopian Amharic language.

The titles that follow are a rather eclectic selection but give a good background to the continent.

A History of Africa, by JD Fage, is comprehensive and digestible and *Africa*, by Phyllis Martin and Patrick O'Meara, is also recommended. *Africa – Dispatches from a Fragile Continent*, by Blaine Harden, is insightful, critical and unsurprisingly banned in a number of African states.

Paul Theroux weaves his overwhelming pessimism and anger about the state of Africa into a great tale of a Cairo to Cape Town trip in *Dark Star Safari*.

My Traitor's Heart is the excellent autobiography of Rian Malan, an Afrikaner trying to come to grips with his heritage and future in South Africa, while *Long Road to Freedom* is Nelson Mandela's unmissable autobiography.

The Ukimwi Road and *South of the Limpopo*, by Dervla Murphy, describe an eccentric and enlightening cycle journey through southern Africa.

It's worth reading anything by Wilfred Thesiger for an insight into colonial and post-colonial Africa, while *Out of Africa*, by Karen Blixen, and *Flame Trees of Thika*, by Elspeth Huxley, are both classic tales.

Travels in West Africa, by Mary Kingsley, is a remarkable account of her travels in 19th-century West Africa.

Africa by Road, by Bob Swain & Paula Snyder, and *Sahara Overland*, by Chris Scott, are invaluable reading for those driving around the continent.

The *New African* is probably the best magazine for politics and economics, although *Focus on Africa* is not far behind and is better with culture. *Africa Today* can also be recommended. *Travel Africa* is a quarterly subscription magazine with great up-to-date travel information.

USEFUL INFORMATION SOURCES
For specific country overviews, the low-down on travel in the region and hundreds of useful links, head to Lonely Planet's website (**W** www.lonelyplanet.com).

For African news and background **W** www.bbc.co.uk, **W** www.newsafrica.net and **W** www.allafrica.com are great starting points. Also try **W** garamond.stanford.edu/depts/ssrg/africa/, an enormous academic resource. It also has literally thousands of links as does Index on Africa (**W** afrika.no).

The Africa Centre (☎ 020-7836 1973; **W** www.africacentre.org.uk; 38 King St, Covent Garden, London WC2E) is a cultural centre, gig venue, education centre for all things African and houses the African Book Centre. The School of Oriental and African Studies (SOAS; ☎ 020-7637 2388; **W** www.soas.ac.uk; Thornhaugh St, Russell Square, London WC1H 0XG) is an academic institution but the general public can use the incredible library (students get discounted entry and the catalogue can be searched online). Events and talks are also held at the school.

Been There, Done That
There were no buses on the border area between Sudan and the Central African Republic (CAR). In fact there were hardly any roads – just sandy tracks through the bush – so in Nyala,

the last town in Sudan, I hitched on a lorry carrying onions to N'Gorou, about 400km away in CAR. 'Shouldn't take long,' said the driver, and we drove out of town just as the sun was setting. 'How splendid,' I thought, as we rumbled through the desert with stars overhead, 'travel in Africa is such jolly good fun.'

Next day, our overloaded Bedford struggled slowly through the sand and it was evening when we reached the Sudanese border checkpoint, to find the immigration office had shut. The following day there were more delays (some other passengers' papers were not in order), so we slept another night at the border – lying on the ground under the lorry.

Day four, and we crossed into the 100km-wide no-man's-land between the border posts. At an innocuous looking river, a few inches of water turned out to be a few inches of mud. We might have been able to push it out of the mud but our driver was a determined man, revving mercilessly until the lorry was neatly buried up to its axles.

It took two days to unload the cargo, dig out the lorry, push it to dry land, and transport the onions across the river. By this time, the onions had started to go mouldy, so we had to spread them in the sun for another day to dry. It then took yet another day to re-fill the sacks and re-load the lorry, then another day to drive to the CAR border post. However, it was Good Friday in Catholic CAR and the fete was celebrated seriously and everybody (including the border guards) had four days off work. By this time, our food had long gone, so we'd started eating the onions, with nothing to do other than wait. Boiled, fried or raw onions were still the only option on the menu.

On the Tuesday after Easter we got through the border, and after another day and night we finally rolled into N'Gorou – it had taken almost two weeks to cover the 400km. N'Gorou had a notoriously difficult checkpoint and I was apprehensive, and sweating profusely but almost entirely pure onion juice. The cop sniffed a few times, then quickly stamped my passport, and couldn't get me out of his office quick enough. Travel in Africa always takes longer than expected.   David Else

The Middle East

Introduction

The Middle East is not so much a place of shifting sands, camels and oases as an arid, varied land with a fascinating heritage and a warm welcome. True it has its problems, and some travellers may find it restrictive, but if you like the kind of travelling that includes a huge number of historical sites and plenty of time sitting in coffee houses (a regional institution) and discussing life, the universe and everything, then the Middle East is for you.

In this book the Middle East includes Jordan, Israel, Lebanon, Syria, Iran, Iraq, Saudi Arabia and the Gulf States. Sometimes Egypt, Libya and Turkey are included in discussion of the Middle East, as much for current political reasons as geographical ones.

Why the Middle East?

Even the keenest fans of the Middle East (and there are many) would have to admit that it gets some bad press. Some of it is justified but, as always, exaggeration, distortion and downright misrepresentation all contribute to a lack of eager travellers packing their bags for Tehrān (Iran) or Damascus (Syria). Shame, shame, shame. While we wouldn't, at present, recommend a fortnight in Nāblus (the West Bank) or a scientific exchange programme with Baghdad University (Iraq), the region's problems tend to be localised and we can heartily recommend the hospitality of Syria, the mountains in northern Iran, the southern deserts of Jordan, exploring by 4WD in Oman and meeting the Bedouin of Israel's Negev desert.

The Middle East is a fascinating place. It's the land of *A Thousand and One Nights* and the Seven Wonders of the Ancient World. Travel here is less about gung-ho outdoor activities or lounging on beaches and more about experiencing a completely different culture and historical landscape. The Middle East is where Africa, Asia and Europe meet, where Christianity, Islam and Judaism were born and where civilisation as we know it developed during more than a dozen sophisticated empires that had risen and fallen before the birth of Christ. What's more, much physical evidence of the Middle East's shared, disputed, and often violent history remains.

Tourism across the region is a diverse picture. The United Arab Emirates (UAE) is a place of lavish and wacky-looking hotels, an exotic and upmarket travel destination with something for independent travellers. Oman, next door, is similar but more adventurous. Jordan and Israel are the most geared up for tourists, and Iraq and Saudi Arabia the least (the Saudi government actively discourages tourism). Accommodation along the Gulf can be fiercely expensive but the region need not cost the earth. The Middle East is not a regular draw for well-heeled clubbers but if you want to party 'Western style' the clubs of Tel Aviv (Israel) give out the most hope, Dubai (UAE) is not bad and Beirut (Lebanon) is reborn as a vibrant, fun and cosmopolitan city. More than adequate compensation for the lack of party towns are festivals and traditional celebrations, majestic deserts, wonderful mountain landscapes and the joy of simply existing in such a vastly different physical and cultural landscape. For those who love to travel with an eye on cultural, political and historical experiences and want a travel experience far removed from the Southeast Asia tourist trail then this is your bag. Don't be scared, take the plunge.

What to Do?

It's pretty unlikely/downright impossible that gappers will cruise into a tax-free, expat job in the Middle East, and volunteer opportunities are not enormous. The things people

Top 10 Must-Sees

Estahban (Iran) – relaxed trading town with superb Islamic architecture.
Maktesh Ramon and Negev Desert (Israel) – try trekking in this stunning natural desert crater.
Petra and Wadi Rum (Jordan) – magical ancient carved-rock city and fantastic slice of desert.
Baalbek (Lebanon) and Palmyra (Syria) – famed Roman cities and wondrous temple complexes.
Muscat (Oman) – enchanting city with fine souks and a great launching point for 4WD wadi bashing.
Musandam Peninsula (Oman) – stark and dramatic beauty of the Middle East's fjords.
Najran (Saudi Arabia) – Yemeni-influenced, fascinating and rarely visited town close to the Empty Quarter.
Damascus (Syria) – one of the oldest cities in the world and an architectural treasure-trove.
Crak des Chevaliers (Syria) – one of the greatest castles in the world.
Dubai (UAE) – the Dubai World Cup is for horse lovers but check out the camel races too.

do in the region are often evocative rather than active. Wandering through bazaars, drinking buckets of mint tea, going to the races (camel and horse – the Dubai World Cup in March is the richest horse race in the world) or exploring the deserts of Israel, Jordan, Oman and the UAE are all popular. One thing's for sure, it's easy to get captivated by the history of the Middle East; there are so many museums, ancient treasures, stunning ruins and historic buildings. For starters there's the amazing ancient city of Petra in Jordan, where huge public buildings were hewn out of rock walls, and then there are the ruins of Byzantine, Persian, Roman and Greek cities with names as famous in legend as in history. Syria, Jordan and Iran are particularly blessed, although arguably it's in Iraq that the greatest treasures of antiquity are found. What's more, in Israel and Jordan between May and September there's the opportunity to work on an archaeological dig.

See Part III for more information on overseas jobs, volunteer work and courses.

GET ACTIVE
Cycling & Mountain Biking
There's no doubt that the Middle East offers some fantastic opportunities for cyclists and mountain bikers. The heat can be a killer (avoid June to September) but mountain biking is common in Israel, Jordan and to some extent in Lebanon. Many people particularly enjoy cycling in Syria and we've heard of people mountain biking in the Mt Lebanon Range and Bekaa Valley in Lebanon but check this out locally.

Skiing & Snowboarding
Not a Middle Eastern activity that immediately springs to mind but there's some skiing on the slopes of Mt Makmal northeast of Beirut in Lebanon and in the Kūhhā-ye Alborz (Alborz Mountains) north of Tehrān where, thanks to the slight liberalisation of the female dress codes, fewer women now ski in a full-length *chador* (a tent-like black outfit).

Trekking, Mountaineering & Climbing

Many of the region's beautiful, arid or desert trekking areas are positively dangerous in the fierce heat of summer so avoid June to August. Wadi Rum (Jordan) is a spectacular place to hike, as is the landscape around Petra. There are some great climbs elsewhere in Jordan. Maktesh Ramon (the world's largest crater) and the canyons and pools of Ein Avdat in Israel's Negev Desert are great trekking areas but the higher, cooler Upper Galilee and Golan regions of the country are also well geared up for trekking.

North of Tehrān is Kūhhā-ye Damāvand (5671m), the highest peak in the Middle East, and the surrounding Kūhhā-ye Alborz offer some marvellous trekking and mountaineering. Trekking infrastructure is not well developed in Iran.

Oman has good trekking and climbing potential, while walking through a landscape punctuated by ancient, fortified mountain settlements around Manakhah and Al-Mahwit is the highlight of many a trip to Yemen.

Watersports

The Red Sea has some world-class coral reefs and underwater geography. At Eilat (Israel) and Aqaba (Jordan) you can dive (courses are available) and pursue a variety of watersports from sailing to water-skiing. Also consider a side trip to Sinai (Egypt; see the Africa chapter), which also has amazing diving. The UAE is also geared up for watersports.

WORK A LITTLE

Job possibilities are limited to teaching English, working in the occasional backpackers hostel (especially Israel) and in the kibbutz or moshav systems in Israel (see the Volunteering, Conservation & Expeditions and Casual/Seasonal Work chapters respectively in Part III for details). If you've specific vocational skills you may be able to join the massive expat workforce in the Gulf but these jobs are usually appointed overseas.

TRAVEL AROUND

Travelling around the Middle East is no big hassle. Buses and minibuses take the lion's share of transport honours. Minibuses tend to be a more chaotic and 'local' experience. Somewhere above or below the minibus in the efficient-transport scale (there are regional variations) are shared taxis, the most common form of public transport in some parts. These run to fixed routes, leave when full, cost a little more than buses (although they can be more frequent and quicker) and stop to pick up/drop off passengers along the way. In wealthy Gulf States extensive car ownership has reduced public transport.

There are a handful of comfortable train lines in the region (most notably in Iran, Israel, Jordan and Syria). Services tend to be slow and infrequent. Flying can be a good option for long journeys and to skip over Iraq and Saudi Arabia. Iran boasts dirt-cheap domestic flights and Emirates offer an Arabian Airpass. Gulf Air and Emirates both have wide regional networks.

There are ferries from Oman and the UAE to Iran and from the UAE to Iraq but surprisingly few other ferry services around the Gulf.

Hitchhiking is never safe and not recommended (unaccompanied women should never hitch) but if you find yourself stranded a raised thumb is an obscene gesture in the Middle East (you work it out). Wave your flattened palm up and down.

Classic Routes

There are three stumbling blocks to overland travel in the Middle East: Iraq for obvious reasons; Saudi Arabia thanks to the difficulty of getting anything other than a transit visa;

and Israel, as an Israeli stamp in your passport prevents entry into Iran, Lebanon, Syria and all Gulf States except Saudi Arabia. But don't fret, you don't necessarily have to fly over these problems. Take a little detour in order to travel in a classic loop: cut up through Jordan and Syria, make a side trip into Lebanon and then loop east through Turkey into Iran before crossing the Gulf by ferry to the UAE for exploration of the Gulf States (Oman is a must). You can then either fly out of Dubai or get a bus across Saudi Arabia to Jordan before flying out of Tel Aviv or cutting down into Egypt (no problems having an Israeli stamp here) and flying out of Cairo.

When to Go?
The best times to visit the Middle East are spring and autumn. Summer is way too hot and winter brings some surprisingly miserable weather to the northern Middle East.

You may also want to avoid Ramadan (see Festivals below) when the whole region is on a go slow and most restaurants and cafés are closed. While other regional festivals cause some disruption they can be great to experience.

CLIMATE
The coasts of the Red Sea, Arabian Sea and the Gulf range from hot to damn hot, often with 70% humidity. Summer daytime temperatures can exceed 50°C, while in winter 30°C is not uncommon. The shore of the Caspian Sea has a milder, central European climate, much like that of the Mediterranean. This doesn't mean that it never gets cold; it does, as much of Iran and Yemen are above 1000m and together with highland areas elsewhere, experience very cold winters, with snow on some peaks.

Much of the Middle East is arid or semi-arid and rarely receives more than 100mm of rainfall annually. The notable exceptions are along the Mediterranean coast and southeast Iran, Yemen and southern Oman. The latter three areas are affected by Indian monsoonal systems from March to May and July to August.

The UAE probably has the best year-round climate.

FESTIVALS
Major festivals in the Middle East tend to be religious. The Islamic ones are celebrated according to the Hegira year or Muslim calendar, which is based on the lunar cycle, just like the Jewish calendar around which all Jewish religious festivals are based. The Christian or Gregorian calendar is used for secular events across the region and is based on the solar cycle making it 10 or 11 days longer than the Jewish or Muslim calendars. So while it was 2003 in the UK at the time of writing it was 5764 in Israel and 1424 in Oman – **W** www.soultospirit.com/calendar/holiday_by_religion.asp lists the dates of many religious festivals. These are some of the region's most important festivals:

Islamic New Year, Ras as-Sana, is getting closer to the Christian New Year, which is also celebrated in some non-Christian parts of the Middle East.

Eid al-Moulid or Moulid an-Nabi is a celebration of the Prophet's birthday.

Ramadan comes at the end of the ninth month of the Islamic calendar and Muslims must fast during daylight hours. Eid al-Fitr marks the end of Ramadan with a three-day feast.

Eid al-Adha marks the time that Muslims make the pilgrimage to Mecca.

Eid al-Kebir or Tabaski commemorates Abraham's willingness to sacrifice his son on God's command, and the last-minute substitution of a ram. Rams are admired across the region and then slaughtered before a big feast.

Nō Rūz, the Persian New Year, is celebrated in Iran and occurs around March 21 causing much merriment but massive transport and accommodation problems.

The Dubai World Cup, the world's richest horse race, is held in the UAE at the end of March.

Easter and Christmas are very important times in Israel, not because there's any sizable Christian population but because of the influx of pilgrims to the Holy sites.

Pesah or Passover celebrates the exodus of the Jews from Egypt and lasts a week. All shops are closed.

Purim or Feast of Lots is one of the happiest of all Jewish festivals. It's held to honour how the Jewish people living in Persia were saved from massacre.

What to Expect?

TRAVELLERS

Historic links mean that British travellers are fairly common in the region, although numbers of Americans, Ozzies, Kiwis and Brits are likely to reduce due to the crises in Israel and Iraq. Traveller hangouts are few and far between in the Middle East but many travellers hang out in Eilat, Aqaba, Dubai and Damascus, a historic city that rightly eats away at many a traveller's time. Oman and southern Jordan (particularly Petra and Wadi Rum) also attract many travellers.

LOCALS

Islamic religious values dominate the societies of the Middle East (Israel aside). It's a very conservative place with strong values of family and hospitality. Women tend to take the back seat to men in almost all matters. That said, there are great cultural differences across the region. For example, there are several very different, nomadic peoples in the region and while restrictions on female dress are severe in Iran, woman are educated equally, serve in parliament and play a role in public life (unlike in Saudi Arabia where women are not permitted even to drive). Certainly there are some generally false misconceptions about women in the Middle East. Many travellers expect local women to be poor, battered and repressed creatures, which is far from the mark. At the same time, Western, solo female travellers are often perceived by locals as loose-moralled harlots and can experience harassment, especially in parts of Israel, Egypt and Turkey, although much less so in strict Muslim states such as Iran.

Showing affection in public, wearing revealing clothes and even holding hands can cause great offence in the Middle East. Women should wear baggy, loose-fitting clothes and have a headscarf handy. Saudi Arabia is an incredibly restrictive place (alcohol, pork, cinema and theatre are all illegal) but at the same time the hospitality of the Middle East is renowned (in Syria it's legendary and at times overwhelming). Any cultural and political differences are more likely to result in an invitation to tea and a good deal of discussion, rather than aggression.

LANGUAGE

Arabic is the official language everywhere accept Iran and Israel, where Farsi (Persian) and Hebrew are spoken respectively. English is widely spoken in the region (some people still speak a little French in Syria and Lebanon) but you're well advised to learn a little of the local language (possible in the Middle East) if you're travelling off the beaten track.

See Courses in Part III for information on language courses. Reading Material, later in this chapter, gives information on Lonely Planet's useful phrasebooks.

HEALTH RISKS

The Middle East is in fact a reasonably healthy place compared with, say, the heart of Africa or deepest Asia. Nevertheless, malaria is endemic in a few rural areas outside Israel and some Gulf States and waterborne diseases are common.

Consult the Health chapter in Part I and seek professional medical advice for more travel health information.

TIME & FLIGHT TIME

The Middle East is divided into three time zones. Israel, Jordan, Lebanon and Syria are two hours ahead of Greenwich Mean Time (GMT). Bahrain, Iraq, Kuwait, Qatar, Saudi Arabia and Yemen are three hours ahead of GMT and Oman four hours ahead. Iran is the odd one out; it's 3½ hours ahead of GMT.

Tel Aviv is a 4¾-hour flight away from London, while Tehrān is 6½ hours away and Muscat eight hours.

ISSUES

Anti-Western sentiment (and anti-American in particular) is certainly increasing in the Middle East largely because of the conflicts in Iraq and the Palestinian Territories (Israel). The latter is an issue that hangs over the whole region and its importance cannot be underestimated. However, the region remains one of the most hospitable and generous in the world and local people are very unlikely to take out any disagreement they have with the government on young British travellers. Acts of terrorism against Western targets in the Middle East are possible but personal safety is pretty good, thanks, in part, to numerous police states and some of the fiercest judicial systems in the world. There's little chance you'll get mugged in Damascus but be careful with whom and where you talk politics – repression is common in the Middle East, the free press a rarity and political dissent can lead to unpleasant consequences.

Places to definitely avoid include parts of the West Bank and Gaza in the Palestinian Territories, Yemen, and the borders of Afghanistan and Iraq in Iran. Likewise rambling around the Israeli-Lebanon border is not a smart move and you're well advised to stay away from political demonstrations.

For further information on travel hotspots, general safety issues and governmental travel advice see Safety in Part I.

INTERNET & COMMUNICATIONS

The internet is banned in Syria and Saudi Arabia. Mobile-phone networks now cover many of the region's more urban areas.

Daily Spend

Costs in the Middle East vary greatly. Transport costs are usually low, thanks to cheap fuel, and the basic necessities of life remain quite reasonable across the Middle East but accommodation costs can be a killer – in some parts of the Gulf you can struggle to find anything under £20 per night. You can get by in Iran for under £10 per day as long as you change money (preferably dollars!) at 'the street rate'. Likewise Syria is good value (around £10 per day) and Saudi Arabia and Jordan surprisingly cheap (around £15 per day). Israel, Oman, Qatar and the UAE are certainly not budget destinations (allow for spending £25–35 a day) but the most expensive place in the Middle East (and with arguably the least to see) is Kuwait (you'll need £40 a day at least).

Getting There

You can cycle, drive, get the bus or take the train to the Middle East from Europe but flying is the most cost-effective way to travel.

AIR

Flying to the Middle East is relatively cheap but, just outside the region, Egypt is an even cheaper destination (see Ticket Costs in the Africa chapter) and you get to see the Pyramids before arriving in the Middle East proper. Cheap deals into Turkey are also a possibility (see No Frills Please, We're British in the Europe chapter). The region's other major hubs are Tel Aviv, Dubai and, to a lesser extent, Amman (Jordan). Cheap fares to Beirut are easy to come by and Dubai is a popular stopover on many round-the-world (RTW) tickets and cheap deals to the Indian Subcontinent. Handily, this stopover traffic means that cheap short stays in swanky hotels are sometimes available.

All the major European carriers offer flights to the Middle East. Alitalia (via Rome), British Airways (BA), Olympic Airways (via Athens) and Lufthansa (via Frankfurt) were some of the outfits offering the cheapest deals at the time of writing. Gulf Air and Emirates were not far behind and have better networks.

Consult the Airlines Appendix at the back of the book for more information on airlines and routes.

Ticket Costs

The best available student/under-26 fares are quoted here. See Passports, Tickets, Visas & Insurance in Part I for more information on how to get the best, most flexible deal.

Return fares to Beirut, Tel Aviv and Dubai are the cheapest (£200/225/280 respectively), while Muscat (£375) is often the most expensive destination. The cheapest open-jaw options are those flying into Cairo and out of Dubai (around £260) but fares don't rise too steeply should you want to fly into Amman and out of Tehrān (around £320), or a dozen other similar combinations.

SEA & OVERLAND

From Cyprus there are ferry sailings to Lebanon and Israel. Ferries to Israel also leave from mainland Greece (and sometimes from Crete and Rhodes), while Egyptian boats head to Saudi Arabia and Jordan. Occasionally ships leave Suez for the Gulf too. Saudi Arabia has ferry links to Sudan and Eritrea.

Land borders are pretty simple; Egypt to the south; Turkey to the north and Turkmenistan, Pakistan and Afghanistan to the east.

SPECIALIST TOUR OPERATORS

Dozens of British tour operators operate trips in the Middle East (see the Global Tour Companies Appendix at the back of the book). Other region-specific operators include:

Arab Tours (☎ 020-7935 3273, fax 020-7486 4237; |e| arabtours@btconnect.com; 60 Marylebone Lane, London W1U 2NZ) is the Middle East specialist with tours to Libya.

Caravanserai Tours (☎ 020-8855 6373, fax 020-8855 6370; |e| caravanserai@music farm.demon.co.uk; |W| www.caravanserai-tours.com; 1–3 Love Lane, Woolwich, London SE18 6QT) specialises in Iran and Libya.

THE MIDDLE EAST & BEYOND

You could easily head east and begin a great overland odyssey down through Africa to Cape Town or just as easily head home through Europe. Adventurous travellers may want to look towards the heady heights of Central Asia (which opens up possibilities to explore both Russia and China) or continue east on the famous hippie trail to Kathmandu, from where Southeast Asia and eventually Australia await.

Further Information

READING MATERIAL

Lonely Planet publishes a single guide to the *Middle East* (which includes Egypt, Libya and Turkey), plus individual guides to a number of countries and cities in the region. There's also a guide to the classic route between Istanbul and Cairo, and Farsi (Persian) and Arabic phrasebooks.

The BBC's *The Fifty Year War: Israel & the Arabs* (co-written by an Arab and Jew) and *The Arab World: Forty Years of Change*, by Elizabeth Fernea & Robert Warnock, provide a great overview to the conflict. *The Middle East*, by Bernard Lewis, is a more comprehensive history of the region. *Living Islam*, by Akbar Ahnted, is recommended reading for all Western travellers to the region.

At the Drop of a Veil is the story of Marianne Alireza who married into a Saudi merchant family in the 1940s, while Geralditte Brooks' *Nine Parts of Desire* is a thorough and balanced investigation into the life of women under Islam. *Black on Black*, by Ana M Briongos, thoroughly dismantles many prejudices about Iran. *Gates of Damascus*, by Lieve Joris, delivers a real insider's look into the Syrian capital. Within the narrative of a love story, Anne Caulfield's *Kingdom of Film Stars* gives a great insight into life with the Bedouin and in Jordan more generally.

Romantic and evocative accounts of the region include Wilfred Thesiger's *Arabian Sands* (the legendary crossing of the 'Empty Quarter' of Saudi Arabia and Oman), *The Marsh Arabs* and *Desert, Marsh and Mountain*.

Seven Pillars of Wisdom, by TE Lawrence, tells of another famous desert adventure and Freya Stark's famous Middle Eastern travels are told in over 20 books including *East is West*, *Valleys of the Assassins* and *Beyond the Euphrates*.

The Middle East is an international monthly magazine covering all aspects of the region.

USEFUL INFORMATION SOURCES

For specific country overviews, the low-down on travel in the region and hundreds of useful links head to Lonely Planet's website ([W] www.lonelyplanet.com).

Other useful starting points include [W] www.arabia.com, [W] www.albawaba.com and [W] www.birzeit.edu (handy for an insight into the Palestinian Territories).

The Royal Asiatic Society (☎ 020-7724 4741, fax 020-7706 4008; [e] info@royalasiatic society.org; [W] www.royalasiaticsociety.org; 60 Queens Gardens, Bayswater, London W2 3AF) is a private, academic organisation and may be able to help you with detailed and specific research. Likewise the School of Oriental and African Studies may also be of use (see the Africa chapter).

Been There, Done That

Everything was going rather well. Steve and I had ridden all the way through Europe and the Bab al-Hawa (gate of wind) on the Turkish-Syrian border without a mishap. We were feeling rather pleased with ourselves and heading for Aleppo when calamity struck and we hit a patch of loose stone; we slid off and the motorbike was hit by a bus (which hurried away). A host of local people immediately rushed to our aid and there was extra surprise and a rush of good will once they realised Steve spoke Arabic. It was amazing. Some very enterprising locals patched up the motorcycle while I was treated to food, buckets of mint tea and great kindness. The motorcycle was (just) roadworthy but after long goodbyes I decided to catch the bus to Aleppo and meet Steve at the bus station. Only when I arrived he wasn't there. Wandering around like a lost sheep I was immediately befriended by a taxi driver but realising my problem and surprised to find a woman travelling on her own, he immediately became my guardian escorting me to the police post where my plight aroused very genuine concern. Apparently there are two bus stations in Aleppo and a search commenced while I was given more food, mint tea and many, many cigarettes. By this time the whole bus station was talking about me so when Steve rode through the gates of the bus station 90 minutes later he was greeted like a conquering hero, with cheers and applause. Nowhere have I encountered anything like Syria's code of friendship and responsibility shown to lost female guests.   Caroline Thorp

Russia, Central Asia & the former Soviet Union

Introduction

The area described here in eight pages is bigger than Africa and Australasia put together. Central Asia (in this instance Armenia, Azerbaijan, Georgia, Kazakhstan, Uzbekistan, Kyrgyzstan, Tajikistan, Turkestan, Turkmenistan and Afghanistan) is about the size of Europe. Together with Belarus, Russia and Ukraine this creates a region of huge contrasts covering everything from permanently frozen tundra to harsh desert, from European Christianity through Middle Eastern Islam to Asian Buddhism. Great cities and historic towns await your gaze and there's enough wildness and wilderness as anywhere on the planet. You'll need patience, tolerance and a good sense of humour for travel in this region but the former realm of the communist bogeyman is a fascinating place nevertheless.

Why Russia, Central Asia & the former Soviet Union?

History, mystery and the opportunity to have a voyeuristic peak at 70 years of communist detritus lures thousands of travellers to the region. Mountainous terrain and wilderness drag in many more. The change since 1989 has been incredible but only slowly is the generosity and interest locals show to travellers manifesting itself in the region's previously grey and humourless tourist and service industries. Capitalism has been embraced with a big, warm-hearted Russian hug in the west, most notably in Moscow where every tourist is cheerfully fleeced just as they would be in London or Paris. Outside the capital, businesses gear themselves towards local people (who are probably not earning more than £30 per month) and prices plummet.

So what's on offer? Well, in the west you could comfortably spend your time checking out museums and historical sites then hang out in cafés when the shear weight of culture wears you down. Fascinating St Petersburg and Moscow are filled with museums, palaces and monuments. The Bolshoi, Red Square and the Kremlin are all wonderful doses of high culture that are happily offset by some of the wildest, most hedonistic (and dangerous) clubbing in the world.

Central Asia offers a completely different travel experience. The landscape has a habit of turning rough and untamed; stunning jagged mountains, expansive deserts, homesteads in alpine valleys and nomadic horsemen all await. Within this hard and often taxing environment are a string of ancient cities and architectural treasures, like the fire temple of Zoroastrian in Azerbaijan or the 14th-century mausoleum of Kozha Akhmed Yasaui in Turkestan, that stretch from Tbilisi to the Silk Road.

Halfway across Russia is Lake Baikal, the deepest freshwater lake in the world, a magnificent place to explore and an essential stop on the famed Trans-Siberian Railway. This is one the great train journeys of the world and a springboard to exploring not only the Siberian wilderness but also Mongolia and northern China.

Beyond the old iron curtain can still feel like a recently rediscovered country. Occasionally you get a full dose of Soviet weirdness, like in Minsk (Belarus), a place that illustrates what living under communism must have been like. At other times the problems thrown up by the collapse of the Soviet Union are only too evident; encounters with poorly paid border guards or police can be expensive and the worst kind of hassle; the logistical difficulty of travelling, poor accommodation and shocking food can be very wearing; massive pollution and the numerous smouldering, pointless little conflicts and major civil wars that have afflicted many countries in Central Asia.

But there are more positives than negatives in a region that could see its fortunes reversed by the exploitation of massive natural resources. The first, tentative escorted tours of Afghanistan began in 2003 and although it'll be a long time before the region as a whole is geared up for common or garden tourists, it's an ideal place for gappers.

What to Do?

Many gappers are taking advantage of the increasing number of voluntary opportunities in the region but most content themselves with travel, often including a trip along the Trans-Siberian Railway.

See Part III for more information on overseas jobs, volunteer work and courses.

GET ACTIVE

Outdoor activities are embraced with enthusiasm in the region. Local inquiries may well turn up a group participating in an activity you're interested in. New adventure travel possibilities are cropping up all the time and there are numerous opportunities for expeditions into the Arctic, Siberian wilderness and mountains of Central Asia.

Cycling & Mountain Biking

Mountain biking is organised by local and international companies in many areas also recommended for walking and trekking. A few hardy people set off to cross Russia by bike but spares are rare and there's a lot to be said for taking the train across much of Siberia.

Horse & Camel Trips

You can immerse yourself in Central Asia's culture of horsemanship in Turkmenistan (the land of the crazy horse-riding desert nomad) and central or eastern Kyrgyzstan. Camel trekking is possible in northern Uzbekistan.

Top 10 Must-Sees

Ashtarak (Armenia) – ancient churches and the majestic Mt Aragats' 4090m.

Atashgah Temple (Azerbaijan) – marvellous Temple of Fireworshippers in Odlar Yourdu, or 'Land of Fires'.

Inylchek Glacier (Kyrgyzstan) – awesome high-mountain landscape and stunning trekking.

St Petersburg & Moscow (Russia) – home to Russia's greatest museums and cultural masterpieces.

Yaroslavl & Nizhny Novgorod (Russia) – classic Russia is found in these 'Golden Ring' towns.

Lake Baikal (Russia) – 'the Pearl of Siberia' is crystal clear, packed with wildlife and surrounded by mountains.

Kamachatka Peninsula (Russia) – live volcanoes, black-sand beaches and a weird rocky landscape.

Odessa (Ukraine) – Viennese-inspired Opera houses, cathedrals and funky nightlife next to the Black Sea.

Bukhara (Uzbekistan) – Central Asia's densest collection of Islamic monuments.

Minsk (Belarus) – seriously odd, Soviet-style city belonging to another era.

Skiing & Snowboarding

Rudimentary ski facilities are found on the Kazakhstan-Kyrgyzstan border. The central Caucasus around Elbrus (5642m) and Dombay-Yolgen (4000m) are better and heli-skiing is possible in both areas. The Kola Peninsula north of Moscow, the Altai Mountains on the Kazakhstan-Russia border and the Carpathians in Ukraine provide cross-country skiing *par excellence*. Cross-country skiing is very popular in Russia and Ukraine where reasonable, cheap, locally made kit is readily available.

Trekking, Mountaineering & Climbing

Mountainous and wild, Central Asia is a fantastic walking and trekking destination. Try the national parks and remote lakes in southern and eastern Kazakhstan and Kyrgyzstan, the alpine valleys of the Fan Mountains in Tajikistan and the heart of the Tien Shan range in eastern Kyrgyzstan, where glaciers and 6000m-plus mountains provide some impressive goals for climbers, trekkers and mountaineers.

Elsewhere the Crimea and Carpathian ranges in Ukraine, Lapland Nature Reserve in western Russia, the Elbrus area of the Caucasus, the Altai Mountains in southern Russia and Western Mongolia, the Ural Mountains in central Russia, the Sayan Mountains on the border with Mongolia and the volcanic and surreal Kamchatka Peninsula all offer some fantastic possibilities.

Other Activities

Rafting and kayaking trips are launched from Tashkent (Kazakhstan) and you can explore Siberia by boat on the Irtysh, Yenisey and Ob rivers. Boating around the Crimea coast on the Black Sea is popular between May and mid-October.

4WD tours are becoming popular in Central Asia, particularly in Kyrgyzstan and Tajikistan and don't discount the region's wildlife, which includes Siberian tigers in the east and some fantastic bird life in the southern Caucasus.

Caving is possible in Kyrgyzstan, Kazakhstan and Armenia, where the Speleological Society takes guided hiking, caving and mountain expeditions. In Siberia a Russian sauna (including a beating with birch twigs and naked roll in the snow) is a unique experience.

WORK A LITTLE

Only spawny gappers find any paid work in the region other than teaching English but many people participate in voluntary student exchange and English-teaching programmes working with kids in summer camps on Lake Baikal. Other Volunteer opportunities need sorting out in advance.

TRAVEL AROUND

Things may have got better for air travel in the region since 1994 when the passengers and crew of an Aeroflot Airbus A310 were killed after the pilot let his kids have a go but on less popular internal routes there are still overloaded crates out there held together with cable ties and gaffer tape. Aeroflot and Transaero ([W] www.transaero.com) are up to international safety standards but check out other carriers when you hit the ground.

Train travel is the best way to get around the region but you'll usually have to buy more expensive 'foreigner's' tickets. Expect anything under second class to be cramped, uncomfortable and insecure. Buses service a huge network cheaply, slowly and with less bureaucratic insanity. Minibus services and shared, or *marshrutnoe*, taxis are sometimes a good alternative. However, like accepting that first shot of vodka, what seemed like a good idea at the time turns into a nightmare. Road conditions are variable and in southern former Soviet republic's fuel shortages and roadblocks detract from the thrill of the open road.

Hitching is never entirely safe but it's common and the distinction between hitching and taking a taxi (shared or otherwise) is often blurred – you pay either way.

In Russia and the west, boat travel on canals, rivers or lakes is a great way to get about. There's also an erratic ferry service from Baku (Azerbaijan) to Turkmenbashi (Turkmenistan).

Most cities have a good public-transport system.

Classic Routes

The seven-day Trans-Siberian Railway links Vladivostok (Russia) on the Pacific to Moscow passing through eight time zones and across 9289 kilometres of mountain, plain, swamp and desert. It's not necessarily a fixed route; you can detour through Kazakhstan and western China, Mongolia and northern China on your way to Beijing. Another alternative is the BAM line, which can act as a springboard for exploration of the Siberian wilderness. You can stop anywhere en route, although you'll have to buy separate tickets as you go along.

The 'Golden Ring' *(Zolotoe Koltso)* allows the exploration of historic old towns (such as Suzdal, Yaroslavl and Rostov-Veliky), Russian Orthodox churches and magnificent monasteries northeast of Moscow. It's not going to take months but will give a real taste of what old Russia must have been like.

The Silk Road is not so much one trail as a network of trade routes linking Xi'an in China and the Mediterranean. This fantastic, difficult route leads from China into Kyrgyzstan via the Torugart pass and is still in use today. Travellers can continue northwest down the Fergana valley to Bishkek and then southwest down to Uzbekistan and the delights of Samarkand and the winding back streets and stunning Islamic architecture of Bukhara and Khiva (a city frozen in time). From there you can work your way down through Turkmenistan to the wondrous Sunday bazaar in Ashgabat via Merv, where no less than five walled cities once stood. Train lines link many of these highlights winding slowly and uncomfortably from Ürümqi in China southwest through Central Asia to the Iranian border.

When to Go?

If you like snow, ice, ludicrous temperatures, fur hats and winter sports then travel in winter. Siberia is at it's best in February, apparently. Not convinced? Then choose spring or autumn but avoid the April spring thaw. The deserts of Central Asia become a riot of colour in April. Summer is the essential time to explore the highest regions of Central Asia (passes are snowbound until May) and provides rain and nice temperatures for western Russia and the Black Sea coast. During June and July you'll be plagued by biting insects in northern Russia and Siberia (August and September are better) and this is also a resoundingly duff time to visit Central Asia's deserts.

CLIMATE

Generally the region has a continental European climate. Summers are very warm but Russia's long, dark, very cold winters are truly extreme – much of the country is well below freezing for over four months of the year (November to March) but in February and March the sun shines, there's a lack of humidity and it doesn't *feel* so cold. The coast bordering the Sea of Japan experiences a northern monsoonal climate, which means there's a 30-40% chance of rain each day between May and September.

FESTIVALS

There are plenty of festivals in the region and a number of national celebrations and obscure anniversaries disrupt bureaucratic life – much of Russia shuts down for the first half of May.

Christian holidays and festivals are widely (and wildly) celebrated by members of the Russian Orthodox Church.

Islamic holidays are celebrated in Central Asia (see Festivals in the Middle East chapter).

Rozhdestvo, the Russian Orthodox Christmas, is held across Russia on January 7 and begins with midnight church services.

Maslenitsa, the Goodbye Russian Winter festival, is held across eastern Russia in late February/early March when folk shows and various games are held.

Navrus, 'New Days', is a huge, official two-day festival and Islamic celebration of the spring equinox in Central Asia (normally fixed on March 21). Banned until 1989 it involves traditional food, music, drama, art and colourful fairs.

Festival of the North is held in eastern Russia in the last week of March – Murmansk and other northern towns hold reindeer races, ski marathons etc.

International Labour Day and the **Spring festival** are celebrated in Russia on May 1 & 2, traditionally with a huge military parade in Moscow.

St Petersburg White Nights takes place in the last 10 days of June and involves cultural events, merrymaking and late-night partying. Many other northern towns have their own version.

The Voice of Asia Rock Festival showcases regional rock groups, not the likes of Ozzy Osborne, during August in Medeu (Kazakhstan).

What to Expect?

TRAVELLERS

While the tourist trail in western Russia is well trodden, the rest of the country and Central Asia (where travel can be hard yards) are the preserve of hardy travellers, many of whom hail from Europe.

Tourist hangouts are difficult to determine. The region has no Ibiza or idyllic Thai islands but you'll find plenty of travellers in Russia's 'Golden Ring', on the Trans-Siberian Railway and, to a lesser extent, beside Lake Baikal and the Black Sea coast.

LOCALS

Despite the often dull, grey face and downright rudeness of the region's bureaucracy and service industry, friendliness and unconditional hospitality are common and sometimes overwhelming. Respond with a small gift and be careful not to take advantage. Vodka is often forced upon guests, even in Muslim Central Asia. 'Vodka terrorism' is also common on train journeys and during other chance social encounters. Saying 'just a small one then' is a one-way ticket to Doomsville but 'I'm an alcoholic' is a plausible excuse.

Immigrants from former colonies make up 20% of Russia's population and Central Asian states all have an ethnic majority bearing their names. The millions of Russians and Ukrainians living in Central Asia are referred to as Slavs.

Generally attitudes are conservative, particularly in Central Asia where care should be taken around religious sites – skimpy clothing is a definite trouble starter. A neat appearance goes far in the region and polite, gentlemanly behaviour is expected by female Russians.

The Christian Russian Orthodox Church is enjoying a revival and, with the notable exception of Georgia and Armenia (which have some of the world's oldest and most spectacularly located churches), Central Asia is staunchly Muslim. Buddhism and Judaism exist in small pockets, although there has been a mass emigration of Jews in recent years.

LANGUAGE

Russian is the second language of most people in Central Asia, where numerous ethnic languages are used locally. Learning the Cyrillic alphabet is a huge help, not only for Russia but for deciphering Central Asian, Ukrainian and Belarusian languages too. English is not widely spoken and in some parts of Central Asia using Russian goes down pretty badly, to say the least, so learn a few words of the local language too.

See Courses in Part III for details on language courses in the region and the UK. Reading Material later in this chapter gives information on Lonely Planet's useful phrasebooks.

HEALTH RISKS

Travellers require the usual armful of jabs and there are a few other health issues to consider. Tick-borne encephalitis, Lyme disease and Japanese encephalitis (spread by mosquitoes) are major problems in eastern Siberia during the summer, especially for trekkers. Cholera is not uncommon in southern regions and you can catch malaria in southern Tajikistan. Diphtheria is on the increase in Ukraine.

Short-term visitors are at little risk from the region's well-known nuclear pollution – it's actually possible to tour Chernobyl!

Consult the Health chapter in Part I and seek professional medical advice for more travel health information.

TIME & FLIGHT TIME

Central Asia is divided into three time zones and Russia 10! Moscow and most of western Russia is three hours ahead of GMT. Many countries in the region operate Daylight Savings Time (moving their clocks one hour forward) in summer.

From London, Almaty (Kazakhstan) is an 8½-hour flight away, while Moscow is 3½ hours away. Vladivostok is 12 hours from London – you fly over the Arctic – while Baku (Azerbaijan) is a relatively short hop in comparison (5¾ hours).

ISSUES

Getting visas for the region can be a big hassle so leave at least three months to organise it all prior to departure – getting them on the road will draw you into a huge web of bureaucratic nastiness. Clusters of countries, snake-like borders, complicated regulations and numerous options make choosing the correct visa difficult, while some countries still insist on an invitation or sponsorship (a hotel reservation will do) before issuing a visa.

Some Central Asian states insist that you register with the police upon arrival in a new town/the country for the first time. This is a pain but registration and visa irregularities can cause expensive problems – officials have a reputation for shaking down travellers. That said, the clamp down on corruption is improving and visa regulations may have changed by the time you read this.

At the time of writing the following were out of bounds to foreigners: Afghanistan, western Azerbaijan, the Kazakhstan-Kyrgyzstan border (thanks to occasional banditry), Tajikistan (although the situation is variable), parts of Georgia, eastern Armenia and some regions within the Russian Federation (Chechnya, Dagestan, North Ossetia, Ingushetia,

Karachai-Cherkassia and Kabardino-Balkaria, including the Elbrus area) plus a number of borders between Central Asia, the Middle East and China.

The casual repression of human rights, a lack of press freedom, massive corruption and Islamic fundamentalism all feature in the colourful life of the region but violent drunks (including the occasional policeman) are more of a problem to travellers.

For further information on travel hotspots, general safety issues and governmental travel advice see Safety in Part I.

INTERNET & COMMUNICATIONS
You'll find plenty of internet cafés but good connections are scarce in Central Asia. The same holds true for mobile communication (don't bother taking your mobile to Kyrgyzstan), the use of which is spreading out of big cities in Russia and Ukraine and into the regions.

Daily Spend
In Russia, Ukraine and Belarus a two-tier pricing policy exists which means tourists pay more for train and air tickets, many hotels and museums/attractions.

Moscow is at least as expensive as your average European city and a dorm bed is going to cost you £10. St Petersburg and Kyiv (Kiev; Ukraine) are only a little better but away from these cities prices plummet. Budget for £20–25 a day in Russia, Belarus and Ukraine and you'll have a fine time.

In Central Asia budget on spending £15–25 a day if you're not living on caviar and hiring 4WDs. A half-decent hotel bed costs around £8 but basic accommodation is a quarter of that. Black markets (US dollars are the currency to carry) in Uzbekistan and Turkmenistan make travel cheaper.

Getting There
You can arrive by road and rail from Iran, China and Europe. Or you can just fly, which given the taxing nature of the region's borders and visa regulations is not a bad way to start your trip.

AIR
The region's major hubs, in ascending order of flight expense, are Kyiv, Moscow, Almaty and Baku. Sadly the region is rarely included in round-the-world (RTW) tickets but open-jaw tickets are offered between a number of major cities.

Moscow is serviced by dozens of airlines but in Central Asia your options are limited – often it's Lufthansa (who have great connections and alliances in the region) and British Airways who offer the best deals. Aeroflot occasionally comes out with some top deals and is the only airline servicing Vladivostok.

Consult the Airlines Appendix for more information on airlines and routes.

Ticket Costs
The best available student/under-26 fares are quoted here. See Passports, Tickets, Visas & Insurance in Part I for more information on ticket pricing and on how to get the best, most flexible deal.

You can often find return tickets to Kyiv for under £200, while flying into Moscow is only a little more expensive. If you're flying into Almaty and Baku you can stumble across tickets for £450 but £550 is more likely. Fares to Tashkent are about 10% more expensive. Ashgabat (Turkmenistan) and Dushanbe (Tajikistan) are two expensive destinations (don't be surprised by a £800 price tag).

Of the 'open-jaw' options into Almaty or Baku and out of Kyiv or Moscow comes out cheapest (about £380). Using more obscure destinations will cost closer to £550.

Vladivostok and destinations in far-eastern Russia are better served from Southeast Asia – a one-way London–Vladivostok ticket is about £550.

SEA & OVERLAND

Despite the amazing network of ship canals and sea ports there are no scheduled services into the region and only a little traffic across the Black and Caspian seas.

By land there are hundreds of routes into the region from east, west, north or south. Trains are the easiest option into the region and are available from all directions.

Before you make any plans, check out the border crossings you want to use carefully.

SPECIALIST TOUR OPERATORS

Dozens of large British tour operators run trips in Russia and Central Asia (see the Global Tour Companies Appendix) out of which Regent Holidays can be recommended and Hinterland Travel is unusual in that it runs trips in Afghanistan. The following companies are regional specialists:

Inntel Moscow (☎ 020-7937 7207, fax 020-7938 2912; e inntelmoscow@inntelmoscow .co.uk; W www.inntel-moscow.co.uk; 167–169 High St Kensington, London W8 6SH) arranges all manner of trips.

Russia Experience (☎ 020-8566 8846, fax 020-8566 8843; e info@trans-siberian.co.uk; W www.trans-siberian.co.uk; Research House, Frasier Rd, Perivale, Middx UB6 7AQ) can organise transport, tours and all-inclusive adventures in Russia, Central Asia and China.

Ukrainian Travel (☎ 0161-652 5050, fax 0161-633 0825; e info@bob-sopel-travel.demon .co.uk; W www.ukraine.co.uk; 27 Henshaw St, Oldham, Lancashire OL1 1NH) is the UK's leading Ukraine specialist, also know as Bob Sopel's.

Russia, Central Asia, the former Soviet Union & Beyond

The world's your oyster from Russia and Central Asia. Overland routes back to Blighty could take in the best of the Middle East or rarely explored parts of Eastern Europe. If you move into western China you could follow the Karakoram Highway (one of the most breathtaking overland trips in the world) down into the Indian Subcontinent. Just as easy would be an exploration of China, ending in Southeast Asia from where Australia is a short plane ride away.

Further Information

READING MATERIAL

Lonely Planet publishes *Central Asia*; *Georgia, Armenia & Azerbaijan*; *Russia & Belarus*; *Moscow*; *St Petersburg*; and *Trans-Siberian Railway*. Travellers will also find Lonely Planet's *Central Asia*, *Russian* and *Ukrainian* phrasebooks invaluable.

For good background information consult Benson Bobrick's *East of the Sun*, *The Rise & Fall of the Soviet Empire*, by Stephen Dalziel, and *Beyond the Oxus: Archaeology, Art & Architecture of Central Asia*, by Edgar Knobloch (a rich, if specialist, text) and *The Silk Road: A History*, by Irene Franck & David Brownstone (a fantastic history of the old trade route).

Mission to Tashkent is the autobiography of British intelligence officer FM Bailey. His greatest tale recounts how after the Russian revolution he was employed as a Bolshevik agent tasked with tracking down himself.

Turkestan Solo, by Ella Maillart, *A Short Walk in the Hindu Kush*, by Eric Newby, and *Journey into Russia*, by Laurens van der Post, are not contemporary texts but still provide intelligence and insight.

A tough river journey is recalled by Frederick Kempe in *Siberian Odyssey: A Voyage into the Russian Soul*, while *Danziger's Travels*, by Nick Danziger, is a classic, contemporary tale of daring do. Colin Thubron's *Among the Russians* is a precise and eloquent account of travelling before the Iron Curtain fell but more humorous is *USSR: From an Original Idea by Karl Marx*, by Marc Polonsky & Russell Taylor. *Red Odyssey*, by Marat Akchurin, is a more blood 'n' guts account of the fall of the Soviet Empire.

Extreme Continental, by Giles Whittell, is one to read when you think you've got it bad in Central Asia. Also check out *Journey to Khiva*, by Philip Glazebrook, plus *Apples in the Snow* and *A Journey to Samarkand*, by Geoffrey Moorhouse.

Trekking in Russia and Central Asia, by Frith Maier, provides a great background for anyone wanting to trek and climb in the region.

USEFUL INFORMATION SOURCES

For specific country overviews, the low-down on travel in the region and hundreds of useful links head to Lonely Planet's website (**W** www.lonelyplanet.com).

Useful starting points for web searches include **W** www.eurasianet.org (a good news source and portal for Central Asia), **W** cesww.fas.harvard.edu (a good academic resource for Central Asia), the academic **W** www.departments.bucknell.edu/russian, **W** www.russia-travel.com (tourist orientated site), **W** www.russianculture.ru (background on Russian culture and museums), **W** www.wps.ru (good links to press and web media), **W** www.brama.com and **W** www.uazone.net/Ukraine.html (Ukrainian information) and **W** www.belarusguide.com (a good start for Belarus).

The Royal Asiatic Society and The School of Oriental and African Studies can also be of use to students before they travel (see Useful Information Sources in the Africa and Middle East chapters).

Been There, Done That

By the end of my three-month stint teaching English in the middle of Siberia, I thought I had come to terms with Russian life. It's an often brutal business, living in a sub-zero climate where the only consolation – for many men, at least – is the vodka bottle. But the father of one of my students got to hear that I was leaving and invited me out to his country dacha for a night I shall never forget.

We whizzed across the icy roads in a 4WD with darkened windows, and slid to a halt outside a low villa. Inside, I was told to strip down to my underpants and ushered into a sauna and instructed to lie down. As I was getting used to the intense heat, the biggest Russian I have ever seen came in with a bucket and a handful of birch branches. Ah, I thought, the famous beating with birch twigs. Actually, it was more of a tickling – the leaves are left on, making the experience a little more gentle. The idea is to stimulate the circulation for what happens next…

All the time I was getting hotter and hotter, until I could bear it no more. 'Count to 10 before you get out, then run outside and roll in the snowdrift.' Thanks to the copious amount of vodka I had consumed, I did just that. Forget the blast of heat you feel when you arrive somewhere tropical – the blanket of Siberian cold wrapping itself around you is a sudden and sensual experience, simultaneously exhilarating and terrifying, and gives a new definition to the word 'invigoration'. You want to scream with pain and yell with delight at the sheer intensity. Life in Siberia is all about extremes, and rolling around in the midwinter snow is the ultimate high.

Benjamin Richards

Indian Subcontinent

Introduction

The Indian Subcontinent stretches even the most well-worn travel clichés about diversity, mysticism and cultural vibrancy. One of the most densely populated regions on earth it has an enormous number of tourist sites, varied landscapes and rather unusual experiences. Sublime and inspiring as it is squalid and frustrating, the Indian Subcontinent can be hard going, but for all the people who can't wait to get their flight home there are others who cannot wait to go back, despite the frayed tempers, bad guts and travel hardships.

Why the Indian Subcontinent?

I can still remember the feeling of panic when I arrived at New Delhi airport for the first time, aged 18, and hundreds of rickshaw wallahs descended on me like a Mogul horde. A few minutes later, on the ride into town, I saw my first cases of leprosy and elephantiasis of the testicles…sounds awful doesn't it? But it does grow on you, I promise. Matt Smith.

For cultural depth and colour there is no place like the Indian Subcontinent, even if arrival can be tricky and is likely to bring on a severe case of culture shock. It's not simply a place to *see*, where a checklist itinerary can be followed and no surprises expected, it's a mind-bending place that should be drunk in and experienced. Let your senses be assaulted, let your travels drift off at a tangent. Nothing in the region is ever quite what you expect and no-one who visits the region comes away with the same travel experience.

The region's plains, deserts and deltas all slope up towards the Himalaya, the mightiest of mountain ranges. Here the craziness of India's massive cities is left behind and you enter a more tranquil Buddhist world blessed with the kind of landscapes trekkers dream about. In the west, Hinduism gives way to Islam and the cultural landscape slowly becomes more Middle Eastern and Central Asian. Nowhere on the planet can you travel for as long as here – the India Subcontinent is cheap as chips. Food hygiene could be better (the Calcutta two-step or Karachi cha-cha is going to get you at some point), bureaucracies could be easier to navigate and touts less in your face but there are more than enough compensations.

India has a continent's worth of attractions. For some people it's *the* main attraction in the Indian Subcontinent and it will sideswipe you with its size, clamour and diversity as well as its hassles, hardships, mishaps and the insane intensity of its cities. Hinduism, one of the oldest religions, permeates everything. The country is one of the most intricate and rewarding dramas unfolding on earth.

Bangladesh is widely perceived as a disaster zone, not a country, but behind the cyclones and floods it's a place with a tremendous number of attractions in a small place but one rather devoid of travellers. Clearly the old slogan of Bangladesh's tourist body – 'Come to Bangladesh before the tourists' – rings true.

The Himalaya bring different treats. Bhutan's Buddhist culture remains unique in its purity, the environment is pristine, architecture awesome and tourist numbers tightly regulated, thus keeping Bhutan somewhat isolated. Nepal has been letting trekkers explore its great heights and timeworn temples for decades. It has some of the best walking trails on earth. Sadly the Maoist uprising in Nepal has intensified, giving trekking trips a dicey edge, though it's still possible to trek (thought communism was dead, eh?).

Pakistan is associated with conflict, lawlessness and Islamic fundamentalism. True, rounds of military coups and skirmishes with India over Kashmir don't help with PR but the country has long been a safer, less hasslesome alternative to India, especially for gappers who want their landscapes mind-blowing, trekking extraordinary and preconceptions shattered. Pakistan has a long tradition of hospitality and is the site of an ancient civilisation rivalling those of Egypt and Mesopotamia but sadly, thanks to the threats of extremist terror, the current advice is to give it a miss.

Marco Polo remarked that Sri Lanka was the finest island of its size anywhere in the world. He'd been around a bit (although he probably hadn't dived off the beautiful coral islands of the Maldives) and clearly knew a place of unique beauty when he saw it – the accessible island has amazing beaches, all sorts of environments, great birdlife, elephant processions, masked devil dances and some stunning ancient architecture.

Some visitors are only too happy to get on an aircraft and fly away but if you thrive on sensual overload stick around, the Indian Subcontinent is for you.

What to Do?

Paid work may be very thin on the ground for gappers but there are thousands of volunteer opportunities. It's possible to undertake all sorts of courses in the region including cookery, local classical instruments, dance, art and craft. The region is also renowned for Hindu and Buddhist courses and retreats that offer instruction in meditation, yoga, reiki and philosophy. Tibetan refugees in northern India and Nepal teach many aspects of their culture.

See Part III for more information on overseas jobs, volunteer work and courses available in the region.

Travelling gappers have many places to see, much to do and cool places to do nothing.

GET ACTIVE

There are loads of activities happening in the region and it's possible to get professional instruction in many.

Cycling & Mountain Biking

The Himalaya attracts mountain bikers like bees to a honey pot. The Thimphu and Paro valleys in Bhutan, the Kathmandu Valley in Nepal and the Karakoram Highway or Gilgit Region in Pakistan are good bets. Then there's the Indian Himalaya.

Pakistan also has good cycling on Potwar Plateau (Islamabad to Peshawar) and the Margalla and Murree Hills (north of Islamabad).

Top 10 Must-Sees

Taj Mahal (India) – as amazing and exhilarating as you've been told.
Kolkata (Calcutta) – India's intense cultural capital.
Puthia (Bangladesh) – contains the amazing Hindu temples of Govinda and Siva.
Varanasi (India) – the Ganges River and city of Shiva; a Hindu holy city.
Jaisalmer (India) – site of the most remarkable fort in the country.
Leh (India) – perched among the Himalaya, this is Tibet in exile.
Sigiriya (Sri Lanka) – a spectacular fortress near to a deserted city.
Kathmandu (Nepal) – a traveller-friendly and relaxing city.
Hunza Valley (Pakistan) – home to some of the world's finest mountain scenery.
Moenjodaro (Pakistan) – ruins mark the site of a remarkable ancient city.

In India and Bangladesh thousands of kilometres of roads lie before you but cycle touring in India is not for the faint- or weak-hearted. You'll have to contend with death-head drivers, a vicious climate and constant curiosity. Think twice about bringing your state-of-the-art 24-speed unless you want it to be poked, probed and perved at every time you stop.

Diving & Snorkelling

Excellent scuba diving and snorkelling are found in Sri Lanka at Hikkaduwa and Unawatuna.

The Andaman and Nicobar Islands in the Bay of Bengal boast India's only real diving and snorkelling opportunities but the Maldives is one of the best diving and snorkelling locations in the Indian Ocean.

Trekking & Mountaineering

Trekking the Himalaya is top of most gappers' activity lists. In Bhutan trekking is the ideal way to experience Bhutanese culture and unspoilt wilderness, while in Nepal it's a major industry. Nepalese treks head out from Kathmandu and include those to Everest Base Camp, the Annapurna circuit and the Jomsom Trek. Less-travelled alternatives include the Kanchenjunga Base Camp trek, the Dolpo region and Mustang (highly recommended). The Indian Himalaya (Ladakh, Himachal Pradesh, Sikkim and Uttar Pradesh) is not as popular but equally rewarding. Trekking near Darjeeling (West Bengal) is lower altitude but still great fun.

Pakistan's fantastic trekking is best in the shadow of K2 (8611m) and the Karakoram Range. Gilgit, Nanga Parbat, Baltistan and Hunza are all launching points for great treks. For something less demanding there are good one-day hikes in the Ziarat Valley, near Quetta.

For trekking in Sri Lanka, try climbing Adam's Peak (2224m) or walking across the strange silent plateau of Horton Plains near Nuwara Eliya to see the 700m (2296ft) drop at World's End.

There are a host of companies offering full-on mountaineering expeditions in the Himalaya both in India and Nepal. Some offer training courses. See When to Go later in this chapter for best trekking times.

Lonely Planet publishes a clutch of guides to trekking in the Himalaya (see Reading Material later in this chapter).

White-water Rafting & Watersports

The Himalaya is one of the world's great rafting destinations. Bhutan has rapids up to class five (the hardest commercially run rapid). Mo Chhu, upstream of Punakha in eastern Bhutan, and the Ema Datse Canyon on the Mangde Chhu in central Bhutan have, potentially, some of the best rafting on earth.

Rafting and kayaking in Nepal, especially on the Trisuli River near Kathmandu and the Sun Kosi in Dolalghat, is more established. Rafting expeditions involving treks to your launching points are also possible. In India white-water rafting trips are possible on the Indus (arrange them in Leh). In Pakistan there's white-water rafting along the Hunza, Gilgit and Indus rivers.

More sedate boating is possible in Sundarbans National Park in Bangladesh, where rowing boats are the only way to get around some areas.

On the Bentota River in Sri Lanka you can windsurf and water-ski.

Wildlife Watching

India is one of the so-called 'megadiversity countries' that between them account for 70% of the world's biodiversity. Elephant, one-horned rhinoceros, lion, panther, monkey, bear, snow leopard, many species of antelope and a huge variety of birds are all found in India's parks. Sri Lanka and Bangladesh are no wildlife slouches either. Jeep safaris are common and you can explore some parks in India by elephant (a better way of getting close to the animals).

Other Activities
There are floodlit village badminton courts all over Bangladesh and games of cricket are played in every available space throughout the region.

In Sri Lanka there are surf breaks at Hikkaduwa, Unawatuna and Arugam Bay (by far the best waves).

Basic Indian ski resorts are found at Narkanda in Himachal Pradesh and Auli in Uttar Pradesh. The season is January to March and there's usually one lift in working order and a place to hire gear.

Gappers can get a bird's-eye view of the Subcontinent from a paraglider or hang-glider in the Himalaya and Goa.

Camel treks can be arranged in the deserts around Jaisalmer and Pushkar in Rajasthan (India) between October and February. Horse safaris are also possible in Rajasthan and in the hill stations of the Indian Himalaya.

WORK A LITTLE
Those gappers who manage to find work in the region usually find it teaching English, although food and board often serves as a salary.

Many gappers undertake some kind of volunteer work and opportunities are hugely varied: behavioural primate research in Sri Lanka; working with mentally handicapped adults in Pakistan; cleaning beaches in Goa, India; and starring as an extra in a Bollywood epic (something of a long shot) are all possible. Some gappers turn up unannounced at hospitals, charities or environmental organisations expecting their services to be of immediate use. This is not always the case, so sort out any placement before leaving home.

TRAVEL AROUND
India (and Delhi in particular) sits at the heart of a cheap regional air network. All flights to Bhutan go via India. Air travel in India can be made cheaper with an air pass from Jet Airways (W www.jetairways.com) and Indian Airlines (W www.indian-airlines.nic.in). In Nepal, the odd, spectacular flight is really worthwhile, both to save time and energy and to enjoy the sheer joy of the landscape. There are cheap flights to the Maldives from Kerala (India).

Bus drivers on the Indian Subcontinent are among the world's most reckless, which if you've been to South America you'll agree is quite an achievement. Buses vary from very crowded, noisy, dirty and unreliable affairs (common on shorter journeys) to comfortable, fast and more expensive coaches (which service long-distance routes). Invariably on cheaper services getting on board is a real scrum.

Trains are a lot easier on the nerves, knees and backside, so long as you're not in (crowded) third class and can negotiate the chaos of buying a ticket and getting on board. The Indian railways system is deservedly legendary and unlike any other sort of travel on earth. The journey between New Jalpaiguri and Darjeeling climbs 2100m from the heat of West Bengal to the famous hill station at the foot of the Himalaya. It is one of only two rail journeys in the world blessed with World Heritage status. Rail passes are available in India but not great value.

International services exist between India and Pakistan but not to Bangladesh where unbridged rivers and differing gauges complicate rail travel.

Bangladesh has a slow but rather wonderful system of water transport – the famous 'Rocket' paddlewheel steamer between Dhaka and Khulna is a must – and there are boats plying the glorious waterways of Kerala (India) plus the famous Mumbai (Bombay) to Goa ferry. Ferries to the Andaman Islands from Chennai and Kolkata are possible but the ferry service across Adam's bridge from India to Sri Lanka has not yet reopened.

In the Himalaya and other remote mountainous areas jeeps and 4WDs act as shared taxis between towns and more rural locations. You can hire a vehicle yourself easily enough but getting a driver is sometimes mandatory and always a good idea.

Motorcycling around India (especially on a locally made Enfield Bullet) is a popular but hazardous endeavour even for experienced two-wheelers.

Taxis, trams, auto-rickshaws, cycle-rickshaws and tongas (horse-drawn carriages) all serve as transport in urban areas.

Classic Routes

Routes through Bangladesh are quite fractured thanks to the delta in the south but from the beaches of Cox's Bazar you can explore many of the country's attractions while heading north towards the Indian border and the delights of West Bengal, Sikkim and Assam. This then leads into a grand tour of India, which could go something like Kolkata, Varanasi, Agra (for the Taj Mahal), Delhi, Jaipur (spring board to the stunning architecture of Rajasthan), Mumbai (Bombay; capital of Bollywood), Goa (which retains a vibrant traveller scene with great beaches), Hampi (visiting the stunning 16th-century ruins of Vijayanagar), the Kodagu highlands, Kerala (whose backwaters should be explored by boat) and then through Tamil Nadu (a region of stunning Hindu temples) to Chennai. For something much shorter there's the Golden Triangle of cultural delight between Delhi, Agra and Jaipur.

Concentrating your efforts in India is a pretty good idea and there are some great regions to choose: Rajasthan (the Land of Kings) with its deserts, Mughal splendour, Hindu temples and Islamic architecture; the Madhya Pradesh and the Mughal heartlands, which includes the Taj Mahal; the Indian Himalaya, which incorporates hill stations, the Kulu Valley and Ladakh; and tranquil (well relatively) Kerala, Goa and the tropical south, including the Maldives and Andaman Islands.

Sri Lanka is but a small hop from Chennai and a loop through the south takes in national parks, surfing beaches, dive resorts and the temples and ancient ruins of the central highlands.

Due to the Nepalese terrain, routes through the country are very difficult without taking the odd flight. Indeed most travellers spend time between Annapurna (8090m) and the country's eastern border with China.

Pakistan is well explored in a long loop leading southwest from Lahore (which has some stunning Mogul architecture) to Karachi via the famous Sufi shrines of Uch Sharif and ruins of the ancient city of Moenjodaro. Then fly up to Islamabad (good for museums and impressive mosques) for exploration of the wild and fascinating Northwest Frontier Province and the Karakoram Range. For information on the remarkable Karakoram Highway see the Northeast Asia chapter.

When to Go?

Many gappers head to the Indian Subcontinent between October and March when the weather is cooler and drier. The Karakoram Range, northern Pakistan, Himachal Pradesh and the rest of the Indian Himalaya are at their most accessible from May to September, despite the occasional storm. Contrastingly October to November, a time of balmy weather and lush vegetation after the monsoon, is probably the ideal time to trek in Nepal and

Bhutan, although high mountain passes are closed in some regions; wild flowers bloom between February and April. The deserts of Rajasthan (India) are at their best during the monsoon (May to August).

Avoid Pakistan and Bangladesh during Ramadan when everything closes down.

Trekking in Nepal is good from September to December, although March and April bring spring flowers.

CLIMATE

There are big regional variations across the Indian Subcontinent, from the arid deserts of Rajasthan to the cool highlands of Assam, allegedly the wettest place on earth. Much of southern India, Bangladesh and Sri Lanka are subtropical and tropical.

The region basically has a three-season year: the 'hot' season of February to May; the monsoon or 'wet' season from May to October (which is preceded by intense humidity and characterised by short and violent thunder storms) and the 'cold' season from October to February (India's northern cities become quite crisp at night in December).

In addition to these generalisations, Sri Lanka and India's southeast coast are affected by a short monsoon from mid-October to January. Rainfall in Sri Lanka is heaviest in the south, southwest and central highlands; the northern and north-central regions are very dry. Bangladesh experiences cyclones in May, June, October and November.

FESTIVALS

The region is jam-packed with Hindu, Buddhist and Muslim festivals. Some are so spectacular that you'd be a fool to miss them if you were remotely close. Check out some of the (nationwide unless stated otherwise) festivals:

Holi Festival (India), or Festival of Colours, is celebrated in February/March and is one of the most exuberant Hindu festivals marking the end of winter. It involves throwing as much coloured water and powder over as many people as possible.

Durga Puja (Bangladesh & West Bengal) is celebrated during October when statues of the goddess Durga astride a lion, with her 10 hands holding 10 different weapons, are placed in every Hindu temple.

Kumbh Mela (India) is a massive festival held every three years (last held at Nasik in 2003) to commemorate an ancient battle between gods and demons. It attracts tens of millions of Hindu pilgrims to Allahabad, Hardwar, Nasik or Ujjain, cities that are alternate hosts.

Rath Yatra (India) commemorates the journey of Krishna from Gokul to Mathura with a June/July spectacle in Puri involving the procession of a gigantic temple 'car' pulled by thousands of eager devotees.

Nehru Cup Snake Boat Races (India) are a big event in Kerala. They take place at Alappuzha (Alleppey) on the second Saturday of August.

Pushkar Camel Fair (India) is a huge, colourful celebration held in Rajasthan during November.

Diwali (or Deepavali) is the happiest festival of the Hindu calendar and is celebrated across the region over five days in November. Sweets, oil lamps and firecrackers all play their part.

Tsechus (Bhutan) take place at dzongs and monasteries in spring and autumn in honour of Guru Rinpoche. The five days of spectacular pageantry, masked dances and religious allegorical plays have remained unchanged for centuries.

Dasain (Nepal) is the most important of all Nepalese celebrations. Held in September/ October, it features the biggest animal sacrifice of the year. During Tihar (October/ November) animals are honoured rather than slaughtered.

Esala Perahera (Sri Lanka), in July/August, is Kandy's most important and spectacular pageant, with 10 days of torch-bearers, whip-crackers, dancers, drummers and elephants lit up like giant birthday cakes.

Kataragama (Sri Lanka) are the daily prayers held at this Hindu, Buddhist and Muslim shrine but in July/August there's a predominantly Hindu festival where devotees put themselves through the whole gamut of ritual masochism.

Basant (Pakistan) is a kite festival in Lahore. People have picnics on their roofs and the skies are full of kites sometime in February/March.

Baisakhi (Pakistan & India) on April 13–15 Sikh Punjabi pilgrims celebrate at the Hasan Abdal shrine near Rawalpindi in Pakistan.

What to Expect?

TRAVELLERS

You'll probably never travel with such a cross-section of travellers as in the Indian Sub-continent. Freaks, do-gooders, adventurers, enlightenment seekers, beach bums, drug fiends, death-march trekkers, and café anthropologists are all found in India and come in all creeds, shapes and sizes. Many travellers, whatever their interests, are drawn at some point to the few places in the region that are perfect for escaping from the stresses and strains of travelling here:

Kulu Valley (India) – highland valley with trekking and rafting.

Goa (India) – famous for its wild parties, now a mainstream hangout; many people now hermit in Hampi.

Pushkar (India) – most popular holy hangout but other places in Rajasthan are less commercial.

Kathmandu (Nepal) – the famous end of the Hippie Trail is still relaxing and traveller-friendly.

Darjeeling (India) – has attracted escapees from the lowlands for centuries.

Pokhara (Nepal) – laid-back lakeside retreat.

Mirissa (Sri Lanka) – clean waters and relaxed island atmosphere.

Madyan (Pakistan) – old hippie hangout and still a fine place to rest up.

Manali & Dharamsala (India) – the seat of Tibetan government in exile plus some great mellow hangouts.

LOCALS

India can be a mind-bender. As a rule its numerous peoples are incredibly friendly, though the experience of 50 people invading your personal space and all trying to be incredibly friendly at the same time can be a little exasperating! Some are genuinely interested in your reasons for visiting India. Some want to practise their English, have their photograph taken with you or find out about the permissive sexual practices in the West (something of a national obsession). However, some people just want to con you out of your money or give you the hard sell for their goods/services and it's just something you have to get used to. Quite a few travellers make the mistake of assuming all Indians are like this, only to be humbled by some random act of kindness later in their travels. The important thing is to keep your sense of humour, accept the departure of peace and quiet, and enjoy the energy and excitement while you can.

Hinduism is practised by over 80% of the population and the religion infuses all aspects of society. Hindus believe in reincarnation, karma (conduct or action and their consequences) and dharma (station in life). The latter two affect how you'll be reincarnated – behave like a cad or get ideas above your station/caste and you'll come back as some filthy, garbage-eating rodent. Be good and you may return in a high caste (or as a man if you're a woman). Caste restrictions are loosening and don't usually affect relations between locals and travellers but play a large part in the life of the region. Nepal, Sri Lanka and Bhutan have strong Buddhist traditions (see Northeast Asia for more information).

Pakistan's and Bangladesh's real social chemistry is within the family, and family and clan are dominant factors in life. Islam is strong in Pakistan, which although secular has allowed the increasing influence of *Shariah* law into politics and Sunni, Shia and Sufi branches of Islam are present in the country. See the Middle East chapter for more information on behaviour in Islamic countries. Despite the reputation given them in the media, Pakistanis are very hospitable and the country is generally less hassle and safer than India.

LANGUAGE

Happily English is widely spoken throughout the region. In each country there are numerous dialects and regional languages. Indian Hindi is the official language and widely spoken but it's only the mother tongue for 20% of the nation. Urdu is spoken by the Muslim population (especially in Pakistan). Tamil and Sinhala are the official languages of Sri Lanka (Tamil is spoken in southern India too). Bengali is spoken in Bangladesh, Nepali in Nepal and Dzongkha (which is related to Tibetan) in Bhutan.

There are loads of language courses in the region and the UK (see Courses in Part III for information). Reading Material, later in this chapter, gives information on Lonely Planet's phrasebooks.

HEALTH RISKS

The Indian Subcontinent is not the healthiest of places and a raft of vaccinations is necessary, including rabies if you're trekking in remote areas. Other health problems include cholera, diarrhoea, malaria, giardiasis and altitude sickness, which kills a handful of travellers each year.

The region is not renowned for excellent kitchen hygiene and a large number of travellers get a bad case of the squits. Dysentery is also common. We cannot stress heavily enough the importance of purifying water and treating all water presented to you with extreme suspicion.

Consult the Health chapter in Part I and seek professional medical advice for more travel health information.

TIME & FLIGHT TIME

Pakistan is five hours ahead of Greenwich Mean Time (GMT), Bhutan and Bangladesh six, India and Sri Lanka 5½ hours and Nepal 5¾ hours.

Islamabad is an 8¼-hour flight away from London, Delhi nine hours away, Dhaka 9½ hours and Colombo 10½ hours away. You must fly via the Gulf or India from London to Kathmandu (totalling at least an 11¼-hour flight).

ISSUES

There is considerable tension along India and Pakistan's northern border (the so-called 'Line of Control') and just one open border bwetween these countries (the Wagah-Attari border) and between India and Bhutan (the Darranga-Samdrup Jongkhar border). Crossing into Bangladesh from India is usually straightforward but travellers have had problems on minor borders. Elsewhere there are no problems crossing between countries in the region. The Indian and Bangladeshi borders with Myanmar (Burma) are closed to foreigners (although the situation may change), as is the India-China border.

Sadly there are numerous areas unsafe for travellers. Such is the terrorist threat to westerners in Pakistan (at the time of writing) that the British government was advising against travel to the country. The Chittagong Hill Tracts in Bangladesh continue to cause concern and Maoist rebels in Nepal have undertaken widespread attacks both in Kathmandu and close to popular trekking routes. No territory is out of bounds yet but in the past Maoists have demanded money and/or equipment from trekkers in the Annapurna circuit and the risk of such an encounter is increasing.

India is not without its problems. Avoid Jammu and Kashmir, areas of Gujarat, Rajasthan and Punjab close to the border with Pakistan, Ladakh close to the Line of Control and the northeastern provinces of Manipur and Tripura. Several other rural areas are still very feudal and there's a strong risk of violent crime.

The north and east of Sri Lanka has been unsafe for many years but a formal ceasefire between the Sri Lankan Government and the LTTE (the Tamil Tigers) gives reason to be optimistic. Certainly travellers have been visiting Trincomalee and Nilaveli but rural northern and eastern Sri Lanka is still deemed too dicey.

Hassle from accommodation touts, rickshaw-wallahs, would-be guides and people peddling a wide array of legal/illegal goods and services gets many travellers down. The constant attention is particularly acute in parts of India, Sri Lanka and Bangladesh, much less so in the Himalaya. Theft is an issue and stories of scams and drugged food and water are common. Outside of Lahore, Pakistan is a reasonably safe place as far as personal property and robbing are concerned.

A lot of these issues are linked to the utter poverty and destitution that's visible everywhere. Travellers must be prepared for the often harsh social realities of travelling in these countries.

Baksheesh is a tip in many instances but the baksheesh system (a way of life in Pakistan) can open doors, smooth the way and get you out of/into a world of trouble. Many bureaucrats and officials are not shy of asking for a little baksheesh from travellers in certain situations.

For further information on travel hotspots, general safety issues and governmental travel advice see Safety in Part I.

INTERNET & COMMUNICATIONS
Cybercafés are very popular in the Indian Subcontinent and spreading faster than rumours. Mobile-phone technology is also becoming more available.

Daily Spend
Bangladesh is easily the cheapest place in the region, and Bhutan the most expensive. In Bangladesh £10 a day ensures a decent hotel and first-class train travel but it's possible to scrape by on as little as £3 a day. Bangladesh is a great place to splurge on a little luxury.

It costs around £125 a day to be in Bhutan but as all travel is part of a tour group this wedge covers all your costs apart from drinks, laundry and cultural stuff like a traditional Bhutanese hot-stone bath.

A hardcore of travellers make it around India and Pakistan on £6–7 a day, subsisting on dhal and rice, staying in flop houses, not moving around much and travelling on crowded buses. £15 brings you into a different class of travel with private bathrooms (around £8 for something decent), a varied diet and a superior class of transport. Converted maharajah's palaces and the like demand five-star prices.

Nepal is a little more expensive than India and offers less variety but you can still trek independently for as little as £15 a day. Private bank exchange rates and a black market make life a little cheaper.

More expensive, but certainly not extortionate, is Sri Lanka, which for just over £10 a day can be explored in pleasant comfort. An extra £5 ensures entry to some delightful rest houses.

Getting There

There's a huge amount of traffic between London and the Indian Subcontinent and fares are cheap. You'll have to go via India or the Middle East for Kathmandu (Nepal). Fantastic overland routes to the Indian Subcontinent from Europe and the rest of Asia are well worth considering.

AIR

The region's major hubs are Delhi, Mumbai and Kolkata in India plus Karachi (Pakistan), Colombo (Sri Lanka) and Dhaka (Bangladesh). Flights from Britain into many other cities are possible such as Chennai in India; Islamabad and Lahore in Pakistan are possible but more expensive. There are no direct flights into Kathmandu (Nepal) and Paro (Bhutan). Many round-the-world (RTW) tickets feature Delhi, Mumbai, Colombo and even the Maldives.

Middle Eastern airlines Royal Jordanian, Kuwait Airways, Gulf Air, Qatar Airways and Emirates were offering the cheapest flights into the Indian Subcontinent at the time of writing. All these deals include a stop in the Middle East which could be extended for as long as you like for no extra charge. A mixed bag of European airlines offer good deals occasionally; at the time of writing it was Lufthansa and Austrian Airlines. Bhutan's national carrier Druk Air is the only airline servicing Paro, the nation's only airport.

Consult the Airlines Appendix at the back of the book for more information on airlines and routes.

Ticket Costs

The best available student/under-26 fares are quoted here. See Passports, Tickets, Visas & Insurance in Part I for more information on how to get the best, most flexible deal.

Karachi, Delhi and Mumbai are the cheapest places on the Indian Subcontinent to fly into (about £390 return). Chennai, Dhaka and Islamabad are all about £100 more expensive but flights into Kolkata and Colombo are around the £450 mark. Flying into Kathmandu is going to cost you £550–600 but an open-jaw flight into Colombo and out of Kathmandu can cost only £510. Flying into Dhaka and out of Colombo costs about the same, whereas into Delhi and out of Chennai is around £450.

SEA & OVERLAND

There's an occasional ferry between Karachi and the United Arab Emirates but it's more like an expensive duty-free shopping trip than an affordable sea route.

The most common overland route is along the old Hippie Trail from London to Kathmandu, via Turkey and the Middle East which, bar a few hundred kilometres in Iran, is a journey possible by train. A number of travellers with their own vehicles and overland truck companies travel this route into Pakistan. An alternative route cuts down through Russia and Central Asia to Iran and then Pakistan or from Kyrgyzstan to China and down the legendary Karakoram Highway into Pakistan.

SPECIALIST TOUR OPERATORS

Heaps of British tour operators run trips to and within the Indian Subcontinent. The major ones are detailed in the Global Tour Companies Appendix at the back of the book. Other region-specific operators include:

Essential India (☎/fax 01225-868544; e info@essential-india.co.uk; W www.essential-india.co.uk; 106a Upper Westwood, Bradford-on-Avon, Wiltshire BA15 2DS) runs trips across the country including some focusing on arts and crafts.

Indian Encounters (☎ 01929-481421; W www.indianencounters.com; Creech Barrow, East Creech, Wareham, Dorset BH20 5AP) offers rather select tours of India and horse-riding safaris in Rajasthan.

The Indian Subcontinent & Beyond

The Indian Subcontinent is at a crossroads of dozens of possible overland trips while air fares to Africa, Europe, the Middle East and Southeast Asia are cheap.

Heading overland to Southeast Asia is a little tricky thanks to Myanmar's closed borders with Bangladesh and India but you could loop around through China via Nepal and then cut into Vietnam or Laos and then head overland/by ferry to Australia. Quite a trip. Alternatively head across the Himalaya on the Karakoram Highway or via Nepal to China, from where the whole of Northeast Asia opens up – and the possibility of getting the Trans-Siberian Railway back to the fringes of Europe.

Further Information

READING MATERIAL

Lonely Planet publishes guides to numerous countries, regions and cities in the Indian Subcontinent plus a guide to the route from Istanbul to Kathmandu. *Healthy Travel Asia & India* and *World Food India* give an excellent background, while *Trekking in the Indian Himalaya*, *Trekking in the Nepal Himalaya* and *Trekking in the Karakoram & Hindukush* are indispensable for trekkers. So are the *Hindu & Urdu*, *Nepali* and *Bengali* phrasebooks. *Chasing Rickshaws*, by Tony Wheeler and Richard l'Anson, is an insightful coffee-table book and *Sacred India* is a beautifully photographed exploration of beliefs in India.

Good background reading is given in *Bangladesh: Reflections on the Water*, by James J Novak, *So Close to Heaven: The Vanishing Buddhist Kingdoms of the Himalayas*, by Barbara Crossette, *Plain Tales from the Raj*, edited by Charles Allen, *Only Man is Vile: The Tragedy of Sri Lanka*, by William McGowan, *People of Nepal*, by Dor Bahadur Bista, *Pakistan: A Modern History*, by Ian Talbot, and *Every Rock, Every Hill: A Plain Tale of the North-West Frontier & Afghanistan*, by Victoria Schofield.

Religious and spiritual themes are examined in *The Tibetan Book of Living and Dying*, by Sogyal Rimpoche and *Hinduism*, by KM Sen. Gita Mehta's witty *Karma Kola* is a suitable antithesis.

Travelogues on the Indian Subcontinent are extremely common. Peter Matthiessen's *The Snow Leopard* is a beautiful account of a search for the elusive cat, while Paul Theroux's *The Great Railway Bazaar*, Alexander Frater's delightful *Chasing the Monsoon*, *The Golden Peak: Travels in Northern Pakistan*, by Kathleen Jamie, *To the Frontier*, by Geoffrey Moorhouse, *Full Tilt*, by Dervla Murphy, *City of Djinns*, by William Dalrymple and Peter Somerville-Large's engagingly dotty *To the Navel of the World* are all worth a read.

John Hunt's *The Ascent of Everest* is a 'by-the-numbers' but fascinating account of the famous first ascent of the mountain. *Into Thin Air*, by Jon Krakauer, is an incredible account of a disastrous set of expeditions on Mt Everest.

USEFUL INFORMATION SOURCES

For specific country overviews, the low-down on travel in the region and hundreds of useful links head first to Lonely Planet's website ([W] www.lonelyplanet.com).

The following portals and useful websites should help you chase down any aspect of interest on the Indian Subcontinent:

[W] **www.travelbangla.com** – Bangladeshi tourism overview.
[W] **www.bhutan.org** – general information on Bhutan.
[W] **www.khoj.com** – good portal for things Indian.
[W] **www.info-nepal.com** – great Nepalese travel site.
[W] **www.bena.com/sherpa1/** – Nepalese trekking site.
[W] **www.south-asia.com** – good Nepalese portal.
[W] **www.pakistanlink.com** – US-based Pakistan news service.
[W] **www.lanka.net** – broad portal into all things Sri Lankan.
[W] **www.lacnet.org** – academic Sri Lanka links galore.

The Royal Asiatic Society and The School of Oriental and African Studies can also be of use to students before they travel (see Useful Information Sources in the Africa and Middle East chapters).

Been There, Done That

It was just after midnight on Christmas night when our plane touched down in Bombay (as it was then). My friend and I each had an open-return ticket and some travellers cheques, and I had a brand-new Lonely Planet guidebook in my rucksack. India lay before us – no bookings, no fixed itinerary. The air was richly scented, the cyclone-wire tunnel that led through the airport and out into the night was lined with staring faces, and the suburbs had never been further away. We got chatting to a German backpacker who seemed to know what she was doing, and followed her onto a bus bound for Colaba, which carried us through ever narrower, more crowded streets and eventually deposited us outside the Taj Mahal Intercontinental.

Undeterred by my guidebook's grim predictions, we set off up the street in search of a cheap place to see out the night. Like scruffy moths we wandered towards a patch of incongruously bright light. Across the road from a floodlit colonnade was a film crew – megaphone-wielding director, cameramen, grips and all – piled high on the back of a battered old truck. The penny dropped: we had walked onto a Bollywood movie shoot. Before we could retreat into the night, an assistant jumped down from the truck, ran towards us and motioned us to stay, and we loitered in the light, a crowd scene of three, while a few moments of celluloid action were consigned to the can. By now it must have been 2am. My journal records that we abandoned our budding film careers and resumed the search for a hotel only to end up, defeated, back at the Taj, very slowly sipping expensive coffee.

Some time before dawn, on a whim, the three of us piled into a taxi and made our way to the docks, where we bought tickets for the steamer to Goa and joined the crowd sweating at the barriers. The sky was lightening when at last the gates opened. We stumbled forwards with the throng, found the potter we'd offered a few rupees to secure us benches on the upper deck, and leaned back on our rucksacks. As the sun rose on day one, we reflected on an opening night that no amount of planning could have bought.   Nick Tapp

Northeast Asia

Introduction

Northeast Asia includes China, Japan, Hong Kong, Korea (North and South), Mongolia, Taiwan and occupied Tibet. This is the mystic East, whose beliefs, traditions and cultures have captivated and perplexed Europeans for centuries. The region is home to some of the world's most and least technologically advanced nations (Japan and Mongolia, the Timbuktu of Asia). These two nations not surprisingly show the huge economic disparities of the region and for travellers Japan is fiercely expensive and Mongolia happy-shopper cheap. At the same time, China is busily reinventing and reasserting itself with seemingly unstoppable economic momentum. Much is changing in the region but along with the fantastic food, incredible temples and shrines, unsurpassed architectural monuments and beautiful landscapes, an undeniable magic remains.

Why Northeast Asia?

Don't pack your preconceptions when coming to Northeast Asia. It's not a uniform place. The economic gap between nations may be getting closer but the austere temples, serene Zen gardens and Blade Runner Metropolis of Tokyo are still a mighty contrast to remote western China and the nomad camps of Mongolia where some of the culture shock comes with bucket showers and tortuous bus rides. Travelling through Japan, South Korea and Taiwan is (language aside) pretty easy-going. At the same time you can still satisfy your desires for stunning Buddhist temples, wonderful broad-roofed buildings, sacred mist-shrouded peaks and cultural experiences like nothing on earth.

China is different but has all of these attractions in spades. In fact it has everything except wonderful beaches (Japan's southwestern, subtropical islands have those) and could easily gobble up a year by itself without even seeing a panda. It's a fascinating time to visit China as the yin of revolutionary zeal is being balanced by the yang of economic pragmatism and there's a physical (in building and infrastructure) and social reincarnation under way. Behind the rampant development lies the same epic landscapes that gave rise to some of the world's greatest dynasties, evidence of which is so wonderfully showcased in the Forbidden City (Beijing), Great Wall of China and Xi'an's (Shaanxi province) terracotta warriors.

Travel in Northwest Asia is not without its problems. Language is the obvious one but in China there continue to be serious limits to personal freedoms, despite the arrival of Starbucks and Coca Cola. Most relevant to travellers are the restrictions on access to parts of western China and the Himalayan splendour and stunning Buddhist traditions of Tibet, where the imposition of Han Chinese culture has been as brutal as the eviction of students from Tiananmen Square.

Still, China isn't North Korea, a totally different bag of travel treats, but entry to the very weird, totalitarian Marxist dictatorship is heavily restricted. Mongolia is far more open, lives up to the hype and is one of the last great adventure destinations in Asia. Ulaan-baatar (the capital of Mongolia) may not seem like the end of the earth but consider it the gateway.

Japan, South Korea and Taiwan perhaps provide examples of how China might turn out. Modernity sits neatly alongside unique ancient culture while between the sanitised shopping malls are strange traditions and unexpected rural festivals. Everyone creates his or her own impression of these countries. Many people will appreciate Japan's many Zen gardens and stunning Shinto shrines but whether you end up trekking the high peaks or immersing yourself in Buddhism, you'd better come with an open mind and prepared to be surprised. Japan has 'love hotels' and vending machines that dispense magic mushrooms. So it isn't all politeness, strict etiquette and raw fish.

What to Do?

Work in Northeast Asia is increasingly possible but the region is not necessarily a great place for voluntary work (at least if you don't speak a local language). Travelling gappers will find these countries teeming with 'sights' but there are also loads of things to do and take part in.

A number of travellers specifically study the regions' beliefs. In Japan Zen Buddhism is taught through exceedingly strict (both mentally and physically) courses. Tibetan Buddhism is less austere but restrictions in Tibet make retreats and courses very difficult if not impossible.

Other courses in regional culture include cooking, language, pottery, traditional medicine, martial arts, music, dance and craft. Kyoto (Japan) is particularly renowned for courses in Japanese arts, and Tai Chi is taught in parks across China. Language courses are widespread throughout the region and in Japan a cultural visa may let you work too.

See Part III for more information on overseas jobs, volunteer work and courses.

GET ACTIVE

In Japan, Korea and Taiwan outdoor activities are pursued with passion and there are associations for most things. In China the leisure industry is booming. New adventure sports possibilities are popping up all the time but doing stuff independently can lead to piles of red tape.

Cycling & Mountain Biking

China is synonymous with the popularity of the bike (300 million cyclists can't be wrong). It's a great way to get around the country but restrictions are imposed on foreigners in some areas. Happily, guided mountain-biking tours are available.

The mountains of Japan, South Korea and Taiwan offer numerous mountain-bike trails. Japanese coastal regions are popular with cycle tourists.

Top 10 Must-Sees

Great Wall of China (China) – still essential viewing on any trip.
Lhasa (Tibet) – the Potala Palace, Jokhang Temple and bruised heart of Tibetan culture.
Kakunodate (Japan) – 17th-century samurai houses and cherry trees.
Tokyo & Shanghai (Japan & China) – welcome to the future metropolises.
Gyeongju (South Korea) – an important historic and religious city.
Kayasan & Songnisan National Parks (South Korea) – combine great trekking with stunning temples and Buddhist relics.
Orchid Island (Taiwan) – underground homes and relatively unspoilt aboriginal culture.
Xi'an (China) – the army of Terracotta Warriors and much more.
Beijing (China) – look beyond the Forbidden City and Summer Palace to the winding hútòng (alleyways).
Kyoto & Nara (Japan) – ancient capitals packed with shrines, temples and culture.

Skiing & Snowboarding

South Korea has some reasonable skiing and Japan more than 300 (pricey) ski resorts split between Honshū and Hokkaidō (which gets some great powder). The season is December to April. Cross-country skiing is very popular and cheaper.

Skiing in northern China is possible but pretty average. No fear, the China Ski Corporation (**W** www.chinaski.com) offers ski and snowboard safaris in Tibet and Qïnghai Province.

Ski tours leave from Ulaanbataar (Mongolia) in January and February.

Trekking & Mountaineering

Scaling sacred mountains is about the extent of most people's walking experience in North east Asia. The trek up Mt Fuji (3776m) is a freezing overnight pilgrimage for many Japanese and Éméi Shān (China) is truly something special – stone steps lead up to a network of Buddhist monasteries linked by mountain paths thronged with pilgrims. However, the region has some classic, very accessible walking areas, particularly in the mountains of Japan, South Korea and Taiwan. Try the 3000m-plus peaks of the Japanese Alps on Honshū and in the heart of Hokkaidō; Songnisan National Park in South Korea; Yangmingsham National Park and Yushan (3952m) and Hsuehshan (3883m) mountains in Taiwan. National parks across these three countries often offer good walking and many routes have campsites and mountain huts.

Walkers in China are largely exempt from bureaucratic shenanigans but mountaineers are not. The most exciting mountaineering terrain lies in western China and Tibet (where you can just about get away with doing a little trekking). The forested alpine valleys of Jiuhài Gōu (Sìchuan) and jungles of Xīshuāngbǎnnà in Yunnan offer some good trekking but there are thousands of other places. Wild China (**W** www.wildchina.com) runs adventurous treks across the country.

Mongolia's 100-plus glaciers and 30 to 40 permanently snow-capped mountains are *the* place for remote, adventurous mountaineering and trekking. Khövsgöl Nuur (a stunning lake that also offers fishing, kayaking and caving), the Kharkhiraa Valley, Gurvansaikhan National Park, the hills of Khovd and the Gobi Desert also offer great trekking. See Climate later in this chapter for when to go.

Other Activities

Taiwan has big snowless mountains so some inventive (and fearless) soul developed grass skiing.

There's good scuba diving around the Japanese islands of Okinawa and Yaeyama, Cheju-do in South Korea (a volcanic location and home of female pearl divers) and Kenting and the Penghu Islands in Taiwan (the cheapest place to learn).

The Hsiukuluan and Laonung rivers in Taiwan have some good white-water rafting runs and there are some surf breaks off Japan and Taiwan but don't make them the target of your travels. Golf is big in Japan but costs a fortune.

Camel rides are popular in Inner Mongolia and the deserts around Dūnhuáng (Gansu Province, China). Horse riding is on the cards in the hills of Xinjiang, outside Sōngpān (Sìchuan Province) and west of Beijing.

Bird-watching in China is most rewarding on Qïnghǎi Hú near Xiníng, Qïnghǎi Province (rare black-necked cranes can be seen March to June).

Mongolia and southwest China also have some good caving, the best in the world according to some.

WORK A LITTLE

There are a growing number of employment opportunities in China but you'll need a work visa and probably some Mandarin Chinese. Common openings include teaching English and marketing and there are possibilities for travel agents, creative English writers, bar staff and secretaries.

Finding work in Japan is possible but the costs of setting up house can be prohibitive (expect to need £3000). Teaching English comes top of the pops again – for information on Japan Exchange Teaching (JET) see the Teaching chapter of Part III. Bartending, hostessing (keep your wits about you – a British backpacker was murdered working as a hostess in Tokyo) and modelling are all possibilities here and in South Korea and Taiwan.

TRAVEL AROUND

Air travel can be a good-value way to cover huge distances. In Japan it's not much more expensive than the train but in China crashed, aged, Russian airliners and terrifying stories can put you off. Things are improving along major routes thanks to Boeing and Airbus but out in the sticks… Regional flights are numerous but you can't fly between mainland China and Taiwan (go via Hong Kong).

A good rail network covers the region. Japan's super-fast bullet trains are an essential experience and rail passes are available (you must purchase these outside Japan). Chinese trains come in all shapes, sizes and comfort levels and offer the only legal way to cross into Mongolia by land.

Buses throughout the region offer good value and huge coverage and in Japan overnight services are a way of saving on hotel bills. Vehicle reliability can be a problem away from major Chinese routes.

In Mongolia, Tibet and southwest China, trucks and 4WD vehicles serve as public transport. Hiring 4WDs is common in remote regions. In South Korea and Taiwan long-distance shared taxis, known as bullet taxis, travel between major destinations but negotiate a price before setting off.

There are daily ferries from Japan to South Korea and regular services to Taiwan and various parts of China. There are ferries from South Korea to China and Taiwan, and from Taiwan to Macau (China).

Within China coastal and river ferry services are decreasing but you can still get to Macau and Hong Kong or to South Korea. Until the Three Gorges Project gets fully underway, a boat trip down the Yangtze River is still a classic.

Classic Routes

With a region so broad and diverse, classic routes are tricky to pin down. Many people start in Japan, explore between Tokyo and Kyoto (which contains a load of attractions in a small area) and then take the ferry from western Honshū to Busan in South Korea. From Incheon near Seoul there's a ferry to Tianjin in China where there's so much to explore you may not get the chance to see Mongolia, though you'd be missing out. Alternatively Korea could be cut out entirely by taking the ferry from Kobe in Japan to Shanghai (China).

Another option is to catch the ferry to Chilung in Taiwan from Okinawa, after hopping through the other southern Japanese islands. You can fly almost anywhere from Taiwan or get the ferry to Macau (China).

Hong Kong to Kunming via Yulin is a favourite backpacker route across China. Yunnan Province is an exotic, beautiful and scenically stunning place rich in Chinese culture, and access to the delights of Southeast Asia is easy from Kunming. Beijing to Tibet via Xi'an is another popular Chinese route, especially among travellers. From Lhasa, the capital of Tibet, there's a wonderful route into Kathmandu and the Indian Subcontinent.

The Karakoram Highway is another breathtaking route into the Indian Subcontinent. Between Kashgar in China and lslamabad in Pakistan is the Khunjerab Pass (4730m; officially open from May 1 to November 30). Stop at the beautiful turquoise Karakul Lake if you can. It's a beautiful spot on the Chinese side of the route sandwiched between the Kongur (7719m) and Muztagh-Ata (7546m) mountains.

Following the Silk Road from Beijing leads through the archaeological delights of Xi'an (the road's historical starting point), the deserts of Xinghai and a host of other attractions until reaching Kashgar where exciting options into Central Asia and along the Karakoram Highway begin. You could also bypass Kashgar and catch the train to Kazakhstan and Russia.

When to Go?

Given the range of climate and attractions you could visit Northeast Asia whenever and have a good time. That said, March to May (spring) and September to October (autumn) are generally considered to be the best times to visit.

Hanami, a celebration of the arrival of plum, peach and cherry blossoms from February to April is a good but crowded time to visit Japan. June and September are probably the best months to visit Tibet and Mongolia and September to October *the* time to consider entering the Gobi Desert. In July (when it's very hot) accommodation and transport are stretched in Mongolia and China (where domestic tourism is booming). In September or November, when skies are clear and the foliage spectacular, visit China and South Korea. South China is pretty nice year round.

Some travellers find winter the perfect time to visit southern areas because temperatures are cool but not prohibitively cold and the crowds of tourists are absent.

CLIMATE

Northeast Asia stretches from the subarctic lands of northern China down past the tropic of Cancer. Generally speaking it experiences four seasons at the same times as in Britain. Temperatures can be extreme and humidity unpleasantly high in summer when Japan, southeast China and South Korea are hit by heavy rains and the odd typhoon.

In Mongolia and north of the Great Wall of China it gets incredibly cold in winter (try -40°C) while the central Yangtze River valley experiences fiercely hot temperatures during long, hot summers. Summer is the only time it's unlikely to rain in central China. Be prepared for any weather in spring and autumn.

Japan has the most diverse climate in the region (thanks to the length of the archipelago and high mountains down its spine), which means it can be snowing in northern Hokkaidō and positively balmy in southern, subtropical Okinawa. Western Japan receives a large amount of precipitation in winter, while the Pacific side is cold but less snowy.

If you're travelling in summer or winter then try and focus on coastal and southern areas, which are more temperate than inland.

FESTIVALS

The region's fascinating festivals are a varied and unusual mix. They can be exuberant or sombre, chaotic or well organised. Travellers should be aware that major celebrations clog up accommodation and public transport. Check out some of the following:

Tsagaan Sar (Mongolia), White Month, is a pocket of merriment held in January and February in the depths of the winter. Booze and food feature heavily.

Yah-Yah Matsuri (Owase, Japan) is an argument contest at the beginning of February. Competitors scream Samurai chants and try to look fearsome. Then take off all their clothes and jump in the ocean.

Sapporo Snow Festival & White Illumination (Japan) are held in February with ice sculpture, other events and an illumination of the park's winter landscapes.

Losar (Tibet) is a colourful New Year Festival of drama, pilgrimage, dressing up and celebration in February/March.

Seokcheonje (South Korea) is held in March and September drawing crowds to Confucian shrines to hear traditional court orchestras and watch costumed rituals.

Water Splashing Festival (China) is held at Xīshuāngbǎnnà in Yunnan around mid-April. As the name suggests, it's about washing away the dirt and sorrow of the old year and bringing in the happiness of the new.

Dragon Boat Festival (Hong Kong) honours the poet Qu Yuan in June with races of ornate canoes and lively festivities.

Naadam (Mongolia) showcases the loves of the country (namely horse racing, archery and wrestling) across the country on July 11 and 12.

Gion Matsuri (Japan) is renowned and commemorates a 9th-century request to the gods for an end to the plague sweeping Kyoto, with an incredible parade of massive man-dragged floats on July 17.

O-Bon (Japan) is the Buddhist Festival of the Dead. The celebration of ancestors takes place in July and August. There's much lantern lighting.

Harvest Moon Festival (Korea) is the most important lunar holiday on the peninsula and falls in early September. People return to their family homes to pay homage to their ancestors.

Birthday of Confucius (China) is celebrated on September 28 with a giant festival in Qufu, Shandong Province, where the great sage was born and died.

What to Expect?

TRAVELLERS

China draws travellers from across the world. Americans and British expats have rushed there to set up businesses (with mixed success), and there are still loads of expats in Hong Kong and more heading into Shanghai. Japan, South Korea and Taiwan are all well used to seeing American tourists, less so Europeans. Seoul and Tokyo have large English-speaking expat communities.

Surrounded by limestone pinnacles and wonderful scenery is Yangshuo (Guangxi Province), a superb backpackers' hangout, while the beautiful old walled town of Dali (Yunnan) sits beside the pleasant Ěrhǎi Lake. Elsewhere in the region it's pretty easy to escape to an island or into the mountains away from the hectic crowds of the cities.

LOCALS

Northeast Asian systems of social etiquette and religious beliefs are way too complex to explain in detail here. However a few generalisations will help: directness is not a common trait. In fact people often tell you what they think you want to hear, especially in China, where a smile doesn't necessarily indicate happiness, sometimes just embarrassment or worry.

'Face' and the avoidance of losing it are very important throughout the region. Try not to make anyone back down directly or look stupid if something goes awry. Smiling negotiation is the order of the day, direct confrontation a last resort. Flattery and self-deprecation are useful traits to polish.

The peoples of Northeast Asia are proud and nationalistic. In Japan you'll find people extremely friendly and courteous, shy and hospitable (there's even a tourist system of evening home visits). The Japanese are most forgiving of social gaffs but long-term residents complain that it's difficult to get beyond being treated as a foreigner and guest.

In South Korea and China the influence of Confucianism is very noticeable. The philosophy delivers a hierarchical system of deference; women defer to men, younger brothers to older brothers, respect flows upwards from subjects to rulers. It's a pretty handy system if you're near the top of the tree but difficult if you're outside these relationships.

China has only been 'open' to foreigners for 20 years and many people have a curious or suspicious attitude to travellers. Chinese people will stare and sometimes prod and travellers often tire of the exclamation of '*lawoai*' (a reasonably polite term for foreigners) and the commonly experienced but unofficial, two-tier pricing system.

The boundaries between religion and philosophy are often blurred in Northeast Asian religions. Shinto, Japan's widest-held religion, is a mix of myths and Gods. It sits easily alongside Zen Buddhism but Mahayana is Northeast Asia's most common form of Buddhism. In Tibet more mystical Tantric or Lamaist Buddhism is practised – it's this branch that the Dalai Lama heads. Taoism, based on wise proverbs, is China's only home-grown religion. Islam has many followers in China, particularly in the west. There are pockets of Christianity across the region and Judaism in China.

LANGUAGE

Chinese business people may know a little English but the language is more widely understood in Japan, South Korea and Taiwan (and especially in Hong Kong). Portuguese is spoken in Macau.

China throws up a mixed bag of languages and dialects. Mandarin (*Putonghua*) is the official language and Cantonese (*Yue*) is spoken in Hong Kong and surrounds. There are six other major dialects. Japanese and Korean are fairly uniform across their respective countries but there are a few obscure dialects. In July 2000 Korea adopted a new method of romanising the Korean language, introducing a few new spellings. You may see some old spellings knocking around – if in doubt go back to the original Korean script (see Lonely Planet's Korea guide for more details). The new spelling is used in this chapter.

An increasing number of signs display names in Western letters as well as Northeast Asian characters but you'll certainly need to understand a few characters in each language, especially Mandarin. Language courses are available in the UK and across the region (see Courses in Part III for more information). Reading Material, later in this chapter, gives information on Lonely Planet's useful phrasebooks.

HEALTH RISKS

A variety of jabs are required for travel in this part of the world. In addition, dengue fever and Japanese encephalitis occasionally occur on Taiwan and are present in rural China, which is a great reservoir of hepatitis B. Dysentery, hepatitis, liver flukes and malaria are relatively common in southwest China. Schistosomiasis (bilharziasis) and typhoid are present in the central Yangtze River basin. However, probably the main health problem for visitors is the incredible pollution in China's cities leading to respiratory ailments.

Dicey food may bring on an emergency toilet dash in China but Japan and South Korea are very healthy places. Mongolia is pretty healthy too, apart from the odd outbreak of meningococcal meningitis and brucellosis from unboiled milk or home-made cheese.

Blood banks in Northeast Asia don't stock Rh-negative blood.

Consult the Health chapter in Part I and seek professional medical advice for more travel health information.

TIME & FLIGHT TIME

Japan and Korea are both nine hours ahead of Greenwich Mean Time (GMT). The whole of China is set eight hours ahead of GMT, which is ideal for Beijing but hopeless in the west where working days and opening hours are adjusted to avoid commuting two hours before dawn and such.

From London it's an 11¾-hour flight to Tokyo, 12 hours to Hong Kong, 11 hours to Seoul and 10 hours to Beijing.

ISSUES

Officially you can only cross from China into Russia and Mongolia by train but it's possible to get a bus to various Russian borders. You cannot cross into Afghanistan, Bhutan or India by land. The Nepalese border can be a hassle but you'll get through.

The shackles are getting looser but there's still a little paranoia about letting foreigners roam around China unchecked or do anything too unusual. A number of areas remain off-limits to foreigners and you'll need an Alien Travel Permit to pass through or enter others (such as Tibet).

The repression of human rights is common in China. The occupation of Tibet and brutal imposition of Chinese rule is the most well-known issue in the country but there is continuing repression of the ethnic Uighur Muslim minority in Xinjiang Province. In response to a number of bombings, thousands of Uighurs have been detained since September 11.

Petty crime is much more of a problem in China than elsewhere in Northeast Asia. 'Hard seat' (essentially third class) train carriages can be insecure at night. If you're planning to cycle bring a good cycle lock. Con artists operate on the street and in offices.

Travellers staying longer than 30 days in Mongolia must register with the Foreign Citizen's Bureau in Ulaanbaatar.

For further information on travel hotspots, general safety issues and governmental travel advice see Safety in Part I.

INTERNET & COMMUNICATIONS

You are in one of the most technologically advanced regions on earth so mobile and web access are no problem except in Mongolia and rural China.

Daily Spend

Northeast Asia is expensive compared with Southeast Asia. The dubious honour of most expensive country goes not to Japan but North Korea, where the few tightly policed tour groups that are allowed in are charged vast sums of hard currency.

Coastal China is surprisingly expensive (at least £30 a day, more in pricey Hong Kong) but moving inland can cut your costs to £15–25 per day. Food is cheap everywhere but unofficial 'tourist prices' are charged for many goods and services.

A Japanese hostel bed costs at least £15, more like £25, in Tokyo and you're looking at at least £40–50 of expenditure every day. Rail passes (only available overseas), overnight buses and the ubiquitous noodle stalls can help cut costs, as does continuing deflation.

South Korea is steadily becoming more expensive. Sniffing out the bargains brings down daily costs to £20 a day but £30 would be more realistic.

You can spend £10 a day bumming around Mongolia's capital Ulaanbaatar but more like £15 out in the wilds thanks to transport costs and expensive traditional ger camps (£15 plus per person). Camping keeps down costs; hiring 4WDs (often essential to get off the beaten track) puts them up to around £60 a day.

Budget for £15 a day bumping along the bottom in Taiwan or £25 away from sweaty dormitories. Taipei can be fiercely expensive.

Cash rules in Japan where international ATMs (automatic teller machines) are rare.

Getting There

Many travellers appear in the region as part of a round-the-world (RTW) trip or after trawling around Southeast Asia. The Trans-Siberian Railway can deposit travellers in Beijing, northeast China and Mongolia.

AIR

Direct flights are possible into Northeast Asian hubs, including Beijing, Shanghai, Hong Kong, Seoul (South Korea), Taipei (Taiwan), Tokyo and Osaka (Japan). Ticket prices are not *that* different between them.

It's no problem getting open-jaw tickets into the region and Beijing, Hong Kong and Tokyo crop up on a number of RTW tickets. Stopovers to the latter two, plus Osaka and occasionally Seoul, are possible on some tickets into Sydney (Australia), with carriers such as Japanese Airlines and Korea Air.

Northeast Asian routes are highly competitive and there's usually a wide choice of fares. European airlines such as KLM, Air France and Lufthansa were offering cheap student fares to Northeast Asia at the time of writing. British Airways (BA), Cathay Pacific, Gulf Air and Turkish Airlines also turn out cheap deals.

Consult the Airlines Appendix at the back of the book for more information on airlines and routes.

Ticket Costs

The best available student/under-26 fares are quoted here. See Passports, Tickets, Visas & Insurance in Part I for more information on how to get the best, most flexible deal.

Beijing is the cheapest destination (return is £400 to £450) but occasionally some good deals for South Korea pop up. Getting to Hong Kong costs £430 to £480 return, about the same as Shanghai. Return fares to Seoul cost £440 to £500, Tokyo £450 to £475 return (Osaka is a little more expensive) and Taipei £530 to £575.

Return tickets to Australia, including a stop in Japan, cost between £550 and £800. An open-jaw ticket into Osaka and out of Shanghai costs between £450 and £475. Into Seoul and out of Beijing is cheaper (£410 and £440) but into Hong Kong and out of Beijing the cheapest of the lot (£400 to £460).

SEA & OVERLAND

Although there's plenty of sea transport between the countries in Northeast Asia, there's only one sea link out of the region, namely the ferries from Nakhodka in Russia (close to Vladivostok, the terminus of the fabled Trans-Siberian Railway) to Yokohama or Niigata in Japan.

A huge number of Central and Southeast Asian countries border China but routes into Afghanistan, India and Bhutan are closed. It's easier to get into the region by train from Russia and Central Asia, although there are some fantastic high road passes and border crossings in the west.

It's still almost impossible to take your own vehicle into China – the authorities don't allow foreigners to drive between cities.

SPECIALIST TOUR OPERATORS
The number of tour operators offering trips in China is increasing but foreign operators are rare in Korea, Taiwan and Japan. Consult the Global Tour Companies Appendix at the back of the book.

Northeast Asia & Beyond
The region borders an enormous number of countries, and flights out of the region's hubs can take you anywhere in the world reasonably cheaply. Heading back home overland is one fabulous possibility: there are four great options by train via Russia and the mouth-watering possibility of crossing into Nepal from China and following the old Hippie Trail from Kathmandu back through the Middle East. Tropical Southeast Asia and the Indian Subcontinent also beckon, as do the toys and joys of Australasia and North America. Circle Pacific airfares allow exploration of the great ocean's islands and coastlines and need not cost the earth.

Further Information
READING MATERIAL
Lonely Planet publishes guidebooks to all the countries in the region, as well as a few cities plus a guide to the Karakoram Highway. Also helpful are *Healthy Travel Asia, Hiking in Japan, World Food Hong Kong, World Food Japan* and phrasebooks to the region's major languages.

For some insight into the current process of change in China check out *China Wakes*, by Kristof and Wudunn, *Evening Chats in Beijing*, by Perry Link, and *Deng Xiaoping and the Making of Modern China*, by Richard Evans. *Japan: a Short Cultural History*, by George B Sansom, is among the best introductions to Japanese history and *Inside Japan*, by Peter Tasker, an excellent insight to contemporary Japan. *Korea, Tradition & Transformation*, by Andrew C Nahm, provides a great up-to-date history of the peninsula.

More personal accounts of the region include *The Private Life of Chairman Mao* written by the man's private physician Zhisui Li, and the fascinating family saga *Wild Swans*, by Jung Chang. Cohn Thubron's *Behind the Wall* and Paul Theroux's *Riding the Iron Rooster* remain the two best recent travel books written about China. *China by Bike*, by Roger Grigsby, covers a journey through Taiwan, Hong Kong and the east coast of China. *To Dream of Pigs*, by Clive Leatherdale, is an excellent travelogue of both North and South Korea.

Alan Booth's *The Roads to Sata* traces a four-month journey on foot across northern Japan. *Lost Japan*, by Alex Kerr, covers 30 years of the author's experiences, while Kare Taro Greenfield's *Speed-tribes – Children of the Japanese Bubble* is an entertaining foray into the drug-peddling, computer-hacking underworld of the disaffected Japanese youth. *Memoirs of a Geisha*, by Arthur Golden, is a classic.

USEFUL INFORMATION SOURCES
For specific country overviews, the low-down on travel in the region and hundreds of useful links head first to Lonely Planet's website (**W** www.lonelyplanet.com).

The following portals and useful websites should help you chase down any aspect of interest on Northeast Asia:

W tour2korea.com – stacks of Korean travel information and links.
W www.japantravelinfo.com – portal of the Japan National Tourist Board.

W **www.hkta.org** – Hong Kong's Tourist Association website.
W **www.cnta.com/lyen** – the portal of the China National Tourism Administration.
W **www.cybertaiwan.com** – a funky and functional Taiwanese site.
W **www.ChinaPage.com** – covers Chinese art, poetry and language.
W **www.tibet.org** – examines Tibet's sad occupation and repression.
W **www.outdoorjapan.com** – a light overview of the outdoor possibilities in Japan.
W **www.silk-road.com** – an insight into culture along the Silk Road.

The Royal Asiatic Society and School of Oriental and African Studies can both be of use to students before they travel (see Useful Information Sources in the Africa and Middle East chapters).

Been There, Done That

You can tell a lot about a culture by its toilets and nowhere is this more the case than in Japan. Just as Japanese communities range from the thatched-roof villages of Hokkaidō to the ultramodern metropolis of Tokyo, so too Japanese toilets run the gamut from stone-age primitive to space-age hi-tech.

I remember visiting my Japanese teacher's house long before I had any real grasp of the written language. After dinner, I begged off to do some business in the bathroom. On opening the bathroom door, I was greeted by a futuristic toilet the likes of which I'd never seen. Instead of the simple flush the toilet had a control panel with an alarming range of functions written in Japanese. Daunting as it was, nature was calling and I figured I could work out these intricacies, so I sat down and did what I had to do.

As I was seated, I noticed that one of the buttons on the control panel had a little picture on it resembling a fountain. 'Ahah,' I thought, 'that must be the bidet function.' Never having tried a bidet, I thought I'd give it a whirl and was immediately hit by a rather surprising jet of hot water that showed no signs of tiring. I searched the control panel frantically for some sort of 'stop the bidet' button but was met by an incomprehensible array of squirls and scribbles. I was well and truly trapped – if I stood up to flee the bathroom would get soaked. Calling for help wasn't really an option here. What could my teacher do, short of invading the bathroom to rescue me?

Finally, in desperation, I gambled and hit a button near the bidet button. To my great relief, the stream stopped and I was free. When I finally made it back to the table, my teacher looked at me a little quizzically. 'Just out of interest,' I asked, 'how do you write "stop" in Japanese?' She's a smart woman, and I think she got the picture.   Chris Rowthorn

Southeast Asia

Introduction

Southeast Asia has been attracting travellers for decades. Together with the Indian Subcontinent it formed the inspiration for the beginning of Lonely Planet and modern guidebooks. Today the region remains a backpacker mecca and attracts huge numbers of gappers, travellers, beach bums and office escapees. There's always someone to travel with, new people to hangout with, somewhere to party. You may think that all this attention has taken the gloss off the Asia experience but happily the coral-ringed islands, stunning temples and dense jungles you've been dreaming about can still be found with a little effort.

Why Southeast Asia?

'Why not?' is probably a better question. The sprawling Asian cities of Bangkok (Thailand), Jakarta (Indonesia) or Kuala Lumpur (Malaysia) can be a bit of a shock to the system but even if you arrive in the chaos of the classic French colonial cities of Hanoi (Vietnam) and Phnom Penh (Cambodia) the unhurried and smiling demeanour of many of the region's people will soon shine through.

There's a well-worn trail through Cambodia, Vietnam, Laos, Thailand and Malaysia (which together form Indochina or mainland Southeast Asia), a route that takes you through a full compliment of tropical traveller attractions. At its centre lies Thailand, which has some of the most tranquil, tropical islands and relaxing beach hangouts in the world (see Travellers later in this chapter). It's a fantastic place to kick back and as cheap as anywhere in a region that's pretty cheap to start with. The seascapes of the coast – palm-fringed islands, coral reefs, tall limestone towers standing high above the sea – usually satisfy the more discerning of travel slackers but the beaches of Thailand and Malaysia are fast getting the package-tour treatment. The search for untouched paradise (that will inevitably go the same way) remains a major topic of conversation among travellers who talk misty-eyed of obscure islands in the Philippines and Indonesia. That said, getting off the tourist trail is still possible and hugely rewarding. The highlands of Laos, Vietnam and Cambodia still offer some great experiences that the sun worshippers on the coast might not find. It's that jungle thing that's the biggest draw – river rides on bamboo rafts, encounters with unique hill tribes, obscure temples and amazing (but sweaty) treks are all deservedly popular.

Conflict still corrupts parts of the continent but just as some places succumb, so others emerge. Cambodia, a place of ancient temples, empty beaches, mighty rivers, remote forests and (outside the famous temples of Angkor) only a handful of tourists, has emerged from the decades of war and isolation to establish itself back on the travel map. Likewise Laos is awakening after what seems like a very long nap. It's the least developed, least hectic and most enigmatic of the three former French Indochinese states (Cambodia and Vietnam are also blessed with some lovely French architecture). The Buddhist temples of this small, quiet country are as stunning as its ancient history. Vietnam has also risen phoenix-like to become a premier backpacker destination. It's a place of sublime natural settings and a dignified and highly cultured society.

Parts of the floating emerald islands of the Indonesian archipelago are sadly going the other way. For centuries the islands have been a magnet to a diverse range of people attracted by its sandalwood and spices, its Bali Hai lifestyle and its magnificent beaches, mountains and volcanoes. Sadly uprisings, coups and terrorist attacks have dented its reputation somewhat.

Also badly treated by the global PR machine is the 7000-island archipelago that is the Philippines. The south may be a little dicey but the north is still ideal for laid-back island-hopping in a tranquil tropical paradise, where many more people speak English than in the rest of Southeast Asia.

The arguments as to whether tourism in Myanmar (Burma) exacerbates or eases the country's problems are hotly debated but check out Amnesty International's website (W www.amnesty.org) before making a decision.

Singapore is a more leisurely, sanitised start to Southeast Asia having traded in its rough-and-ready opium dens and pearl luggers for towers of concrete and glass. Parts of Malaysia are showing the same inclination but the country remains one of the most pleasant, hassle-free destinations in Southeast Asia as well as one of the most politically stable and economically buoyant. It's a vibrant fusion of Malay, Chinese, Indian and indigenous cultures and customs, with a burst of spectacular wildlife, awe-inspiring jungle and wonderful cultures in Sarawak and Sabah in Malaysian Borneo.

Thailand probably receives more visitors than anywhere else in Southeast Asia and no other regional nation has so many historical relics, so if you're interested in ruins, temples and abandoned cities, this is the place to go. Bangkok lives up to its billing for good or ill and Thailand is easy to travel in and cheap.

What to Do?

There are a few volunteer opportunities in Southeast Asia but finding work is a little hit and miss. Consequently kicking back on beautiful tropical beaches, drinking Thai whiskey cocktails from a bucket and searching for the perfect banana pancake takes up a serious amount of gappers' time in Southeast Asia, no matter how pious their intentions seemed back home. And why not? Islands and beaches around the region provide perfect back-packer hangouts and party venues. Should, God forbid, it cloud over on the coast there are dozens of adventure activities, hundreds of amazing cultural sites and loads of courses to undertake. You can study *vipassana* (insight meditation) in Vientiane (Laos) and Yangon (Myanmar), while there are numerous meditation centres dotted around Thailand (instruction is sometimes in English and accommodation free, although donations are expected). Tuition in full-contact Thai boxing is available in Bangkok and Naklua, and Chiang Mai is a centre for classes in Thai cooking and traditional massage. Arts and crafts are taught in some parts of Indonesia and Malaysia's cultural centres offer classes in traditional Malaysian handicrafts and cookery courses can be found in Kuala Lumpur and Penang.

See Part III for more information on overseas jobs, volunteer work and courses available in the region.

GET ACTIVE

Most of the activities in the region are available year round. The weather plays the largest part in deciding when to travel (see Climate later in this chapter).

Caving

In Sarawak, Gunung Mulu National Park has a number of spectacular caves, including the 51km-long Clearwater Cave, one of the longest in the world. Not to be out done, Palawan's Underground River in the Philippines sports an 8km-long meandering network of caves. Adventure tours into both systems can be arranged.

In Vietnam spelunkers (cavers) should head for the spectacular Phong Nha river caves, northwest of Dong Hoi. The network of tunnels and chambers at Cu Chi (35km from Ho

---

Top 10 Must-Sees

Pha That Luang (Vientiane, Laos) – a stunning Buddhist temple.
Angkor Wat (Cambodia) – famed ancient and abandoned Khmer capital.
Hanoi (Vietnam) – Indochina's finest French colonial architecture.
Ayuthaya & Lopburi (Thailand) – wonderful Thai capitals of the past.
Baliem Valley (Papua, Indonesia) – amazing cultures and jungle trekking.
Batang Rejang River (Sarawak, Malaysian Borneo) & Sungai Mahakam River (Kalimantan, Indonesia) – longhouses, longboats and long river journeys.
Banaue (Philippines) – stunning rice terraces, a wonder of the country.
Luang Nam Tha (Laos) – unique hill country with a former royal capital.
Hué (Vietnam) – a royal city with citadels, elegant tombs and exquisite cuisine.
Kyaiktiyo Paya (Myanmar) – a remarkable, stupa-topped gilded boulder.

Chi Minh City) and Vinh Moc (near the old border between North and South Vietnam) enable visitors to experience the claustrophobic life led by villagers and guerrillas during the war.

Cycling & Mountain Biking

Vietnam is the major cycle-touring destination of Southeast Asia. The country's flat coastal areas are particularly popular and light traffic flows (once off the main highways) a real boon. Mountain biking is a great way to take advantage of Laos' terrain (there are bikes for hire in Vientiane and Luang Prabang) and Cambodia. Lonely Planet's *Cycling in Vietnam, Laos & Cambodia* covers these areas in further detail.

Malaysian bicycle-touring routes are up the east coast of the peninsula and a cross-peninsula route from Butterworth to Baling. Malaysia is a fine place to cycle, as is Thailand, where the flat terrain and lush river scenery beside the Mekong River is popular.

Mountain biking is pretty big in the Philippines, especially around Moalboal on Cebu. Also investigate Guimaras Island and rugged Camiguin Island off the north coast of Mindanao.

Diving & Snorkelling

Beautiful beaches, fantastic coral and clear seas make the region a fantastic dive destination, although dive operators vary in quality. If you're just interested in snorkelling then you can pick up gear at all the most popular beaches in Southeast Asia.

Indonesia offers great diving and snorkelling off Bali (try Nusa Dua, Sanur and Padangbai), between Komodo and Labuanbajo in Flores, around the Banda Islands and off Pulau Biak north of Papua. The sea gardens of Sulawesi, particularly around Manado, are legendary.

Diving and snorkelling enthusiasts can take their pick from Malaysia's excellent east-coast islands, including Tioman, Pulau Kapas, Pulau Redang and Perhentian Islands.

The Philippines has a wealth of underwater opportunities around Boracay, Alona Beach (Bohol), Puerto Princesa (Palawan) and the island of Apo. There is also some fantastic diving around the WWII shipwrecks in Subic Bay (Luzon) and Coron (Busuanga Island).

In Thailand diving and snorkelling are particularly popular around Pattaya but the diving opportunities around Phuket are more diverse. The islands of Chumphon Province and the Khao Lak islands are less developed and the reefs practically undisturbed.

Also try Sihanoukville (Kompong Som; which also has the country's finest beaches) in Cambodia, the Myeik archipelago in Myanmar and Nha Trang in Vietnam.

Surfing & Windsurfing

Indonesia is the biggest surf destination in Southeast Asia. Renowned spots include Ulu Watu in Bali, Grajagan in Java, Nias off Sumatra and the Nusa Tenggara islands. Windsurfing is possible in the southern resorts of Bali.

The breaks off Siargao Island in the Philippines can reach Hawaiian scale between October and May. Boracay is the Philippine windsurfing mecca.

Trekking

Trekking in Southeast Asia is about jungles, scaling mountains and volcanoes, or both.

There's limited trekking (and elephant rides) in Ratanakiri and Mondulkiri in Cambodia but Sumatra in Indonesia has better jungle treks, particularly in Gunung Leuser National Park (get organised in Berastagi or Bukit Lawang). Java has good walking in its national parks; Gunung Merapi (2911m) is a taxing climb – Gunung Bromo (2329m) less so. The volcano that dominates Lombok, Gunung Rinjani (3726m), is a strenuous but worthwhile three-day jaunt. More adventurous jungle-trekking opportunities are available in Kalimantan and Papua (Irian Jaya).

The highlands of Laos make perfect, adventurous trekking territory (although there's little set up for travellers). Try Bokeo, Champasak, Khammuan, Luang Nam Tha, Luang Prabang and Vientiane provinces.

Despite intense logging in Malaysia there's still great jungle trekking in the Taman Negara National Park and beautiful Tasik Chini in Pahang. In Sarawak there's a great four-day hike to the summit of Gunung Mulu (2377m) and adventurous treks in the Kelabit Highlands. Many visitors to Sabah climb Mt Kinabalu (4101m; it takes two days).

You can climb various (often active) volcanoes in the Philippines including Mayon (2450m; the world's most perfect volcanic cone) and Mt Taal. There are wonderful trekking opportunities along Luzon's Pacific Coast, especially in Bikol and Quezon provinces.

Chiang Mai, Mae Hong Son and Chiang Rai in northern Thailand are very popular centres for jungle treks into the mountainous hill-tribes regions. Trekking is possible in many of Thailand's national parks and is a little further from the beaten track.

There's good hiking in a few Vietnamese national parks and the beautiful countryside around Da Lat and Sapa (also popular for horse riding).

Wildlife Watching

Southeast Asia has a fair amount of wildlife and a huge amount of birdlife. Malaysia's Taman Negara and Kenong Rimba national parks are excellent spots and other parks across the region can be rewarding.

Malaysia's Turtle Islands National Park is a good place to see green turtles between July and October. The Terengganu coast, Pulau Pangkor off Lumut, and Selingan Island north of Sabah are other favoured turtle-watching locations.

On Don Khong, a Laotian island in the Mekong River, you can see Irrawaddy dolphins between December and May.

In Indonesia the most accessible national park is Gunung Leuser in Sumatra but more famous are the 'dragons' on the nearby islands of Komodo and Rinca.

Other Activities

Rafting is offered on Bali's Ayung River and near Beaufort in Sabah. Boatmen steer tourist-filled canoes through the rapids in Pagsanjan southeast of Manila in the Philippines – if it looks familiar in places, that's because Coppola filmed parts of *Apocalypse Now* on the river. Rafting trips on large bamboo 'house-rafts' can be taken on a number of rivers in north and central Thailand. Popular waterways are the Mae Klong River in central Thailand and the Pai River in Mae Hong Son Province.

In Malaysia there's great fishing in Taman Negara National Park (which has wonderful bird-watching) and canoeing and fishing trips in beautiful Tasik Chini.

Touring the islands and coastal limestone formations around Phuket and Ko Phang-Nga in Thailand (which are very popular with adventurous climbers) by inflatable canoe has become an increasingly popular activity. The typical sea-canoe tour seeks out half-submerged caves, timing excursions so that it's possible to paddle into the caverns at low tide.

WORK A LITTLE

There are a few employment opportunities in the region but work seems to be a pretty hit-and-miss affair. Where you do find work it's usually teaching English – there's quite a lot of work in Cambodia, Thailand and Vietnam plus to a lesser extent Laos – but don't expect much in the way of wages.

In Laos the amount of work from NGO organisations is increasing for those with volunteer experience, and elsewhere there's quite a variety of volunteer opportunities, ranging from working in orang-utan orphanages in Borneo to teaching English in Thailand.

TRAVEL AROUND

Air travel around Southeast Asia can be a real bargain. The best fares are found in Bangkok, Singapore and Penang (Malaysia). If you've flown into Southeast Asia with one of a cluster of regional carriers then the Asean airpass is available (£75 per flight coupon).

Train travel is an option in Java, Malaysia, Myanmar, Thailand and Vietnam. Cambodia's train network is up and running very, very slowly. The train journey between Bangkok and Nam Tok is one of the most emotive in the world as it follows the route first forged by allied prisoners in WWII. It cuts through some of Thailand's most beautiful scenery.

Bus transport varies greatly in quality, speed and safety (the latter two are not always interlinked). In Malaysia, Indonesia, the Philippines and Thailand long-distance buses range from cheap and cheerful to air-con luxury. Thailand even has women-only buses. On remote routes and elsewhere in the region buses tend to be neither swift nor comfortable – Vietnam's buses are as bad as Cambodia's roads. Long-distance shared taxis are available in some countries.

With some 1180 miles of navigable waterways boat transport is common in Cambodia. In jungles of Kalimantan, Sarawak and Sabah there's plenty of river transport. Hundreds of ferries and boats service islands in the Indonesian and Philippine archipelagos but safety is often slap-dash. Don't board anything *really* shonky or overcrowded.

Local transport includes taxis, minibuses, pick-up trucks with rows of seats along each side, auto rickshaws, bicycle rickshaws and horse-drawn carts. Most are ridiculously cheap but agree on a fare in advance. Original to the Philippines are *jeepneys*, highly ornate, originally reconstructed jeeps.

Classic Routes

Many travellers heading to Southeast Asia content themselves with exploring Thailand, Laos, Cambodia and Vietnam. This makes pretty good sense as flights into Bangkok are cheap and there's a neat circuit through all these countries.

If you want something a little more taxing then there's a great route through the whole of the region ending in Australia. Phnom Penh is the best starting point from where travellers head east into Vietnam (although there's also a border crossing into Laos beside the Mekong River). Most travellers head north along the Vietnamese coast to Hué before cutting west into Laos at the Lao Bao-Kaew Neua border (possibly after a side trip up to Hanoi). The main crossing into Thailand is close to the capital Vientiane. The route then heads down through Thailand and Malaysia via Bangkok, Kuala Lumpur and some of the best beaches and tropical islands in the region to Singapore.

Huge ferry and domestic air networks service Indonesia, and both offer ways of avoiding long, difficult road journeys. From southern Malaysia ferries lead to Sumatra but from Singapore it's possible to leapfrog a string of smaller Indonesian islands to Sumatra or Kalimantan. From either island all routes lead to Java and Jakarta, the Indonesian capital. The route now splits; either pootle through Java to Bali (which has cheap flights to Australia) or cut up to Sulawesi and push on to Papua. In any case the end of the route is in Kupang, West Timor, from where there are flights to Darwin, Australia. In future it may be possible to travel overland to East Timor (which also has flights to Darwin) but at present the Timorese militia make this journey dangerous for westerners.

This Southeast Asian 'Grand Tour' misses out Myanmar and the Philippines. In the case of Myanmar this is largely because the Thai-Myanmar land border is closed but flights to Yangon are cheap from Bangkok. Flights to Manila, the capital of the Philippines, are possible from across the region but cheapest from Bangkok. It is possible to get a ferry to the southern Philippines island of Mindanao from Kalimantan and Sabah but sadly Mindanao is too dicey for Western tourists. The rest of the Philippines, however, is worthy of six months' exploration in itself.

When to Go?

There are few really bad times to visit Southeast Asia. Even during the monsoon, downpours are sudden, torrential, short and usually followed by sunshine. They're rarely an impediment to travel except in remote areas (Cambodia and Indonesia are most susceptible to washed-out roads).

As a rule of thumb, hit mainland Southeast Asia in the cool and dry of November and March, then escape to the archipelagos of the Philippines and Indonesia between April and October. If you're hitting the hill stations of Myanmar or highlands of Laos and Thailand, March to May can be pleasant.

Ramadan causes disruption in Indonesia, Brunei and Malaysia, while various celebrations in the rest of the region affect accommodation and transport. The peak tourist months in mainland Southeast Asia are December and August. The Christmas and Easter periods can also be busy but these holidays bring waves of migratory Australians to Indonesia and cause transport nightmares in the Philippines. For more information on Islamic festivals see the Middle East chapter.

There are bagfuls of festivals in both May and November (see Festivals later in this chapter).

CLIMATE

With the exception of northern Myanmar, all of Southeast Asia lies within the tropics. Warm or downright hot weather with high humidity is common in lowland areas. Head to the highlands and mountains to escape the heat – it's been known to snow on Puncak Jaya (5030m) in Indonesia!

Typhoons occasionally strike the Philippines and north and central Vietnam between June and early October.

Mainland Southeast Asia (Three-Season Countries)

North and central Thailand, Cambodia, Laos, Myanmar and Vietnam have a relatively cool dry season (November to March), followed by a hot dry season (March to May). A hot rainy season begins around June, petering out by October. Highland areas are significantly cooler than the lowlands and temperatures can get down to freezing in winter.

Oceanic Southeast Asia (Two-Season Countries)

Southern Thailand, Myanmar, Brunei, Indonesia, Malaysia and Singapore experience two yearly monsoons: one from the northeast (usually between October and April) and one from the southwest (between May and September). Rain is usually heavier during the northeast monsoon but often you'll find better weather simply by crossing from one side of the island or country to the other.

The climates of the Philippines and Maluku (Indonesia) are more complex and share aspects of both mainland and oceanic climates.

FESTIVALS

The region is jam-packed with religious festivals (Buddhist and Muslim mostly, but also Chinese and Christian) and wild celebrations of a more irreligious nature. Make sure these events don't pass you by:

Black Nazarene Procession (Philippines) involves the transporting of a life-size, black-wood statue of Jesus through the streets of Quiapo on January 9.

Ati-Atihan (Philippines) is a three-day Filipino 'Mardi Gras' celebrated on Panay in the third week of January.

Chinese New Year is widely celebrated by the region's numerous Chinese communities in January/February (try Kuala Lumpur) but many nations (such as Vietnam where Tet is the country's most important festival) also celebrate the new lunar year.

Khmer New Year (Cambodia) brings the country to a standstill in mid-April – a fair amount of water and talcum powder gets thrown around. Similar is the three-day Thingyan (water festival) in Myanmar and Songkran in Thailand.

Tamu Besar (Malaysian Borneo) is a huge tribal gathering in Kota Belud featuring a massive market, ornately decorated horsemen and medicine men. It's held in May at Kota Belud in Sabah.

Bun Bang Fai (Laos), the rocket festival, is an irreverent pre-Buddhist May celebration of processions, merriment and firing of bamboo rockets (to prompt the rains for the new rice season). Similar is the Rocket Festival in northeast Thailand.

Tiet Doan Ngo (Vietnam), Summer Solstice Day, in June sees the burning of human effigies to satisfy the need for souls to serve in the God of Death's army.

Trung Nguyen (Vietnam), Wandering Souls Day, is held on the 15th day of the seventh moon (August) when offerings are given to the wandering souls of the forgotten dead.

Festival of Light (Myanmar) celebrates Buddha's return from heaven with fire balloons, paper lanterns and offerings at the local pagoda.

Bon Om Tuk (Cambodia) is the most important Khmer festival and celebrates the end of the wet season in early November.

That Luang (Laos) offers fireworks, candlelit processions and music in Vientiane during November.

The Elephant Roundup (Thailand) is held in Surin during November where lumbering pachyderms indulge in races, tug-of-war and football.

In Brunei, Indonesia and Malaysia, Islamic festivals are widely celebrated (see the Middle East chapter for details).

What to expect?
TRAVELLERS
Southeast Asia attracts veteran travellers, greenhorn gappers and every kind of traveller in between. Once you've tasted the delights of Southeast Asia, it has a habit of dragging you back and there's always a high number of gappers and graduates on the road. Southeast Asia is an almost compulsory stop on many round-the-world (RTW) routings from the UK so there are very many Brits in the region, along with Europeans of all shapes and sizes (particularly Scandinavians, Dutch and Germans).

Southeast Asia is particularly blessed with places to hang out, due largely to the combination of great beaches and low costs. If the constant round of stunning religious buildings, fascinating peoples and beautiful national parks is getting to you, head down for one of the following:

Gili Islands & Bali (Indonesia) – cheap, coral-fringed specks of paradise.
Yogyakarta (Java, Indonesia) – relaxed, lively Javanese city.
Bukittinggi (Sumatra, Indonesia) – cool, easy-going mountain retreat.
Danau Toba (Sumatra, Indonesia) – huge crater lake and tranquil rest stop.
Ko Phang Nga, Ko Tao, Ko Chang and the **Phi Phi islands (Thailand)** – renowned hangouts and good-time islands.
Mae Hong Son & Mae Sai (Thailand) – highland hangouts and trek/rafting bases.
Luang Prabang (Laos) – for lovers of Buddhist temples and monasteries.
Angkor (Cambodia) – rightly famed for the nearby ancient Khmer temples.

LOCALS
The Thais are often depicted as fun-loving, happy-go-lucky folk and certainly in Thailand, Malaysia and Indonesia you'll never meet such a smiling, friendly and tolerant bunch. However, Southeast Asian people are also characterised as very strong-minded and have struggled for centuries to preserve their spirit of independence. The antics of some young travellers can really grate with local people. Some travellers report that Cambodia and Vietnam are less laid-back than Thailand but then where isn't?

It may seem on the surface that the region is pretty westernised but ancient cultural traditions and perceptions do influence the lives of most people.

Southeast Asia can be divided into the Buddhist cultures of mainland Southeast Asia; the Islamic cultures of oceanic Southeast Asia; the Chinese culture of Singapore and other ethnic Chinese; and the ancient cultures of hill tribes across the region.

The cultures of the Philippines and Vietnam resist easy categorization. While extremely traditional in many ways, the culture of the Philippines still bears the unmistakable stamp of Spain and the United States; and that of Vietnam is an interesting mix of Chinese and Southeast Asian influences, with the odd French touch.

Across Southeast Asia, the life of the family, extended family and the village take precedence over the life of the individual. Modesty (including in dress) is a prized social virtue and traditional codes of conduct are retained. In the case of the Islamic cultures of oceanic Southeast Asia *adat*, the ancient social code of the village, still governs life, and non-Muslim traditions have influenced local Islam. In Buddhist cultures status and social obligation (traditions that predate even Buddhism) are all-important and a high percentage of males are Buddhist monks at some point during their lives. Similarly, Southeast Asia's ethnic Chinese still live their lives according to Confucian principles. Up in the hills, you'll find that the ancient animist religions of the tribal peoples are still very much alive but keep in mind that by visiting tribal peoples you may be destabilising or damaging their culture simply by your presence.

Attitudes towards women vary greatly across the region. Gender equality is reasonable in Thailand and the Philippines but Indonesia is almost a 'pre-feminist state'. In Buddhist Indochina women travellers are often perceived as a little odd though this doesn't lead to too many hassles. In Indonesia the sight of solo women travellers can be seen as provocative and Western women are perceived as 'loose'.

Although Thai backpacker havens aren't exactly good adverts, discrete dress is very important throughout the region, especially when visiting religious sites. Sandals are okay but flip-flops are too casual for many places. There are plenty of other dos and don'ts to consider, all outlined in Lonely Planet's guidebooks.

LANGUAGE

With an estimated 1000 spoken languages, Southeast Asia is one of the world's most linguistically diverse regions. For visitors to Southeast Asia the most useful local language to learn is either Thai (which is understood in Thailand, most of Laos and parts of Vietnam but difficult to speak as it's a tonal language) or Bahasa Indonesian/Bahasa Malaysian (these are almost identical and not dissimilar to Filipino). Mandarin and Cantonese will also come in handy for conversing with ethnic Chinese across the region.

A few pleasantries in the local language are always appreciated but English is by far the most common second language of the region – most in the tourist industry understand a little.

It's possible to take a language course in the region or in the UK (see Courses in Part III for information). There are numerous Lonely Planet phrasebooks available (see Reading Material later in this chapter).

HEALTH RISKS

You'll need a good many vaccinations prior to travel in Southeast Asia. It's not as unhealthy as India but it ain't Switzerland. Once you've had your jabs watch out for dengue fever and malaria in rural areas (both are transmitted by mosquitoes), liver flukes (one of the joys of raw fish or swimming in the Mekong River) and schistosomiasis (bilharziasis), which is found in many lakes and rivers. Rabies is another nicety found in Indonesia and Laos.

HIV/Aids is a huge and increasing problem in Southeast Asia, and the sex industry the main (though not exclusive) source of infection for British travellers.

Consult the Health chapter in Part I and seek professional medical advice for more travel health information.

TIME & FLIGHT TIME

Cambodia, Laos, Thailand and Vietnam are seven hours ahead of Greenwich Mean Time (GMT); Brunei, Malaysia, the Philippines and Singapore are eight hours ahead and Myanmar, slightly awkwardly, 6½ hours ahead. Indonesia is divided into three time zones, seven, eight and nine hours ahead of GMT.

Bangkok is 11½ hours' flying time from London. Singapore (12¾ hours) and Kuala Lumpur (12½ hours) also have non-stop flights from London but destinations like Manila (16 hours) and Jakarta (17 hours) require a change of planes.

ISSUES

Visitors to Myanmar may venture only into officially designated tourist areas and there have been military conflicts and instances of banditry on the border with Thailand.

Sporadic outbreaks of violence still occur in Cambodia and many provinces remain heavily land mined (Cambodia is one of the world's most heavily mined countries). The Thailand side of the Cambodian border is no picnic either.

There's strong anti-Western sentiment in some parts of the Indonesian archipelago and Western interests have been and continue to be targeted. Sulawesi, East Kalimantan, Papua, Aceh, West Papua and West Timor had pockets of unrest at the time of writing. You should not visit Maluku or East Timor.

The Saisombun Special Zone in Laos is not safe and permits are required to visit Xaysomboune special province. In Xieng Khuang Province (Plain of Jars) and along the Lao-Vietnamese border there's a huge problem with land mines and unexploded ordnance.

The Philippines-based Abu Sayyaf militants have taken hostages from the islands of Sipadan and Pandanan that lie off the eastern coast of Sabah (Malaysian Borneo). A real risk of kidnap remains in this area and in the Mindanao and Sulu archipelagos in the Philippines itself. Kidnappings and bombings have occurred elsewhere in the Philippines.

In Vietnam, Dak Lak and Gai Lai have seen passionate protests by ethnic minorities. Land mines and unexploded ordnance are major problems in the country.

For the last few years a smoke haze caused by rampant wildfires and slash-and-burn agriculture has plagued the skies over Malaysia, Singapore and Indonesia during the second half of the year.

INTERNET & COMMUNICATIONS

Myanmar is the biggest slouch in the internet stakes but the rest of the region is pretty up to speed. Mobile communications are still in an early stage of development.

Daily Spend

The economies of Southeast Asia have been on a roller-coaster ride recently and currency collapses are not uncommon, which, generally speaking, make the place even cheaper.

Brunei takes the dubious honour of most expensive Southeast Asian country. It's almost devoid of backpacker accommodation. The norm for a decent hotel room is £30.

Malaysia is not the cheapest place in the region and is going to cost you £15 a day, which means staying in Chinese hotels (£5) and eating cheap on the street. Sabah and Sarawak are about 30% more expensive than Peninsular Malaysia. The Philippines is about the same sort of money, perhaps a little more expensive but is not in Singapore's league (the most westernised place in Southeast Asia is going to cost you £20 a day at least).

Laos offers some top cheapness. A bed in Vientiane costs about £4 but you can find accommodation elsewhere for under £2. Even a room in a relatively flashy hotel costs only a tenner, roughly your daily budget up-country. Cambodia is only mildly more expensive but Vietnam is closer to the costs of Thailand where £10–15 a day will do you nicely, although there are plenty of opportunities to spend much more (Bangkok costs more like £25 a day).

Getting There

There's a huge amount of traffic between London and Southeast Asia but only fares into the major hubs are cheap. Many travellers bound for Australia arrive on cheap RTW tickets or stopovers but there are some fantastic, if taxing, overland routes worth considering (see Southeast Asia & Beyond below).

AIR
The major hubs are Bangkok, Kuala Lumpur and Singapore. Direct flights into these cities are possible from the UK but if you're heading to Manila (Philippines), Jakarta or Bali (Indonesia), Hanoi (Vietnam) and Phnom Penh (Cambodia) you'll have to change planes at least once, most likely at one of the region's three hubs or Hong Kong.

Singapore Airlines and Cathay Pacific are the region's major carriers and a joy to fly with. Other major players servicing the region include British Airways (BA), Qantas, Malaysia Airlines and Thai Airways International. Garuda Indonesia is perhaps not the world's favourite airline. A host of Middle Eastern and European carriers regularly offer cheap deals, usually via a hub somewhere else.

Consult the Airlines Appendix at the back of the book for more information on airlines and routes.

Ticket Costs
The best available student/under-26 fares are quoted here. See Passports, Tickets, Visas & Insurance in Part I for more information on how to get the best, most flexible deal.

Tickets into Bangkok and Jakarta are cheapest (£400 return), followed smartly (in increments of around £40) by Singapore, then Kuala Lumpur and Manila. Fares are more expensive to Hanoi (£500–600), Phnom Penh (£680) and Vientiane (£720). Open-jaw tickets into Bangkok and out of a host of Southeast Asian cities can be found for under £500, roughly the same amount as a ticket into Manila and out of Jakarta. Getting an open-jaw fare including Hanoi or Phnom Penh you're looking at £800, which is more expensive than a cheap RTW ticket.

SEA & OVERLAND
There are no ferries to the region other than the irregular ferry to Papua from Papua New Guinea. Occasionally gappers pick up berths on yachts heading to Southeast Asia from Darwin and elsewhere in Australia. The Darwin to Bali Yacht Race in July/August is a good time to look around.

SPECIALIST TOUR OPERATORS
Heaps of British tour operators run trips within Southeast Asia. The major ones are detailed in the Global Tour Companies Appendix, or you could contact:

Symbiosis (☎ 0845 123 2844, fax 0845 123 2845; e info@symbiosis-travel.com; W www .symbiosis-travel.com; Studio 1b, 101 Farm Lane, London SW6 1QJ) offers tailor-made trips. 'Something beyond the normal package tour,' apparently.

Southeast Asia & Beyond
There are a couple of taxing but exhilarating overland routes into Northeast Asia from where all roads lead west towards Europe (the Trans-Siberian Railway is just one possibility). Heading into the Indian Subcontinent means leapfrogging Myanmar, which is possible with a loop up through China and down through Nepal. Many travellers take advantage of cheap RTW tickets and use Southeast Asia as a staging post on the way to Australia. You can also get cheap flights from Bali and Timor to Darwin and other cities across Australia.

Further Information
READING MATERIAL
Lonely Planet publishes a huge number of guides to countries, provinces and cities within the region. Add to this dozens of phrasebooks, books on the region's cuisine, guides to some of Southeast Asia's best dive sites and *Healthy Travel: Asia & India* and you have a comprehensive background.

There are dozens of books on the history and culture of Southeast Asia. Detailing the region's more troubled contemporary history are *Sideshow: Kissinger, Nixon & the Destruction of Cambodia*, by William Shawcross (the Vietnam War era), *Air America: The Story of the CIA's Secret Airlines*, by Christopher Robbins (focuses on the infamous gun- and drug-running activities of the CIA in Laos), *The Politics of Heroin in Southeast Asia*, by Alfred W McCoy, *Timor: a People Betrayed*, by John Dunn and *For Every Tear A Victory*, by Hartzell Spence, reckoned to be the definitive biography of former Philippine president Marcos. *Dispatches*, by Michael Herr, is a cold, hard, correspondent's view of the Vietnam War. Bao Ninh gives a North Vietnamese perspective in *The Sorrow of War*.

Tim Page's *Derailed in Uncle Ho's Victory Garden* is a great travelogue by a former war photographer revisiting the sites of the Vietnam War. Norman Lewis' *A Dragon Apparent* is a classic tale set in Indochina. Christopher Kremmer's *Stalking the Elephant Kings: In Search of Laos* is insightful, while Redmond O'Hanlon's *Into the Heart of Borneo* is a wonderfully funny account of jungle travel. Other travel tales include Spalding Gray's *Swimming to Cambodia*, *Drums of Tonki*, by Helen & Frank Schreider, Paul Theroux's *The Great Railway Bazaar*, Pico Iyer's *Video Night in Kathmandu*, *In Search of Conrad*, by Gavin Young, and *Under the Dragon: Travels in a Betrayed Land*, by Rory McLain.

USEFUL INFORMATION SOURCES
For specific country overviews, the low-down on travel in the region and hundreds of useful links head first to Lonely Planet's website (**W** www.lonelyplanet.com).

The following portals and useful websites should help you chase down any aspect of interest in Southeast Asia:

- **W** **www.cambodia.org** – a great site with a comprehensive list of links.
- **W** **indonesia.elga.net.id** – a great introduction to Indonesia.
- **W** **www.visit-mekong.com** – general site on Laos and Cambodia.
- **W** **www.vientianetimes.com** – not the official government mouthpiece it first appears.
- **W** **www.filipinolinks.com** – impressive set of links relating to the Philippines.
- **W** **www.thaiindex.com** – includes general information and loads of links.
- **W** **www.vietnamadventures.com** – details more than just adventure travel.
- **W** **www.thingsasian.com** – good portal to the whole of the region.

The Royal Asiatic Society and The School of Oriental and African Studies can also be of use to students before they travel (see Useful Information Sources in the Africa and Middle East chapters).

Been There, Done That
At the end of my first big overseas trip – three months in the UK and Europe – I decided to break my journey on my way back to Australia with a two-week stop-off in Bali. I only had £60 left but figured I could make it stretch at a pinch.

The lack of ready cash imposed on me a not unwelcome enforced leisure: I didn't have enough money to tear around visiting temples and sights, so I slipped into a routine of walking along the beach in the early morning, spending a good part of the day lying on the beach, and reading in the evening after buying my supper from a roadside trolley. On one occasion, as I was sitting on the beach, I was invited to join a group of Balinese women who were engaged in a thanksgiving ritual beneath a makeshift bamboo shelter. Before them was spread a sumptuous feast – fresh fruit, seafood and rice. On another evening I watched as an entire village walked to the water's edge, brightly dressed in ceremonial sarongs, and the male elders carried offerings into the sea.

I have travelled quite a bit since that first trip but some of my best travel memories are of that quiet two weeks in Bali. There are as many different types of travellers and reasons for travelling as there are destinations: there are those who feel they've let themselves down if they don't visit every single sight mentioned in their guidebook, those who revel in the camaraderie of 'the road,' and those who simply want to get a great suntan. All of these 'ways' of travelling are legitimate. As for me, I learned during those two weeks in Bali that a culture reveals itself in subtle, unexpected ways, and if you sit back quietly, often you'll find that it will unfold without any concerted effort on your part. Michelle Coxall

Australia, New Zealand & the Pacific

Introduction

Travelling in Australasia is unique. The region is as diverse and physically stunning as North America but accessible at a fraction of the cost, and Australia and New Zealand are, in places, as laid-back and indulgent as the paradise islands of Thailand. Pacific Papua New Guinea (PNG) and the South Pacific islands offer varied travel and cultural experiences but backpacking around Australia and New Zealand is largely about having fun, partying and packing in as many new and exciting experiences as possible. Many, many gappers end up in Australia and New Zealand, two of the most hassle-free backpacking destinations in the world.

Why Australia, New Zealand & the Pacific?

Australia and New Zealand are geared up for backpackers like nowhere else. Travel is easy and relatively cheap and around every corner someone seems to be offering a new kind of exciting activity. Australasia is a huge 'outdoors' destination. This has something to do with the sheer size of the place (Australia alone has over 7.5 million sq km of sparsely populated territory). It's also because travelling here is not all about visiting ancient relics and old churches. Indigenous culture may be gaining considerable prominence but over the last 200 years Ozzies and Kiwis have created their own culture built on an enjoyment of the outdoors, an influx of numerous cultures and the cosmopolitan vibrancy of 'new' cities like Sydney, Melbourne and Auckland.

Most people harbour a particular image of Australia, such as the Opera House or blood-red Uluru (Ayers Rock). Yet these famous icons do scant justice to the richness of Australia's natural treasures and its cultural diversity. Australia offers a wealth of travel experiences, from the vastness and drama of the outback, to the spectacle of the Great Barrier Reef and its islands, the cosmopolitanism of Sydney, and some of the best beaches in the world. This vast country and the friction between the ancient land steeped in Aboriginal lore and the New World cultures being heaped upon it, gives Australia much of its character.

New Zealand is like a microcosm of all the world's attractions. Thrill seekers and anyone interested in wide-open spaces will love this country of rare seismic beauty. You can climb active volcanoes, see glaciers descending into rainforests and enjoy the abundant forest reserves, long deserted beaches and unique varieties of endemic fauna, such as the kiwi. Any number of outdoor activities – trekking, skiing, rafting and, of course, that perennial favourite, bungee jumping – await the adventurous. You can swim with dolphins, gambol with newborn lambs, whale watch or fish for fattened trout in the many streams. The people, bound in a culture that melds European with Maori ancestry, are resourceful, helpful and overwhelmingly friendly.

The Pacific Ocean is huge, as large as the world's other oceans put together, and its paradise islands are just tiny dots separated by enormous distances. It's hardly surprising then that the cultures of the Pacific – conveniently divided into Polynesia (Many Islands), Melanesia (Black Islands) and Micronesia (Small Islands) – are so diverse. What *is* surprising is that they have anything in common at all other than mountain rainforests, perfect beaches, stunning underwater geography and thriving coral reefs.

The South Pacific can be the paradise you thought it was going to be but you'll have to put aside many myths and preconceptions before you arrive. The paralysis that afflicts Pacific travellers is legendary but it is often a place of conservative dress, not loose morals and grass skirts.

Papua New Guinea (PNG) is raw and untamed. Fascinating clans of prosaic hill people, tiny tree kangaroos and enormous Queen Alexandra birdwing butterflies are typical of the type of diversity that has, for so long, excited explorers, anthropologists and travellers. But PNG is not without its problems and in comparison Australia and New Zealand really are lands of carefree travel, a giant adventure playground that's beyond comparison.

What to Do?

There's so much to do in Australia and New Zealand that you really need two gap years to do it justice. Many gappers work at some point, either as a fundamental part of their gap year or to rustle up extra beer money.

Australia and New Zealand offer some wonderful opportunities to learn new skills, be they Aboriginal language and culture, or sheep sheering and the trade of a jackeroo/jillaroo.

See Part III for more information on overseas jobs, volunteer work and courses available in the region.

Travelling gappers have numerous wonderful options.

GET ACTIVE

You can get up to all sorts in Australasia, there seems to be no limit to possibilities. Australia and New Zealand are absolutely rammed with action-packed national parks and while the South Pacific is more limited there's plenty to do (although on Christian islands many activities aren't appropriate on Sunday unless you're in a resort accustomed to heathen Western tourists).

Top 10 Must-Sees

The Overland Track (Tasmania) – Australia's most famous bushwalk; Cradle Mountain, serene glacial lakes and windswept plains.

Sydney (Australia) – a vibrant, cosmopolitan city and stunning harbour.

Great Barrier Reef (Queensland, Australia) – an unforgettable marine environment of iridescent coral reefs studded with idyllic islands.

Kakadu National Park (NT, Australia) – outstanding Aboriginal art in a magnificent landscape packed with wildlife.

Uluru (Ayers Rock; NT, Australia) – the iconic heart of the outback.

The Pilbara (WA, Australia) – haunting red-dust landscape cut through with gorges.

Rotorua (North Island, New Zealand) – rich Maori culture and a landscape of geysers and bubbling mud pools.

Tongariro National Park (North Island, New Zealand) – tramp or ski in the volcanic landscape of this World Heritage area.

Waitomo Caves (North Island, New Zealand) – magical limestone caves complete with glow worms and black-water rafting through a series of underground rivers.

Aitutaki Atoll (Cook Islands, South Pacific) – laid-back paradise beaches; a fantastic stopover.

Cycling & Mountain Biking

Traffic is relatively light in Australasia and cycling is a great (and cheap) way to get around South Pacific islands. Australia has some fine cycling touring (around the wineries in the Yarra Valley, Victoria or Barossa Valley, South Australia, or along the Murray or Murrumbidgee rivers for example) but only the very hardy and experienced should tackle the outback. There are some excellent cycle routes and mountain-bike trails in cities and national parks across the country.

Many travellers describe New Zealand as a cyclist's paradise: it's clean, green, uncrowded and unspoiled, and there are plenty of places where you can camp or find cheap accommodation. Bicycle rental can be daily, weekly or monthly and is inexpensive. Several tour operators offer mountain biking trips starting at the top of various precipitous summits.

Diving & Snorkelling

Putting aside the obvious joys of Queensland's Great Barrier Reef, diving spots include South Australia's Kangaroo Island (which has a few shipwrecks) and Esperance, Rottnest Island, Ningaloo Reef and Carnarvon in Western Australia (WA). Diving in the southern waters around Melbourne, Adelaide, Perth and Tasmania brings shipwrecks, seals and dolphins. Australia is a great place to learn to dive and courses typically cost between £125 and £200.

The Poor Knights Island near Whangarei (North Island) is reputed to have the best diving in New Zealand. Good diving can also be had in the Bay of Islands Maritime & Historic Park, the Hauraki Gulf Maritime Park and the Sugar Loaf Islands reserve in the North Island, plus the Marlborough Sounds Maritime Park and Fjordland in the South Island.

South Pacific dive sites are largely uncrowded, undisturbed and offer diving for all levels in warm, clear water. Dramatic drop-offs, caves, wrecks and coral arches are found among dive sites on the Cook Islands, French Polynesia, Fiji, Tonga and New Caledonia. The Solomon Islands and Vanuatu have some remarkable WWII wrecks. Diving in PNG is reputed to be among the best in the world – try Kavieng, Lorengau and the sublime Wuvulu Island.

Sailing

Yachts offer a way of getting around in the South Pacific (see Travel Around later), as well as a specific activity in Vava'u (Tonga) and Fiji, two brilliant sailing destinations.

Group sailing trips are popular around Australia's Great Barrier Reef (the Whitsunday Islands in particular). In New Zealand, sailing trips are offered in the Bay of Islands (and Whangaroa to the north), the southern lakes (Te Anau and Wakatipu) and the cities of Auckland (the City of Sails) and Dunedin.

Skiing & Snowboarding

New Zealand has some of the best skiing in the southern hemisphere (June to early November). The North Island (near Ohakune) and South Island (west of Christchurch and around Queenstown) both have numerous ski resorts. In addition to downhill skiing, cross-country, ski touring, ski mountaineering and off-piste heliskiing are all possible on the virgin snow and glaciers of the Southern Alps.

In Australia, Thredbo and Perisher ski resorts in New South Wales' (NSW) Snowy Mountains, and Falls Creek and Mt Hotham in Victoria enjoy a short and sometimes sweet season between mid-June and early September.

Surfing & Windsurfing

South Pacific surfing destinations include Guam, Tonga, French Polynesia, Fiji and PNG.

There are a few great breaks but many unreliable dogs. Several islands have set up beach huts as very cheap accommodation for the surf crowd.

Australia boasts many world-class surf breaks, some close to Sydney and Perth, some in beach towns like Lorne in Victoria, Byron Bay in NSW and the Gold Coast in Queensland. However, much of the most legendary surf is found in rather remote areas: in southwest WA is Margaret River, off the Great Ocean Road in Victoria lies Bells Beach, while Cactus Beach is found near Penong in South Australia (SA). Geraldton (WA) is a windy windsurfing mecca.

There's good surfing to be found *somewhere* in New Zealand year round; Ragland is rightly famed and Dunedin has the best spots in the South Island. Other southern locations include Greymouth, Kaikoura and Westport. Up north, Matakana Island, Tauranga and Whangamata have possibilities.

Trekking & Mountaineering

The South Pacific is not renowned for jungle trekking but it's possible on some larger islands. The best-known walking trail in PNG is the Kokoda Trail but the entire country is criss-crossed by tracks.

Australia and New Zealand have fantastically well-organised trekking and trail infrastructures. Tasmania's trekking is rightly famed. The Overland Track (plus plenty of other walks in Cradle Mountain-Lake St Clair National Park) and the tough South Coast Track are tremendous highlights. Elsewhere in Australia don't discount rugged, arid, rewarding hikes in the West MacDonnell Range (Northern Territories; NT), the Flinders Ranges (SA), the Thorsborne Trail (Hinchinbrook Island, Queensland), the Blue Mountains and Snowy Mountains (NSW & Victoria) and the long and winding Bibbulmun Track that offers one of the best ways to see WA's southern forests.

Many of these regions offer fantastic rock climbing but also check out Victoria's Mt Arapiles and the High Country (Mt Buffalo), Warrumbungle National Park in NSW and Karijini National Park in WA.

Tramping (Kiwi lingo for hiking or trekking) in New Zealand is possible along thousands of kilometres of marked tracks serviced by a network of back-country huts. Much of New Zealand's best trekking is in the national parks of the South Island and includes the Abel Tasman Coastal Track, Routeburn Track, Milford Track and Kepler Track. On the North Island there are the Tongariro Northern Circuit and Whanganui Journey. All will be fairly crowded in summer and Christmas. The best weather is from January to March but any time from November to April should be OK. The Mt Cook region is one of many outstanding mountaineering and climbing areas; others are Mt Aspiring National Park, Lake Taupo, Cambridge around Christchurch, north of Dunedin and Fjordland.

White-water Rafting & Other Watersports

Sea kayaks can be rented on several South Pacific islands including Tonga and Fiji where multi-day trips are available. A couple of hundred people canoe down the Sepik in PNG each year but you'll need some experience and good equipment. There's some fabulous rafting down PNG's turbulent mountain rivers.

Australia's best white-water rafting trips are probably on the upper Murray and Nymboida rivers in NSW and the Tully River in Queensland. Canoeing is possible at Coffs Harbour (NSW) and you can paddle a canoe up Katherine Gorge in Nitmiluk National Park (NT), on the Glenelg River (Victoria), the Ord and Blackwood rivers (WA), Barrington Tops National Park (NSW), the Coorong (SA), the quiet waters of the Murray River National Park (SA) and the Franklin (Tasmania).

New Zealand's rafting highlights include the Rangitata River (one of best), Shotover Canyon and the Kawarau River in the South Island. In the North Island, the Wairoa River is popular, so are the Kaituna Cascades. Cave or black-water rafting involves donning a wetsuit then floating along underground rivers (sometimes filled with eels!) such as the Waitomo, Westport and Greymouth. Canoeing is popular on the Whanganui River and Lake Taupo in the North Island and numerous lakes in the South Island. Renowned areas for sea kayaking are the Hauraki Gulf, Bay of Islands and Coromandel in the North Island plus the Marlborough Sounds, Fjordland, along the coast of Abel Tasman National Park and Milford Sound in the South.

Jet-boats are ideal for shallow and white water and the Shotover and Kawarau rivers near Queenstown are renowned jet-boating locations.

Canyoning (heading through tough rapids, waterfalls and the like by jumping and abseiling) is possible near Queenstown.

Wildlife Watching
Migrating humpback and southern right whales pass close to Australia's southern shores between May and November. Popular whale-watching spots include Eden (NSW), Warrnambool (Victoria), Albany (WA), and Hervey Bay and Fraser Island in Queensland. Dolphins can be seen year round at many places on the east coast (Jervis Bay, Port Stephens, Byron Bay), WA (Bunbury, Rockingham, Esperance, Monkey Mia) and Victoria (Sorrento, Gippsland). Kangaroo Island (SA) is another great wildlife-watching destination.

Kaikoura on the South Island is New Zealand's centre for marine-mammal watching. You can swim with dolphins and seals, while sperm whales can be seen here October to August. You can swim with dolphins at Whakatane, Paihia, and Tau or cage dive with sharks at Kaikoura. There are numerous opportunities to dive with sharks in Australia – whale sharks (and other species) can be seen at Ningaloo Reef (WA) but strict rules forbid you from touching or riding the sharks!

Other Activities
There's excellent horse riding in the Snowy Mountains and Great Dividing Range (NSW). There are also extended horse treks out of Alice Springs (NT) and in the Kimberley (WA), where supported multi-day treks are possible. In New Zealand great horse trekking destinations include Taupo, the Coromandel Peninsula, Pakiri, Kaikoura, around Mt Cook, Dunedin, and the West Coast national parks. Camels are alternative animal transport in Australia and two-week adventures are possible out of Alice Springs plus shorter trips in Broome (WA) and SA.

Fraser Island is just one of the places in Australia where you can test your 4WD driving skills. Rap jumping takes place near Cairns, among other places – it's basically running down a cliff tied to a rope and pulley (it's brown-trouser stuff).

The best places for caving in New Zealand are around Auckland, Westport and Waitomo (which offers a spectacular 100m abseil into the 'Lost World').

Bungee-jumping is big near Cairns and on the Gold Coast of Australia but the biggest jumps are in New Zealand – the Nevis Highwire (134m) is the region's highest jump but the Pipeline on the Shotover River is no slouch (102m).

There are numerous places where you can try tandem skydiving on the Queensland Coast. You can have a go at paragliding and hang-gliding near Queenstown and Te Mata Peak or Hawkes Bay in New Zealand, plus near Tamworth (NSW) in Australia.

WORK A LITTLE

God bless those 18-30 working visas (you can still work when you're 31 but you need to apply shortly after your 30th birthday). Australia and New Zealand are not without their unemployment problems and at the time of writing Australia was suffering one of its worst ever droughts which has heavily affected farming, but there are loads of work opportunities if you're not that fussy. Fruit-picking (often poorly paid) is a good one (January to April in New Zealand, year round in Australia) and there are always options in the service industry (bar work, working in a ski resort etc), staffing the desk of some backpackers' hostel (you'll get board and lodging at least), working on a cattle/sheep station as a jackeroo/jillaroo and the crappy jobs you may be all too familiar with. As English is the first language there's plenty of office work, especially for those with secretarial or computer skills.

If you want to get some experience in a particular field or volunteer for work in a particular sector there's no better place to do it. There are loads of volunteer opportunities in Australia including working on organic farms, helping conserve the environment or working in community-run roadhouses. There are some volunteer opportunities in the South Pacific but work is as elusive as Lord Lucan.

Remember that if you're found working illegally in any of these nations you'll be banned from the country and probably deported.

TRAVEL AROUND

Australia is so vast (and so empty in places) that a huge number of long-distance trips are made by air. Qantas is the major domestic player and offers the Boomerang Pass (which can include the South Pacific) but new boy Virgin Blue (W www.virginblue.com.au) regularly offers cheaper deals (and makes Qantas' airpass uneconomical). A number of small airlines emerged from the wreckage of Ansett (now defunct). Air New Zealand dominates the Kiwi domestic market but Origin Pacific (W www.originpacific.co.nz) sometimes offers cheaper fares.

Cheap discounted internal flights are becoming the norm in Australia and New Zealand but also check out round-the-world (RTW) tickets that include internal flights. If you've booked a ticket into, say, Melbourne you can sometimes get a free stopover in Sydney if your flight touches down there first.

In PNG and the South Pacific air travel is the only realistic way of getting around the region. Happily Polynesian Airlines (W www.polynesianairlines.com) and Air New Zealand form the backbone of a number of air passes and there are many others covering the whole region and individual island groups that can help cut costs (see W www.southpacific.org/air.html for details).

The major long-distance bus companies in Australia are Greyhound Pioneer (W www.greyhound.com.au) and McCafferty's (W www.mccaffertys.com.au). Tackling the main routes and a few tourist attractions off major roads are Oz Experience (W www.ozexperience.com; they have a huge network), and The Wayward Bus (W www.waywardbus.com.au), two of many companies offering a more 'alternative' bus network. Various bus passes are available for these services.

InterCity (W www.intercitycoach.co.nz) is the biggest Kiwi bus company, with Kiwi Experience (W www.kiwiex.co.nz) offering a hop-on hop-off bus service. There are loads of other shuttle buses racing around the country.

In PNG and the South Pacific, bus services are rarely ruthlessly efficient and are often family run operations using small Japanese minibuses.

Australia and New Zealand have skeletal rail networks. In Australia trains are usually slower and more expensive than buses. In New Zealand trains are modern, quick and expensive. Rail passes are available in Australia, where the Ghan service between Adelaide and Alice Springs is a classic.

Many visitors group together and hire or purchase a car/4WD/campervan and there are some wonderful 4WD outback tracks in Australia. Some hire companies run cheap 'drive away' vehicle-delivery services, which can be an economical way of getting from A to B. Lift sharing is a better bet than hitching (which is not completely safe) across the vast distances of Australia but in New Zealand many travellers find hitching a good way of getting around.

There are ferries between Melbourne and Tasmania and between the North and South islands of New Zealand and that's about it other than the odd river pleasure cruise. Passenger ships, freighters, charters, outboard dinghies and canoes are used to get around PNG and individual South Pacific islands. Boat travel between South Pacific island groups is surprisingly rare and passages on freighters expensive (about the same, if not more, than flying). However, one for adventurous souls is the rarely used canoe route from Nukumanu in PNG to the Ontong Java in Malaita Province in the Solomon Islands.

From May to October experienced sailors can find some crewing in Samoa, Fiji, Tonga and Auckland. Scout around Sydney in April but watch out for male 'single handers' who insist on female crew only.

Classic Routes

Routes in the South Pacific are dominated by potential RTW ticket routings and air-pass variations. Things are much easier in Australia and New Zealand.

The most popular route in Australia is up the east coast from Melbourne to the rainforest beyond Cairns. You could add to this the wonderful section of coastal road in Victoria, west from Melbourne to Warrnambool known as the Great Ocean Road before continuing into NSW for the cosmopolitan splendour and good times of Sydney, temperate Blue Mountains and chilled out (yet action-packed) Byron Bay. Heading north into Queensland is the great sands of Fraser Island, the Whitsunday Islands, the Great Barrier Reef and the remarkable rainforest of Cape Tribulation.

This classic east-coast route can be extended into NT by cutting west through Mt Isa to Tennant Creek and then north to the canyons, water wonders and Aboriginal rock paintings of Nitmiluk (Katherine Gorge) National Park near Katherine. East of Darwin is Kakadu National Park, one of the most wonderful environments and centres of Aboriginal culture in Australia.

Of course the most comprehensive way to 'do' Australia is to make a loose, lop-sided figure of eight around the country in an extension of the east-coast route. Once into the NT, cut down from Tennant Creek to Uluru (Ayers Rock) and the wonderful MacDonnell Ranges near Alice Springs before heading north to the treasures of northern NT. From there go southwest into sparsely populated Western Australia (WA), through the Kimberley to Broome, then south through the Pilbara, Shark Bay and Geraldton. South of Perth you may want to visit Margaret River and the old-growth 'tall forests' in the far south, before crossing the Nullarbor Plain to Port Augusta in SA where the Flinders Ranges are a great distraction. Once back in Melbourne you can catch the ferry to Devonport and explore the majestic trekking region that is Tasmania.

A great alternative for your travels through Australia would be to use Lonely Planet's excellent *Aboriginal Australia & the Torres Strait* or *Watching Wildlife: Australia*. You'll certainly get a totally different perspective on the country than most gappers do.

Getting to New Zealand from Australia can be expensive (£220 return) so consider building it into a RTW ticket. New Zealand is more manageable than Australia but many gappers don't allow enough time for the country. If time is short it's still worth planning a route or concentrating on either North Island or South Island. From Auckland the first stop could be the Bay of Islands before moving through the centre of the North Island (taking in Rotorua, Lake Taupo and Tongariro National Park) to Wellington. The South Island can be pretty well explored in a large loop but be sure to visit the Nelson area and Abel Tasman National Park before heading along the west coast (taking in the delights of the Southern Alps) to Milford Sound. Queenstown then beckons, or you could head around the remote southern coast before turning to the east coast to Christchurch.

When to Go?

Any time is a good time to be in Australia and the weather in New Zealand is never so miserable that there's no point in visiting: there's stuff happening year round. Overall, spring (September to October) and autumn (April to May) are probably the best times to travel – the weather is reasonably mild everywhere, and spring brings out the wildflowers in the outback. In autumn it's particularly beautiful around Canberra and in the Victorian Alps.

In Papua New Guinea many roads are impassable in the wet season (December to March), while in the South Pacific the shoulder seasons, October and May, have fewer crowds and lower prices (most visitors arrive with higher prices in the dry season, May to October). Around Christmas flights get booked out as islanders return home. This festive traffic affects the rest of Australasia too (local accommodation and transport is very busy) and there's a surge of interest in tickets to the region from Britain once autumn arrives.

CLIMATE

Summer (December to February) brings warm pleasant weather to New Zealand and turns many parts of Australia (especially the southern states) uncomfortably hot. In northern Australia this is the wet season, when it's very, very humid and when the sea swarms with box jellyfish. The North Island of New Zealand can be quite pleasant at anytime of year, although the west of the country is generally wetter than the east. New Zealand has a changeable maritime climate and winters (June to August) are a lot harsher than in Australia but snow is seldom seen near sea level. Australian winters can be quite miserable in NSW but this is the perfect time to visit Queensland, NT (which will have dried up) and the outback.

In the South Pacific, south of the equator the dry season runs from May to October and the wet season is November to April. North of the equator (ie, Micronesia) the seasons are more or less reversed. It's always hot but during the wet season, heat, humidity and rain can make things uncomfortable, and in some places there's a risk of cyclones.

FESTIVALS

Australasia is not normally a place you'll need to look far for a party but if you can, check out some of the following:

Festival of Sydney (Australia) includes open-air concerts, street theatre, fireworks and loads of other stuff in January.

Rugby Sevens Tournaments (Fiji, Samoa & the Cook Islands), hugely popular annual Pacific rugby competitions (January/March), feature much dance and celebration as well as rugby .

Summer City Programme (New Zealand) is essentially a series of festivals around Wellington in January/February.

Marlborough Food & Wine Festival (New Zealand) sanctions the consumption of great quantities of quality food and booze in mid-February in Blenheim.

International Festival of the Arts (New Zealand) brings an entire month of national and international culture to Wellington in February (even-numbered years only).

Womadelaide (Australia) is Adelaide's outdoor festival of world music and dance held during February/March in odd-numbered years.

Gay & Lesbian Mardi Gras (Australia) is Sydney's massive, outlandish celebration in February/March. Rivalled by Melbourne's Midsumma Festival in January/February.

Golden Shears Sheep-Shearing Contest (New Zealand) is a must for lovers of sheep, scat and sweat. It's held in Masterton in March.

Beer Can Regatta (Australia) is an August series of boat races in Darwin open to craft constructed entirely of beer cans.

Mt Hagen Show (Papua New Guinea) is a big gathering of clans, with traditional dances and dress, in late August.

Henley-on-Todd (Australia) is Alice Spring's unusual boat race 'run' on a dry river bed in September.

Canterbury Show Week (New Zealand), with agricultural exhibits, rides, local entertainment and livestock in Christchurch during November.

Festival of Pacific Arts is held in October every four years (the next one is 2004) in a different Pacific country. It's a celebration of art, crafts, dance and song.

Hawaiki Nui Va'a (French Polynesia) draws canoes from many Pacific nations to a race between the islands of Huahine, Raiatea, Tahaa and Bora Bora in October.

Stompen Ground Festival (Australia) is held in Broome during October to celebrate Aboriginal arts and culture. Similar is Barunga Wugularr Sports & Cultural Festival held near Katherine in June.

Melbourne Cup (Australia) is the country-stopping horse race on the first Tuesday in November.

South Pacific Games are held every four years in a different location around the Pacific. The 2003 games were in Fiji.

Christian festivals are a big deal in the South Pacific, so if you're around for Christmas or Easter prepare for much merriment.

What to Expect?
TRAVELLERS
Australia and New Zealand attract a huge range of travellers to their backpacker paradises and you're sure to find some like-minded souls among the wide range of creeds, colours and personalities. At some point most travellers are drawn to one of the following backpacker hangouts and traveller magnets. Not all of them are places to chill:

Cook Islands & Tuvalu (South Pacific) – the most laid-back slices of paradise you're likely to find.

Wellington (New Zealand) – a major good-time town and travel crossroads.

Nelson (New Zealand) – great base for beach life and top tourist activities.

Queenstown (New Zealand) – the resort/party town of the South Island, with heaps of high-octane adventures.

Sydney (Australia) – there's a high gapper count in this city that's great for job-seekers and beach bums alike.

Byron Bay (Australia) – one of the most laid-back and cosmopolitan spots on the east coast.

Cairns (Australia) – humid, buzzing and gregarious place and launching point for so much

Airlie Beach, Magnetic Island and **Mission Beach (Australia)** – renowned traveller hangouts on the glorious Whitsunday and North Queensland coasts.

Melbourne (Australia) – refined, cosmopolitan Sydney rival and a great town for dining and generally enjoying oneself.

Cape Tribulation (Australia) – great, tranquil piece of rainforest paradise in Northern Queensland.

Kalbarri and Broome (Australia) – remote but popular west-coast bases for adventure.

LOCALS

Australia and New Zealand are essentially multicultural societies. Until WWII, Australians were predominantly of Anglo-Celtic descent but that has changed dramatically as people from Greece, Italy, Yugoslavia, Lebanon and Turkey arrived after the war. Australasian populations have been supplemented by more recent influxes of immigrants from Polynesia and Asia. There are about 380,000 Aborigines and Torres Strait Islanders in Australia and 530,000 Maoris in New Zealand.

Sport is the Australasian religion (the Ozzies are world beaters in far too many of them) and many Australians and Kiwis occasionally take the opportunity to take the mick out of us Poms (which comes from POME, Prisoner of Mother England), especially about British sporting failings. People are friendly, gregarious and will often go out of their way to help you (especially in New Zealand). There are a lot of preconceptions about Australasians. Certainly they are not wage slaves, there's a strong emphasis on the quality of life and they like a good drink (and/or smoke) but not everyone is a surfing beach bum. Generally the work/life balance is about right and society is very wide ranging.

The South Pacific has some pretty diverse codes of social behaviour and, as in PNG, Christian missionaries have been extraordinarily influential and in some cases reinforced already conservative (contrary to popular belief) social traditions. Tahiti and the Cook Islands remain pretty easy-going but covering up is a rather uncomfortable requirement in island nations like Tonga and modest dress appreciated generally. The peoples of PNG and the South Pacific are proud and nationalistic. Their societies have a strong clan and hier-archical structure with a noble class at the top. Some people are, at best, pretty ambivalent about travellers although a clean and presentable appearance goes a long way to ensuring a warm welcome.

LANGUAGE

English is the dominant language of the region. Lonely Planet's phrasebook to *Australian* allows you to understand the hotchpotch of Ozzie slang as well as some of the many Aboriginal and Torres Strait languages.

English and Maori are the two official languages in New Zealand. English is more widely spoken, though the Maori language is making a comeback. A mellifluous, poetic language, Maori is surprisingly easy to pronounce if spoken phonetically and each word split into separate syllables.

Over 750 languages (about 30% of the world's indigenous languages) are spoken in PNG. Pidgin (or Neo-Melanesian) is the popular lingua franca. Covered in a Lonely Planet phrase-book, Pidgin is primarily derived from English and German but only covers about 1300 words. Many educated people prefer to speak English. Another popular language is Motu (or 'Police Motu'), the local second language of the Port Moresby coastal area.

The South Pacific is a similar mass of languages but French or English are usually spoken wherever you go. Lonely Planet's *South Pacific Phrasebook* covers some of these languages, plus Maori.

HEALTH RISKS

Australia and New Zealand are very healthy places. A few cases of mosquito-borne diseases (such as dengue fever, Ross River fever and Murray Valley encephalitis) are reported in northern Australia. You can get amoebic meningitis from bathing in New Zealand's natural hot thermal pools and a few unclean lakes and rivers transmit giardia but that's about it.

The most unhealthy countries in the region are PNG, the Solomon Islands and Vanuatu where malaria is endemic and a raft of vaccinations are required.

Putting aside the sharks, snakes, spiders, box jellyfish and other poisonous Australian creatures, the weather poses the greatest risk to health in the region. The sun is fierce and heat exhaustion, dehydration and sunburn a constant threat. Prolonged sun exposure causes cancer, as many Australians will testify to. In New Zealand, exposure and hypothermia are real dangers to unprepared trekkers at high altitude. Also be aware of the strength of the sun (you can burn in as little as six minutes in some places).

Consult the Health chapter in Part I and seek professional medical advice for more travel health information.

TIME & FLIGHT TIME

Australia is divided into Eastern Standard Time (Greenwich Mean Time, GMT, + 10 hours) Central Time (GMT + 9½ hours) and Western Time (GMT + eight hours). New Zealand is 12 hours ahead of GMT. Both Kiwi clocks and most areas of Australia's clocks are put forward one hour between October and March. South Pacific nations are split by the International Date Line, which puts Tonga 13 hours ahead of GMT while Samoa, a short hop to the north, is 11 hours *behind* GMT and therefore exactly one day behind.

There are no direct flights into the region, all aircraft stop at least once. This means that Sydney is a 22-hour flight away from London. Darwin (19 hours) and Perth (21 hours) are closer, Auckland farther away (26½ hours). If you want to fly direct to Nadi (Fiji) a cheap ticket often involves 35 hours and two stops.

ISSUES

There are few tricky borders or hotspots in the region but PNG and the Solomon Islands still give cause for concern, while events in Fiji seem to have calmed down. You're advised not to visit the Southern Highlands Province of PNG and in other Highlands Provinces, Port Moresby and Lae the law-and-order situation remains very poor. Assaults, robbery, vehicle hijacks, random shootings and serious sexual assaults are common. However, while it has its problems PNG has been the subject of considerable negative reportage and most travellers experience no problems. We recommend listening to local advice and, above all, making friends with the people who live in the area you are visiting.

The Solomon Islands have been a dog's breakfast since the coup in June 2000, and although the MEF (representing ethnic Malaitans on Guadalcanal Island) and the IFM (representing natives of Guadalcanal) are technically still at peace there are problems with lawlessness. You should not venture into parts of rural Guadalcanal, or onto the island of Malaita without checking the situation locally. Visits to other provinces in the Solomon Islands are generally trouble-free.

For further information on travel hotspots, general safety issues and governmental travel advice see Safety in Part I.

INTERNET & COMMUNICATIONS

Internet access, pay-as-you-go mobile phones and cheap-as phonecards (call the UK for less than 5p a minute!) are widely available in Australia and New Zealand. In the Pacific things are a little more hit and miss but islands are slowly getting connected to mobile phones and the internet.

Daily Spend

From a UK perspective Australia looks pretty cheap. Food, in particular, is great value (a good feed in a food court costs around £3) and £6 is going to get you a pretty reasonable dorm bed. Conceivably you could get by on £20 a day but the social nature of travelling in Australia adds greatly to your costs (a *pot*, half pint, of beer costs about 90 pence). New Zealand is, if anything, a little more expensive.

If camping or staying in hostels you can often self-cater and while not all the good things in life cost money (walking, swimming, bird-watching or sitting under palm trees is free!), many enjoyable activities are expensive and can end up making a big dent in your budget. Running a vehicle can save you money (especially if you find paying passengers) or be a milestone around your neck, so think hard before buying one.

Costs in the South Pacific vary greatly but it's certainly not a budget destination and is a little more expensive than Australia or New Zealand (you could scrape by on just over £20 a day). If you're on a short stopover and not intending to move around that much you will save some cash but some islands extract small fortunes from tourists – French Polynesia and New Caledonia are very expensive. Imported goods like film and packaged foods are always expensive but local food and lodging can be reasonably priced – Samoa and the Cook Islands aren't too bad. PNG has no tradition of cheap hotels and restaurants, so the towns can be very expensive.

Getting There

AIR

Virtually all gappers arrive in the region by air. RTW tickets with a couple of stops in Asia are very popular but there are a number of simple return fares that offer stopovers in South America and the Middle East as well as Asia. More than one 'on-line' stopover is permitted by some airlines (see the Round the World chapter for details) and some airlines offer more stopovers, open-jaw options and general flexibility on this route than others.

The main international hubs are Sydney, Melbourne, Perth and Auckland, although some airlines offer connections into Brisbane, Darwin, Wellington, Hobart, Cairns, Canberra and Adelaide. In the South Pacific, Nadi (Fiji), Papeete (French Polynesia) and Apia (Samoa) are regular stop-offs for jets coming from the USA (Air New Zealand flights from Los Angeles stop in a number of South Pacific islands) but many South Pacific destinations are serviced via Sydney or Auckland.

The major airlines servicing the long haul from Britain are Qantas, British Airways (BA), Singapore Airlines, Cathay Pacific, Emirates, Malaysian Airlines, Royal Brunei, Korean Airlines, Virgin, Thai Airways and Air New Zealand. Shop around; this is a highly competitive route.

Consult the Airlines Appendix at the back of the book for more information on airlines and routes.

Ticket Costs

The best available student/under-26 fares are quoted here. See Passports, Tickets, Visas & Insurance in Part I for more information on how to get the best, most flexible deal.

At the time of writing the cheapest return fare into Sydney (£575) was with Korean Airlines and included a stop in Seoul. However, the cheapest flights into the region were with Royal Brunei (£570) who allowed several 'on-line' stopovers en route to Perth – you could also fly out of Darwin at no extra cost. The cheapest flights into Melbourne were with Austria Airlines (£630) via Vienna and Kuala Lumpur.

Open-jaw tickets using Australasian cities cost around £640, sometimes less depending on the combination of cities. Malaysia Airlines were offering more expensive deals to Australia but with good stopover options in a couple of Southeast Asian destinations.

The cheapest fares to Auckland were with Korean Airlines (£625) but a better deal is with Air New Zealand which allows a stop in Los Angeles (£594) and for another £100 you can stop in Rarotonga (Cook Islands) too. Tickets to Nadi (Fiji) cost £625 with Korean Airlines.

SEA & OVERLAND

Hard-travelling gappers can make it all the way to Australia by surface transport via the Middle East and Southeast Asia. You could even avoid the short plane journey from Bali or Timor into the region by heading to PNG from Papua (Indonesia). Currently the most common way of doing this is to charter a boat (£30 per person) from Jayapura in Papua to Vanimo in PNG. The regular ferry service seems a thing of the past and the land border is sometimes open, usually closed.

SPECIALIST TOUR OPERATORS

Loads of British tour operators would be only too happy to book you onto one of their many trips within Australasia (see the Global Tour Companies Appendix at the back of the book) but with so many top-quality local operations (all listed in Lonely Planet's guidebooks) this is not necessary and often more expensive.

Australia, New Zealand, the Pacific & Beyond

Tickets to Africa, South America, North America and Asia are all reasonable from Australia and New Zealand. However, cheaper visits to these countries could be arranged through a RTW ticket bought in the UK.

If you've just bought a one-way to Australia (which is perfectly possible) there are some great overland trips back home. You could get a flight to Indonesia and follow the old Hippie Trail or head north to China and take the Trans-Siberian Railway from Beijing to Moscow.

Further Information
READING MATERIAL

Lonely Planet publishes guides to numerous islands, nations, regions and cities in Australasia. There are also excellent guides to *Aboriginal Australia & the Torres Strait Islands*, *East Coast Australia*, *Healthy Travel Australia*, *New Zealand & The Pacific* and *Watching Wildlife: Australia* plus a number of walking, diving and cycling guides.

A sympathetic account of Australia's Aboriginal peoples is given by Richard Broome in *Aboriginal Australia* and *Kings in Grass Castles*, by Dame Mary Durack, paints a picture of the early cattle-station pioneers. *Te Ao Hurihuri: Aspects of Maoritanga*, by Michael King, concerns Maori culture.

Sean & David's Long Drive, by Sean Condon, is an amusing tale of two ill-equipped urban Australians faced with the vastness of their own country. Bill Bryson's *Down Under* offers more amusing anecdotes. *My Place*, by Sally Morgan, is a disturbing account about the stolen generation of Aboriginal children. *Tracks*, by Robyn Davidson, is an amazing tale of one woman, the western deserts and camels, *Songlines*, by Bruce Chatwin, is a classic travelogue about Australia and Howard Jacobson recounts a circuit of the country in *In the Land of Oz*.

A great account of travels through the South Seas is *Slow Boats Home*, by Gavin Young, the sequel to *Slow Boats to China*. Paul Theroux's *The Happy Isles of Oceania – Paddling the Pacific* is a downbeat/miserable account of his travels through the region but *Tonga Islands: William Mariner's Account*, by Dr John Martin, is a fascinating read. *Wanderings in the Interior of New Guinea*, by Captain JA Lawson, is an implausible but entertaining travelogue of never-again-seen Mt Hercules (higher than Mt Everest), waterfalls larger than Niagara, the New Guinea tiger, giant daisies, humungous scorpions and other curiosities.

USEFUL INFORMATION SOURCES

For specific country overviews, the low-down on travel in the region and hundreds of useful links head first to Lonely Planet's website (**W** www.lonelyplanet.com).

The following portals and useful websites should help you chase down any aspect of interest in the region:

- **W** www.pacificislands.com – useful and factual travel information.
- **W** www.sidsnet.org/pacific/sprep – information on the South Pacific Environment Programme.
- **W** www.aboriginalaustralia.com – covers culture, art and tourism.
- **W** www.australiaonline.com.au – off-beat site packed with information.
- **W** www.csu.edu.au/education/australia.html – a mine of useful information with links to government organisations.
- **W** www.bushwise.co.nz – women-specific information about accommodation and activities.
- **W** www.doc.govt.nz – Department of Conservation site with practical information.
- **W** www.kiwinewz.com – up-to-date and packed with information about Queenstown and the Southern Lakes.

Been There, Done That

Apparently only 3% of people fail to 'find romance' after leaving Sydney for the East Coast Trail. This information was passed on to me while playing a quiz in a bar in Alice Springs, which required drinking lots and taking your clothes off. I'm not sure if I was a winner or loser. Certainly Rick, who I was with, was a definite loser and got nabbed by the police coming home from the pub – he was doing a dying fly in the road with all his cards and money spread over the pavement. Classic form. He later pissed off everyone in the dorm by playing disco with the light switch. Somehow we managed to get up and make it to Kings Canyon the next day, which was just incredible, although the heat and the sun dehydrated us completely.

At Uluru we splashed out on Pioneers Lodge, went on an Aboriginal guided walk and spent time watching the rock at sunset. Unfortunately it was one of the 8 to 12 times a year it rains. Still learnt a Top Tip to scam free food, namely smuggling your own paper plates and meat into the hostel BBQ and then eating your fill of self-service salad, spuds etc.

Five days later we'd done a free-fall parachute jump near Cairns, spent two nights fruitlessly socialising in the Woolshed and then fled further north to Cape Trib where we met Big Mick, Snake Catcher and whole bunch of real Ozzie characters full of stories. Rick and I both did two scuba dives on the reef going down about 8 to 10 metres. A magic day, saw loads of fish, we are completely addicted and can't wait to do it again.   Bando Sharratt

North America & the Caribbean

Introduction

TV and cinema have made North America seem familiar but the scale of the place and scope of possibilities will stagger you. There's so much space, such a diversity of environments and an overwhelming number of fast-food outlets. The Caribbean is a very different proposition, unique in attitude and atmosphere but influenced strongly by its great neighbour. Love it or hate it, North America has left its mark on us too but to understand the place, forget what you think you know and instead immerse yourself in it. North America is one huge, wonderful playground for those who can afford the entrance fee.

Why North America & the Caribbean?

The USA is the greatest success story of the modern world – a nation fashioned from an incredibly disparate population whose desire to choose their own paths to wealth or heaven, forged the richest, most inventive and powerful country on earth. It's quite a story, although Canada would have to be a pretty hefty sub-plot. It can be hard work dismantling your preconceptions about North America. So much of the country has been filmed, photographed, painted and written about that you need to peel back layers of representation to stop it from looking like a wonderful stage set.

Bumbling around America and Canada is just about the antithesis of travelling in India. It's not even like touring Europe. There aren't piles of ancient monuments, churches or relics of ancient cultures to visit. Instead, historical sites often relate to the pioneers of a great continent and the monuments are about triumph over a new land. However, arguably it's the natural wonders that are the real highlights; the Grand Canyon, Niagara Falls, Yosemite National Park, Monument Valley, the Florida Everglades, Hawaii's volcanoes and the fjords, islands and glaciers of the inside passage in Alaska. What's more there's virtually no activity you can't partake in. Looking to devote your gap year to hip-hop? No problem. Have a desire to become a skateboard guru or nude freefall parachutist? Go right ahead, you won't be alone and someone will show you how.

Despite polemicists who justly cite the destruction of Native American cultures, racism and imperialism at the top of a long list of wrong-doings, half the world still remains in love with the idea of America, a land where some of the world's most exciting cities and mind-blowing landscapes are found, and where anything is possible.

Most people's concept of Canada goes little beyond appreciating its vastness and recognising its flag but this nation has a complex three-dimensional character influenced by English, French (Québec is definitely more croissants than hamburgers) and Native American culture. Those expecting Canada to be a blander counterpart of the USA should check their preconceptions at the door. Canada's wild northern frontier has etched itself into the national psyche, and its distinct patchwork of peoples has created a country that is decidedly different from its southern neighbour.

What both nations have in common is a strong sense of regionalism, a trenchant mythology, more history than you'd think and some of the most approachable natives in the world.

The march of time has not flattened the myths about Greenland. The aurora borealis (Northern Lights), the vast tundra, the glittering columns of ice and the monstrous glaciers are one part of the picture; igloos, dogsleds and proverbially tight-lipped Inuit are another.

But any land that has a mirage-inducing atmosphere capable of turning a dog turd on the horizon into a sailing ship has got to be worth visiting.

The Caribbean provides a suitable antithesis to North American go-getting. Laid-back was invented here but it is not just package-tourist heaven. Jamaica has deep social problems that have their roots in colonialism and slavery. The Dominican Republic is a pretty good advert for Caribbean paradise (white-sand beaches, impressive mountains and exotic fish and wildlife) and you can just about survive as an independent traveller. Communist Cuba struggles on and you pay for the privilege of seeing this great country with the currency of the oppressor, the US dollar. Haiti is out of the gapper's loop, along with much of the Eastern Caribbean, where £500-a-night resorts and private beaches are pretty common, but the Caribbean region does offer a little hope for the gapping traveller.

What to Do?

Many gappers start their North American adventures working in a summer camp or on a student work programme before spending a few months travelling around. Others go for it big style, buying a car and travelling the highways and byways for as long as their money holds out.

North America is a great place to pursue a single interest (eg, charity work, conservation, teaching) or activity but getting a visa for training or a course is getting difficult. See Part III for more information on overseas jobs, volunteer work and courses.

GET ACTIVE

North America and the Caribbean have world-class locations for just about any activity you care to mention. No matter what you're into you'll find a perfect spot to do it and folks to do it with in America.

Caving

North America is big underground. Caving is possible in New Mexico's beautiful Carlsbad Caverns, the Lehman Caves in Nevada or Mammoth Cave in Kentucky (one of the world's largest cave systems with 540 kilometres of passages). Jamaica is honeycombed with limestone caves and caverns, particularly in the west, and experienced cavers have the extensive underground sections of the Camuy River to explore in Puerto Rico.

Top 10 Must-Sees

The Grand Canyon (USA) – it'll blow you away whatever your preconceptions.
New Orleans (USA) – music, Mardi Gras and Creole culture.
Monument Valley (USA) – the desert parks and landscape of the Southwest are a must.
Inside Passage (Alaska) – some of the continent's most stunning scenery.
Niagara Falls (Canada) – premier tourist attraction, marvellous and garish.
Vancouver Island (Canada) – fantastic wilderness, beauty and adventure activities.
Havana (Cuba) – faded glory, Spanish colonial architecture and '50s American cars.
Kingston (Jamaica) – reggae, cultural vibrancy and great cricket.
Death Valley (USA) – the second-hottest place on earth.
Badlands South Dakota (USA) – rugged, beautiful landscapes in the Dakotas and Nebraska.

Cycling & Mountain Biking

Mountain biking is huge, particularly in California (where it was invented). Cycle touring in the forests of New England, the islands off the Atlantic coast, southern Louisiana and California's Wine Country can be recommended. In Canada, the Laurentian Mountains of Québec and the Rockies of Alberta and British Columbia are great mountain-biking locations. Cycling is a great way to get around Caribbean islands.

Diving

Diving is good year round in Hawaii where underwater caves, canyons, lava tubes, vertical walls, sunken ships and the sunken volcanic crater of Molokini await exploration. Elsewhere in the USA, the Great Lakes, Florida Keys (where you can dive with sharks) and southern California have great potential. The Caribbean is where the diving really rocks, St Lucia, Dominica, Tobago, St Vincent and the Grenadines being among the regular favourites. Cuba has world-class dive sites and 30-odd dive centres. Diving among the shipwrecks along the Dominican Republic's north coast and coral gardens on the warmer southern coast is deservedly popular. Haiti has black coral and stunning underwater geology and there are hundreds of picture-postcard coral reefs off islands in the Eastern Caribbean.

Skiing & Snowsports

Alaska, Canada, Greenland and the USA have an incredible amount of cross-country skiing. The main alpine ski centres in Canada are in Ontario, Québec, Alberta and around Whistler in British Columbia. In the USA, the Rocky Mountain states (Colorado in particular) host the most popular ski fields, including Aspen, Vail, Jackson Hole and Big Sky. Lake Tahoe is Sierra Nevada's major ski destination.

Dog-sledging is very popular in Alaska, Canada and Greenland. Trips can last for a few hours or a few weeks. Ice-skating and ice hockey are popular Canadian pastimes.

Surfing & Windsurfing

Surfing is king in Hawaii. Waves reach monstrous proportions between November and February but beginners can learn the basics at Waikiki and then watch the professionals on Oahu's North Shore. Maui draws top international windsurfers like moths to a candle. California also has a few surfable breaks – Malibu, Rincon, Trestles and Mavericks among them. There are a hundred other decent breaks along the US coastline.

Canada has some chilly surfing off Nova Scotia and in the warmer waters off Melmerby and Caribou near New Glasgow.

There are a few surf spots in Cuba and some excellent breaks along the north and east coasts of the Dominican Republic.

Trekking, Mountaineering & Climbing

Alaska is pretty out-there when it comes to trekking, climbing and mountaineering. Even in summer the weather can quickly turn harsh and cold. Great tracks include the Chilkoot Trail near Skagway, the Resurrection Pass Trail on the Kenai Peninsula and the Pinnell Mountain Trail near Hyder.

Trekking in Greenland is equally serious but intrepid hikers have spectacular scenery and serious mountaineers a lifetime's supply of rock and ice to get into. Trips onto the ice cap are possible.

In Canada, Killarney Park has a long-distance trail around the tops of its rounded mountains. Other impressively vertical regions include Gaspésie Park and Mont Tremblant Park

(Québec), Gros Morne National Park in Newfoundland and Cape Breton National Park in Nova Scotia. More hardcore trekking can be had in Pukaskwa National Park and the partially completed Trans Canada Trail (can you spare 750 days?).

The USA has even more trekking options ranging from the alpine meadows of the High Sierra to the forested byways of the Appalachian Trail. Also consider desert trails and canyons in the Southwest (it's possible to walk the mile down into the Grand Canyon) and Pacific Crest Trail in the Sierra Nevada. In Hawaii there are Haleakala and Volcanoes national parks, plus a stunning trek along Kauai's Na Pali Coast.

The Caribbean is not renowned for trekking but Cuba has some good options such as the three-day trek over the Sierra Maestra via 2000m-high Pico Turquino. The Central Highlands in the Dominican Republic and most of the country's national parks; embryonic trails in the Blue Mountains in Jamaica; in the rainforest of El Yunque, in the Karst region of Río Camuy Cave Park in Puerto Rico; and cloud forests, alpine meadows and complex limestone cave systems of Macaya and La Visite national parks in Haiti are all interesting possibilities.

Rock climbing and mountaineering are popular in the Sierra Nevada, Rockies and Yosemite National Park (El Capitan and Half Dome are both legendary big wall climbs). Canadian climbing venues include Collingwood, Sault Ste Marie and Thunder Bay in Ontario, Banff and Jasper in Alberta and Squamish in British Colombia. Mt McKinley (6096m) in Alaska is the highest mountain in North America but is the preserve of organised expeditions.

Watersports

In the USA explore the wetlands of Georgia, Louisiana and Florida by boat or take a boat to check out the bioluminescence at Phosphorescent Bay and Esperanza in Puerto Rico. Alaska has some great kayaking opportunities at Misty Fjords, Glacier Bay and Katmai national parks. In Canada try Nova Scotia's Kejimkujik National Park.

Sea kayakers will never look back after paddling Muir Inlet in Glacier Bay National Park or Tracy Arm Fjord, south of Juneau in Alaska. British Columbia and Vancouver Island in Canada and the Pacific Northwest and Maine Atlantic coast in the USA are similarly blessed. In Greenland kayaking trips come with the added excitement of icebergs.

White-water rafting on Idaho's Snake and Colorado rivers are just two among many rafting locations in the Rockies, Sierra Nevada and Appalachian Mountains. 'Tubing' (heading down a river in an old truck tyre), kayaking and canyoning are all popular in the USA and there's white-water rafting on Canada's Ottawa River.

Wildlife Watching

Baby seals await your cooing adoration on the Magdalen Islands of Québec.

Whale-watching is popular in New England and in numerous places around the Caribbean. Killer whales can be seen off Vancouver Island and plenty of other spots in Canada.

Bear-watching is popular in Canada (check out the polar bears in Churchill, Manitoba) and you can see buffalo in Wichita Mountains Wildlife Refuge in Oklahoma. Wolves, mountain lions and bears are found in North American national parks.

Manatees can be seen in Florida, a good place to dive with sharks (if there is a good place).

Other Activities

Some fantastic deep-sea fishing is found off Hawaii and various ports around the USA and Cuba. Most anglers come to North America to fish for rainbow and cut-throat trout, Dolly

Varden, Arctic char and grayling in the remote lakes and rivers of Alaska and Canada. Floatplanes are used to drop anglers at the best spots. Wonderful trout streams are also found in the Rockies, both sides of the border.

Horse riding in Cuba takes place in special tourist ranches at Baconao and Trinidad. In the big sky country of Wyoming, Colorado and Montana, horse riding is cowboy style on huge cattle ranches. Horse riding is a great way to explore Jamaica and most resorts have stables.

The Caribbean is a first-rate sailing destination between November and May. In the USA, New England, North Caroline, Florida and San Francisco are popular sailing locations.

The USA is a cheap place to learn to fly and parachute.

WORK A LITTLE

Getting a work visa is very difficult unless you're part of a student work programme like those run by Bunac (British Universities North America Club). There are loads of opportunities in summer camps, ski resorts and cattle ranches and for au pairing (which is not possible in Canada but booming in the USA – there are five different government programmes). Working illegally is an option but the pay is often terrible and you'll get deported *tout de suite* and be in big trouble if caught. Don't have anything in your luggage to do with job-hunting when you enter North America.

Crewing on yachts in southern USA and the Caribbean is a real possibility (rich folks regularly need deck hands) but in British Caribbean dependencies you'll need a job offer before getting a work visa.

TRAVEL AROUND

Air travel in North America is not as cheap as many people believe, but given the distances involved and vast network this is not surprising. When you look at dollars per mile it's not bad value, but book in advance and try to use Southwest Airlines ([W] www.southwest.com; these guys invented no-frills flying) and Jet Blue ([W] www.jetblue.com). Flying around Greenland, Northern Canada and Alaska can be very expensive but the only way into some remote places. From the USA the cheapest Caribbean flights are into Puerto Rico or the Bahamas. You cannot fly directly between the USA and Cuba – go via Canada. Within the Caribbean flights are costly but like North America a number of air passes are available.

North America's limited train network is a great (if rather expensive) way to get around. Two classic journeys include Toronto to Vancouver and the California Zephyr, which runs through the whole gamut of US environments between Chicago and San Francisco. Toronto is linked to New York and Chicago by train and Montreal to New York.

North America's bus network is extensive. Greyhound ([W] www.greyhound.com) is the biggest player. The bus is derided by many (wealthier) Americans but 'riding the dog' provides an unvarnished view of life in relative comfort and at a decent price (bus passes are available). In rural areas local bus services are often less than adequate.

The Green Tortoise ([W] www.greentortoise.com) provides alternative bus transport around the USA but their services are more like a group-orientated tour. Moose Travel ([W] www.moose network.com) runs a hop-on, hop-off bus service in Canada.

In the Caribbean, buses and minibuses are hit and miss, ranging from air-conditioned luxury to crowded squalor. Jamaica's bus 'system' is the epitome of chaos.

Driving in the USA is a cultural and sensual experience as well as the best way to get off the beaten track. However, if you're under 25 hiring a car is often impossible and insuring your own car can be expensive for under-21s.

Drive-aways are an option for over-21s (see Work Your Route in Part III). Basically you deliver someone's car across some vast distance in a set time.

Car shares are rather casual in the USA (check out hostel noticeboards) and more official in Québec, thanks to the lift-sharing organisation Allo Stop (**W** www.allostop.com).

Hitching is never entirely safe and not recommended (never do it in the USA). However, many travellers happily hitch around Canada and Alaska. If you decide to hitch don't over-stretch yourself – distances between towns are often massive. Hitching in Cuba is pretty common and government vehicles are legally required to pick up hitchhikers if they have the room.

Ferries operate along the Pacific coast of Canada and Alaska. Ferries from Bellingham, Washington take 2 to 4½ days to make the scenic, tranquil trip to Juneau, Alaska. Travelling by boat is an essential option in Greenland; a fleet of coastal ferries runs up and down the west coast from Aappilattoq in the south to Uummannaq in the north.

Jamaica is an easy yachters' hop from neighbouring islands and the eastern seaboard of North America and much of Eastern Caribbean is linked by ferry and freighter services.

Classic Routes

Routes through the Caribbean are pretty easy if you've got money – head down to Florida, across to the Bahamas and then south. Obviously a yacht would be handy but hopping between islands in the Eastern Caribbean is pretty easy.

A good route around Canada follows the Trans Canada Highway (with camp grounds and picnic spots at intervals) from Newfoundland to the Rocky Mountains of Alberta and British Columbia where more options open up. These include the Alaska Highway (the Alcan) or Top-of-the-World Highway (an adventurous option) up into US territory or a thorough exploration of British Columbia, including the wonders of Vancouver Island.

In the USA your route is pretty much a matter of taste. You could make a huge loop around the country, heading up the west coast from California, taking in Yosemite National Park and San Francisco en route to Seattle or Vancouver, before heading east via the Great Lakes and Chicago to New England. From New York you could make your way through the Mid West to the magnificent desert lands and ranges of the Southwest. Alternatively you could head down the Atlantic coast to tropical Florida, before looping around the Gulf of Mexico to the Rocky Mountains. From the Rockies, Las Vegas and the Grand Canyon are relatively close by American standards.

Of course you may want to restrict yourself a little and explore more thoroughly the parks and deserts of the Southwest and Texas; the Rockies, their foothills and surrounding states; or the rivers and forests of New England. Heck, you could do anything, but as fans of American movies know, some of the best Americana is experienced by going on a road trip. Classic routes include:

Route 40 'The National Road' – 952 kilometres of American heritage along the original American highway that stretches from Cumberland, Maryland, to Vandalia, Illinois.

Route 66 'The Mother Road' or **'Main St, USA'** – a classic route from Chicago to Los Angeles (LA). The Great Plains, deserts, old frontier towns, mountains and heaps of Americana all await. Interstate routes have superseded much of the original route that now exists in small sections.

Highway 1 – a classic, winding coastal road that links LA to San Francisco and continues all the way to Seattle.

Highways 163 & 261 – two relatively short but magnificently scenic roads through sandstone monoliths of Utah's Valley of the Gods and Monument Valley.

When to Go?

The comfortable days of June to August are when most tourists flock to Alaska, northern Canada and Greenland. At this time the tundra is a riot of wild flowers and red berries but plagues of mosquitoes and insects can be a problem until September. The 24-hour daylight of high summer brings a wave of slightly unhinged behaviour and loads of festivals in the north. The more remote roads in Alaska and Canada can be driven comfortably between May and September. October brings the aurora borealis, the Northern Lights, and the beginning of cross-country skiing and dog sledging.

For the rest of North America be a little more selective about when to visit, ideally hitting the road in spring or autumn. In this 'shoulder season' (a cheap time to travel in May and September) the summer mobs that descend upon the national parks and other attractions are absent and off-season discounts are available. Autumn is an especially good time to visit New England and the upper Great Lakes because of the totally spectacular autumn foliage. Spring is ideal for the arid Southwest.

The Caribbean, Hawaii and tropical southern USA are pleasant places to visit in winter and autumn but do attract thousands of tourists at this time.

CLIMATE

Most of North America experiences four distinct seasons, the same as Britain, although their time of arrival varies. In the middle third of the continent, summers and winters are extreme.

East of the Rockies the USA is nastily hot and humid during summer, especially in the south. North America's northernmost, western and eastern coasts are very wet, though much of the rain falls during winter. The great North American prairies are fairly dry year round and stay well below freezing in winter. Still, Florida has a tropical climate and California's southern coast is comfortable year round. Hawaii's climate is fantastic, balmy and warm, with northeasterly breezes – the rainiest period is between December and March. Alaska's climate is not known for its consistency but you can be sure that, like northern Canada, temperatures of -45°C aren't uncommon in midwinter. High rainfall and moderate temperatures dominate summer (15–21°C) and there's an unpleasant thaw in May.

George Washington referred to the Bahamas as the 'Isles of Perpetual June,' which pretty much sums up the climate of most of the Caribbean – warm and humid. Generally there's a rainy season running from May to November when the Caribbean and southern USA gets a battering from the occasional hurricane.

FESTIVALS

Festivals and events in small towns and giant cities are common across North America. Many Caribbean towns celebrate various saints and hold colourful and vibrant carnivals. Check out some of the following:

Québec City Winter Carnival (Canada) takes place in mid-February and features parades, ice sculptures, dances and music .

New Orleans' Mardi Gras (USA), a rowdy, touristy, bacchanalian knees-up, takes no prisoners in February/March.

Caribbean Carnivals (Cuba) – Havana parades and indulges in much merriment during late February/early March. Santiago de Cuba is in late July. Santo Domingo's (Dominican Republic) raucous carnival straddles Independence Day (February 27). A second Carnival begins August 15.

Drambuie World Ice Golf Championship (Greenland) is a decidedly wacky golf tournament in late March – Uummannaq Fjord is its stage. Shout 'Fjord!' not 'Fore!'

Kentucky Derby (USA) is Louisville's hugely lucrative horse race held in May.

Summer Solstice (Alaska) brings on midnight baseball, log-chopping, axe-tossing and tree-climbing competitions across the country in almost continuous daylight on June 21.

Moose Dropping Festival (Alaska) is high-class poo chucking held in Talkeetna at the beginning of July.

Vodou Pilgrimages (Haiti) include one to the sacred waters of Saut d'Eau in Ville-Bonheur on July 16 and another one to Plaine du Nord on July 25. The next day many pilgrims move to the town of Limonade, where the feast day of St Anne doubles as a day of respect for the Vodou spirit Erzulie.

Merengue Festival (Dominican Republic) – in July/August Santo Domingo is the epicentre of the Haitian and Dominican dance form.

Reggae Sunsplash and **Reggae Sumfest (Jamaica)**, held about one week apart in July/August in Ocho Rios and Montego Bay respectively, are the biggest beach parties on the island.

National Hobo Convention (USA) is held in Britt, Iowa, in August and is one for truly inveterate travellers.

Antigua Sailing Week (Antigua) is a massive yachting festival in late April and a highlight of the Caribbean.

Burning Man (USA) is a massive, wild, alternative festival held in the Black Rock Desert of Nebraska in the last week of August.

What to Expect?

TRAVELLERS

Your travelling buddies are just as likely to be locals as other visitors but there are a fair number of Northeast Asian, European and antipodean travellers in North America. You'll find very few backpackers in the Eastern Caribbean (it's just too expensive unless you're very selective). There are more travellers in Jamaica and the Dominican Republic and a lot of package tourists too.

Back in North America, California attracts loads of travellers looking for a place to chill. San Antonio attracts country-music fans, Haight-Ashbury in San Francisco drifting alternative types and Venice Beach in Los Angeles all sorts of folks. Certainly San Francisco features pretty heavily in many a gapper's plans but hangouts are tricky to find. Elsewhere New Orleans, Seattle and Vancouver attract many travellers, while Alaska and northern Canada draw those looking for peaceful pastimes. For a cheap, relaxed time head to the free campsites in obscure national forests or go trekking in any of the national parks.

LOCALS

North Americans suffer from some cracking stereotypes, and you're likely to encounter your share of portly, car-obsessed gung-ho and parochial people, who've never been outside of their country. But you'll also find kindred spirits in the most unlikely places and you'll struggle to find a more polite, friendly and helpful people (handy when you go into a café to be presented with 50 choices of bread and coffee).

Immigration (forced or otherwise) is one of the defining characteristics of America's national identity, although this neatly sidesteps Native Americans. In the well-organised society that is the USA, the eastern seaboard is more formal than the west and many people hold strong Christian beliefs. Don't underestimate the scale of national pride, which has grown considerably after September 11. Afro-American culture is strongest in the south, just as Mexican and Latin American culture has an increasing influence in Texas, New Mexico, Arizona and California.

Canadian national identity has been shaped by the harsh realities of life on the northern frontier. Canadians are still discovering their modern identity but for sure it's distinctly different from the character of the USA. Some people see them as a little more reserved, more laid-back, amazingly hospitable, more *sensible* and far from boring.

You may not meet any native peoples travelling randomly through North America but if you make the effort to visit a reservations or tribal land be respectful, polite and don't take photographs without permission.

The Caribbean is relaxed and laid-back, a place of many influences. Populated by the descendants of African slaves, to some extent Africa still influences society and the family but the region also shows the influences of France, Britain and the USA and is home to a high number of expats.

LANGUAGE

English is the dominant language but it can be difficult to understand in the Deep South and Caribbean. French and English are both official languages in Canada but in Québec you'll need to rely on French, which is also spoken around Louisiana in the USA. Spanish is spoken in Cuba, the Dominican Republic and Puerto Rico and immigration from Latin America means that Spanish is increasingly spoken in the USA. There are pockets of other languages.

Reading Material, later in this chapter, gives information on Lonely Planet's useful phrasebooks.

HEALTH RISKS

North America is really pretty healthy, which is just as well as being ill costs a fortune. Gappers should be aware of the small risk of tick-borne diseases (such as Rocky Mountain fever and Lyme disease), giardiasis caught by drinking contaminated water (known locally as 'beaver fever') and the odd case of rabies in the northern wilderness. Sharks are an occasional health risk in Florida.

In the Caribbean a few more travel precautions and vaccinations are required. Some fresh water is contaminated with schistosomiasis (bilharzias) or leptospirosis and be aware that mosquitoes in some areas carry dengue fever.

Consult the Health chapter in Part I and seek professional medical advice for more travel health information.

TIME & FLIGHT TIME

The USA is divided into five time zones: Eastern Time (Greenwich Mean Time – GMT – minus five hours), Central Time (GMT minus six hours), Mountain Time (GMT minus seven hours) and Pacific Standard Time (GMT minus eight hours). Alaska is nine hours behind GMT. Time in Canada starts 3½ hours behind GMT in Newfoundland stretching to US Pacific Standard Time in the west. Clocks go forward an hour during Daylight Saving Time (April to October). Greenland is three hours behind GMT and most of the Caribbean is four hours behind.

Montreal is the closest hub to London (a seven-hour flight), followed smartly by Boston and New York. LA is 11¼ hours away, St Lucia 8½ hours and Montego Bay (Jamaica) 10½ hours.

ISSUES

Borders are pretty easy-going in the region, although upon arrival gappers should be prepared for thorough questioning by the US Immigration & Naturalisation Service (INS). If anything is out of order or they suspect you of intending to work illegally they'll send you straight back to Blighty.

You need to jump through an increasing number of hoops to get a visa for the USA, although short-stay visas of up to 30 days are issued upon arrival. When you get to a US city it's a good idea to find out which areas are too dangerous to venture into (even during the day).

The political situation in Haiti remains troubled, kidnapping of foreign nationals (for ransom money) is increasingly common and you're advised not to spend you're hard-earnt gap year here.

The vast majority of visits to Jamaica are trouble-free but gappers should be aware that there are high levels of crime and violence, particularly in Kingston, and you should avoid certain routes.

Crime and guns freak out a few gappers in the USA but once you've been there a while you'll realise that these are pretty well localised to 'bad neighbourhoods' and rural America is very safe.

For further information on travel hotspots, general safety issues and governmental travel advice see Safety in Part I.

INTERNET & COMMUNICATIONS

Internet cafés are found all over the place but access is cheapest in public libraries.

The North American mobile-phone system is a few years behind Britain and only tri-band phones can be used. Pay-as-you-go mobiles are not available. They just don't get it when it comes to mobile phones.

Daily Spend

If you want to do North America in style, welcome to the world of credit and consumerism. You're not going to get much change from £30 a day (more like £60 if you're partying in the city). The US Bureau of Land Management (BLM) and national forest areas often have very basic free campsites (which cost if you have a car). A similar system of camp/picnic sites operates in Canada and discrete campers will have no problem in rural areas. More up-together camping costs about £7 a tent, hostels £8–18 a night and cheap motel rooms about £25. In Hawaii you can squeeze by on £20 a day if camping and self-catering. Canada costs about the same as the USA, perhaps a little less but in Alaska and Greenland it's much more expensive (like £40 a day).

Cars and fuel are cheap in North America but insurance for gappers under 21 can be expensive in the USA, less so in Canada (Vancouver is the cheapest state to get insured). Cars are cheaper in California and have less rust and are therefore valuable once you come to sell them in New York.

Be aware that taxes and tips can add 20% to advertised costs but a number of plane, train and bus travel passes can reduce costs.

Cuba is pretty cheap for the Caribbean but you're still looking at £30 a day having fun in Havana (some businesses demand US dollars but using pesos is much cheaper). Jamaica is a bit cheaper (£20 a day) but Haiti and the Dominican Republic are more difficult for independent travellers. In the rest of the Caribbean accommodation can be frighteningly expensive. Trinidad and Tobago is not bad costs wise but forget about visiting St Kitts on a shoestring budget.

Getting There

Unless you're a transatlantic sailor or plan to swim the Bering Strait you'll be flying to North America and the Caribbean.

AIR

Vancouver, Toronto and Montreal are the major air hubs in Canada. Chicago, LA, New York, Miami and Washington are the major hubs in the USA but flights into other cities are rarely frighteningly more expensive.

Getting to Greenland is very expensive from Britain (less so from Canada) and most flights go via Iceland.

There are direct flights from London to a few former British colonies in the Caribbean and flights from Paris to Guadeloupe and Martinique. The cheapest way to visit the Caribbean is often as part of a package deal, at least initially.

Transatlantic alliances and code-share agreements mean that reaching many major North American destinations can require at least one change of planes (at least in order to get the cheapest deal). Flying into Anchorage, Alaska and many Caribbean destinations certainly requires this.

Virgin Atlantic, British Airways, Kuwait Airways and United Airlines were offering the best deals into New York and LA at the time of writing. To destinations elsewhere in the country a mighty raft of US airlines can offer good deals and American Airlines often delivers the best open-jaw deals within the USA.

Consult the Airlines Appendix at the back of the book for more information on airlines and routes.

Ticket Costs

The best available student/under-26 fares are quoted here. See Passports, Tickets, Visas & Insurance in Part I for more information on how to get the best, most flexible deal.

The cheapest way into North America is to fly into Boston (£190) or New York (£210 return). For a ticket into LA you're looking at £265, the same as Miami fares. Toronto costs £310 and Vancouver £380. Fares into Anchorage Alaska are about £500.

Return flights to Port of Spain (Trinidad) are the most expensive in the region (£605). Montego Bay in Jamaica is better value (£473), although St Lucia is not that much more expensive (£500).

Open-jaw tickets can make a lot of sense. Into LA and out of New York costs just £240, or £360 if you fly into Anchorage, Alaska. If you want to see some of Central America too then a ticket into New York and out of Mexico City or San José (Costa Rica) will cost £425 and £455 respectively.

There are no direct flights from the UK to Greenland. However, there are flights from Copenhagen (£570; mostly western and southern Greenland) and Reykjavík (£290; mostly eastern Greenland). Both cities can, with a little cunning, be reached from the UK for under £120 (see No Frills Please, We're British in the Europe chapter).

SEA & OVERLAND

If you really got lucky you could work your passage across the Atlantic on a cruise ship or yacht (see Work Your Route in Part III). Getting to Iceland by ferry from the Shetlands hoping for a boat to Greenland is another optimistic notion and any sea journey is likely to cost more than a flight.

SPECIALIST TOUR OPERATORS

There are hundreds of tour operators running activity and sightseeing tours in North America. Of particular interest to sea-worthy gappers may be the numerous sailing operators in the Caribbean and southern USA. See the Global Tour Companies Appendix at the back of the book and check out:

Trek America (☎ 01295-256777, fax 01295-257399; W www.trekamerica.com; 4 Waterperry Court, Middleton Rd, Banbury, Oxon OX16 4QB) offers lodging, camping and trekking tours aimed at those aged 18 to 38 travelling in 12- to 14-seater vans.

North America, the Caribbean & Beyond

You can get from the Eastern Caribbean to Güiria in Venezuela by ferry and then the whole of South America is before you.

It's occasionally possible to get a boat from Jamaica and other Caribbean islands to Central America (Belize, Honduras and Panama normally). Hitching a berth on a yacht is another option and might take you through the Panama Canal into the Pacific. May is the turnaround time in the Caribbean – people leave before the hurricanes arrive.

Border crossings between the USA and Mexico are efficient and busy. From Mexico the whole of Central America can be explored by land.

Further Information

READING MATERIAL

Lonely Planet publishes a range of guidebooks to countries, regions and cities in North America, as well as Cuba, Jamaica and Eastern Caribbean. Trekkers are spoilt with *Hiking in Alaska*, *Hiking in the Rocky Mountains*, *Hiking in the Sierra Nevada* and *Hiking in the USA*. *Cycling Cuba*, *Cycling USA – West Coast*, numerous diving guides, a couple of food guides and phrasebooks complete the comprehensive background.

There's a very rich literary background to North America. Fiction is often as insightful as travelogue but if you're happy with random recommendations try *Coming into the Country*, by John McPhee (about Alaska), *Native Peoples & Cultures of Canada*, by Allan Macmillan, *Dread: The Rastafarians of Jamaica*, by Joseph Owens, *Che Guevara: A Revolutionary Life*, by Jon Lee Anderson, Peter Matthiessen's *Indian Country*, Dee Brown's seminal *Bury My Heart at Wounded Knee* and *The Autobiography of Malcolm X*.

Zora Neale Hurston's classic *Tell My Horse: Voodoo and Life in Haiti and Jamaica* is well worth a look as is Pico Iyer's *Cuba and the Night*, Peter Stark's *Driving to Greenland*, Tete-Michele Kpomassie's *An African in Greenland*, Mark Twain's *Roughing It*, Jack Kerouac's *On the Road* and *Dharma Bums* and Edward Abbey's wonderful *Desert Solitaire* (the last three are real classics). *Into the Wild*, by Jon Krakauer, is an apocryphal tale of wilderness misadventure but also try Bill Bryson's *The Lost Continent*, VS Naipaul's *A Turn in the South*, Jonathan Raban's *Old Glory*, Sean Condon's *Drive Thru America* and *Ghost Riders: Travels with American Nomads*, by Richard Grant.

USEFUL INFORMATION SOURCES

For specific country overviews, the low-down on travel in the region and hundreds of useful links head first to Lonely Planet's website (W www.lonelyplanet.com).

The portals and useful websites listed on the following page give a different slant on the countries.

W www.roadsideamerica.com – the 'online guide to offbeat attractions'.

W www.historic66.com/index.html – slightly anal Belgian site about the 'Mother Road'.

W www.uq.edu.au/~zzdonsi/us_tips.html – helpful Ozzie hints on travelling in the USA.

W www.travel.org/na.html – huge travel directory for North America.

W www.canoe.ca – Canadian news and culture portal.

W www.caribseek.com and W www.caribbean-on-line.com – general portals into all things in the Caribbean.

Been There, Done That

Acting on the advice of so-called mates, once we arrived in Canada we invested a sizable but not incredibly large amount of money in what's euphemistically entitled an RV, or recreational vehicle.

They are not. Our problems started almost straight away. We picked up the RV from where these 'friends' had stored it, some warehouse on the outskirts of Vancouver. It was rush hour as we set off to cross the city to the nearest RV Park and after discovering we had no map we were negotiating the rush hour on a wing and a prayer. Luckily enough by the time we had got lost in an industrial estate for the best part of an hour the traffic was beginning to subside. We were also helped by the low speed limits and the odd phenomenon (for Londoners) of people actually respecting them.

The problem with the RV was its size. We picked the next size up from the smallest and it was huge. It had a giant air-conditioning unit on the top that we almost took off going under a bridge with millimetres to spare and all the passers-by waving at us. I thought they were just being friendly. Also, when we travelled up the 'sunshine coast' (in March it rained all the time) the overhang over the back wheels grounded out getting on and off the ferries. It was also made of flimsy stuff; one of our friend's blessed children put a boot through the wall and had it not been for a tube of wood filler and some judicious end-of-trip repairs we would have lost a heap of money when we sold it on (which was easy enough).

Having said that, the temperate rainforest and Pacific Ocean were fantastic, as was the skiing, and the Canadians couldn't be more kind and helpful. But if you want a carefree time or want to go up small bumpy roads don't buy an RV.   Karen Crawford

Mexico, Central & South America

Introduction

South America is fast becoming one of the world's most popular gap-year travel destinations. It has the beaches and coral archipelagos of Thailand, the historic and cultural resonance of Central Asia, and wildlife attractions and national parks to rival Africa. The seven nations of Central America plus Mexico and 13 South American nations make up a region that stretches across almost the whole gamut of climatic zones, terrain and environments from lowland deltas to mountains that soar to a smidgen below 7000m. Parts of the region remain relatively unexplored and you can add to the travel mix remarkable ancient cultures and some of the world's wildest parties. It's a wonder the place isn't overrun with eager young backpackers.

Why Mexico, Central & South America?

With the sad exception of Colombia, the days of coups, civil war and conflict are just about over and even countries like El Salvador and Nicaragua, once bywords for terror and death squads, are now evolving tourist destinations. There's never been a better time to visit the region.

From pampas to penguins, massive glaciers to rainforest, the region is blessed with an amazing array of natural riches. In Central America the number of national parks is stunning (27% of Costa Rica is protected in one way or another) and the idyllic islands on the Caribbean coast, white-sand beaches and the world's second-largest barrier reef (Belize) provide plenty of places to dive, party and lounge around.

In South America, the vast Amazon rainforest dominates most people's thoughts and the odd horrendous bus ride or tricky river trip into the heart of the rainforest are always worth making. In Paraguay, the Chaco is a remarkable area of almost featureless plain but one of South America's last frontiers and a great bird-watching destination. The pampas of Argentina is the rangeland of the legendary *gauchos* (Latino cowboys), while in Peru the Nazca Lines (enormous geoglyphs of shapes and figures) are etched in the pampas. Ecuador has amazing biodiversity but if you've got the money (or can beg, borrow or steal it) head to the Galápagos Islands, an area of unique and well-protected wildlife that you'll see nowhere else on earth.

At the end of the continent, well beyond the awesome falls of Foz do Iguaçu on the border of Brazil and Argentina, is Patagonia, an area of mountainous terrain, glaciers, fjords, whales, elephant seals and penguins that finally arrives in Tierra del Fuego, the last stop before Antarctica.

Like its bossy northern neighbour, the region's character has been formed through waves of migration, conquest and development. But unlike the USA, Central and South America display many architectural relics of fallen civilisations, and indigenous peoples still play a major part in regional cultural life. The colonial influences of Spain and Portugal are obvious physically and socially. A huge percentage of the people are *mixoes* (of mixed European and indigenous origin) but in Buenos Aires (Argentina) and Santiago (Chile) you could easily think you've been transported to Madrid. It's a very different experience to stroll among the indigenous Quechu and Aymara peoples of La Paz (Bolivia), which lies at over 3600m.

In Central America, ancient Aztec and Mayan architectural relics are stunning and very accessible, while breathtaking Inca cities and monuments of South America are equally accessible. Visiting the *moai*, the huge stone heads of Easter Island, never fails to impress but a trip to this isolated island is expensive unless you've added it to your round-the-world (RTW) ticket. A more accessible man-made marvel is the Panama Canal.

By and large Mexico, Central and South America is an affordable travel destination and various economic calamities have actually made some countries (like Argentina) even more affordable. Despite the economic flightiness, the region's infrastructure is improving, along with the average standard of living, although you wouldn't think it by looking at the *favelas* (shanty towns) of Río de Janeiro (Brazil) or Lima (Peru). There's a huge disparity between rich and poor.

Central and South America is where you can make your travel fantasies come true. Snaking through the Andes perched on the roof of a train; gliding through the Amazon admiring the landscape from a hammock; traversing high regions of granite spires, ice and snow; or simply kicking back on tropical beaches and partying like a maniac at the Brazilian carnivals of Río, Salvador, Recife and Olinda are dreams that can come true – they certainly know how to enjoy themselves in Brazil!

What to Do?

Paid work is thin on the ground but volunteer opportunities are bountiful. Many gappers find themselves being drawn into the local culture and will find loads of things to learn in the region. Everything from weaving lessons in Guatemala to samba lessons in Brazil are available and tonnes of gappers learn Spanish. You can go on archaeological digs in Costa Rica or be taught to windsurf in Honduras. See Part III for more information on overseas jobs, volunteer work and courses available in the region.

While many gappers have a target in mind when they touch down, there is so much to see and do and there are so many cool places to do nothing.

GET ACTIVE

The region offers loads of activities and it's possible to get professional instruction in many. The rainy season is the main obstacle to participation in most activities (see Climate later).

Caving

Guatemala has a growing number of caving opportunities, the most famous of which are in Verapaces. Sotano de las Golondrinas near Tancanhuitz (Mexico) is one of the world's great caving destinations. Speleologists should also check out the Cueva del Guácharo (inland from Cumaná), the most spectacular of Venezuela's many cave systems. Possibilities in Brazil are found around Bonito and Parque Nacional de Ubajara.

Cycling & Mountain Biking

The highlands of Guatemala, Honduras and Costa Rica are popular mountain-biking areas, along with the gorges and desert around San Pedro de Atacama (Chile) and the mountains around La Paz (Bolivia). The Patagonian Andes provides some tough cycle touring (including strong winds and harsh weather), especially around the Lake District (Chile and Argentina), good cycling destinations themselves. Cyclists have tackled Brazil's Trans-Amazon Highway and the Panamericana (the north-south highway on South America's west coast) but strewth that's a serious undertaking.

Top 10 Must-Sees

Tikal (Guatemala) – the country's most spectacular Mayan archaeological site.

Belizean Cayes (Belize) – fantastic diving and snorkelling amongst pristine coral.

Parque Nacional Corcovado (Costa Rica) – virgin coastal rainforest, stunning beaches and loads of wildlife.

Archipiélago de Bocas del Toro (Panama) – laid-back villages, coral reefs, jungle and deserted beaches.

Parque Nacional Torres del Paine (Chile) – turquoise lakes, towering granite pillars, glaciers and God's own trekking country.

Salar de Uyuni (Bolivia) – amazingly stark, one of the world's largest salt flats.

Machu Picchu & the Inca Trail (Peru) – a classic trek to one of the wonders of the ancient world.

Teotihuacán (Mexico) – wonderful Mexican Mayan site with pyramids and temples.

Foz do Iguaçu (Argentina & Brazil) – awesome waterfalls, more than 2km wide.

Easter Island (Chile) – the *moai*, those famous stone heads, are just one of the attractions.

Diving & Snorkelling

The region's top diving is along the Caribbean coast, particularly off the Belizean barrier reef around Caye Caulker and Ambergris Caye. The Bay Islands of Honduras (renowned for cheap PADI open-water dive courses), Yucatán Peninsula and many parts of Costa Rica, Nicaragua and Panama also have excellent dive sites.

South America's best diving is off Venezuela, Colombia (including the island of Providencia) and the Galápagos islands, which are arguably the best dive destination on the Pacific coast – although dodgy between September and November, hammerhead sharks and great undersea landscapes are fair compensation. The Pacific coast and Mar de Cortés (the Gulf of California between Baja California and mainland Mexico) is renowned for pelagic fish – huge shoals of hammerhead sharks, enormous whale sharks and manta rays can be seen.

Skiing & Snowboarding

The continent's best downhill-ski areas are in Argentina (Las Leñas, Chapelco and Cerro Catedral) and Chile (El Colorado, La Parva and Valle Nevado near Santiago and Termas de Chillán in the south). The season is from June to September.

Bolivia has the world's highest (and possibly most dilapidated) ski resort at Chacaltaya (operating February to late April). The altitude (4900m to 5320m!) will leave you gasping. You could also engage in some challenging ski touring in the high Andes.

Surfing & Windsurfing

There are some world-class breaks in Costa Rica's Parque Nacional Santa Rosa and at Zunzal in El Salvador (where there's an international surfing competition). Check out the 'Mexican Pipeline' at Puerto Escondido in Baja California, a great surfing destination.

In Brazil, home to South America's best surf, great breaks are found near Florianópolis (Santa Catarina State). There are a few other good spots dotted around, including off Easter and Galápagos islands.

Windsurfing in Brazil is good in Búzios and simply splendid on the Ceará coast. Jericoacoara and Icaraizinho attract hardcore windsurfers, while Los Barriles is Mexico's windsurfing capital.

Trekking & Mountaineering

The Andean countries of South America (Ecuador, Chile, Peru and Bolivia) provide some stunning trekking. A good quarter of Bolivia (the Nepal of South America) is over 3500m and from La Paz Inca trails lead into the dramatic Yungas region or you could take on the challenge of the remote Cordillera Quimsa Cruz and Cordillera de los Frailes before perfecting your snow mountaineering techniques on the 6000m peaks. In Chile, San Pedro de Atacama is just one of many launching points for treks, while in Ecuador Quito is a great trekking base. You could also trek around Chimborazo (6310m; some mountaineering experience is needed for the climb) or venture into the *páramo*, high-altitude grassland.

Huaráz is at the heart of Peru's best trekking country and there are some great opportunities in Parque Nacional Huascarán – mountaineers can scale Huascarán (6768m). Cusco is the launching point for the Inca Trail to Machu Picchu – the four-day trek to the amazing 'lost' Inca city. In Brazil, the Bahia Highlands and Parque Nacional da Serra dos Órgãos near Río offer good trekking. Colombia's Sierra Nevada de Santa Marta has some potential but Argentina and Chile are really blessed with the Patagonian Andes, God's own trekking country. Chile's Torres del Paine and Argentina's Nahuel Huapi national parks both have good trail infrastructure and some stunning routes.

The mountaineering in South America is exceptional. Ecuador's volcanoes, Peru's Cordillera Blanca, Bolivia's Cordillera Real and Argentina's Mt Aconcagua (6962m, the highest peak in the region) all offer exciting possibilities. Argentina's Fitz Roy range has good technical climbs.

Jungle treks can be arranged at Rurrenabaque in Bolivia, Iquitos in Peru, and Manaus in the heart of Brazilian Amazonia, and Venezuela has some well-signposted jungle trails.

Volcano climbing is popular in Central America (El Salvador has 25 extinct volcanoes) and the region's wonderful national parks offer great, short-duration walking and longer treks. In Nicaragua trekkers can crisscross the dense cloud forest of Selva Negra near Matagalpa (look out for howler monkeys) and explore Volcán Mombacho. The Petén region of northern Guatemala is good for jungle trekking and the country is a climber's paradise – there's some good mountaineering on Volcán Tajumulco (4220m; the tallest peak in Central America) and in the Cuchumatanes Range. Intrepid gringos trek around Copper Canyon in northwest Mexico and Barranca del Cobre in Baja California. Honduras' best walks are in Parque Nacional Pico Bonito (which has trails around the reserve) and Parque Nacional Celaque, which contains the country's highest peak and lush cloud forest.

White-water Rafting & Other Watersports

In Central America there's some fine rafting on the Reventazón and Pacuare rivers in Costa Rica, while Honduras and Guatemala (which has class IV rapids) have recently developed rafting industries. Honduras also has gentle rafting and boating trips. Veracruz State is the epicentre of Mexico's white-water rafting industry.

Chile has some of the best white-water rafting in South America with good rapids on the Maipó, Trancura and Futaleufú rivers. There's also some rafting in Peru (the Río Colca canyon is particularly difficult), Argentina (best around Mendoza and Bariloche) and Ecuador.

Venezuela's Delta del Orinoco offers plenty of fun for river and boating enthusiasts. Yarinacocha in Peru has good canoeing and while going boating in the Golfo do Fonseca (El Salvador) you may see dolphins and sea turtles. Sea kayaking in the Gulf of California (Mar de Cortés) off Baja California is very popular.

Wildlife Watching

Central America has some wonderful national parks, protected areas and bird habitats, packed with all kinds of flora and fauna. Costa Rica has been quickest to realise the potential of eco-tourism (there are even some fantastic rainforest canopy-top walkways) but don't discount the wonders of the national parks and bio-reserves elsewhere – Panama is a fantastic bird-watching destination (940 species and counting).

In South America there are some great trips into the Ecuadorian and Brazilian Amazon plus Venezuela's national parks (Henri Pittier is a great place for bird-watching). Then, of course, there's the Galápagos Islands, an outstanding and pristine wildlife habitat. If you can get to the Falkland Islands or Tierra del Fuego in the far south you'll see some pretty remarkable wildlife (elephant seals, sea lions, penguins, six species of dolphin and killer whales). The marshlands called Esteros del Iberá in Corrientes (Argentina) rival the biodiversity of the Amazon.

Other Activities

There's great rock climbing close to Río de Janeiro (over 350 routes). Horse riding is very popular in Costa Rica, Uruguay, Paraguay and Argentina where many *estancias* (working ranches) take in paying guests. Paragliding and hang-gliding are popular in Mérida State (Venezuela) and there's some hang-gliding around Pedra Bonita close to Río. Sailing is big in Búzios (Brazil) and off the larger resorts along the coast and at Carmelo and Mercedes in Uruguay. Monteverde (Costa Rica) is the best place for zip-lining (zipping across the top of the jungle canopy on a wire or 'flying fox').

WORK A LITTLE

Teaching English is again top of the working pops but there's also scope to crew on foreign yachts that stop along the coast of Guatemala, Costa Rica, Venezuela, Ecuador and Peru. Deck hands are occasionally taken on by yachts either end of the Panama Canal. In popular tourist areas there are sometimes adverts for tour leaders, trekking guides, hostel managers, bar hands or shop workers.

This region has loads of volunteer work. Opportunities include teaching, organic farming, conservation, community projects and working with street kids. The Costa Rican national park system even pays its volunteers! Chile, Peru and Ecuador have organised volunteering structures.

TRAVEL AROUND

Air travel is popular in Central and South America both with big-capacity national airlines and smaller outfits dedicated to transporting well-heeled tourists to various attractions and national parks.

Grupo TACA (W www.taca.com), an alliance of regional airlines, offers a couple of useful air passes to foreign travellers in Central America. Flying is refreshingly cheap in the Andean countries of South America. Single-country and multi-country air passes are available (see W www.lastfrontiers.co.uk/airpass.htm) making the high life a little cheaper. Remember that open-jaw tickets can avoid unnecessary (and expensive) backtracking, while airline alliances sometimes mean that getting a flight to your farthest destination may enable a stopover elsewhere on the continent.

Most of the main roads in Central and South America are paved (the Panamericana runs down the west coast of South America and the Interamericana from Mexico to southern Panama) but highland Peru, Bolivia and Ecuador have some terrible roads. It's the bus that takes the strain in the region. Between major cities smart, air-conditioned vehicles are often used but on local routes or in remote areas buses remain the rickety chicken capsules of yore, propelled by bus drivers without the best reputation for safety. Converted flatbed trucks or pick-ups (with rows of wooden benches for passengers) are used on really bad roads. Small, private shuttle buses are sometimes available between popular destinations.

Mexican and South American railways, though reduced in recent years, are invariably cheaper (but slower) than buses. Argentina, Brazil, Bolivia, Chile, Ecuador, Mexico and Peru all have classic train journeys – Peru's Inca Line from Puno on the shores of Lake Titicaca to Aguas Calientes winds through some fantastic scenery and brings you within spitting distance of the route to Machu Picchu. Trains vary from short, diesel-powered trains with dining cars to *mixtos* freight/passenger trains that transport everything and stop everywhere. Trains in Chile and Argentina are generally more modern than elsewhere.

Hire cars are expensive and often unavailable to under-25s. One option is buying a car, possibly in the USA before exploring Central America, or in South America (Santiago, Chile, is the best place). However, there are big paperwork hassles to consider and you can't physically drive between Central and South America.

Hitching is not really safe but in remote areas where there's little public transport it's a serious option. Expect to pay for your lift.

There are numerous boat services along the coast of Central and South America, out to nearby islands, up various rivers and across the region's lakes. This transport ranges from speedy motor launches and motorised dugouts to large ferries and freighters. Classic river journeys are found on the Amazon or Orinoco but you can be literally miles from the shore. Smaller rivers like the Mamoré on the Brazil-Bolivia border, or Plátano in Honduras make for more evocative and idyllic journeys. A hammock and sleeping bag are essential items for cheap river travel (cabins are costly). Classic boat journeys in the region include the following:

Puerto Montt to Puerto Natales (Chile) – a ferry journey down the wonderful fractured coast to Parque Nacional Torres del Paine.

Largo General Carrera (Chile) – Coyhaique to Chile Chico and Puerto Ingeniero Ibáñez.

Lake Titicaca (Peru & Bolivia) – there are great journeys to Isla del Sol and Isla de la Luna.

Río Manu (Peru) – from Cusco charter a river trip into Manu Biosphere Reserve in the heart of Amazonia.

Río Negro (Brazil) – amazing trip up to Leticia (Colombia) from Manaus (Brazil).

The Darién Gap separates Panama and Colombia, and so Central and South America. It's very dangerous to cross by land, slightly safer by boat transport along the Caribbean coast but this may currently also be too dangerous. See Issues later for more details. Freighters occasionally head between Colón (Panama) and Barranquilla (Colombia) and expensive yachts between Cartagena (Colombia) and Colón. You can get a boat to the Colombian island of San Andrés (off the coast of Nicaragua). However, most people cross the Darién Gap using a combination of small boats from Colón to Turbo (Colombia) or overfly the whole sorry section from Panama City.

Classic Routes

The region lends itself to linear travels and over the years the Gringo Trail has developed as travellers move through Central America and down the west coast of South America to Tierra del Fuego. You could start this popular journey by getting a cheap flight into Los

Angeles (LA) before crossing into Mexico and exploring down to the remarkable Reserva de la Biosfera Montes Azules before cutting up to Cancún on the Caribbean Coast.

Central America is manageable enough to be explored on its own – it would be a tidy way to spend a year. Mexico has the most diverse range of environments but the jungle and forest of the other seven countries will not leave you bored. The Pacific and Caribbean coasts have great beaches and magical islands. From Mexico head down to the remarkable reefs and islands of Belize then move west into Guatemala, a country whose historic and natural attractions are bound to take up plenty of your time. El Salvador is an option before/after exploring Honduras and heading down through Nicaragua to the eco-tourist capital of the region, Costa Rica. Panama is the last country in Central America and leaves you with a tricky choice, how to cross the Darién Gap and, more fundamentally, whether to enter Colombia (see Travel Around earlier).

Many travellers pick up the Gringo Trail in Ecuador, where the Galápagos Islands are an expensive but worthwhile diversion. Once you've cut down to Lake Titicaca in Peru a number of options present themselves. You could continue south through the natural glories of Chile to Tierra del Fuego, or northeast into the heart of the Amazon, head east into the (very) highlands of Bolivia, or southeast through Paraguay to Argentina.

From Tierra del Fuego you may be tempted to think that it'd be a blast to head all the way back up the east coast through Brazil to Venezuela but that's a big, big ask. It's better to condense your attentions on, say, exploring among the indigenous peoples and heights of Bolivia, Peru and Chile; the wonderful national parks and coastline of Argentina and Chile; the stupendous biodiversity of Central America; having a truly hedonistic time in Brazil; or taking on La Ruta Maya, a great exploration of the archaeological treasures of Central America concentrating on Guatemala, Belize, the Yucatán (Mexico) and the majestic Mayan ruins at Copán in Honduras. Trekking, bird-watching, snorkelling, surfing, kayaking, undertaking a conservation survey, learning Spanish or Portuguese, studying Incan culture or organising a nutty expedition into the jungle are all worthy themes for a trip.

When to Go?

This vast region has many 'best' times to travel, which gives you all the more reason to be selective about which regions you visit. In South and Central America the peak tourist seasons are December to January and March to April. While much of Central America also has a peak season in July to August, October to May is generally the best time to visit.

Things are a little more complicated in South America due to huge climate variation. Generally speaking March to May and September to November are the best times to travel in South America. These are shoulder seasons so costs are generally lower and it's not too hot or too cold.

If you're going to attempt the whole Gringo Trail you could start in Mexico in October and then work your way down to Patagonia. Bear in mind that arriving any later than about April is going to preclude normal (ie without mountaineering equipment) trekking in the Patagonian Andes, which can be snow-bound by June.

CLIMATE

Central and South America stretches south from the Tropic of Cancer over the Equator to within spitting distance of the Arctic Circle.

Central America sits firmly in the tropics but thanks to considerable variations in altitude the region has a real selection of climate. The coastal lowland regions are hot and humid (around 30°C) but go up to between 1000m and 2000m and the climate becomes temperate, almost spring-like (about 25°C). Above 2000m things can get cold at night (temperatures of inland Mexico can approach freezing during December to February) and some areas above 4000m have an alpine climate. The main seasons of the region are not governed by temperature but by rainfall. The rainy season (*invierno* or winter) runs from around April to mid-December (October in Mexico) with the May to September period being quite hot and humid. The rest of the year is the dry season (*verano* or summer), although the Pacific Coast experiences less rain than the Caribbean side. Hurricane season reaches its peak in Central America in August to October.

South America has all sorts of climates and there are also variations within individual countries. Latitude and altitude are the biggest factors. The top two-thirds of the continent is essentially tropical and experiences little variation in temperature but some variation in rainfall during the year; in rainforests there's less variation. Below the Tropic of Capricorn, South America becomes more temperate with mild winters (June to August), warm summers (December to February) and progressively more marked seasons. Parts of northern South America experience wet weather between January and May, while the Andean Highlands are dry and cold between June and August (when many people choose to visit). This is the best time to visit Patagonia but not southern Brazil, which is beset by interminable downpours.

Greater seasonal extremes are experienced the farther south you venture. In the Patagonian Andes the cold, amount of snow and severity of the climate should not be underestimated. The large rain shadow of the main Andes range creates arid areas in Patagonia, northern Chile and Peru.

FESTIVALS

From sacred indigenous ceremonies in Peru to Carnaval in Río, the region is chock-full of exciting festivals and observances. Try to wangle at least one into your itinerary:

Carnaval (Brazil) – the country's carnivals in Río, Olinda, Recife and Salvador are some of the most hedonistic parties on earth. Parades, dancing, music and good old debauchery abound in February.

Festival Internacional de Música del Caribe (Colombia) – in Cartagena the second half of March is given over to Caribbean music by groups from around the world.

Los Diablos Danzantes (Venezuela) is held on Corpus Christi (usually the ninth Thursday after Easter) in San Francisco de Yare. A fiery parade and devil-dancers cap off the festivities.

Inti Raymi (Peru) – the 'sun festival' of Cusco (June 24) culminates with a re-enactment of the Inca winter solstice observance at Sacsayhuamán.

Rabin Ajau (Guatemala) is an impressive festival of indigenous traditions (especially the Kekchi Indians) held in highland Cobán from July 21 to 26.

Chu'tillos (Fiesta de San Bartolomé; Bolivia) is a rocking weekend festival of Bolivian culture held during August/September in Potosi. Musical and dance groups from around the world also take part.

Festival of Yamor (Ecuador) is Otavalo's biggest shindig (early September) and supplies fireworks, parades and an all-round party atmosphere. The Queen of the Fiesta procession is a highlight.

Día de Los Muertos (Day of the Dead; Mexico), on November 2, is when Mexicans usher the souls of their dead back to earth across the country (Pátzcuaro is especially colourful).

Día del Tango (Argentina) is an informal celebration of the birthday of tango great Carlos Gardel (December 11) and a good time to hit Buenos Aires for tango events and a pilgrimage to the singer's grave. Also check out the Día de la Muerte de Carlos Gardel on June 24.

Día de Nuestra Señora de Guadalupe (Mexico) is the day (December 12) of Mexico's patron saint, Guadalupe. Festivities culminate with a huge procession and party at the Basilica de Guadalupe in Mexico City.

What to Expect?

TRAVELLERS

You'll find plenty of your fellow gappers kicking around. Headline tourist attractions draw in many and the linear nature of the Gringo Trail means that a pretty regular selection of travellers are/were travelling in your footsteps.

Spanish travellers make up a fair number of backpackers but other European, Northeast Asian and antipodean nationals are present. In Central America there's a large number of North American travellers but in South America there's a good chance you'll be travelling with Argentineans, Chileans and Brazilians (regional tourism is growing).

In some places travellers are drawn together by either attractions or the chance to step into a slower pace of travel. Here are a few of the many backpacker hangouts:

San Pedro de Atacama (Chile) – sleepy, groovy backpacker hangout in the arid Chilean Andes.

Jericoacoara (Brazil) – a small fishing village, one of Brazil's most in resorts with hip Brazilians, backpackers and windsurfers.

Lake Titicaca (Bolivia & Peru) – a massive lake with some tranquil and accessible islands in the middle.

Tikal, Quetzaltenango, Panajachel and **Antigua (Guatemala)** – Mayan delights, activities and other attractions draw buckets of backpackers.

Pucón (Chile) – must-visit, happening town on the Gringo Trail with loads of activities on offer.

Montañita (Ecuador) – a bohemian little place with the best surf in the country.

La Palma (El Salvador) – a tranquil mountain retreat with good trekking and plenty of art.

San Juan del Sur (Nicaragua) – a magnificent Pacific bay and holiday-party town with great July 16 Fiesta.

Isla Montecristo (El Salvador) – a peaceful community on the Pacific peninsula.

Cusco (Peru) – a powerful draw for travellers, due more to its mountain location than urban charms.

LOCALS

A large proportion of the population are *mestizos* (of mixed Spanish and Indian descent), although a good chunk (up to 50%) of Guatemalans, Peruvians, Ecuadorians and Bolivians are self-identified indigenous peoples. Brazilians are a mix of all sorts of heritages, Portuguese, Indian, Spanish and most notably African. Some countries on the Caribbean coast have Creole and African heritage and there are pockets of the strangest immigrant populations, particularly in the south (Argentina still has Welsh and Syrian pockets). The population is growing quickly (30% of the population are under 15) and over three-quarters of South Americans live in cities. Central America still has an agrarian economy and cultures tied to the traditions of the land. The family is the basic unit of society.

With such a diversity of peoples it's not easy to generalise about locals other than to say that Central and South Americans are a gregarious bunch, not easily offended, and they want to exchange pleasantries before engaging in conversation. Some obviously broad-brush generalisations are that: Ecuadorians behave politely; Paraguayans are renowned for their warmth and hospitality; Chileans are really open and warm; Argentineans are very European in outlook (Buenos Aires is a pretty fashionable and Western place); Costa Ricans are quite North American; the indigenous peoples of the Andes are reserved and do not always appreciate the presence of tourists; Latin South Americans can display intense emotions, particularly about football; Peruvians may be offended by skimpy clothing, Brazilians probably will not; Brazilians display a real lust for life, and drinking *mate* tea is a way to make friends with Uruguayans.

Central and South America are strongly Catholic lands but among indigenous peoples allegiance to Catholicism has been something of a veneer hiding traditional beliefs and practices. There's sometimes an undercurrent of racism against indigenous peoples or folks of African origin – often it's the whites and people of European descent who have the money and power.

Machista attitudes, stressing masculine pride and virility, are fairly widespread in the region and leads to exaggerated attention towards women, even serious aggression (much less so among indigenous peoples). Alas, rude putdowns or witty one-liners often wind up these men who are keen not to lose face.

LANGUAGE

Spanish is the language of the region but it's a little different from classical Castilian and can be tricky for new speakers (Lonely Planet has a separate phrasebook for *Costa Rican* and *Latin American Spanish*!). There's also a little variation in vocabulary between countries. English is understood in the tourist areas of Belize and Costa Rica but without a little Spanish you'll struggle in the region. Portuguese is spoken in Brazil but it's a little different to European Portuguese and there are a number of regional dialects. If you understand Spanish you'll pick up Portuguese reasonably quickly.

There are some great places to learn Spanish including Antigua and Quetzaltenango in Guatemala (a good place for home stays), Quito in Ecuador, Cusco in Peru and San José in Costa Rica. There are loads of places to learn Portuguese in Brazil.

There are hundreds of indigenous Indian languages and in some Andean regions Quechua or Aymara are the first language. In La Paz and Cusco there are courses in these tongues.

For more information on Language Courses see Part III.

HEALTH RISKS

Central and South America have plenty of health hazards and although you're advised to get a string of vaccinations, you're unlikely to get anything more serious than a dose of the squits.

Outbreaks of meningococcal meningitis and cholera sometimes crop up and yellow fever is endemic in Panama and most of the top half of South America (Argentina, Chile and Uruguay are fever-free). Malaria is less widespread in South America but occurs all the way up the southwestern coast of Mexico.

Jungles are thoroughly unhealthy places for Europeans and insect bites can afflict travellers with dengue fever, Chagas' disease, typhus and various other unpleasant nasties. Altitude sickness can easily be fatal and care should be taken when ascending in the Andes.

Consult the Health chapter in Part I and seek professional medical advice for more travel health information.

TIME & FLIGHT TIME

All of Central America is six hours behind Greenwich Mean Time (GMT), with the exception of Panama (which is five hours behind GMT). South America is divided into zones; three, four and five hours behind GMT. Brazil is divided between three- and four-hour zones behind GMT.

There are only a few direct flights to the region from London, most notably Mexico City (an 11½-hour flight), São Paulo (Brazil; 11¾ hours), Buenos Aires (14 hours) and Caracas (Venezuela; 10 hours).

ISSUES

Colombia has gone from bad to worse since the end of peace negotiations between the government and FARC (the Revolutionary Armed Forces of Colombia) rebels and the US-backed 'War on Drugs' began in earnest. The Choco (including the Darién Gap), Putumayo, Meta and Caquetá regions are completely out of bounds. British backpackers have been kidnapped and killed trying to trek between Panama and Colombia but there is a safer (but not trouble-free) route by boat along the Caribbean coast. Political/narcotic violence occurs elsewhere in Colombia and at the time of writing the USA and Australian governments advised against travel to the country and the Colombian border with Ecuador.

Elsewhere there is still tension in parts of the Mexican State of Chiapas. Inquire locally before heading into Oaxaca too.

Political instability in Argentina, Bolivia, Ecuador and Venezuela shouldn't really affect gappers, unless society goes completely belly up, but you should avoid political demonstrations.

The police and military are corrupt and a law unto themselves in many countries. A clean-cut, neat appearance goes a long way to ensuring an easier encounter with all forms of officialdom.

Sexual assaults against women and violent crime are a problem in Mexico (especially Mexico City), El Salvador (especially outside San Salvador at night), Nicaragua (don't travel to the North Atlantic Autonomous Region), Guatemala (don't drive to Panajachel via Patzun) and Honduras. These problems are the legacy of civil and guerrilla warfare and an abundance of guns. Crime is also a big problem in Brazil, Colombia and Peru (long regarded as a hazardous country, Peru has greatly improved in recent years).

The El Niño weather phenomenon was already affecting certain regions in Peru in 2003. There's likely to be an extended and oppressive summer around Lima and other coastal areas while the rest of the country may receive torrential rainfall that could lead to flooding, landslides and general destruction.

For further information on travel hotspots, general safety issues and governmental travel advice see Safety in Part I.

INTERNET & COMMUNICATIONS

Internet access is becoming more common across the region, both in hostels and at specific cybercafés. Mobile-phone technology is also spreading, although it's more prevalent in the region's wealthier countries.

Daily Spend

Latin America ranges from the delightfully cheap to 'are you taking the mick?' expensive. French Guiana and the Galápagos Islands are the most expensive destinations – you'll need £30 a day just to get by. Belize (the most expensive place in Central America) and Brazil drain about £20 a day from the budget (a good hostel bed costs £10) but expenditure tumbles if you're camping or right out in the sticks. Panama, Costa Rica, Chile, Paraguay, Uruguay, Venezuela and Peru fill that £15–20 a day bracket, then come the bargains like Guatemala, Honduras, Bolivia and Ecuador where £15 a day is enough (a cool place to stay costs under £5). Entry to Latin America's national parks costs between £3 and £10.

There are ways to keep costs down other than travelling slowly and living on bread and fruit. Travelling with a hammock saves money. On beaches and other natural attractions there's sometimes a *palapa* (a simple thatched structure/shade) or beach bar where you can sling a hammock, while on long river journeys hammock space is much cheaper than a cabin. There are also numerous air passes for individual countries and regions.

Once off the well-established tourist trails prices drop, although facilities are really not geared up for tourism.

Getting There

You're going to have to fly but getting a ticket into the USA and then travelling down into Mexico is not a bad idea – in fact this is how many travellers dip their toe into Latin America across the San Diego-Tijuana border, one of the busiest border crossings in the world. Buying (not hiring) a car in the USA and then exploring Central America can be a good option.

AIR

South America is covered by many RTW tickets and some Australian fares offer a South American stopover (notably with Aerolineas Argentinas). Some tickets to the region also allow stopovers in the USA.

US carriers like American Airlines and United Airlines often offer the cheapest deals into Central America but you'll be lucky to get into the region in less than 16 hours. Iberia, Lufthansa and Air France also offer good deals and quicker journeys.

Consult the Airlines Appendix at the back of the book for more information on airlines and routes.

Ticket Costs

The best available student/under-26 fares are quoted here. See Passports, Tickets & Visas in Part I for more information on how to get the best, most flexible deal.

The cheapest cities to fly into are Mexico City (£425) and Caracas (£420). The most expensive destinations are Lima, San José and Guatemala City where a return ticket costs at least £550. There are some good-value open-jaw options for the continent, namely into Mexico City and out of Panama City for £525; into Caracas and out of Lima, Santiago or Buenos Aires costs £530; and into Mexico City and out of São Paulo is about £450. UK travel agents can book you a flight across the Darién Gap, between Panama City and Quito in Ecuador, for about £120.

European airlines such as Iberia, Lufthansa and Air France offer most of the cheap deals into South America, while US carriers like American Airlines, Continental and United Airlines offer some good deals with stopovers in North America and the best access to Central America.

SPECIALIST TOUR OPERATORS

Heaps of British tour operators run trips within Latin America. The major ones are listed in the Global Tour Companies Appendix. Other region-specific operators include:

Journey Latin America (☎ 020-8747 3108, fax 020-8742 1312; W www.journeylatin america.co.uk; 12–13 Heathfield Terrace, Chiswick, London W4 4JE) runs tours using public transport and upmarket options with private vehicles across the continent. It also offers cruises to Antarctica.

South American Experience (☎ 020-7976 5511, fax 020-7976 6908; e info@south americanexperience.co.uk; W www.southamericanexperience.co.uk; 47 Causton St, Pimlico, London SW1P 4AT) organises tours, flights and accommodation in selected countries.

Trips Worldwide (☎ 0117-311 4400, fax 0117-311 4401; W www.tripsworldwide. co.uk; 14 Frederick Place, Clifton, Bristol BS8 1AS) runs small-group and tailor-made tours to select and pretty environmentally sound resorts including the Amazon Basin.

Mexico, Central & South America & Beyond

There are plenty of flights to Australia and New Zealand from Chile, Brazil and Argentina. You may get a stop-off in the South Pacific en route but obviously the cheapest way to arrange this is with a RTW ticket. Flights up to North America (Miami is the cheapest destination) are numerous and some good deals can be found.

In São Paulo and Buenos Aires you can occasionally find a cheap deal to Johannesburg but don't hold your breath.

A real travel goal would be to fly into Chile or Argentina, head down to Tierra del Fuego and then strike north making for Alaska. It's quite a trip, and Tim Cahill drove it in 231/2 days, a trip he describes in his book *Road Fever.*

Further Information

READING MATERIAL

Lonely Planet publishes guides to numerous countries, regions and cities in Latin America. *Healthy Travel: Central & South America*, *World Food Mexico*, *Trekking in the Patagonian Andes*, and diving guides to *Belize, Baja California* and *Honduras' Bay islands* provide excellent background. The *Brazilian, Costa Rica Spanish, Latin American Spanish* and *Quechua* phrasebooks are very handy.

Cocaine Politics: Drugs, Armies & the CIA in Central America, by Peter Dale Scott and Jonathan Marshall, provides a new perspective on the US 'war on drugs'.

Peter Matthiessen describes part of the Gringo Trail in *The Cloud Forest*; Alex Shoumatoff's *In Southern Light* explores firsthand Amazonian legends; *Tales of a Shaman's Apprentice*, by Mark Plotkin, is part travelogue, part botanical guide; *The Old Patagonian Express*, by Paul Theroux, tells of a train journey from the USA to Patagonia; *In Patagonia*, by Bruce Chatwin, is an observant and insightful picture of the place and people; *Through Jaguar Eyes*, by Benedict Allen, tells of a perilous 3600-mile trans-Amazon journey; *When the Dogs Ate Candles*, by Bill Hutchinson, is an anecdotal account of El Salvador's civil war; *The Fruit Palace*, by Charles Nicholl, is a good introduction to the craziness of Colombia.

Also try *Inca-Kola*, by Matthew Parris, *Eight Feet in the Andes*, by Dervla Murphy, Sara Wheeler's *Travels in a Thin Country* and Charles Darwin's *Voyage of the Beagle.*

USEFUL INFORMATION SOURCES

For specific country overviews, the low-down on travel in the region and hundreds of useful links head first to Lonely Planet's website (W www.lonelyplanet.com).

The following portals and useful websites should help you chase down any aspect of interest on Central and South America:

W www.larutamayaonline.com – concentrates on Guatemala and Central America.

W www.centralamerica.com – reasonably detailed site on Costa Rica with lots of links.

W www.lanic.utexas.edu/ – great link to some fantastic academic resources, mostly in Spanish.

W www.saexplorers.org – travel-club site with bulletin board and volunteer information.

W www.southamericadaily.com – a good place for a low-down on the region's news.

W www.gosouthamerica.about.com – multifaceted portal to Latin America.

W www.latinworld.com – gateway to loads of information, some in Spanish.

Been There, Done That

'Hey, look at that massive rucksack!' the pint-sized schoolboy shouted to his friend. They gawped admiringly at my rather average-sized backpack as if they had never seen anything like it before. They probably hadn't. Strangers in this isolated part of Quiché, Guatemala, are rare; gringos even more so – the occasional United Nations human rights overseer (probably more sparsely loaded)…and me.

As a volunteer for an agricultural NGO supporting poverty-stricken rural communities, I was a lucky exception. I had joined a team of mechanics to help maintain corn-grinding mills funded by our organisation.

The maintenance bit was a stroll in the park compared with the travel. Our 4WD took us literally to the end of the road, through villages where dogs doze in the middle of the street without fear. Just when friends back in London were sleeping off the stresses of another Monday at the office, we began a mud-spattered climb in darkness to one of the remotest inhabited places imaginable.

My constant comedy falls were the main entertainment during the four-hour trek over the mountain. Our night's lodging, welcome relief from such 'merriment,' had no electricity. Rows of corn dangled from its wooden ceiling. A family of seven lived in a space roughly the size of my parent's front room, all helping to serve our rice-and-corn dinner, which we ate by candlelight. The day before, through friends of a friend, I had dined in luxury at one of Guatemala's most exclusive private clubs. Tonight's simple fare somehow seemed more special. Later, the whole family slept on their kitchen floor so we could be more comfortable.

In the morning, we serviced the corn-grinding mills to the backdrop of a spectacular mountain range. Ironically, these tranquil surroundings witnessed some of the ugliest fighting of the 1980s. Today's battle is against shocking poverty. Despite this, the simple lifestyle and generosity of the people, largely untainted by Western consumerism, enchanted me.

When the kids admired my backpack, I realised no guidebook could offer such privileged insights. Voluntary work had opened my eyes to a world I would otherwise never have known.

Jolyon Attwooll

Part III

Volunteering, Conservation & Expeditions

Gap-Year Organisations

Looking for something to do in a gap year can be rather overwhelming. You're probably thinking where shall I go? What should I do? How can I arrange a project abroad without contacts or a foreign language? One solution is to use a gap-year organisation. Often these groups have grown out of youth-development activities and have recognised that gappers want to take on a challenge but need some support to do it.

You can go abroad for up to a year with these organisations, often helping developing communities with teaching, health care or conservation. These programmes are intended to give a far greater degree of support and direction than volunteering with a charity or aid agency (see Volunteering Abroad later in this chapter). Richard Oliver of the Year Out Group (see the boxed text later in this section) says:

Employers and universities favour structured gap years. Young people naturally want their gap year to be fun but we encourage them to leave their comfort zone and learn something about the world.

PROS & CONS

As a rule, gap-year organisations offer a package programme that takes care of almost everything. You pay a flat fee and won't need to spend months trying to arrange everything in an unknown country from afar (see Costs later in this section for further information). Your travel, accommodation, local support and the project itself will all be arranged for you.

If you take this route you'll get a structured experience while abroad and there will be plenty of help provided so that you don't feel as if you're being chucked in at the deep end. Some gappers may be leaving home for the first time or might never have lived abroad and so there's plenty of value in getting a leg up.

Gap-year organisations usually have years of experience and enjoy good working relationships with countries and local communities. Often a party of gappers, accompanied by a team leader, will get taken abroad to accomplish a particular goal such as building a community health centre or refurbishing a school, and also get to enjoy activities such as trekking and camping. Team leaders tend to be experts in survival techniques and are accompanied by trained medical staff.

Another major advantage of using a gap-year specialist is that as you'll be around other gappers at the same stage in life, either school leavers or postgrads, who will become new friends and surrogate family while you're far from home.

Many gap-year organisations pride themselves on what's known in the field as 'inter-cultural exchange'. This basically means that they will help you discover the local culture and language so that you have something lasting to take away with you. Similarly, it is expected that you will make a valuable contribution to the community where you live for several months. Groups such as AFS UK, i-to-i, Project Trust, VentureCo and Inter-Cultural Youth Exchange (ICYE) all have induction programmes along these lines so that you'll be equipped with some prior knowledge of the place you're visiting and gain some understanding of the local language so you can communicate with the locals. This is especially useful if you are living with a local family and working on a community project such as an orphanage or school.

An organised gap-year trip might also help with your career choices. As Diane Clasby explains, a gap year can have a profound influence on your professional direction:

On the Cultural Destination Nepal programme I met people from all over the world and they gave us loads of different things to do. I stayed with a Nepalese family and at first there was some awkwardness as we watched each other and I tried to watch and learn how they did things. Initially they were watching to see me eat with my hands, which is the local custom.

I taught in Kathmandu, mainly English conversation. It was challenging as I had no teaching experience and I continually needed to come up with new ideas in the classroom. Everyone was so grateful that I was there speaking English with them. It was so rewarding for me personally. I used to stay on in the evenings and talk with the teachers to help them too because their grammar and punctuation weren't great.

The whole trip really inspired me. I was all set to come back to study psychology but I changed to studying environmental science at another university. I just found the issues I encountered so interesting. I'm now writing a dissertation on solar energy in Nepal and rural electrification. My gap year and the experience in Nepal made me reassess what I wanted to do in the future.

But going with a gap-year organisation might not be the right thing to do for some people. The cost is one major disadvantage to think about, as often you'll need to raise over £2500 for three months (see Costs later in this section). You'll have to judge whether this kind of sum provides value for money or whether you could put together a similar experience on your own for less. Having said that, many gappers enjoy raising the money and come back from their trips claiming to have had the time of their lives. Ultimately, it's a question of priorities.

There are some other downsides though. Sometimes a group-based gap year might not really provide you with much exposure to the local culture. Are you sure you want to be surrounded mostly by other British people when you go abroad? If you're serious too about helping a charity in a poorer part of the world, it might be better volunteering with an organisation that's focussed on world development rather than your own personal development (see Volunteering Abroad later).

For the more independent, particularly postgrads with previous experience of living and working abroad, a gap-year organisation might provide too much 'hand-holding' and seem a little too institutionalised. However, school leavers may need more support than those who travelled a lot during university.

You also need to think about how long you want to be away for. Some companies such as Project Trust and GAP Activity Projects (GAP) Projects send you away for up to a year while many other gap-year activities are for much less. Once you arrive a placement might begin to feel too short or too long so bear in mind that because you'll have paid a fee upfront you won't get a rebate if you want to leave early or extend your stay.

Whether or not to use a gap-year organisation and its specially designed projects depends on your individual needs and priorities. Weigh up the choices by talking to each group. They welcome inquiries and will happily put you in touch with former gappers who travelled with them. Ask for as much information as you need. These specialist groups serve a purpose and continue to be popular but there are variations among them and you should do your homework first before making any commitment.

Almost every gap-year organisation runs one or several open days each year where you can go to meet the staff and former gappers. Often they will also give talks in schools and colleges. To summarise:

Pros:

- You will be assigned a structured project.
- You will have a thorough introduction to your destination and the project.
- Gap-year organisations are experienced in creating programmes geared towards 'personal development' so that your gap year is both challenging and educational.
- You will be mixing with other people your own age and at the same stage in life.
- Experienced team leaders and in-country reps will provide support in an unfamiliar culture.
- Paying one fee upfront will cover all your basic needs in advance.
- You will not need to worry about arranging accommodation and food.
- A gap-year organisation has experience working with gappers and local communities on an ongoing basis.
- There are established procedures in case of emergency.
- You will be travelling with experts who are concerned with safety and survival, especially in extreme environments.

Cons:

- The cost may seem excessive.
- You might feel locked into a pre-paid commitment and end up feeling trapped.
- Sometimes there may not be enough interaction with local culture and people.
- An organised gap-year activity might begin to feel too short or too long.
- Coming out of school or college, you might feel that everything is too managed and institutional.
- You may not get on with or respect the staff managing the projects.
- To some individuals gap-year organisations may seem too concerned with personal development and not enough with improving the communities they visit.

TYPES OF TRIP

There are hundreds of activities, projects and programmes to choose from. For example, you can help in a Japanese hospital, teach English in China or the Ukraine, trek through the Andes, track lions in South Africa, or conserve the Amazonian rainforest. These gap-year programmes are designed to provide an educational challenge for you far away from the routines of home. They will be placing you in remote areas of the world and setting you to work among people with different languages, religions and cultures.

Many offer a combination of an outward-bound adventure such as trekking, climbing or rafting, with a community-based conservation or social project such as repairing trails or teaching in schools and orphanages. Agencies working like this include Adventureworks, Madventurer, Raleigh International and VentureCo.

On team-based trips you will be travelling and working in a group of about 10 to 15 of your peers. With a Raleigh programme you may also be working with disadvantaged young people from Britain and also local youngsters in the host country.

Hannah Durden appreciates the direction and the variety of different experiences her team-based gap year gave her but she believes that you need to put in the work in order to really enjoy it:

Originally I was a defiant teen, believing I could take a gap year on my own. But then I realised that I wasn't really that sure. VentureCo offered me culture, the chance to learn a language and a volunteering opportunity. The project I joined worked in the rainforest and we built food storage for a village and cleared a jungle trail. I loved it but some of the others didn't work hard enough to enjoy the experience. Some were moaning that they wanted to be on the beach.

The travel expedition afterwards was excellent too. We followed the coast of Peru down to Chile and then went into the Bolivian salt flats.

I was very glad to have taken a structured gap year otherwise I could have ended up bumming around. My advice is if you don't know what to do, do something structured but don't be half-hearted about it.

Year Out Group

The Year Out Group (☎ 07980-395789, fax 01380-812368; e info@yearoutgroup.org; W www.yearoutgroup.org; Queensfield, 28 Kings Rd, Easterton, Wilts SN10 4PX) was formed in 1998 to promote the concept of organised gap-year programmes and to ensure good practice among its members. It is a not-for-profit organisation. All members have to sign up to the following code:

Accurate Literature Brochures and briefing packs have to be clear and accurately describe what is on offer.

Professional Support and Welfare Programmes are vetted and monitored to make sure that first-class security and safety procedures are followed. This includes good briefing of participants before they embark on their trip and in-country support once they're there. Companies also have to ensure that their staff are well trained.

Standards Programmes must be continually evaluated and improvements made where necessary.

Ethical Considerations Sensitivity to social, environmental and local issues has to be shown, particularly in the programmes' host countries.

Financial Security Compliance with UK statutory financial regulations, including systems in place to protect payments from clients.

Membership All new members must agree to these criteria.

The Year Out Group came about because founding members got fed up with operating in an unregulated environment. This doesn't mean that if you decide to go with a company not in the group that you're stuffed, because there are plenty of good gap-year companies out there who haven't joined up. However, it does give you another layer of protection and guarantees. Whatever, do check out their website (W www.yearoutgroup.org) as there's some useful information and suggestions on it in terms of all your gap-year options.

Current Year Out Group members are: Academic Year in the USA & Europe, Africa & Asia Venture, African Conservation Experience, Art History Abroad, BSES Expeditions, BUNAC, CESA Languages Abroad, Changing Worlds, Coral Cay Conservation, Council on International Educational Exchange, CSV (Community Service Volunteers), Flying Fish, Frontier Conservation, GAP Activity Projects, Gap Challenge/World Challenge Expeditions, Greenforce, i-to-i, Outreach International, Project Trust, Quest Overseas, Raleigh International, The Smallpeice Trust, SPW – Students Partnership Worldwide, Teaching & Projects Abroad, Travellers, Trekforce Expeditions, The International Academy, The Year in Industry, Year Out Drama, VentureCo.

Groups such as Project Trust and GAP Activity Projects (GAP) concentrate on long-term volunteering assignments. Usually their gappers are sent to placements working in schools, orphanages and medical clinics for up to a year. These are deliberately challenging but with plenty of support and advice available close at hand. Chris O'Rourke joined GAP Activity Projects (GAP) and taught English to Tibetan monks, which he found challenging and educational:

My placement was hard going but rewarding. I especially enjoyed learning how to teach. The cultural references are very different but tiny things are oddly very similar. They have the same expression 'red sky at night, shepherd's delight.'

I had seen poverty before but to live in it is quite different. It's important to keep an open mind. Don't be judgmental and keep a sense of humour. I got lots wrong and yet they remained very polite to me.

I picked the right organisation but it is possible to go by yourself. If I went again, I'd probably just do an online search. There are lots of monasteries with websites and you could contact them directly offering to teach there for a few months. If they need help, they will provide food and lodging. There are always lots of other gappers around for company.

Other groups such as i-to-i and Teaching & Projects Abroad specialise in acting as 'sending' agencies by gathering a large range of worldwide opportunities so that you'll have as much choice as you could wish for. For example, i-to-i runs placements teaching English in a kick-boxing school or living in a village that adopts stray elephants. Teaching & Projects Abroad has 260 placements alone in medical facilities such as helping doctors and nurses in a Mongolian hospital. Unusual placements might have restrictions but if you don't fit the criteria there are hundreds of other esoteric options.

Some organisations such as AFS UK and ICYE are situated around the world. They're keen on 'inter-cultural exchange', which means that volunteers are expected to learn a local language and live with a host family.

As an alternative to using a UK-based agency you might want to apply directly to groups based overseas that run gap-year programmes for foreign visitors. Cultural Destination Nepal runs a volunteering and adventure programme for visitors to Nepal, and Timeless Excursions does the same in India. They have designed a structured experience, combining a period spent in community development with tours and expeditions to show gappers their spectacular natural resources. And Kwa Madwala offers three months' safari-conservation training in South Africa.

Trade Aid recruits gap-year volunteers to research, set up and then create a project that will leave a lasting effect on a Tanzanian village. In 2003 the gappers were asked to establish a honey-bearing bee swarm that could then be handed over to a village resident to maintain in the future.

See Contacts later in this chapter for further details on all these organisations.

COSTS

Using a gap-year organisation to find you a placement will cost you anything between £750 and £4500 depending on what you choose to do, where you choose to do it and what the price includes. The Government recognises that this is a substantial amount and in May 2003 it piloted a Young Volunteer Challenge scheme to encourage young people from lower income backgrounds to volunteer.

What is included in the fee will vary so it's important to ask in advance. A fee of £4500 might seem steep but it will cover flights, language tuition, a volunteering placement and an outward-bound adventure such as trekking through the Andes, plus it'll include a contribution to the social project you end up working for. If you add up what you'll receive it might begin to seem like a lot of bite for your buck.

Any adventure component in a gap-year programme such as trekking, mountaineering or rafting is also bound to be considerably more financially demanding because you'll need more supervision and equipment. There might also be equipment you need to bring yourself.

Raleigh International uses the fees it charges to bring some disadvantaged young people on the teams. It also, like many gap-year groups, funds the local projects that benefit the poor communities visited by the gappers.

Gap Challenge charges from £2000 for a placement and an open-ended return ticket allowing you to arrange your own travel provided you return within one year.

Project Trust will charge you £3850 for a year's placement inclusive of all costs and regardless of where you go in the world. By contrast, GAP Activity Projects' (GAP) flat fee of £750 doesn't include the cost of flights.

One alternative to paying a UK-based organisation is to find a locally based company such as Cultural Destination Nepal or Timeless Excursions in India, which charge significantly less than British organisations. Inevitably, their overheads are less but remember that many UK-based organisations believe that the fundraising process is part of the challenge and many of them channel part of your fee into the local projects gappers go to help. Diane Clasby took this alternative route because it seemed better value:

I originally got a place with Raleigh International but I was sceptical about the amount of money I was expected to pay. Cultural Destination Nepal organised everything for me, all I had to do was get on the bus and enjoy it. Because it was a locally based group I only had to pay around £380 and we were offered so much. On the jungle safari I rode on elephants! But other volunteers do need to be careful because when I went back to Nepal in summer 2002 I met some people who felt they were being ripped off by another local group working with volunteers.

Drawing up a budget is a practical way of planning a gap year. After you've done your research and found a placement you want, establish approximately how much you will need to raise in order to finance your time abroad. You know from the start that you have to raise the fee but what is more difficult to estimate is how much cash you may need for day-to-day living expenses. Most placements will provide food and lodging as part of the fee but you will need some spending money for drinks, phone calls, film and additional travel. The cost of all this is quite tricky to establish in advance but if you speak to the staff they'll give you a rough idea about local prices and suggest what you might like to budget for.

Naturally you may encounter a situation that calls for an unbudgeted expense so it's worthwhile setting aside some money for an emergency or on-the-spot temptation. You might need to buy a set of clothes if your backpack is lost or stolen, or you might simply want to make a detour while travelling.

John Locke of Teaching & Projects Abroad says:

The problem I find is that people's expectations in terms of how they should live keep rising. In India volunteers are sometimes spending £20 to £30 per week when they could be living on £10. If you're wise you'll spend your pocket money on activities with the family who host you, as it's the best cultural exchange. The closer you get to the family you live with, the more they'll tell you about their country and culture.

TIMING & APPLICATIONS

Timing is a crucial aspect of joining an organised gap-year project. Places fill up fast. Africa & Asia Venture says that places in Kenya are so popular that they start filling a year ahead and sometimes individuals will even apply two years before they plan to go. So if you're thinking of taking a gap year after school or college you'll give yourself the greatest number of choices if you start thinking about it at least a year in advance, despite the pressure of looming exams.

But things don't always go according to plan and you might end up deciding to take a gap year at the last minute. Despite the popularity of some activities there are always some unfilled places on the books, plus you can apply to an organisation such as i-to-i, which claims to find a gap-year project for anyone applying at short notice.

Each gap-year organisation develops its own application and selection procedures and tries to develop particular selling points, for example, all i-to-i volunteers wanting to teach receive a TEFL course, which is included in the fee. Contact the organisations by phone or email and ask for more information and a brochure. Most also publish fairly extensive information on a website. Then if you like what you read you can fill out a printed or online application form. You will also be asked to provide references.

Nearly everyone who applies will be asked to attend a 'getting to know you' session where you will be checked to see if you have the right 'attitude' to go and work in a different culture and function well in a team. Effectively it's just a safety net to ensure that every gapper and project is going to benefit. Applicants are rarely turned down but if they are they'll be encouraged to reapply. Ivan Wise of GAP Activity Projects (GAP) says:

Our selection process aims to get to grips with how tough an individual is, to see whether they could cope with being sent to remote placements in a less-developed country. We turn down applicants if they've applied for the wrong reasons, perhaps where a parent or teacher has suggested they apply. It won't work if you're shy by nature and you're sent to a busy classroom in China. At the end of a scheme we hope volunteers will be confident, organised and resourceful.

The selection process for Project Trust is rigorous and involves five-day exercises in the Scottish Hebrides. Despite the taxing selection procedure, up to 85% of applicants are still accepted. They are matched with a project that suits their level of experience and interests. On acceptance, volunteers undergo a training programme.

CHECKLIST

If you're considering a gap-year placement ask yourself, what do I want to achieve in my time abroad? Does a project suit my temperament? Do I feel instinctively comfortable with my decision? There is plenty of experienced advice and guidance to steer you. Gap-year groups actively encourage inquiries and are familiar with every type of doubt you might want to throw at them.

Such organisations are becoming very professional at selecting, placing and then supporting their volunteers while overseas. It is rare to hear of any serious disappointment. Usually gappers have earned a distinct sense of personal achievement, which they are grateful for. Any hardships or mishaps tend to be funny afterwards.

Before making any financial commitments, ask to speak to former gappers who used the same company. They will tend to be honest about the challenges you will face and how you can prepare. If you speak to several people who've had positive experiences in the recent past then the organisation you're checking must be doing something right.

However, occasionally things will go wrong. When difficulties arise on a gap-year placement it's usually because expectation doesn't match reality and because individuals are finding themselves out of their normal comfort zone. Working in many developing countries might be rather uncomfortable at times but if you establish before you go the kind of board and food you'll find on arrival then there's less likely to be disappointment.

Inevitably for some, there will be frustration, homesickness and illness. The unexpected may happen but treat it all as an adventure and a time to learn. With the right attitude you can make the most of tricky situations.

Don't put up with anything that makes you feel persistently uncomfortable and unhappy. The point of going on an organised placement is that you have the backing of an agency staffed by experienced people.

Use the following checklist when applying to gap-year organisations:

- Who qualifies to take part and how are they selected? When are the application deadlines?
- What activities are available? Are there choices?
- Who are the beneficiaries of these activities? How will I benefit?
- Where are the placements? How long are these placements for?
- What is the cost? Is there a deposit to pay and is it refunded later?
- Is there advice and help with fundraising?
- What are the organisation's goals?
- Is there any help with medical preparation such as advice on vaccinations? Are there any days set aside for an induction?
- What support systems are in place? Is there a local representative in place to provide assistance on the spot? What medical care is available?
- Does the organisation provide help with travel and visa requirements? Is insurance included?
- How will volunteers be living? Will other volunteers be living nearby?
- Do gappers receive an induction to the country and project?
- Is there any training provided in local languages, teaching techniques or with specialised equipment?
- How can gappers keep in touch with friends and family?
- Are support and a debriefing given on return home?

FURTHER INFORMATION

Most, if not all, gap-year organisations hold regular open days around the country where they'll make a presentation, which usually includes speeches by former volunteers. Increasingly gap-year groups are also making appearances at travel exhibitions such as The Daily Telegraph Adventure Travel & Sports Show (W www.adventureshow.co.uk), Destinations (W www.destinationsshow.com) and Independent Traveller's World (W www.itwshow .com). These usually take place in London from January to March each year. VSO (see that section later) also organises an annual volunteering fair called Volunteering World, which usually takes place in February. Lectures at such exhibitions will cover many relevant issues for gappers hoping to spend time abroad on a volunteering project or other venture. Past topics include Travel & Teach, Tropical Health and Preparing for the Big Trip.

On the net you'll find a huge amount of information on an organisation or destination. Lonely Planet publishes a bulletin board called the Thorn Tree where travellers share tips and information. The *Independent* publishes a special gap-year guide on its website (W www .independent.co.uk), which includes tips on buying insurance and advice for parents on letting go of their children. Other useful sites to visit are W www.isco.org.uk, W www.yearout group.org, W www.gapyear.com, W www.gapwork.com and W www.gap-year.com, which all aim to help gappers prepare a trip and find an organisation to help them, and give advice often drawn from others who've gone before you.

Volunteering Abroad

If you want to work abroad during a gap year without going with an organisation that arranges everything for you, there are alternatives. It's possible to work for a charity working in the developing world. These aid and development charities are often called non-governmental organisations, or NGOs for short, meaning that they raise their own funds and are independent of any government. NGOs set up and run projects that bring direct benefit to local people who might be suffering from poverty and a lack of resources such as healthcare and education. There are literally hundreds in the UK working in international development, transferring skills and resources to the poor areas of the world. Some actively recruit young and enthusiastic volunteers to donate their labour and abilities.

Enthusiasm and dedication are always appreciated by these charities. You might even have a favourite cause you want to help. But bear in mind that these volunteering programmes might be tougher than volunteering with a gap-year organisation. This is simply because a gap-year organisation is run to provide an experience to educate young people and give them an introduction to different cultures in a dependably safe way. There is some overlap between volunteering with a gap-year organisation and an NGO but working for the latter puts the work of the charity and the people it serves first.

As a volunteer for a charity you'll still have in-country support, but you'll be expected to be fairly resilient and self-sufficient. Sometimes you might be living and working in a village without running water or electricity. You might also be working alone without other volunteers from the UK. Still, if you're eager enough and understand the commitment needed it might be right to volunteer for an NGO, especially if you're a postgrad with more experience of travel and of life in general.

These NGOs are mainly small organisations that recruit by word of mouth because they tend to be run on a shoestring. On average you should apply at least three months in advance but each charity has its own deadlines (for full details of each volunteering programme see Contacts later). Once you fill out a printed or online application form you will usually be invited in to talk to the charity to see if you are suitable for a placement. Some of them put on age restrictions and you might need to be 21 or a postgrad to become a volunteer. Others will take school leavers but you'll need to convince the recruiters that you are sufficiently dedicated to its work and that you have the maturity to cope with the challenges. So try to do some research about any charity you approach. When you go for an interview you'll need to be able to talk about the work and where it takes place.

Each organisation will charge a fee, which usually includes a programme charge and administrative costs. Fees range from £500 to £3300 and it varies widely as to whether the fee includes a flight. With the exception of VSO's subsidised programme, most NGOs ask volunteers to be self-funding, meaning that you'll need to carry all your own costs. Sometimes the volunteering programme fee is one source of fundraising for the charity but ask what your money is used for if you have any doubts about what you're paying for. The Muyal Liang Trust, which sends teachers to Sikkim (India), does not believe in charging a fee and simply asks you to pay for your travel and living costs. Where food and accommodation are provided you'll sometimes be asked to make a contribution, which might be as low as £1.50 per day because local prices are usually so much lower.

The options you have for international volunteering are enormous. You might start by asking yourself what kind of work you want to do. For example, if you want to work with children you might apply to the Batemans Trust working with the marginalised Anglo-Indian children living in an orphanage in southern India, or to help Casa Alianza, which tries to educate and shelter the poorest street children of Central America. They both accept volunteers and arrange the placement with accommodation, provided you can demonstrate a serious commitment. These are just two examples of small charities working in limited locations on specific goals.

Alternatively, you can work in social development. Student Partnership Worldwide (SPW) runs programmes promoting health education such as teaching nutrition and hygiene, and an environmental programme supporting organic farming and irrigation. When Stephen Bell graduated from college he joined SPW and went to Zimbabwe to be a peer educator within a secondary school, working in adolescent health and HIV prevention. He explains that a volunteer from the UK in the developing world faces the challenge of being accepted and their work being taken seriously:

I was paired up with a local volunteer and we held informal classes outside the usual curriculum. We did drama, sports and role-playing to help empower the students to protect themselves. I was thrown in at the deep-end because where I lived was the real country without running water or electricity. We cooked over fires. There were only four walls and a floor.

In Zimbabwe teaching is a highly respected profession and teachers demand respect, so it was difficult to ask them to participate in our work. But at one meeting we told them to take off their ties and got them to dance in a circle. Even the headmaster was persuaded to join in. We were trying to break through their boundaries.

Sexuality is not something talked about much in Zimbabwe and it remains a taboo to have sex before marriage. Our aim was to open the subject up to discussion.

If you're prepared to make an effort you'll be accepted. In time I became something other than just a visiting English guy. It could be tough and it took time to adjust but it was completely rewarding.

One way of simplifying the process of finding a volunteering placement with a charity is to apply to agencies that place volunteers with local projects around the world. They are becoming increasingly popular. You'll pay a fee and they will set up a placement for you. They resemble gap-year organisations but are working with a broader age range and don't offer the same level of support. But it's a happy medium between going with a gap-year organisation and joining a small grass-roots group without much support at all. International Voluntary Service publishes a booklet in April so that's a good time to apply as there will be the greatest choice of opportunities. Experiment in International Living and Involvement Volunteers take requests for placements year round but it's recommended that you apply at least one to three months before departure in order for all the paperwork to be completed.

Involvement Volunteers is a good example because you pay a registration fee of £80, send in a profile with preferences for the type of work that interests you and they will send back some matching placements. The final charge will depend on how many placements you choose. For example, three volunteering positions in Australia will cost £380 to arrange. You'll pay for the flights but commonly food and accommodation will be provided (in very poor countries such as India you'll be expected to make a daily contribution). Options run the entire spectrum from saving turtles to working on an old steam railway. One advantage of volunteering this way is that with a round-the-world ticket you could string several placements together in different locations.

. Work camps are yet another option and recruit volunteers to start and complete a project in less than a month. Habitat for Humanity is one such group, building affordable housing around the world in short bursts of three weeks. You would join an international team of volunteers to build two hundred houses. You'll be asked to raise £2000 and all your personal costs such as travel too. Another example of volunteering in this way is going to a work camp with Aid Camps, which will charge £550 for three weeks, excluding flights, and half the fee goes towards purchasing building materials.

There are many different permutations in international volunteering. Some are for a few weeks while others such as L'Arche learning disability centres ask volunteers for a commitment of a year. In between is a happy medium of three- to five-month volunteering placements such as Volunteer Africa or the Himalayan Light Foundation.

Some organisations use volunteering experience as a way of promoting international understanding. Cross-Cultural Solutions has similarities with a gap-year organisation but it is working with a wider age group and the volunteering aspect is a serious commitment. Nevertheless, it recognises the importance of teaching volunteers about the countries and peoples they work with, running lectures and visits during the placement. Camille Shah worked with Cross-Cultural Solutions in a Peruvian home for HIV-positive mothers and children after finishing a degree:

You need to be realistic. A volunteer is not going to change the planet but I was told that I had made an impact on their lives. I'm still in touch with the home and I remember the smiles on the kids' faces.

I helped organise teaching activities, group games and excursions. These children are illiterate because they're not allowed to go to state schools.

I also helped out in a community centre for the elderly within a pioneering shantytown, which had built their own schools, lighting and sewage systems. The people are impoverished but they have strength of character.

The educational aspect of the programme was crucial because you're learning about the global issues that affect the people you're working with. My time in Peru was a life-changing experience for me.

Those of you with two years' professional experience might think of applying to VSO (see separate section later) or Skillshare International, which recruit trained specialists such as medics, engineers and administrators. These tend to be people taking a career break who might be asked to work for two years but if you meet the criteria, it's one more option to look at.

The appeal of volunteering is that you can find one or several opportunities that meet your own priorities and interests. You don't have to work on conventional development or social projects. For example, the Glencree Centre for Reconciliation takes on volunteers in a unique attempt to resolve the conflict in Northern Ireland. Ecologia Trust sends help to an experimental commune in Russia where 30 families care for orphans and grow all the food on an ecofriendly farm.

Financial cost needn't be a problem either. Even the most ardent eurosceptic can be grateful for European Voluntary Service, funded by the EU, which covers travel and living costs. The hosting organisation you work for even pays pocket money of £120 per month, which is more than enough to support a social life abroad. There are roughly 600 places each year for British citizens and it's recommended that you apply at least six months in advance.

Here is a checklist of questions to consider before volunteering abroad:

* How much time do you want to commit?
* Do you know what kind of work to do?
* Do you need to work in a team or would you prefer to work individually?
* Do you want to live and work in one country or region of the world?
* How much can you afford to pay for travel, living costs, a placement fee and charitable contribution?
* Do you know what your money will be used for?
* Do you have any special skills, eg, vocational training, foreign languages and professional experience?
* How much tolerance do you have for limited facilities, eg, running water or electricity?
* Are you adaptable? Are you willing to learn another language?
* Will your efforts genuinely be of use to the people you work with?
* Are you sensitive to other cultures and tolerant of difference?
* Do you have a sense of humour?

VOLUNTARY SERVICE OVERSEAS (VSO)

VSO is justly famous for its pioneering work in sending volunteers to the developing world. The organisation recruits experts in medicine, engineering, small businesses, agriculture etc to assist projects run by partner organisations such as ministries of education. The main programme requires professional experience and you will need to make a two-year commitment. This usually rules out gappers and tends to be popular among those taking a career break. Some graduates over the age of 21 are recruited to teach English but the majority on VSO's main programme are over 25 years old.

But don't be put off because there are two youth programmes, which are ideal for school leavers and undergraduates aged 17 to 25.

The World Youth Millennium Awards provide the opportunity for young people in the UK to work with exchange visitors from abroad. Twice a year nine individuals are paired with nine visitors to spend three months in the UK and three months abroad working on a practical project. On each leg of the exchange the pair live with a host family. You'll be expected to raise £500 as a contribution to the scheme but you will be heavily subsidised so you won't need to worry about any other expenses. Once accepted, you have the choice of working with visitors from and returning to Cameroon, Ghana, India, Indonesia, Nigeria, Sri Lanka, South Africa, Tanzania and Thailand.

Ruth Unstead-Joss joined the World Youth Millennium Awards and was particularly impressed by the unique cultural exchange that occurs on the programme:

I had graduated from college and wanted to find practical volunteering work. The scheme appealed to me because it promoted diversity. My exchange partner was Bukky from Nigeria who was Muslim and the same age as me, 22. We had a good relationship and lived with the same family. It was difficult but that's not the point.

In the UK we worked at a centre for learning disabilities in Lowestoft, helping out with drinks, art sessions, teaching literacy and numeracy. It was poignant to see Bukky learning sign language and become better at communicating with the visitors than the staff.

In Nigeria I went to north of Lagos to work in a relief agency. Every day something would surprise me. Once the father in my host family got a goat out from the boot and the following morning I saw it being cut up for meat because we would be eating it that night.

The whole experience taught me what I could do because it opens you up and pushes you to achieve more than you can imagine.

Another programme aimed at undergraduates is called Youth for Development. This 'sandwich year' programme sends university students between the second and third year on an overseas attachment for 10 to 12 months to gain practical work experience abroad as an introduction to development work. You will obviously need your university department's approval for this scheme but VSO has designed it specifically for students in higher education. Once again the fee is subsidised so it remains manageable at £500.

Application forms for both programmes are sent out in August and volunteers are then sent out the following July after post-selection training in January/February. Assessment days take place in regional cities around the country where candidates are considered for their suitability after participating in a series of group exercises and an interview. Essentially the day is designed to assess whether you have the appropriate degree of commitment and ability to work well with other people.

Acceptance is further conditional on the right placement being found, passing a medical and paying the fee. On returning from the placement volunteers are encouraged to stay involved by offering to give advice to new volunteers and by sharing their experiences in training courses.

KIBBUTZIM

Any tourist aged between 18 and 45 is allowed to work as a volunteer on an Israeli kibbutz. These co-operatives are famous worldwide for their pursuit of a communal ideal where all members jointly work the land and own everything in common. Similarly, all the members act as an assembly to make the governing rules. This kind of idealism has proved popular to visitors from around the world who have found the experience to be one of the purest and most successful forms of communal living.

Volunteers from all backgrounds (provided their country of origin has diplomatic relations with Israel) are welcomed to join the community. A kibbutz has on average about 600 people living on it and there are about 270 of these communities spread throughout the country. The kibbutz movement is non-religious and pluralistic. While you are living in the community everything is shared with you but in return you will be expected to pull your weight and make a proper contribution to the communal life.

In the UK you must apply through Kibbutz Reps in London (for further details see Contacts later in this chapter), which will then assign you a place on a kibbutz. A minimum commitment of two months is expected and it's possible to live and work there for up to eight months. You can apply all year round but you should apply a minimum of six weeks in advance. It's possible to state a preference for the kind of work you want to do but the placement depends upon the needs of the individual communities at the time. The fee of £300 includes the flights, visa and programme fee. While working as a volunteer you will receive roughly £50 per month as spending money plus your food and bed. Your health is protected with a medical insurance policy.

The work is physically hard and volunteers are expected to work six-and-a-half hours a day, five days a week. Work tends to be divided into three areas: agriculture, tourism and services. In the agriculture area you might be picking citrus fruits, avocados, bananas, dates, melons etc; maintaining irrigation systems; or working with chickens and eggs or farmed fish. Some kibbutzim derive income from tourism so you might work in a guesthouse, restaurant, health spa or shop, or in a nature reserve or historical site. The third branch of work is on the service side helping in the kitchen, laundry or in a factory making irrigation equipment.

For some people working on a kibbutz is the chance to become integrated into a fully functioning community without a great deal of cost. Essentially you will be earning your keep as you work. Volunteers are welcomed into the social life of the community and they are free to use the cinema, swimming pool and join the sports teams. This produces a friendly atmosphere that many volunteers remember fondly. You're also likely to meet other volunteers from countries all over the world. Normally you will share a room with another person, who might be from Brazil, Australia or the Czech Republic.

There is plenty of time for leisure and travel, particularly at the weekend, which in Israel is Friday and Saturday while Sunday is a normal working day. Every three weeks volunteers are given an extra two days' holiday, which is often used to travel within the country.

To volunteer on a Moshav or village farm see the Casual/Seasonal Work chapter.

RELIGIOUS ORGANISATIONS

Much of the work bringing relief and aid to the world's poorest people is carried out by religious or faith-based organisations. This continues a long tradition of religious charitable work overseas. In Britain volunteer programmes are essentially run by Christian-based groups, with the exception of one Jewish agency (neither Muslim Aid nor the Islamic Relief Fund send volunteers abroad).

Much like other charities working in world development, volunteers are expected to be self-funding. Likewise you will be charged a programme fee, which contributes to the development work. These fees range from £700 to £4000 and tend to be all-inclusive packages so you won't need to pay for travel too (for more details see Contacts later in this chapter). Volunteers are usually expected to fund-raise the costs and many churches will help potential volunteers with collections and back sponsored activities.

Some religious organisations have deadlines for applications while others such as the sending agency Christians Abroad (see Contacts at the end of this chapter) can be more flexible, assigning volunteers to placements year round. But as a rule of thumb you should apply for limited places at least three months in advance. The Church Mission Society (CMS) and Experience Exchange Programme have set training times in July and December so you'll need to give yourself enough time to get onto one of these courses.

Most faith-based charities and NGOs describe themselves as non- or inter-denominational, meaning that it doesn't matter if you're Greek Orthodox or Baptist provided that you support the Christian basis of faith. However, some of these charities will be affiliated to particular churches in Latin America, Africa and Asia so it's best to learn more about the distinct religious culture of each organisation. Africa Inland Mission (AIM) asks that volunteers belong to one of the Protestant churches. Some will have an evangelistic mission meaning the promotion of faith is important, for instance you might be teaching in Sunday schools, while others focus more on specific development projects.

The kind of work resembles that of other charities working in development, including activities such as teaching, caring for children or working in a medical centre. For example, The Toybox Charity works with street children in Central America while the Church Mission Society (CMS) works around the world on a spectrum of social projects. If you're unsure about where to apply but want to work in a faith-based environment you could contact Christians Abroad, which acts as a sending agency, recruiting volunteers to work on faith-based grassroots projects, mainly in Africa.

Beth Tash, who joined a Latin Link Step Team in Peru after A levels, tells us that:

Serving people is a big thing for me and a test of faith. This gave focus to the work I did in Peru. In the UK we have plenty of food and money but life there is really hard.

Our team of 11 built a school at 14,000 feet up in the Andes in the middle of nowhere but it was very beautiful. It was hard work, consisting mainly of moving mud. You learn so much. The people there have so much hope and trust, it was inspirational and they were so welcoming. I'd say to anyone thinking of doing something similar, just go. It's brilliant fun and very challenging.

Do-it-yourself

There are specialist services to help you find what you want to do. They don't arrange placements but simply act as an information service opening up the possibilities for voluntary service, particularly by telling you about grassroots projects based in other countries that might be otherwise hard to find. For a small fee you'll send in your interests and they'll try to find a suitable indigenous group working in social development or conservation. It will then be up to you to contact the group and arrange a placement yourself. In this way you might save yourself a lot of money but perhaps more usefully you'll be finding an extraordinary opportunity that you might not otherwise find.

Worldwide Volunteering (W www.worldwidevolunteering.org.uk) is a reference database comprising a massive 250,000 placements in over 900 volunteer organisations. It is possible to search the database at a local library, career centre or university. Alternatively you can search the database on the website three times or send a request to the office for a fee of £15. The information is updated every six months. 'We're like a marriage bureau,' says Jacqueline Dingle. 'There are fabulous projects in our database which will make you leap out of your desk with excitement.'

WorkingAbroad (W www.workingabroad.com) is another database and matching service and specialises in environmental, humanitarian and educational grassroots work. 'Some of the projects we keep information on are literally one man and his dog,' says the director Andreas. 'Our database is great for people with certain passions. They might want to work with one type of flower.'

By paying a fee of £29 to correspond by email or £36 by post, WorkingAbroad will compile an individual report after assessing each profile to determine what placement is most suitable, taking into consideration education, skills and personal interests. The service is probably better for university students and postgrads than for school leavers but it all depends on the individual. One 17-year-old gapper lived as a volunteer in Bangladesh for eight months where she also learnt the language.

World Service Enquiry (W www.wse.org.uk), produced by Christians Abroad, is another reference service for potential volunteers. About 60% of the entries are faith-based organisations, which largely work with volunteers professing the same faith. However, you'll also find here many of the major volunteering groups working at community level around the globe. World Service Enquiry is published on the web and can be purchased as a printed edition. Any postgrads thinking of a career in aid work might want to use their One to One service where for a fee of £120 you'll receive a one-hour advisory session and written report outlining where best to use your skills and education.

Another group who can provide advice is Returned Volunteer Action (☎ 020-7278 0804, fax 020-7278 70129; e retvolact@lineone.net; 1 Amwell St, London EC1R 1TH), an association of former volunteers who provide support and advice to anyone hoping to offer their services abroad. It publishes a series of titles such as *Volunteering and Overseas Development: A Guide to Opportunities* and *Thinking About Volunteering Overseas*.

The net is obviously great for finding community and voluntary work. Without national boundaries, many websites collate information from around the world. For instance, TimeBank (W www.timebank.org.uk) publishes a searchable overseas directory containing contacts for hundreds of worldwide organisations looking for volunteers; the service is free to use.

Another site with lots of good reference material on it is W www.idealist.org. It lists over 32,000 international organisations and on any given day over 6000 volunteering opportunities. It is aimed at Americans so it's best to use it to find out information rather than sign up with it. You can use the site for free.

Volunteering in the UK

You don't need to travel to the ends of the earth in order to volunteer your time and education. That old saying 'charity begins at home' is very true. Some individuals might need to stay at home after school to resit exams or to earn money for gap-year adventures, university fees or student debts.

There are lots of areas at home that provide challenging experiences. Some opportunities for voluntary work include working with recovering drug addicts, the homeless, the disabled, the elderly, youth groups, women's groups, the mentally ill, hospitals and hospices, animals, children and families, prisoners and ex-offenders, human rights, law, historic conservation, the arts, sports, environmental conservation, political campaigns, refugees and literacy. The list is almost endless; take your pick.

Some charities and organisations may even offer formal training and qualifications such as an NVQ (National Vocational Qualification). At the very least you should be able to obtain a reference outlining what you did and, with luck, what a valuable contribution you made. If you're going to be doing something entirely motivated by the need to raise cash, such as working in a call centre or supermarket, finding an interesting volunteering project might provide relief for part of the week.

A postgraduate might be thinking of a career in social work or medicine so time spent volunteering in a hospital or prison might help steer professional choices.

One of the best places to start looking for a position is your local volunteer bureau. To find your nearest volunteer bureau use the website at W www.navb.org.uk or look in the local Yellow Pages. There are about 400 individual volunteer bureaux throughout the UK with, on average, connections to 200 organisations or projects looking for help in your area. Even if you have no clear idea what you'd like to do, an adviser can make suggestions by assessing your interests and abilities. Then the bureau will come up with three of the most suitable matches.

If you don't live near a big town try to find a Council for Voluntary Service, which tend to operate in smaller communities (see W www.nacvs.org.uk for a full list), or Rural Community Councils (W www.acre.org.uk), which operate in country areas.

Volunteering opportunities for those in the gap-year age group are continually improving. One recent innovation is the Millennium Volunteers (MV) scheme, which aims to change the appeal of volunteering in the UK over the coming years by encouraging young people aged 16 to 24 to devise their own projects based on what they enjoy doing. There is a network of 160 local projects that supervise MV volunteering in England alone, aiming to attract 100,000 volunteers per year (see W www.mvonline.gov.uk for contacts). The scheme is run separately in Scotland (W www.mvscotland.org.uk), Wales (W www.wcva.org.uk) and Northern Ireland (W www.volunteering-ni.org).

For example, a DJ might teach children, find a slot on a local radio station, teach literacy or organise a conservation project. If you have an idea that you believe can benefit your local community, approach your nearest MV project for help.

Stephanie Stasiuk wanted to work for Camp America. However, although she had spent time in theatre groups she was asked to gain more experience working with children. So she organised some local activities in Milton Keynes through the Millennium Volunteers scheme. She says:

I was working three days a week with kids excluded from school, helping them learn and take work experience. I also helped a local college, discussed youth issues on the local radio station, started a local magazine, got involved with a street-dancing project and raised money on Red Nose Day. So I was very busy. On top of that I also had two part-time jobs to earn money for my trip to the States.

The scheme is really good to young people and supported me with all my projects. If you want to do something locally just go for it as Millennium Volunteers can help you out.

If you are looking for a structured assignment in your gap year, which resembles an international placement, then you should contact Community Service Volunteers (CSV; **W** www .nacvs.org.uk) who attach volunteers aged 16 to 35 to residential projects for four to 12 months, largely in social services for young offenders, the homeless, children in care and the disabled. CSV particularly welcomes interest from gap-year students. Food and accommodation are provided and an allowance of £27 paid per week. Placing 2500 volunteers at any one time, CSV runs one of the UK's largest programmes for volunteers.

TimeBank (**W** www.timebank.org.uk), in partnership with the BBC, is a web-driven resource encouraging people to give time to their local communities. Simply register your interests online, stating how much time you can donate, and TimeBank will try to find you a compatible local posting. The search engine enables users to be quite specific about what they want; for instance, you can either look for faith-based charities or filter them from the search. In 2003 TimeBank will be publishing a series of new pamphlets about how to take a gap year and how to fundraise.

Another web-based database is **W** www.do-it.org.uk, published by YouthNet UK, listing opportunities including residential posts (where you live on site) in the UK. There's also volunteering news and discussion boards.

Most reference libraries have directories of charities and bodies who take on volunteers. The *Voluntary Agencies Directory* is especially relevant. Libraries also have notice boards where local community groups post up requests for help. On Wednesday each week, the *Guardian* lists volunteering opportunities in the jobs section. Local hospitals are frequently looking for additional help and a convenient way of finding a way to help is to contact the National Association of Hospital & Community Friends. Schools too need classroom assistants and reading helpers. Another route is to work in a charity fundraising shop, found on almost every major high street. Oxfam (**W** www.oxfam.org.uk) is just one of many charities running a national network of shops run by volunteers.

Conservation Programmes Abroad

Saving turtles or orang-utans, rainforests or coral reefs, is now widely available to keen amateurs on a gap year hoping to donate some muscle in return for the experience of living in some of the world's most untouched areas.

Many groups working in this field actively recruit volunteers to help out because it's a source of income and they genuinely need extra help to gather scientific data. This type of scientific expedition tends to be based in one place, such as a rainforest camp or beside a coral reef, unlike an overland expedition (see the Overland Expeditions section later) and some volunteering programmes that move around.

Charities such as Biosphere Expeditions, Coral Cay, Frontier and Greenforce take volunteers for two to 12 months to assist scientists working in the field. You'll be trained to identify plant and animal species and record your observations. So you'll be an integral part of any scientific expedition. Winning the support and co-operation of local communities is crucial to the success of conservation work so you might be asked to do some educational work with the local community and explain the nature of the scientific project and what is being achieved.

Rebecca Crossland explains how volunteers earn a genuine sense of achievement and become a valuable part of the team:

I graduated in Marine Biology and joined a Frontier expedition in Tanzania surveying the coral reefs, tropical and commercial fish. We did other work too with local fishermen on marine ecosystems and the mangroves.

We lived in bandas, shelters made with dried palm-tree leaves. The only problem was the roof leaking during a storm but I wouldn't class that as a disaster, and occasionally we couldn't dive because of the weather.

In the tropics you do need to check for ulcers, which develop from small scratches. It becomes a routine to check your body every day so you can clean any wounds.

The food was basic, local staples such as rice, beans, fresh fruit and some fish.

The expedition had volunteers from lots of different backgrounds and it was good fun. The average age was about 23 but there was a range of ages. I made friends with people I'm still in touch with.

Going on a Frontier expedition is not a holiday because it has a serious purpose. It's even been known for volunteers to discover new species.

Volunteers on a conservation expedition can be working and living in quite tough conditions such as high humidity, extreme cold, out at sea or among lots of insects far from the common comforts of home. Before joining a team, you will be asked to produce a medical certificate from your doctor confirming that you are in good health, reasonably fit and have had the relevant vaccinations.

After you sign up you'll be sent a dossier outlining what equipment to bring and where to buy it. Generally, any period spent diving will require you to bring a wet suit, fins, mask, snorkel and diving watch but any special equipment such as cylinders, weights and buoyancy devices will be provided. If you're going to be working in tropical jungle then you'll need loose clothing, a mosquito net, a light blanket instead of a sleeping bag and trekking boots. On the other hand, mountain work will usually require trekking poles, good walking boots, waterproof clothes, lots of clothing layers, water carriers and a day pack. Camping gear, when needed, will be provided by the conservation charity.

Selection for a conservation expedition, aside from being healthy, simply depends on the ability to pay, because volunteers on a conservation expedition are working in a team under instruction from the scientists. However, conservation charities stress that these expeditions do not represent a holiday. The scientific research is serious and team members need to be dedicated.

Expeditions can be quite expensive because the locations are remote and the research needs substantial funds. Prices range from £950 excluding flights for three months to £1000 excluding flights for two weeks. Sometimes discounts are available if you extend your stay. Simple accommodation and food is normally provided for the team. Dive training will sometimes cost an extra £400 if you don't have the PADI diving certificate or similar dive qualification, while other groups may charge more for a marine expedition but the dive training will be included.

Volunteering on a conservation project can sometimes be expensive but you're paying for the privilege of working with rare wildlife such as researching the habitat and behaviour of the snow leopard in Russia's isolated Altai region.

Instead of going on a two-month programme it's also possible to take a shorter trip of two to three weeks such as the 130 choices provided by Earthwatch, a specialist in conservation working holidays. You'll have the choice of projects in 45 different countries spanning research on the medicinal plants of antiquity to the small predators of Madagascar.

For something a little different contact Archaeology Abroad for the chance to work on a dig in Kazakhstan or Guatemala where you'll join a team of professional archaeologists who need voluntary help. Or consider volunteering at the Sunseed Trust in southern Spain where they are discovering new applications for solar power to help the developing world (see the Contacts section later for more details).

Conservation Programmes in the UK

If you're looking to stay at home during a gap year and want to work in conservation then the best bets are the British Trust for Conservation Volunteers (BTCV) or the National Trust (NT), which work to save natural landscapes and historic monuments. They run 'working holidays' for one to two weeks. Choices for an NT holiday in 2003 included herding goats, creating a sculpture trail, setting up a music festival and clearing ancient woodland. It's possible to go on one or several working holidays in a row but these are usually taken by people in careers who want an unusual holiday out in the open protecting the environment, so there will be a cross-section of ages. A team of say 12 people will, for example, repair dry-stone walls or hedges or restore sand dunes.

On a working holiday you'll usually get fed and given a bed all for a small fee. The NT charges £55 for a week. So it's a cheap way of getting stuck into conservation work with a group of other enthusiastic people for a short period of time. It's also an introduction to the spectrum of conservation work. The NT's working-holiday programmes even include the chance to work on an archaeological dig.

Another gap-year alternative would be to take on a role as a volunteer officer at either the BTCV or the NT for six to 12 months. These officer roles are residential, meaning you'll be living away from home while you work at a protected or historical site. No fees are charged and no wage paid. BTCV even offers an NVQ in environmental management. This work experience and training can be used as a first step to a career in conservation.

If you want to work with wildlife then the Royal Society for the Protection of Birds (RSPB) is a good place to start because it runs a formal volunteering scheme for up to 100 people at its 33 reserves around the country. You'll work as a warden running the bird sanctuaries and in return receive professional training in bird conservation.

But if you want to learn about experimental conservation you might want to find a place working at the Centre for Alternative Technology in Wales, on either a working holiday or as a six-month volunteer working on various conservation, recycling and renewable-energy projects. There are only 18 of these places so it's a case of getting your foot in the door early on.

Another option is to offer help to charities working in the field of environmental campaigning. One of the most energetic is Friends of the Earth, which depends on support from volunteers. While there isn't an official scheme as such, roughly 50 volunteers are running the London HQ at any one time. Contact the volunteering co-ordinator and demonstrate your enthusiasm. Even if you don't work at HQ there are 250 Friends of the Earth local groups raising money and campaigning on environmental issues throughout the year.

Overland Expeditions

The term 'expedition' is commonly used by gap-year organisations and conservation charities to cover all kinds of adventure travel, charitable work or scientific research. It can mean several things but here it refers to an overland journey with an outward-bound character, moving from A to B through challenging landscapes. These expeditions tend to be two to six weeks of travelling in the spirit of traditional exploration.

While these adventures can be physically demanding, the sense of achievement can be exhilarating, as Cate Vinton describes:

I went with an expedition team to Zimbabwe. It was my first visit to a developing country and a complete culture shock and eye opener. We trekked up Mt Binga, the highest mountain in the country, for over a week. You realise what you're capable of. Teamwork too is so important. All the kit was shared and we had to carry everything because there were no porters.

You need to have a decent level of fitness but we never got the impression that anyone was holding us back. We didn't run up the mountain and everything was very much done as a group. My advice is don't wear yourself down. It helped that I had time to prepare for several months in advance.

There were the usual mosquitoes and nibbling insects but nothing serious. The only problem was that some people came down with a stomach bug, including the team leader, just as we were going to push for the top. The experience in all was very rewarding. It was fantastic.

Overland expeditions can vary according to the kinds of landscape crossed. For example, Jagged Globe specialises in mountaineering, combining both rock climbing and trekking. There's even the chance to climb Mt Everest but you'll have to raise a jaw-dropping £30,000 to achieve that. Most expeditions cost between £1500 and £3000 for two to six weeks as a package, where all your needs including flights are included.

The British Schools Exploring Society (BSES) and the Dorset Expeditionary Society each specialise in taking young people aged under 21 on journeys through wilderness environments to give them adventure and an educational challenge. Expeditioners are taught about ice work, camping, hill walking and living outdoors.

If you're feeling really adventurous you could even organise your own expedition with a group of friends. The Royal Geographical Society runs an Expedition Advisory Centre, which provides resources for planning an expedition or field research abroad. The society also makes small grants to scientific expeditions working in remote and challenging conditions. Each November there's a seminar called Explore where you can find contacts and inspiration. There is also a programme of workshops and lectures throughout the year with titles such as 'Land Rover Driver Training' and 'Wilderness Medical Training'. In addition, the centre publishes a list of handy books for budding explorers such as the *Expedition Planners' Handbook*, *Joining An Expedition* and *Caving Expeditions*, among many others.

Even if you don't possess the leadership gene to organise your own trip, the centre publishes a *Bulletin of Expedition Vacancies* listing trips that are looking for team members, so the centre is a great source of advice for the explorer in you that might want to paddle up the Amazon or reach the polar caps.

Contacts

GAP-YEAR ORGANISATIONS

Adventureworks

The Foundry Studios, 45 Mowbray St,
Sheffield S3 8EN
☎ 0845 345 8850
fax 0114-276 3344
e info@adventureworks.co.uk
w www.adventureworks.co.uk

Adventureworks (youth arm of mountaineering company Jagged Globe) runs a gap-year programme combining a three-week adventure in the mountains with a community-based project. Adventure activities include climbing, trekking, mountain biking and rafting. You then have the option to help a community conservation or social project, which largely involves teaching in schools. Training is given to all expeditioners. The programme fulfils the expedition requirements of the Duke of Edinburgh's Gold Award and the Queen's Scout and Guide Awards.

Timing & Length of Placement: Three-week adventures with the option to join a community project with a one- to three-month commitment. Applications should be sent six to 12 months in advance of departure. Expeditions to Ecuador & Tanzania leave in July/August (and December for Tanzania), and to Nepal in April/May or October/November.

Destinations: The mountainous regions of Ecuador, Nepal & Tanzania.

Costs/Pay: The adventure phase costs between £1500 and £2000, flights and all in-country costs included. The volunteering phase costs roughly an additional £200 per month.

Eligibility: Aged 18 to 25 but applicants are predominantly school leavers.

Africa & Asia Venture

10 Market Place, Devizes, Wilts SN10 1HT
☎ 01380-729009
fax 01380-720060
e av@aventure.co.uk
w www.aventure.co.uk

For motivated students and graduates who want to teach in the developing world. Comprehensive training is provided in local language, religion, culture and history. Throughout the placement local staff give full support and backup.

Timing & Length of Placement: Apply as early as possible; places in Kenya start to fill up a year in advance. Departures take place in September, January and May. Placements are for four to six months.

Destinations: Tanzania, Kenya, Uganda, Malawi, Botswana, Nepal & India.

Costs/Pay: Costs £2490, including accommodation, food and an allowance.

Eligibility: Applicants must be aged 18 to 24.

African Conservation Experience

Applications Department, PO Box 9706,
Solihull, West Midlands B91 3FF
☎ 0870 241 5816
e info@conservationafrica.net
w www.conservationafrica.net

Offers conservation placements in game and nature reserves in southern Africa. These are ideally suited to anyone interested in botany, biology, environmental sciences and veterinary science, especially school leavers and students considering a career in conservation and the environment. Postgrads are able to carry out specific field research.

Timing & Length of Placement: One to three months.

Destinations: Southern Africa.

Costs/Pay: Costs £3500 for three months, flights and full board included. Fundraising is supported and encouraged.

Eligibility: School leavers, university students and postgrads.

AFS International Youth Development

Leeming House, Vicar Lane, Leeds LS2 7JF
☎ 0113-242 6136
fax 0113-243 0631
e info-unitedkingdom@afs.org
w www.afsuk.org

With 50 years of experience in volunteering and community work around the world, AFS offers a large variety of opportunities. AFS prides itself on the extent of support it offers international volunteers. Cultural exchange and immersion are as important as the development work itself. Volunteers live with a local family.

Timing & Length of Placement: Six months.

Destinations: Over 50 different member countries of the AFS network around the world.

Costs/Pay: Costs from £2950.

Eligibility: Applicants must be aged 18 to 29.

Changing Worlds

11 Doctor's Lane, Chaldon, Surrey
CR3 5AE
☎ 01883-340960
fax 01883-330783
W www.changingworlds.co.uk

Changing Worlds offers a wide variety of volunteering experiences for a gap year across the globe. Opportunities include teaching or working in an orphanage.

Timing & Length of Placement: Placements are usually for three months but can be extended at no extra cost. Apply a minimum of three months in advance.

Destinations: Chile, India, Nepal & Tanzania.

Costs/Pay: Costs from £2185 including flights, insurance, food and accommodation.

Eligibility: Applicants must be aged 18 and over.

Cultural Destination Nepal

GPO Box 11535, Kathmandu, Nepal
☎/fax 00 977 1 426996
e cdnnepal@wlink.com.np
W www.volunteernepal.org.np

Runs a programme called Volunteer Nepal, which aims to introduce participants to Nepal's diverse geographical and cultural environment. Volunteers live with local families and become involved in local volunteering such as teaching English. Everyone is given a cultural induction and language training. In addition to the two-month volunteering phase there is a trekking expedition to observe traditional life and to see natural fauna and flora. The placements end with a jungle safari and white-water rafting.

Timing & Length of Placement: Placements start in February, April, August and October and last two to four months.

Destination: Nepal.

Costs/Pay: Costs from £380, accommodation and two meals a day provided. Air fare and insurance not included.

Eligibility: Applicants must be aged at least 18.

GAP Activity Projects (GAP)

44 Queen's Rd, Reading, Berks RG1 4BB
☎ 0118-959 4914
fax 0118-957 6634
e volunteer@gap.org.uk
W www.gap.org.uk

With 30 years of experience, GAP Activity Projects (GAP) is a well-established name in the gap-year market. Experiences offered include TEFL placements, caring for the disadvantaged, working in medical clinics and conservation. GAP prides itself on offering good-value placements and runs a bursary scheme for those individuals who need help with the fees. Preparation includes teaching skills if required and introductions to each country. There is also a Business Partnership Scheme, where a number of large UK businesses give former volunteers preferential consideration for summer jobs while at university.

Timing & Length of Placement: Placements mirror the academic year and run from September to September but can be from four to 12 months.

Destinations: 32 different countries.

Costs/Pay: Flat fee of £750, flights not included.

Eligibility: Applicants must be aged 18 or 19.

How to Apply: Phone or email for an application form. Interviews take place in regional centres around the UK.

Gap Challenge

World Challenge Expeditions, Black Arrow House, 2 Chandos Rd, London NW10 6NF
☎ 020-8728 7200
fax 020-8961 1551
e welcome@worldchallenge.co.uk
w www.world-challenge.co.uk

Gap Challenge runs expeditions and gap projects around the world intended to educate and develop skills among young people. The organisation sees raising the cost of an expedition as an integral part of the gap experience. Gap-year placements include medical support, conservation, teaching and care work. Travel is encouraged with 12-month return air tickets. In-country support is provided. See Expeditions later for information on the company's World Challenge Expeditions.

Timing & Length of Placement: There are no official deadlines as applications can be approved and arranged in nine days but earlier applications lead to greater choice. Three-, six- and nine-month gap-year challenges leave in September, January and April.

Destinations: The 13 different destinations include Australia, Canada, Costa Rica, Peru & Ecuador's Galápagos Islands.

Costs/Pay: Prices start at £2000, 12-month return flights and board and lodging included. Travel insurance needs to be bought separately.

Eligibility: Applicants must be aged 18 to 25.

i-to-i

England: 9 Blenheim Terrace, Leeds LS2 9H2
☎ 0870 333 2332
fax 0113-242 2171
Ireland: Main St, Ardmore, Co. Waterford
☎ 024 94889
e info@i-to-i.com
w www.i-to-i.com

i-to-i is a leading force in international volunteer and teaching placements. There are over 1000 opportunities worldwide. Placements are available in teaching English, conservation, health and other professions. A TEFL course is included for those hoping to teach English, which you can take online. Alternatively you can attend one of the weekend courses held in 16 cities around the country. It's also possible just to take the TEFL course alone and arrange independent travel. In South America and Thailand free lessons in the local language are included in the package.

Timing & Length of Placement: Applications can be sent in at the last minute because i-to-i specialises in organising late placements. But places are filled on a 'first come, first served' basis so it's advisable to book early. Placements are from two weeks to a year.

Destinations: Include Australia, Bolivia, Costa Rica, Ecuador, Honduras, China, India, Mongolia, Nepal, Sri Lanka, Thailand, Ireland, Ghana & South Africa.

Costs/Pay: Placements cost from £750 to £1795. TEFL courses taken alone cost £195.

Eligibility: Open to anyone aged 17 to 70.

Inter-Cultural Youth Exchange (ICYE) UK

Latin America House, Kingsgate Place, London NW6 4TA
☎/fax 020-7681 0983
e info@icye.co.uk
w www.icye.co.uk

ICYE UK belongs to an international federation of 35 members. Their international programme places volunteers on social and environmental projects. In Latin America many volunteer-assisted programmes provide education, housing and welfare for street children. On arrival volunteers are given a 10-day language induction. Accommodation is either residential or with a host family. Potential applicants are asked to attend a monthly information day in London.

Timing & Length of Placement: Six or 12 months.

Destinations: Many around the world including Bolivia, Brazil, Columbia, Costa Rica, Ghana, Kenya, Nepal, New Zealand, Nigeria & Thailand.

Costs/Pay: £2850/£3250 for a six-/12-month placement, international flights and living costs included.

Eligibility: Open to those aged 18 to 30 but volunteers tend to be postgrads or people on career breaks.

Kwa Madwala

PO Box 192, Hectorspruit, 1330, Mpumalang Province, South Africa
☎/fax 00 27 13-792 4219
e gazebog@mweb.co.za
W www.kwamadwala.co.za

This organisation's object is to give gap-year students a broader outlook on conservation, wildlife and life in general. The three-month gap experience will appeal to the 'all-rounder' seeking a challenging adventure and a unique holiday in the bush. A shorter option of 25 days is also on offer. You'll learn how to track lions, identify snakes and survive in the bush. At the end of the experience you'll receive a certificate in conservation competency. The reserve will also help find work in South Africa for any gappers hoping to use their new skills in employment there. Using the email address is the best means of contact.

Timing & Length of Placement: Three months.

Destinations: Kwa Madwala Private Game Reserve in South Africa, located south of Kruger National Park.

Costs/Pay: The experience costs 50,000 South African Rand (roughly £3800). Pocket money of £300 is suggested.

Eligibility: Open to anyone aged over 17. You need to be fit, healthy and able to work in a team; 'not for the faint hearted'.

The Leap

The Trainers Office, Windy Hollow, Lambourn, Berks RG17 7XA

☎ 0870 240 4187
fax 01488-71311
e info@theleap.co.uk
W www.theleap.co.uk

The Leap specialises in ecotourism and has an impressive choice of placements in different types of environment such as game parks, ranches, deserts, rainforests, mountains, beaches and coral reefs. Seventy-five per cent of volunteers are on a gap year.

Timing & Length of Placement: Placements are all for three months. Departures are flexible but usually take place in September, December, March and June. You need to apply at least a month before you leave.

Destinations: Botswana, Kenya, Namibia, Nepal, Malawi & South Africa.

Costs/Pay: Placements cost from £2100, flights excluded but all other costs included.

Eligibility: You must be aged at least 18 at time of departure.

Link Overseas Exchange

25 Perth Rd, Dundee DD1 4LN
☎ 01382-203192
fax 01382-226087
e info@linkoverseas.org.uk
W www.linkoverseas.org.uk

Gappers are mainly asked to teach conversational English and to interact with children in schools and orphanages. Other options include working in Tibetan monasteries and a women's development centre. These experiences are intended as a prelude to knowledgeable and culturally sensitive travel at the end of the placement. As a registered charity, Link can provide you with a charity number to help fundraise.

Timing & Length of Placement: Placements are for six months, which can be extended to 12 months. Applications are taken year round but departures are limited to February and August. If you want to fundraise you should give yourself several months.

Destinations: China, India & Sri Lanka.

Costs/Pay: The package costs £2250, which includes all your needs.

Eligibility: Applicants must be aged 17 to 25.

Madventurer

Adamson House, 65 Westgate Rd, Newcastle upon Tyne NE1 1SG

☎ 0845 121 1996

fax 0191-261 9010

e team@madventurer.com

w www.madventurer.com

Madventurer combines volunteering activities with a travel adventure. You can choose from a variety of options in respect of how long you volunteer and how long you travel to create a bespoke, individual package. Volunteering tends to involve refurbishing or building schools and teaching in them. You'd join a group of five to 12 people but solo opportunities are also available. Adventure travel on offer includes travelling the entire length of Africa or going to see the mountain gorillas of central Africa. If you're a university student then you can opt for one of the summer programmes, which allow you to volunteer and travel during the summer holiday.

Timing & Length of Placement: You need to apply 'the sooner the better' in order to take full advantage of fundraising help. You can volunteer for five weeks to a year. Adventure travel is from 15 to 77 days.

Destinations: Ghana, Guatemala, Kenya, Peru, Tanzania & Uganda.

Costs/Pay: A five-week volunteering placement costs £1180, which can be extended another five weeks for an extra £315. An adventure trip ranges from £370 to £900 depending on the number of weeks taken.

Eligibility: Open to those aged 18 and upwards.

Outreach International

Bartlett's Farm, Hayes Rd, Compton Dundon, Somerset TA11 6PF

☎/fax 01458-274957

e info@outreachinternational.co.uk

w www.outreachinternational.co.uk

Outreach International is keen to promote cross-cultural exchange and education, combining the desire to travel with the possibility of assisting local community projects. Conservation, education and social-work programmes are the principle focus.

Timing & Length of Placement: Projects are for three to nine months. Departures are in January, April, July and September. You should apply at least three months before although last-minute applications can still fill any empty places.

Destinations: Ecuador, Mexico & Cambodia.

Costs/Pay: Placements cost £3100 for three months plus £400 for each additional month, including travel, insurance, living and support.

Eligibility: Open to those aged 18 to 25.

Personal Overseas Development (PoD)

7 Rosbury House, Lytton Grove, Putney SW15 2EY

☎ 07880-707736

e info@thepodsite.co.uk

w www.thepodsite.co.uk

PoD specialises in short-notice programmes for students who change their plans when they get their exam results in August. It offers two gap-year experiences – working in an orphanage or teaching in an African village and helping with ecotourism. An adventure such as a safari, white-water rafting or trekking is taken at the end of the placement. Four to 12 gappers live together on one site and are supervised at a distance, unlike some gap-year placements where you tend to work with team leaders all day.

Timing & Length of Placement: Programmes lasts for three to six months. Ideally you should apply at least two months in advance of departure dates but empty places can be filled at the last minute.

Destinations: Africa, Asia & South America.

Costs/Pay: The gap programme costs £2500, flights excluded.

Eligibility: Applicants must be school leavers aged 18 and 19. Volunteers need a degree of self-sufficiency and independence.

Project Trust

The Hebridean Centre, Isle of Coll, Argyll, Scotland PA78 6TE
☎ 01879-230444
fax 01879-230357
e info@projecttrust.org.uk
w www.projecttrust.org.uk

The philosophy of Project Trust is to provide young people with an opportunity to understand an overseas community by immersing themselves in it by living and working there for a full year. Two hundred placements are made every year. All volunteers attend a one-week training course on the Scottish island of Coll where you'll be taught about your destination, enrolled on a survival course and given specific vocational training such as care work and teaching. Project Trust will provide advice and administrative help in fundraising. Opportunities exist in fields such as teaching, social/care work, outdoor education and conservation,

Timing & Length of Placement: Gappers are sent abroad for one year. Departures are August/September (January for winter programme). You need to apply as early as possible as places for autumn departures tend to be filled by the previous December; you can apply over a year ahead. Training courses are in July for autumn placements.

Destinations: 24 different destinations including China, Chile, Cuba & Malawi.

Costs/Pay: The price of £3850 includes all costs.

Eligibility: Applicants must be aged between 17 and 19.

Quest Overseas

32 Clapham Mansions, Nightingale Lane, London SW4 9AQ
☎ 020-8673 3313
fax 020-8673 7623
e emailingyou@questoverseas.com
w www.questoverseas.com

Runs gap-year environmental expeditions and projects for school leavers, undergraduates and graduates, ranging from a six-week summer expedition or project to a three-month programme, which is split into three phases to encompass a language course, a period spent volunteering and time spent on an expedition. Projects include working with an animal-rescue centre in Bolivia and a youth club in a Lima shantytown.

Timing & Length of Placement: Gap-year programmes are for three months but there's also a six-week expedition option. Applications can be processed 18 months in advance but tend to start coming in about a year before departure. Expeditions leave between December and April.

Destinations: South America & South Africa.

Costs/Pay: Prices range from £1150 to £3985 for a three-month expedition, flights and insurance excluded. A fee of £47 for training days is extra.

Eligibility: School leavers, undergraduates and graduates aged 18 to 23.

Raleigh International

27 Parsons Green Lane, London SW6 4HZ
☎ 020-7371 8585
fax 020-7371 5116
e info@raleigh.org.uk
w www.raleigh.org.uk

Raleigh International is one of the oldest gap-year organisations and runs expeditions that incorporate conservation work and community programmes such as building schools and clinics. Each expedition is split into three groups, which rotate so that everyone spends some time on a different project. Expeditioners are given training and introduced to the wider global issues of development and sustainability. Raleigh runs a Youth 'At Risk' Programme for young people who have, for example, suffered long-term unemployment or are in recovery from addictions. This ensures that expeditions include people from a diverse social background.

Timing & Length of Placement: There are 10 expeditions per year, each lasting three months. You need to apply three to 15 months in advance.

Destinations: Costa Rica, Chile, Ghana, Namibia & Malaysia.

Costs/Pay: £3500, including training, flights, food, accommodation and in-country support.

Eligibility: Open to those aged 17 to 25.

Teaching & Projects Abroad

Gerrard House, Rustington, W Sussex BN16 1AW

☎ 01903-859 911

fax 01903-785 779

e info@teaching-abroad.co.uk

W www.teaching-abroad.co.uk

Teaching & Projects Abroad offers a range of gap-year opportunities including teaching English, journalism, medicine, archaeology, conservation and animal care. In each destination there are paid and trained staff to provide support to volunteers. For every three months of voluntary work it's possible to take two weeks off for travel. Alternatively, it's possible to travel independently either before or after a placement.

Timing & Length of Placement: Placements are usually for 10 weeks. For popular programmes such as conservation in the Amazon it's best to apply 18 months in advance.

Destinations: Many countries around the world including Bolivia, China, India, Mexico, Mongolia, Nepal, Peru, Russia, Thailand & Papua New Guinea.

Costs/Pay: Placements of up to three months cost £895 to £2295, food and lodging included. Travel costs are extra.

Eligibility: For those aged over 18.

Timeless Excursions

340 Somdutt Chambers - II, 9 Bhikaji Cama Place, New Delhi 110066, India

☎ 00 91 11-6161198

fax 00 91 11-6161200

e timeless@vsnl.com

W www.timelessexcursions.com

Timeless Excursions organises gap-year placements in India teaching conversational English, art, music, drama, history, geography and maths. Other options include conservation projects in wildlife reserves, restoration of historical monuments and providing support in orphanages. Volunteers are given 24-hour support throughout the placement.

Timing & Length of Placement: One to four months.

Destination: India.

Costs/Pay: Placements cost from around £350 per month, flights excluded.

Eligibility: Applicants must be aged 17 to 23.

Trade Aid

Burgate Court, Burgate, Fordingbridge, Hants SP6 1LX

☎ 01425-657774

e tradeaid@netcomuk.co.uk

W www.mikindani.com/tradeaid

The Trade Aid project is based in Mikindani, Tanzania. In February and September each year Trade Aid takes four gap-year students to work in the community. Each group is set a specific project that necessitates special research and training before leaving the UK. In 2003 one group established a swarm of bees to produce honey, which was then handed over to the care of a local beekeeper.

Timing & Length of Placement: Placements are for five months, leaving twice a year in February and September. You should apply at least six months in advance.

Destination: Tanzania.

Costs/Pay: There's no placement fee but food and lodging are provided; volunteers need to pay for travel, insurance and vaccinations. A local wage is paid each week equivalent to £8.

Eligibility: Those aged 17 to 20 can apply for gap-year placements but older professionals are also taken.

Travellers Worldwide

7 Mulberry Close, Ferring, W Sussex BN12 5HY

☎ 01903-700478
fax 01903-502595
e info@travellersworldwide.com
w www.travellersworldwide.com

Travellers Worldwide offer placements involving teaching, conservation, work experience, learning a language and cultural exchange. See later chapters for further information on a specific field. Most volunteers are on a gap year but some will be more mature and taking career breaks. Choose from rehabilitating orang-utans to teaching drama.

Timing & Length of Placement: One- to three-month placements with the possibility of an extension or taking more than one placement. Applications can be submitted up to one month in advance. They are running programmes throughout the year so you can leave when you want.

Destinations: Argentina, Brazil, China, Cuba, Ghana, India, Kenya, Malaysia, Nepal, Russia, South Africa, Sri Lanka & Ukraine.

Costs/Pay: Placements cost from £895, including food, accommodation and support. Flights and insurance are excluded from the cost so that volunteers can have flexible travel plans. Extra months cost £200 to £500.

Eligibility: Open to those aged 17 to 70. Generally qualifications aren't required but there are some exceptions, particularly in medicine and law.

VAE Volunteer Teachers Kenya

Bell Lane Cottage, Pudleston, nr Leominster, Herefordshire HR6 0RE
☎ 01568-750329
fax 01568-750636
e harris@vaekenya.co.uk
w www.vaekenya.co.uk

A gap-year teaching programme designed to assist poor primary and secondary schools in the central Highlands area of Kenya, overlooking the Great Rift Valley. Volunteers are sent in pairs and live with Africans in a rural setting where houses have no water or electricity. On average 20 volunteers are sent out each year but demand for help is huge so there is some flexibility on numbers.

Timing & Length of Placement: Volunteers have the option of either a three- or six-month placement. Departure is usually in January.

Destination: Kenya.

Costs/Pay: A fee of £3100 includes flight, insurance and accommodation. Volunteers earn the basic salary of a local teacher. Part of the cost pays for local support staff and a programme for street kids.

Eligibility: School or university leavers.

VentureCo Worldwide

The Ironyard, 64–66 The Market Place, Warwick CV34 4SD
☎ 01926-411122
fax 01926-411133
e mail@ventureco-worldwide.com
w www.ventureco-worldwide.com

Every year teams of 16 people head off to join ventures combining a month's local language study and cultural orientation with a period spent working on a local aid project and at the end a two-month challenge of a transcontinental expedition. Volunteers can learn Spanish, work on an agri-conservation project on the Pacific Coast or with orphans, or join an expedition from the headwaters of the Amazon to the heights of Machu Picchu. VentureCo makes the distinction between school leavers and graduates on gap years.

Timing & Length of Placement: Four months.

Destinations: South & Central America, Nepal & India.

Costs/Pay: Prices from £4200, including flights, all in-country costs and a contribution to the aid project. Some pocket money is recommended on top.

Eligibility: Gap Year Ventures are for school leavers aged between 17 and 19; Career Gap Ventures are for those taking a career break or sabbatical from work or university.

Volunteer Study Abroad

PO Box 4784-00200 City Square, Nairobi, Kenya

☎ 00 254 2-722607178

e info@volunteerstudyabroad.org

w www.volunteerstudyabroad.org

A chance to spend a gap year working in a school, an orphanage, a health clinic, animal welfare or HIV education. If you only have a month or so to spare, you might want to choose a cultural-exchange programme allowing you to live with a Kenyan family and join them in their daily activities.

Timing & Length of Placement: Projects are for a week up to a year. There's no application deadline.

Destinations: Kenya but expanding to Malawi & Tanzania.

Costs/Pay: From £710 for one month, flights excluded.

Eligibility: Applicants must be aged over 16.

VOLUNTEERING ABROAD

Africatrust Networks

Beaufort Chambers, Beaufort St, Crickhowell, Powys NP8 1AA

☎/fax 01873-812453

e wales@africatrust.gi

w www.africatrust.gi

The volunteer programme is with disadvantaged young people in African rural and urban communities. Teams of 10 to 15 travel out and work together.

Timing & Length of Placement: Three to six months.

Destinations: Ghana, Mali & Morocco.

Costs/Pay: Volunteers are asked to raise £500 for three months, £750 for longer.

Eligibility: Post-university volunteers preferred.

Aid Camps

28a Stondon Park, London SE23 1LA

e info@aidcamps.org

w www.aidcamps.org

Aid Camps projects include building schools and health centres.

Timing & Length of Placement: Projects

are only for three weeks. Posts are filled on a 'first come, first served' basis but it's advisable to apply six to eight months in advance.

Destinations: Cameroon, Kenya & India.

Costs/Pay: The fee is £550, food and accommodation included. Half of the fee is used to finance the project.

Eligibility: For those aged 18 and over. No skills/experience needed.

L'Arche

10 Briggate, Silsden, Keighley, W Yorks BD20 9JT

☎ 01535-656186

fax 01535-656426

e info@larche.org.uk

w www.larche.org.uk

An international network of residential communities for adults with learning disabilities. Volunteers are needed to live with the residents and share their lives. You'll be asked to accompany residents to college, assisted workplaces or therapeutic workshops. L'Arche in the UK does not arrange international placements but will handle inquiries and can provide a list of contacts.

Timing & Length of Placement: Volunteers are asked to devote at least a year. There are always vacancies.

Destinations: Many European countries, Australia, Canada, New Zealand & the US.

Costs/Pay: There's no fee. You'll have your own room and earn some pocket money.

Eligibility: Assistants must be at least 18.

ATD Fourth World

48 Addington Square, London SE5 7LB

☎ 020-7703 3231

fax 020-7252 4276

e atd@atd-uk.org

w www.atd-uk.org

ATD sends volunteers to support human rights and alleviate extreme poverty around the world. It asks for a high level of commitment both in terms of training and time spent abroad. Assignments are drawn up according to interests and skills.

Timing & Length of Placement: Training alone takes three months. One to two years are spent abroad. Assignments take place in Europe and the developing world.

Destinations: 25 countries on five continents.

Costs/Pay: Travel is self-funded.

Eligibility: Volunteers must be 18 and over.

The Batemans Trust

Stocks Lane Farm, nr Steventon, Abingdon, Oxon OX13 6SS
☎/fax 01235-832077
e info@batemanstrust.org
w www.batemanstrust.org

The Batemans Trust was set up to help educate Anglo-Indian children, descendants of former Anglo-Indian marriages over several generations. This substantial community continues to be treated like outcasts and the families suffer many social problems. Volunteers who can teach English or extra-curricular activities such as music, drama and art are sent out to help. Trained medical staff such as nurses are also needed.

Timing & Length of Placement: Commitment needed for at least one of the school terms, which run June to September, October to December and January to April.

Destinations: Chennai (Madras) & other parts of India.

Costs/Pay: Volunteers need to cover their own flights and either raise £500 or pay a weekly charge for their food and lodging.

Eligibility: For postgrads aged over 23 with TEFL, PGCE or medical training.

British-Romanian Connections

PO Box 86, Birkenhead, Liverpool CH41 8FU
☎/fax 151-512 3355
e brc@pascu-tulbure.freeserve.co.uk

Sends volunteers to Romania to teach English and take part in school activities.

Timing & Length of Placement: Volunteers are expected to stay at least three months, which is the length of a school term. You need to apply at least two months in advance but can leave throughout the year.

Destination: One town in Romania.

Costs/Pay: Volunteers need to cover their air fare but accommodation and food is provided.

Eligibility: School leavers, students and postgrads welcome.

Casa Alianza

Unit 2, The Business Exchange, Rockingham Rd, Kettering, Northants NN16 8JX
☎ 01536-526447
fax 01536-526448
e casalnza@gn.apc.org
w www.casa-alianza.co.uk

Casa Alianza provides care and support for Central American street kids. The work is challenging and often emotionally difficult. The charity picks applicants who can demonstrate a serious and mature commitment.

Timing & Length of Placement: Minimum of six months but a year is preferred.

Destinations: Guatemala, Honduras, Nicaragua & Mexico.

Costs/Pay: There's no fixed fee but you'll need to be self-funding.

Eligibility: For university students and postgrads with a high level of dedication.

Casa Guatemala

☎ 0151-606 0729
e pete_rachel@lineone.net
w www.casa-guatemala.org

Volunteers are needed to help out in a large orphanage teaching and caring for the children. Other types of work are also possible such as working on the farm or the hotel, which raises income. Ask for their information pack.

Timing & Length of Placement: A stay of at least three months is requested.

Destination: Guatemala.

Costs/Pay: Volunteers need to arrange their own transport. Allow roughly $2 a day to cover food and accommodation.

Eligibility: Applicants must be over 18.

Challenges Worldwide

☎ 0131-332 7372
e Helen@challengesworldwide.com
w www.challengesworldwide.com

A recruitment agency for worldwide local NGOs working on constructive and sustainable project opportunities. Volunteers usually live with host families.

Timing & Length of Placement: Year-round opportunities with no application deadline. Placements are for three months to a year.

Destinations: Antigua, Bangladesh, Belize, Dominica, Ecuador, Gambia & Tasmania.

Costs/Pay: From £1650 for three months, food and accommodation included but excluding flights.

Eligibility: Minimum age of 18.

Children on the Edge

PO Box 319, Chichester, W Sussex PO19 1WJ
☎ 0845 458 1656
fax 0845 458 1657
e office@childrenontheedge.org;
w www.childrenontheedge.org

Children on the Edge has been running play schemes for orphans for 12 years. During 2003 the programme is being changed but volunteers will be needed for 2004. Check with the office or website for further details.

Destinations: East Timor, Kosovo & Romania.

Costs/Pay: From £1200, flights included.

Eligibility: Applicants must be 18 or over.

Concern

248–250 Lavender Hill, London SW11 1LJ
☎ 020-7738 1033
fax 020-7738 1032
e infolondon@london
.concernworldwide.org
w www.concern.net

Working with the world's poor, Concern runs voluntary assignments without any formal structure, which are suitable for the independent-minded. Twenty per cent of volunteers have no professional experience but skills such as nursing, accountancy, IT and administration are preferred. There are 10 to 20 places a year for people without vocational qualifications or professional experience.

Timing & Length of Placement: A commitment of two years is standard but it's possible to do a year.

Destinations: Around the world.

Costs/Pay: There's no cost and sometimes an allowance is paid.

Eligibility: Applicants must be 21 or over.

Concordia

2nd Floor, Heversham House, 20–22 Boundary Rd, Hove, E Sussex BN3 4ET
☎ 01273-422218
fax 01273-421182
e info@concordia-iye.org.uk
w www.concordia-iye.org.uk

Concordia is a not-for-profit charity committed to international youth exchange. The International Volunteer Programme offers the opportunity to join international teams working on a community-based project. Project types include conservation, renovation, archaeology, construction, youth work, special needs, arts and culture.

Timing & Length of Placement: Two to four weeks.

Destinations: Over 40 different countries.

Costs/Pay: Registration fee of £80 to £115 plus travel costs.

Eligibility: Anyone aged 16 to 30 can apply.

Cross-Cultural Solutions

PO Box 7127, Quorn, Loughborough LE12 8ZX
☎ 01509-414558
e infouk@crossculturalsolutions.org
w www.crossculturalsolutions.org

Cross-Cultural Solutions offers volunteer programmes all over the world. Placements are in social development. Emphasis is put on cultural exchange so you'll have the chance to learn about the society you work in through seminars and travel.

Timing & Length of Placement: Placements are for two to 12 weeks and can be extended. Apply 60 days in advance.

Destinations: Latin America, Asia, Africa & Eastern Europe.

Costs/Pay: The cost of £1200 includes board, lodging and insurance but excludes flights.

Eligibility: Anyone under 18 needs their parents' permission.

Cuba Solidarity Campaign (CSC)

The Red Rose Club, 129 Seven Sisters Rd, London N7 7QG
☎ 020-7263 6452
fax 020-7561 0191
e office@cuba-solidarity.org.uk
w www.cuba-solidarity.org.uk

CSC organises volunteers for the International Work Brigade camps in Cuba. British contingents are mixed with groups from other countries. Volunteers carry out light agricultural or construction work and visit schools and hospitals.

Timing & Length of Placement: Three-week camps are organised twice a year in summer and winter. Apply four months in advance.

Destination: Cuba.

Costs/Pay: The cost of the trip will be around £850, which includes flights, accommodation and food.

Eligibility: There are no age limits.

The Daneford Trust

45–47 Blythe St, London E2 6LN
☎/fax 020-7729 1928
e dfdtrust@aol.com
w danefordtrust.org

Runs an international Young Worker Exchange Programme with 25 places a year.

Timing & Length of Placement: Up to a year.

Destinations: The Caribbean & Africa.

Costs/Pay: Applicants need to raise money to cover travel and living expenses. Assistance is given in fundraising.

Eligibility: Restricted to residents of the London boroughs aged 18 to 28. Multicultural applications encouraged.

Ecologia Trust

The Park, Forres, Moray, Scotland IV36 3TZ
☎ 01309-690995
fax 01309-691009
e all@ecologia.org.uk
w www.ecologia.org.uk

Ecologia sends volunteers on gap years to Kitezh (Russia), an ecovillage that acts as foster parents to orphaned children. You'll live with a Russian family, teach English and help with the pioneering play therapy.

Timing & Length of Placement: Volunteers can go for two to 12 months year round but August and New Year are popular times. You'll need to apply a minimum of two months in advance so that visas can be arranged.

Destinations: Kitezh, 300km south of Moscow. Ecologia also runs summer camps at Kitezh and an ecological camp in the Urals.

Costs/Pay: Volunteers pay £625 for two months, flights excluded.

Eligibility: Applicants must be 16 or over.

European Voluntary Service (EVS)

c/o Connect Youth, British Council, 10 Spring Gardens, London SW1A 2BN
☎ 020-7389 4030
fax 020-7389 4033
e connectyouth.enquiries@british council.org
w www.connectyouthinternational.com

Funded by the EU, EVS is designed to enable young people to volunteer in another European country. Opportunities include working in conservation, or with children, the disabled, the elderly or young people. You'll need to find a 'sending' organisation in the UK that's affiliated with the scheme, which will then send you to a 'host' organisation in one of the participating countries. These include EIL, ICYE, Project Trust and UNA Exchange, which are listed separately in this chapter.

Timing & Length of Placement: Voluntary service lasts six to 12 months. Applications should be made a minimum of six months in advance.

Destinations: Member countries of the EU plus Norway & Iceland. Additionally, some limited opportunities in Latin America & Africa.

Costs/Pay: Volunteers receive an allowance of £120 per month plus board and lodging. Basic expenses, insurance and training are reimbursed.

Eligibility: Applicants should be aged between 18 and 25. No qualifications are required.

Experiment in International Living (EIL)

287 Worcester Rd, Malvern, Worcs WR14 1AB
☎ 0800 018 4015/01684-562577
fax 01684-562212
e info@eiluk.org
w www.eiluk.org

EIL sends volunteers abroad to help with social, environmental and civic activities in the developing world. Language training is included as part of the programme. Volunteers travel alone but join teams of international volunteers.

Timing & Length of Placement: Three months is the average length but this can be extended. Applications should be in at least 10 weeks in advance. Most departures are during the academic summer holidays but volunteers can be placed throughout the year.

Destinations: Twelve countries largely in Latin America but also Africa & Asia.

Costs/Pay: From £430 to £1800, travel and insurance excluded.

Eligibility: Applicants must be 18 and over. A willingness to work in a team and take language lessons is important. Pre-existing knowledge of any languages is an asset, especially Spanish.

Global Vision International (GVI)

Amwell Farmhouse, Wheathampstead, Herts AL4 8EJ
☎ 01582-831300
e info@gvi.co.uk
w www.gvi.co.uk

GVI offers conservation and community projects. Choices include working with street children in Ecuador to working in a New Zealand ecosanctuary. GVI provides monthly volunteer workshops to give prospective volunteers an idea of what they will be doing, plus full training upon arrival at the host project.

Timing & Length of Placement: Expeditions leave every month. You need to apply at least one month in advance.

Destinations: Ten countries including Honduras, Nepal, South Africa & the USA.

Costs/Pay: £350 to £5000, flights and insurance excluded.

Eligibility: Anyone from 17 to 70 is welcome to apply but volunteers tend to be post-grads. No experience needed.

Habitat for Humanity

11 Parsons St, Banbury OX16 5LW
☎ 01295-220184
fax 01295-264230
e enquiries@hfhgb.org
w www.hfhgb.org

Teams of 10 to 15 leave the UK to join other international teams to build housing for the poor, which are sold at cost without interest on the loan. When you apply as an individual you'll be assigned to an open team.

Timing & Length of Placement: Projects are for two to three weeks.

Destinations: Forty-five different countries.

Costs/Pay: You'll need to raise £2000, which contributes to building costs. Flights, vaccinations and visa are extra.

Eligibility: Volunteers must be 18 and upwards.

Hands Around The World

PO Box 25, Coleford, Glos GL16 7YL
☎/fax 01594-560223
e info@handsaroundtheworld.org.uk
w www.handsaroundtheworld.org.uk

Groups go from specific areas of Britain to build and refurbish schools and clinics.

Projects will be advertised in your local press. Or you can apply as a skilled volunteer, eg, a medic or IT specialist.

Timing & Length of Placement: Projects last two to three months. Teams go out year round.

Destinations: Brazil, Kenya, India & Zambia.

Costs/Pay: Costs are £200 per member and the group needs to raise £1500 per person.

Eligibility: For those aged 18 plus.

Himalayan Light Foundation (HLF)

GPO Box 12191, Kathmandu, Nepal
☎ 00 997 1 425393
fax 00 997 1 412924
e info@hlf.org.np
w www.hlf.org.np

HLF is an NGO working to improve the quality of life for Nepal's remote Himalayan population by introducing renewable energy technologies. Volunteers are needed to develop and coordinate the programmes by working with local NGOs and donor agencies. You'll live with a local family, have your own room and receive two meals a day. Volunteers are also requested to bring their own laptop computer to work on.

Timing & Length of Placement: Volunteers are asked to give a five-month commitment.

Destination: Nepal.

Costs/Pay: A £95 contribution is charged. Living with a local family will cost approximately £51 per week.

Eligibility: More suited to undergrads or postgrads. Computer literacy is required, especially knowledge of MS Word, Excel and Outlook. You'll also need a Bachelor's degree, or to have at least enrolled in a university programme.

HiPACT

PO Box 770, York House, Empire Way, Wembley, Mddx HA9 0RP
☎ 020-8900 1221
fax 020-8900 0330
e enquiries@hipact.ac.uk
w www.hipact.ac.uk

HiPACT is an association of British universities working to develop educational resources. Each year it takes between 50 and 80 volunteers to support the work in Nigeria. Volunteering ranges from help on the TV show to setting up community education projects.

Timing & Length of Placement: From five to 10 weeks, which can be extended by request.

Destination: Nigeria.

Costs/Pay: There's no fee. You'll pay for your flights and sometimes you'll be asked to contribute towards food and accommodation.

Eligibility: You must be an undergrad or postgrad.

ICA:UK

PO Box 171, Manchester M15 5BE
☎/fax 0845 450 0305 or 0161-232 8444
e ica-www@ica-uk.org.uk
w www.ica-uk.org.uk

Placements are with local development organisations worldwide. First determine whether or not to volunteer at a Volunteer Orientation Weekend. Then you must attend the 12-day Volunteer Foundation Course. It's possible to apply to a scholarship fund for help with course costs.

Timing & Length of Placement: Placements are for nine to 15 months. Try to plan a year ahead.

Destinations: Around the world.

Costs/Pay: The foundation course costs £990. Placements generally provide accommodation and sometimes a modest living allowance. Volunteers are responsible for flights.

Eligibility: Everyone over 18 is welcome but you need to be independent by nature and able to 'land on your feet' in a new environment.

India Development Group

68 Downlands Rd, Purley, Surrey CR8 4JF
☎ 020-8668 3161
fax 020-8660 8541
e idguk@clara.co.uk
w www.idguk.org

This group works in rural development helping villagers learn new economic skills and self-sufficiency. Any technical expertise is particularly useful.

Timing & Length of Placement: Placements are for a minimum of six months. There's no set deadline for applications but it's best if volunteers go in September.

Destination: India.

Costs/Pay: Volunteers pay for travel and living costs. Accommodation with breakfast is available, plus evening meals and lodging for around £3 a day.

Eligibility: For those aged over 21.

International Voluntary Service (IVS)

Old Hall, East Bergholt, Colchester
CO7 6TQ
☎ 01206-298215
fax 01206-299043
e ivs@ivsgbsouth.demon.co.uk
w www.ivsgbn.demon.co.uk

IVS attaches volunteers to short-term work camps, which assist conservation, inner-city kids, orphanages, community arts and people with disabilities. You'll be joining teams made up of six to 20 volunteers from around the world. There are over 700 activities to choose from every year.

Timing & Length of Placement: A booklet comes out every April so it's best to register before then so you can have the greatest choice. Placements are for two to four weeks but you can join different work camps back-to-back for as long as you want.

Destinations: All around the world.

Costs/Pay: The registration fee is £105, food and accommodation provided. Volunteers cover their own travel costs.

Eligibility: Volunteers need to be at least 18.

Involvement Volunteers

7 Bushmead Ave, Kingskerswell, Newton Abbot, Devon TQ12 5EN
☎ 01803-872594
fax 01803-403154
e ivengland@volunteering.org.au
w www.volunteering.org.au

This Australian international group runs a huge programme of volunteering opportunities around the world. Choices include saving turtles, working on a steam railway, living with indigenous families or helping on horse trails. The advantage of this programme is that you can choose as many placements as you want. Each prospective volunteer states a preference for a country or region and the kind of work they want to do. Then a special programme is built around them.

Timing & Length of Placement: Applications are taken year round but you need to give at least one month's notice. Placements can range from three weeks to a year.

Destinations: Forty different countries, including Argentina, Australia, Fiji, Japan, India, Nepal & New Zealand.

Costs/Pay: Registration costs £80. The programme fee depends entirely on how many placements you choose and where you go. If you plan to volunteer in Australia on three placements you're looking at paying about £380. You're responsible for all your other costs although often food and accommodation are provided. In some very poor countries such as India you'll be expected to make a contribution to the people you're living with.

Eligibility: Anyone aged 18 and beyond.

Karen Hilltribes Trust

Midgley House, Heslington, York
YO10 5DX
☎ 01904-411891
fax 01904-430580
e penelope@karenhilltribes.org.uk
w www.karenhilltribes.org.uk

Volunteers help with teaching English and installing clean water systems for the indigenous Karen Hilltribes of Thailand. Fifty to 70 volunteers are recruited annually to assist the ongoing work of the charity but this is not a programme with the needs of volunteers first in mind.

Timing & Length of Placement: Applications are taken year round but the trust prefers a six- to nine-month commitment in order to coincide with much of the Thai school year.

Destination: Northern Thailand.

Costs/Pay: There's a fee of £1250, which goes to the work of the charity, but you'll need to raise approximately £3000 in total to cover all your costs such as travel and food.

Eligibility: For anyone aged 18 and over but graduates preferred. Dedication to the work of the charity is important. You'll also need to make the effort to learn both the Thai and Karen languages while you're there.

Kibbutz Reps

1a Accommodation Rd, London
NW11 8ED
☎ 020-8458 9235
fax 020-8455 7930
e inquiry@kibbutz.org.uk

This is the official representative of the Kibbutz movement in the UK. You'll need to register with Kibbutz Reps, which will then arrange your volunteering placement in Israel.

Timing & Length of Placement: It's recommended that you apply at least four weeks in advance but last-minute arrangements are sometimes possible. Volunteers are asked to make a minimum two-month commitment and can stay for up to eight months.

Destinations: Israeli Kibbutzim.

Costs/Pay: The fee is roughly £300, including administration, insurance and the flight to Israel. Spending money of approximately £50 per month is paid to volunteers.

Eligibility: For those aged 18 to 35.

Marlborough Brandt Group (MBG)

1a London Rd, Marlborough, Wilts
SN8 1PH
☎ 01672-514078
fax 01672-514992
e info@mbg.org
W www.mbg.org

Named after the famous Brandt Commission Report advocating support for the developing world, MBG runs an aid and education project in Gambia. Younger volunteers leave in groups of four to stay with local families and work as teaching assistants in secondary schools. Postgrads with skills can find a placement according to their expertise. Volunteers should apply in writing and they will receive an information pack.

Timing & Length of Placement: Placements are for three months; skilled volunteers can stay longer.

Destination: Gambia.

Costs/Pay: The fee is £1500, which includes flights and living expenses.

Eligibility: Applicants must be 18 or over.

MondoChallenge

Galliford Bldg, Gayton Rd, Milton Malsor,
Northampton NN7 3AB
☎ 01604-858225
fax 01604-859323
e info@mondochallenge.org
W www.mondochallenge.org

MondoChallenge sends volunteers to teach English, maths and science to primary and secondary schools in the developing world.

Timing & Length of Placement: Stays are normally from two to four months. You can travel out at any time of the year and there's no deadline for application.

Destinations: Chile, Gambia, India, Kenya, Nepal, Sri Lanka & Tanzania.

Costs/Pay: Volunteers pay £800 for three months, travel costs excluded. Part of the fee is channelled into the school.

Eligibility: For those aged 18 and over. TEFL isn't required.

Muyal Liang Trust

53 Blenheim Crescent, London W11 2EG
☎ 020-7229 4774
e jjulesstewart@aol.com

Volunteers are needed to teach English at a school in Sikkim (India) run by the Trust. Four to five teachers are needed from March to December, the local school year. It's best to email your interest and in return you'll receive a factsheet explaining the project in detail.

Timing & Length of Placement: You need to commit to two months, which can be extended provided the Indian government agrees to a new visa. There's no application deadline.

Destination: India.

Costs/Pay: No fee required but volunteers must fund their travel and costs.

Eligibility: For those aged 18 and above but older postgrad volunteers preferred. A school leaver would need to demonstrate enough maturity.

Nepal Kingdom Foundation/ Muirs Tours

Nepal House, 97a Swansea Rd, Reading, Berks RG18HA
☎ 0118-950 2281
e info@nkf-mt.org.uk
W www.nkf-mt.org.uk

At any one time 45 to 50 volunteers are working in rural areas of Nepal teaching English, working in conservation and permaculture, and helping support the development of tourism as a source of local income. Muirs Tours is the sister non-profit organisation, which arranges volunteering opportunities. For example, it's possible to work in Tanzania training local people to work as tourist guides.

Timing & Length of Placement: Placements are for two months plus. Applications are taken year round.

Destination: Nepal.

Costs/Pay: There's a registration fee of £100 plus a daily living cost. In Nepal you'll pay £5 per day to cover all accommodation and food.

Eligibility: For those aged 18 and over.

Nicaragua Solidarity Campaign (NSC)

129 Seven Sisters Rd, London N7 7QG
☎ 020-7272 9619
fax 020-7272 5476
e nsc@nicaraguasc.org.uk
W www.nicaraguasc.org.uk

NSC operates short trips to help Fair Trade agricultural cooperatives grow and harvest coffee, sesame oil and vegetables. If a volunteer wants to stay longer than the usual three weeks, NSC will help provide a 'tailor-made' placement for several months. Volunteers live with host families.

Timing & Length of Placement: Trips are usually for three weeks. Apply by April to be sure of a place on the one certain trip that leaves each year.

Destination: Nicaragua.

Costs/Pay: The approximate cost is £1000, which covers everything except spending money.

Eligibility: For those aged 18 and over.

Rokpa UK Overseas Projects

Kagyu Samye Ling Eskdalemuir,
Langholm, Dumfriesshire DG13 0QL
☎ 01387-373232
fax 01387-373223
e charity@rokpauk.org
W www.rokpauk.org

There are a few places each year teaching English in Tibet and working in a Nepalese soup kitchen.

Timing & Length of Placement: You can apply any time for placements in Tibet but the Nepalese soup kitchen only opens mid-December to the end of March so you need to apply before then.

Destinations: Tibet & Nepal.

Costs/Pay: Both schemes require self-funding. In Tibet food and accommodation are provided but in Nepal volunteers are asked to find local lodging.

Eligibility: Applicants should be aged 21 and over.

Rural Centre for Human Interests (RUCHI)

Bandh, Bhaguri 173233, Dist. Solan,
Himachal Pradesh, India
☎ 00 91 1792-82454
fax 00 91 1792-82516
e totem_volunteer_India@yahoo.com
W www.ruchi.org

RUCHI, a development charity in the Himalayan foothills, runs the Totem volunteer programme. You can choose to work in social development, environmental management, improving water facilities or all three.

Timing & Length of Placement: You can travel out year round although October is the best time of year for the weather. There is space for 20 volunteers at any one time. Volunteers usually come for three weeks but it's possible to stay longer by arrangement with the charity.

Destination: India.

Costs/Pay: Volunteers pay £700 for food, board and programme costs. Flights are excluded.

Eligibility: For those aged 18 plus.

Save the Earth Network

PO Box CT 3635, Cantonments, Accra, Ghana

☎ 00 233 21-667791

fax 00 233 21-669625

e ebensten@yahoo.com

This African-based group recruits volunteers to build schools and libraries, teach English and maths, and care for street children and orphans. Conservation work is also an option. You'll live with a local family but have your own room. Cultural and environmental tours are also on offer to volunteers so they can learn about Ghana in depth.

Timing & Length of Placement: Placements are from one month to a year. You can join year round.

Destination: Ghana.

Costs/Pay: Each month costs £158, food and lodging included. Anyone wanting to stay more than two months receives a 25% discount. Ecotours cost £126 per week.

Eligibility: Applicants must be 18 plus.

Skillshare International

126 New Walk, Leicester LE1 7JA

☎ 0116-254 1862

fax 0116-254 2614

e info@skillshare.org

W www.skillshare.org

Skillshare only recruits people with professional experience such as finance, project management, small business, health, teaching or conservation.

Timing & Length of Placement: Training takes place over six months and you'll then need to commit for at least one year.

Destinations: Eastern & southern Africa, & India.

Costs/Pay: Recruits must pay for their own travel and expenses but usually a small allowance equivalent to a local wage is paid. Accommodation tends to be provided.

Eligibility: You need to have two years' professional experience and be aged at least 25.

Student Action India (SAI)

c/o HomeNet, Office 20, 30–38 Dock St, Leeds LS10 1JF

☎ 07071-225866

e info@studentactionindia.org.uk

W www.studentactionindia.org.uk

SAI runs volunteer placements in 'social development', teaching Indians basic literacy and numeracy, and health skills. Volunteer work might be with street children, women's credit unions or rural development projects.

Timing & Length of Placement: There's a two-month summer programme for July to August and a five-month placement for September to February.

Destinations: India – placements in Bangalore, Delhi, Mumbai & Indore.

Costs/Pay: Two months cost £475 and five months cost £950, flights and insurance excluded. Budget for roughly £50 per month living expenses.

Eligibility: Applicants must be 18 plus. Volunteers should try to demonstrate an awareness of development and an interest in India although first-time visitors are welcome.

Student Partnerships Worldwide (SPW)

17 Dean's Yard, London SW1P 3PB

☎ 020-7222 0138

fax 020-7233 0088

e spwuk@gn.apc.org

W www.spw.org

SPW offers the chance to work with African and Asian volunteers in rural communities, developing life skills and changing attitudes to health, social and environmental issues. There are two programmes: health education and environment. Volunteers from the UK are paired with a volunteer from the host country.

Timing & Length of Placement: Volunteers leave every September, January, February and March for four- to nine-month assignments. There's no application deadline.

Destinations: India, Nepal, Uganda, South Africa, Tanzania & Zimbabwe.

Costs/Pay: Fees are £2900 to £3300 and cover everything.

Eligibility: Applicants should be aged 18 to 28 and have a serious commitment to development issues.

Sudan Volunteer Programme (SVP)

34 Estelle Rd, London NW3 2JY
☎/fax 020-7485 8619
e davidsvp@aol.com
w www.svp-uk.com

SVP recruits 20 to 30 native English speakers a year as teachers of the language, preferably with TEFL.

Timing & Length of Placement: SVP likes people to volunteer for at least four months. Volunteers mainly leave in September, January and July.

Destination: Northern Sudan.

Costs/Pay: Accommodation is provided as well as a monthly stipend equivalent to US$100. Volunteers cover the flights.

Eligibility: For undergraduates upwards.

TANZED

80 Edleston Rd, Crewe, Cheshire
CW2 7HD
☎ 01270-509994
e enquiries@tanzed.org
w www.tanzed.org

Volunteers are needed to work as English teachers in Tanzanian rural primary schools. You'll live in pairs within a village. There's unlikely to be electricity and certainly no running water although you'll be within reach of a well.

Timing & Length of Placement: You need to commit to a minimum of six months but preferably 12, which can be extended by agreement. Departures are in January and June/July but there is some flexibility. Applications should be made six months in advance.

Destination: Tanzania.

Costs/Pay: The fee is £1750, which covers flights, insurance, training and accommodation.

Eligibility: Applicants must be postgrads aged 21 and over with either a TEFL or PGCE certificate.

Task Brasil Trust

PO Box 4901, London SE16 3PP
☎ 020-7394 1177
fax 020-7394 7713
e info@taskbrasil.org.uk
w www.taskbrasil.org.uk

Task Brasil works with the street children of Rio de Janeiro, where it runs a shelter and several outreach projects. Volunteers are encouraged to use all of their skills to help out with teaching, cooking, cleaning and generally caring for the children. In 2003 it opened an organic farm in the country to take children out of the harsh urban environment and teach them agricultural skills. Volunteers can spend alternating weeks in the city and the farm or choose to remain just on one project.

Timing & Length of Placement: Placements run from a few weeks to a year. You can join Task Brasil year round but do need to apply three months in advance.

Destinations: Rio de Janeiro, city and state, Brazil.

Costs/Pay: Costs cover flights, food and accommodation and are £1200 for one to three months, £1800 for three to six and £2500 for six to 12.

Eligibility: Applicants must be 21 plus.

Tukae

22 Hilgrove Rd, Newquay, Cornwall
TR7 2QZ
☎ 07880-707736/01637-874188

e aas@tukae.org

W www.tukae.org

Tukae is just beginning to actively recruit gappers, mainly to teach English in primary schools but if volunteers have any particular skills these can be put to good use. A new educational resource centre is being planned for the project. Applicants should first contact Personal Overseas Development (PoD; see Gap-Year Organisations earlier), which handles recruitment.

Timing & Length of Placement: A six-month commitment is preferred, which can then be extended. Apply at least three months in advance but places depend on the availability of accommodation.

Destination: Northeastern Tanzania.

Costs/Pay: The programmes cost from £3000, which covers everything.

Eligibility: Everyone aged 18 and over. No skills required but any are welcome.

UNA Exchange

Temple of Peace and Health, Cathays Park, Cardiff CF10 3AP

☎ 029-2022 3088

fax 029-2066 5557

e info@unaexchange.org

W www.unaexchange.org

UNA Exchange arranges International Volunteering Placements (IVPs) and Medium Term Volunteering (MTV), and is also a sending agency for the European Volunteer Service (EVS; see separate entry earlier). Assignments include environmental and social work such as working in an orphanage. Some projects require an orientation weekend.

Timing & Length of Placement: Long-term EVS projects are for six to 12 months, MTV is for one to 12 months and IVPs are for two to three weeks.

Destinations: Over 50 countries.

Costs/Pay: The registration fee for MTV and IVPs is £120 (£100 for members), excluding travel costs but usually including food and accommodation. A contribution to the local project of around £100 to £150 is also required. See the website for EVS fees.

Local projects may pay a small allowance.

Eligibility: IVPs are for anyone aged 15 plus. EVS volunteers must be 18 to 25.

Village Education Project (Kilimanjaro)

Mint Cottage, Prospect Rd, Sevenoaks, Kent TN13 3UA

☎ 01732-459799

e info@kiliproject.org

W www.kiliproject.org

Volunteers teach English to primary-school children and organise extra-curricular activities. There are 10 places each year.

Timing & Length of Placement: Teaching assignments last eight months. The deadline is October for departure in January.

Destination: Mshiri village on the slopes of Mt Kilimanjaro, Tanzania.

Costs/Pay: £2000, flights and accommodation included but food excluded.

Eligibility: For those aged 18 and over.

Volunteer Africa

W www.volunteerafrica.org

Volunteers work with local people in Tanzania to build community resources such as schools or health centres, which is '...hard work and hard living but fun'. There's full pre-departure and overseas support. Anyone interested is asked to contact Volunteer Africa through the online application form.

Timing & Length of Placement: You have the choice of four-, seven- or 10-week assignments. Ideally you should apply six months in advance, particularly if fundraising (advice and help is provided).

Destination: Singida Region, Tanzania.

Costs/Pay: From £970 to £1810, food and accommodation included but excluding flights and insurance.

Eligibility: For anyone over 18.

Voluntary Service Overseas (VSO)

317 Putney Bridge Rd, London SW15 2PN

☎ 020-8780 7500

e enquiry@vso.org.uk

W www.vso.org.uk

See the VSO section earlier in this chapter for detailed information.

Timing & Length of Placement: The World Youth Millennium Awards (WYMA) programme begins February and August and lasts six months.

Destinations: Cameroon, Ghana, India, Indonesia, Nigeria, Sri Lanka, South Africa, Tanzania & Thailand.

Costs/Pay: You'll need to raise at least £500 for the WYMA, which will cover travel, accommodation and food.

Eligibility: WYMA programmes are for anyone aged 17 to 25.

Winant Clayton Volunteer Association (WCVA)

The Davenant Centre, 179 Whitechapel Rd, London E1 1DU

☎ 020-7375 0547

e wcva@dircon.co.uk

w www.wcva.dircon.co.uk

For 50 years WCVA has been placing British volunteers in social projects such as working with the homeless, HIV sufferers and the elderly. There are about 20 places each year. All visas are arranged by WCVA.

Timing & Length of Placement: Placements are for two months from late June to July. Applications should be in by the end of January.

Destination: East coast of the USA.

Costs/Pay: You need to buy your own flights but accommodation and a weekly stipend for food are provided.

Eligibility: For British and Irish passport holders aged 18 and over.

Youth Action for Peace (YAP)

8 Golden Ridge, Freshwater, Isle of Wight PO40 9LE

☎ 01983-752557

e yapuk@ukonline.co.uk

w www.yap-uk.org

YAP is an international movement promoting human rights, sustainable development and youth exchanges. At any one time it holds information on thousands of projects and work camps looking for short-term volunteers. If you join YAP you'll be sent out to join a team of international volunteers building schools and clinics or refurbishing existing community facilities.

Timing & Length of Placement: Most camps last two to three weeks but it's possible to do a series of camps for up to a year. There's no deadline but most of the camps take place in summer. It's best to join in March when the annual directory is published.

Destinations: Many in Europe but opportunities are global.

Costs/Pay: A registration fee of £95 entitles you to receive the directory and access it online. Travel costs are your responsibility but food and accommodation are usually provided.

Eligibility: Applicants must be 18 or over.

RELIGIOUS ORGANISATIONS

Africa Inland Mission (AIM)

3 Halifax Place, Nottingham NG1 1QN

☎ 0115-950 1199

e uk@aim-eur.org

w www.aim-eur.org

AIM recruits members of Protestant churches to teach in African schools.

Timing & Length of Placement: Three-month to two-year placements. You need to apply by March 30 for departures the following September and January.

Destinations: Kenya, Lesotho, Mozambique & Uganda.

Costs/Pay: Volunteers are expected to raise from £1500 to £4000 to cover all expenses.

Eligibility: You need to be at least 18 and a member of a Protestant church.

Assumption Lay Volunteer Programme (ALVP)

23 Kensington Square, London W8 5HN

☎ 020-7361 4752

e cburns@rayouth.freeserve.co.uk

w www.assumptionreligious.org

ALVP is an ecumenical volunteering opportunity run by the Assumption Sisters for mature, adaptable and willing people. It's mainly used by professionals on a career break or direction change but gappers above the age limit are welcome to apply. The work revolves around education in its broadest sense.

Timing & Length of Placement: You need to apply at least six months in advance to join the part-time training course.

Destinations: Many countries around the world.

Costs/Pay: Volunteers are asked to raise £700. The balance for the full cost is covered by the Order.

Eligibility: Professional skills aren't essential but you must be aged 22 to 40.

BMS World Mission

PO Box 49, 129 Broadway, Didcot, Oxon
OX11 8XA
☎ 01235-517700
W www.bmsworldmission.org

This Baptist missionary group arranges gap-year service placements for 'action teams' in three phases: training in September; six months spent volunteering abroad; and an educational tour on return. Volunteers will be matched to a placement according to their skills and experience. Work involves street kids, teaching English, evangelism, construction and youth work.

Timing & Length of Placement: The mission is for 10 months from September and you need to apply by the end of February.

Destinations: Brazil, Kosovo, India, Italy, Nepal & Uganda.

Costs/Pay: The cost for gappers is around £3200 but this varies.

Eligibility: You must be aged 18 to 25.

Christians Abroad

233 Bon Marché Centre, 241–251
Ferndale Rd, London SW9 8BJ
☎ 0870 770 7990
fax 0870 770 7991
e admin@cabroad.org.uk
W www.cabroad.org.uk

Christians Abroad is a 'faith-based' Christian ecumenical recruitment agency working with locally based projects that don't have links to other British organisations. Volunteers are expected to profess Christianity because the schools and hospitals they are sent to expect that, but denomination is not relevant. All volunteers are also asked to attend a pre-departure briefing. An ability to adapt to isolation and challenging conditions such as rudimentary services is recommended. Volunteering vacancies are regularly published on the website.

Timing & Length of Placement: Two months to a year plus.

Destinations: Around the world but mostly in Africa.

Costs/Pay: There's a £150 administration fee. Volunteers are expected to buy their flights and health insurance through Christians Abroad because they can claim the tax back to fund its work.

Eligibility: Applicants must be aged 21 and over.

Christian Aid

PO Box 100, London SE1 7RT
☎ 020-7960 2703
e gapyear@christian-aid.org
W www.christian-aid.org.uk/gapyear

Christian Aid's gap-year scheme uses gappers to promote international development in British schools and youth groups.

Timing & Length of Placement: The scheme runs from September to June. Apply early in the calendar year.

Destinations: The UK, with a two-week trip to one of the overseas projects.

Costs/Pay: Volunteers are asked to raise £1800, including food, board and overseas trip.

Eligibility: Open to those aged 18 to 25. Non-denominational but practising Christians are preferred as much of the work takes place in church groups.

Church Mission Society

157 Waterloo Rd, London SE1 8UU
☎ 020-7928 8681

fax 020-7401 3215
e info@cms-uk.org
w www.cms-uk.org
The Church Mission Society is a voluntary society within the Church of England. It welcomes Christian volunteers of all denominations. The 'Make A Difference' programme operates around the world in cross-cultural missions such as helping refugees, schools and hospitals.
Timing & Length of Placement: Training sessions take place twice yearly in July and December. Applications need to be in at least two months before either session. Placements are for six to 18 months.
Destinations: 21 different countries.
Costs/Pay: Placements are self-financed. A one-year placement is usually around £3000. Sometimes an allowance will be paid.
Eligibility: Applicants must be aged 18 to 30.

Experience Exchange Programme (EEP)

USPG, 157 Waterloo Rd, London SE1 8XG
☎ 020-7803 3416
e habibn@uspg.org.uk
w www.uspg.org.uk
Volunteers 'need to be able to explore the concept of faith and work in a Christian environment' but the programme is not evangelistic. The EEP is jointly run by USPG and the Methodist Church and recruits volunteers using its massive network of contacts to match individuals to indigenous social projects.
Timing & Length of Placement: Placements are for six to 12 months. Twelve-day training programmes take place in July and December. Apply at least three months in advance.
Destinations: All over the world.
Costs/Pay: Volunteers need approximately £2000. EEP has some financial resources to help those who find it difficult to raise the necessary finances.
Eligibility: Applicants must be at least 18.

Jesuit Volunteer Community (JVC)

23 New Mount St, Manchester M4 4DE

☎ 0161-832 6868
fax 0161-832 6958
e staff@jvc.u-net.com
w www.jesuitvolunteers-uk.org
JVC mainly runs a gap-year scheme in the UK but it also places individuals within sister projects in Europe. Volunteers live in communal houses and work on inner-city projects following four guiding principles: spirituality, simple living, social justice and community.
Timing & Length of Placement: You need to apply by the end of April in order to qualify for the scheme, which takes place from September to July. Contact JVC to find out the European application deadline.
Destinations: France, Germany & the UK.
Costs/Pay: You only need to cover travel costs.
Eligibility: Applicants must be aged 18 to 35. You must be fluent in either French or German for a European placement.

Latin Link

175 Tower Bridge Rd, London SE1 2AB
☎ 020-7939 9000
fax 020-7939 9015
e step.uk@latinuk.org
w www.stepteams.org
Latin Link operates Step Teams, volunteers who go out to Latin America to work on social projects such as building community resources, helping with street kids or working in soup kitchens. Volunteers work in a non-denominational Christian ethos.
Timing & Length of Work: Spring programmes last four months, summer programmes seven weeks. These can be taken back-to-back. Application deadlines for these are December and May.
Destinations: Argentina, Brazil, Bolivia, Cuba, Ecuador, Peru & Spain.
Costs/Pay: Fees start from £1800 and include flights, food and accommodation. Spending money of £350 or more is also needed.
Eligibility: For those aged 17 and over. Most volunteers sit in the 18 to 30 age group.

Oasis Trust

The Oasis Centre, 115 Southwark Bridge Rd, London SE1 0AX
☎ 020-7450 9000
fax 020-7450 9001
W www.oasisteams.org

Oasis runs several different programmes for volunteers to work in 'social action' around the world, helping to provide shelter, food and education for the vulnerable and socially excluded.

Timing & Length of Placement: Placements are generally for a month to a year. Most teams and individual placements leave in September. Applications should be sent in at least three months in advance.

Destinations: 16 countries on five continents.

Costs/Pay: From £1000 to £5000 inclusive of all costs except vaccinations. Taking additional spending money is recommended.

Eligibility: For those aged 18 or over. Anyone younger can apply for under a month's work.

Time for God (TFG)

2 Chester House, Pages Lane, Muswell Hill, London N10 1PR
☎ 020-8883 1504
fax 020-8365 2471
e recruit@timeforgod.org
W www.timeforgod.com

TFG offers people-based community work around the world such as in schools and inner-city projects.

Timing & Length of Placement: You can volunteer for 10 to 12 months. There are two start dates: September and January. Applications should be in at least two months beforehand.

Destinations: Around the world.

Costs/Pay: Volunteers need to raise £700/£1000 for UK and international projects respectively, which will cover accommodation, food and pocket money.

Eligibility: Applicants must be aged 18 to 25.

The Toybox Charity

PO Box 660, Amersham, Bucks HP6 5YT

☎ 01494-432591
fax 01494-432593
e info@toybox.org
W www.toyboxhomes.org.uk

Toybox is a small charity that offers four to six places each year working with street kids in Guatemala.

Timing & Length of Placement: Apply anytime but volunteers leave in September.

Destination: Guatemala.

Costs/Pay: You need to raise £3000 for a year's placement, flights included.

Eligibility: For those aged 18 to early 30s.

Transform (Tearfund)

100 Church Rd, Teddington TW11 8QE
☎ 020-8977 9144
fax 020-8943 3594
e transform@tearfund.org
W www.tearfund.org/transform

There are approximately 42 places for volunteers to work mainly with children in areas such as AIDS, disability and teaching English. Work is with Christian partners and volunteers are expected to support the evangelical basis of faith.

Timing & Length of Placement: Apply by November to depart in March and return in July.

Destinations: Malawi, Mexico, Lesotho & Thailand.

Costs/Pay: The cost includes everything except vaccinations and starts from £2550.

Eligibility: For those aged 18 to 24.

UK Jewish Aid & International Development (UKJAID)

44a New Cavendish St, London W1G 8TR
☎ 020-7224 3788
e ukjaid@talk21.com
W www.ukjaid.org

UKJAID is a channel into 'non-sectarian' international development for the Jewish community. The volunteering scheme was being developed during 2003. Contact the office for the latest details.

Timing & Length of Placement: Placements are for three to six months.

Destinations: Dependent on the needs of

partner agencies. Contact the organisation for current opportunities.

Costs/Pay: Contact UKJAID directly for up-to-date costs.

Eligibility: For those aged 21 to 23.

World Exchange

St Colm's International House, 23 Inverleith Terrace, Edinburgh EH3 5NS

☎ 0131-315 4444

fax 0131-315 2222

e we@stcolms.org

w www.worldexchange.org.uk

World Exchange is an ecumenical aid project run by Scottish churches. Placements are within a Christian environment and volunteers will work in education, health or community projects. Younger volunteers have full support from a host and the UK office. Recruits are sent abroad in pairs.

Timing & Length of Placement: Most departures are in January and August but increasingly individuals leave when it suits them. Most go for one year but a shorter experience of two to five months is available.

Destinations: Cuba, Kiribati, India, Malawi & Pakistan.

Costs/Pay: The cost of around £2500 includes travel, insurance, accommodation, food and a modest living allowance.

Eligibility: You need to be a British citizen aged 17 to 75.

World Vision UK

599 Avebury Boulevard, Central Milton Keynes MK9 3PG

☎ 01908-841000

fax 01908-841025

e studentchallenge@worldvision.org.uk

w www.worldvision.org.uk

The Student Challenge programme puts small teams of highly motivated Christians to work in one of World Vision's long-term development programmes for the summer.

Timing & Length of Placement: Applications must be received by February 20. Interviews take place in March/April. Placements last four to six weeks during July and August and on return there's a debriefing session.

Destinations: Armenia, Ghana & Zambia.

Costs/Pay: The cost is estimated at £900 to £1400, which includes flights, food and accommodation. Visas and vaccinations are extra.

Eligibility: For supporters of the Christian basis of faith aged 18 to 30.

DO-IT-YOURSELF

TimeBank

The Mezzanine, Elizabeth House, 39 York Rd, London SE1 7NQ

☎ 020-7401 5420

fax 020-7401 5421

e feedback@timebank.org.uk

w www.timebank.org.uk

Timebank is a web-driven database for anyone looking to volunteer overseas. It lists more than 500 British and indigenous aid and development projects that recruit volunteers. Submit an online profile and the database will match you with suitable placements.

Destinations: Global.

Costs/Pay: No fee.

Eligibility: Depends on each placement.

WorkingAbroad

59 Landsdowne Place, Hove, E Sussex BN3 1FL

☎/fax 01273-711406

e info@workingabroad.com

w www.workingabroad.com

A referral service linking volunteers to hundreds of small-scale indigenous projects, including excavating archaeological sites in France, assisting scientists in the Indonesian rainforest, working with street children in Central America and providing medical assistance in Sudan. Or if you have an interest in, say, protecting one particular flower then WorkingAbroad can help. This is a useful agency if you want to find small, grassroots projects and don't want to pay a large fee. The affiliated WorkingAbroad Projects sets up and organises several programmes largely working in permaculture (sustainable development) and indigenous rights.

Timing & Length of Placement: Send in your application and the results can be produced in two weeks.

Destinations: 150 countries worldwide.

Costs/Pay: There's a fee of between £29 and £36. Some of the projects pay a small salary.

Eligibility: Each placement has its own restrictions.

World Service Enquiry

233 Bon Marché Centre, 241–251 Ferndale Rd, London SW9 8BJ

☎ 0870 770 3274

fax 0870 770 7991

e wse@cabroad.org.uk

W www.wse.org.uk

This agency provides guidance for individuals hoping to volunteer abroad. It publishes *Opportunities Abroad*, a monthly list of vacancies, and offers 'One to One', a vocational guidance service for graduates thinking of a career in overseas development.

Destinations: Global.

Costs/Pay: There's a fee of £120 for 'One to One', which includes research, a 90-minute interview and a report outlining the best course of action for each individual.

Eligibility: Depends on the placement you're looking at.

WorldWide Volunteering

☎ 01935-825588

fax 01935-825775

e www.worldvol@worldvol.co.uk

W www.worldwidevolunteering.org.uk

Apply online for a volunteering match with 900 organisations and 250,000 placements.

Destinations: Global.

Costs/Pay: It costs £15 for three searches of the online database.

Eligibility: Depends on each organisation and placement.

VOLUNTEERING IN THE UK

Community Service Volunteers (CSV)

237 Pentonville Rd, London N1 9NJ

☎ 020-7278 6601

e information@csv.org.uk

W www.csv.org.uk

CSV's national network challenges young people to volunteer away from home. The emphasis of CSV placements is on social work such as working with the homeless, young offenders and at-risk youth, children with learning disabilities or children in care. CSV runs one of the UK's largest programmes, with 2500 full-time volunteers.

Timing & Length of Placement: Four to 12 months.

Destinations: Anywhere within the UK.

Costs/Pay: Residential volunteers receive food, accommodation, travel and an allowance of £27 per week.

Eligibility: For anyone aged 16 to 35.

Glencree Centre for Reconciliation

Glencree, Enniskerry, Co. Wicklow, Ireland;

☎ 00 353 1-282 9711

fax 00 353 1-276 6085

e info@glencree-cfr.ie

W www.glencree-cfr.ie

Glencree is a unique centre for reconciling the conflicts in Northern Ireland. Volunteers are needed to help run the centre by looking after visitors, cooking and cleaning. A study trip to Belfast is included in the work.

Timing & Length of Placement: You can volunteer for three to 12 months. Most volunteers start in September so applications should be in by June. It is also possible to start in March.

Destination: The Republic of Ireland, 20 miles south of Dublin.

Costs/Pay: Pocket money to cover basic costs is paid to volunteers but it's recommended that you bring £600 to cover extra costs.

Eligibility: There are no age limits.

National Association of Hospital and Community Friends (NAHCF)

2nd floor, Fairfax House, Causton Rd, Colchester, Essex CO1 1RJ

☎ 01206-761227

fax 01206-560244

e ladan@hc-friends.org.uk
w www.hc-friends.org.uk
NAHCF represents 800 local groups who work in the community supporting medical patients. Traditionally Friends staffed shops, tea bars, tea trolleys and made ward visits. Now half of their activities are more hands on and include working in mental health, with people with disabilities, on HIV projects, in A & E departments and with children. The association is a good starting point for anyone wishing to volunteer at home in the medical field and is especially valuable for anyone interested in a medical career. Aspiring volunteers will be matched with a local charity.
Timing & Length of Placement: Negotiable with the local project.
Destinations: Local hospitals and community health projects.
Costs/Pay: No costs are involved.
Eligibility: For anyone aged 16 and above.

Millennium Volunteers (MV)
MV Unit, Room E4b, DFEE, Moorfoot, Sheffield S1 4PQ
☎ 0800 085 1624
e millennium.volunteers@dfes.gsi.gov.uk
w www.mvonline.gov.uk
Millennium Volunteers is a UK-wide initiative to encourage young people to volunteer their time for the benefit of others. Using the strapline 'build on what you're into', MV allows young people to get involved in an activity that involves issues that they care about, using their interests or hobbies as a starting point. Volunteers who complete 100 or 200 hours of work earn certificates recognising their achievement.
Timing & Length of Placement: As long as you choose but within the upper age limit.
Destinations: Local British communities.
Costs/Pay: There are no fees. Some funds are available to sponsor new projects.
Eligibility: Volunteers must be aged 16 to 24.

TimeBank
The Mezzanine, Elizabeth House, 39 York Rd, London SE1 7NQ
☎ 020-7401 5420
fax 020-7401 5421
w www.timebank.org.uk
TimeBank's web-driven directory offers diverse opportunities to help out in your community. First register your interests and then search the database for a local match.
Destinations: Countrywide.
Costs/Pay: No Fee.
Eligibility: Depends on each scheme.

CONSERVATION PROGRAMMES ABROAD

Archaeology Abroad
31–34 Gordon Square, London WC1H OPY
e arch.abroad.ucl.ac.uk
w www.britarch.ac.uk/archabroad
Archaeology Abroad provides information about excavation opportunities both for experienced and inexperienced diggers. Email or write for the contacts booklet, which lists projects around the world that recruit unpaid help. In early 2003 these included the British School in Rome, digging camps in Kazakhstan and Mongolia, and a Mayan excavation in Guatemala. In your applications to a dig director try to demonstrate any skills you have such as linguistic abilities or prior experience. Most archaeological work involves manual labour.
Timing & Length of Placement: Most excavations ask for a minimum commitment, usually two weeks. Apply as early as possible but even if you miss a deadline it's still worth applying because some volunteers may have dropped out.
Destinations: Around the world.
Costs/Pay: You need to take out your own travel insurance. Participation fees are sometimes required to cover digging costs. Some projects, largely in Europe, are free to join or only require a small fee. Accommodation is often provided but you should ask first.
Eligibility: Check to see if you need a local visa. Usually you need to be at least 18.

Atlantic Whale Foundation

59 St Martins Lane, London WC2N 4JS
☎/fax 020-7240 5795
W www.whalefoundation.org.uk

There are two conservation programmes working with whales and dolphins – volunteering on the tour boats or helping scientists with research. Application forms are on the web.

Timing & Length of Placement: It's possible to participate year round. You can stay as long as you wish but for a minimum of two weeks.

Destinations: Tenerife (Canary Islands).

Costs/Pay: The volunteer programme is £100 per week or £500 for eight weeks, including basic accommodation and half board.

Eligibility: For those aged 16 and over.

Azafady

Studio 7, 1a Beethoven St, London W10 4LG
☎ 020-8960 6629
fax 020-8962 0126
e mark@azafady.org
W www.azafady.org

Volunteers help with grassroots conservation and sustainable development in Madagascar such as protecting lemurs and turtles and setting up income-generating schemes for the villagers.

Timing & Length of Placement: Assignments last 10 weeks and start in January, April, July and October.

Destination: Madagascar.

Costs/Pay: The fee is £2000, excluding flights, vaccinations and visa.

Eligibility: For those aged 18 and over.

Biosphere Expeditions

Sprat's Water, nr Carlton Colville, The Broads National Park, Suffolk NR33 8BP
☎ 01502-583085
fax 01502-587414
e info@biosphere-expeditions.org
W www.biosphere-expeditions.org

Biosphere Expeditions emphasises the genuinely scientific nature of its expeditions and discourages any impression that they are 'tours'. They are not specifically aimed at gap-year students but young school leavers are welcome to apply. Expeditions in 2003 included researching the movements of snow leopards, cheetahs, monkeys, macaws and wolves.

Timing & Length of Placement: Places go very fast and 2003 places were almost solidly booked by February so book far in advance, ie, eight to 10 months. Expeditions are usually for two weeks but can be extended to two months maximum.

Destinations: Altai (Russia), Azores & Poland.

Costs/Pay: Around £1000 for two weeks, flights excluded. Discounts apply for multiple bookings up to a maximum of 40%.

Eligibility: Open to all.

Conservation Volunteers Australia (CVA)

e info@conservationvolunteers.com.au
W www.conservationvolunteers.com.au

The Conservation Experience offers you the opportunity to contribute in a practical way to the conservation of the Australian environment. Projects include tree planting; erosion and salinity control; seed collection; construction and maintenance of walking tracks; endangered flora and fauna surveys and monitoring; weed control; habitat restoration; and heritage restoration. You can apply directly through the website. A visitor's visa for Australia is appropriate for the Conservation Experience because you are regarded as simply being on holiday and covering all your own costs. You'll be joining a team of six to 10 other volunteers. There are CVA offices across Australia – see the website for contact details.

Timing & Length of Placement: Four- or six-week programmes. Additional weeks cost around £75 each. You can start any Friday you choose.

Destination: Australia.

Costs/Pay: £300 to £450, including all meals, accommodation and project-related transport. You'll need to arrange your own flights and travel insurance.

Eligibility: For anyone aged 15 to 70.

Coral Cay Conservation (CCC)

The Tower, 13th floor, 125 High St, London SW19 2JG

☎ 0870 750 0668

fax 0870 750 0667

e info@coralcay.org

w www.coralcay.org

Volunteers are assigned to expeditions to survey some of the world's most endangered coral reefs and tropical forests. Volunteers are expected to pay a fee to join and you'll encounter a diverse group of people and wide age range. Prior scientific experience is not required as training takes place in situ.

Timing & Length of Placement: You need to apply three months before an expedition is set to leave. Thirteen expeditions start throughout the year. Teams work for three months, which can be extended by request for up to a year.

Destinations: Fiji, Malaysia, Honduras, the Philippines & Tobago.

Costs/Pay: Fees do not include flights, insurance or equipment. There's a handy online calculator to help give you an idea of how much each expedition will cost.

Eligibility: All ages from 16 upwards.

Earthwatch Europe

267 Banbury Rd, Oxford OX2 7HT

☎ 01865-318838

fax 01865-311383

e info@earthwatch.org.uk

w www.earthwatch.org/europe

Earthwatch supports more than 130 expeditions, sending volunteers to work side by side with scientists. Subjects include archaeology, biodiversity, global change and oceans.

Timing & Length of Placement: One- to three-week trips are possible throughout the year.

Destinations: 45 countries.

Costs/Pay: From £1200, flights included.

Eligibility: Some expeditions are restricted to individuals aged 21 and over.

Ecovolunteer

c/o WildWings, 1st floor, 577/579 Fishponds Rd, Bristol BS16 3AF

☎ 0117-965 8333

fax 0117-937 5681

e wildinfo@wildwings.co.uk

w www.ecovolunteer.org.uk

Ecovolunteer provides working conservation holidays, often run by research scientists. You'll be working hands-on to collect information and help out in animal sanctuaries. Some of the choices include working with elephants in Thailand, wolves in Russia, monkeys in Mexico and river otters in Brazil. Ecovolunteer is based in the Netherlands but bookings are taken through the WildWings travel agency.

Timing & Length of Placement: Volunteering can last from one week to six months. Some places are year round but others are seasonal. Apply several weeks in advance; certain popular programmes such as the one based in Mongolia require at least four months' notice in advance.

Destinations: Brazil, Columbia, India, Malaysia, Mongolia, New Zealand, Russia, Thailand & others.

Costs/Pay: From £89 to £2000, flights excluded.

Eligibility: You need to be aged over 18 to participate.

Frontier

50–52 Rivington St, London EC2A 3QP

☎ 020-7613 2422

fax 020-7613 2992

e info@frontier.ac.uk

w www.frontier.ac.uk

Frontier offers keen volunteers the opportunity to make an effective contribution to global conservation by working on research projects in remote tropical environments. Frontier also offers the opportunity to gain a BTEC Advanced Diploma in Tropical Habitat Conservation during an expedition, which is the equivalent of an A level.

Timing & Length of Placement: Trips are for four, 10 or 20 weeks.

Destinations: Madagascar, Tanzania & Vietnam.
Costs/Pay: Fees range from £1850 to £3650.
Eligibility: For those aged 17 and over.

Greenforce

11–15 Betterton St, Covent Garden, London WC2H 9BP
☎ 0870 770 2646
fax 0870 770 2647
e info@greenforce.org
w www.greenforce.org
Greenforce runs a series of environmental projects around the globe, focusing on wildlife conservation. The work ranges from tracking elephants in Zambia to climbing trees in the Amazon and diving on coral reefs. All training is provided, including scuba diving for marine volunteers. Open days are held once a month in London. Teams comprise 16 people.
Timing & Length of Placement: Programmes last 10 weeks. There are four departures per year in January, April, July and October.
Destinations: Marine expeditions in the Bahamas, Borneo & Fiji. Terrestrial expeditions to Zambia & the Peruvian Amazon.
Costs/Pay: A terrestrial expedition costs from £2550 and a marine expedition from £2750, including dive training. A deposit of £250 is required with your application. You will need to cover flights.
Eligibility: For those aged 18 to 70.

Orangutan Foundation

7 Kent Terrace, London NW1 4RP
☎ 020-7724 2912
fax 020-7706 2613
e info@orangutan.org.uk
w www.orangutan.org.uk
Prompted by the popularity of visits and offers of help, the Orangutan Foundation now runs a programme for volunteers to help save this rare Asian ape. Skills are not required because volunteers are not used for research work but will participate in activities such as clearing trails and maintaining the education centre.

Timing & Length of Placement: Places are very popular so you are advised to apply up to eight months in advance. Volunteers stay for six weeks and owing to visa restrictions this cannot be extended. Teams of 12 volunteers leave 14 times a year.
Destination: Kalimantan (Borneo).
Costs/Pay: The fee of £500 covers all in-country expenses but you'll need to buy and arrange the flights.
Eligibility: For anyone aged 18 to 70.

Nautical Archaeology Society (NAS)

Fort Cumberland, Fort Cumberland Rd, Eastney, Portsmouth PO4 9LD
☎/fax 023-9281 8419
e nas@nasportmouth.org.uk
w www.nasportsmouth.org.uk
NAS can provide contacts and information about nautical archaeology at home and abroad. Diving is not essential because some excavations take place on the foreshore or in tidal waters. NAS also provides training courses ranging from diving to IT for archaeology.

Project Africa

African Conservation Trust
PO Box 310, Linkhills, South Africa 3652
☎/fax 00 27-31-2016180
e info@projectafrica.com
w www.projectafrica.com
Project Africa offers volunteers the chance to participate in conservation projects in South Africa such as working with hippos, caracals (African lynx) or cheetahs.
Timing & Length of Placement: Projects are ongoing without start and end dates.
Destinations: Malawi & Botswana.
Costs/Pay: Three months will cost £950, which includes food, accommodation and in-country travel costs but excludes flights, visas and inoculations.
Eligibility: No skills are needed as training is given but you do need to be relatively fit and healthy and aged 18 and above.

Rainforest Concern

27 Landsdowne Crescent, London W11 2NS

☎ 020-7229 2093
fax 020-7221 4094
|e| info@rainforestconcern.org
|w| www.rainforestconcern.org
Rainforest Concern runs two projects to protect breeding turtles and works to conserve rainforest habitats.
Timing & Length of Placement: Apply by New Year to join the turtle programmes that run from February to August. To help in the Ecuadorian rainforest you can leave whenever you want without any significant lead time.
Destinations: Costa Rica & Panama for turtle conservation, Ecuador for rainforest protection.
Costs/Pay: You need to buy your flights and pay between £10 and £16 per day for bed and board.
Eligibility: For anyone aged 18 and above.

Scientific Exploration Society (SES)
Expedition Base, Motcombe,
Shaftesbury, Dorset SP7 9PB
☎ 01747-853353
fax 01747-851351
|e| enquiries@ses-explore.org
|w| www.ses-explore.org
SES shares the same ethos as Raleigh: to take up a challenge and build teamwork. Expeditions have a scientific purpose, for example, mapping reefs or conducting an archaeological survey. Often SES is invited in by host governments and local communities to achieve a specific goal. All teams have an expert related to the project and also a doctor.
Timing & Length of Placement: Expeditions leave throughout the year. Applications need to be in at least two to three months before departure so volunteers can attend a briefing weekend six weeks before departure.
Destinations: Bolivia, Botswana, Guyana, India, Madagascar, Tibet & many more.
Costs/Pay: The cost of £3000 includes all needs.
Eligibility: No skills required. Applications welcomed from anyone aged 18 and over.

For fit, healthy individuals who are happy working in a team.

Sunseed Trust
☎ 0118-956 7190
fax 0118-961 2069
|e| adrian@windisch.co.uk
|w| www.sunseed.org.uk
Sunseed is a charity researching sustainable energy sources for application in environments with little rainfall. Recently it developed a solar-powered oven for use in Rwanda. Volunteers are needed to help run the research project in southern Spain. You can get involved in testing solar cookers, helping in the nursery and constructing buildings from sustainable materials. The trust does not give out the address to deter volunteers just showing up without booking.
Timing & Length of Placement: Ideally you should book four to six weeks in advance. Volunteers can come for short periods of less than a month or stay on as working volunteers for up to a year by developing their own research project.
Destination: Almeria (Spain).
Costs/Pay: The fee covers food and accommodation but excludes flights. From October to April (low season) it costs roughly £65 per week. From May to September (high season) it costs £90 per week.
Eligibility: Those aged 16 and 17 need their parents' permission.

Trekforce Expeditions
34 Buckingham Palace Rd, London
SW1W 0RE
☎ 020-7828 2275
fax 020-7828 2276
|e| info@trekforce.org.uk
|w| www.trekforce.org.uk
Trekforce Expeditions aims to save endangered rainforests by working with local communities. Conservation can be combined with a teaching option. Most volunteers are on a gap year but some volunteers can be in their late 20s and 30s. Trekking groups of 18 are always accompanied by four staff, including one doctor.

Timing & Length of Placement: There's no official deadline for applications but it's advisable to give yourself time to fundraise (two to five months depending on the location and whether or not you want to teach).
Destinations: Belize, Guatemala, Guyana & Malaysia (Borneo).
Costs/Pay: Eight-week expeditions cost £2570 and 17-week expeditions cost £3800. Flights need to be purchased separately.
Eligibility: For those aged 18 to 32.

CONSERVATION PROGRAMMES IN THE UK

British Trust for Conservation Volunteers (BTCV)
36 St Mary's St, Wallingford, Oxon OX10 0EU
☎ 01491-821600
fax 01491-839646
e information@btcv.org.uk
W www.btcv.org.uk
BTCV is the UK's largest practical conservation charity, annually involving 10,000 volunteers in projects to protect and enhance the environment. The organisation offers Millennium Volunteer placements and Volunteer Officer (VO) posts, which combine leadership training with work experience. These fall into two categories: practical conservation, and marketing and administration. Some VOs can work towards NVQs in environmental management. BTCV doesn't organise foreign placements but it can put you in touch with sister NGOs such as the Australian Trust for Conservation Volunteers. BTCV also organises working holidays for two weeks both in the UK and abroad, which tend to involve traditional conservation work such as drystone walling, hedging, and sand-dune restoration.
Timing & Length of Placement: VOs are asked to commit to approximately six months or more to justify the cost of training. Working holidays are for two weeks.
Destinations: National parks, coasts, urban parks, wildlife parks.

Costs/Pay: VOs don't need to pay anything. Working holidays cost from £40 for a weekend in the UK to £600 for a holiday in Latin America.
Eligibility: VOs need to be 18 and over. Working holidays are for those aged 16 or 17.

The Centre for Alternative Technology (CAT)
Machynlleth, Powys SY20 9AZ
☎ 01654-705950
fax 01654-702782
W www.cat.org
Each year 18 volunteers are taken on for six-month stints working in one of nine departments working with conservation, recycling and renewable energies. Some accommodation is available on site and volunteers are expected to make a contribution of about £5.50 per day for food. CAT also runs short-term volunteering programmes each summer. Contact volunteer co-ordinator Rick Dance.
Timing & Length of Placement: Short-term (two weeks) or long-term (six months) placements are available.
Destination: Powys (Wales).
Costs/Pay: Volunteers make a contribution of £5.50 per day for their food. Accommodation is provided.
Eligibility: For those aged 18 and over.

Friends of the Earth (FOE)
26–28 Underwood St, London N1 7JQ
☎ 020-7490 1555
fax 020-7490 0881
e info@foe.co.uk
W www.foe.co.uk
FOE campaigns for the protection of the environment. As well as a national office, FOE has regional offices and a network of over 200 local groups, all of which rely on volunteer help. At the London HQ there are roughly 50 volunteers at any time but you need to contact your local group or the head office at the time you're free to see if new volunteers are needed because there's no formal scheme. Activities include helping

with press cuttings to assisting with research.
Timing & Length of Placement: Volunteers can work for as long or little as they like and there's no application deadline.
Destinations: London & regional offices.
Costs/Pay: There's no costs or pay.
Eligibility: Open to anyone.

The National Trust (NT)

Rowan, Kembrey Park, Swindon SN2 8YL
☎ 0800 609 5383
fax 01793-496815
e volunteers@ntrust.org.uk
W www.nationaltrust.org.uk

The NT conserves many of Britain's historical buildings and landscapes, from Roman sites to contemporary houses, and industrial architecture, mountains, woodland and coast. The trust offers an assistant warden scheme, which is ideal for gappers, and which will train you to work as a manager on one of the properties. Working conservation holidays are available too, where teams of 12 clear beaches, survey flowers, work on archaeological digs etc.
Timing & Length of Placement: Assistant warden posts are usually for six to 12 months. Positions are posted monthly on the website and there's no deadline for applications. Working holidays are from a weekend to a week.
Destinations: Countrywide.
Costs/Pay: Assistant warden positions don't require a fee and will sometimes provide accommodation and some expenses. Working holidays cost £29 for a weekend and £55 for a week.
Eligibility: The assistant warden scheme is for anyone aged 18 plus. The minimum age for working holidays is 17.

Royal Society of the Protection of Birds (RSPB)

The Lodge, Sandy, Beds SG19 2DL
☎ 01767-680551
e volunteers@rspb.org.uk
W www.rspb.org.uk

The RSPB runs a voluntary wardening scheme in its 33 reserves around the UK.

There are 60 to 100 places each year. Apply with three or four preferred locations and starting dates.
Timing & Length of Placement: A six- to 12-month commitment is required. There's the possibility of moving to another reserve after three months.
Destinations: Around the UK.
Costs/Pay: The only costs are travel and food as training, support and lodging are all provided.
Eligibility: Volunteers must be aged 18 plus.

OVERLAND EXPEDITIONS

Brathay Exploration Group

Brathay Hall, Ambleside, Cumbria
LA22 0HP
☎ 015394-33942
e admin@brathayexploration.org.uk
W www.brathayexploration.org.uk

Brathay has 55 years of experience organising educational and challenging expeditions for young people. If you're looking for a short-term expedition then Brathay might provide the ideal answer. These trips may be shorter than most but they resemble other expeditions in providing a challenging overseas adventure that is not just a holiday. Some expeditions focus on fieldwork, others on trekking.
Timing & Length of Placement: Expeditions are for one to five weeks.
Destinations: The Alps, Malaysia, Mongolia, Morocco, New Zealand, North America, Norway, South Africa & Tanzania.
Costs/Pay: Expedition costs range from £185 to £1950, flights excluded.
Eligibility: Expeditioners are aged 15 to early 20s.

BSES Expeditions

The Royal Geographical Society, 1 Kensington Gore, London SW7 2AR
☎ 020-7591 3141
fax 020-7591 3140
e bses@rgs.org
W www.bses.org.uk

BSES (British Schools Exploring Society) was

founded in 1932 by a surviving member of Scott's Antarctic Expedition. It aims to provide opportunities for young explorers to join exploratory projects in remote areas of the world. There are 72 places on each expedition.

Timing & Length of Placement: Expeditions last from four weeks to three months.

Destinations: Traditionally expeditions have been to arctic and sub-arctic destinations but over the last 14 years BSES expeditions have been expanded to include trips to Kenya, Papua New Guinea, India, Morocco & the Peruvian Amazon.

Costs/Pay: A three-month gap-year expedition will cost in excess of £5000. Shorter expeditions of four to six weeks cost between £2400 and £3000.

Eligibility: Applicants must be aged 16 to 20. However, recent college graduates aged 21 to 24 can apply to be assistant team leaders. Some experience of camping, hill walking and outdoor activities is recommended.

Dorset Expeditionary Society (DES)

Chickerell Rd, Weymouth, Dorset DT4 9SY
☎/fax 01305-775599
e dorsetex@wdi.co.uk
W www.dorsetexp.co.uk

The DES runs several expeditions a year, which teach skills such as ice work and rock climbing. Full training is given.

Timing & Length of Placement: Applications begin in September and continue to be accepted until all places are filled. Expeditions last three or four weeks, leave in July and return in August.

Destinations: Ecuador, India, Italy, Kenya, Scotland & the US.

Costs/Pay: From £400 to £2000 all-inclusive. Pocket money should be taken.

Eligibility: The general age range is 15 to 21 but some expeditions may have specific age requirements within that range. Expeditioners must first win a place during a selection weekend where they need to demonstrate a capacity for teamwork.

Expedition Advisory Centre

Royal Geographical Society, 1 Kensington Gore, London SW7 2AR
☎ 020-7591 3030
fax 020-7591 3031
e eac@rgs.org
W www.rgs.org/eac

If you're thinking of organising your own expedition with a friend or want advice about how to find one that suits your interests and ambitions then the BAC is the best place to start. It also publishes the guide *Joining an Expedition* (£7.50), which lists expedition companies and supplies advice about fundraising.

Timing & Length of Placement: Applications for grants for geographical research must be applied for by January 25 for the following summer or autumn and by August 25 for the following winter or spring.

Eligibility: BAC mainly works with undergraduates and older.

The Expedition Company

PO Box 17, Wiveliscombe, Taunton, Somerset TA4 2YL
☎ 01984-624780
fax 01984-629045
e info@expedition.co.uk
W www.expedition.co.uk

This company specialises in arranging expeditions across jungle, mountain and safari terrain.

Timing & Length of Placement: Expeditions last from four weeks to six months and in order to secure a place it's best to apply well in advance. For a tailored expedition it's best to propose the idea six months in advance.

Destinations: Latin America, East Africa & Europe.

Costs/Pay: £1500 to £3500 depending on the project and destination, flights included. The price also includes a token for an adventure such as a safari or diving trip.

Eligibility: Gap-year expeditions are for those aged 17 to 21. Adult expeditions are for those aged 22 and over.

Jagged Globe
The Foundry Studios, 45 Mowbray St,
Sheffield S3 8EN
☎ 0845 345 8848
fax 0114-276 3344
e climb@jagged-globe.co.uk
w www.jagged-globe.co.uk
Jagged Globe specialises in mountaineering expeditions around the world. Choose between the gentler option of climbing in the Scottish Highlands or ascending mighty Mt Everest.
Timing & Length of Placement: Expeditions run from two weeks to 70 days but most from three to four weeks. There are no application deadlines, places are filled on demand.
Destinations: The world's peaks and mountain ranges.
Costs/Pay: Most expeditions cost under £3000, flights included, but if you want to climb Everest you'll need to find £30,000.
Eligibility: For those aged 17 and above.

Wind, Sand, Stars
6 Tyndale Terrace, London N1 2AT
☎ 020-7359 7551
fax 020-7359 4936
e office@windsandstars.co.uk
w www.windandstars.co.uk
This organisation runs an annual summer expedition in the desert and mountains of Sinai to develop new desert survival skills while working with the local Bedouin people. Future Sinai projects include regeneration of Bedouin fruit gardens and archaeological surveys at the nawamis, the oldest roofed buildings in the world.
Timing & Length of Placement: The expedition is for four weeks in July/August.
Destination: The Sinai desert (Egypt).
Costs/Pay: The cost is £1300.
Eligibility: Applicants must be aged 16 to 25.

World Challenge Expeditions
Black Arrow House, 2 Chandos Rd,
London NW10 6NF
☎ 020-8728 7200
fax 020-8961 1551
e info@world-challenge.co.uk
w www.world-challenge.co.uk
Shorter than most gap-year placements, these expeditions are designed to promote team building and personal development. The teams all have an experienced leader and participants are all assigned a specific role with responsibilities such as looking after the food.
Timing & Length of Placement: Application deadlines are flexible because expeditions are conditional upon demand. Call for an application pack or use the online form. All expeditions leave in July for four weeks, except those to the Amazon and the Andes, which last six weeks.
Destinations: The Andes, the Amazon, Borneo, East Africa, Central America & the Himalayas.
Costs/Pay: The average price is £2900, which includes flights and all in-country costs.
Eligibility: Applicants must be aged 16 to 22.

Proper Jobs

What Kind of Work?

There are as many kinds of gap year as there are kinds of people. While some gappers crave exotic travel, others are just as happy boosting their savings or working towards their dream job. Although it's not as glamorous as hiking across the Serengeti, working in your gap year will demonstrate to future employers that you are a mature, forward-thinking individual. This could win you valuable Brownie points when you apply for a proper job further down the line.

There are some brilliant opportunities out there for budding entrepreneurs. You might think about doing work experience with a local company. Or maybe recharging your savings with some temp work. You could always take your first steps as a freelance journalist. Or how about embarking on a fully paid work placement in Europe or America? A lot will depend on how much time and money you have at your disposal.

Of course, you could always apply for a proper long-term job and leave at the end of the year but few companies will be impressed if they invest time and training in you and you leave and take those skills elsewhere. Among other things, you'll be writing off your chances of a good reference and you'll also have to come up with a creative answer if anyone asks you why you left your last job.

Fortunately there are loads of ways to work in a temporary position and get paid without damaging your career prospects. If you do decide to spend a year working in the UK or overseas, this chapter covers some of the choices that lie ahead.

WORK PLACEMENTS IN THE UK

OK, so you've decided you want to work in the UK during your year out. Your next choice is whether to do unpaid work experience or apply for a proper paying job. There are some great industrial placement schemes out there that pay a good salary but you'll usually have to sign up for the whole year. Work experience is usually unpaid but you can do it for a few months and still see a bit of the world before you start university.

Industrial placement schemes are usually aimed at students taking a gap year *during* their degree such as those on sandwich courses. However, there are a handful of schemes specifically targeted at both pre-university gappers and graduates. The best opportunities are in engineering, IT and business but if you look around you can find placements in almost any field.

Many companies offer both yearlong placements and short summer placements lasting eight to 12 weeks. Pay is based on an annual salary – typically £10,000 to £13,000 for the year. Office-based placements are usually open to people studying for any degree but some placements ask for specific subjects. Competition can be fierce and you usually need at least 24 UCAS points to apply.

The website W www.prospects.ac.uk is the official website for graduate careers advice in the UK and is an excellent place to start looking for work placements. The website has a search engine for work placements, managed by the National Council for Work Experience (NCWE). The websites W www.europe.hobsons.com/placements.html and W www.doctor job.com/workexperience/search.asp also have great listings.

Another good place to get information is your school or university careers service. The careers websites for most universities and colleges in the UK are listed on W www.prospects .ac.uk. Alternatively try visiting the website of any company you might like to work for. Some of the larger placement schemes are covered under Contacts at the end of this chapter but there are hundreds of other schemes out there waiting to be discovered.

The Year in Industry programme (W www.yini.org.uk) is the main scheme for school leavers who want to do paid work experience before university. Placements can be found for aspiring engineers, scientists, IT professionals and businesspeople, and, if a company takes a shine to you, it may offer you future vacation work or even sponsorship through university. The Year in Industry has an arrangement with the gap-year organisation Raleigh International (see Contacts in the Volunteering, Conservation & Expeditions chapter), allowing you to combine working in industry with travel – contact them for more details.

Another possibility is the British Army, which provides a variety of training programmes for school leavers. There are plenty of jobs that don't require guns or shooting, and in some cases the Army will sponsor you for the rest of your studies. However, there's a definite Faustian element to these schemes – any freebies you get from the Army will have to be repaid with active service sooner or later.

If you're prepared to work for nothing then most companies will be happy to give you work experience and you won't have to sign away your whole year out. Work experience is usually arranged on a case-by-case basis and you can often find a position just by telephoning a company you'd like to work for and talking to someone in the Human Resources department. Your school or university careers service can also help you arrange a placement. Students are usually paid an allowance for lunch and transport but it's a good idea to choose a company close to home so you can stay with family or friends while you work.

If you have artistic leanings you could try asking for work experience at a local gallery or theatre – the Royal Opera House in London (see Contacts) takes on lots of budding set designers, costume makers and lighting technicians. If you're interested in getting some experience of social work, Community Service Volunteers (CSV; W www.csv.org.uk) arranges voluntary community projects around the UK – see Contacts in the Volunteering, Conservation & Expeditions chapter for more details. Work experience is also often available in local government offices (see the website W www.lgjobs.com/workplacements.cfm).

People hoping to study medicine or nursing often volunteer at local hospitals. There are also loads of voluntary healthcare programmes available in the developing world – see the Volunteering, Conservation & Expeditions chapter for some suggestions. If you're a qualified nurse you can easily find temporary paid work in the UK or overseas. The website W www .nursingnetuk.com has excellent advice on nursing in the UK and overseas plus a worldwide search engine for jobs. There's a global nursing shortage and countries such as Australia and the USA often have special immigration programmes to entice nurses from abroad. See the websites W www.bluchip.com and W www.australiannursingsolutions.com.au for some ideas of what's out there.

WORK PLACEMENTS ABROAD

You don't have to stay in Britain to gain experience of real work. Work placements are available all over the world. In Europe placements are usually known as *stages* or *traineeships*, while in the US they're almost always called *internships*.

As with UK placements, most foreign schemes pay a salary or a monthly allowance, which should cover your food, accommodation and travel. Some will also pay for the costs of your travel to the placement. If you're thinking of taking an unpaid traineeship abroad you'll need to cover your living expenses while you work. The Leonardo da Vinci programme (W www .leonardo.org.uk) provides funding for vocational training in more than 30 countries but you have to apply through your school or university – inquire at the careers service.

To participate in an overseas training scheme you may also need a work permit or visa. This can be difficult on your own but fortunately a whole industry has sprung up sponsoring foreign students on traineeships around the world. The British Universities North America

Club (BUNAC) and a host of similar organisations offer various organised work-placement programmes to America and further afield. They handle all the paperwork, arrange your work permit and ensure that the training scheme or internship meets the approval of the immigration authorities. Foreign companies offering traineeships are also much more likely to offer you a job if they know there's a big organisation behind you. See Contacts for information on some of the more popular schemes.

The USA is the most popular destination for work placements overseas and a year spent working for an American company is likely to bowl over potential employers back home. There are thousands of internships available every year in the USA and many are published in annual lists, which you can buy over the internet or in bookshops (see the list of internet resources at the end of this section for a few suggestions).

Some programmes let you work for 18 months, while others give you six months or a year. Some are open to students, others just to graduates. Many restrict you to certain types of job – usually management, business, finance and commerce. One interesting option is the Mountbatten Internship programme (see Contacts for details), which lets you work in New York for a year. David Marshall from London has the following to say about working for a New York investment bank on the Mountbatten programme:

The Mountbatten team were really professional. Any problem at all while we were in New York and they were on hand to help – even moving interns who were unhappy in their jobs to new placements. The accommodation was also great – just 25 minutes from downtown Manhattan – though I did have to share a room with two other boys for a year. The only downside was that some employers didn't treat the Mountbatten staff as real graduate-level employees. I'd just finished an MA in English Literature but my tasks at the office included picking out lost documents from the dustbin and washing the boss' apple before he left for a flight...

Whatever you end up doing, you usually need to be studying a subject that directly relates to the internship you apply for. You'll have to complete a detailed training plan, stating what you hope to gain from your traineeship. A wishy-washy plan is going to go straight into the 'return to sender' pile so it's worth thinking about what you hope to gain when you look for an internship. Similar programmes are sometimes available in Australia, South Africa and South America.

Another good source of overseas traineeships is the European Union (EU). Many organisations in Europe take on paid interns or *stagiaires* every year. Conducting a *stage* is a great way to learn about international economics and politics, and working in a foreign-language environment will really beef up your CV come graduation.

Most *stages* last around five months. You can work in fields such as translating, journalism, finance, politics, economics, human rights and engineering. To apply for these positions you usually need to be able to speak at least one other EU language apart from English.

Most European organisations offer a monthly cash allowance to cover your living and travelling expenses, and you'll be asked to produce a report or research project during your *stage*. The main centres of European politics – and therefore the best places to find placements – are Brussels (Belgium), Geneva (Switzerland), Frankfurt (Germany) and Luxembourg.

The website **W** www.eu-careers-gateway.gov.uk/finding/stage.htm is the European recruitment gateway for the British Civil Service and has links to internship programmes at all sorts of European institutions. Another fantastic website for EU traineeships is **W** www.eurodesk.org/euinfo/euenbody.htm.

Many international organisations around the world offer similar programmes. The website **W** http://missions.itu.int/~italy/vacancies/internships.htm lists internships as far afield as

Tanzania and the Philippines. Some gap-year organisations can also fix you up with a paid or unpaid internship in an exotic location. Several options are covered under Contacts.

If you're thinking of a career in the development or charity business, you might think about joining a voluntary project overseas. Lots of ex-participants end up working for the companies they spent their gap year with so it's worth asking about job opportunities. Some companies are described in the Volunteering, Conservation & Expeditions chapter. Be aware that you usually have to pay a substantial fee for these programmes. Some gap-year companies also offer projects where you do work experience in business or journalism in the developing world.

If you aren't sure about whether a work placement overseas is for you, there are several websites that offer advice – useful resources include:

[W] **www.careerseurope.co.uk** – A resource centre for the International Careers Information service.

[W] **www.europe.hobsons.com** – A great careers site with advice on work placements and internships.

[W] **www.internjobs.com** – A member of the AboutJobs.com group, with a huge database of internships around the world.

[W] **www.internships.com** – Publishes a variety of guides to US internships.

[W] **www.internships-usa.com** – Publishes information on over 3000 internships in the USA.

[W] **www.jobpilot.co.uk** – Lists work experience/internships worldwide.

RECRUITMENT AGENCIES

Although you can sometimes find a job by simply turning up and saying how great you are, most jobs are filled through recruitment agencies and job adverts in the national papers. The UK has literally hundreds of recruitment agencies. Most specialise in certain types of jobs – engineering, IT, hospitality, sales or secretarial work for example – and offer both permanent jobs and temporary positions. For gap-year work or work overseas you'll probably be looking at temporary work rather than a permanent job.

Jobcentres are run by the government and offer everything from cleaning jobs all the way up to management positions. Unfortunately they can be rather gloomy places. As an alternative there's a countrywide job-search facility on the Jobcentres website [W] www.job centreplus.gov.uk, or you can search for jobs all over Europe at [W] www.europa.eu.int/eures. This site also has links to job centres across the EU.

Private recruitment agencies tend to be more upbeat and have a reputation for providing better-paid, more skilled jobs. There are links to loads of private agencies on the website [W] www.rec.uk.com. Some of the more useful agencies are covered in the Contacts section. In theory, agencies will match you with a job that matches your skills, though this isn't always the case, as John Rose from Leicester found out in Chicago:

I registered with one of the big recruitment agencies as soon as I arrived in Chicago and took a series of computer and typing tests. My scores were high so I was expecting to walk into an office job almost immediately. A few days later the agent called up and told me she had a job for me, but she wanted to know how tall I was. When I told her five foot eight, she said, 'That's great, you'll be ideal.' What was the job? Working in an office with a low ceiling perhaps? Nope. They wanted me to dress up as the smallest Animaniac from the children's cartoon and hand out fliers. Needless to say, I didn't take the job.

If you prefer not to go through an agency there are hundreds of websites where you can search for jobs online from the comfort of your own PC – see the Appendix for listings.

TEMPING

Many people still imagine that all temps are like the original 'Kelly Girls' – ie, prim secretaries with horn-rimmed glasses. However, these days you can temp in almost any job, from engineering to web design, and there are just as many 'Kelly Guys' out there. Some people even make a full-time living moving from temp job to temp job.

The first step is to find a temp agency that recruits staff for the kind of job you want to do. In the UK a good starting point is the website **W** www.agencycentral.co.uk, which has links to hundreds of British recruitment agencies.

You'll need to register and have an interview, which will be followed by a series of aptitude tests. For general office work, this usually involves a typing test and an assessment of how good you are at using computers.

Temporary staff are employed directly by the agency rather than individual companies and wages are typically paid a week in arrears with tax deducted. Temping used to get a bad rap for long hours and poor pay but the 'temp slave' image is pretty out of date. These days, you should be entitled to fair pay, reasonable working hours and paid holidays. As a rough indication, wages for office temps start at around £7 an hour in the UK, £5 an hour in America and £7 an hour in Australia. You can usually earn more if you can touch-type or have a specific skill such as web design or computer programming.

Most temp jobs are nine-to-five positions but you can work over the weekend or only on specific days if this suits you better. Lots of people use office temping as a way to pay the rent while they establish careers in all sorts of unrelated fields. If you do decide that the business world is for you, many agencies offer temporary-to-permanent positions where you come on board as a temp and can move into a full-time position if you like what you see.

The downside of temping is that you often end up doing tedious, repetitive jobs such as data entry and photocopying. If you have specific skills or experience you can often find something a bit more challenging but even skilled staff sometimes end up doing jobs that are far beneath their abilities, giving rise to the popular temp joke:

Temp to Agent: 'I want to complain – I'm a trained secretary but a monkey could do this job!'
Agent to Temp: 'That's why we're paying you peanuts.'

Katharine Wrobel from Belfast came up against this side of temping:

I joined a recruitment agency in Sydney and ended up working there as a receptionist. I was the first person to meet the would-be temps and I screened all the phone calls so I was always being asked to give my opinions of the people who came through the door. Regardless of what I said, the recruitment agent's assessment usually came down to what the temp was wearing and whether or not she liked their hairdo! I never had the nerve to tell her that, being a paltry backpacker, my entire wardrobe, minus the underwear, was the result of early morning closet-and-laundry-basket plundering in my flatmate's room.

Our advice is to approach things with a positive attitude. Even if an assignment is boring, you won't be doing it forever, and if you seem keen, employers will often try to find you something more interesting to do. If you do a good job they may even ask for you again or offer you a full-time job. Temping also has its perks, such as cheap lunches and free internet access. If you're working for more than a few weeks you may also get some vocational training which can go straight down on your CV.

Loads of people use temp agencies to find work overseas. You can often register with a recruitment agency in the UK before you leave and they'll pass on your details to one of their branches abroad. Reed, Hays Personnel and Adecco all have offices around the world – see Contacts for details. There are also hundreds of job-search sites where you can hunt for jobs abroad without ever leaving your desk. Remember that you may need a work permit to work outside Europe – permits are covered in detail under Red Tape later in this chapter.

FREELANCING

If you have a skill such as writing, editing, photography, translating or web design, you might consider freelancing during your year out. However, this is a highly competitive business and you'll need to be self-motivated to succeed. It can take time to build up a network of contacts and even experienced freelancers sometimes struggle to make ends meet financially. That said, freelancing is a good way of building up a portfolio of work, which can help you get a job later on.

Journalism is probably the best known freelance occupation and if you've got a good idea for a story you have as much chance of selling it as the next freelancer. The important thing is to target the right person. When you call a magazine or newspaper, try to talk to the editor of the specific section where you think the article might go (eg, the Travel Editor for a travel story). It can all seem pretty daunting at first but editors get dozens of these calls every day and just because they don't like one idea it doesn't mean they won't like the next one. Jane Roddick from Chester still remembers the nerves of pitching her first story idea to an editor:

I could barely speak because I was so nervous, and the first couple of times I actually put the phone back down before anyone picked up. But eventually I worked up the courage to wait until the editor answered. I introduced myself as a freelancer and pitched my story idea and to my surprise he said he would take 1000 words on the subject right away. The funny thing was that I wasn't a freelancer when I picked up the phone but by the end of the phone call I was.

The rates of pay for freelance writers, editors and photographers depend on the publication – national newspapers and glossy magazines usually pay more than local papers, the free press or websites. Writers usually get around £200 per 1000 words, photographers get £100 to £200 for a day or around £150 per photo, and editors get £60 to £100 for a day's work.

The National Union of Journalists (NUJ) is the body responsible for issuing press cards in the UK but you have to earn a certain amount of your income from journalism to qualify. Media and journalism students can get a temporary press card for £10, which is valid for the duration of their course. There's more information on the NUJ website **W** www.nuj.org.uk. Sadly, the fake press cards available in places such as Bangkok aren't worth the paper they're printed on.

For some ideas of publications to approach see the listings of newspapers, magazines and news websites at **W** www.world-newspapers.com. Many English-language newspapers overseas are desperate for writers and editors. It may be worth visiting their offices with some examples of your work and seeing if you can get a job. Journalist Peter Arnett – who won a Pulitzer Prize – got his first big break by walking into the offices of the *Bangkok World*. If you are going somewhere exotic you might also think about contacting editors at travel magazines and websites and offering to file reports back home while you travel, or talking to backpacker magazines such as TNT.

As a freelancer you technically require a work permit to work outside Europe but many people get around this by only writing for publications back home or arranging to be paid electronically into their bank account at home. However, you still have to pay tax on these earnings unless you're registered as a nonresident (see Taxation later in this chapter).

Journalism isn't the only way to freelance. Many web designers and IT professionals also fund their travels by taking on short computer jobs around the world. Translating is another skill you can use almost anywhere and you can usually charge around £50 per 1000 words translated. The websites **W** www.foreignword.biz and **W** www.proz.com are good places to register your skills and pick up contract work.

Whatever your field, people need to be able to reach you. A roaming email account and a mobile phone are essential. A digital copy of your CV and some photocopies of anything you've had published will also come in handy. You might also think about setting up your own website, listing your skills and contact details and giving some examples of your work. Having your own business cards will also add a touch of professionalism.

If you have a car, bicycle or motorcycle, you might consider working as a dispatch driver – try approaching courier and dispatch companies directly or by phone. Teaching is another skill you can freelance almost anywhere in the world – see the Teaching chapter for more information.

Other useful resources for journalists and other freelancers include:

W **www.freelance-proofreaders.co.uk** – A site for freelance proofreaders and editors where you can post your skills online for £75 per year.

W **www.freelancers.net** – A listings service for freelance writers, designers and IT staff. You can post your skills and contact details online for free.

W **www.journalism.co.uk** – An excellent journalism and editing site. You can advertise in their database of freelancers for £50 a year.

W **www.journalismuk.co.uk** – Has extensive resources for British journalists, including jobs listings.

W **www.despatch.co.uk** – Has extensive listings for courier companies in the UK.

W **www.translatortips.net** – An American site with useful tips for freelance translators.

W **www.worldwidefreelance.com** – Has listings of potential markets for writers around the world.

Eligibility

In an ideal world anyone would be able to work anywhere but in reality you often have to jump through all sorts of hoops before you can work overseas. Europe is the easiest place to work due to harmonisation of labour rules across the EU. To work almost anywhere else you usually need to be sponsored by an overseas employer, and they have to prove that they couldn't find a local person to do the job.

Fortunately many countries have special immigration programmes that allow students from Britain to visit and work on educational exchanges. In return, students from these countries get to work in Britain. To be eligible you usually have to be a student or graduate and you'll need to apply through a designated sponsor such as BUNAC (see the Work Permits & Regulations section for details).

Wherever you are going, speaking the local language will increase your chances of finding work. In countries such as France and Germany, being able to speak the local language is almost essential. Computer skills will also make it easier to find work. If you're entering another country on an exchange programme, the skills you need will depend on the work placement.

To get the most out of working overseas, it's important to be enthusiastic, flexible and open-minded. Employers are looking for people who can adjust quickly to a different way of doing things and are happy working with new people.

Red Tape

There is much more red tape associated with working overseas than there is with just visiting for a holiday. Applications take longer and usually cost more and you have to satisfy certain conditions before a work permit will be issued. The point of all this is to ensure that a) you aren't working illegally and b) you will pay your taxes. Things have got even tougher since the events of September 2001 – anyone applying for a visa to enter the USA must now have an interview at the US embassy in London or Belfast.

WORK PERMITS & REGULATIONS

If you intend to work abroad you'll need to get a work permit. This is just a formality within the European Economic Area (EEA) – ie, Austria, Belgium, Denmark, Finland, France, Germany, Greece, Ireland, Italy, Luxembourg, the Netherlands, Portugal, Spain, Sweden and the United Kingdom (the nations of the EU), plus Iceland, Norway and Liechtenstein – but it can be harder elsewhere.

Brits are allowed to look for work in any EEA country for up to three months without restrictions though you may need to register on arrival. After this time you have to apply for a residence permit, which usually involves taking your passport and job contract down to the local town hall. The exact procedure varies slightly from country to country. Rules for every European nation are listed on the website [W] www.europa.eu.int/scadplus/citizens/en/inter.htm. Most EU countries require you to take out medical insurance before you can start working.

In contrast, America can be harder to get into than Fort Knox. Fortunately you can get around most of the red tape if you join an educational exchange programme with an organisation such as BUNAC (see Contacts for more information). They can fix you up with an internship and sponsor you for a J-1 visa, which will allow you to work in the US for six to 18 months. To apply you have to be a university student or graduate, or have two years of work experience and there's a £67 fee. You can only work for the company you were placed with but you're allowed to travel for about a month at the end of your placement. Some organisations can also arrange work placements in South Africa and Brazil.

For some jobs you may need to have a medical, which usually has to be carried out by a doctor approved by the immigration authorities. You may also need to show a clean criminal record. In the UK this information resides with the Criminal Records Bureau. You can apply for a certificate of your criminal record, known as a 'disclosure', on the website [W] www.disclosure.gov.uk. The fee is £12.

Australia, New Zealand and Japan offer useful working-holiday visas that allow you to work and travel for up to a year. The idea behind these schemes is that you take on casual jobs to pay for your travel, but plenty of people use them to get a serious job. See the Casual/Seasonal Work chapter for more on working-holiday visas.

Up-to-date information about work permits and visa restrictions can be found on the websites of many embassies in London, eg, [W] www.usembassy.org.uk or [W] www.australia.org.uk. Handy guides to working conditions across the world are published by the website [W] www.goinglobal.com.

TAXATION

Taxation is a very personal subject. Even in Europe, every nation has its own rules for income tax. But as the old saying goes, it's the one thing you can't avoid. In the UK single people can earn up to £4615 a year tax-free. After that you have to pay tax at the prevailing rate. Tax and National Insurance contributions are usually deducted at source. The UK tax year runs from April 6 to April 5 the following year and you'll have to file a tax return at the end of the year (see the Inland Revenue website **W** www.inlandrevenue.gov.uk for more information). If you've overpaid tax you can claim a refund at the end of the year.

If you work overseas you'll be liable to pay local income tax. You often need to register for tax when you arrive. In Australia you should apply to the Australian Taxation Office (**W** www.ato.gov.au) for a tax file number (TFN) before you start work. In the USA, exchange visitors only pay federal and state taxes and not social security. However, you still need to apply for a social security card – the sponsoring organisation will usually help with this. You need to present some ID that you've had for at least two years.

Details of the tax laws in numerous countries can be found by following the links on the website **W** www.taxsites.com/international.html#countries. Alternatively do a search on the internet for 'income tax' and the name of the country you're interested in. If you're working overseas for a whole year you can declare yourself *nonresident* in the UK to avoid paying tax twice. Some countries have specific tax deals with Britain to make this easier – more information is on the Inland Revenue website.

Red tape can also work in your favour, particularly if you've paid too much tax while working overseas. Exchange organisations such as BUNAC have well-established schemes where you can claim back any overpayments before you leave. Alternatively the company ESS Tax Refunds (**W** www.taxback.com) can help you reclaim tax you've paid overseas for a fee.

Spec Letters & Applications

You don't always have to wait until someone advertises a job to apply for work. Many companies are impressed by people who take the initiative and approach them on spec. However, large corporations usually insist that people only apply for advertised jobs. Your careers service can give you advice on whether or not to approach specific companies.

Many companies prefer you to approach them first by phone. Once you've established that they accept speculative applications you can then approach them by letter asking for an interview. Try to address the letter to a specific person (and make sure you spell their name correctly!) and tailor the letter to the company you are approaching. You want to grab their attention – try an opening such as:

Dear (name of the person you're writing to),

I am very interested in finding out how I could come and work for your organisation. I'm currently studying for a business studies degree at Southampton University and I will be graduating in June 2003. In my final year I have specialised in investment banking in the new states of the EU. As Bancorp is one of the pioneers in this area I feel the work I have done on this subject would make me a real asset to your organisation...

Aim to keep the letter short and punchy and say when you are available for an interview. Make sure you include your contact details in the letter and attach a copy of your CV. If you are applying to a foreign company the letter should be in the local language. Your careers service can advise you on how to write a good covering letter.

If you are applying to an advertised position there will usually be an official application form. This can often be printed off the internet. Once you've filled it out it's a good idea to take a photocopy so you can remember what you said come interview time. Many companies now use online application forms and you can usually revise what you've written before you decide to officially submit.

Contacts

WORK PLACEMENTS ABROAD

Alliances Abroad

702 West Ave, Austin, Texas 78701, USA
☎ 00 1 512-457 8062
fax 00 1 512-457 813
e inbound@allianceabroad.com
w www.alliancesabroad.com
Alliances Abroad organises paid and unpaid internships in America and Brazil. You can either find your own internship or take a pre-arranged placement. For its seasonal work programmes in the USA and Australia see the Casual/Seasonal Work chapter.

Types of Work: Hospitality, management, finance, business and IT.

Timing & Length of Work: Internships last six to 18 months.

Destinations: The USA & Brazil (São Paulo).

Costs/Pay: US internship fees start at £1205 for six months, including insurance but excluding flights and visa fees. The Brazil programme starts at £470. Wages depend on the placement.

Eligibility: Applicants must be 18 to 30 and current university students (graduates accepted for USA programme). Portuguese speakers are preferred for the Brazil option.

How to Apply: Download an application pack from the website. You must provide four passport photos and a reference and there's a phone interview.

Association for International Practical Training (AIPT)

10400 Little Patuxent Parkway, Suite 250, Columbia, Maryland 21044-3519, USA
☎ 00 1 410-997 2200
fax 00 1 410-992 3924
e aipt@aipt.org
w www.aipt.org
AIPT has been arranging work placements in the USA since 1950. You can either find your own placement or AIPT will match you with a traineeship that matches your studies or career plans. See the Casual/Seasonal Work chapter for information on its short summer work exchanges.

Types of Work: Work placements must be in a field that relates to your studies or future career plans.

Timing & Length of Work: Six to 18 months.

Destination: The USA.

Costs/Pay: Fees range from £500 for six months to £1130 for 18 months, including insurance but excluding flights and visa fees. Pay varies with the job you do.

Eligibility: Applicants must be at least 18 and must either be a full-time university student or have two years' work experience in the relevant field.

How to Apply: Download an application from the website. Once you register for a programme you must sign up for a presentation where you'll have an interview.

BUNAC

16 Bowling Green Lane, London EC1R 0QH
☎ 020-7251 3472
fax 020-7251 0215
e enquiries@bunac.org.uk
w www.bunac.org
BUNAC offers an Overseas Practical Training Programme that allows you to work on long-term paid or unpaid internships in the USA. Up to 30 days' travel is usually permitted at the end of your training. For its seasonal work and summer camp programmes, see the Casual/Seasonal Work and Au Pairing & Working with Kids chapters.

Types of Work: Business, management, finance, commerce, education, social science, library science, counselling, social services, health (excluding nursing or medical internships) and arts & culture (within a gallery or museum).

Timing & Length of Work: Traineeships can last up to 18 months and departures are possible year round.

Destination: The USA.

Costs/Pay: Registration fees range from £325 (for three months) to £875 (for 18 months); flights, compulsory insurance and visa fees are extra. Wages depend on the type of work you do.

Eligibility: Applicants must be at least 19. Students and non-students are accepted.

How to Apply: Download an application form from the website. Applicants must arrange a full-time traineeship before they apply – BUNAC can provide assistance with this – and also provide references and a training plan.

Càlédöñiâ Languages Abroad

The Clockhouse, Bonnington Mill, 72 Newhaven Rd, Edinburgh EH6 5QG

☎ 0131-621 7721/2

fax 0131-621 7723

e unitedkingdom@ccusa.co.uk

w www.caledonialanguages.co.uk

Càlédöñiâ offers language courses (see Contacts in the Courses chapter for details) that can be combined with voluntary work experience. You need to take a minimum three-week language course before your work experience placement (the Peru placement includes language lessons).

Types of Work: Placements include conservation and social projects, and work in cultural institutions.

Timing & Length of Work: The minimum placement time is eight weeks (six weeks in Peru).

Destinations: Cuba, Costa Rica, Bolivia, Peru & Brazil.

Costs/Pay: The placement fee is £294. The Peru programme costs £825.

Eligibility: Applicants must be at least 18.

How to Apply: Call or see the website for language course options. Apply with a CV and covering letter in Spanish (Portuguese for Brazil).

CCUSA

Green Dragon House, 64–70 High St, Croydon, Surrey CR0 9XN

☎ 020-8688 9051

fax 020-8680 4539

e info@ccusa.co.uk

w www.ccusa.com

CCUSA offers a Practical Training Scheme that allows you to work on paid or unpaid traineeships in the USA. You'll find your own traineeship and have it approved by CCUSA, who then arranges the paperwork. For its seasonal work programmes and summer camp jobs, see the Casual/Seasonal Work and Au Pairing & Working with Kids chapters.

Types of Work: Management, finance, commerce or business.

Timing & Length of Work: Traineeships can start at any time of year and last 12 months.

Destination: The USA.

Costs/Pay: Registration costs £300, plus £415 for compulsory insurance. Visa fees, flights and accommodation are extra. Pay will depend on the position.

Eligibility: Applicants must be at least 20 and have two years' college/university study or work experience in the same field as the proposed training programme.

How to Apply: Applicants must find a traineeship and have it approved by CCUSA. Application forms can be downloaded from the website; apply at least two months before you want to start work.

CDS International

871 United Nations Plaza, New York NY 10017-1814, USA

☎ 00 1 212-497 3500

fax 00 1 212-497 3535

e info@cdsintl.org

w www.cdsintl.org

CDS offers a Professional Development Programme that lets you visit the USA on a career-related internship. You have to arrange your own placement but CDS will handle the paperwork and provide an orientation on arrival in New York or Los Angeles.

Types of Work: Placements in business, technical and engineering companies, and hotel administration.

Timing & Length of Work: Programmes begin monthly year round and last three to 18 months.

Destination: The USA.

Costs/Pay: Participants pay £315 and must take out compulsory health insurance. Flights and visa fees are extra.

Eligibility: Applicants must be aged 21 to 35 and have completed at least two years of a university degree. One year of work experience is an asset.

How to Apply: Download an application form from the website. Applicants must provide a US-style resume (CV), photo, copy of passport identity pages and evidence of qualifications or student status.

CIEE (Council on International Educational Exchange)

52 Poland St, London W1F 7AB
☎ 020-7478 2000
fax 020-7734 7322
e infouk@councilexchanges.org.uk
W www.ciee.org.uk

The CIEE operates a Professional Career Training Programme for graduates. You can work on any paid traineeship in the USA but you must have a confirmed position before you leave. The CIEE offers help finding traineeships, including an online job search service, and arranges your visa, insurance and other paperwork. The CIEE also offers various language courses and casual work programmes – see the Courses and Casual/Seasonal Work chapters for details.

Types of Work: Any career-related traineeship is allowed, subject to approval by CIEE.

Timing & Length of Work: Traineeships may last for up to 18 months.

Destination: The USA.

Costs/Pay: Programme fees start at £320 for two months, increasing by £35 for each additional month. Flights, visa fees, compulsory insurance and accommodation are extra. Wages depend on your job.

Eligibility: Applicants must be between 20 and 40 and have A levels and a university degree or equivalent qualifications.

How to Apply: Download the application pack from the website. All applicants must complete a training plan showing how the traineeship will aid their career and provide proof of qualifications and two references.

Civil Service EU Recruitment

EU Staffing, Room G6, Admiralty Arch, The Mall, London SW1A 2WH
☎ 020-7276 1609
fax 020-7276 1652
e eustaffing@cabinet-office.x.gsi.gov.uk;
W www.eu-careers-gateway.gov.uk

This Civil Service department provides information on jobs at European institutions. You can register and they'll pass on free information about *stages* (traineeships) and full-time positions at organisations such as the European Parliament and European Commission.

Council of Europe

Temporary Unit (Traineeships), Directorate of Human Resources, Council of Europe, F-67075, Strasbourg, France
☎ 00 33 3 88 41 20 00
fax 00 33 3 88 41 27 10
e recruitment@coe.int
W www.coe.int/t/e/human_resources/jobs/10_traineeship_opportunities

This large European institution offers unpaid traineeships for graduates who are interested in European politics. Trainees take an induction course and can attend meetings of the European Parliament and European Assembly during the traineeship.

Types of Work: Admin, eg, taking minutes at meetings, drafting reports and carrying out research in council offices.

Timing & Length of Work: Three months from January, April or October.

Destination: Strasbourg (France).

Costs/Pay: Traineeships are unpaid and trainee must pay all transport and accommodation costs.

Eligibility: Applicants must be university graduates and a good knowledge of French is desirable.

How to Apply: Download the application from the website. Apply by September.

Don Quijote

2/4 Stoneleigh Park Rd, Epsom, Surrey KT19 0QT
☎ 020-8786 8081
fax 020-8786 8086
e info@donquijote.co.uk
W www.donquijote.org

This Spanish language school offers a programme where you complete an advanced Spanish course and then take a business orientation and do an unpaid work placement for three months in Barcelona or Madrid.

Types of Work: Mainly admin roles in businesses and government organisations.

Timing & Length of Work: The length of the Spanish course will vary depending on your ability (typically six to 12 weeks). Business orientations last for two weeks and internships last three months, starting on set dates throughout the year.

Destination: Spain.

Costs/Pay: Courses start at £631 for six weeks (£1086 for 12 weeks), business orientation costs £129 and the internship is £1199. Students pay a £26 enrolment fee. Accommodation is extra.

Eligibility: Applicants must be at least 18.

How to Apply: Call for an application pack or fill in the online enrolment form.

Earthwise Living Foundation (ELF)

PO Box 108, Thames 2815, New Zealand
☎/fax 00 64 9 353 1558
e info@elfnz.com
w www.elfnz.com

ELF organises custom-made internships and work-experience programmes in New Zealand. Accommodation is provided with a New Zealand family or in an apartment. You can arrange a placement to match whatever you are studying.

Types of Work: Possible internships include marketing, finance, law and conservation.

Timing & Length of Work: Placements are for one month to one year.

Destination: New Zealand.

Costs/Pay: Fees start from £1230 for six weeks, including accommodation. Flights and insurance are extra. Most positions are unpaid.

Eligibility: Applicants must be aged between 16 and 50, and paid interns must have a Working Holiday visa.

How to Apply: Download the application from the website. There's a phone interview and you should provide two references and a CV. Apply three months before you want to start.

The English-Speaking Union

Dartmouth House, 37 Charles St, London W1J 5ED
☎ 020-7529 1550
fax 020-7495 6108
e esu@esu.org
w www.esu.org

This registered charity offers unpaid internships for 12 students a year in the offices of the US Congress. Former participants have worked in the offices of Edward Kennedy and the White House. An orientation and training session is provided and you can travel in the USA at the end of the internship.

Types of Work: Admin work in the offices of politicians.

Timing & Length of Work: June to August.

Destination: Washington DC, USA.

Costs/Pay: £200 administration fee and £1400 for accommodation. You cover your own flights, insurance and living expenses.

Eligibility: Candidates must be in the penultimate or final year of their degree (any discipline) when they apply.

How to Apply: Send a detailed CV and 250-word statement by post explaining how the internship will benefit your future career plans by November 28. Interviews are held in December. Political experience is an advantage.

Euro Academy

67–71 Lewisham High St, London SE13 5JX
☎ 020-8297 0505
fax 020-8297 0984
e enquiries@euroacademy.co.uk
w www.euroacademy.co.uk

This European language school offers unpaid work placements in Europe. Participants take a two- or four-week residential language course (see Contacts in the Courses chapter for details) and must reach at least intermediate level before the internship starts.

Types of Work: Placements are in admin, tourism, marketing and teaching.

Timing & Length of Work: Work placements last four to 24 weeks.

Destinations: France, Spain, Italy & Germany.

Costs/Pay: Fees start at £350. The language course, flights and accommodation are extra.

Eligibility: Applicants must be aged 18 and must have reached intermediate language level.

How to Apply: Call or see the website for an application form. You must provide a CV in the appropriate foreign language and a letter of motivation. There may be a phone interview to test language skills. Allow two months' notice when applying.

European Central Bank
Recruitment & Staff Development Division, Postfach 16 03 19, D-60066 Frankfurt am Main, Germany
☎ 00 49 69 1344 0
fax 00 49 69 1344 7979
e recruitment@ecb.int
W www.ecb.int

Europe's leading financial institution offers a wide range of internships at its headquarters in Frankfurt. Vacancies are listed on the website.

Types of Work: Auditing, translation and financial services.

Timing & Length of Work: Internships last three to six months.

Destination: Frankfurt (Germany).

Costs/Pay: Interns get a stipend. Travel costs to/from Frankfurt will be reimbursed.

Eligibility: Applicants must have a relevant academic background and computer skills. Translators must have a university degree and be fluent in English and at least one other European language.

How to Apply: See the website for current vacancies. Apply by post with at least two references, a covering letter and CV in English, and evidence of qualifications.

European Commission
Traineeships Office, B100 1/7, European Commission, B-1049 Brussels, Belgium
☎ 00 32 2 299 2339
fax 00 32 2 299 0871
e eac-bureau-des-stages@cec.eu.int
W europa.eu.int/comm/stages

Twice a year the European Commission offers around 600 trainee positions in various roles at its central offices in Brussels and Luxembourg. Selection is a two-stage process – the best candidates are added to the 'Blue Book', which is then passed to the various departments in the EC. Translating internships are also available – see the separate website W www.europa.eu.int/comm/dgs/translation/index_en.htm.

Types of Work: Admin work, taking minutes of meetings, researching and assessing projects etc.

Timing & Length of Work: Five months from March and October.

Destinations: Belgium (Brussels) & Luxembourg.

Costs/Pay: *Stagiaires* get £500 per month, which must cover food, accommodation and transport.

Eligibility: Applicants must be under 30, have a university degree, be fluent in one European Community language and speak at least one other.

How to Apply: Apply by August 31 for the March *stage* or by March 1 for the October *stage*. Forms must be completed on the website and you have to send in evidence of qualifications and a signed paper application.

European Parliament
Traineeship Office, KAD O2C007, L - 2929 Luxembourg
☎ 00 352 43 00 3697
fax 00 352 43 00 248 82
e stages@europarl.eu.int
W www.europarl.eu.int/stages

The European Parliament offers a variety of paid and unpaid traineeships at its Luxembourg headquarters, useful for people hoping to work in politics or international economics. Competition for positions is tough and applicants who can demonstrate an interest in European politics are preferred.

Types of Work: Admin jobs in economics, law, political science, journalism and translating.

Timing & Length of Work: Five months from February or September (one to four months for unpaid traineeships).

Destinations: Luxembourg & Brussels.

Costs/Pay: Paid interns earn around £680 per month; accommodation is extra. You'll be reimbursed for costs of travel to the internship.

Eligibility: Applicants must be aged 18 to 45, university graduates, fluent in one European community language and competent in another. This must be your first EU internship. University students can apply for unpaid internships.

How to Apply: Download the application from the website. You must provide a reference and proof of qualifications. Apply by October 15 for February traineeships or June 15 for September traineeships.

ESA (European Space Agency)

ESA Education Office, Personnel Department, 8–10 rue Mario Nikis, 75738 Paris Cedex 15, France
☎ 00 33 1 53 69 76 54
fax 00 33 1 53 69 75 60
e maileduc@hq.esa.fr
w www.esa.int/hr/educational/index.htm

ESA has a paid Young Graduate Trainee Scheme (YGTS) for science and technology graduates. You can work at the European Space & Technology Center in the Netherlands, the European Space Operations Center in Germany, the ESA Center in Italy or the ESA Headquarters in Paris.

Types of Work: Interns do hands-on technical work relating to their field of study.

Timing & Length of Work: The YGTS lasts for one year. End-of-studies training of one to six months is also available.

Destinations: The Netherlands, France, Germany & Italy.

Costs/Pay: Trainees get a monthly stipend for living expenses. End-of-studies trainees are unpaid.

Eligibility: Applicants for the YGTS must

be recent graduates from a science or technology degree.

How to Apply: See the website for current vacancies and apply online. There's an interview and you have to take a medical. Apply at any time for sandwich traineeships by submitting a CV and covering letter to the relevant department (see the website for addresses).

Foreign & Commonwealth Office (FCO)

Recruitment Section, Room 2/98, Old Admiralty Bldg, Whitehall, London SW1A 2PA
☎ 020-7008 0762
fax 020-7008 0638
e recruitment.public@fco.gov.uk
w www.fco.gov.uk

Part of the British diplomatic service, the FCO arranges around 40 short work placements at British consulates around the world every year as part of the Overseas Undergraduate Attachment Scheme.

Types of Work: Trainees work mainly in admin jobs in the economic, commercial, management, visa or consular sections at embassies and consulates.

Timing & Length of Work: Attachments are for two weeks to two months starting in July.

Destinations: Participants can be posted wherever there is a British consulate.

Costs/Pay: Traineeships are unpaid but travel to the placement and accommodation are provided.

Eligibility: Applicants must be university students in their penultimate year. Applicants can be studying any degree but must show a genuine interest in diplomatic work.

How to Apply: Download the application from the website. Apply before January with a CV, covering letter and two references. There's a telephone interview in February and an in-depth security check.

GLS Sprachenzentrum Berlin

Kolonnenstr 26, 10829 Berlin, Germany

☎ 00 49 30 78 00 89
fax 00 49 30 787 41 92
e germancourses@gls-berlin.com
w www.german-courses.com

GLS is a German language school with an unpaid work experience programme. You do a four-week residential German course and then an internship with a company in Berlin.

Types of Work: Past placements have been in marketing, banking, insurance, travel and tourism.

Timing & Length of Work: Language courses last a minimum of four weeks; work experience placements last six to 12 weeks.

Destination: Berlin (Germany).

Costs/Pay: The placement fee is about £305; a four-week residential course is £460. Work experience is unpaid but accommodation can be arranged in home-stays or shared apartments for around £63 per week.

Eligibility: Applicants must be at least 18, speak some German and have reached intermediate level before the internship can start.

How to Apply: Apply with a CV and covering letter in German. There's an online booking form on the website.

Grampus

Libby Urquhart, Grampus Heritage & Training Ltd, Olney Bank, The Ross, Comrie, Perthshire PH6 2JU
☎ 01764-670653
e libby@grampus.co.uk
w www.grampus.co.uk

This educational organisation offers work-experience placements in Europe for art students as part of the Leonardo da Vinci programme. Projects have a heritage or environmental focus.

Types of Work: Art, heritage, archaeology and environmental projects are available.

Timing & Length of Work: Projects last four weeks and are available year round.

Destinations: Germany & Poland.

Costs/Pay: Costs are covered by the Leonardo da Vinci grant; travel, accommodation, meals and insurance are included.

Eligibility: Applicants must be at least 18, have a current passport and demonstrate an interest in the project applied for.

How to Apply: Download an application from the website. You'll need to provide two references.

International Association for the Exchange of Students for Technical Experience (IAESTE)

Education & Training, British Council, 10 Spring Gardens, London SW1A 2BN
☎ 020-7389 4771
fax 020-7389 4426
e iaeste@britishcouncil.org
w www.iaeste.org.uk

Run in conjunction with the British Council, IAESTE provides thousands of engineering and industrial placements with companies around the world.

Types of Work: Mainly technical and engineering.

Timing & Length of Work: Eight to 12 weeks from June.

Destinations: Placements are possible in 80 countries.

Costs/Pay: Participants get an allowance for accommodation, food and work travel; flights are extra. There's a £60 IAESTE administration fee.

Eligibility: Applicants must be full-time university students and have completed at least one year of study.

How to Apply: Download the application from the website and apply by December 10 to register. A list of placements is sent to registered students in January. You then have to provide a CV, reference and statement of your reasons for taking the internship.

International Association for Students of Economics and Management (AIESEC)

2nd floor, 29–31 Cowper St, London EC2A 4AT
☎ 020-7549 1800
fax 020-7336 7971

e| national@uk.aiesec.org
W| www.workabroad.org.uk

AIESEC is the world's largest student organisation and arranges overseas work-exchange programmes for around 100 students a year from member universities – see the website for current members. They provide an orientation before you go and a reintegration session on your return.

Types of Work: Management, technical, development and education traineeships are on offer.

Timing & Length of Work: Placements are for eight weeks to 18 months.

Destinations: Placements are possible in more than 85 countries.

Costs/Pay: The registration fee is £160. Placements pay a subsistence salary. You cover your own transport, insurance and living expenses.

Eligibility: Applicants must have graduated within one year or be an undergraduate at an AIESEC member university. Candidates aged under 27 are preferred.

How to Apply: Apply online. There will then be an assessment and interview.

International Exchange Centre (IEC)

35 Ivor Place, London NW1 6EA
☎ 020-7724 4493
fax 020-7724 0849
e| isecinfo@btconnect.com
W| www.isecworld.co.uk

The IEC organises paid internships in the USA and France. In America you can arrange your own internship or take an organised work placement that relates to your future career. Interns are assisted with all paperwork and have an orientation on arrival. The French programme includes an orientation on arrival and 20 hours of French lessons. For details of seasonal work and summer camp programmes see Contacts in the Casual/Seasonal Work and Au Pairing & Working with Kids chapters.

Types of Work: Internships can be in any career-related field.

Timing & Length of Work: Internships are from June or December, for four to 18 months (for eight to 12 weeks in France).

Destinations: The USA & France. Other destinations are planned.

Costs/Pay: American internships cost from £210 for four months if you arrange your own internship, or from £1190 if you take an organised work placement. French internships cost from £550. Transport and visa costs are extra. Pay depends on your job.

Eligibility: For US programmes applicants must be aged between 18 and 28, and be a graduate or have experience. For French programmes applicants must be between 18 and 30 and have intermediate-level French; non-students are accepted.

How to Apply: Email or phone for an application form three months before you want to start.

Interspeak

Stretton Lower Hall, Stretton, nr Malpas, Cheshire SY14 7HS
☎ 01829-250641
fax 01829-250596
e| enquiries@interspeak.co.uk
W| www.interspeak.co.uk

Interspeak has been arranging unpaid work placements or *stages* in Europe since 1981. Traineeships are tailor-made to match your interests and you stay with a host family.

Types of Work: Categories include law, IT, journalism, tourism and marketing.

Timing & Length of Work: Mini-*stages* last up to two weeks; maxi-*stages* last three to 24 weeks.

Destinations: France, Germany, Spain & the UK.

Costs/Pay: For mini-*stages* there's an £80 registration fee and £320/540 for one/two weeks, including accommodation and meals. For maxi-*stages* there's a £320 placement fee and accommodation and food cost £140 per week.

Eligibility: Applicants must be aged 17 to 19 for mini-*stages* and 18 or older for maxi-*stages*, with some knowledge of the local language.

How to Apply: See the website or call for an application form. Applications are accepted year round but February/March is the best time to apply.

i-to-i UK
9 Blenheim Terrace, Leeds LS2 9HZ
☎ 0870 333 2332
fax 0113-242 2171
e info@i-to-i.com
W www.i-to-i.com

i-to-i offers dozens of teaching and volunteering projects plus unpaid work-experience programmes in journalism and business in lots of interesting destinations. Journalism projects are English-speaking and can be in TV or print journalism. Homestay accommodation is provided (except in Ireland) and there are orientations, language lessons and local support once you arrive.

Types of Work: Journalism (radio and TV), marketing, advertising and tourism.

Timing & Length of Work: Placements are for four to 12 weeks.

Destinations: Bolivia, China, Ghana, Honduras, India, Ireland, Mongolia & Sri Lanka.

Costs/Pay: Fees range from £995 to £1695, excluding flights and visa fees.

Eligibility: You must be aged at least 17 and provide a copy of your CV. Intermediate Spanish is required for Latin American projects.

How to Apply: Call first to discuss suitability for projects. You then register online, pay a £195 deposit and an application is sent out to you.

Japan Exchange & Teaching (JET) Programme
JET Desk, Embassy of Japan, 101–104 Piccadilly, London W1J 7JT
☎ 020-7465 6668
fax 020-7491 9347
e jet@embjapan.org.uk
W www.jetprogramme.co.uk

This is mainly geared towards teachers (see the Teaching chapter for more details) but also has openings for graduates with good written and spoken Japanese as Coordinators for International Relations (CIR). Visas, flights and training are provided and you get a salary and in-country support.

Types of Work: Admin tasks in English and Japanese, interpreting at local events and coordinating international events.

Timing & Length of Work: The programme lasts one year from July/August.

Destination: Japan.

Costs/Pay: There are no fees. Wages for the year are around £19,000 after taxes but you pay for accommodation and compulsory medical insurance.

Eligibility: Applicants must be under 40, have a university degree and be able to speak and write Japanese to an intermediate level.

How to Apply: Download an application form from the website. Apply from September/October (closing date is in late November). You must provide two references and fill in a medical declaration. Interviews are held in London in February.

Mountbatten Internship Programme
5th floor, Abbey House, 74–76 St John St, London ECIM 4DZ
☎ 020-7253 7759
fax 020-7831 7018
e info-uk@mountbatten.org
W www.mountbatten.org

Founded in 1984, Mountbatten offers business-focused internships with companies in New York City. Participants are awarded a Certificate in International Business Practice. Mountbatten will match you with an internship and make all the visa, insurance and accommodation arrangements.

Types of Work: Clerical or administrative work at financial firms or other city businesses.

Timing & Length of Work: One year from January, April/May or September.

Destination: The USA.

Costs/Pay: The total cost is £1745, plus air fares. Participants are paid about £560 per month, with a possible £315 bonus.

Eligibility: Applicants must be university or college graduates aged between 21 and 28.

A typing speed of 45 words per minute is preferred.

How to Apply: Download an application pack from the website. Applicants must provide a digital copy of their CV, a personal statement giving their reasons for applying and at least two references. Applicants are interviewed in London. Apply by March 15 for the September programme, by July 31 for the January programme or by October 31 for the April/May programme.

Office of the United Nations High Commissioner for Human Rights (OHCHR)

8–14 Av de la Paix, 1211 Geneva 10, Switzerland
☎ 00 41 22 917 9000
fax 00 41 22 917 9024
e personnel@ohchr.org
w www.unhchr.ch

Europe's leading human rights institution has unpaid internships for graduates at its headquarters in Geneva. Graduates in International Law, Political Science, History and Social Sciences are preferred and applicants must demonstrate an interest in human rights and current affairs.

Types of Work: Research, drafting reports and other admin tasks.

Timing & Length of Work: Three to six months from May/June or November/December.

Destination: Geneva (Switzerland).

Costs/Pay: Positions are unpaid and you must make your own travel arrangements.

Eligibility: Applicants must be university graduates in a relevant field and speak two of the following languages: English, French, Spanish, Arabic, Russian and Chinese.

How to Apply: Print off the application form from the website. You must provide three references. Apply by April 30 for May/June internships or by October 31 for November/December internships.

The Smallpeice Trust

74 Upper Holly Walk, Leamington Spa, Warks CV32 4JL

☎ 01926-333200
fax 01926-333202
e gen@smallpeicetrust.org.uk
w www.smallpeicetrust.org.uk

Partly funded by the EU, this independent educational trust offers a gap-year programme of engineering training at a UK university, followed by a language course at a European university and an unpaid work-experience placement with a European engineering company.

Types of Work: Engineering.

Timing & Length of Work: Programmes run from September to May. Engineering training and work placements last for three months; the language course lasts one month.

Destinations: Training is at a UK university; the language study and work placements sectors can take place in one of nine European nations.

Costs/Pay: The programme costs from £4950, including tuition, full-board accommodation and flights.

Eligibility: Applicants must be aged at least 18 and need to have just finished secondary education and to have a deferred place at university to study engineering.

How to Apply: Send a SAE to the office or go online to get an application form. There will be an interview as part of the selection process.

Teaching & Projects Abroad

Gerrard House, Rustington, W Sussex BN16 1AW

☎ 01903-859911
fax 01903-785779l
e info@teaching-abroad.co.uk
w www.teaching-abroad.com

Teaching & Projects Abroad is mainly a teaching and volunteering organisation but also offers an impressive range of unpaid work-experience projects in a variety of unusual destinations. Participants get local support and there's a travel agent to help you book flights. For volunteering projects and teaching opportunities see Contacts in the

Volunteering, Conservation & Expeditions and Teaching chapters.

Types of Work: Journalism, veterinary medicine, law, accountancy and architecture.

Timing & Length of Work: Placements are for three months (can be extended for an extra fee).

Destinations: China, Ghana, India, Mexico, Mongolia, Romania, Russia & South Africa.

Costs/Pay: Fees range from £1595 to £2495 for three months, including insurance, accommodation and meals but not visa fees or flights.

Eligibility: Applicants must be aged at least 18 and have finished their A Levels or equivalent. Spanish is needed for the Mexico programme.

How to Apply: Complete the online application form and pay £195 deposit.

Travellers Worldwide

7 Mulberry Close, Ferring, W Sussex
BN12 5HY
☎ 01903-700478
fax 01903-502595
e info@travellersworldwide.com
W www.travellersworldwide.com

Travellers organises work-experience placements in a variety of unusual destinations. Placements are tailored to suit your interests. For information on voluntary work and teaching overseas, see Contacts in the Volunteering, Conservation & Expeditions chapter.

Types of Work: Journalism, media and law.

Timing & Length of Work: Placements are for at least three months.

Destinations: Argentina, Ghana, India, Russia, South Africa, Sri Lanka & the Ukraine.

Costs/Pay: Costs start from £1195, including accommodation and all meals but excluding flights.

Eligibility: Applicants must be aged at least 17.

How to Apply: Call for a brochure or apply online. There will then be a telephone interview.

WORK PLACEMENTS IN THE UK

ABN AMRO

Graduate Recruitment Dept, 250 Bishopsgate, London EC2M 4AA
☎ 020-7553 9118
fax 020-7678 2588
W www.graduate.abnamro.com

This international bank accepts large numbers of interns at its European offices.

Types of Work: Management and global finance.

Timing & Length of Work: Three months.

Destinations: London, Paris & Amsterdam.

Costs/Pay: Wages are based on entry-level salary.

Eligibility: Applicants should be in their penultimate year of university with 24 UCAS points and a predicted 2:1 degree.

How to Apply: Apply online using the form on the website.

BBC

W www.bbc.co.uk/jobs

The BBC offers short unpaid internships in various different disciplines relating to TV and radio. Some positions are in regional centres such as Birmingham, Bristol and Manchester. All inquiries are handled via the website.

Types of Work: Journalism, programme making, sound engineering, lighting, costumes and business support.

Timing & Length of Work: Internships last one to four weeks and can start any time.

Destination: The UK.

Costs/Pay: Placements are unpaid.

Eligibility: The minimum age varies from 15 to 18 years.

How to Apply: See the website for upcoming vacancies and apply online.

British Telecom (BT)

☎ 0800 731 6835
e placement@abraxas.com
W www.ragtime.com

BT has openings for summer and year-long placements at its offices around the UK, including regional opportunities in

Scotland, Northern Ireland and Wales. All recruitment inquiries should be made through the website, by email or by phone.

Types of Work: Telecommunications, finance, marketing, IT etc.

Timing & Length of Work: Summer placements are for three months, industrial placements are for six to 12 months.

Destination: The UK.

Costs/Pay: The weekly salary starts at around £260.

Eligibility: Applicants should be penultimate year degree students with grade C or above in English at GCSE. Specific skills may be required for individual positions (see the website).

How to Apply: See the website for vacancies and apply online to specific positions. Summer placements are advertised from November.

Civil Service

W www.careers.civil-service.gov.uk

The Civil Service offers large numbers of paid and unpaid work-experience placements every year. You can work in government departments all over the country, from the Scottish Executive to the Ministry of Defence.

Types of Work: Most positions involve admin in government offices.

Timing & Length of Work: Placements vary from short summer placements to long-term projects.

Destination: The UK.

Costs/Pay: Paid placements earn either a stipend for living expenses or a full wage based on around £12,000 per year.

Eligibility: Applicants should be graduates or undergraduates studying for a relevant degree.

How to Apply: See the website for current vacancies and then apply to the relevant department.

Corus Group

Ashbourne Hill Management College, Leamington Spa, Warks CV33 9PY

☎ 01926-488033

fax 01926-488024

e recruitment.web@corusgroup.com

W www.corusgroupcareers.com

Formerly British Steel, the Corus Group offers large numbers of internship placements around the UK.

Types of Work: Engineering, technology, finance, HR, business etc.

Timing & Length of Work: Placements are for three months from June or one year from July.

Destination: The UK.

Costs/Pay: Wages are from £200 to £250.

Eligibility: Applicants must be university students (first-year or above for summer placements, penultimate year for industrial placements). Preferably you'll be on track for 2:2 degree.

How to Apply: See the website for vacancies and to register. Application packs are then sent out for specific jobs.

Euromoney Institutional Investor PLC

Nestor House, Playhouse Yard, London EC4V 5EX

☎ 020-7779 8888

fax 020-7779 8842

e information@euromoneyplc.com;

W www.euromoneyplc.com

This financial publisher offers graduate training courses in journalism, which can potentially lead to full-time work.

Types of Work: Journalism, sales and marketing.

Timing & Length of Work: Openings are available year round and last six months.

Destination: The UK.

Costs/Pay: Wages are based on £12,000 a year.

Eligibility: Courses are open to all graduates.

How to Apply: Apply using the online form. There will then be an interview.

IBM UK Ltd

Student Employment Officer, Recruitment Dept, PO Box 41, North Harbour, Portsmouth, Hants PO5 3AU

☎ 02392-289111

e student_pgms@uk.ibm.com
w www-5.ibm.com/employment/uk/students

This computer giant offers a variety of trainee schemes for students. You can do short summer placements or longer schemes for up to a year. The Pre-University Employment programme is specifically targeted at gap-year students.

Types of Work: IT design, software development, marketing, admin, finance, HR, sales etc.

Timing & Length of Work: Summer placements last three months from June/July. Other traineeships last nine to 12 months from July/August.

Destinations: North Harbour (nr Portsmouth), Hursley (nr Winchester), Warwick, Basingstoke, South Bank (Central London), Bedfont & Sunbury (Greater London).

Costs/Pay: Wages are based on £12,000 per year.

Eligibility: For Pre-University Employment applicants' predicted A-level results must be at least A, A, B and they must have a deferred place at university. See the website for other trainee programmes.

How to Apply: Apply using the online form (by the end of April for Pre-University Employment).

KPMG

☎ 0500 664665
w www.kpmgcareers.co.uk

This large accountancy multinational offers paid work-experience placements across the UK and special gap-year placements for pre-university gappers. All recruitment inquiries should be made through the website or by phone.

Types of Work: Placements are in various financial and accountancy sectors.

Timing & Length of Work: Gap placements last six to nine months from October. Vacation placements last eight weeks from June. There are also one-year business placements for sandwich students.

Destination: The UK.

Costs/Pay: All positions are paid based on £12,500 per year.

Eligibility: For the gap programme applicants must have A-grade GCSE maths and 24 predicted UCAS points. For other programmes applicants must be students in their penultimate year with at least 24 UCAS points, an A in GCSE Maths and C or better in GCSE English.

How to Apply: See the website for vacancies and apply online.

PricewaterhouseCoopers (PwC)

The Graduate Recruitment Centre,
PO Box 5885, Birmingham B4 6FB
☎ 0808 100 1500
e careers.three@uk.pwcglobal.com
w www.pwcglobal.com/uk/eng/careers/main/index.html

This leading management consultancy offers summer and long-term internships at its offices around the UK. There's also a specific scheme for pre-university gap-year students.

Types of Work: Business advice, tax, law and finance.

Timing & Length of Work: Summer internships last for six weeks from July. The gap-year programme lasts six months from September. Six-month sandwich placements can start year round.

Destination: The UK (the gap programme is in London and the Southeast only).

Costs/Pay: Pay is based on an entry-level salary.

Eligibility: Applicants for internships must be in their penultimate year of university study. Gap-year applicants should have good A-Level prospects and be interested in the financial world.

How to Apply: See the website for current vacancies. Apply on the website or call for an application.

Reuters

85 Fleet St, London EC4P 4AJ
w about.reuters.com/careers/graduate

This international news agency has short internships and yearlong work placements in journalism and other aspects of their business. All recruitment inquiries are handled through the website.

Types of Work: Business, finance & legal, journalism, sales & marketing and technology.

Timing & Length of Work: Three-month summer internships or 12-month placements are available.

Destination: The UK.

Costs/Pay: Interns are paid according to an entry-level salary.

Eligibility: This varies according to internship.

How to Apply: See the website for current vacancies and apply online from November.

Rolls-Royce plc

PO Box 31, Derby DE24 8BJ

☎ 01332-244309/15

ⓔ erika.aubrey-rees@rolls-royce.com

ⓦ www.rolls-royce.com/careers

Rolls-Royce offers around 100 internships and 50 summer placements per year in mechanical engineering and business.

Types of Work: Engineering, logistics, purchasing and finance.

Timing & Length of Work: Internships last four to 12 months and start year round. Summer placements run from June to September.

Destination: The UK.

Costs/Pay: Wages are based on an entry-level salary.

Eligibility: Applicants must be in their second year of study or above and on track for a 2:1 degree or higher.

How to Apply: Apply using the online form. This will be followed by an assessment.

Royal Opera House

Covent Garden, London WC2E 9DD

☎ 020-7212 9410

fax 020-7212 9441

ⓔ education@roh.org.uk

ⓦ www.royaloperahouse.org/education

The Royal Opera House offers work experience in most of its departments, including the press, costume and technical departments.

All work is done at the main Covent Garden building.

Types of Work: Mostly technical and costume-related roles, plus some admin jobs.

Timing & Length of Work: Placements are available year round except August/September. Most people stay for two weeks to a month.

Destination: The UK.

Costs/Pay: Positions are unpaid.

Eligibility: Applicants must be over 16 for admin roles and over 18 for other positions. Students or graduates from a theatre or art-management background, or people with previous theatre work experience are preferred.

How to Apply: Apply in writing with a CV and covering letter.

Sir Robert McAlpine

Eaton Court, Maylands Ave, Hemel Hempstead, Herts HP2 7TR

☎ 01442-233444

fax 01442-230024

ⓔ information@sir-robert-mcalpine.com

ⓦ www.sir-robert-mcalpine.com

One of Britain's leading construction companies, Sir Robert McAlpine offers summer and industrial placements in engineering and construction at its headquarters in Hemel Hempstead. It also offers a sponsorship scheme where outstanding students receive funding through university and summer work if they sign up to join the company on graduation.

Types of Work: Construction and civil engineering.

Timing & Length of Work: Summer programmes are for eight to 12 weeks and industrial placements are for one year.

Destinations: Around the UK.

Costs/Pay: The salary is based on £13,500 per year (£11,250 for summer placements).

Eligibility: Applicants should be in the penultimate year of a construction-related degree.

How to Apply: Apply on the website or write requesting an application form.

STEP Enterprise Ltd

2nd floor, 11–13 Goldsmith St,
Nottingham NG1 5JS
☎ 0870 036 5450
fax 0115- 950 8321
e enquiries@step.org.uk
w www.step.org.uk

STEP offers more than 1500 paid summer placements for students at British businesses and technology companies. The main STEP programme runs in the summer but you can do placements for up to a year if you take a gap year during your university course. See the website for your local STEP representatives and projects.

Types of Work: Accounting, business, community work, engineering, education, health, IT, law, media, manufacturing, retail, tourism and web design.

Timing & Length of Work: The STEP programme lasts eight weeks; specialised industrial placements can last up to a year.

Destination: The UK.

Costs/Pay: Students on STEP programmes get a weekly stipend of £170. The stipend varies for longer projects.

Eligibility: Applicants must be second- or penultimate-year students on full-time degree courses at university or equivalent. You can't apply if you have more than six months' work experience.

How to Apply: Fill in an online application form.

Thames Water

Graduate Recruitment Team, Thames Water, Clearwater Court, Vastern Rd, Reading, Berks RG1 8DB
☎ 0118-373 8582
e undergraduate.placements@thameswater.co.uk
w www.twgraduaterecruitment.com

Thames Water offers summer placements in engineering and operations and year-long placements in IT, research, technology and business. Other regional water companies have similar schemes.

Types of Work: Placements involve hands-on training in engineering, technology and admin.

Timing & Length of Work: Placements are for three months or one year. See the website for start dates.

Destination: The UK (Southeast).

Costs/Pay: Wages are based on around £13,000 per year.

Eligibility: Applicants must be in their penultimate year of a relevant degree.

How to Apply: See the website for current vacancies. Apply from October.

Unilever

Unilever Graduate Recruitment, 2nd floor, 20 Park Way, Newbury, Berks RG14 1EE
☎ 0870 154 3550 or 01635-584138
e enquiry@go-ucmds.com
w www.ucmds.com

One of Britain's most decentralised companies, Unilever is an umbrella organisation for all sorts of businesses (eg, Lipton tea, Ben & Jerry's ice cream) and offers work placements at offices all over the UK.

Types of Work: Management, marketing, human resources, IT etc.

Timing & Length of Work: Placements are for two months from July.

Destination: The UK.

Costs/Pay: The pay is £250 a week.

Eligibility: Applicants should be in the penultimate or final year of their degree (science or technology required for some placements).

How to Apply: Apply online by February, using the form on the website.

Year in Industry (YINI)

w www.yini.org.uk

This is the main scheme for school leavers in the UK. It places around 800 students in industrial work placements every year. Participants get 20 days of formal training during the year. See the website for your nearest YINI representative.

Types of Work: Placements are mostly in engineering, science, IT and business.

Timing & Length of Work: Jobs usually start in August and finish the following July.

Destination: The UK.

Costs/Pay: The minimum salary is £150 a week.

Eligibility: Applicants should have a confirmed offer at university for the following year.

How to Apply: Apply online or download the application form from the website. Once you have registered there will be an interview.

RECRUITMENT AGENCIES

Adecco

Elstree Way, Borehamwood, Herts
WD6 1HY

W www.adecco.co.uk

This international recruitment agency has more than 5000 offices in 62 countries and specialises in temp and office work. You can upload your CV, register and search for jobs online. Other fields include education, engineering, health and construction. See the website for your nearest Adecco branch.

Drake Employment

W www.drakeintl.com

Drake has offices in the UK, the USA, Canada, Australia, New Zealand, South Africa, Hong Kong, Singapore, Malaysia and Switzerland. You can submit your CV, register and job search online. See the website for your nearest Drake office.

Hays Personnel

1 Southampton St, Covent Garden, London WC2R OLR

☎ 020-7520 5988
fax 01279-642096

W www.hayspersonnel.com

Hays is a leading recruitment agency that specialises in various types of office staff and IT, education, engineering and construction staff. It has offices in Britain, Europe, Canada, Australia and New Zealand. See the website for your nearest office. You can register and search for jobs online and you can even do a virtual interview over the web.

Kelly Services

e kellyinfo@kellyservices.co.uk
W www.kellyservices.co.uk

The original temp agency, Kelly has offices in the UK, Europe, the USA, Canada, Asia and Australia. It offers temp and permanent office, technical, engineering, IT and education jobs around the world. See the website for your nearest Kelly office.

Monster

W www.monster.co.uk

Monster is a leading recruitment company with operations in the UK, Australia, New Zealand, India, Hong Kong, Singapore and most European countries. You can register, create a digital CV and contact job experts on the website. Many leading banks and corporations get all their temporary and permanent staff through Monster. It is a digital service and all inquiries go through the website.

Reed Executive plc

W www.reed.co.uk

Reed is another recruitment multinational, with hundreds of offices in the UK, Europe, Canada, South Africa, Australia and New Zealand. See the website for your nearest Reed office. Reed specialises in temporary and permanent office and engineering/construction jobs. You can register online.

Teaching

Congratulations! You've opened this book and presumably understand what you're reading so you already possess the prime qualification needed to join the ranks of one of the world's largest industries, that of English-language teaching (ELT). As the language of computing, international law and global business, and of Michael Jackson, Britney Spears, Eminem and the all-branded, fast-edit, monied-up world they represent, everybody and his sister wants to learn English. From the backstreets of Khartoum (Sudan) to the high-rises of Kyoto (Japan), proficiency in English is seen as a key to a better future, whether that future hinges on dreams of a taxi-driving gig in New York or simply the ability to communicate better with foreign business partners. There is almost nowhere that English teaching is not in demand and few countries, no matter how dicey, are considered out of bounds. When rents began to show in the Iron Curtain in the late 1980s, first through the breaches were the English-language schools, often up and running long before the diplomats arrived to secure political connections. We've met far-from-home Brits, Irish, Aussies, Kiwis and Americans employed teaching English in the oil fields of Libya, in hotel-management schools in Vladivostok (Russia) and in medical faculties in Colombia.

Closer to home, every city to small town throughout countries such as France, Italy and Spain – and most of the rest of Europe, Eastern and Western – has its English-language schools, where it's possible to combine paid work with exotic locales, attractive scenery and, if you choose the right destination, a bit of sun. Teaching English as a foreign language, or TEFL (pronounced 'teffle') for short, offers a whole world, a career and a lifestyle – if you want it that way. Alternatively, it can just be a great paying way to travel for 12 months.

Teaching opportunities abroad beyond TEFL are thin on the ground. Language is an obvious barrier. How are you going to teach art in Italy, for instance, if you don't speak Italian? There are a few ways around this and these are described under Other Teaching later in this chapter. The options are slightly broader for university graduates and this is also discussed later. For voluntary teaching work abroad also see the Volunteering, Conservation & Expeditions chapter earlier and for teaching sports and summer camps in the United States see the Casual/Seasonal Work chapter.

Pros & Cons

The major appeal of teaching, whether English or otherwise, is that it can actually be the means to travel, unlike bar work, fruit picking, staffing the desk at a hostel or similar, all of which typically involve rolling up in a place then seeking employment. Armed with the right qualifications (and obtaining these can take as little as a month of your time – see Training later in this chapter) it's often possible that a school overseas will pay your way there and then help with matters such as accommodation and, where necessary, work permits. Once you've entered the world of ELT you'll find that it operates like a superhighway with overlapping networks of connected schools worldwide. It's possible to move from one country to the next remaining in steady employment, gaining experience and status as you go, which can be parlayed into increased responsibility and more dosh. Pamela Smith's tale is typical of many:

I'd just finished uni and I wanted to travel the world and sidestep the immediate issue of choosing a career. I intended it to be a couple of years before 'settling down'. I didn't have any qualifications and I couldn't afford to do CELTA but through a chance meeting with an Italian at a dinner party in Hull I was put in touch with the boss of a small school in

Novara just outside Milan. After a bit of faffing, I was offered a job with accommodation and pocket money at the end of the week. I had two or three painful but character-building years – which were fun actually – of cowboy schools, managing to get all the way to Singapore. There the British Council employed me based on my experience – four years by then.

Six years on and Pam is still with the British Council, regularly jetting to places as far flung as Ankara (Turkey) and Tashkent (Uzbekistan) to host training courses. She's in the process of negotiating a move to lecturing in Australia and happily accepts that in ELT she has the career she once sought to sidestep. She has no complaints.

Teaching doesn't have to be a life sentence. It can work equally well as a short-term arrangement. A teaching post provides initial security (a flat, cash, people around to help if things go wrong) on arriving fresh in a new country, easing your way into what could be a confusing new society. You are working with fellow teachers who are likely to be a diverse and international bunch and probably willing providers of boozy initiations into local customs and peculiarities. William Haynes of his time spent teaching in Bangkok recalls:

We had Irish Jim whose accent was so 'tick' nobody in the staff room could understand him let alone the students, Randy who lived in a seedy hotel room with his pet rabbit, John the ex-mercenary from Louisiana and Kevin the serial Thai marrier who'd been in Southeast Asia five years and got hitched three times.

And then there are the students – a fantastic and often overlooked resource for experiencing the country.

Not everybody takes to teaching. It can be arduous and frustrating work requiring great patience, especially if the students are beginners and have zero language ability. Day after day of parroted drilling of 'My name is,' 'Her name is,' 'Your name is,' can be totally dispiriting. Schedules are often split between morning and evening classes (to fit around students' working hours) stretching out your own working day. Added to which there's the preparation time. Newly qualified teachers will find that for every hour in the classroom there's at least the same spent in preparing lessons. Being pinned down to five, possibly six days a week in the classroom doesn't leave much chance for travelling around either. Most of the time it's as much as you can do to get out and explore the town or city in which you're based. For all of these reasons teaching is not the best job to fund a hardcore travel habit but it can provide an excellent means of getting to experience and know one place extremely well.

Teaching English as a Foreign Language (TEFL)
TRAINING
Speaking English is the bottom-line entry requirement and rarely enough of a qualification on its own. These days it's likely only to lead as far as employment at a dubious cowboy school, where teaching standards are as poor as the cash-strapped students who can't afford better. Such places can provide a first foothold in the world of English teaching but it will be a shaky foothold and one with little job security attached. The vast majority of TEFL teachers take some form of training to gain a recognised professional English-language teaching qualification. This is no longer quite the passport to guaranteed work that it once was (too many people chasing the same jobs) but it does provide solid foundations and it's a minimum requirement for work with the main ELT employers.

There are two standard qualifications for TEFL teaching. The best known is CELTA, which is the Cambridge Certificate in English Language Teaching to Adults, administered by the University of Cambridge ESOL (English for Speakers of Other Languages) department. The other is TESOL, which stands for Teaching English to Speakers of Other Languages, and is overseen by Trinity College London.

There are no special qualifications required to get a place on one of these courses but all applicants go through a strict screening process. This begins with candidates being sent a Language Awareness Task with questions about things such as vocabulary, grammar and phonology. According to Simon Marshall, an ELT Teacher Training Consultant, *'If the applicant makes a reasonable and serious attempt to do this they're then invited for an interview. If their task is hopeless then they are not.'* At the interview applicants are given further written tasks *'...to check that they can spell and didn't get someone else to do their original task.'* Applicants also get a good chatting to, either on a one-to-one basis or in a group. The aim is to examine language awareness and to judge how well the applicant will be able to stand up to the stress of publicly observed teaching practices. Assessors are also looking for an ability to work cooperatively with others. As Simon says, *'It is not a course for prima donnas.'*

Applicants for the intensive four-week course should be free of any outside commitments. Those with jobs are advised to follow a three-month, six-month or one-year course. At the end of the interview it's made plain that candidates have to pass the course through their efforts and that attendance alone is not sufficient to be awarded the certificate.

It's a process that seems to work well as only about five per cent of candidates fail the course or drop out worldwide. Simon adds that *'...most find the course a hugely enjoyable experience'* and a frequent comment from those who successfully complete is *'It has been the best learning experience of my life.'*

Both the CELTA and TESOL courses involve about 100 hours of tuition. In their most intensive form this is four crammed five-day weeks, or it can be done part time, stretched over several months. Either way involves rigorous training during which course attendees (typically eight to 12 people on a course) are taught how to teach through example. Passes are awarded based on written work and the all-important and nerve-racking observed lesson, where the candidate fronts a class of real students and conducts a lesson of their own devising for the examiners.

Course costs vary greatly depending on the institution but expect to pay from around £650 up to £1080 at International House (IH) in London, one of the premier teacher-training centres in the country, where courses are run on a monthly basis. There are literally hundreds of places throughout the UK running TEFL courses, from specialised language institutes to local night-school centres and further-education colleges. For a list of those offering CELTA send a large SAE to Cambridge ESOL, TEFL Unit, 1 Hills Rd, Cambridge CB1 2EU (☎ 01223-553 355; ℮ efl@ucles.org.uk; Ⓦ www.cambridge-efl.org) or follow the links on the website; for TESOL-affiliated courses write to Trinity College London, 89 Albert Embankment, London SE1 7TP (☎ 020-7820 6100, fax 020-7820 6161; ℮ tesol@trinity college.co.uk; Ⓦ www.trinitycollege.co.uk). Alternatively, another fantastic resource is the VSO website (Ⓦ www.vso.org.uk/volunteering/education_tefl.htm) where you'll find an excellent 80-page document listing course centres in the UK complete with dates, durations, prices and full contact details.

A more interesting option might be to take the TEFL course abroad. Several of the larger schools and institutions have branches or affiliates overseas where fully accredited courses are held several times a year. Teaching standards are every bit as high as in the UK and there may be a chance of a job at the school afterwards (see the following Jobs section). Although there are flights and accommodation to be paid for, given the lower wages and living costs in some cases flying off to do a TEFL course in some appealing foreign location can work out cheaper than doing it at home. For example, the one-month CELTA course taught at the IH affiliate in Cairo costs the equivalent of £650. Add another £250 for flights and it's still £200 cheaper than enrolling at the London HQ. Other centres offering TEFL abroad are listed in the Contacts section. You can also visit the Cambridge ESOL website (see earlier in this section), which lists centres offering TEFL courses in over 40 different countries.

JOBS

Once qualified, the next step is finding a job, something that's no longer quite as easy as it once was. Just how easy or difficult depends on how flexible you are. Being prepared to consider any place going, from Addis Ababa (Ethiopia) to Zaporizhzhya (it's in Eastern Ukraine and, yes, it does have an English-language school), greatly improves your employment prospects. Conversely, a fixation on Rome, Florence or Barcelona will only make life difficult because everybody wants plum postings such as these. Timing plays a role too; the majority of recruitment takes place between May and August for academic years starting in September.

Schools typically offer contracts for one full year and usually cover the cost of a return flight and help out with finding accommodation. They don't usually cover your rent – that's down to you – but levels of pay for qualified TEFL teachers are usually fairly good, and most teachers live a very comfortable life style. Teachers who break their contract before the year's up will normally forfeit their return flight and may have to pay back the cost of the outward journey too. Many schools also offer summer contracts lasting three months. Hiring for these goes on around January/February. In all cases you are unlikely to be able to pick up a job where you can just pack your bags and head off immediately; that does sometimes happen but more realistically you need to allow a lead time of perhaps around three months from the time you apply.

Note that taking a TEFL course abroad gives a head start in looking for a job; schools often offer teaching positions to one or two of those who have just successfully completed their CELTA/TESOL in-house.

Two of the biggest employers of TEFL teachers overseas are the British Council and International House (IH). The Council is the cultural wing of the Foreign & Commonwealth Office and is devoted to spreading the good word about the UK across the globe. Part of that includes teaching the locals our language and almost every major city worldwide has a British Council with a teaching centre. All appointments are dealt with by the main office at Spring Gardens in London and vacancies are posted on the website (W www.britishcouncil.org). The British Council is fussy about who it employs and it typically requests a first degree, a TEFL certificate and one or (more often) two years of teaching experience. However, we have known of fresh-off-the-cert-course teachers to be offered jobs so it's always worth checking.

IH (see Contacts) is a network of over 110 schools (at last count) based in over 30 countries around the world, from Azerbaijan to Vietnam. Their central recruitment office is in London and deals with about 500 placements a year. You can download a 'Recruitment Programme' booklet from their website. Minimum requirements are CELTA, TESOL or equivalent and, unlike the British Council, IH encourages newly qualified teachers to apply.

The advent of the internet has made finding out just what's available so much easier – gone are the days when the surest method was to make weekly visits in person to scour the notice board at IH on London's Piccadilly. Aside from the British Council and IH websites, both of which have job sections, try some of the following:

AAA EFL
W www.aaaefl.co.uk

A directory resource for teachers of EFL. Hit the 'Employment' link for lists of jobs broken down by region and then country. Very much oriented towards Asia.

Dave's ESL Cafe
W www.eslcafe.com

Dave Sperling's informal online 'meeting place' for students and teachers of English. It's a great place for the newly qualified to hang out and has good links to job-vacancy sites. Especially good if you fancy China, Japan or the Middle East. Read the 'Job Information Journal' postings before you go.

EduFind ELT Job Centre
W www.jobs.edunet.com

Also known as the 'TEFL job centre'. Search for jobs by country or subscribe to the 'Job Emailing List'.

EL Gazette
W www.elgazette.com

A well-established online journal (previously the EFL Gazette). Click on 'prospects' for job vacancies.

EFL WEB
W www.eflweb.com

A website for teachers and students of English and a great resource for people who are just starting or who want to start a career in EFL; just follow the 'Current Vacancies' link.

ELT News
W www.eltnews.com/eltnews.shtml

A website for English teachers in Japan, with a daily-updated jobs page (vacancies in Japan only).

Europa Pages
W www.europa-pages.com/www_write/eltoffers.html

An international ELT job board with vacancies of all kinds, some requiring highly qualified professionals, others accepting of motivated enthusiasts; requests are from schools, businesses and private individuals. Ads list salaries and give direct contacts.

Guardian TEFL
W www.educationunlimited.co.uk/tefl

A part of the Guardian Unlimited website that is devoted to ELT. It carries every job posted in the paper along with those from the *Observer*, plus online-only job ads.

The *Times Educational Supplement* occasionally has jobs but these are usually for experienced practitioners, possibly with MAs in the field. You could also try contacting schools directly, particularly if you are set on a particular destination. For addresses consult the *EL Gazette Guide to English Language Teaching around the World* (Short Books, £13.95), the 11th edition of which was published in 2002, or Susan Griffith's superbly comprehensive *Teaching English Abroad* (Vacation Work, £12.95).

Graduates

Beyond the standard TEFL route there are several other options available to graduates. VSO (Voluntary Service Overseas; see Volunteering, Conservation & Expeditions chapter earlier for further details) offers English-teaching positions to graduates with a BA and a TEFL qualification, although there is a scheme whereby suitable graduate applicants who can't afford TEFL can apply for course sponsorship with the VSO. Other kinds of overseas teaching posts are also available to graduates, for which no teaching qualification is required. At the time of writing the VSO website was offering opportunities for graduates of science (especially chemistry and physics), as well as accountants, engineers and computing specialists (two years' experience required in all cases). Although it now offers all kinds of gap-year placements, from animal care to journalism, Teaching & Projects Abroad began life providing opportunities for university students to go and teach English in Moldova. It continues to offer postings for gappers and postgrads to work as TEFL teachers in primary, secondary and special schools, and in universities and adult education centres. Besides English language, there are opportunities for teachers of French, German and Spanish, and of drama, music and sports. According to the Teaching & Projects Abroad website, students with qualifications in geography, history, chemistry, physics, biology, economics, zoology and geology can also be fixed up with worthwhile placements. However, unlike most gap work where you can expect to earn a salary, you have to pay Teaching & Projects Abroad for your placement; see Contacts.

Similarly, the Centre for British Teachers (CfBT) is an organisation that supplies British teachers to schools overseas, although these positions come with a salary.

JET stands for Japan Exchange and Teaching, and it's a government programme that invites university graduates from overseas to go to teach in Mexico. Just joking. Japan. Most participants go over as Assistant Language Teachers (ALTs) and are placed in cities, towns and villages throughout the country, where they work in a state junior or senior school assisting the Japanese class teacher in teaching English. You work a normal 35-hour Monday to Friday week and draw an annual salary, out of which you cover your own rent and expenses (a round-trip flight is provided). In addition to academic qualifications (see Contacts) applicants must have some sort of an interest in Japan, exhibited presumably during an interview. A TEFL qualification is not required.

In addition to ALT positions, there are also a few vacancies for Sports Exchange Advisors – basically sports coaches. To qualify you have to be recommended by an official body and have a

---

On the Spot

It's risky to hope that you can just roll up in some foreign place and land a job. Which is not to say it never happens. Debbie Smith was holidaying in Cairo when she was approached on the streets by a tout and introduced to the manager of a makeshift English-language school desperate for native-speaking staff. Eager to extend her stay in the city she accepted. Voilà! A job. But the school would do nothing to secure a legitimate work permit, overcrowding led to classes frequently being taught in kitchens and hallways, and finally the meagre wages stopped being paid altogether. This story is unfortunately all too common when dealing with cowboy schools. Reputable places tend to do their recruiting from the UK. Your hope lies in the rare smaller, private schools that, while decently run, don't have any UK representation and are not part of the great ELT network (see Pamela Smith's story in the earlier Pros & Cons section). To improve your chances, when looking for work dress smartly and go armed with a typed CV and proof (copies) of any qualifications such as GCSEs, A levels or your degree. Destination also plays its part. Schools in developing countries tend to be less picky and opportunities are greater. Also, places where demand for English is high often reap easier rewards, eg, in Japan or South Korea employment seems relatively easy to come by.

recognised and 'prestigious' (their wording, so a note from the Wallasey Snooker Club presumably won't do it) coaching certification, or three years' experience of coaching in your specialised field.

Other Teaching

It is possible to get other tutoring work abroad aside from teaching English but it's not easy and language remains a key issue. We have met native English speakers teaching accounting in Moscow, leading aerobics sessions in Bangkok and giving instruction in elocution in Hong Kong but all these jobs have come as a result of living in the cities in question and spotting an opportunity. This sort of thing cannot be planned for. You could try lugging around your acoustic guitar in the hope that the youth of India is just dying to learn – and willing to pay for – the chord sequence to *Wonderwall* but don't count on it.

One solution is to look for work in a school abroad where English is the main language of instruction. In regions such as Africa, large parts of Asia, and the Middle East, where educational standards are deemed deficient, independent 'American' and 'British' schools often exist to provide education for the children of expats, diplomats and wealthy aspirational locals. These schools typically cater for children from five years old through to mid-teens (ie, infants, juniors and seniors) and typically follow curriculums set by American or British examination bodies (including GCSEs). There's no central body for these schools and each will have its own application procedures and qualification requirements – and these will vary depending on how desperate the staffing situation is at any given time. Recognised teaching qualifications such as a PGCE (Postgraduate Certificate in Education) will always be desirable but a place on a teacher-training course at home or even relevant A-level results may be enough, sometimes more than enough. Stuart Kinloch had been teaching English at a language school in Karachi (Pakistan) when he applied for a job at a school affiliated to a major embassy:

The ad said 'English teachers required' so I went for an interview taking along my CV and my TEFL certificate. It turned out they didn't want people to teach English but teachers who were English and could teach other subjects. It was a misunderstanding, so I was about to leave when the director who was interviewing me said, 'But you have an O level in mathematics and we're looking for a mathematics teacher.' And so for an academic year I taught maths to a bunch of 14- and 15-year-olds, preparing them for an exam that I'd only just scraped a D pass in. Some of the kids knew more than I did.

Finding addresses of such schools is a chore as there's no published directory; the best bets are to consult *Teaching English Abroad* (Vacation Work, £12.95), check out the fortnightly newspaper *Overseas Jobs Express* or, if you know which cities you're interested in, contact the relevant US or UK embassy or consulate for a schools list.

In addition to employing qualified TEFL tutors the British Council also operates an English Language Assistant (ELA) scheme where a TEFL teaching qualification is not required. ELAs work in schools or colleges abroad helping local class teachers with the teaching of English. The assistants' role varies but they're a kind of teachers' resource on legs, typically required to provide conversation practice with the students and to talk on aspects of the UK and its culture. To qualify as an ELA you must have native level fluency in English and have completed your secondary education and at least two years of higher education. You also need an A level, Higher Grade or equivalent in the language of the country to which you're to be posted (unless it's China, where there's no foreign-language requirement). For more details visit the British Council website (**W** www.britcoun.org/education/assistants/index.htm).

For teaching placements organised by gap-year companies see Gap-Year Organisations in the Volunteering, Conservation & Expeditions chapter earlier.

Contacts

The following list includes some of the major international ELT organisations with multiple schools and teaching centres abroad.

Bell

Hillscross, Red Cross Lane, Cambridge CB2 2QX
☎ 01223-212333
fax 01223-410282
e info@bell-centres.com
W www.bell-schools.ac.uk

Bell has four language-learning centres in the UK (Cambridge, Norwich, London and Saffron Walden). It runs full-time CELTA courses at its Cambridge and Norwich centres. It's also possible to do the course in either Geneva or Poland.

TEFL Training Offered? CELTA.
Qualifications Required for Work: To work at a Bell centre the minimum requirements are usually a university degree, DELTA (Diploma in English Language Teaching to Adults) and at least one year's teaching experience.
Destinations: Bell operates language centres in Prague, Geneva & Malta, and has associated schools in Bulgaria, Italy, Latvia, Malta, Poland, Romania, Spain & Thailand.

Berlitz UK

Lincoln House, 296–302 High Holborn, London WC1V 7JH
☎ 020-7915 0909
fax 020-7915 0222
e teaching@berlitz.co.uk
W www.berlitz.com

Berlitz is one of the largest ELT employers in the world and has more than 400 locations worldwide.

TEFL Training Offered? No. However, successful applicants will be enrolled on a Berlitz training course.
Qualifications Required for Work: Applicants must be aged at least 21 and have a degree. Teaching experience is not essential.

Timing & Length of Work: Placements are available year round. Contracts are indefinite.
Destinations: There are over 400 centres in 40 countries.

British Council

10 Spring Gardens, London SW1A 2BN
☎ 020-7930 8466
fax 020-7839 6347
e general.enquiries@britishcouncil.org
W www.britcoun.org

The British Council is the largest ELT employer in the world. It recruits around 300 English-language teachers each year but standards are high and inexperienced teachers are rarely hired. For a complete list of overseas offices and for vacancy postings check the website or contact 'Educational Enterprises' at the above address.

TEFL Training Offered? No.
Qualifications Required for Work: CELTA/TESOL and a degree, plus a preferable two years' teaching experience.
Timing & Length of Work: Placements are available year round. Contracts are usually for two years and renewable.
Destinations: There are teaching centres in over 70 countries, from Argentina to Yemen.

English First (EF)

Teacher Recruitment Centre, 36–38 St Aubyns, Hove, E Sussex BN3 2TD
☎ 01273-201431
fax 01273-746742
e recruitment.uk@englishfirst.com
W www.englishfirst.com

Headquartered in Shanghai, EF has two bases in the UK (Hove and Manchester), both offering teacher training and recruitment. Candidates who successfully complete TEFL courses are typically offered contracts in China and Indonesia.

TEFL Training Offered? EF does its own non-accredited TEFL course (monthly), which is equivalent in content to CELTA and TESOL. From summer 2003 it will also offer accredited TESOL courses in Manchester.

Qualifications Required for Work: CELTA/TESOL.

Timing & Length of Work: Year-round placements with one-year minimum contracts are on offer, as well as two-month summer teaching contracts in China.

Destinations: Franchise schools are mainly in China & Indonesia, plus Russia & Eastern Europe & a foothold in Thailand.

Inlingua

Rodney Lodge, Rodney Rd, Cheltenham, Glos GL50 1HX
☎ 01242-253171
fax 01242-253181
e recruitment@inlingua-cheltenham.co.uk
w www.inlingua-cheltenham.co.uk

Five-week-long TEFL courses are run continuously back-to-back and successful candidates are helped to find a teaching position overseas. Qualified teachers can also use the website for job searching – links put job-hunters directly in touch with the schools without going through any kind of Inlingua induction or screening.

TEFL Training Offered? CELTA.

Qualifications Required for Work: CELTA/TESOL, although teachers with specialist experience (eg, working with children) can sometimes find work without having the cert.

Timing & Length of Work: Entirely dependent on the country and institution. European contracts tend to be nine months to a year, while in somewhere like South America you shouldn't expect to have any kind of contract at all.

Destinations: There are over 300 affiliated schools worldwide in approximately 22 countries.

International House (IH)

106 Piccadilly, London W1J 7NL
☎ 020-7518 6970
fax 020-7518 6971

e hr@ihlondon.co.uk
w www.ihlondon.com

Established in 1953, IH is the mother of all language institutes, with over 120 carefully monitored affiliates in more than 30 countries. There's a fantastic transfer system whereby teachers can move from country to country within the network. Follow the recruitment link on the website for teaching vacancies.

TEFL Training Offered? CELTA at the London central office and at numerous affiliate schools overseas.

Qualifications Required for Work: CELTA/TESOL.

Timing & Length of Work: Placements are available year round. Contracts are usually for one year and renewable. Three-month summer contracts are also offered.

Destinations: Everywhere – see the website for a full list.

Language Link

21 Harrington Rd, London SW7 3EU
☎ 020-7225 1065
fax 020-7584 3518
e languagelink@compuserve.com
w www.languagelink.co.uk

Language Link has a network of more than 50 schools where its students can teach after successfully completing one of its courses. It can also provide contact details of other international schools.

TEFL Training Offered? CELTA.

Qualifications Required for Work: CELTA, TESOL, PGCE or prior teaching experience.

Timing & Length of Work: Placements are available year round. Contracts are usually from 36 weeks to two years.

Destinations: China, the Czech Republic, Russia, Slovakia & Vietnam.

Linguarama

Oceanic House, 89 High St, Alton, Hants GU34 1LG
☎ 01420-80899

fax 01420-80856
e personnel@linguarama.com
w www.linguarama.com
Linguarama finds placements for around 80 to 100 teachers annually in its language schools abroad. Applicants must be graduates.
TEFL Training Offered? No. However, successful applicants will be enrolled on a Linguarama induction course.
Qualifications Required for Work: CELTA/TESOL or equivalent and a degree.
Timing & Length of Work: One academic year (nine months) minimum but a two-year commitment is preferred.
Destinations: Schools in more than 20 European cities in France, Germany, Italy & Spain.

Saxoncourt
124 New Bond St, London W1S 1DX
☎ 020-7491 1911
fax 020-7493 3657
e recruit@saxoncourt.com
w www.saxoncourt.com
Saxoncourt is one of the largest UK recruiters of ELT teachers, filling around 400 teaching vacancies a year.
TEFL Training Offered? Monthly courses are held at teacher-training centres in central London and Bromley.
Qualifications Required for Work: CELTA/TESOL, although this can be waived for jobs in hard-to-recruit-for China, Japan and Taiwan if the applicant has the right aptitude (lived abroad before, worked with kids etc). Note that a degree is required to secure the necessary work permit.
Timing & Length of Work: Contracts are for an academic year (nine months) in Western Europe; one full year elsewhere.
Destinations: Most recruiting is done for Saxoncourt's affiliated schools in the Far East but there are also jobs in Western and Eastern Europe and South America.

Centre for British Teachers (CfBT)
60 Queens Rd, Reading, Berks RG1 4BS
☎ 0118-902 1000

fax 0118-902 1434
e enquiries@cfbt.com
w www.cfbt.com
CfBT is a non-profit-making registered charity placing British teachers (EFL, primary and secondary) in posts abroad.
TEFL Training Offered? No.
Qualifications Required for Work: CELTA/TESOL plus two years' experience for Malaysia; PGCE and three years' experience for Brunei.
Timing & Length of Work: Contracts are for a minimum of two years.
Destinations: The main ongoing teaching programmes are in Malaysia & Brunei, although posts in Afghanistan & the Xian province of China were being offered on its website when we last checked.

JET Programme
JET Desk, Embassy of Japan, 101–104 Piccadilly, London W1J 7JT
☎ 020-7465 6668
fax 020-7491 9347
e jet@embjapan.org.uk
w www.jetprogramme.co.uk
JET places graduates in teaching positions in Japan. In 2002, 631 British graduates took part. No teaching qualifications or Japanese-language skills are necessary.
TEFL Training Offered? No.
Qualifications Required for Work: A Bachelor's degree in any subject by July of the year of departure.
Timing & Length of Work: Contracts are for one year (July to July), renewable for two years.
Destination: Japan.

Teaching & Projects Abroad
Gerrard House, Rustington, W Sussex BN16 1AW
☎ 01903-859911
fax 01903-785779
e info@teaching-abroad.co.uk
w www.teaching-abroad.co.uk
Teaching & Projects Abroad is the leading organised volunteer placement company in the UK. There are opportunities for TEFL

overseas, and also drama, science and many other subjects. Prices start at around £1000, which covers three months' food and accommodation with a local host family, plus insurance and the back up of the local Overseas Director who can be contacted 24 hours a day.

TEFL Training Offered? No.

Qualifications Required for Work: Varies depending on placement.

Timing & Length of Work: Placements are for a few weeks to several months.

Destinations: The line up currently includes Bolivia, Chile, China, Ghana, Mexico, Peru, Romania, Thailand, Togo & Ukraine.

Casual/Seasonal Work

If you want to make a bit of money in your gap year without signing up for a proper job, then casual work is the way to go. Working on a casual basis has lots of advantages. You can start and leave whenever you want. You can do any job that takes your fancy. And on top of this, you'll walk away with money in your pocket.

Lots of people take on casual jobs to earn a bit of cash before embarking on a gap-year project overseas but there are loads of exciting ways to travel and do casual work at the same time. The only real obstacle is getting a visa that will allow you to work where you want to work.

Luckily for gappers, Britain has special immigration agreements with various countries that allow young Brits to travel and work in casual jobs for a summer or even a whole year. We'll cover these up front, as you can do any job you like once you have the appropriate paperwork.

With a work permit, a whole world of casual work opens up. You could do bar work in Amsterdam or New York. Or maybe spend a winter ski-instructing in the Rocky Mountains. Or how about picking bananas on the tropical coast of Australia? Whatever you feel like doing, this chapter should give you some pointers.

Work Permits for Casual Work

British citizens can work wherever they want within Europe (see Red Tape in the Proper Jobs chapter for more information). However, working in America or Australia is another matter and under normal circumstances you have to go through all sorts of rigmarole to get a work permit. Fortunately young people are eligible for special treatment.

The UK has special arrangements with a number of countries that allow people of a certain age to visit each other's countries to work. Currently gappers from the UK can use these schemes to visit the USA, Canada, Australia, New Zealand, South Africa and Japan.

To do casual work in the USA you have to get sponsorship from an educational exchange organisation such as the British Universities North America Club (BUNAC), who will sort out all the paperwork you need to get a J-1 visa. This lets you work for up to four months over the summer and travel for up to a month after you finish work. You need a confirmed job offer before you start but you can change jobs once you reach America.

To be eligible you must be at least 18 and a student on a degree course (or equivalent) or a gap-year student with a confirmed offer of a university place. Some of the bigger sponsorship schemes are covered under Working-Holiday Organisations under Contacts at the end of this chapter. Similar schemes in Canada and South Africa are valid for up to a year.

Another way to work in the US is on an H-2B visa. The company that wants to hire you must arrange this and you have to work in the same job for your entire stay. The most common companies sponsoring gappers are ski resorts (see later in this chapter for more information). You need to have an interview at the American embassy in London or Belfast to get any US visa.

Working in Australia, New Zealand or Japan is more relaxed. You can apply for a yearlong working-holiday visa yourself at the appropriate embassy and then do whatever job you like when you arrive.

The working-holiday scheme in Australia and New Zealand is open to those aged 18 to 30 but you can only participate in the scheme once for each country. The Australian visa restricts you to a limit of three months' work for any particular employer but you can work for as many people as you want to during the year.

The visa fee is £65 for Australia and £30 for New Zealand. You must show evidence of a return plane ticket (or the money to pay for one) and savings of around £2000. More information can be found on the websites **W** www.immigration.govt.nz (for New Zealand) and **W** www.immi.gov.au (for Australia). Many of the organisations listed under Working-Holiday Organisations (see Contacts) can also arrange working-holiday visas for a fee.

Japan issues about 400 yearlong working-holiday visas a year to Brits aged between 18 and 25. You must have a return plane ticket (or money to pay for one) and £1500 in savings. See the website **W** www.embjapan.org.uk for more information. Most of the work available in Japan is TEFL teaching but Japanese speakers can also find hospitality and office jobs.

We generally don't recommend working without a work permit or visa. If you work illegally and get caught you'll probably be deported at your own expense and you may never be able to visit that country again.

RESOURCES FOR JOBSEEKERS

Once you've got your work permit or visa, the next step is to find a job. The best starting place is the web. There are hundreds of job-search and recruitment websites that specialise in seasonal jobs and, with a bit of luck, you can arrange a job almost anywhere in the world from the comfort of your own PC. Some of the better websites include:

- **W** **www.aboutjobs.com** Umbrella site for several American job sites, including summer jobs.com, overseasjobs.com and resortjobs.com.
- **W** **www.abroadnaway.com** Useful for people wanting to work in the USA, this site has listings of seasonal jobs, internships etc.
- **W** **www.anyworkanywhere.com** Another good work-abroad site with worldwide job listings and an email job bulletin.
- **W** **www.alseasonsagency.com** Hospitality recruitment agency in Australia that provides work for working-holidaymakers at certain times of year.
- **W** **www.backdoorjobs.com** Excellent US site with listings of outdoor, artistic and adventure jobs.
- **W** **www.berkeley-scott.co.uk** UK recruitment agency for temporary hospitality, leisure and office jobs worldwide.
- **W** **www.caterer.com** A huge catering website with a worldwide job search for chefs, waiters, kitchen and bar staff.
- **W** **www.coolworks.com** Excellent US site dedicated to outdoor and adventure jobs.
- **W** **www.hospitalityadventures.com** Large US hospitality recruitment site.
- **W** **www.jobmonkey.com** US site with excellent listings of outdoor jobs, ski work and other casual jobs.
- **W** **www.jobpilot.co.uk** Europe-wide job-search site.
- **W** **www.jobsabroad.com** A decent American job-listings site.
- **W** **www.jobs-in-europe.net** Listings of jobs across Europe, broken down by country.
- **W** **www.leisureopportunities.co.uk** Good for leisure jobs in the UK and Europe.
- **W** **www.netrecruituk.com** Has links to specialist recruitment websites for all sorts of seasonal and adventure jobs.
- **W** **www.nzjobs.go.to** Specialises in jobs for working-holidaymakers in New Zealand.

W www.overseasjobsexpress.com Fortnightly print and online newspaper for seasonal and full-time job listings worldwide.

W www.payaway.co.uk An excellent website with jobs and info for gappers – you can sign up for a regular email jobs bulletin.

W www.thehospitalitysite.com.au Has a job search for hospitality jobs across Australia.

W www.voovs.com Has sites devoted to ski and snowboard jobs, hospitality jobs and leisure jobs worldwide.

Employment agencies are also useful weapons in your job-search arsenal. Many covered in the Proper Jobs chapter also provide seasonal jobs. If you look in the phonebook wherever you are, you should be able to find an agency close to you. Another option is temping, which falls somewhere between proper jobs and casual work.

In Australia several backpacker organisations run job searches specifically for people on working-holiday visas. Worldwide Workers (**W** www.worldwideworkers.com) runs internet cafés and recruitment centres in Sydney, Melbourne and Cairns, and provides work for around 10,000 travellers a year in bars, restaurants, hotels, shops and offices and on farms.

Hospitality

Your bags are packed and you're ready to go. Now you need to decide what kind of job you want to do. Many people turn to the hospitality industry. Hotels, restaurants and bars are huge employers worldwide and there is usually loads of work to do over the summer and winter holiday seasons. The best time to apply is around a month before the start of the season, though there are always new openings once the season starts as people drop out. Keep an eye out for any new restaurants that look like they might be opening soon.

Tourists always need places to stay and eat, so holiday resorts are great places to pick up hospitality jobs. These are generally unskilled and you can learn on the job, so you don't necessarily need any previous experience. Places to think about include: the Greek Islands and Cyprus; Ibiza; the Spanish Costa Brava; the French Alps; the east coast of Australia; New Zealand (both North and South islands); the Rocky Mountains (both Canada and the USA); and the east coast of America.

You can often pick up hospitality work by responding to signs in restaurant windows or local ads. Your best chance of finding a job is just walking in and asking if they have any work. Working-holiday companies such as BUNAC (see Contacts) can often fix you up with a hospitality job in the USA or Canada. Tour operators also take on loads of hospitality staff every season – this is covered later in this chapter. There are also numerous specialist recruitment agencies for hospitality jobs. See Resources for Jobseekers earlier in this chapter for places to start searching for a hospitality job on the net.

The local minimum-wage laws usually cover hospitality jobs. In the UK, for example, those aged 18 to 21 must be paid at least £3.80 an hour. Note that European companies usually prefer you to speak the local language.

HOTELS & RESTAURANTS

Hotel and restaurant jobs are normally easy to find in seaside resorts, tourist towns and big cities. However, competition for jobs is often fierce so you may have better luck in a quiet, out-of-the-way place. If you don't already have experience, you may get stuck doing jobs such as dish-washing, cleaning or working in the kitchen.

Hotel work typically involves working in reception or cleaning rooms and making beds. Some more upmarket hotels also have jobs for lift operators and old-fashioned bellboys. You generally need admin skills to work on reception but anyone can be a maid, and that includes you guys out there. Wages reflect the unskilled nature of the work – you can earn around £3.50 to £5 per hour in the UK, £3 to £4.50 in the USA and £3.50 to £4.50 in Australia.

A good fun – though less well-paid – option is to work in a backpacker hostel. Accommodation is usually thrown in and there's often a chance to lead tours or pub crawls in the local area. Backpacker hostels can be found all over Europe, Australia, New Zealand, Canada and the USA. In Britain try approaching the YHA (**W** www.yha.org.uk) – it takes on around 400 staff every year for its hostels around the UK.

Restaurants may be looking for waiters and waitresses, kitchen assistants, chefs (if you have catering qualifications), short-order cooks (if you don't), plus door staff to find people tables and busboys to clear tables at the end of meals. Typical hourly wages are £3.50 to £5 in the UK and £3 to £4.50 in Australia, plus tips. US wages are usually lower – typically £2 to £3 an hour – but you earn loads of tips on top of this. Megan Dorcas had this to say about her experience of working as a waitress in the French part of Switzerland:

The resort where I worked was really small and beautiful – it was just like living on the front of a chocolate box. It was packed with people like me – there to work a season – and we all made friends really easily. I learned how to serve Raclette *(huge melting Swiss cheeses scraped onto potatoes and gherkin); how to carry* Fondue Chinoise *without spilling boiling oil over myself or the customers, plus I helped organise the carnival in the village. At the end of my stint I also ended up with quite a bit of saved money because the tips were really good and this pretty much financed the rest of my gap year.*

The 'Gap Packs' published by **W** www.gapwork.com have useful listings of hotels and restaurants that employ backpackers around the world. If you aren't fussy, fast-food outlets are invariably on the lookout for staff.

BARS & CLUBS

Bar work is a great way to earn money while you travel. There are all kinds of bar jobs, from pulling pints in a village pub to mixing cocktails, Tom Cruise style, in a trendy bar downtown. The work is easy and very sociable but the pay isn't great and the hours don't suit everyone (though late risers will feel right at home).

These days many places expect you to have some experience behind the bar (this is where that Saturday job at the Crown & Anchor comes into its own). As well as serving drinks you'll have to change barrels of beer, clean up spilt drinks and persuade people to go home at the end of the night. Many people tell a few white lies to get their first bar job and, if you pick things up fast, you can often get away with it. Alternatively Shaker UK (**W** www .shakerbartending.co.uk) offers a course in *mixology* (bar-tending and cocktail-making), which will give you some extra clout when looking for a bar job – see the Courses chapter for details.

The kind of bar work you do will partly depend on where you are. Rural pubs can be pleasantly chilled-out but time can crawl by. At the other end of the scale, nightclubs and bars often have a great vibe but the pace is fast and furious and you can end up knackered at the end of the night. There are some daytime bar jobs but most places will ask you to work at least a few nights. There is always more competition for jobs at trendy nightspots so it's often easier to find work in a local drinking hole in the suburbs.

As far as wages go you can earn £4 to £7 an hour in the UK and Europe and £3 to £6 in Australia. American bar wages are quite low – typically £2 to £4.50 – but most people tip at least a dollar every time they buy a round so the tips can really add up. It's often easier to find a job on the door or as a glass clearer.

The easiest places to find bar work are big cities and coastal resorts. Pubs often put signs up in the windows or on backpacker hostels' notice boards. By far the best way to get a bar job is to walk in and ask if they are hiring but there are also specialist recruitment agencies for hospitality and bar jobs – see Resources for Jobseekers earlier. Women can also find work in promotional sampling, which involves roaming bars handing out complimentary drinks or other freebies. The male equivalent – handing out fliers for clubs and bars – is also popular.

To serve alcohol you have to be over the legal drinking age. In the UK, Australia, New Zealand, Canada and parts of Europe this is 18. In America it's 21. If you want to do bar work in the Australian states of Victoria and New South Wales you'll need a Responsible Service of Alcohol (RSA) certificate. You can get this at the end of a one-day course for around £35 – contact the Restaurant & Catering Association offices (**W** www.restaurant cater.asn.au) in Victoria and New South Wales for details.

SPECIAL EVENTS

Conferences, exhibitions, sporting events and festivals are all great sources of temporary work. Staff at special events are usually supplied by specialist recruitment agencies – see Special Events under Contacts later for some suggestions – but you can often get a job by approaching the organisers directly. Many businesses that have nothing to do with the event itself also need extra staff to deal with all the extra people in town.

Sporting events provide some great opportunities. You might want to consider the Melbourne Grand Prix, the Australian Indy Car World Series, the Wimbledon tennis championships in London and the Superbowl in America. The Olympics is set to take place in Athens in 2004 and is still recruiting staff, though Greek-speakers are preferred – see the website **W** www.athens2004.com.

Kelsall McEwen of Pierowall, Orkney, went to Canada with BUNAC and landed a job at the Calgary Stampede:

I went out to Canada with a pre-arranged job as a painter in Vancouver but when I arrived the job fell through so I started working as a chambermaid (not very dignified!). Then I heard from someone at the youth hostel where I was staying that there were jobs going at the Calgary Stampede, the biggest wild-west show in the world. I ended up sweeping sand off a walkway on an artificial beach at a themed bar. The wages were pretty low but the work was easy and we had loads of time off to go and see the shows at the Stampede, which were fantastic – loads of people in denim cowboy outfits riding real bucking broncos and lassoing horses! I made loads of friends and earned enough money in the three months I was working to buy an old car and tour around the rest of Canada.

Exhibitions and conferences also employ huge numbers of people. Try contacting art galleries and museums directly to see if they have any openings. There are also specialist recruitment agencies for exhibitions but you'll have to find a local agency wherever you are, as few companies supply staff for overseas events. If you search on the internet for 'event staff' or 'promotional personnel' in the country you want to work in, you should be able to find a handful of agencies to call.

Big music events such as the Glastonbury Festival (**W** www.glastonburyfestivals.co.uk) in the UK take on staff every year to clean up the site in exchange for free tickets but most paid staff are supplied by agencies. Cultural festivals are often a better bet. The Edinburgh International Festival (**W** www.eif.co.uk) takes on lots of temporary staff every August. Listings of major festivals around the world can be found on the website **W** www.festivals .com.

Tour Operators

The holiday trade is the most seasonal business of all. Almost all tour operators take on some extra staff during the holiday season and gappers make up a sizable proportion of the intake. Holiday companies usually specialise in either summer sun or winter snow but quite a few cover both seasons and have jobs year round.

The most common job openings at holiday companies are for reps and couriers. Basically, reps are the people who greet holidaymakers at the airport and rush around organising activities, while couriers work on the resort taking care of people's day-to-day needs. This often involves taking care of children while the adults are off having fun. The minimum age for couriers is usually 19 but you usually need to be over 21 to be a rep. If you work for a camping holiday company you'll also have to help with *montage* and *démontage* – putting up and taking down tents.

Tim Saunders from London rated his experience as a camp courier very highly:

I went with Keycamp to Camping Castell Montgri in northern Spain, which has to be one of the finest campsites in the world. There was a cinema, several bars and restaurants and one of the largest pools on the Costa Brava. Before the customers arrived we had to clean the mobile homes and put up all the tents. Then the campsite exploded into a ferocious melee of holiday-makers. Life as a courier was very busy and when I was on site I was never really off duty. The pay wasn't great – around £80 per week – but accommodation and cheap food were provided and we had free run of the facilities. On our time off we went into the nearby town where there were special bars just for couriers. The drinks were cheap and dancing on tables was positively encouraged! Overall I had a fantastic time; it was a summer that will live in my memory forever.

Other possible jobs include adventure-activity instructors (watersports and skiing instructors are most in demand), entertainers, bar and restaurant staff and domestic staff and cleaners for hotels and ski chalets. Various types of holiday company work are covered in this section.

The easiest way to get work is to apply directly to holiday companies – see the listings for PGL, Holidaybreak, Club Med and others under Contacts. Wages are fairly low – typically £50 to £150 per week – but accommodation is always included and most companies offer free or cheap meals and free transport to and from the resort.

SKI RESORTS

If skiing every day and partying every night sounds like your cup of tea, there are loads of opportunities for work at ski resorts around the world. For most jobs you work one shift in the morning and another in the early evening, so you can usually get a few hours on the slopes every afternoon. Winter work is usually available from November to April. In the summer many ski resorts reinvent themselves as 'Mountain and Lake' resorts, so there may be summer vacancies as well.

France is the most popular destination for British skiers, followed by Austria, Switzerland and Italy. Skiing in the USA and Canada is concentrated in the Rocky Mountains. More unusual places to ski include the Czech Republic, Australia, New Zealand and Japan. A useful source of ski information is the Ski Club of Great Britain (☎ 0845 458 0780; W www.skiclub.co.uk). It costs £15 a year to join if you are under 24, and membership entitles you to all sorts of perks.

Working on the Slopes
Ski resorts offer plenty of work for experienced skiers and snowboarders. If you have the right qualifications, working as a ski instructor or ski guide will maximise your time on the slopes. There are also plenty of openings for ski couriers – basically babysitters on skis – and staff at ski shops.

Although these jobs are undeniably cool, the wages are not as high as you might expect. Instructors in Europe tend to earn £60 to £100 per week, including all meals, accommodation, ski gear and ski pass. In the USA you can earn £5 to £6.50 per hour but accommodation is extra. You may be able to make extra cash offering private lessons in your time off. Ski staff usually stay with other workers in resort chalets. Of course being an instructor does have its perks, as Jeanine Stanier from Hull found out when she worked as a ski instructor at Meribel in France:

I've been skiing since I was little and I found an instructor job at Meribel on the internet. It was probably the most fun I've ever had, though it was frustrating at times. There were some students who couldn't put on their skis or had no sense of balance. One day a blizzard came in and one of the students lost his hat so I had to give him mine and I froze all the way down the mountain. The best bit was having time to ski off-piste when I wasn't teaching. And the après-ski was fantastic. I don't know if it was anything to do with the job but I was certainly in demand!

To work as a ski or snowboard instructor or guide you usually need international qualifications. In Britain these are awarded by the British Association of Snowsport Instructors (BASI; W www.basi.org.uk). There are three grades of qualification but you usually only need the lowest grade (Grade III) for seasonal instructing or guiding jobs. Some schools offering ski instructor courses are covered in the Courses chapter.

Other jobs you might end up doing out on the slopes include working on a snow-making machine, operating ski lifts or working in a ski-repair clinic.

Chalet Staff
Obviously, given the choice, you'd be a ski instructor. But if your skiing skills aren't quite there yet, there are plenty of other jobs you can do at ski resorts. Probably the easiest work to find is behind the scenes in a ski chalet. Chalets work like mini hotels and the same kinds of jobs need to be done every day – ie, changing the sheets, cleaning, cooking meals etc.

The majority of chalets rely on 'chalet boys' and 'chalet girls' to do the cooking and cleaning. If there is any cooking involved the company will test your skills before signing you up. The Murray School of Cookery (see Contacts in the Courses chapter) in Farnham offers a specialist course just for chalet chefs. Lots of people prefer to stick to just cleaning; the pay is lower but so are the responsibilities!

Chalet staff work long hours and you usually have to share accommodation with other workers. On the other hand the sense of camaraderie can be great and you have loads of free time to ski. In most chalets, every night ends up being party night. Victoria Thwaites gave us the following appraisal of her time as a chalet cook in the Alps:

Chalet work is bloody hard! The cooking was the main part of the job and I was on my own in a tiny kitchen. It got easier once we got into the season as by then I was familiar with the dishes I was cooking and could relax a bit more. Cleaning was the worst part. I was usually so hungover that every morning when I cleaned the loo, all I wanted to do was be sick in it, and every time I made a bed I just wanted to get in and sleep in it. But then you finish your work, go outside, and all you want to do is go up the mountain!

The majority of chalet jobs are arranged through agencies or big holiday companies – see Contacts for details. Transport to the resort and accommodation and meals are usually free, plus ski and boot hire and a ski pass are often thrown in. Wages range from £60 to £165 per week.

Applying

Competition for jobs on the pistes can be fierce. If you're serious about ski or chalet work you should start your job hunt as early as possible. The big recruitment push usually begins in the summer but jobs also come up later in the year as people drop out for one reason or another. You might consider taking a ski-instructor course in the summer to improve your chances of finding work when the snow starts to fall. If you want to find a job at short notice you'll have a better chance at one of the more obscure resorts – in Romania or the Czech Republic for example.

To work at resorts in Europe, you usually just need to be an EU passport-holder. Working-holiday visas are fine for ski work in Australia and New Zealand. For the US and Canada you'll usually need to go through BUNAC or a similar company. Alternatively there are a few ski companies who will sponsor you on an H-2B visa directly – one reliable option is Aspen Snowmass (**W** www.aspensnowmass.com) in Colorado.

The best place to start your search for ski work is the web. The agency Ski Staff (see Contacts for details) recruits for over 100 companies in the Alps. There are hundreds of other great ski websites out there – try pointing your browser towards:

- **W** www.coolworks.com Has listings for ski-resort work worldwide.
- **W** www.freeradicals.co.uk Recruits for ski companies all over Europe and America.
- **W** www.natives.co.uk A fantastic online recruitment agency with listings of ski and resort work year round.
- **W** www.payaway.co.uk Has excellent listings for ski jobs.
- **W** www.skiconnection.co.uk Has a large database of ski jobs worldwide. There's a £9.99 registration fee.
- **W** www.voovs.com An excellent ski site with listings of current ski jobs around the world.

ACTIVITY HOLIDAYS

While some holidaymakers just want to relax, others are looking for a bit of a thrill. Companies such as Sunsail, Acorn Adventure and the Kingswood Group offer activity holidays around the world and almost all take on seasonal instructors for watersports and other adventure activities – see Contacts for their details. You usually have to be qualified to teach but some companies let you train as an instructor while you work. Instructor courses for watersports and other activities are covered in the Courses chapter.

Coastal resorts may have openings for windsurfing, sailing, water-skiing, jet-skiing, scuba diving or traditional surfing instructors. At holiday centres inland you might be able to teach canoeing and kayaking, rock climbing, bungee jumping, skydiving…the list goes on and on. If you have a favourite adrenaline sport, you can often train to be an instructor and then work all over the world.

The easiest way to get work is to apply directly to a tour operator – various companies that take on adventure activity staff are listed under Contacts. Some industries – scuba diving in particular – have a huge turnover of staff and you may be able to find work by just turning up and offering your services. Dive schools in Australia and Asia often provide free training to dive master or instructor level if you promise to work on their dive boats when you qualify.

Companies that train watersports instructors can often find work around the world for their graduates – talk to Flying Fish (**W** www.flyingfishonline.com), the United Kingdom Sailing Academy (**W** www.uksa.org) or the International Academy (**W** www.international-academy.com) – some of these courses are covered in the Courses chapter.

Theme parks and other big tourist attractions also take on thousands of staff every summer. Accommodation is usually provided and you can ride on as many roller-coasters as you want during your time off. Disneyland Resort Paris (see Contacts for information) is probably the most obvious choice in Europe. In the UK try Alton Towers in Staffordshire (**W** www.alton-towers.com) – they take on 1500 staff every year. Other good places to pick up theme-park work are America and the Gold Coast of Australia. Theme parks across the world are listed on the website **W** www.themepark city.com.

Down & Dirty

If you don't mind getting your hands dirty there are loads of jobs out there that let you work outdoors in the summer sun and improve your tan while you work. Some gappers earn money to go travelling by working on a fruit farm or building site in the UK. Others pack their bags and pick up farm work on the road – grape-picking in France is a legendary year-out activity.

You don't need any particular skills to do most casual building and farm jobs but you should be prepared to put in some hard physical work. Previous experience will always increase your chances of finding work in either field. You usually have to do some training before you can do potentially dangerous jobs such as operating heavy machinery or working with power tools.

Farm wages are generally low but food and accommodation is often thrown in and you'll have few opportunities to fritter away your earnings out in the sticks. In most places you should be able to earn at least £150 per week. Building sites often pay better, and jobs such as laying concrete floors can pay more than office work.

FRUIT-PICKING

As a casual job, fruit-picking has tons of advantages. You can work outside. You don't need any previous experience. Work is often cash in hand. You can wear whatever you want. However, it's quite hard work and you usually have to get up at the crack of dawn to get the fruit to market on time.

Depending on where you are in the world, you might end up picking apples, grapes, strawberries, lettuces or even bananas. You can find harvest timetables for various countries on the website **W** www.anyworkanywhere.com/jg_farms.html. You usually get paid according to the amount of fruit you pick. Most people manage to take home £20 to £30 per day. Many farms will let you camp on the grounds or provide hostel accommodation for workers, which can cut down your expenses.

If you want to earn a bit of quick cash to fund your gap year, fruit and vegetable farms in Kent and East Anglia take on pickers between March and October. Jobs are often advertised in Job Centres, or try calling the farms direct. You'll need to apply early as hundreds of migrant workers flock to the UK from Eastern Europe every harvest season.

Grape-picking – known in France as *vendange* – is probably the best known fruit-picking job in Europe. The two-month season kicks off in September. This is one of the cushier fruit-picking jobs as most vineyards lay on a huge French lunch with copious quantities of wine for their workers. The largest centre of grape-growing in France is the beaujolais region in Burgundy, just north of Lyon. The organisation Appellation Contrôlée (see Contacts for details) can arrange grape-picking in France, as well as other fruit-picking jobs around Europe.

Dorothea Benatar has the following to say about her experience as a fruit-picker in France:

I went to the Dordogne to pick raspberries but when I got there it turned out that the crop had failed because there wasn't enough sun. Luckily I found a strawberry-picking job through a friend of a friend. The work was back-breakingly hard and we had to crawl up and down the rows on all fours in the baking heat for about £3 an hour. When the strawberries ran out we moved on to plum-picking, which was pretty nasty too – the boys got the nice job of shaking the trees while the girls had to scramble around on their knees picking up the plums. I finally ended up picking grapes, which was great. You could work standing up and you got a proper two-hour French lunch break with loads of delicious food and wine. We were usually totally drunk by the time we went back to work in the afternoon!

The east coast of Australia is another good place to find fruit-picking work. Timetables for the fruit and vegetable harvest are published on the web every year – try searching for 'Fruit-picking Timetables' using the search engine W www.google.com. As well as more conventional fruit and veg, you can pick unusual crops such as cotton, bananas and ginger and there are even opportunities for harvesting *fruits de mer*, ie, shellfish!

Other good places to look for picking work include New Zealand, the USA and around Cape Town in South Africa. The website W www.pickingjobs.com has a search page where you can find fruit- and vegetable-picking jobs around the world. See Contacts for some companies that specialise in picking work.

FARM WORK

Fruit-picking is just one of a thousand jobs that need doing on a farm. Seasonal workers are hired to plant crops, repair fences, drive tractors, shear sheep and a host of other farming chores. You'll have to work hard but you'll be out in the open air and it's easy to save money. There are lots of specialist companies who can place you in a farm job overseas with other foreign workers for a fee. See Contacts for some examples. Wages typically start at around £150 per week.

Much of the work on Australian farms is done on horseback or off-road motorcycles and working as a jackeroo or jilleroo can be a great way to spend a season. The Visitoz scheme (see Contacts) will provide you with the skills you need to be an Aussie farm hand and provide you with a guaranteed job at the end of it. The other jackeroo and jilleroo courses listed in the Courses chapter may also be able to help you find work at the end of your course.

It used to be possible to work on a *moshav* (community farm) in Israel but the Moshav Movement has closed its volunteer offices due to the current security situation. Try contacting Project 67 (☎ 020-7831 7626) in London to see if things have changed by the time you read this. For information on working on a kibbutz see the Volunteering, Conservation & Expeditions chapter.

BUILDING WORK

The construction industry has always relied on contractors so short-term building work is easy to find in most countries. It can also pay surprisingly well, particularly if you have experience working with heavy machinery. There are openings around the world for labourers, steelworkers, heavy-vehicle drivers, electricians, plumbers, carpenters, furniture makers, civil engineers and surveyors.

The easiest way to find work is to go through one of the established recruitment agencies. Kelly Services, Adecco and Hays Personnel all recruit construction staff and have offices worldwide (see Contacts in the Proper Jobs chapter for details). Construction is usually union-controlled so there isn't much point approaching building sites directly. Building work can range from completely unskilled jobs, such as labouring, to structural engineering. Many people take on unskilled labourers for short-term projects such as site clearing.

You'll have to adjust to the local way of doing things, as Tom Bindloss from Leeds found out during his year out in Australia:

I was living in Manly, Sydney, working as a labourer for a man owning several houses on the peninsula. In general it was a good job, well paid, and we got free beers every Friday on the beach. One day we were demolishing an old wall when I noticed a huge brown spider, about two inches across, less than a foot from my hand. Both my mate and I scrambled up the wall and whimpered until the boss came over and shouted, "What the hell is up with you, that's just a house spider!" and he shooed it away with his foot. Twenty minutes later I turned over a brick and there on the other side was another great hairy spider. Hearing our cries for help, the boss ran over again, and was again unimpressed. "It's just a huntsman," he said. "You see them all the time."

Later the same day we were digging out the wall foundations when the boss came over and grabbed my elbow mid-shovel. I looked down the handle past my hand and less than six inches away was yet another large black spider, looking angry. So I asked what the big deal was, by now totally unfazed by the whole spider issue. Scottie (my boss) said, "Now hold up Tom, that one will kill you." It was a Sydney funnel-web, one of Australia's most poisonous spiders!

Good resources for anyone thinking about building or construction work include:

W **www.constructor.co.uk** A good construction and civil engineering site with lots of UK jobs.

W **www.ukconstruction.com** Has extensive listings of UK jobs and other construction resources.

W **www.buildersplanet.com** Worldwide resources for working in construction.

W **www.careersinconstruction.com** Useful resource and jobs site for construction careers.

W **www.constructionjobs.com** US site with lots of job listings.

Contacts

WORKING-HOLIDAY
ORGANISATIONS

Alliances Abroad
702 West Ave, Austin, Texas, 78701, USA
☎ 00 1 512-457 8062
fax 00 1 512-457 8132
e workandtravelusa@allianceabroad.com;
W www.alliancesabroad.com
Alliances Abroad offers a Work & Travel Programme in the USA over the summer for students, and a Seasonal Work Programme on a H-2B visa that is open to students and non-students. Work placements are provided or you can find your own job with their approval. It also offers farm work – see later in this section – and work-experience programmes (see Contacts in the Proper Jobs chapter).
Types of Work: Participants are placed in unskilled seasonal jobs, particularly in hospitality and catering.
Timing & Length of Work: The Work & Travel Programme runs for four months from mid-May. The Seasonal Work Programme runs for three to 10 months from March or November.
Destination: The USA.
Costs/Pay: Fees and wages vary – call or email for the latest rates. Insurance is included but flights are extra.
Eligibility: For the Work & Travel Programme you must be aged 18 to 28 and a current university/college student or have a guaranteed place at university. For the Seasonal Work Programme you can be 18 to 40.
How to Apply: Download the application form from the website. You must provide two references, a copy of your passport and have a telephone interview. Apply about four months in advance.

Association for International Practical Training (AIPT)
10400 Little Patuxent Parkway, Suite 250, Columbia, Maryland 21044-3519, USA
☎ 00 1 410-997 2200
fax 00 1 410-992 3924
e aipt@aipt.org
W www.aipt.org
AIPT offers the Experience USA Programme where you work for four months over the summer on a J-1 visa. It handles the paperwork, arranges a job placement and provides insurance and an orientation before and after you fly. See the Proper Jobs chapter for its career-related work programmes.
Types of Work: AIPT offers jobs in hospitality, shops, sports camps and offices.
Timing & Length of work: Placements are for four months from June.
Destination: The USA.
Costs/Pay: Placement cost around £570, excluding flights and visa fees. Wages depend on the placement.
Eligibility: Applicants must be at least 18 and be either full-time university students or have two years' relevant work experience.
How to Apply: Download an application form from the website. Apply by October 15. Once you register for the programme you can sign up for a presentation where you'll have an interview.

BUNAC
16 Bowling Green Lane, London EC1R 0QH
☎ 020-7251 3472
fax 020-7251 0215
e enquiries@bunac.org.uk
W www.bunac.org
BUNAC has a popular scheme where you work in a support role at an American summer camp. Visas, paperwork and travel arrangements are handled by BUNAC. There are also flexible work and travel programmes around the world, where you can do any job you like for a set period of time. Orientation sessions are held before departure and when you arrive, and help is provided with job hunting. For information on working with children or professional

work programmes see the Au Pairing & Working with Kids and Proper Jobs chapters.

Types of Work: Kitchen and cleaning work, general maintenance and office work are on offer at summer camps. Participants on other schemes can do any kind of job.

Timing & Length of Work: Summer Camp USA programmes last eight to nine weeks from early/mid-June. Other programmes last 12 months and start on set dates throughout the year.

Destinations: The USA, Canada, Australia, New Zealand & South Africa.

Costs/Pay: Summer Camp USA costs £252, including visa fees, return flights, in-country transport, food and lodging. Camp participants are paid around £570 at the end of camp. Costs and wages vary for other programmes – see the website for details.

Eligibility: You must be aged at least 18 and be a student on a full-time course or have an offer of a university/college place the following year.

How to Apply: Apply from September for Summer Camp USA programmes. You'll have to take a telephone interview, provide two character references and most camps require a medical. Forms for all programmes can be downloaded from the website.

Camp America

American Institute For Foreign Study (AIFS), 37a Queen's Gate, London SW7 5HR
☎ 020-7581 7373
fax 020-7581 7377
📧 enquiries@campamerica.co.uk
🌐 www.campamerica.co.uk

Camp America offers various work packages in the USA. All visas, travel and paperwork are handled by Camp America and there's a pre-departure and arrival orientation and training session. Country-wide job fairs and interview sessions are held between January and March – check the website for details. For information on working as a camp counsellor see Contacts in the Au Pairing & Working with Kids chapter.

Types of Work: Camp America offers catering, maintenance and admin work at summer camps, resorts, theme parks, hotels and country clubs.

Timing & Length of Work: Placements are typically for nine to 16 weeks from May or June.

Destination: The USA.

Costs/Pay: Summer camp and resort programmes cost around £315, including flights, accommodation, in-country transport and food (but not visa fees). Wages start at £450. Other work-experience programmes cost £405 plus air fares (plus £210 if you want a job placement) and wages vary.

Eligibility: Applicants must be aged at least 18 by June 1. You must be a full-time student or gap-year student with a confirmed college/university place for the following year.

How to Apply: Apply from October. Download the application form from the website. You'll have to arrange an interview and show a clean criminal record, two character references and two passport photos.

CCUSA

Green Dragon House, 64–70 High St, Croydon, Surrey CR0 9XN
☎ 020-8688 9051
fax 020-8680 4539
📧 unitedkingdom@ccusa.com
🌐 www.ccusa.com

CCUSA offers support jobs at American summer camps and various work-experience programmes around the world. For camp work, orientation sessions are held in the UK during April and May, and all visas, paperwork and travel arrangements are handled by CCUSA. For other programmes you can find your own job (in the USA, Australia and New Zealand) or take a placement (in the USA and Brazil). For information on its professional work programmes or working as a camp counsellor see Contacts in the Au Pairing & Working with Kids and Proper Jobs chapters.

Types of Work: Summer-camp jobs include kitchen, cleaning and office work. Jobs in Brazil include office work, hotel work and teaching beach sports. Participants on other work programmes can do any kind of job.

Timing & Length of Work: US programmes run for nine to 11 weeks from May or June. Brazil programmes last for three or six months and begin on set dates in January, April, July and October. Australia and New Zealand programmes start monthly.

Destinations: The USA, Australia, New Zealand & Brazil.

Costs/Pay: The US summer-camp programme costs £275, including flights, visas and accommodation; support staff can earn up to £630. Fees and wages vary for other programmes – see the website for details.

Eligibility: Applicants must be aged at least 18. For all US programmes you must be a full-time student or a gap-year student with an unconditional offer at university. The Brazil programme requires a working knowledge of Portuguese.

How to Apply: Download an application form from the website. Apply by mid-April for US programmes; then there's an interview. Country-wide job fairs for summer-camp positions are held in March and April.

Changing Worlds

11 Doctors Lane, Chaldon, Surrey CR3 5AE
☎ 01883-340960
fax 01883-330783
🄴 welcome@changingworlds.co.uk
🅆 www.changingworlds.co.uk

Changing Worlds organises work placements in Australia and New Zealand. It sorts out your work placement, paperwork and flights, and provides an orientation on arrival. You can either work on farms or in hotels, or do unpaid crewing on an old-fashioned tall ship in New Zealand. Accommodation is provided for all placements.

Types of Work: Work is available in hotels, on farms and on tall ships (unpaid, men only).

Timing & Length of Work: Placements are for three to six months from September or

January (also from March for Australia).

Destinations: Australia & New Zealand.

Costs/Pay: Fees are £2395 for Australia and £2495 for New Zealand, including flights but not insurance or visa fees. Wages are paid except for ship work.

Eligibility: Applicants must be aged 18 to 30.

How to Apply: Apply using the website or call for an application form. There will then be an interview and you'll need to provide two references and two passport photos.

CIEE (Council on International Educational Exchange)

52 Poland St, London W1F 7AB
☎ 020-7478 2000
fax 020-7734 7322
🄴 infouk@councilexchanges.org.uk
🅆 www.ciee.org.uk

CIEE offers various work programmes overseas. It will arrange your working visa, insurance and other paperwork and provide an orientation before you leave. You arrange your own flights and accommodation. Participants can do any kind of work and CIEE can help you find a job before you go. There's a job fair in February where you can arrange work directly with US employers. CIEE also offers professional work programmes, language courses and teaching programmes – see the Proper Jobs and Courses chapters for more details.

Types of Work: You can do any job you want for the time period specified on your visa.

Timing & Length of Work: US programmes last for four months from June to October. Australia and New Zealand programmes last up to a year and can start any time.

Destinations: USA, Australia & New Zealand.

Costs/Pay: Work & Travel USA costs £335, plus a £67 visa fee (paid directly to the visa-issuing authority). Australia and New Zealand programmes cost from £320 for three months to £500 for a year, plus visa fees. Wages will depend on the job you do.

Eligibility: For the USA, applicants must be aged at least 18 and be either a full-time student or have an unconditional offer at university. For Australia and New Zealand applicants can be aged 18 to 30.

How to Apply: Download the application pack from the website. Participants in US programmes are interviewed by phone.

International Exchange Centre (IEC)

35 Ivor Place, London NW1 6EA
☎ 020-7724 4493
fax 020-7724 0849
e isecinfo@btconnect.com
W www.isecworld.co.uk

The IEC organises work placements all over the world. You can work and study in Russia (with four weeks of Russian lessons in Moscow) or work in America in support roles on summer camps or doing other casual jobs. The South Africa programme lets you do any casual job. For information on internship programmes or working as a camp counsellor see the Au Pairing & Working with Kids and Proper Jobs chapters.

Types of Work: You can do hospitality work in Russia, and cleaning, kitchen and maintenance work on American summer camps. Participants on other work programmes can do any job.

Timing & Length of Work: American programmes last for up to four months from June. Programmes in South Africa and Russia last 12 months and can start at any time.

Destinations: USA, Russia & South Africa.

Costs/Pay: Summer camp placements cost £115, including flights, meals and accommodation; wages vary from £315 to £440. Other US programmes cost £370 with a job placement or £280 if you arrange your own job; wages vary and air fares are extra. See the website for costs of other programmes.

Eligibility: Applicants must be at least 18 (19 for South Africa). For US and South Africa programmes you must be a full-time student.

How to Apply: Email or phone for an application form three months in advance. Apply before end of April for American programmes. Following your application

there will be a phone interview. People on summer camps or job placements may have to provide two or more references, a clean criminal record and a medical.

Japanese Association of Working Holiday Makers (JAWHM)

Sun Plaza 7f, 4-1-1 Nakano, Nakano-ku, Tokyo Japan 164-8512
☎ 00 81 3 3389 0181
fax 00 81 3 3389 1563
W www.jawhm.or.jp

JAWHM offers a job referral service and support for people visiting Japan on working-holiday visas. There are branches in Tokyo, Osaka and Fukuoka. Visit the offices with your passport and two passport photos to register. You then have an orientation and can apply for the positions on their jobs list. Most jobs last three months or more.

Village Camps

Personnel Office, Dept. 1000, 1260 Nyon, Switzerland
☎ 00 41 22-990 9405
fax 00 41 22-990 9494
e personnel@villagecamps.ch
W www.villagecamps.com

Village Camps has openings for support staff at summer camps across Europe. For information on becoming a camp counsellor see Contacts in the Au Pairing & Working with Kids chapter.

Types of Work: Positions include chefs, kitchen workers, bar staff, receptionists and drivers.

Timing & Length of Work: Placements are from April/May to June or June to August.

Destinations: Switzerland, France, Holland, the UK & Austria.

Costs/Pay: Wages start at £140 per week. You pay for transport to camp.

Eligibility: Applicants must be aged at least 18 to 23 depending on the job. All staff need a first-aid certificate and a driving licence is preferred.

How to Apply: Download the application, applicant-release and authorisation forms from the website.

WorldNetUK

Avondale House, 63 Sydney Rd,
Haywards Heath, W Sussex RH16 1QD
☎ 01444-457676
fax 01444-440445
e info@worldnetuk.com
w www.worldnetuk.com

WorldNetUK offers support jobs on US summer camps in partnership with Inter-Exchange/Camp USA. It handles all visas and paperwork, and flights, transport etc are included in the cost. For details on working as a camp counsellor see Contacts in the Au Pairing & Working with Kids chapter.

Types of Work: Catering, domestic and general maintenance work is available.

Timing & Length of Work: Placements are for eight to 10 weeks from June.

Destination: The USA.

Costs/Pay: The programme costs from around £300, including flights, medical insurance and administration. Workers earn around £550 for the season.

Eligibility: Applicants must be at least 18 by June 1. You must be a full-time university student.

How to Apply: Call/email for a brochure. There will be an interview and a medical and criminal-record check. Apply from October.

SPECIAL EVENTS

Event Staff

Unit 5b/5c, Chosen View Rd, Kingsditch,
Cheltenham GL51 9LT
☎ 01242-530055
fax 01242-511001
e jobs@event-staff.co.uk
w www.event-staff.co.uk

This is an agency providing stewards and other staff for concerts and other special events across the UK. It also supplies sound, lighting and video engineers.

Recruit Event Services Ltd

2nd floor, Elvin House, Stadium Way,
Wembley HA9 0DW
☎ 020-8585 3794
fax 020-8903 3056
e editor@recruiteventservices.co.uk
w www.recruiteventservices.co.uk

Recruit Event Services specialises in finding staff for UK sporting events, air-shows, concert venues, festivals, premier-league football matches and other special events. See the website for vacancies. Call or email to register.

TOUR OPERATORS & ACTIVITY HOLIDAYS

3D Education & Adventure

Osmington Bay Centre, Shortlake Lane,
Weymouth, Dorset DT3 6EG
☎ 01305-836226
fax 01305-834070
e admin@3d-jobs.co.uk
w www.3d.co.uk/jobs

3D hires instructors in adventure sports and camp monitors (ie, couriers) on summer camps for its centres on the south coast of England and the Isle of Wight. It also places staff on projects at Pontin's resorts around Britain. It takes on around 500 instructors and 750 camp staff annually.

Types of Work: Roles include watersports instructors, IT instructors, activity-sport instructors, lifeguards and couriers.

Timing & Length of Work: Instructors work from mid-January to mid-November. Summer camps last six weeks from July.

Destination: The UK.

Costs/Pay: Wages start at around £70 per week, including food and accommodation.

Eligibility: Applicants must be at least 18. You need to have relevant qualifications for instructor jobs.

How to Apply: Apply online or download the application form. You must provide three references. Successful applicants are invited on a six-day assessment.

Acorn Adventure

Acorn House, 22 Worcester St,
Stourbridge, W Midlands DY8 1AN
☎ 01384-446057
fax 01384-378866

e topstaff@acornadventure.co.uk
W www.acorn-jobs.co.uk
Acorn is one of Britain's leading adventure-holiday companies and has seasonal openings for around 300 staff every year at centres around Europe. A one- or two-week training course is held in March where you gain skills relevant to the job (eg, sailing, canoeing, how to work as a rep). Transport is provided to resorts.
Types of Work: Positions available include instructors in adventure sports (eg, canoeing, rock climbing, sailing, windsurfing), camp reps, catering staff and drivers.
Timing & Length of Work: Placements are from April to September.
Destinations: The UK, France, Spain & Italy.
Costs/Pay: Wages vary from £40 to £200 per week, depending on your level of responsibility. Food and accommodation are free.
Eligibility: Watersports and other instructors need relevant qualifications (see the website for details). Drivers/loaders need a clean driving licence and experience of driving large vehicles. Applicants must be aged at least 17.
How to Apply: Call or download the application form from the website or apply online. You must provide two references and evidence of qualifications. Apply from October.

Camp Beaumont
Kingswood House, 11 Prince of Wales Rd, Norwich, Norfolk NR1 1BD
☎ 01603-284266
fax 01603-284250
e clare.trett@kingswood.co.uk
W www.campbeaumont.com
Camp Beaumont organises summer camps for kids around the UK and takes on seasonal staff every year.
Types of Work: Couriers (some childcare involved).
Timing & Length of Work: Placements are from June to August.
Destinations: London & Southeast England.

Pay: Staff earn above the minimum wage, and room and board are provided.
Eligibility: Applicants must be aged 18 to 30.
How to Apply: Apply online with addresses of two references.

Canvas Holidays Ltd
East Port House, Dunfermline, Scotland KY12 7JG
☎ 01383-629018
fax 01383-629071
e recruitment@canvasholidays.co.uk
W www.canvasholidays.co.uk
Canvas Holidays takes on seasonal couriers at around 100 holiday camps across Europe. Work includes looking after campers and children and putting up and taking down tents. Transport from a UK port and accommodation in shared permanent tents are provided.
Types of Work: Opportunities are as couriers.
Timing & Length of Work: Placements are from March to October.
Destinations: France, Italy, Spain, Holland, Germany, Austria & Switzerland.
Costs/Pay: Wages start at £100, accommodation included; meals are extra.
Eligibility: Applicants must be at least 18 (19 for France) and have a clean criminal record.
How to Apply: Fill in the online application form on the website. Successful applicants are invited to an interview.

Club Med
Club Med Recrutement, 11–12 Place Jules Ferry, 69458 Lyon Cedex 06, France
☎ 0845 3 67 67 67
e recruit.uk@clubmed.com
W www.clubmed-jobs.com
This huge holiday company has 120 holiday villages around Europe and the Mediterranean and offers temporary work placements for the summer and winter seasons.
Types of Work: Work includes sports coaching, entertainment, childcare and hospitality work.

Timing & Length of Work: Placements are for three to eight months from April to October (summer resorts) or December to April (winter resorts).

Destinations: France, Italy, Spain, Portugal, Morocco, Tunisia & Turkey.

Costs/Pay: Total wages start at £500. Room, board and transport to resorts are provided.

Eligibility: Applicants must be aged 20 to 35. French speakers are preferred.

How to Apply: You must include a CV, covering letter and photo. Following your application there will be an interview in London.

Disneyland Resort Paris

Service net Recrutement, B.P. 110, 77777 Marne La Vallée Cedex 4, France
☎ 00 33 1 64 74 40 00
fax 00 33 1 60 45 52 20
e dlp.casting.fr@disney.com
W www.disneylandparis.com/uk/employment

This huge theme park just outside Paris employs huge numbers of seasonal staff, from professional cartoon characters to waiters and office staff. Actors, circus staff and performers should see the website for casting details. Yearlong gap work may also be available.

Types of Work: Seasonal staff are employed as receptionists, sales and public-relations staff, ride attendants, business support and entertainers.

Timing & Length of Work: Placements are from March to October.

Destination: France.

Costs/Pay: The starting salary is £760 per month. Accommodation can be provided for £160 per month.

Eligibility: Applicants must be aged at least 18.

How to Apply: Apply by email or post well in advance.

Haven Europe

Haven Europe HR, 1 Park Lane, Hemel Hempstead, Herts HP2 4YL
☎ 01442-203970
fax 01442-241473
W www.haveneurope.com

Haven Europe operates around 40 holiday camps in Europe and takes on large numbers of seasonal staff. Accommodation and transport to resorts is provided but workers take care of their own food. Family members can visit on discounted Haven holidays.

Types of Work: Seasonal staff are taken on as bar, hospitality, maintenance and reception staff, reps and lifeguards.

Timing & Length of Work: Placements are from March to June and July to October.

Destinations: France, Spain & Italy.

Costs/Pay: Seasonal staff receive from £95 or £105 per week, depending on the camp.

Eligibility: Applicants must be aged at least 18. Previous experience and conversational French, Spanish or Italian is preferred. Lifeguards need relevant qualifications.

How to Apply: See the website or call for an application form. Following your application there will be an interview.

Holidaybreak

Hartford Manor, Greenbank Lane, Northwich CW8 1HW
☎ 01606-787522
fax 0870 366 7640
e overseas-recruit@holidaybreak.co.uk
W www.holidaybreakjobs.com

Holidaybreak is the owner of the Eurocamp and Keycamp holiday companies. It employs around 2000 staff a year for its holiday camps in Europe. Most people work as couriers or reps and the camps all have restaurants, bars and sports facilities. For some jobs there's a training session before you go off to camp; couriers are normally trained on camp.

Types of Work: Jobs include couriers, reps, tent erectors and guides.

Timing & Length of Work: Placements are from May to September.

Destinations: France, Spain, Italy, Austria, Germany, Netherlands, Luxembourg, Belgium & Croatia.

Costs/Pay: Wages start at £100 per week,

including accommodation; meals are subsidised.

Eligibility: Applicants must be aged at least 18 (21 for some jobs). Language skills and a clean driving licence are preferred.

How to Apply: Apply from October using the online application form or call for an application pack. You'll need two references, and some jobs require a clean criminal record. There will be an interview and orientation.

The Kingswood Group

Kingswood House, 11 Prince of Wales Rd, Norwich, Norfolk NR1 1BD

☎ 01603-284266

fax 01603-284250

e clare.trett@kingswood.co.uk

w www.kingswood.co.uk

Kingswood organises educational camps for kids around the UK and takes on instructors and general staff every season. There are regular assessment weekends where you can see how they operate and apply. As part of the job, staff are trained for National Governing Body (NGB) qualifications in various activities, including fencing, climbing, archery and lifeguarding. The same organisation offers seasonal jobs at summer camps in the UK – see the Camp Beaumont entry earlier in this section for details.

Types of Work: Kingswood takes on instructors, catering and maintenance staff.

Timing & Length of Work: Placements are from September to June.

Destination: The UK.

Costs/Pay: Wages start at £250 per month for the first season but accommodation and meals are included (wages increase for repeat seasons).

Eligibility: Applicants must be aged 18 to 24.

How to Apply: Apply online with addresses of two references.

PGL People

Alton Court, Penyard Lane, Ross-on-Wye, Herefordshire HR9 5GL

☎ 01989-767833

fax 01989-767760

e pglpeople@pgl.co.uk

w www.pgl.co.uk/people

PGL specialises in holidays for children and recruits over 2500 people a year. Seasonal support jobs are available at its residential centres around Europe (19 centres in the UK, 12 in France and one in Spain). For information on working with children on PGL camps see Contacts in the Au Pairing & Working with Kids chapter.

Types of Work: PGL employs seasonal support staff (hospitality staff, administrators and maintenance).

Timing & Length of Work: Placements are from February to October or May to September.

Destinations: UK, France & Spain.

Costs/Pay: All jobs pay £60 per week, and board, lodging and travel are free.

Eligibility: Applicants must be at least 18 with language skills and relevant qualifications.

How to Apply: Recruitment starts in October. Download the application form from the website. You need to provide two referees and show a clean criminal record.

Solaire Holidays

1158 Stratford Rd, Hall Green, Birmingham B28 8AF

☎ 0870 054 0202

fax 0121-778 5065

e holidays@solaire.co.uk

w www.solaire.co.uk

This small camping-holiday company hires summer staff at its European holiday camps.

Types of Work: Solaire employs seasonal camp couriers, and bar, cleaning and maintenance staff.

Timing & Length of Work: Placements are from May to September.

Destinations: France & Spain.

Costs/Pay: Wages start at £70 per week; travel and accommodation are free.

Eligibility: Applicants must be aged at least 18.

How to Apply: Send in your CV with a covering letter stating when you are free to work. There will then be an interview.

Specialist Holidays Group (SHG)

UK Recruitment, Tui UK & Specialist Holidays Group, Greater London House, Hampstead Rd, London NW1 7SD
☎ 0870 888 0028
fax 020-8541 2492
e overseasrecruitment@s-h-g.co.uk
w www.shgjobs.co.uk

SHG recruits seasonal staff for Thomson Ski/Lakes & Mountains, Crystal Holidays & Jetsave, Simply Travel and Specialist Sun.

Types of Work: SHG employs seasonal hotel and waiting staff, couriers, reps, ski and chalet staff.

Timing & Length of Work: The summer season runs from March/April to September; the winter season runs from November to April.

Destinations: France, Italy, Austria & Andorra.

Costs/Pay: The wages package is competitive and includes accommodation and food (plus skis, boots and ski passes for winter workers).

Eligibility: Applicants must be at least 18; reps must be 21 or over and should speak their destination's language.

How to Apply: Fill in an online application on the website. Successful applicants will have an interview. You must provide two references.

Sunsail

The Port House, Port Solent, Portsmouth, Hants PO6 4TH
☎ 023-9222 2222
fax 023-9221 9827
e hr@sunsail.com
w www.sunsail.com

This holiday company employs around 1700 staff on its yachts and beach resorts around the globe. As well as watersports instructors, there are openings for catering staff and couriers. Transport to work, accommodation and food are provided.

Types of Work: Sunsail employs sailing and boat maintenance staff, watersports instructors, hosts, activity staff (ie, couriers) and hotel, bar and catering staff.

Timing & Length of Work: Most jobs run between March and November. Some winter opportunities are available at ski resorts.

Destinations: Most jobs are in the Mediterranean but there are also openings in the Caribbean, Thailand & Malaysia etc.

Costs/Pay: Wages range from £65 to £100, including accommodation and board.

Eligibility: Applicants must be aged at least 19 (21 for yacht staff), with the relevant qualifications for instructor jobs.

How to Apply: Download the application form from the website. You have to provide a passport photo and proof of qualifications, then there's an interview.

SKI RESORTS

Inghams Travel

Overseas Reps Department, Inghams Travel, 10–18 Putney Hill, London SW15 6AX
☎ 020-8780 4400
fax 020-8780 8805
e travel@inghams.com
w www.inghams.co.uk

Inghams is a well-regarded ski company with openings for staff at its ski resorts in Europe every winter. Room, board and transport to the resorts are provided and you get a ski pass for your time off. It also has openings for hotel staff at some of its summer resorts in Europe.

Types of Work: Inghams recruit chalet and hotel staff, bar and waiting staff, managers, reps etc.

Timing & Length of Work: Placements are for December to April.

Destinations: France, Italy, Switzerland & Austria.

Costs/Pay: Wages are from £300 per month.

Eligibility: Applicants must be at least 18 (23 for rep and management jobs). Reps should ideally speak French, German, Italian or Spanish.

How to Apply: Download the application form from the website. Apply from April.

There will be an interview and you'll need to provide a reference.

Jobs in the Alps
17 High St, Gretton, Northants NN17 3DE
☎ 07050 121648
fax 01536-771914
e enquiries@jobs-in-the-alps.com
w www.jobs-in-the-alps.co.uk
Jobs in the Alps provides around 100 ski and chalet jobs every winter and around 80 hospitality jobs every summer, all in the Alps.
Types of Work: Chalet and hotel jobs.
Timing & Length of Work: Placements are from December to April and mid-June to mid-September.
Destinations: Switzerland & France.
Costs/Pay: Applicants are invited to join the Jobs in the Alps club; the subscription/membership fee depends on the length of placement. Workers earn from £350 per week.
Eligibility: Applicants must be aged at least 18 and should have studied A-level French or German.
How to Apply: Register on the website to get a list of vacancies.

Mark Warner
Resorts Recruitment Department, George House, 61–65 Kensington Church St, London W8 4BA
☎ 020-7761 7300
fax 020-7761 7301
e recruitment@markwarner.co.uk
w www.markwarner-recruitment.co.uk
Mark Warner is a major tour operator with 27 years of experience. Winter jobs are available at seven ski resorts in the Alps, including jobs as chalet and ski hosts (ie, ski couriers). Summer positions are available at nine resorts in the Mediterranean and Aegean. Transport, meals and accommodation are provided for all jobs.
Types of Work: Catering, housekeeping and ski/snowboard hosting are available in winter. Hotel, restaurant and waterfront positions are available in summer.

Timing & Length of Work: Winter jobs are for six to seven months from November and summer jobs are for six to seven months from April.
Destinations: France, Italy & Austria (winter); Greece, Turkey, Sardinia, Corsica & Italy (summer).
Costs/Pay: Rates of pay depend on the position but the minimum wage is around £50 per week.
Eligibility: Applicants must be aged at least 19 (you must be older for jobs with more responsibility). Ski/snowboarding staff and watersports instructors must have relevant qualifications.
How to Apply: You can apply year round. Download the application form from the website. Successful applicants are called for an interview.

PGL Travel
Ski Personnel Dept, Alton Court, Penyard Lane, Ross-on-Wye, Herefordshire HR9 5GL;
☎ 01989-767311;
fax 01989-767760;
e skipersonnel@pgl.co.uk;
w www.pgl.co.uk/people
PGL specialises in holidays for children and offers around 100 short-term seasonal winter jobs at resorts around Europe. For information on working with children on PGL camps see Contacts in the Au Pairing & Working with Kids chapter. For summer jobs see Tour Operators & Activity Holidays earlier in this section.
Types of Work: Jobs as instructors, reps and couriers (working with small groups of children) are available.
Timing & Length of Work: Placements are for one to five weeks around February or the Easter holidays.
Destinations: France, Italy, Switzerland & Austria.
Costs/Pay: All jobs pay £165 per week. Board, lodging and travel are all free.
Eligibility: Applicants must be aged at least 20 (18 for instructors) and be able to speak conversational French, Italian or German.
How to Apply: Recruitment for the following

year starts in October. Download the application form from the website. You'll need to provide two referees and show a clean criminal record.

Ski Staff

Peers Manor, Dane Court Manor, School Rd, Tilmanstone, Kent CT14 0JL
☎ 0870 432 8030
fax 0870 011 0719
e work@skistaff.co.uk
w www.skistaff.co.uk

Ski Staff is a recruitment agency that provides staff for over 100 British ski companies operating in the French, Swiss, Austrian and Italian Alps. Jobs can be found for instructors, ski hosts and chalet staff, and there's a CV-matching service if you can't find anything that suits you right away. See the website for vacancies.

Total Holidays Ltd

3 The Square, Richmond-Upon-Thames, Surrey TW9 1DY;
☎ 0870 161 3613;
fax 0870 168 7687;
e recruitment@skitotal.com;
w www.skitotal.com

Ski Total is a British ski company with 20 years of experience. It hires staff every season for ski resorts around Europe. You pay a refundable deposit of £100, which covers your outbound transport.

Types of Work: Ski hosts, technicians, reps, nannies, chalet and catering staff are hired.

Timing & Length of Work: Placements are from November to April.

Destinations: France, Italy, Austria & Switzerland.

Costs/Pay: Wages are from £50 per week, including meals, accommodation and ski pass.

Eligibility: Applicants must be aged at least 21 (18 for nannies).

How to Apply: Call, email or see the website for an application form.

World Challenge Expeditions (WCE)

Black Arrow House, 2 Chandos Rd, London NW10 6NF

☎ 020-8728 7200
fax 020-8961 1551
e welcome@world-challenge.co.uk
w www.world-challenge.co.uk

WCE's Gap Challenge offers paid work placements at hotels and ski resorts in Canada's Banff and Jasper National Parks. WCE arranges the visas, flights, paperwork and orientations before and after arrival. Resort workers receive a free ski pass. Six months' travel time is allowed after the placement. You can also do an extended programme that includes a three-week adventure course.

Types of Work: Placements are in hotels and ski resorts and jobs range from housekeeping to lift operators.

Timing & Length of Work: Placements are for six months from November (hotel work is also available in March and September).

Destination: Canada (Banff).

Costs/Pay: The total fee is £1577 (£3000 for the extended programme). Insurance and accommodation are extra (estimated cost £150 per month). Participants earn £60 to £150 per week.

Eligibility: Applicants must be aged 19 to 24. You must be a full-time student or a gap-year student with a confirmed offer of a university place.

How to Apply: Download the information pack and application form from the website. The interview and selection takes place at the company's residential centre in Buxton, Derbyshire.

FRUIT-PICKING & FARM WORK

Agriventure

Ave M, National Agricultural Centre, Stoneleigh Park, Kenilworth, Warks CV8 2LR
☎ 02476-696578
fax 02476-696684
e uk@agriventure.com
w www.agriventure.com

Agriventure arranges paid work exchanges for aspiring farmers in five different countries. It arranges all the paperwork and provides a guaranteed farm job, transport

and visas, plus support in the host country. The host farm provides board and lodging.
Types of Work: Work is on arable or mixed farms.
Timing & Length of Work: Placements are for four months to one year. Work in the USA, Canada and Japan starts between February and April. Work in Australia and New Zealand begins August/September.
Destinations: Australia, New Zealand, Canada, the USA & Japan.
Costs/Pay: Fees start from £1930, including flights, visa fees and insurance. Wages vary depending on the job and host country.
Eligibility: Applicants must be aged 18 to 30 and have practical farming experience.
How to Apply: Apply using the online form on the website. You'll then be sent an application pack. You must provide two references.

Alliances Abroad

2423 Pennsylvania Ave NW, Washington DC, 20037, USA
☎ 00 1 202 467 9467
fax 00 1 202 467 9460
e work@alliancesabroad.com
w www.alliancesabroad.com
This American company organises work placements on farms in rural Australia. The programme includes three days' orientation at Rainbow Beach near Brisbane and five days' farm training. Participants go on to work on rural farms around Australia. Horses and motorcycles are used for some jobs and you can expect to work hard and have plenty of adventures.
Types of Work: Jobs are on farms or in rural hospitality.
Timing & Length of Work: Participants are allowed to work and travel in Australia for up to 12 months. You can start at any time.
Destination: Australia.
Costs/Pay: The programme fee is £850, including room and board. Flights, visa fees and compulsory insurance are extra. Farm wages are typically £450 per month.
Eligibility: Applicants must be aged 18 to

30. You must not have previously held a working-holiday visa for Australia.
How to Apply: Download the application form from the website. There's a phone interview and you must provide four passport photos and two references. Apply three months before you want to start.

Appellation Contrôlée (APCON)

Ulgersmaweg 26c, 9731 BT, Groningen, Holland
☎ 00 31 50 549-2434
fax 00 31 50 549-2428
e project2@bart.nl
w www.apcon.nl
This Dutch organisation places seasonal workers on farms across Europe. You make your own way to the farms.
Types of Work: Options include fruit-picking near Lyon and farm work across northern Europe.
Timing & Length of Work: Grape-picking is in September/October. Other jobs run approximately from May to September.
Destinations: France, Denmark & Holland.
Costs/Pay: Registration costs from £65. Workers are paid around £23 per day and food and accommodation are usually included.
Eligibility: Applicants must be aged at least 18.
How to Apply: Fill in the online form and send in the payment.

Fruitfuljobs.com

Unit 3, Honeybourne Industrial Estate, Evesham, Worcs WR11 7QF
☎ 01386-832555
fax 01386-833960
e info@fruitfuljobs.com
w www.fruitfuljobs.com
This is a recruitment service for jobs in the British soft-fruit industry. It can put you in contact with farms needing workers throughout the harvest season. Most jobs involve supervising and managing the crop rather than actually picking fruit.
Types of Work: Jobs can be found as field supervisors, packing supervisors, tractor

drivers, and in crop management (laying plastic sheeting for strawberries etc).

Timing & Length of Work: Placements are for April to October.

Destinations: Around the UK.

Costs/Pay: Workers earn around £5 per hour. Accommodation is normally provided on the farms for a small supplement.

Eligibility: Applicants must be aged at least 18.

How to Apply: Fill in the online registration form. You will then be contacted to discuss matching you with a grower.

International Exchange Centre (IEC)

35 Ivor Place, London NW1 6EA
☎ 020-7724 4493
fax 020-7724 0849
e isecinfo@btconnect.com
W www.isecworld.co.uk

The IEC organises a variety of long and short-term work placements around the world, including farm placements in Europe. Casual options include strawberry-picking in Denmark, farm work in Norway and paid training programmes for agricultural students in Finland, New Zealand and the USA.

Types of Work: Fruit-picking, planting and harvesting and other agricultural jobs are on offer.

Timing & Length of Work: Strawberry-picking runs from June to July. Other positions start year round. Traineeships last up to 12 months.

Destinations: Denmark, Norway, Finland, the USA & New Zealand.

Costs/Pay: Programme fees range from £150 for Denmark to £640 for agricultural training in the USA. Wages vary from country to country.

Eligibility: Applicants must be aged at least 18. You must be an agricultural student or have two years' practical experience for training programmes.

How to Apply: Email or phone for an application form three months in advance.

Visitoz

Grange Cottage, 6 Shipton Rd, Ascott-under-Wychwood, Oxon OX7 6AY
☎ 01933-831972
e julesmith@aol.com
W www.visitoz.org

Visitoz organises work on outback farms in Australia. The package includes an orientation at Rainbow Beach near Brisbane and a training course in the skills you need in order to work on an Australian farm such as horse-riding and managing livestock. Work placements are then provided on around 950 farms across Australia. You have to apply for a working-holiday visa but Visitoz will help with all the paperwork and travel arrangements and meet you at Brisbane airport when you arrive.

Types of Work: Work is on arable and livestock farms. Jobs include mustering cattle, harvesting or planting crops and building fences.

Timing & Length of Work: The training course lasts four days. Farm work is then available in three-month blocks for up to a year.

Destination: Australia.

Costs/Pay: The fee is £595, including the training course and orientation. The host farms provide accommodation and food. Flights, insurance and visa fees are extra. Wages start at around £150 a week.

Eligibility: Applicants must be aged 18 to 30. A tidy appearance is required as workers stay with farming families.

How to Apply: Call or email for an application pack. There will then be an interview in person or by phone.

World-Wide Opportunities on Organic Farms (WWOOF)

PO Box 2675, Lewes, E Sussex BN7 1RB
☎/fax 01273-476286
W www.wwoof.org

WWOOF arranges unpaid farm work at organic farms around the world. You stay with a host family and do about six hours' work a day in exchange for room and board. You must make all your own travel arrangements.

Types of Work: Volunteer farm work on organic arable and mixed farms.

Timing & Length of Work: Placements can range from a few days to a year.

Destinations: WWOOF represents host farms in many countries around the world, from Britain to Costa Rica.

Costs/Pay: Work is unpaid but room and board are provided.

Eligibility: Applicants must be aged at least 18.

How to Apply: Join the local WWOOF organisation where you want to work (see the website for contact details); it costs around £15 to join and members get a regularly updated list of WWOOF host farms.

BUILDING WORK

Hill McGlynn

Prospect House, Meridians Way, Ocean Way, Ocean Village, Southampton SO14 3TJ

☎ 0800 169 0863

e resource@hillmcglynn.com

w www.hillmcglynn.com

Hill McGlynn is a leading construction recruitment agency with worldwide connections. The Resource Centre can advise you on finding temporary construction work abroad.

Hill McGlynn – Australia

Suite 214, 566 St Kilda Rd, Melbourne, Victoria 3004, Australia

☎ 00 61 3 9526 8188

fax 00 61 3 9526 8176

e melbourne@hillmcglynn.com.au

w www.hillmcglynn.com.au

The Australian side of Hill McGlynn specialises in finding work in the construction industry and welcomes those on working holidays.

Work Your Route

Travel, the actual process of getting from A to B, can be one of the most expensive elements of any gap year. But some people travel the world for free and some even get paid for it. Several of the options looked at here are highly suited to gap-year travel, such as crewing a yacht or doing a summer season as a tour guide. Others are better suited to a post-university gap year because they'll either eat into more of your time or demand more than a year's commitment.

Crewing a Yacht

The world really opens up for you on a yacht – you get to see so much more of it than is usually possible by public transport (and wind in your sails is much more exotic than leaves on the line). Many gappers say it is the *only* way to experience the islands of the Aegean, the Pacific, the Indian Ocean and the Caribbean. And they're right – you get to go places in a private boat that the rest of us only dream about.

There's a real camaraderie at sea with everyone helping everyone else out. It's a small world and you bump (hopefully not literally) into the same people all the time. You work hard and you play hard – the social life at marinas is more full on than anyone ever bargains for.

Crewing a yacht also looks good on your CV. Many of the skills you need at sea are also needed in business – teamwork, preparation, attention to detail, anticipation, keeping cool in a crisis and working efficiently under pressure.

These days, though, competition for crewing jobs is strong so the more sailing experience you've got the easier it'll be to get that first job. To maximise your chances why not do a Competent Crew Course in the UK before you leave (see Watersports, Sailing & Crewing under Contacts in the Courses chapter)? If you're really serious then think about a five-day intensive Day Skipper Shore-Based Course (from around £350) followed by a five-day intensive Day Skipper Practical (from around £390). A first-aid course is also a good idea, as anyone with any medical training is always useful at sea.

Before you leave the UK you could also check out the annual boat shows in London (January; **W** www.londonboatshow.net/) and Southampton (September; **W** www.southampton boatshow.com), which will give you a good feel for the industry and maybe some crewing leads or contacts.

If you only have limited experience then the job you're most likely to get is deckhand, right at the bottom of the pile. As Claire Harrison explains, this is what she started off doing:

My first job crewing was in the Greek Islands as a deckhand. At sea this meant I washed the decks, cleaned and tidied up, did some cooking and took my turn on watches. At port I helped fix up the boat so it stayed in top condition (sanding down, varnishing etc), ran errands and generally helped prepare the boat for the next leg of its voyage. What I didn't have to worry about was navigation, crew management, passage planning and departure dates. That was basically the skipper's job, though I learnt as much of this as I could from him.

If you're working your passage as a deckhand then you'll probably be asked to contribute a little towards your upkeep. Usually skippers/owners ask for up to £10 a day towards costs – but not always.

Before running away to sea, though, it's worth considering whether this is a lifestyle that will suit you. A private yacht is a very small place to live and you need to get on with everyone;

when you're at sea you're together 24 hours a day. Your sleep is disrupted because of night watches, meal times are shifted to fit in with these, you'll encounter bad weather and possibly life or death situations, you'll be seasick and you'll never feel really clean because all washing is done with sea water. Your skipper is always in absolute charge, will order you about and he/she will lay down all the rules; after all, it is their home that you're living in. If you like a drink and a smoke it's worth sounding out the skipper's views on these habits, particularly when at sea.

If you want to tee up a crewing position before leaving the UK then yacht delivery is a good deal (see Crewing a Yacht under Contacts at the end of this chapter). It will also give you valuable sailing experience. Otherwise, try the classified ads in magazines such as *Yachting Monthly* (**W** www.yachtingmonthly.com) and *Yachting World* (**W** www.yachting-world.com). Females should watch out though as sometimes lonely old sea dogs sniffing around for company rather than crew place these ads. Then there are the specialist crewing agencies where, for a fee, your requirements are matched with those of a skipper – see Crewing a Yacht under Contacts. However, word has it that relatively inexperienced crew rarely get jobs with these agencies and that some are simply online bulletin boards that few skippers bother to read.

Most gappers are usually on the road when they decide to try a little crewing. Although there are usually crewing agencies wherever there's a decent-sized marina, many gappers are better off finding their own jobs.

A good place to hang out or work is the repair yard because this is where you'll meet all the skippers fixing up their boats for a long-distance voyage. And getting a crewing job is all about who you meet, who you know and who will recommend you. This means that any job in the marina (usually washing and cleaning boats) or in the local chandlery – basically the yachtie equivalent of a car-accessories store – is worth going for. It'll bring you into contact with the right people. In the evenings check out the main yachtie bars – there's always one or two near any marina – and you could be introduced to skippers needing crew. Otherwise, there's no harm in putting up notices in the local yacht club, on marina notice boards or at chandleries.

If none of that works then ask from boat to boat if there's any work going. Richard Thomas wrote in with this tip:

Target the larger yachts (30ft to 50ft), as they'll be the ones going long-distance. Also, the bigger the boat the more crew is needed. Don't bother with the boats anchored out at sea as they're likely to be in the middle of cruising and so will already have their crew. To begin with you'll usually be taken on to work the odd day and if the skipper likes you then you'll be asked to join the crew. Getting your first job is a hundred times more difficult than the next one.

A word of warning though: while the captain is checking you out, check out the captain. Ensure that any job you get is with an experienced, responsible skipper.

Yachting is totally seasonal. This means that if you're in the right place at the right time then getting a job will be much easier. A table showing where you need to be when follows:

Months	From	To
January to March	South Africa (Cape Town)	The Caribbean, the Mediterranean, South America
March to April	Gibraltar	Greece, Turkey
March to May	The Caribbean	USA (East Coast), the Mediterranean, Panama Canal

Months	From	To
March to June	USA (West Coast)	South Pacific (particularly Tahiti)
March to May	Northern Europe	The Mediterranean
April	New Zealand	Australia, USA (West Coast) via Pacific Islands
April to June	USA (East Coast)	The Mediterranean
May to July	South Africa (Durban)	Islands of Indian Ocean
June to August	Australia (Darwin)	Indonesia, Indian Ocean
August to September	Fiji	New Zealand
September to October	Greece, Turkey	Gibraltar
October to November	Gibraltar	The Caribbean via the Canary Islands
October to November	USA (West Coast)	Mexico
November	Islands of Indian Ocean	South Africa (Durban)
November	USA (East Coast)	The Caribbean
November to December	The Canary Islands	The Caribbean

The two main sailing seasons are from April to October in the Mediterranean and from October to May in the Caribbean. In the Mediterranean boats usually sail west to east in the spring ending up in the Greek Islands or the Turkish coast. In October they all head back to Gibraltar before congregating in the Canary Islands for a November/December Atlantic crossing to catch the season in the Caribbean. If you want to crew in the Mediterranean then good yachting centres to try are Gibraltar, the Balearics or the Greek Islands. In the Caribbean, Barbados or St Lucia are usually the first ports of call after crossing the Atlantic.

Another good bet are the hundreds of worldwide amateur long-distance races or regattas. The most famous is the Atlantic Rally for Cruisers (ARC; W www.worldcruising.com), which starts in November from Las Palmas in the Canaries and finishes in St Lucia in the Caribbean. Another big yachting event is Antigua Sailing Week (W www.sailingweek.com) at the end of April. Yacht owners are often looking for crew at these times either to be an extra pair of eyes and hands or to help contribute to costs.

When crewing you need a passport with more than a year to go on it, and either a ticket home from your final destination or enough money to buy that ticket plus additional funds. Basically, immigration authorities want to ensure that you're not going to stay in their country and that you're definitely not going to be a drain on their resources. When you join a boat you'll be signed on as crew and you can only be signed off, or assigned to another boat, if you can fulfil these requirements. When you arrive somewhere like the Caribbean or the US Immigration will usually give you a couple of days to make onward plans.

And, finally, drugs are a huge NO-NO on boats. Skippers are really big on this because they stand to lose almost everything if drugs are found on their ship. And, as you can imagine, US coastguards are very hot on this when boats arrive in American waters from the Caribbean.

Cruise Ships

Cruising has always been big in North America but Europeans now have the bug and can't get enough. More than 12 million people worldwide took a cruise in 2003 and another 30 new ships will set sail before 2005 to keep up with demand. Around 120,000 people are currently employed on cruise ships: a number only set to grow.

Cruising is a year-round business and so cruise lines are constantly looking to fill vacancies. Some of the larger ships have up to 1000 crew, and the turnover of staff is high.

Most people choose to work on cruise ships to see the world. The Mediterranean and the Caribbean are the main stomping grounds but the Far East and round-the-world (RTW) itineraries are also popular. Many then stay on because it's a good way to save money as you get free board and lodging. It is also a real opportunity to make international friends – cruise lines hire from all over the world and some ships will have over 50 nationalities working on board. The leading supply is from the Philippines, India (particularly Goa) and the countries of the former Soviet Union (particularly Ukraine).

Most cruise ships are like floating towns with every convenience you'd expect on a trendy high street. This means that the variety of jobs on board is enormous: there are casinos needing dealers, retail outlets needing sales assistants, officers needing secretaries, and ship newspapers needing journalists. For the stage-struck, some of the best jobs on board are as entertainers – singers, musicians, dancers etc – but the standards are as high as the kicks in a can-can. In contrast, you don't have to be David Bailey to become a ship's photographer because all training is normally given on board – see Contacts for details. And, in the land of the Midnight Buffet, there are always loads of jobs for catering and waiting staff. In all there are between 150 and 200 different positions on board a decent-sized cruise ship.

The top jobs pay anything from £20,000 per annum upwards but the majority of positions pay around £1000 a month. If you're in the service front-line then you will get less because most of your income will come from tips – some waiters, bar or cabin staff make more than £300 a week from the paying guests. Don't forget, you don't stump up for the rent or weekly shop and, on top of this, most cruise employees are classed as self-employed, which means that wages are paid tax-free.

But it's not all plain sailing. Ian Smith, who worked six months on a cruise ship in the Caribbean, mentions some of the downsides:

The hours are long – sometimes up to 14 or 15 a day. I often had to work seven days a week (which rather scuppers shore leave) and my living conditions were very cramped as I had to share a cabin with two others. A cruise ship is also a very class-ridden society with officers on top and everyone else below in order of seniority. (Saying that also reminds me of how much bonking went on!) Many of the lowliest and worst paid positions are taken by crew from developing countries and so there's often an innate racism on board too.

In September 2002 the charity War on Want and the International Transport Workers' Federation wrote a report called *Sweatships – what it's really like to work on board cruise ships* highlighting the situation of these workers. It can be downloaded from **W** www.war onwant.org.

If you're thinking of working on a cruise ship during your gap year then there are a couple of things to bear in mind. Firstly, cruise ships aren't really interested in gap-year students. They're looking for professionals with good communication skills, often with a minimum of two years' relevant experience and qualifications in their field. As a result, most jobs are advertised with a minimum age of between 20 and 23, with 21 being the norm. Many positions with passenger contact also prefer you to speak at least one other language. All of this is not to say you won't get a job on a cruise ship during your gap year; many people do, but the selection process is rigorous and usually only those with the right attitude win through.

It is unusual for cruise lines to hire direct. Recruitment is mostly handled by agencies or by 'concessionaires' – companies who own and run their own facilities on a ship (eg, shops, gyms, hairdressers). A lot of recruitment agencies or concessionaires are based in the US but interview and hire worldwide, so it's definitely worth applying to them. Those listed under Cruise Ships in the Contacts section all have UK offices. For a list of international agencies check out the private website at [W] www.geocities.com/thetropics/shores5933.

Start applying at least two months before you want to start. The best time for a newcomer to get their first job is around Christmas and New Year when experienced crew want to be at home (they also know what hell festive cruises can be to work). Most contracts last from between four to 10 months, but six months is the most usual. You then get two months' unpaid leave (or you quit altogether). When you're at the contractual stage it's important to understand what you'll be paying for and what the cruise line or concessionaire will pick up. For instance, most ships won't depart from or arrive at Britain; so who's going to pay your air fare? Steer clear of agencies that charge upfront fees or internet sites trying to sell you a list of current vacancies – both are usually an expensive waste of time.

To work at sea you'll need a passport with more than a year to go on it, a clear criminal record (you can even run into trouble with a jaywalking fine) and travel insurance. This is also a good time to get your yellow fever vaccination. If you intend to work in US waters, where so much of the cruise industry is based, you will also need a C1/D visa (see [W] www .usembassy/org.uk/cons_web/visa/niv/crew.htm for details). If any other visas are needed once you're on board then the crew purser will sort this for you. Sometimes agencies or concessionaires require other bits from you like a Basic Sea Survival Certificate and a medical examination (you'll have to jump through several medical hoops to work for an American cruise company). When you're offered a job the cruise line will help you sort all of this out and will pay for these.

There are lots of websites about working on cruise ships, often written by those who've been there and done that. Two good ones are: [W] www.geocities.com/thetropics/cabana/ 1590 and [W] www.cruiseman.com/cruiseshipjobs.htm. Also worth looking at for catering staff are [W] www.payaway.co.uk/dircatering.htm and the more general [W] www.cruise-community.com where recruitment for the job section is handled by Berkeley Scott Selection (see Cruise Ships under Contacts).

Tour Guiding

Independent travel isn't everyone's cup of tea. Plenty of people sign up for guided tours and there's bags of variety. Some are run on a shoestring where you sleep in tents and cook your own food; others stay in top-class hotels and eat in Michelin-starred restaurants. Some cater for school children, others for groups of 20- and 30-somethings, and many are for older people. The type of customer and their expectations will be very different in all these cases and it is important to work for the company that best suits your personality and style of travelling. You also have to decide how long you want to spend doing this sort of job. Many tour operators want you to sign up for a minimum of two seasons or 18 months. This is because training costs are high and they want a decent return on their investment.

What is initially attractive about tour guiding is being paid to sightsee in a foreign country. What you get out of it, though, is much deeper than that. You get under the skin of the countries where you lead. The experience of working day-to-day with the local people means you form relationships and understandings that simply aren't possible as a traveller or tourist. Working as a tour guide also looks great on your CV due to the job's high levels of responsibility and pressure.

As a tour guide you are responsible for the smooth running of a trip and the overall satisfaction of your group. This means that you're not only a leader and motivator but also a facilitator and manager, ensuring that all hotel and restaurant reservations, sightseeing opportunities, and group needs and requests are met. You will also look after company funds, keep expense accounts, handle a string of stressful events from stolen passports to serious illnesses, and write tour reports. Many companies will expect you to spout educational commentary, some will use local guides for this, or there'll be a good mixture of the two. At the end of the trip your performance will be assessed by the group when they fill in feedback forms – now that's a scary thought!

Life isn't easy being a tour guide. As Laetitia Northmore-Ball, who worked for American Council of International Studies (ACIS), put it:

On my first 10-day tour I lost 4lbs in weight; I was so busy and anxious about doing a good job that I forgot to find time to eat. I was on call 24 hours and that's exhausting. I was running around all the time, permanently on edge, with no time for myself just organising what we were going to do next. I'd be up before my tour group arranging things, and then last to bed. Even then I wouldn't sleep, as I'd revise my tour-guiding spiel for the next day and usually end up dreaming about the job.

But she also says:

At the end of the trip when my first tour group left I felt bereft. I never thought I'd get so used to holding up that umbrella and it felt weird walking away from the airport with no group behind me. I'd got used to the constant company and to performing, and I loved it.

Quite often trips run back-to-back, which means that as one group goes home the next one arrives. It also means that you could be working abroad, with very little time off, doing a succession of tours for up to six months. Being with new people all the time gives great variety but also means you constantly have to prove yourself.

To work as a tour guide you must enjoy being with people and find it easy to get on with them, while remaining in charge. You need to have confidence in yourself and inspire confidence in others, especially when things go wrong, as it did for tour guide David Else. He turned up in Aswan, Egypt, with a tired group of 15 who'd just stepped off the overnight train from Cairo to find they had no hotel reservations:

I was straight up with my group and immediately told them we had a problem but said that I'd sort it. Being a lovely day I took them to a park and organised a local lad to bring everyone cups of tea. I then arranged for them to use the loos at a nearby hotel. When I knew the group was comfortable I rushed off around town looking for alternative accommodation. It was Christmas though, and everywhere was booked out. In the end I rang HQ and they said they'd try to pull some strings for me. It turned out that we did have rooms at the original hotel but they had been booked under the company's local name and not the international one. So, we were fine in the end. But as a Tour Guide, I'm constantly thinking on my feet, showing resourcefulness and making a plan so that everything keeps moving. It's when there are problems that your training and skills come in. You're definitely at your most valuable when there's a crisis.

Tour companies often require their guides to speak a foreign language. Excellent communication skills are also essential, as well as a love of public speaking. It's also important to be able to see the funny side of a situation and to have fun with your group while doing a good job.

You won't be doing this job for the pay but whatever you do get is on top of free accommodation, return air fare and sometimes free meals – see Tour Guiding under Contacts for details. In addition, many tour guides earn good tips. You should share these with your driver (if you have one). Also, it is traditional for tour guides to make a profit on the side by getting free meals at the restaurants where you take the group or commission at some of the shops the group visits. Obviously, these tactics need to be used with discretion and in moderation.

In terms of work visas, you'll be expected to have a passport from one of the EU countries allowing you to work in Europe. The tour operator will arrange work visas for outside of Europe.

Jobs are often advertised in the free London magazine, *TNT* (**W** www.tntmagazine.com/uk/), or the independent travel magazine, *Wanderlust* (**W** www.wanderlust.co.uk). They are also pinned on notice boards in the languages department of universities, or the careers office. Sometimes, they turn up in **W** www.payaway.co.uk. Otherwise many are advertised on the tour operator's website and on notice boards at travel fairs.

A word about industry jargon – tour guides who don't give educational commentary are called 'tour leaders'. This is doubly confusing when the overland companies in the following Behind the Wheel section often call their drivers 'tour leaders' too.

Behind the Wheel

Coach and overland companies estimate that 90% of their drivers are male. This ratio reflects the proportion of applications, not the selection process; all companies would love to hire more female drivers. So, girls, how about seeing the world this way?

Insurance cover requires drivers to be aged at least 23 and often 25 years old.

OVERLAND COMPANIES

Practically all drivers who work for overland companies are called tour leaders although there's a lot of 'tour guiding' in their job description (see the preceding Tour Guiding section for more information. This makes the job twice as difficult or twice as rewarding depending on whether you see your billycan as half empty or half full.

It's got to be said that the overland companies would really prefer gap-year students as paying customers rather than paid employees. It often takes between six and 18 months to become a fully qualified overland driver/tour leader and so they want you to stay in the job for at least a couple of years. The minimum age also means that this is probably a post- rather than pre-university option, which might free you up to spend more time doing it.

Overland drivers will always tell you they have the best job in the world. They love travelling in challenging environments, seeing extraordinary things every day, being their own boss, the high levels of responsibility, making a difference to the developing countries they visit, and being on the road for much of the year.

These days the 4WD trucks that overland companies use are pretty sophisticated. They're rough and tough but more comfortable than they look, with padded seats, a stereo, safe, camp oven, retractable awnings, reference library, roof racks, lighting and sometimes a fridge/freezer. They seat around 25 passengers. As tour leader your main job is to look after the vehicle, know the routes, and drive safely through them. You'll also have to fix the truck if it breaks down. Many of the overland routes run through Africa, Asia or South America, and sod's law dictates you always break down in the middle of nowhere. So sound mechanical knowledge has to be matched by the wily thinking of a bush mechanic. This applies to both the truck and to your group who'll not be best pleased with any hold-up, as

Paul Goldstein explains:

We broke down in the middle of the Serengeti. I got out and so did the local Kenyan guide. We opened up the bonnet and one look told us that this was serious and we'd be stuck for ages. I was about to go and give the bad news to the group when the more experienced Kenyan guide told me to wait a while. He then dipped his hand into the engine and smeared my face, hands and arms with black grease. 'Now go and tell them,' he said, 'they'll be a lot more understanding.'

The other important part of the job is the leading and tour guiding. One moment you're a driver and mechanic and the next you're a cultural and wildlife expert, crew manager, local fixer, social secretary, medical doctor, love counsellor, and international peacemaker (not all groups exist in perfect harmony). For these reasons, on most overland trips there are two tour leaders, and often a cook, who can share the responsibility of keeping the group safe, happy and well.

The health of your passengers is crucial. Gary Ashdown, a tour leader for Guerba, writes to say:

The truck broke down in the Cameroon, West Africa. I was busy fixing it when one of the passengers came down with severe malaria. We needed to get her to hospital quickly and, ideally, to a hospital out of the country. There were two of us leading the trip and we weren't sure of the fastest way to reach Calabar in Nigeria, the nearest airport town, so I hitched and the other tour leader took the bicycle. The roads were so bad that George Kiama, the cyclist, got there first and arranged medical help and evacuation. I then had to hitch back to the truck and continue fixing it.

Despite this story, the roads on many overland trips are better than they used to be. Many are now sealed, although they all still compete in the pothole Olympics. Importantly, there's no night driving when you're overlanding (unless there's an emergency) and rare are the days when you're driving for nine hours at a stretch.

To drive for overland companies you need a LGV-C (Large Goods Vehicle) licence (the old HGV or Heavy Goods Vehicle licence). It takes between five and eight days to train for this at around £135 a day – see Miscellaneous Contacts in the Courses chapter. Often, as mentioned, you need to be a trained mechanic or bush mechanic.

You don't do it for the pay, is what everyone says, you'll do it for the excitement – as you'll see under Behind the Wheel in the Contacts section, many companies were a little cagey about salary. But, your pay does increase with seniority, and all your day-to-day costs are met, as well as flights to and from the UK. In addition, there's not much time to spend what you do earn and so much of your wages can go into savings.

The overland company sorts your visas or immigration documents. But you do need to know how to get yourself and your group through some dodgy border crossings where petty bribery and corruption is often part of everyday life.

Under Behind the Wheel in the Contacts section the details of a few overland companies are given. For a full list see **W** www.go-overland.com. This site also looks at the various posible overland routes, the history of overland travel and some of the companies in more depth.

COACH-TOURING COMPANIES

Driving for a coach company is a very different ball game. For starters you'll just be doing the driving, as there'll be an on-board guide. This is just as well because most coach companies tour Europe and you'll need all your concentration to negotiate the traffic.

You'll also need a PCV-D (Passenger Carrying Vehicle) licence (the old PSV or Public Service Vehicle licence). The course for this concentrates more on passenger comfort but costs about the same as the LGV – see Overland Companies earlier in this section and Miscellaneous under Contacts in the Courses chapter. Often you'll also need some mechanical knowledge, although this isn't so crucial in Europe where garages are as common as red traffic lights.

In many cases, coach drivers are paid better than the tour guides. One of the reasons for this is that they have less opportunity to earn any unofficial extras, although good tour guides (or those savvy enough to realise they need to get on with you) will share their passenger tips.

OTHER WORK
Drivers are always needed. With a LGV or PCV licence under your belt you'll be able to pick up driving work abroad. Good bets are the local temp agencies for drivers; otherwise a short contract or full-time job with one of the freight-forwarding or road-haulage companies is quite possible.

DRIVEAWAY CARS
If you're spending part of your gap year in the USA then think about registering with one of the many driveaway car companies who need drivers to move cars from one place to another.

You must be over 21 and have a valid driving licence, personal references and between £120 and £245 in cash as a deposit that's refundable when you deliver the car safely. You pay nothing for the use of the car, the company stumps up for insurance, but you have to cover the petrol. The car's got to be delivered to its destination at a specified time – six hours of driving per day is usually allotted. Maximum mileage is also stipulated, so you have to follow the shortest route. Obviously, availability depends on demand but coast-to-coast routes come up a lot and at the start of winter many cars need delivering to Florida. Joe Calder from Scotland picked up a car in Miami and had to deliver it to Oakland, across the bay from San Francisco. He told us:

It was such a thrill to be zipping along 'Alligator Alley' through the Everglades in a 'free' MGB, with the roof down. Then the gearbox gave out and suddenly I didn't feel so great. Fortunately, the tow truck reached me before the alligators, and the problem was fixed amazingly quickly considering that old British sports cars are a minority sport in Florida. But it wasn't looking good for the remaining 3500 miles to California, and took a day out of the week I had been allowed.

A driveaway is a great way to see some of America: especially the highways (only joking). If you have always imagined yourself in a road movie, or following in the tyre tracks of Jack Kerouac, then the experience is exhilarating. Even though I had to rush a little to make up time, I started my days real early and finished them real late, which meant I still got to see plenty of sights off the main drag. I'm glad I did it – I saw so much more than I would have done if I'd flown with Southwest or JetBlue.

Driveaway car companies are listed in the Yellow Pages under 'Automotive Transport and Driveaway Companies' (phone a week or two before you want to travel).

Contacts

All companies listed in this section can be contacted online, or by phone or email, unless stated otherwise.

CREWING A YACHT

Blue Water

La Galerie du Port, 8 Blvd d'Aguillon, Antibes 06600, France

☎ 020-7829 8446 (re-directed to France at local rate)

fax 00 33 4 93 34 35 93

ⓔ crew@bluewateryachting.com

Ⓦ www.bluewateryachting.com

This is a training school and crew-placement centre that matches crew with yachts worldwide. Most vacancies occur from December to April and May to July. Register via the website where there's a one-off registration fee of £10. Call or email every couple of days to see if you've got a placement. Terms will then be negotiated separately with the individual owner/skipper. Most crew using this service are experienced. Boats depart worldwide.

Crewseekers

Hawthorn House, Hawthorn Lane, Sarisbury Green, Southampton SO31 7BD

☎/fax 01489-578319

ⓔ info@crewseekers.co.uk

Ⓦ www.crewseekers.co.uk

This is the largest crewing agency in Europe. A six-month membership costs £50 and 12 months is £75. There are three levels of crew: Leisure Sailing, where crew fund their return fare to the boat and usually pay up to £10 a day towards costs; Boat Delivery for more experienced crew, where expenses are paid but there's no salary; and Professional Crew where all positions are paid. Vacancies occur year round if you're prepared to travel; the Late Availability section on the website is particularly useful. To register go online.

The Cruising Association (CA)

CA House, 1 Northey St, Limehouse Basin, London E14 8BT

☎ 020-7537 2828

fax 020-7537 2266

ⓔ office@cruising.org.uk

Ⓦ www.cruising.org.uk

The CA was founded in 1908. It has a large nautical library, a cruise-planning section and a crewing service that runs from February to June. During these months, five lists are published of skippers looking for crew and crew looking for a berth. On the first Wednesday of each month between February and June there's a meeting for skippers and crew. If you're not a member of the CA, the Crewing Service fee is £34 for skippers and £24 for crew. Many skippers will take novice crew.

Professional Yacht Deliveries Worldwide (PYD)

Witherslack, Grange-over-Sands, Cumbria LA11 6RQ

☎ 01539-552140

fax 01539-552131

ⓔ crew@pydww.com

Ⓦ www.pydww.com

PYD is one of the largest UK yacht deliverers, in need of hundreds of crew each year.

Types of Work: Deckhands & mates.

Timing & Length of Work: Boats are delivered year round; journey times depend on the route.

Destinations: Worldwide.

Costs/Pay: There's no registration fee. Crew are unpaid but all on-board expenses are covered. Travel to the boat is sometimes included, dependent on experience and qualifications.

Eligibility: Applicants must be aged at least 17. PDL will take relative beginners but expects some experience or a Competent Crew Certificate.

How to Apply: Send in your CV and the contact name of someone who has sailed with you to vouch for character and ability.

Reliance Yacht Management
1st Floor Suite, 127 Lynchford Rd,
Farnborough, Hants GU14 6ET
☎ 01252-378239
fax 01252-521736
e crew@reliance-yachts.com
w www.reliance-yachts.com
Reliance is one of the largest yacht deliverers in the world and needs 400 crew each year. Current vacancies are on the website. The office keeps in regular touch with the boats and can talk to concerned parents, if necessary.
Types of Work: Deckhand.
Timing & Length of Work: Boats are delivered year round; journey times depend on the route.
Destinations: Routes are mostly from Europe or South Africa to the Caribbean, North America, Central America, the South Pacific, the Seychelles, New Zealand & Australia.
Costs/Pay: There's a registration fee of £35 for one year. This will be returned if you don't get any work during this time. Crew are unpaid but all expenses are covered (ie, air fare to boat, board and lodging).
Eligibility: There's a minimum age of 17. Reliance will take relative beginners but expects some experience or a Competent Crew Certificate.
How to Apply: Download the registration form from the website or ring the office.

CRUISE SHIPS

The Agency Excellent Entertainment Ltd
Suite 2, The Business Centre, 120 West Heath Rd, London NW3 7TX
☎ 020-8458 4212
fax 020-8458 4572
e theagency@excellententertainment.biz
w www.excellententertainment.biz
The Agency supplies entertainers and entertainment staff to the cruise-line industry worldwide. It is the sole UK supplier to Disney Cruise Line and 12 others. Send your CV with a photo. If you get through this stage you will then be invited to an audition. The minimum age is between 18 and 21, depending on the cruise line.

Berkeley Scott Selection
11–13 Ockford Rd, Godalming, Surrey GU7 1QU
☎ 01483-791291
fax 0870 137 2169
e cruise@bsgplc.co.uk
w www.berkeley-scott.co.uk
Berkeley Scott recruits hotel positions from Assistant Waiter to Hotel Director, Chef de Partie to Restaurant Manager, for all the major international cruise lines, including Carnival, Celebrity, Costa, Cunard, Disney, Hebridean Island Cruises, Norwegian Cruise Line, P&O, Royal Caribbean and Silversea. It also recruits sales staff for retail outlets, entertainers, health & beauty staff, and handles all the casino staff for the Carnival Corporation (who own nine cruise lines). Most positions require one year's experience in a similar role; additionally, casino staff need experience in two card games and one dice game.

Crew's People International
c/o Harding Bros, Avonmouth Way, Avonmouth, Bristol BS11 8DD
☎ 0117-982 5961
fax 0117-982 8100
e sc@hardingbros.co.uk
w www.hardingbros.co.uk
Concessionaire for around 25 ships covering all the major cruise lines and supplying gift-shop staff, fitness instructors, spa consultants, beauticians and hairdressers. Retail staff must be aged at least 21, with three years' full-time retail experience. The minimum age for other positions is 19 and you must have relevant qualifications. If you're offered a job you'll need to obtain a number of safety and medical certificates before taking up the post.

Cruise Service Center Ltd (CSC)
19 Westfield Rd, Edgbaston, Birmingham B15 3QF

☎ 0121-454 2932
e office@cruiseservicecenter.com
W www.cruiseservicecenter.com
CSC recruits for middle to senior management, in positions within the hotel operation, for six top cruise lines. This includes the purser's office, food & beverage department, housekeeping and shore excursions. You need to have three years' full-time experience working in a 5-star hotel or similar.

CTI Group UK

Princes Exchange, Princes Square, Leeds LS1 4HY
☎ 0113-280 5930
fax 0113-280 6080
e cti-uk@cti-usa.com
W www.cti-usa.com
CTI is a worldwide hospitality recruitment agency specialising in the cruise industry. Most positions are within hotel operation (kitchen, bar, restaurant, purser's office and housekeeping). There are some entry-level positions but you'll still need around two years' experience in a high-quality environment.

Ocean Images UK

7 Home Farm Business Centre, Lockerley, Romsey, Hants SO51 0JT
☎ 01794-341818
fax 01794-341415
e jobs@ocean-images.com
W www.ocean-images.com
Ocean images works with 40 cruise ships across all the main cruise lines and has openings for over 180 ship photographers. All levels are considered and beginners are trained on board. Personality and sales skills are important, as all pay is commission-based. To apply, download the application form from the website.

VIP International

17 Charing Cross Rd, London WC2H 0QW
☎ 020-7930 0541
fax 020-7930 2860
e cruise@vipinternational.co.uk
W www.vipinternational.co.uk
VIP supplies housekeeping, food & beverage, pursers' office, culinary department and hotel operations staff to 10 leading cruise lines. You'll need at least three years' experience in a similar position with either a 4-star or 5-star international hotel or equivalent on a cruise liner.

TOUR GUIDING

American Council for International Studies (ACIS)

TM Department (Recruitment), AIFS (UK) Ltd, 38 Queen's Gate, London SW7 5HR
☎ 020-7590 7474
fax 020-7590 7475
e tmdepartment@acis.com
W www.acis.com
ACIS is an educational travel company working in partnership with US teachers to provide educational tours for them and their students. Most of the students are first-time travellers. Recruitment starts each autumn for the spring season and in spring for the summer season. There's a weekend training course and extensive back-up while on the road (24-hour emergency line).
Types of Work: ACIS offers jobs as tour managers.
Timing & Length of Work: Tours last between one week and 10 days, and the seasons run February to May (busiest at Easter) and early June to end of July.
Destinations: Either one European country, one European city or all over Europe, depending on the tour.
Costs/Pay: Daily rates are discussed at interviews. On top there are tips, plus ACIS pay for in-country expenses and return travel.
Eligibility: The minimum age is 21. Applicants must be graduates or students who can speak a second European language (French, German or Spanish preferred).
How to Apply: Apply online. There will then be a panel interview.

Busabout

258 Vauxhall Bridge Rd, London
SW1V 1BS
☎ 020-7950 1661
fax 020-7950 1662
e recruitment@busabout.co.uk
w www.busabout.com

Busabout offers a hop-on hop-off coach transportation service for independent travellers in Europe. Recruitment starts in January for the summer season. If you're successful you'll get a four-week training course around Europe. You will be expected to work more than one full season.

Types of Work: On-board guides.
Timing & Length of Work: The summer season runs from April to October.
Destinations: Nine countries in Europe.
Costs/Pay: The £300 training bond is refundable after working two full consecutive seasons. Pay is around £150 gross per week, including all accommodation.
Eligibility: The minimum age is 25. Familiarity with Europe is important and a second European language helpful.
How to Apply: Download the application form from the website and send it in with a colour photo. There's a group interview where you give a short talk to the panel, followed by a longer private one.

Casterbridge Tours

Salcombe House, Long St, Sherbourne,
Dorset DT9 3BU
☎ 01935-810810
fax 01935-815815
e tourops@casterbridge-tours.co.uk
w www.casterbridgetours.com

Casterbridge runs educational and cultural tours for US and UK schools, colleges and adult groups, mostly in the UK and Europe. The trekking division has tours worldwide. Training takes place over a weekend.

Types of Work: Tour guides.
Timing & Length of Work: Tours of around 10 days run year round. The busiest time is March to June.
Destinations: Worldwide.

Costs/Pay: The daily fee depends on experience and the number of languages you speak. The rate is negotiated at interview.
Eligibility: Applicants must be aged at least 21.
How to Apply: Positions are advertised in national newspapers but you can also phone or email the office.

Contiki Holidays For 18-35s

Wells House, 15 Elmfield Rd, Bromley,
Kent BR1 1LS
☎ 020-8290 6777
fax 020-8225 4246
e liesa.bissett@contiki.co.uk
w www.contiki.com

Contiki is a tour operator offering 'soft adventure' coach holidays in the UK, Europe, the USA, Canada, Australia and New Zealand for those aged 18 to 35. Offices recruit regionally, so this office only deals with Europe, from October to March for the following summer and winter seasons. Six weeks of on-the-road training is given during February, March and April.

Types of Work: Tour managers.
Timing & Length of Work: Trips range from five to 46 days and run year round. Tour managers usually work from April to October in their first year. Short summer contracts are also available where you train in May and finish at the beginning of August.
Destinations: Europe.
Costs/Pay: The daily rate is from £40 for your first year, plus accommodation, meals and transport.
Eligibility: The minimum age is 23.
How to Apply: Email for an application pack.

Exodus Travels

9 Weir Rd, London SW12 0LT
☎ 020-8675 5550
fax 020-8673 0779
e info@exodus.co.uk
w www.exodus.co.uk

Exodus runs overland trips as well as a variety of biking, walking, trekking, snow-based, European and adventure tours. Recruitment takes place in February. Training takes around three weeks and usually includes a first-aid course, a summer mountain-leadership training course, and an overseas training trip shadowing an experienced tour leader.

Types of Work: Tour leaders.

Timing & Length of Work: You can be away working from six weeks to three months at a time. The busiest times are Easter, May to October, and Christmas. There's usually six to seven months' of work a year.

Destinations: Africa, Asia, Europe, Antarctica, Australasia & the Americas.

Costs/Pay: Pay on average is around £140 a week, plus good tips, accommodation and food. You're not paid when you're not leading.

Eligibility: The minimum age is 25. Applicants need independent travel experience, language skills, people skills and a strong interest in outdoor pursuits.

How to Apply: Job vacancies are placed on the website year round. Ads are also placed in TNT and Wanderlust. Please apply for specific positions, although CVs sent on spec will be looked at.

Explore Worldwide

1 Frederick St, Aldershot, Hants
GU11 1LQ
☎ 01252-760200
fax 01252-760201
e info@exploreworldwide.com
w www.exploreworldwide.com

Explore is a small-group adventure travel company. It recruits year round but mostly in early spring for the summer season and late summer for the winter season. All vacancies are advertised on their website. The three- or four-week training course includes a two-day wilderness first-aid course, followed by on-the-road training with an experienced tour leader. Explore is looking for a minimum commitment of one year but ideally more.

Types of Work: Tour leaders.

Timing & Length of Work: Trips last from a weekend to one month. A leader can be

overseas working on back-to-back tours for up to six months.

Destinations: 100 countries worldwide.

Costs/Pay: There's a £200 training bond, refundable after the first season. The basic starting salary is around £25 a day, including accommodation, tips and often meals.

Eligibility: The minimum age is 23. Independent travel experience is essential and a second language is preferable.

How to Apply: The application form is six pages long and has problem-solving sections on it. There's a two-hour individual interview testing your descriptive powers and problem-solving skills. You can download the application form from the website.

High Places Ltd

Globe Centre, Penistone Rd, Sheffield
S6 3AE
☎ 0114-275 7500
fax 0114-275 3870
e treks@highplaces.co.uk
w www.highplaces.co.uk

High Places is a small independent tour operator specialising in treks and mountaineering worldwide. It recruits year round. Training consists of shadowing an experienced leader on an overseas trip. It is expected you'll do at least two consecutive seasons.

Types of Work: Tour leaders.

Timing & Length of Work: Trips are for 18 to 27 days. A leader would normally do two or three back-to-back trips, which comprises an average year's work.

Destinations: Peru, Ecuador, Bolivia, Patagonia, Iceland, the Himalayas, Eastern Europe, New Zealand, Africa & Canada.

Costs/Pay: The daily rate depends on experience and the nature of the trip. Accommodation, meals and transport are included.

Eligibility: The minimum age is 21. You'll need a Summer & Winter Mountain Leadership Certificate (see Gap Year, Wilderness & Jungle Survival under Contacts in the Courses chapter) and a current first-aid certificate.

The Imaginative Traveller

1 Betts Ave, Martlesham Heath, Suffolk
IP5 3RH
☎ 01473-636066
fax 01473-636016
e jobs@imtrav.net
W www.imaginative-traveller.com
This is an adventure travel operator specialising in small-group travel to the Middle East, Asia and Europe. Recruitment is year round but main times are January and May. Training comprises two days in the UK followed by three to four weeks overseas. Most tour leaders do their first contract in Egypt. The initial contract is for 12 months; subsequent contracts are shorter if required.
Types of Work: Tour leaders.
Timing & Length of Work: One-week to four-week trips run year round.
Destinations: Europe, the Middle East, Asia & Europe.
Costs/Pay: Pay is £13.50 a day, plus meals and accommodation.
Eligibility: The minimum age is 22. Travel experience is essential.
How to Apply: Use the application form on the website.

Kumuka Expeditions

40 Earls Court Rd, London W8 6EJ
☎ 020-7937 8855
fax 020-7937 6664
e humanresources@kumuka.com
W www.kumuka.com
Kumuka is a specialist in adventure holidays and overland travel. It recruits year round. Tour leaders are usually employed on annual contracts, although there's seasonal work in Europe between April and October. Four to six weeks of training takes place in London and overseas.
Types of Work: Tour leaders.
Timing & Length of Work: Trips last from four days to 15 weeks. Tour leaders will work for a maximum of six months overseas.
Destinations: Europe, South & Central America, Africa, the Middle East & Asia.

Costs/Pay: Pay depends on experience and on which trip you take. Accommodation, food and excursions are normally included.
Eligibility: The minimum age is 23. A second language is preferred, and you must have travelled in at least two continents.
How to Apply: Apply via the website or email the office.

Top Deck

7 Cambridge Court, 210 Shepherds Bush Rd, London W6 7NJ
☎ 020-7371 3232
fax 020-7751 1204
e ops@topdecktravel.co.uk
W www.topdecktravel.co.uk
Top Deck is a budget adventure travel company. Tours travel by coach or public transport. Recruitment details are on the website. Interviews are held from August to December. Training trips last six weeks, starting late March. Crew are expected to work with the company for at least 18 months.
Types of Work: Tour leaders.
Timing & Length of Work: Trips run year round but the majority are March to October. They range from weekends to 50 days.
Destinations: Europe & Turkey.
Costs/Pay: The training trip costs £325; £175 of it is refundable after two calendar years with the company. Pay starts from £150 per week (including a performance-related bonus). Accommodation and food is included.
Eligibility: You must be at least 23. Travel experience is essential.
How to Apply: Download the application from the website and return it with a photo. Group interviews, where you have to give a speech, are followed by individual interviews.

Travelbag Adventures

15 Turk St, Alton, Hants GU34 1AG
☎ 01420-541007
fax 01420-541022

e jobs@travelbag-adventures.com
W www.travelbag-adventures.com
Travelbag is an adventure tour operator with a worldwide programme for small groups. Most recruitment takes place in April and May. Office-based training takes place over a long weekend followed by a one- or two-week training tour with an experienced tour leader. Tour leaders are employed on short fixed-term contracts.
Types of Work: Tour leaders.
Timing & Length of Work: Trips last from one to three weeks; back-to-back trips mean you could be out in one country for up to six months. Trips run year round but there's less work in winter.
Destinations: Spain, Greece, France, India, China, Japan, Mexico, Argentina, Chile, Morocco, Libya, Egypt, Uganda & Ethiopia.
Costs/Pay: You'd be a self-employed sub-contractor on a basic day rate that depends on experience. Accommodation and meals are provided as per the group itinerary (ie, if your tour is B&B then you get B&B only).
Eligibility: The minimum age is 25. Travel knowledge is essential, a university degree and languages preferable and outdoor experience/certificate useful.
How to Apply: Travelbag is happy to receive on-spec CVs. It usually advertises in *Wanderlust* magazine.

Venture Abroad
Rayburn House, Parcel Terrace, Derby DE1 1LY
☎ 01332-342050
fax 01332-224960
e charlottel@rayburntours.co.uk
W www.ventureabroad.co.uk
Venture Abroad's tours are aimed at scouts and guides. Recruitment takes place in February for the summer season. One or two training days take place in the office then the rest takes place in the overseas resort around Easter or early June.
Types of Work: Tour leaders.
Timing & Length of Work: Trips are between 10 to 12 days. Tour leaders live out in the destination from June to August.
Destinations: Switzerland, Belgium, France, Canada, Malta & Iceland.
Costs/Pay: Pay is £180 per week, accommodation and all transport provided.
Eligibility: Applicants must be undergraduates or postgraduates aged at least 18. German-language skills preferred.
How to Apply: Ads are placed in careers' offices or language departments of universities. Otherwise ring or email the office.

BEHIND THE WHEEL

Busabout
See under Tour Guiding earlier for contact details. Busabout has 18 buses in Europe during the summer. Drivers are expected to work more than one summer season. There's a five-week training course, most of which takes place in Europe where you learn the routes.
Types of Work: Drivers.
Timing & Length of Work: The summer season runs from April 1 to the end of October.
Destinations: Nine countries in Europe.
Costs/Pay: There's a £300 training bond that's refundable after the first season. Pay is approximately £300 gross a week, increasing annually.
Eligibility: The minimum age is 24. You'll need to have a PCV licence.
How to Apply: Download the application form from the website and mail it with a copy of your licence and a current photograph. There are usually two interviews for successful candidates.

Contiki Holidays For 18-35s
See under Tour Guiding earlier for contact details. All information for tour managers is the same for tour drivers except the following:
Costs/Pay: The package is available on request and is dependent on experience.
Eligibility: The minimum age is 23. You'll need a PCV licence plus on-the-road experience.

Dragoman Overland Travel Ltd

Camp Green, Kenton Rd, Debenham,
Suffolk IP14 6LA
☎ 01728-861133
fax 01728-861127
e info@dragoman.co.uk
W www.dragoman.co.uk

Dragoman is the largest overland company in the UK, offering a slightly more up-market experience. Recruitment takes place year round – vacancies are advertised on its website. The 12- to 14-week training course is held at Camp Green and then you're a trainee for the first six months on the road. There are always two drivers on a trip. They work as tour guides too.

Types of Work: Leader drivers, co-drivers, leader mechanics & co-driver mechanics.

Timing & Length of Work: Trips are for two to 42 weeks and run year round.

Destinations: South America, Africa & Asia.

Costs/Pay: There's a daily rate, which increases annually. Pay also depends on experience and skills. Accommodation, meals and transport are provided.

Eligibility: The minimum age is 25. A PCV licence and first-aid certificate are essential.

How to Apply: Contact the office for an application form.

Encounter Overland

Camp Green, Kenton Rd, Debenham,
Suffolk IP14 6LA
☎ 01728-862222
fax 01728-861127
e wild@encounter.co.uk
W www.encounter.co.uk

This is a budget overland company aiming directly at the student market. All recruitment contact details are the same as for Dragoman. One big difference is that there's only one driver who doubles as a tour guide.

Types of Work: Leader mechanics.

Exodus Travels

See under Tour Guiding earlier for contact details. Exodus runs overland expeditions and recruits expedition leaders who drive the trucks and tour guide as well. You will be expected to work for a minimum of two years. Three months' training in the UK is followed by six months' training on the road. There are always two drivers on overland trips who guide as well.

Types of Work: Expedition leaders.

Timing & Length of Work: Trips run year round and last from three to 30 weeks.

Destinations: Worldwide.

Costs/Pay: Pay is between £4000 and £6000 per annum depending on experience, all living expenses apart from beer money included.

Eligibility: Applicants must be aged at least 25 and have a PCV or LGV licence, mechanical skills, travel experience and people skills.

How to Apply: Job vacancies are placed on the website year round. Apply for specific positions rather than sending in your CV speculatively. Related experience is looked on favourably.

Guerba World Travel Ltd

Wessex House, 40 Station Rd, Westbury,
Wilts BA13 3JN
☎ 01373-826611
fax 01373-858351
e info@guerba.co.uk
W www.guerba.com

Guerba offers adventure and discovery holidays, including overland trips. Training involves 18 months on the road with a qualified leader driver. There are two drivers, doubling as tour guides, on any overland trip. Recruitment takes place year round.

Types of Work: Leader drivers & trainee drivers.

Timing & Length of Work: Trips are for one to 12 weeks. Drivers will normally be on the road for 18 months.

Destination: Africa.

Costs/Pay: Pay is from £60 to £250 a week, depending on experience. All expenses are paid.

Eligibility: Applicants must be aged 25 or over and have a LGV licence (no mechanical skills necessary).
How to Apply: Send in your CV and then there'll be questionnaires and interviews.

Kumuka Expeditions

See under Tour Guiding earlier for contact details. Overland trips have a separate driver and tour guide/leader. All information for tour guides is the same for drivers except the following:
Destinations: Central & South America, Asia, Africa & the Middle East.
Eligibility: Applicants must be aged 25 or over, have a LGV or PCV licence and sound mechanical knowledge.

Top Deck

See under Tour Guiding earlier for contact details. All information for tour guides is the same for drivers except that the training includes a couple of days at Top Deck's Dutch coach company studying coach maintenance. Also:
Costs/Pay: The training trip costs £325; £175 is refundable after two calendar years with the company. The first year's pay starts from £190 per week, accommodation and food provided.
Eligibility: Applicants must be aged 23 or over with a European or International Coach licence and some mechanical knowledge. Travel experience is essential.

Au Pairing & Working with Kids

Working with children during your gap year means spending anything from two to 12 months in one country. This is a great opportunity to get to know a foreign culture and people really well, especially if you're an au pair and living with a family.

Other people's children – you either love them or hate them! Before you decide to spend either part of your gap year or the whole thing working with them, it'd be wise to know which category you fall into. Get some experience working with kids either at a local nursery or school, or spend time with your relatives' children when they're awake (very important, baby-sitting the little terror(s) when sleeping doesn't count). Does the time go quickly and everyone have fun or does every minute seem like an hour and every missed poo in the potty a drag to clean up?

You'll have to show varying degrees of time spent caring for children when you apply for these types of jobs, anyway. The programmes in America are particularly hot on this – and good for them. Working with youngsters is one of the most responsible jobs you could ever do in your gap year and no-one wants a repeat of the 1998 Louise Woodward case where a British au pair was found guilty of shaking an eight-month-old baby to death (the verdict of second-degree murder was later reduced to manslaughter).

This chapter looks at working abroad as an au pair, au pair plus, mothers' help and with children on holiday camps in return for pocket money. It does not cover voluntary work with children in orphanages or on the streets – see the Volunteering, Conservation & Expeditions chapter for this.

Working as an Au Pair

According to Council of Europe guidelines, to work as an au pair you should be single and aged between 17 and 30. In reality, though, many countries prefer au pairs to be at least 18, and the upper age limit is sometimes 27.

You pay to travel out to your host family. Once there you will be expected to work up to 30 hours a week (often six hours a day over five days) and baby-sit two nights a week. Usually an au pair will stay with a family for a year (September to June), although contracts can be anything from three months upwards. Both sides are usually entitled to end the contract by giving at least a week's notice. In return you get pocket money of around £45 a week – this can vary slightly depending on the generosity of your family and also the country (you get less in Spain or Italy). You should also expect your own room, three meals a day, two days off a week plus time to attend classes. It is also usual to get a week's holiday for every six months worked. If you work more than 30 hours a week then you should get paid for it.

The words 'Au Pair' mean 'on an equal footing'. This means that au pairs should live and be treated like a member of the family. Because of this, it is a good idea to sit down with your family when you arrive and work out exactly what they will expect from you and vice versa. Au-pair duties vary but include either some or all of the following:

- Waking the children and getting them dressed.
- Preparing or helping to prepare breakfast.
- Clearing up the children's rooms.

- Picking up and tidying away toys from every room in the house, constantly (remember that other people pay personal trainers to devise this type of exercise).
- Taking and/or picking the children up from nursery or school.
- Some shopping.
- Playing with the children.
- Helping to prepare the children's tea.
- Bathing the children and putting them to bed.
- Sweeping up (there's enough mess under a toddler's high chair after meals to top a family-sized pizza), vacuuming, or ironing the children's clothes.
- Accompanying the family on outings or on holiday.

If you want to earn a little more money then there's the option of being an Au Pair Plus. This is similar to being an au pair except that you work more hours – usually seven hours a day, five days a week. Or you could work even longer as a Mother's Help or Nanny: both are full-time positions. A mother's help is expected to work between 45 to 50 hours a week and does a lot more housework and cooking. You need to have a little more experience of childcare but no professional qualifications. The pay is around £150 to £200 per week. Nannying is probably not an option for your gap year because it takes time to get the proper qualifications and experience so that you can take sole charge of children. The pay, though, can be good at around £175 to £350 a week, usually live-in. Nannies are also in demand by holiday resorts and companies.

The best and safest way to get a job as an au pair abroad is to go through a UK agency. Although there are lots of them specialising in matching foreign au pairs with British families, there are fewer and fewer doing it the other way around. This is because the industry is in a bit of a mess. Currently, an agency cannot charge more than £40 for finding you a job and this fee is only charged once you have accepted a family. This means that you can register with lots of agencies that will all work to find you a job but only one of them will be paid. In addition, £40 doesn't really cover the time and effort needed to place you with

---

Is it a Man's World?

For the reserved British male, working as an au pair in Europe requires something of an adjustment. I had no experience of childcare and was surprised by the hands-on nature of the job; not only was I expected to bathe and dress the children but I also found myself in the unenviable position of having to insert suppositories and clean up vomit and diarrhoea. I also discovered that children in France are generally much more affectionate than they are in the UK and the constant kissing and cuddling they expect of you can take some getting used to.

In the family, I was shocked to discover that some sexist attitudes still prevail. Unlike their previous au pairs I wasn't expected to do the ironing – instead I was responsible for the suitably manly task of chopping wood for the log fire.

The two young boys wanted to build dens, go for long bike rides and play rough and tumble. I came to enjoy endless afternoons running around the forest restaging epic battles using branches and sticks for guns.

When my year was over I was immensely sad to leave the children; my year with them had not only improved my French but it had also taught me important lessons about myself. And I'm sure the wood-chopping and suppository-inserting skills I learned will come in handy one day!

Matt Cain

a suitable family. And, if this wasn't enough, it is expected that sometime in 2003 the government will bring in legislation making it illegal to charge this £40 fee. For the au pair wanting to work abroad this means two things: a) many agencies will refuse to find you work because it isn't financially viable; and b) those that do will not be able to spend as much time as they'd like matching students with families. Having said this, most of the agencies listed under Contacts at the end of this chapter are members of the International Au Pair Association (IAPA; W www.iapa.org) and will definitely help you find a family through their partner agencies in the organisation. The majority of placements work out well, like Lydia Rae's in Vienna:

I loved my family and we got on like a house on fire right from the start. The children bought me little welcome presents for when I arrived (thank goodness I thought of bringing them some toy London red buses from home too). The parents had given a lot of thought to local buddies for me and had a list of people my age for me to contact and try to make friends with during my stay. They really made me feel like one of the family and I didn't want to leave when it was time to go; I especially didn't want to say goodbye to the children. I loved the city too – the coffee houses (Starbucks doesn't come close), the apfelstrudel, the music, the art. In my room at uni I have lots of Klimt posters on the wall reminding me of my time there.

However, despite the best au pair and family vetting, some things don't get picked up on and this was the case with 21-year-old Patricia Howton's family:

I worked as an au pair for a French family in Brittany. There was a lot of tension in the house – they had three children: a girl of six, a boy of nine and a newborn baby. The parents didn't get on and the children were really naughty and refused to do anything I asked. At first I wasn't happy but I tried to make the most of it. The father taught me how to windsurf and the mother started to see me as a friend; even the children behaved better as they got to know me. My French really improved, so did my cooking (one evening for a dinner party we had to cut some sweet little red crabs open while they were still alive – that was horrible), and I learnt a lot about caring for babies. It was a summer placement so I only stayed with the family for three months but at the end of this time we were all sad to part – I think I had made a difference in everyone's lives at a difficult time. I kept in touch with the mother and a year later found out that the parents had separated.

Surprisingly, the au pair industry is unregulated, which makes choosing an agency a bit of a minefield. Many of the good ones are members of IAPA, the Recruitment & Employment Confederation (REC; W www.rec.uk.com) or the newly founded British Au Pair Agencies Association (BAPAA; W www.bapaa.org.uk). All three have lists of their members online.

If you want to get a job through an agency then it's best to apply two or three months before you want to travel. If you're a bloke it could take longer because, sorry to say it, you're not in such demand. Most families also prefer a nonsmoker and often want a car driver. Agencies will also need you to provide two character references, two childcare references and the results of a medical. You'll then be given a telephone interview.

You need to match your family as well as the family matching you. This means thinking carefully about what type of family you want. Looking after one child is obviously much easier than two, and once you've got more children than hands it can get tricky. The age of the children is also important – Pauline Almond had this to say of the children she looked after in Australia:

Helen was five and the boy was just six months. Helen went to school and so she wasn't around during the day but needed getting ready in the mornings; I also collected her from school and did activities with her. She was so easy to entertain: we read together, chatted a lot, visited her friends' houses and went to cafés and museums. We did all the things that I find interesting and she found them interesting too, so time with her went really quickly. You really had to keep your eye on her though. One time at a big playground I lost her for a few minutes because I'd turned away to talk to someone. They were the longest minutes of my life and I was frantic.

The boy, Mathew, was totally different. If I were honest I'd say he was a bit boring because I couldn't do much with him and he lost interest in everything really quickly. One real bonus, though, was that if you put him down somewhere he stayed where you put him because he couldn't crawl yet.

You can, of course, fix up an au pair placement yourself. There are ads for au pairs in *The Lady* magazine (**W** www.lady.co.uk), published on Tuesdays (top tip: if reading it in public, wrap it inside a copy of *Heat* magazine). Also try London's ads paper *Loot* (**W** www.loot .com), published on Wednesdays. In addition, there are internet sites like Au Pair Wizard at **W** www.au-pairs.com and Au Pair Job Match at **W** www.aupairs.co.uk where au pairs and families can go online to find each other. These options all have risks attached to them on both sides – no-one has vetted you and no-one has properly vetted the families. If you don't want to go through a UK agency then you can always register direct with a foreign one, either in the UK or when abroad (refer to the IAPA listing of overseas agencies on their website).

So, where can you go as an au pair? You can work in any country in the European Economic Area (EEA). New members are continually being considered but at the moment they include:

Austria	Germany	Liechtenstein	Spain
Belgium	Greece	Luxembourg	Sweden
Denmark	Iceland	Netherlands	UK
Finland	Ireland	Norway	
France	Italy	Portugal	

You can also work in the countries included in the official au pair scheme. There's an up-to-date list on the Home Office website at **W** http://194.203.40.90/default.asp?pageID=110. At present these are:

Andorra	Faroe Islands	Monaco
Bosnia-Herzegovina	Greenland	Poland
Bulgaria	Hungary	Romania
Croatia	Latvia	San Marino
Cyprus	Lithuania	Slovak Republic
Czech Republic	Macedonia	Slovenia
Estonia	Malta	Turkey

Despite the long list of countries, in reality most placements are found in Western Europe (except Portugal) and very few in Eastern Europe, as they don't really have the culture of in-coming au pairs. Turkey, France, Spain and Italy are desperate for British au pairs and some of the Scandinavian countries, as well as Holland, are on the up. You can also au pair in Australia and New Zealand for three months on a Working Holiday visa. Au pairing in America is booming – see the following Working in North America as an Au Pair section for more details. In general you don't need a visa for most of the countries where you can au pair but do check with the embassy or your agency before departure.

Working in North America as an Au Pair

Au pairing in America is big business. Each year thousands of British gappers go to the USA to au pair on US government-sponsored programmes. The deal is so different to au pairing in Europe or elsewhere that it really needs covering separately.

These programmes are represented through any UK agency that says it can place you in the USA – see Contacts. All the programmes are much of a muchness but the biggest is run by Au Pair in America, part of the American Institute for Foreign Studies – see Contacts. The options and requirements for this programme are as follows and will be similar to any programme you go on:

Duration of Stay: One year. There are up to four departure dates a month.

Age: 18 to 26.

Standard Programme: Up to 45 hours of work a week at around £85 per week. There's also a study allowance of £300 provided by the host family because under the rules of your visa you need to study for a minimum of three hours a week. If you complete your one year then your flights to/from the USA are free; if you don't then you need to pay your own homeward airfare. You'll need to show proof of 200 hours recent childcare for non-family members and have had a driving licence for at least six months. There's a £45 non-refundable placement fee, a £60 contribution towards insurance, and a £245 good faith payment returnable upon completion of your one year.

Au Pair Extraordinaire: Up to 45 hours of work a week at around £122 per week. You need to have completed a full-time two-year academic course in childcare or be 19 and have two years' full-time experience as a nanny, childcare provider or nursery school teacher. You also need to have had a driving licence for around six months. All the fees are the same as on the Standard Programme.

EduCare: Up to 30 hours of care a week at around £65 per week. This programme is mostly for families with school-age children and au pairs who want to do more studying. Students usually arrive late July/August or December. The study allowance is £612 and you're placed in areas where you can attend a good college or university. You'll be expected to study for at least six hours a week. You need a minimum of 200 hours childcare experience and to be an experienced car driver. Your fees include £45 for placement, £460 for the programme and £153 for comprehensive insurance. All the other conditions are the same as for the Standard Programme.

What else can you Expect: A private room, three meals a day, time off to attend classes, one weekend off per month and one weekend per month holiday.

When to Apply: Usually three months before departure but that depends on how long it is taking the American embassy to process J-1 Visitor Exchange visas.

Selection Process: This is rigorous. You will be interviewed in person and need to have three written references (two childcare and one character). You will need to show a clear police record, submit a medical form and be psychometrically tested. It is good to know that the selection process for the host families is just as rigorous.

Visas: A J-1 Visitor Exchange visa is valid for 12 months but includes a one-month grace period after the visa has finished. This means that if your visa expires on August 28 then you don't need to leave the country until September 28, allowing you one month's travel in the USA. Due to security concerns, J-1 visas are currently taking longer to process and a personal interview in London or Belfast is now part of the process.

Orientation & Training: Before you join your family there's a four-day Orientation Programme, which includes basic first aid, 24 hours of child-development training and eight hours of child-safety training. After settling in the home, au pairs are also encouraged to complete an Infant/Child CPR and First Aid certification programme, paid for by Au Pair America and run with the American Red Cross.

In-country Support: A community counsellor is allocated to every au pair and he/she will either see or call you within 28 hours of arriving. There are then monthly cluster meetings where all the au pairs in the area get together to bond and chat.

Going to the USA to au pair is really popular, perhaps because you hear so many good reports back from gappers who've taken this option, like Alison Marriott. She says:

I was offered a job in Seattle looking after a two-year-old boy. This involved general care during the day whilst his parents went to work at Boeing, and some housework and occasional cooking for the family. My weekends and evenings were free. I was immediately welcomed as part of the family and I quickly made friends. I joined a gym, played tennis and gradually enjoyed a busy social life. I was taken on holiday to Disneyland with the family and also managed a trip to Canada. After 12 months of work I had one month left to do what I liked. This I spent living on an Indian Reservation. The American way of life is fast and they are very patriotic but they are also incredibly friendly and go out of their way to make you feel welcome. My whole experience in the USA was a memorable one. I learnt a lot about myself and other people and still remain in contact with friends I made there. I would encourage anyone who has this opportunity to grab it with both hands.

On the other hand, au pairing in Canada is not easy. Canada's version of the au pair scheme is the Live-in Caregiver Programme regulated by the Canadian Government. To qualify you'll need to have completed six months' full-time training in a field related to your job in Canada or 12 months of full-time paid employment in a related field.

Children's Holidays

An integral part of American life is sending their kids to camp. There are over 12,000 summer camps in the USA for children aged between six and 16. They spend from one to eight weeks at these residential centres following a packed multi-activity agenda during the day and sleeping in tents or cabins at night. Most camps are in the countryside, beside a lake or in the mountains, so the emphasis is on outdoor life. For many American children camp is heaven on a stick.

These camps are run by thousands of adults who come from all over the world. Most jobs are as a general counsellor or a specialist counsellor. Both involve looking after the children's welfare, being mother, father, sister, brother and friend to them, as well as helping out with morning, afternoon and evening activities. As a specialist counsellor, though, you'll be instructing them in your speciality, whether it is drama or watersports. A typical day looks something like this:

- 7am: Get the children up and dressed, and tidy tent or cabin.
- Supervise breakfast.
- Help with morning activities or teach.
- Supervise lunch.
- Help with afternoon activities or teach.

- Supervise dinner.
- Help with evening activities or teach.
- 9.30pm: Bedtime routine with youngsters, including cabin/tent chat.
- 10.30pm: Bedtime routine with older campers.
- Fall exhausted into bed yourself.

The list of camp activities is endless but includes all sorts of team sports (eg, football, basketball), watersports (eg, water-skiing, sailing), arts & crafts (eg, pottery, painting), entertainment (eg, drama, singing), outdoor pursuits (eg, horse riding, orienteering), music, science and IT. Julia Ferguson's special interest was horses and she writes:

I had the time of my life at camp. I was working all day in the sun, getting a tan, and being paid for it. Don't get me wrong, I worked harder than I have ever done before but with great people and I made so many good friends. I was a general tent counsellor and looked after three lots of girls aged 12 or 13. We all lived in platform tents. My speciality was horse riding so I helped to look after 24 horses in the stables. We taught riding, took the youngsters out on trail rides, and sometimes dressed the horses up like Disney characters.

Life at camp for adults isn't all fun and games though. You practically spend 24 hours a day with the kids, living and sleeping in the same tent or cabin. The days are long and physically demanding. Being responsible for a group of children, particularly their safety, is also very tiring. And you can't relax at the end of the day with a ciggie or a beer because smoking and drinking are usually prohibited. In addition, you'll only get around six days off during your nine-week stint. On the plus side, though, this means you'll be able to save all your pay to go towards your free travel time afterwards.

In terms of money, some camps and some programmes pay better than others but that has to be weighed up against their costs – see Contacts for full details. Once you've done the sums you'll usually still end up in credit but as pocket money often depends on your age (you get more if you're older), school-leavers may only have as little as £50 left over. But, don't forget that this is on top of free flights, accommodation and food.

To work at a camp, get in touch with the companies listed in the following Contacts section. Many ask you to apply in the autumn before you want to go and competition for jobs can be fierce. Peter Ritchie offered this tip:

I put quite a lot of effort into my application. I made a collage out of photos of me doing various activities (canoeing, swimming, spear-carrier in school play) and submitted it. I thought this really made the point that I was willing to turn my hand to anything and that I enjoyed doing all the things that go on at camp. I also put some pics in there of me doing stuff with my uncle's children so that they knew I was child-friendly.

Although many gappers will be after the American experience of camp, many of the camps in Europe, Russia or the UK are modelled on the American type. In Russia, though, they're more basic and less organised. The pay is also atrocious (you'll be lucky to earn £1 a day) and sometimes you also pay for your return flights. But, hey, you're not doing it for the money – the opportunity to work in this part of the world is very unusual.

Contact details for European and Russian opportunities follow. In the UK, try contacting Barracudas (☎ 0845 123 5299; W www.barracudas.co.uk) or Kids Klub (☎ 01449-742700; W www.kidsklub.co.uk).

Contacts

WORKING AS AN AU PAIR

Almondbury Au Pair & Nanny Agency
4 Napier Rd, Holland Park, London
W14 8LQ
☎/fax 01288-359159
e admin@aupair-agency.com or
e admin@nanny-agency.com
w www.aupair-agency.com or
w www.nanny-agency.com
This is one of Europe's largest internet-based agencies for au pairs and nannies. There's full agency backup if things go wrong.
Types of Work: Au pairs, nannies and mother's helps.
Timing & Length of Work: Placements of between six to 12 months are available year round.
Destinations: Europe, the USA, Canada, Russia, Japan & Hong Kong.
Costs/Pay: There's no agency fee.
Organisation Memberships: Universal Au Pair Association.

Anderson Au-Pairs & Nannies
86 High St, Hythe, Kent CT21 5AJ
☎ 01303-260971
fax 01303-230276
e andersonau-pairs@clan-anderson
.freeserve.co.uk
w www.childcare-europe.com
Founded in 1996, au pairs are provided with contact lists, emergency telephone numbers and full support through their international partner agencies.
Types of Work: Au pairs, au pairs plus, nannies and mother's helps.
Timing & Length of Work: Placements of three months to two years are available year round.
Destinations: Western Europe, USA or Canada.
Costs/Pay: There's an agency fee of £40 until the law changes.
Organisation Memberships: IAPA, founding member of BAPAA.

A-One Au Pairs & Nannies
Top Floor, Union House, Union St,
Andover, Hants SP10 1PA
☎ 01264-332500
fax 01264-362050
e info@aupairsetc.co.uk
w www.aupairsetc.co.uk
Founded in 1997, A-one places au pairs in the UK and abroad. It's southern England's regional coordinator for Au Pair in America, covering Hampshire, Dorset, Devon, Cornwall and parts of Wiltshire.
Types of Work: Au pairs, au pairs plus, nannies and mother's helps.
Timing & Length of Work: Placements are available year round, for a maximum of one to two years. There are also some summer-holiday placements.
Destinations: All EU countries, Switzerland, Turkey, the USA, Canada, Australia, New Zealand & South Africa.
Costs/Pay: There's no agency fee.
Organisation Memberships: IAPA, founding member of BAPAA.

Au Pair in America
American Institute for Foreign Studies
37 Queen's Gate, London SW7 5HR
☎ 020-7581 7311
fax 020-7581 7355
e info@aupairamerica.co.uk
w www.aupairamerica.co.uk
Au Pair in America has placed over 48,000 au pairs since 1986 and is the largest programme of its kind. See Working in North America as an Au Pair earlier for full details.
Organisation Memberships: IAPA.

Au Pairs Direct
7 Little Meadow Rd, Bowdon, Cheshire
WA14 3PG
☎ 0161-941 5356
fax 0161-929 0102
e enquiries@aupairsdirect.co.uk
w www.aupairsdirect.co.uk
Founded in 1989, this is northwest England's regional coordinator for Au Pair in America.

Types of Work: Au pairs, au pair extraordinaires and nannies.

Timing & Length of Work: Placements are available year round. They are for one year in the USA and a minimum of six months in Europe.

Destinations: The USA, France & Spain.

Costs/Pay: There's a placement fee of £40 for European placements, until the law is changed.

Organisation Memberships: IAPA, founding member of BAPAA.

Au Pair Network International (APNI)
118 Cromwell Rd, London SW7 4ET
☎ 020-7370 3798
fax 020-7370 4718
e sam@apni.org.uk
w www.apni.co.uk
Founded in 1992, APNI has long-standing relationships with international agencies.

Types of Work: Au pairs, au pairs plus, nannies and mother's helps.

Timing & Length of Work: Placements are available year round and are usually for one academic year. There are some summer-holiday placements of around three months.

Destinations: Europe & the USA.

Costs/Pay: There's a placement charge of £40, until the law changes.

Organisation Memberships: IAPA, Federation of International Youth Travel Organisations (FIYTO), founding member of BAPAA.

Bunters Ltd
The Old Malt House, 6 Church St, Pattishall, nr Towcester, Northampton NN12 8NB
☎ 01327-831144/99
fax 01327-831155
e office@aupairsnannies.com
w www.aupairsnannies.com
Founded in 1994, this is a hands-on, owner-run business with good contacts abroad.

Types of Work: Au pairs.

Timing & Length of Work: Placements

are available year round. There are some summer-holiday placements; otherwise the maximum stay is one to two years.

Destinations: All EU countries.

Costs/Pay: There's no agency fee.

Organisation Memberships: IAPA, founding member of BAPAA.

Childcare International
Trafalgar House, Grenville Place, London NW7 3SA
☎ 020-8906 3116
fax 020-8906 3461
e office@childint.co.uk
w www.childint.co.uk
Founded in 1986, over 600 au pairs per year are placed in in-bound and out-bound programmes.

Types of Work: Au pairs, au pairs plus, nannies, mother's helps.

Timing & Length of Work: Placements are available year round. There are some summer holiday placements; otherwise the maximum stay is one to two years.

Destinations: Europe, the USA, Canada & Australia.

Costs/Pay: There's a placement fee of £40 for Europe, Canada and Australia, until the law is changed.

Organisation Memberships: IAPA, FIYTO, Recruitment & Employment Confederation (REC), founding member of BAPAA.

theChildCareSolution
Avondale House, 63 Sydney Rd, Haywards Heath, W Sussex RH16 1QD
☎ 01444-453566/0845 458 1550
fax 01444-440445
e southernoffice@thechildcare solution.com
w www.thechildcaresolution.com
Founded in 1989, this is one of the largest UK agencies. It also handles nannies and nursery nurses for the ski resorts and summer beach resorts, but you've got to be qualified.

Types of Work: Au pairs, au pairs plus, nannies, mother's helps.

Timing & Length of Work: Placements are available year round. There are some summer-holiday placements; otherwise the maximum stay is one to two years.

Destinations: Europe & the USA.

Costs/Pay: There's no agency fee.

Organisation Memberships: IAPA, REC, founding member of BAPAA.

Just Au Pairs

35 The Grove, Edgware, Mddx HA8 9QA

☎ 020-8905 3355

fax 020-8905 3838

e sam@aupairs.freeserve.co.uk

W www.aupairsandnannies.co.uk

Founded in 1996, this is a family-run business with multilingual staff.

Types of Work: Au pairs, au pairs plus, nannies, mother's helps.

Timing & Length of Work: Placements are available year round. There are some summer-holiday placements of three months; otherwise stays are for six or 12 months.

Destinations: All over Europe & the USA.

Costs/Pay: There's no agency fee.

Organisation Memberships: IAPA, founding member of BAPAA.

Matchmaker Au Pair Agency (MMAPA)

Rosewood, Leigh Gardens, Chelford Rd, Knutsford, Cheshire WA16 8PU

☎ 01565-651703

fax 01565-631726

e mmaupair@aol.com

W www.matchmakeraupairs.co.uk

Founded in 1996, MMAPA is a small owner-run agency.

Types of Work: Au pairs, au pairs plus, mother's helps.

Timing & Length of Work: Placements are available year round. There are some summer holiday placements; otherwise the maximum stay is one to two years.

Destinations: Europe.

Costs/Pay: There's no agency fee.

Organisation Memberships: IAPA, founding member of BAPAA.

Quickhelp Agency

307a Finchley Rd, London NW3 6EH

☎ 020-7794 8666

fax 020-7433 1993

e quickhelp@clara.net

W www.quickhelp.co.uk

Founded in 1975, Quickhelp is an owner-run agency with trained assistants.

Types of Work: Au pairs.

Timing & Length of Work: Placements are available year round. There are some summer-holiday placements of at least three months; otherwise six to 12 months is preferred.

Destinations: France, Spain & Germany.

Costs/Pay: There's no agency fee.

Organisation Memberships: IAPA, founding member of BAPAA.

CHILDREN'S HOLIDAYS

The Boy Scouts of America (BSA)

The Scout Association, Gilwell Park, Bury Rd, Chingford, London E4 7QW

☎ 020-8433 7119

fax 020-8433 7114

e international@scout.org.uk

W www.scoutbase.org.uk/inter/jambo/campusa/ics.htm

BSA runs the International Camp Staff Program (ICSP) in conjunction with the Scout Association. You can work in one of the 400 US boy-scout camps where a version of the scouts' uniform is worn at all times. One week's training is given. You are responsible for arranging your own visa with support from The Scout Association.

Types of Work: Counsellors.

Timing & Length of Work: Placements are for six to 12 weeks from mid-June.

Destination: The USA.

Costs/Pay: You pay a £30 application fee. You also pay for the visa cost, travel insurance, flights and transport to and from camp. Accommodation and food are free. The average pay is from £370, dependent on experience.

Eligibility: Applicants must be aged at least 18 and be members of The Scout Association.

How to Apply: Applications are processed from September to February. There will be a local interview and a medical.

BUNAC
16 Bowling Green Lane, London
EC1R 0QH
☎ 020-7251 3472
fax 020-7251 0215
e enquiries@bunac.org.uk
w www.bunac.org

The British Universities North America Club has run work/travel programmes worldwide since 1962. Over 3500 students go on its Summer Camp USA programme each year. Orientation programmes are held before departure and upon arrival at camp. All visas, paperwork and travel arrangements are handled by BUNAC. You get up to six weeks of free travel time after camp. Participants on soccer-coaching programmes can also apply through BUNAC and are placed on summer soccer camps. For information on the other programmes it runs and jobs at camps not directly related to children see the Proper Jobs and Casual/Seasonal Work chapters.

Types of Work: Camp counsellor, and waterfront (sailing, swimming etc), entertainment (dance, stage performances etc), music, arts & crafts, pioneering (outdoor pursuits), science and sports staff.

Timing & Length of Work: Placements are for eight to nine weeks from early/mid-June to mid-August.

Destination: The USA.

Costs/Pay: The application fee is £62, insurance costs £119 and the visa fee is £67. Return flights, in-country transport costs, food and lodging are free. Pay ranges from £422 for under-21s to £460 if you're over 21. You get paid at the end of the camp.

Eligibility: Applicants must be between 18/19 and 35, and have experience of working with children in a leadership capacity.

How to Apply: Contact the office in September for a brochure and then book

yourself an interview. These are held nationally from November to May. You'll need two character references, one childcare one, a clear criminal record and sometimes a medical.

Camp America
American Institute For Foreign Study (AIFS), 37a Queen's Gate, London
SW7 5HR
☎ 020-7581 7373
fax 020-7581 7377
e enquiries@campamerica.co.uk
w www.campamerica.co.uk

Around 10,000 young people from all over the world travel with Camp America each year. Countrywide recruitment fairs and road shows are held in January and February – check its website for details. All visas, travel and paperwork are handled by Camp America. There's pre-departure and arrival orientation, training days and a 24-hour emergency freephone number for you to call at anytime during your stay in the USA. You can travel for 10 weeks after the camp. For information on jobs at camp not directly related to children see Contacts in the Casual/Seasonal Work chapter.

Types of Work: Camp counsellors and special needs counsellors.

Timing & Length of Work: Placements last for nine weeks from May or June.

Destination: The USA.

Costs/Pay: There's a refundable deposit of £51, £235 to be paid upon acceptance of a place, European airport tax of £14, a visa administration fee of £67, and a passport-processing fee of £15. Flights, accommodation, in-country transport and food are then free. Pay ranges from £280 for under-21s to £430 for over-21s for the nine weeks. Pay goes up to £550 if you've already done a season.

Eligibility: Applicants must be aged at least 18 by June 1 and have some child-care experience.

How to Apply: Apply from October. Download the application form from the website. At the interview you'll need to show a clean criminal record and two references (one character and one child-care).

CCUSA

Green Dragon House, 64–70 High St, Croydon CR0 9XN
☎ 020-8688 9051
fax 020-8680 4539
e] united kingdom@ccusa.co.uk
W] www.ccusa.com

CCUSA has been a summer-camp specialist since 1986. You can choose from eight different types of camp. Job fairs are held in March and April – see the website for details. Group orientation sessions are held in the UK during April and May and training is given when you arrive at camp; waterfront staff take the American Red Cross Lifeguard Course (for those aged 19 or over). All visas, paperwork and travel arrangements are handled by CCUSA. After camp you can travel for up to 30 days. There's also a 24-hour emergency telephone hotline for your time in America. For information on jobs at camp not directly related to children see the Proper Jobs and Casual/Seasonal Work chapters.

Types of Work: General counsellors, specialist counsellors, ropes course instructors (training given), waterfront staff and, in the Russian camps, English/American culture instructor.

Timing & Length of Work: Placements in the USA are from nine to 11 weeks from early June. In Russia it's four or eight weeks from June or July.

Destinations: The USA & Russia (Lake Baikal, Siberia, Black Sea, St Petersburg & around Moscow).

Costs/Pay: The total cost of the US programme is £275. The Russian four-week programme costs £669, eight weeks costs £699. Pay in the Russian camps is £15 a month and in America it's from £334 to £455, depending on age. Flights, board and lodging are free.

Eligibility: Applicants must be aged at least 18 by June 1 and be enthusiastic about working with children.

How to Apply: Apply in October. Download the application from the website. There's then an interview where you'll need to provide two references, show a clean criminal record and take a medical.

French Encounters

63 Fordhouse Rd, Bromsgrove, Worcs B60 2LU
☎ 01527-873645
fax 01527-832794
e] admin@frenchencounters.com
W] www.frenchencounters.com

French Encounters is a small company employing eight gap-year students a year to work with school children aged between 10 and 13 on language and education field trips. There's two weeks of training, including a first aid and presentation skills.

Types of Work: Animateurs (ie, children's entertainers, commentators, supervisors and organisers).

Timing & Length of Work: The four-month season is from mid-February to mid-June.

Destinations: Two Normandy chateaux in France.

Costs/Pay: Pay is from £70 a week, including all accommodation, food, travel and insurance.

Eligibility: Applicants must be aged at least 18 and have A-level French.

How to Apply: Contact the office for an application form. Interviews are held from August.

International Exchange Centre (IEC)

35 Ivor Place, London NW1 6EA
☎ 020-7724 4493
fax 020-7724 0849
e] isecinfo@btconnect.com
W] www.isecworld.co.uk

IEC organises work placements worldwide (see Contacts in the Proper Jobs chapter). It also offers work with children on various camps. All visas and paperwork for the American programme are provided; you need to apply independently for Russian and former Soviet Union programmes.

With the American programme you can travel for at least one month after your placement.

Types of Work: General and special counsellors (a special counsellor teaches something like swimming or music).

Timing & Length of Work: Placements run from June and are for one, two or three months in Eastern Europe and Russia. American placements run from mid-June and last nine weeks.

Destinations: Latvia, Lithuania, Belarus, Ukraine, Russia & the USA.

Costs/Pay: The placement fee for Eastern Europe and Russia is £85, plus you pay for your visa and return flights. The placement fee for American camps is £115, with free flights. The salary in eastern European and Russian camps is between £6 and £30 a month; in America it's from £310 to £425 depending on age. Accommodation and meals are free.

Eligibility: For eastern European and Russian camps applicants must be aged 18 to 30 and have basic knowledge of Russian. For American camps you need to be aged 18 to 28.

How to Apply: Email or phone for an application form. Apply in April for the Russian camp programme and before January 15 for the American one. Interviews are usually over the phone. You have to show 2 to 4 references and have a clean criminal record, plus some camps require a medical.

MLS Camps (UK)
Malmarc House, 116 Dewsbury Rd, Leeds LS11 6XD
☎ 0113-272 0616
fax 0113-277 1100
e employment@mlscamps.com
w www.uk.mlscamps.com

MLS provides football coaches to US day camps. The children are aged from two to 18 years; the core market is those aged seven to 11. Coaches move from camp to camp each week. MLS sorts out your visa, paperwork and travel arrangements.

Coaching assessment days are held in various national locations and there's a two-day induction held in the Midlands.

Types of Work: Soccer coaches.

Timing & Length of Work: Contracts range from four weeks to 10 months. Short contracts start in June or July; longer ones start in January.

Destinations: Every US state, including Hawaii and Alaska.

Costs/Pay: There's a £310 membership fee, which includes your background check, visa processing, flights, accommodation, training, car hire and kit (three sets). You also have to pay £110 insurance. Inexperienced coaches earn between £15 and £45 a day, depending on the hours worked. Accommodation is with host families; meals are sometimes provided.

Eligibility: Applicants must be aged at least 19, have attained a football-coaching award (contact MLS camps if you don't have this and they can point you in the right direction) and be a reasonable standard of player. A driving licence is preferred.

How to Apply: Apply five or six months before you want to travel. Recruitment takes place from August to the end of January. Apply online. You'll then have to attend a recruitment day, fill in a medical form and hand over all the info needed for a background check.

PGL People
Alton Court, Penyard Lane, Ross-on-Wye, Herefordshire HR9 5GL
☎ 01989-767833
fax 01989-767760
e pglpeople@pgl.co.uk
w www.pgl.co.uk/people

Over 100,000 children aged between six and 18 take a PGL holiday each year. Over 2500 staff are needed annually. There are 19 residential centres in the UK, 12 in France and one in Spain.

Types of Work: Group leaders (pastoral and social welfare), instructors (watersports) and support staff (administrators and maintenance).

Timing & Length of Work: From February to October or May to September.

Destinations: France & Spain.

Costs/Pay: All jobs pay £60 per week with a £10 weekly bonus if you've got an instructors' qualification. All board, lodging and travel is free.

Eligibility: Applicants must be aged at least 18, and have language skills and relevant qualifications.

How to Apply: Recruitment starts in October. Download the application form from the website. You'll need to provide two referees and show a clean criminal record. There's no interview.

Village Camps

Personnel Office, Dept. 1000, 1260 Nyon, Switzerland

☎ 00 41 22-990 9405

fax 00 41 22-990 9494

e personnel@villagecamps.ch

W www.villagecamps.com

This is a Swiss-run company specialising in European children's camps. Seven days' training is given at camp. Any visa arrangements (ie, for Switzerland) need to be done by you. For details on facilities and administrative positions (ie, no direct contact with children) see Contacts in the Casual/Seasonal Work chapter.

Types of Work: All sorts of counsellors – activity, house, assistant, junior, outdoor education, ski/snowboard, language – and group leaders.

Timing & Length of Work: Placements are from five to eight weeks beginning April/May, June/July and August/September.

Destinations: Switzerland, Holland, England, France & Austria.

Costs/Pay: Allowances are paid in local currency and vary depending on the position and location. On top of pocket money you get free accommodation and meals. You pay to get yourself out to the camps.

Eligibility: Assistant and junior counsellors are aged between 18 and 20. Group leaders are aged 23 plus. The minimum age is 21 for all other positions. All counsellors need experience of caring for children; a first-aid certificate and driver's licence are preferred. Relevant qualifications are needed for teaching or specialist counsellor positions.

How to Apply: Apply at least eight months in advance. Download the application, applicant release and authorisation forms from the website. Complete and send by mail along with photocopies of any qualifications, two passport-sized photos, names of two referees and a photocopy of your passport. Interviews are by phone.

WorldNetUK

Avondale House, 63 Sydney Rd, Haywards Heath, W Sussex RH16 1QD

☎ 01444-457676

fax 01444-440445

e info@worldnetuk.com

W www.worldnetuk.com

This is the UK representative for Inter-Exchange/Camp USA, placing young people in American summer camps. It handles all visas and paperwork. Training is given on camp. You can travel for up to a month afterwards on your visa. For details of support staff positions see Contacts in the Casual/Seasonal Work chapter.

Types of Work: Camp counsellors.

Timing & Length of Work: Placements are for seven to nine weeks from June.

Destination: The USA.

Costs/Pay: Programmes cost from around £200, including flights, medical insurance and administration. Pay starts at £400 and goes up with age and experience.

Eligibility: Applicants must be aged at least 18 and have experience in sports, arts & crafts, drama, IT etc.

How to Apply: Call/email for brochure. Apply from October. There will be an interview, medical and criminal-record check.

Courses

Taking a course is usually only one component of a gap year. Often it's combined with travelling or working abroad either before or afterwards. Unless you're very rich, it is rarely combined with a volunteer placement, as it's hard enough trying to find the funding for one, let alone the other. Having said that, there are some specific courses that do offer language learning followed by a volunteer project – see Contacts later in this chapter.

A course can be anything from one week to a year long, although most gappers go for one lasting between two and three months. A yearlong course is a big commitment (both in time and money) but there are some fabulous ones out there such as the 'Introduction to Film and Television Production' at the Film School in Wellington, New Zealand, or a year at a US high school, completely immersed in the American way of life.

There are millions of courses out there, from learning French in France to taking a jungle leadership course in Indonesia. All are either taught by multilingual instructors or in English (apart from the language courses). Many courses are also run by UK-based organisations that'll either travel with you in groups abroad or meet you out there. This can be reassuring, particularly if it's going to be your first big sortie abroad, and it'll certainly be reassuring for the parents!

Why Do a Course?

You've just finished studying at school or university and now you're ready for a break. Why on earth would you want to sign up for another course? That's easy: an investment in yourself, your skills and your knowledge will always be worth your time and money. And, if you have the opportunity to do this abroad then your experience will be a hundred times more rewarding. When you do a course in a foreign country there's a load more you learn than what's being taught in the classroom. You can really get to grips with the country's culture and people. You get to meet a lot of like-minded students from around the world and often make lifelong international friends. Living and studying abroad will also engage other parts of your brain; having to integrate yourself into a new social environment in a different country does wonders for your self-reliance, independence, maturity and self-confidence.

Let's also not forget that the more you know, the more valuable you'll be to a prospective employer. That course on your CV might help you stand out in a pile of job applications and get you an interview. It will certainly be looked upon favourably by a university, particularly if it is linked to the undergraduate course you want to do. Ross Magdalani did a Spanish-language course in Barcelona and agrees completely:

I had the time of my life. I wish every day that I could go back there and live the experience again. During my time there I made so many friends from around the world. I also grew up immensely as I lived through so many situations that were all new to me. And because of this I believe that it put me in a much better position to go on to university.

Your gap year is the ideal time to learn new things, precisely because you do have *the time*. When you start working and progressing in your career it's really hard to take a proper break and do something for yourself like learn a language or learn how to become a ski and snowboarding instructor. And, although it might be the farthest thing from your mind right now, it is pretty much impossible to find time to do anything like this if/when you have kids.

What Course?

Now all you have to do is decide what you want to study.

It could be that you want to indulge a passion or an interest you've always had and learn circus skills in Australia or how to play flamenco guitar in Spain.

You might choose a lifestyle course and learn Tai Chi in Thailand or meditation in Greece. It is very likely that the relaxation and stress-busting skills you learn on courses like these will be put to good use in a year or two, either at university or once on the career ladder.

A smart choice is to do a course that will help you get a job abroad during the rest of your gap year. You could train as a jackaroo or jillaroo in Australia and work on a farm, take a cookery course leading to work in a ski chalet or become a watersports instructor like Gennaro Serra. This was how he decided what course to take:

My alarm went off one morning during my art foundation course and like many of us it suddenly struck me: why am I here? I was doing something I didn't enjoy for the benefit of a boring career. I needed to get out! The next day I was on the phone to Flying Fish, a company offering courses in watersports and instructor qualifications worldwide. I wanted to do a course that would give me a sense of achievement, be educational and offer a different lifestyle, where I'd meet a wide range of people and where, above all, I'd have FUN! As a young lad, having fun is an essential part of life. I thought I'd do the course at the beginning of my gap year, and work for the rest of the year on beaches around the globe teaching a wide range of people how to windsurf, and get paid for it. What a hard life!

Many gappers decide to take a course that will help with their university study or enhance their future career prospects. For most this means learning a new language or brushing up on an old one. These days the most popular language to learn is Spanish because over 300 million people speak it in 23 countries. As language courses are so popular, you can often find them combined with a cultural activity such as cooking, dancing or art.

Another way to immerse yourself in the culture of a foreign country and experience its way of life is to live abroad with a family in a homestay – see Living Abroad with a Host Family in the Contacts section later.

Finding out about all the possible courses you could do would almost fill a gap year by itself. Apart from this book, the internet is obviously a great resource and the following organisations can give you loads more information about courses in their own country:

DAAD German Academic Exchange Service (☎ 020-7235 1736; **W** www.daad.de/ london) 34 Belgrave Square, London SW1X 8QB. Ask for their book on summer courses in Germany.

Italian Cultural Institute (☎ 020-7235 1461; **W** www.italculture.co.uk) 39 Belgrave Square, London SW1X 8NX. It's best to visit in person if you can. It's open 10am to 1pm and 2pm to 5pm Monday to Friday and offers loads of leaflets on various courses all over Italy.

The Canning House Education and Cultural Department (☎ 020-7235 2303; **W** www .canninghouse.com) 2 Belgrave Square, London SW1X 8BJ. This is the UK's largest library for all things Spanish, Portuguese and Latin American. There's lots of information on courses here, some of which can be mailed to you.

It is also worth logging on to Studyzone (**W** www.hothousemedia.com/studyzone), a continually updated online magazine for students wanting to learn a language or study overseas.

And, for potential language students, there's the annual London Language Show (**W** www .language-show.com) that's held on the second weekend in November. It's free to get in.

Whichever course you choose, it is important to find out what accommodation options come with it. Often there are three: living with a host family; halls of residence (often on-site); and shared apartments or houses. The cheapest option is to live with a host family. This is also one of the best and fastest ways to assimilate the local culture and language, as Nadia Karavias, who did two language courses, one in Nice (France) and one in Quito (Ecuador), found. She writes:

Seriously think about host families, even if you have reservations. If you don't like your family once out there, you can move and it won't be a problem, but it is the best way to integrate yourself fast and practise with local native speakers.

Last but not least, you'll have to think about whether you want a recognised qualification at the end of your course. This will often mean taking an exam. Most gappers aren't that keen on more exams during a gap year but if you feel you can bear it then it will look good on your CV.

Where?

Once you know what you want to study, you need to decide where you want to go, which school you want to attend and how you're going to book.

If you're doing a language course then the first bit is a no-brainer – you'll want to study in the countries that speak the language you want to learn. If that's Spanish and you're up for some real adventure as well as good schools then think about studying in Latin America. Argentina, Costa Rica and Peru can be cheaper than Spain (even with the air fare). Bolivia, Ecuador and Guatemala have traditionally been the bargain-basement places to learn but they are becoming pricier. If you want to live in Spain then Seville is the most popular destination for gap-year language students. There are thousands of places to study Spanish in the USA, of course, but getting a student visa can be a hassle and also English-speakers will surround you so your progress will be slower. If you're thinking about French, Italian or German, don't forget about Switzerland, if you can afford it. Also, Taiwan and Hong Kong are interesting places to study Mandarin Chinese.

Language students will also need to decide whether to book a school direct or through an agency. An agency is usually based in the UK and so is easy to contact and talk to about your requirements. They also only work with the best schools, frequently visiting them to make sure they're up to scratch. An agency can book your course and your accommodation, and help with visas and any problems when you're abroad. On the downside, going through a third party can sometimes cost more but according to gapper Nadia Karavias it's worthwhile:

Booking with a reputable agency might be more expensive but it is worth it because you are well and truly looked after in the case of any mishaps. It wasn't such an issue for me when I was studying in France but when I was in Ecuador, somewhere totally different to Europe, the agency really gave me a helping hand. If (let's hope not) you are robbed, injured or anything happens you will be taken to hospital and cared for, and they will deal with the system for you. In the end it's just one less thing for yourself or your parents to be worrying about.

If you want to bypass the language agencies you run the risk of booking a dodgy school in a seedy part of town. To avoid this, look for schools that belong to one of the national or international associations that monitor standards. There's a list of them at **W** www .language-learning.net. Most language schools recommended in this chapter belong to the International Association of Language Centres (IALC; **W** www.ialc.org) or International House (IH; **W** www.ihworld.com). Otherwise, find ones that are recognised by the country's ministry of education.

If you fancy choosing your school and booking it all on the web then visit **W** www.language course.net, the only online language agency. You also get a 5% discount on the tuition fees charged by the language school.

Whatever you want to study you'll need to think about your environment. Will you be happier in a large city or a smaller town? Do you want a school by the sea or inland? Can you stand the sweltering heat or do you prefer to be cool? Wherever you decide to go, you'll need to ask some basic questions of the place where you might study:

- How large are the classes?
- Where do most of your students come from?
- What age group do you usually attract?
- How many hours of teaching are there a week?
- Is there any one-to-one tuition?
- Is the course very academic or more recreational?
- Are there any exams and are they optional?
- What exactly is included in the price?
- What activities do you organise outside of lessons and do they cost extra?
- Will my accommodation be far from the school?

For many courses there are often 'centres of excellence', such as in Italy: Florence for art courses and Milan for fashion and jewellery making. There are also particular schools that have an outstanding reputation for certain subjects like the New York Film Academy for filmmaking. Otherwise, you might make your choice on cost – if you plan to work in a ski resort then it's more expensive to live in France, Switzerland and Austria than in Italy, Eastern Europe or North America (and the après-ski is very cheap in duty-free Andorra). Sometimes your choice will depend on where the company you go with holds its courses. For instance, some ski and snowboarding instructor courses only run in Europe, whereas others offer the USA and Canada. This is because it can sometimes be hard to find a job in Europe with a qualification from the Americas or New Zealand.

It is also worth remembering that the bureaucracy involved in getting a visa to study in the US is becoming increasingly difficult. There is now an interview process, which you may find off-putting.

Funding

There's no denying it – many courses are expensive. Not only do you fork out for tuition fees but also flights, accommodation, meals, general living expenses and sometimes equipment. In general, though, most gappers spend around £2500 all up on a course lasting three months, although you can spend much less and also much more. See Contacts for specific details on course costs.

Although there are quite a few grants, funds and scholarships for postgraduate research or study abroad, there isn't much for pre-university students except the following:

The Arvon Foundation: See The Arts in the Contacts section later for contact details. The foundation's writing courses are subsidised by the Arts Council of England and the Scottish Arts Council; grants are available to anyone who can't afford the fees.

Association of Sea Training Organisations (ASTO; ☎ 023-8062 7400; fax 023-8062 9924; e training@rya.org.uk; W www.asto.org.uk) c/o The Royal Yachting Association, RYA House, Romsey Rd, Eastleigh SO50 9YA. This is the umbrella organisation for the tall-ship charities. Around £200,000 each year is distributed to the individual charities to help fund students who can't afford to sail. For a full list of tall-ship charities see the ASTO website; a few are listed under Watersports, Sailing & Crewing in the Contacts section later.

Career Development Loan: See Fundraising in Money & Costs for full details. It may be possible to get one of these loans to help fund your course.

DAAD German Academic Exchange Service: See What Course? earlier in this chapter for details. Each year 80 grants are available to do summer courses in German. The catch is that they're not for pre-university students but those in the middle of a university course that has German as a component. You need to apply in the autumn of the previous year.

Peter Kirk Scholarships: For full details see Miscellaneous under Contacts later.

Lions Clubs International: Contact your local club (get the address from W www.lions .org.uk or call ☎ 0121-441 4544) to see if they participate in the Youth Exchange Programme for those aged 15 to 21.

Rotary International in Great Britain and Ireland: Contact your local club (get the address from W www.ribi.org) to see if they participate in the Rotary's educational programmes.

As you'll probably end up having to fund-raise for your course, it's best to start as early as possible. There are loads of good tips in the Fundraising section of the Money & Costs chapter, and saving up should be seen as part of your gap-year challenge. If you need to supplement your income while studying then try babysitting, English coaching or even busking. Otherwise, if your course trains you to do a paid job during the rest of your gap year, you could borrow the money up front and then pay it back as you earn. Whatever you do, though, it's a really bad idea to start university or a proper job with a gap-year debt hanging over your head.

UK Learning

There are thousands of courses on every possible subject at colleges, universities and adult-education centres all over the UK. A useful resource for finding out what's available in your area is Learndirect (☎ 0800 100 900; W www.learndirect.co.uk), a government scheme, which has details on 500,000 courses nationwide. If you live in London then the official booklets to part-time and full-time study in Greater London are: *Part-time Floodlight, Summertime Floodlight*, and *Full-time Floodlight*. These are available at almost every London newsagent or you can look for a course at W www.floodlight.co.uk.

For more detailed advice about UK gap-year study (as well as help with university, a gap year abroad, and postgraduate career options) there's Gabbitas Educational Consultants (☎ 020-7734 0161; e consult@gabbitas.co.uk; W www.gabbitas.co.uk). Initial phone advice is free, or you can book a phone consultation at £60 for 20 minutes. Don't waste time: this works out at 5p per second.

Two useful courses to do in the UK are Business Studies or Business Administration & Secretarial Skills. Apart from anything else, touch-typing (it only takes 40 hours to learn) is an invaluable skill at university, in temp work, or a future career. These courses are offered at almost all local education centres or local business schools.

Other good courses to do in the UK are those that train you for a job abroad during the rest of your gap year. For instance, a bartending and cocktail-mixing course sets you up to work almost anywhere in the world. Otherwise, getting your Competent Crew Certificate in the UK would be wise if you intend to work your passage on a yacht (see the Work Your Route chapter). Details of all these options are listed under Contacts.

A good UK course to ask your parents to pay for as a birthday or Christmas present is one of the gap-year survival courses. See Gap Year, Wilderness & Survival Courses under Contacts for details. Mother of gap-year twins Sarah and Penny Bundy said:

In some ways your children going off abroad on a gap year is every parents' nightmare but deep down you know it is absolutely the right thing for them to do. However, that won't stop you worrying night and day. When Sarah and Penny broached the subject of me paying for a gap-year survival course I was only too pleased. It made me feel as if I was constructively helping towards their safety and I couldn't think of a better way to spend my money.

Contacts

Most courses in this section take place abroad unless they are a) teaching you a skill for later use in a gap year abroad; or b) so good, despite being a UK course, that they couldn't be left out.

LANGUAGE AGENCIES

AmeriSpan Unlimited

PO Box 40007, Philadelphia PA 19106 USA
☎ 00 1 215-751 1100
fax 00 1 215-751 1986
ⓔ info@amerispan.com
Ⓦ www.amerispan.com

AmeriSpan offers 30 total-immersion language courses in over 50 countries.

Types of Course: All standards of Croatian, Hebrew Arabic, Indonesian, Taiwanese, Thai, Vietnamese, Moroccan, Czech, Hungarian, Dutch, Polish & Ukrainian.

Timing & Length of Course: Courses are from one week to nine months long. Many courses start weekly but some are summer programmes only.

Destinations: Worldwide.

Costs/Pay: Courses cost from £300 for two weeks and from £1396 for 12 weeks, including half-board accommodation.

Eligibility: The minimum age for applicants is 16.

Accommodation: AmeriSpan prefers to sell language courses and host-family accommodation together.

How to Apply: Call a UK agent to book: STA (☎ 0870 160 6070) or Journey Latin America (☎ 020-8747 8315). You can also call them direct in the USA.

Cactus Language

4 Clarence House, 30–31 North St, Brighton, E Sussex BN1 1EB
☎ 0845 130 4775
fax 01273-775868
ⓔ enquiry@cactuslanguage.com
Ⓦ www.cactuslanguage.com

Cactus offers tailor-made language holidays worldwide, which can combine a language course with activities such as salsa dancing, diving, cooking and volunteer work.

Types of Course: All standards of all Western European and Middle Eastern languages, Chinese, Russian, Japanese, Greek, Turkish & Thai.

Timing & Length of Course: Courses are from one week to 12 months long; most start weekly.

Destinations: Central & South America, Europe, the Caribbean, Asia, Russia & the Middle East.

Costs/Pay: One month costs from £299, 12 months from £2500, tuition only.

Eligibility: The minimum age is 18.

Accommodation: Courses can be booked with or without accommodation. You can stay with a host family, in a shared or private student apartment, or at a student residence or hotel.

How to Apply: If you apply and pay online you get a £5 discount, or ring the office.

Càlédöñiâ Languages Abroad

The Clockhouse, Bonnington Mill, 72 Newhaven Rd, Edinburgh EH6 5QG
☎ 0131-621 7721/2
fax 0131-621 7723
ⓔ courses@caledonialanguages.co.uk
Ⓦ www.caledonialanguages.co.uk

Càlédöñiâ offers a large range of straight language courses, as well as language and volunteering, or language combined with a cultural interest. See Health & Exercise later in this section for more details.

Types of Course: All standards of Spanish, French, Italian, German, Portuguese & Russian. Some Spanish courses in Latin America are combined with volunteer work.

Timing & Length of Course: Courses are from one to nine months long; most start every Monday but more specialist courses start at specific times.

Destinations: Spain, France, Italy, Germany, Portugal, Russia, Central & South America.

Costs/Pay: One-month courses range from £350 to £750, three months from £925, tuition only.
Eligibility: Applicants must be aged at least 17.
Accommodation: You can book your course with or without accommodation.

CESA Languages Abroad

CESA House, Pennance Rd, Lanner, Cornwall TR16 5TQ
☎ 01209-211800
fax 01209-211830
e info@cesalanguages.com
w www.cesalanguages.com

CESA is a booking agency with courses in more unusual languages and destinations.
Types of Course: All standards of Western European, Russian, Japanese, Chinese, Hebrew, Moroccan, Latin American Spanish, including Cuban.
Timing & Length of Course: Courses are from two to 16 weeks long, with extensions if required. Beginner courses have set start dates but anyone else can begin any Monday.
Destinations: Western Europe, Russia, Japan, Taiwan, Central & South America, Cuba, Israel & Morocco.
Costs/Pay: Two weeks cost from £357, 16 weeks from £2280 with accommodation.
Eligibility: There's a minimum age of 16.
Accommodation: Mostly flat-share, student apartments or college residences.

Challenge Educational Services

101 Lorna Rd, Hove, E Sussex BN3 3EL
☎ 01273-220261
fax 01273-220376
e enquiries@challengeuk.com
w www.challengeuk.com

Challenge Educational Services provides total-immersion courses in French, which can be combined with art courses. Also see High Schools/Colleges in the US, Canada or Europe later in this section.
Types of Course: All levels of French.
Timing & Length of Course: Courses are from one to 32 weeks, starting most

Mondays year round.
Destinations: Eight locations in France.
Costs/Pay: One month costs from £1645, including accommodation.
Eligibility: Applicants must be aged at least 17.
Accommodation: Usually with a host family or in halls of residence.

CIEE (Council On International Educational Exchange)

52 Poland St, London W1F 7AB
☎ 020-7478 2020/00
fax 020-7734 7322
e infouk@councilexchanges.org.uk
w www.ciee.org.uk

Founded in 1947, CIEE provides many different work and cultural programmes, including Language Study Abroad courses.
Types of Course: All levels of Spanish, French, Italian & German.
Timing & Length of Course: Courses are from two to 36 weeks, starting every couple of weeks.
Destinations: Europe, Mexico & Latin America, including Cuba.
Costs/Pay: Courses cost from £350 for two weeks, including accommodation.
Eligibility: There's a minimum age of 16.
Accommodation: Courses can be booked with or without accommodation. Options include staying with a host family, in a self-catering apartment, or at a hotel or student residence.

Don Quijote

2/4 Stoneleigh Park Rd, Epsom, Surrey KT19 0QT
☎ 020-8786 8081
fax 020-8786 8086
e info@donquijote.co.uk
w www.donquijote.org

Don Quijote specialises in Spanish language courses.
Types of Course: All levels of Spanish.
Timing & Length of Course: Courses are from one to 40 weeks, with weekly start dates.
Destinations: Spain, Peru & Mexico.
Costs/Pay: One month costs from £439,

40 weeks from £3505, tuition only.
Eligibility: The minimum age is 18.
Accommodation: Courses can be booked with or without accommodation. Options are homestay, or student flats and residences.

EF International Language Schools
74 Roupell St, London SE1 8SS
☎ 08707 200735
fax 08707 200708
[e] gapyear@ef.com
[w] www.ef.com
EF offers up-market language courses, which can sometimes be combined with a TEFL course and a teaching placement.
Types of Course: All standards of Spanish, French, German, Italian, Russian & Chinese.
Timing & Length of Course: There are two start dates a month except in July and August when courses begin weekly. Courses are from two weeks to 9 months.
Destinations: Western Europe, Ecuador, Russia & China.
Costs/Pay: Two weeks with half-board costs from £680, nine months from £5750, including flights.
Eligibility: There's a minimum age of 16.
Accommodation: Host-family or university-residence accommodation comes with each course.

Euro Academy
67–71 Lewisham High St, London SE13 5JX
☎ 020-8297 0505
fax 020-8297 0984
[e] enquiries@euroacademy.co.uk
[w] www.euroacademy.co.uk
Euro Academy offers language courses abroad, sometimes combined with cookery, dance and unpaid work placements.
Types of Course: All levels of French, German, Italian, Spanish, Portuguese, Greek & Russian.
Timing & Length of Course: Courses are from one week to one year, and most have weekly start dates.

Destinations: Mexico, Ecuador & Cuba.
Costs/Pay: Two weeks costs from £300, 16 weeks from £1500, tuition only.
Eligibility: The minimum age is 15.
Accommodation: Accommodation is most often with host families or in university residences but hotels or apartments can be requested. Courses are offered with or without accommodation.

Gala Spanish In Spain
Woodcote House, 8 Leigh Lane, Farnham, Surrey GU9 8HP
☎/fax 01252-715319
Gala specialises in sending students to Spain.
Types of Course: All levels of Spanish.
Timing & Length of Course: Courses are from two weeks to nine months and start at two-weekly intervals.
Destinations: Eight cities in Spain.
Costs/Pay: Two weeks costs from £300, 12 weeks from £1400, including accommodation.
Eligibility: The minimum age is 16.
Accommodation: Courses always come with half- or full-board accommodation with a host family, or in a student flat or residence.
How to Apply: Gala prefers telephone inquiries.

Goethe Institut
50 Princes Gate, London SW7 2PH
☎ 020-7596 4004
fax 020-7594 0210
[e] german@london.goethe.org
[w] www.goethe.de
Goethe is a worldwide organisation promoting German language and culture. There are institutes all over Germany where you can learn the language.
Types of Course: All levels of German including intensive, super intensive and business.
Timing & Length of Course: Courses are from two to 12 weeks and run year round at one or another of its locations.
Destinations: 16 centres in Germany.
Costs/Pay: Four-week intensive courses

cost from £638, 12 weeks from £1580, tuition only.

Eligibility: The minimum age is 18.

Accommodation: Goethe can arrange accommodation, usually in student halls of residence or with a family.

Language Courses Abroad Ltd/Spanish Study Holidays

67 Ashby Rd, Loughborough, Leics LE11 3AA

☎ 01509-211612

fax 01509-260037

e info@languagesabroad.co.uk or

e info@spanishstudyholidays.com

W www.languagesabroad.co.uk or

W www.spanishstudyholidays.com

Offers languages courses, volunteer and work-experience programmes. Some courses are combined with cookery, wine courses or archaeology etc.

Types of Course: All levels of Western European, Spanish & Russian.

Timing & Length of Course: Courses are for one week to nine months; most start weekly, depending on the location.

Destinations: Western Europe, Russia, Central & South America (including Cuba).

Costs/Pay: Two weeks costs from £241, 40 weeks from £2289, tuition only.

Eligibility: The minimum age ranges from 14 to 18, depending on the course.

Accommodation: You can stay with a host family, or in a shared apartment, private studio apartment, student residence or hotel.

Language Studies International (LSI)

19–21 Ridgmount St, London WC1E 7AH

☎ 020-7467 6506

fax 020-7323 1736

e fl@lsi.edu

W www.lsi-learnlanguages.com

LSI specialises in language courses abroad and also offers work-experience programmes.

Types of Course: All levels of French,

German, Spanish, Italian, Russian, Chinese & Japanese.

Timing & Length of Course: Courses are for one week to one year. They usually start every Monday but beginners' courses are monthly.

Destinations: Central & South America, Europe & China.

Costs/Pay: Two weeks cost from £200, 34 weeks from £2565, tuition only.

Eligibility: The minimum age is 16, except for courses in Latin America and China where it's 18.

Accommodation: Accommodation is normally with a host family, although other options are available.

Living Spanish

The Barley Mow Centre, 10 Barley Mow Passage, London W4 4PH

☎ 020-8747 2018

fax 0870 056 0706

e info@livingspanish.com

W www.livingspanish.com

Living Spanish sends students to all parts of Spain.

Types of Course: All levels of Spanish.

Timing & Length of Course: Courses are from one week to 40 weeks and start every Monday.

Destinations: All major cities in Spain.

Costs/Pay: Two weeks cost from £200, 40 weeks from £2000, tuition only.

Eligibility: The minimum age is 16.

Accommodation: Accommodation is with a host family or in a shared student flat.

OISE Intensive Language Schools

90 Great Russell St, London WC1B 3PS

☎ 020-7631 3674

fax 020-7631 3679

e info@oise.com

W www.oise.com

OISE is a specialist in intensive-language training, teaching either one-to-one or in groups of four and eight.

Types of Course: All levels of French, German & Spanish.

Timing & Length of Course: Courses are from one week to 36 weeks and start weekly.
Destinations: Paris, Heidelberg & Madrid.
Costs/Pay: Two weeks cost from £480, 36 weeks from £14,220, including accommodation.
Eligibility: The minimum age is 17.
Accommodation: OISE always sells courses with half-board host-family accommodation.

SIBS Ltd

Beech House, Commercial Rd, Uffculme, Collompton, Devon EX15 3EB
☎ 01884-841330
fax 01884-841377
e trish@sibs.co.uk
w www.sibs.co.uk
SIBS offers language courses abroad, often combined with art, cookery or work experience.
Types of Course: All levels of Russian, Japanese and Western European languages including Dutch, Greek & Swedish.
Timing & Length of Course: Courses are from one week to one year; most start weekly but some start monthly.
Destinations: Western Europe, Mexico, South America, Russia & Japan.
Costs/Pay: Courses cost from £200 per week, including accommodation.
Accommodation: All accommodation options are offered but students can opt for tuition only.

Society For Co-operation in Russian and Soviet Studies (SCRSS)

320 Brixton Rd, London SW9 6AB
☎ 020-7274 2282
fax 020-7274 3230
e ruslibrary@scrss.org.uk
w www.scrss.org.uk
SCRSS offers language courses in Russia, as well as an information service and library. It can arrange visas if required.
Types of Course: All levels of Russian.
Timing & Length of Course: Courses are

from one week to one year and usually start weekly.
Destinations: Moscow & St Petersburg.
Costs/Pay: One week costs from £370 for tuition, visa support, transfers and hostel accommodation.
Eligibility: The minimum age is 16.
Accommodation: Hostel or family accommodation can be booked if required.
How to Apply: Two months' notice must be given.

Vis-à-Vis

2–4 Stoneleigh Park Rd, Epsom, Surrey KT19 0QT
☎ 020-8786 8021
fax 020-8786 8086
e info@visavis.org
w www.visavis.org
The French-language partner of Don Quijote offers French-language courses in Europe and Canada.
Types of Course: All levels of French.
Timing & Length of Course: Courses are from one to 40 weeks and start weekly.
Destinations: France, Belgium & Canada.
Costs/Pay: Two weeks cost from £193, 12 weeks from £797, tuition only.
Eligibility: The minimum age is 16.
Accommodation: A homestay or student flats and residences are all options.

LANGUAGE SCHOOLS ABROAD

Austria

Actilingua Academy

Gloriettegasse 8, A-1130 Vienna
☎ 00 43 1-877 6701
fax 00 43 1-877 6703
e info@actilingua.com
w www.german@actilingua.com
Actilingua is situated in central Vienna. Courses for beginners start once a month, intermediary level courses start weekly.
Accreditation/Organisation Memberships: International Association of Language Centres (IALC), Federation of International Youth Travel Organisations (FIYTO).

Canada

LSC Language Studies Canada
1610 Sainte Catherine Street West, Suite 401, Montreal, Québec H3H 2S2l
☎ 00 1 514-939 9911
fax 00 1 514-939 2223
e montreal@lsc-canada.com
w www.lsc-canada.com
Established in 1962, LSC teaches seven levels of French. There are 13 start dates a year and there's a good range of excursions and cultural visits.
Accreditation/Organisation Memberships: IALC, Private English Language Schools Association Canada.

Central & South America

Academia de Español Guatemala
7a Calle Oriente 15, Antigua, Guatemala
☎ 00 502 832 5057/60
fax 00 502 832 5058
e aegnow@guate.net
w www.acad.conexion.com
This school owns two colonial buildings with gardens; many lessons are taught outside. It specialises in one-to-one tuition and classes at all levels start weekly.
Accreditations/Organisation Memberships: Endorsed by Ministerio de Educaciõn and Instituto Guatemalteco de Turismo.

Argentina ILEE
Av Callao 339, 3rd floor, Buenos Aires 1022, Argentina
☎/fax 00 54 11-4782 7173
e info@argentinailee.com
w www.argentinailee.com
Bookshops and cafés surround this school. Classes at all levels start daily, with optional tango lessons. It also has schools in Cordoba and Patagonia.
Accreditations/Organisation Memberships: Institute of International Education (USA).

Estudio Sampere, Cuenca
Calle Hermano, 3–43 (Escalinata), Cuenca, Ecuador
☎ 00 593 7-820460
fax 00 593 7-820462
e cuenca@sampere.es
w www.sampere.com
Cuenca is a beautiful colonial town with cobbled streets. Most courses start every Monday. All standards welcome.
Accreditations/Organisation Memberships: IALC.

Excel Spanish Language Center
Cruz Verde 336, Cusco, Peru
☎ 00 51 84-235298
fax 00 51 84-232272
e info@excelinspanish.com
w www.excel-spanishlanguage programs-peru.org
The school is a five-minute walk from Cusco's main plaza. It has a beautiful courtyard. Courses at all levels start weekly on Mondays.
Accreditations/Organisation Memberships: Recognised by Peru's Ministry of Tourism.

Fast Forward Language Training
Rua Dep. José Lages 499, Ponta Verde, Maceió, Brazil
☎ 00 55 82-327 5213
fax 00 55 82-241 5036
e info@fastforward.com.br
w www.fastforward.com.br
Spanish courses start monthly either in the beach city of Maceió, in the northeast of Brazil, or in São Paulo, South America's largest city. All standards welcome.
Accreditations/Organisation Memberships: Among others, IALC, American Chamber of Commerce.

Forester Instituto Internacional
Los Yoses, del Automercado, 75 Metros Sur, San José, Costa Rica
☎ 00 506 225 3155
fax 00 506 225 9236
e forester@sol.racsa.co.cr
w www.fores.com
Twenty minutes' walk from downtown San

José, the school has a garden and a swimming pool. Beginner to advanced courses start monthly. There are daily free Latin dance classes.

Accreditations/Organisation Memberships: IALC.

France

BLS Bordeaux
42 rue Lafaurie de Monbadon, 33000 Bordeaux, France
☎ 00 33 556 51 00 76
fax 00 33 556 51 76 15
ⓔ info@bls-frenchcourses.com
ⓦ www.bls-bordeaux.com
BLS is housed in a 19th-century building set in the heart of town. Classes for beginners start monthly and for other levels weekly.

Accreditations/Organisation Memberships: Groupement Professionnel des Organismes d'Enseignement du Français Langue Étrangér (SOUFFLE).

ELFE Paris
8 Villa Ballu, Entrance 23, rue Ballu, 75009, Paris, France
☎ 00 33 148 78 73 00
fax 00 33 140 82 91 92
ⓔ contact@elfe-paris.com
ⓦ www.elfe-paris.com
In a mansion house close to the Arc de Triomphe, ELFE general and intensive courses start weekly. Beginners are welcome. You can also combine language with a Civilization Course.

Accreditations/Organisation Memberships: IALC, SOUFFLE.

France Langue
22 Av Notre-Dame, 06000, Nice, France
☎ 00 33 493 13 78 88
fax 00 33 493 13 78 89
ⓔ nice@france-langue.fr
ⓦ www.france-langue.fr
Six blocks from the Mediterranean, courses for all levels run year round. There is also a school in Paris, not far from the Arc de Triomphe.

Accreditations/Organisation Memberships: IALC.

Germany

BWS Germanlingua
Bayerstrasse 13, D-80335 Munich, Germany
☎ 00 49 89-599 89200
fax 00 49 89-599 89201
ⓔ info@bws-germanlingua.de
ⓦ www.bws-germanlingua.de
Established in 1984, courses at all levels start weekly and get booked up quickly around Oktoberfest, which begins mid-September. There is also a BWS school in Berlin.

Accreditations/Organisation Memberships: IALC.

Colon Language Center
Colonnaden 96, 20354 Hamburg 36, Germany
☎ 00 49 40-34 58 50
fax 00 49 40-34 68 54
ⓔ info@colon.de
ⓦ www.colon-language-center.de
This old school, founded in 1952, is in the middle of Hamburg and owns its own foreign-language bookshop. Beginner courses start monthly and all others weekly.

Accreditations/Organisation Memberships: IALC, National Association of German Private Schools.

GLS Sprachenzentrum Berlin
Kolonnenstrasse 26, 10829 Berlin, Germany
☎ 00 49 30-78 00 89/00
fax 00 49 30-787 41 92
ⓔ germancourses@gls-berlin.com
ⓦ www.german-courses.com
In the school opposite Marlene Dietrich's former home, beginner courses start monthly and other courses every Monday.

Accreditations/Organisation Memberships: Among others, IALC, European Association for Quality Language Services (EAQUALS).

Greece

The Athens Centre
48 Archimidous St, Athens 11636, Greece
☎ 00 30 210-7012268
fax 00 30 210-7018603
e info@athenscentre.gr
w www.athenscentre.gr
Established in 1969, this is one of the leading places to study Greek. New classes start monthly and there's also a three-week summer course on the island of Spetses each year. All levels are welcome.
Accreditations/Organisation Memberships: Recognised by Greek Ministry of Education.

Ireland

National University of Ireland, Galway
University Road, Galway, Ireland
☎ 00 353 91-595101/595038
fax 00 353 91-595041
e treasa.uilorcain@nuigalway.ie
w www.mis.nuigalway.ie
Situated in an Irish-speaking area of the country, this school has courses for more advanced students from Easter to September. For complete beginners a four-week course starts mid-July. Lonely Planet author Steve Fallon did the beginner course and subsequently wrote *Travels With Alice* (Lonely Planet Travel Literature).
Accreditations/Organisation Memberships: Part of the National University of Ireland, Galway.

Italy

Istituto Italiano, Centro di Lingua e Cultura
Via Machiavelli 33, 00185, Rome, Italy
☎ 00 39 06-704 52 138
fax 00 39 06-700 85 122
e istital@uni.net
w www.istitutoitaliano.com
Ten minutes' walk from the Colosseum, beginner courses start monthly and other courses each Monday.
Accreditation/Organisation Memberships: IALC, Association of Schools teaching Italian as a Second Language (ASILS).

Istituto Michelangelo
Via Ghibellina 88, 50122, Florence, Italy
☎ 00 39 055- 240975
fax 00 39 055-240997
e michelangelo@dada.it
w www.michelangelo-edu.it
Housed in the 15th-century Palazzo Gherardi, close to the famous Santa Croce church, most classes start weekly. You can also study cookery, art history and fine art in the afternoons. All standards are welcome.
Accreditation/Organisation Memberships: IALC.

Linguadue
Corso Buenos Aires 43, 20124, Milan, Italy
☎ 00 39 02-2951 9972
fax 00 39 02-2951 9973
e admissions@linguadue.com
w www.linguadue.com
In a beautiful Art-Nouveau building in the centre of town, beginner courses start monthly and other courses weekly. The school has its own garden.
Accreditations/Organisation Memberships: Among others, IALC, authorised by the Italian Ministry of Education, ASILS.

Japan

LIC Kokusai Gakuin
Noa-Dogenzaka Building, 12 F 2-15-1 Dogenzaka, Shibuya-ku, Tokyo 150, Japan
☎ 00 81 3-3770 5344
fax 00 81 3-3770 5478
e lictko@netlaputa.ne.jp
w www.lic-net.co.jp
The school year is divided into four terms with start dates at the beginning of each. All standards welcome.
Accreditations/Organisation Memberships: IALC.

Mexico

Center for Bilingual Multicultural Studies
San Jerónimo 304, Colonial San Jerónimo, Cuernavaca, Morelos 62179, Mexico
☎ 00 52 777-3171087
fax 00 52 777-3170533
e admission@bilingual-center.com
w www.bilingual-center.com
Called the 'City of Eternal Spring', Cuernavaca is 50 miles south of Mexico City. The school is set in dramatic landscaped gardens with fountains and swimming pools. Courses start every Monday.
Accreditations/Organisation Memberships: IALC.

Portugal

CIAL Centro de Linguas
Avenida da República 41-80, 1050-187, Lisbon, Portugal
☎ 00 351 217 940 448
fax 00 351 217 960 783
e Portuguese@cial.pt
w www.cial.pt
Courses start monthly in Lisbon, Porto or Faro. At the Porto school you can combine your language course with one on culture. All levels are welcome.
Accreditations/Organisation Memberships: Among others, IALC, recognised by the Portuguese Ministry of Education, American Association of Teachers of Spanish and Portuguese.

Russia

Liden & Denz Language Centre
Transportny per. 11, 5th floor, 191119, St Petersburg, Russia
☎ 00 7 812-325 22 41
fax 00 7 812-325 12 84
e lidenz@lidenz.ru
w www.lidenz.ru
Situated in the heart of this beautiful city, beginner courses start monthly and most

other courses weekly. The school has an in-house travel agency that can help with visas.
Accreditations/Organisation Memberships: IALC.

Spain

ABC-Instituto Español de Cultura
Guillem Tell 27, 08006 Barcelona, Spain
☎ 00 34 93-415 5757
fax 00 34 93-218 2606
e info@ambricol.es
w www.ambricol.es
With a penthouse terrace overlooking Barcelona, beginner classes start monthly and all other classes every Monday.
Accreditation/Organisation Memberships: IALC, accredited by the Instituto Cervantes, FIYTO.

Estudio Sampere
Lagasca 16, E-28001, Madrid, Spain
☎ 00 34 91-431 4366
fax 00 34 91-575 9509
e sampere@sampere.es
w www.sampere.com
Founded in 1956, beginner classes start monthly and all other classes weekly. There are also schools in Salamanca, Alicante, El Puerto de Santa Maria and Cuenca in Ecuador.
Accreditation/Organisation Memberships: Many, including IALC, NAFSA (Association of International Educators).

Malaca Instituto
C/Cortada 6, Cerrado de Calderon, 29018, Malaga, Spain
☎ 00 34 95-229 3242
fax 00 34 95-229 6316
e espanol@malacainst-ch.es
w www.malacainst-ch.es
The school is 15 minutes' walk from the beach. It has a cinema, two sun terraces and a swimming pool. The intensive Spanish course starts every two weeks. Hispanic Studies is also offered. All standards are welcome.

Accreditation/Organisation Memberships: Among others, IALC, EAQUALS.

Switzerland

ASC International House
72 rue de Lausanne, 1202 Geneva, Switzerland
☎ 00 41 22-731 85 20
fax 00 41 22-738 21 58
e admin@asc-ih.ch
W www.asc-ih.ch
ASC is located four blocks from Lake Geneva, in the French-speaking part of Switzerland. A range of courses for all levels start on Mondays.
Accreditations/Organisation Memberships: Affiliated to International House World Organisation.

Taiwan

Taipei Language Institute (TLI)
Taipei Roosevelt Center 4F, No 50 Roosevelt Rd, Sec 3, Taipei, Taiwan
☎ 00 886 2-2341 0022
fax 00 886 2-2363 4857
e tli.Taipei@msa.hinet.net
W www.tli.com.tw
Founded in 1956, TLI has five centres in Taiwan. You can transfer between them in order to see more of the country while you study. There are also three centres in mainland China and one in Tokyo. Beginners are welcome.
Accreditations/Organisation Memberships: None, they used to be a member of the IALC, but they outgrew their membership. They have an excellent reputation.

UK

The Language School
School of Oriental and African Studies, Thornhaugh St, Russell Square, London WC1H OXG
☎ 020-7898 4888
fax 020-7898 4889

e languages@soas.ac.uk
W www.soas.ac.uk
Unfortunately for travellers, this is the best place to study the more unusual languages of African, Near and Middle Eastern, East Asian, Southeast Asian and South Asian countries. There are courses for all standards.
Accreditations/Organisation Memberships: Part of London University.

LIVING ABROAD WITH A HOST FAMILY

En Famille Overseas
4 St Helena Rd, Colchester CO3 3BA
☎ 01206-546741
fax 01206-546740
e marylou_toms@btinternet.com
W www.enfamilleoverseas.co.uk
Founded in 1945, students stay with families in Europe. Language tuition is optional.
Timing & Length of Stay: Stays are from one week to 12 months and are available year round.
Destinations: France, Spain & Italy.
Costs/Pay: Two weeks cost from £279, 12 weeks from £1250, full board.
Eligibility: The minimum age is 15.

Experiment in International Living (EIL)
287 Worcester Rd, Malvern, Worcs WR14 1AB
☎ 0800 018 4015
fax 01684-562212
e info@eiluk.org
W www.eiluk.org
EIL is a registered charity that offers many gap-year programmes, including homestays with urban or rural families, farms and ranches etc.
Timing & Length of Stay: Stays are from one week upwards.
Destinations: 25 worldwide destinations in all continents, including Thailand, India, Ghana & Nigeria.
Costs/Pay: Two weeks to four months in Guatemala costs from £175 (yes, this price

is correct). Five weeks in Thailand cost from £433 and two weeks on an American ranch from £528. All prices include full-board accommodation.

Eligibility: The minimum age is 18.

Homestay New York
630 East 19 Street, Brooklyn, New York, 11230 USA
☎/fax 00 1 718-434 2071
e helayne@homestayny.com
W www.homestayny.com
Experience life in the Big Apple by staying with real American families.

Timing & Length of Stay: If you're on a tourist visa you can stay from three days to two weeks. If you're on a student visa then you can stay for up to six months.

Destination: New York.

Costs/Pay: From £56 per night for B&B.

Eligibility: The minimum age is 18.

How to Apply: Online reservations are preferred. A prior appointment is needed if you want to visit the office.

San Francisco Homestay
1670 South Amphlett Blvd, Suite 214, San Mateo, CA 94070, USA
☎ 00 1 650-378 8572
fax 00 1 650-378 8592
e info@sfhomestay.com
W www.sfhomestay.com
Places students with American families in San Francisco, Berkeley and Silicon Valley.

Timing & Length of Stay: Stays from one week upwards are available year round.

Destinations: San Francisco, Silicon Valley, Berkeley & Stanford.

Costs/Pay: It costs from £78 a week for an economy homestay (shared room and shared bathroom), from £125 a week for a standard half-board homestay (own room, own bathroom). Various discounts are detailed online so check out the website. There's a one-off placement fee of £112.

Eligibility: The minimum age is 18.

How to Apply: Online.

COOKERY & COCKTAIL-MAKING IN THE UK

Cookery at the Grange
The Grange, Whatley, Frome, Somerset BA11 3JU
☎/fax 01373-836579
e info@cookery-grange.co.uk
W www.cookery-grange.co.uk
This is a very popular place for gap-year students to study. The courses are residential, with 24 students living on site. The social life is good.

Types of Course: The Essential Cookery Course and Chalet Course.

Timing & Length of Course: The Essential Cookery Course runs for four weeks, eight times a year. The Chalet Course is for five days in October each year.

Costs/Pay: The Essential Cookery Course costs from £2290, the Chalet Course from £650, including accommodation.

Eligibility: The minimum age is 18. You can only do the Chalet Course if you've done the Essential Cookery Course first.

How to Apply: It's advisable to book one year in advance.

Edinburgh School of Food & Wine
The Coach House, Newliston, Edinburgh EH29 9EB
☎ 0131-333 5001
fax 0131-333 5041
e info@esfw.com
W www.esfw.com
You can take courses in practical cookery, wine appreciation or basic food-handlers' hygiene, plus there's a six-month diploma course. There's also a special course for gap-year students.

Types of Course: Intensive Cook Certificate Course.

Timing & Length of Course: The course lasts five weeks and runs six times a year.

Costs/Pay: The course costs from £2500, including your essential cook's kit. Accommodation is extra.

Eligibility: The minimum age is 17.

Leiths School of Food & Wine

21 St Alban's Grove, Kensington, London
W8 5BP
☎ 020-7229 0177/020-7937 3366
fax 020-7937 5257
e info@leiths.com
W www.leiths.com

Founded in 1975, Leiths offers three main courses geared towards gap-year students (see below).

Types of Course: The Foundation Course, Basic Certificate in Practical Cookery and Beginners Certificate in Food & Wine.

Timing & Length of Course: The Foundation Course lasts from two to four weeks and starts mid-July, the Basic Certificate runs for four weeks from the end of August and the Beginners Certificate is for 10 weeks and starts at the end of September.

Costs/Pay: The Foundation Course costs from £979, the Basic Certificate from £2000 and the Beginners Certificate from £4150. All courses are non-residential.

Eligibility: The minimum age is 17.

Murray School of Cookery

Glenbervie House, Holt Pound, Farnham, Surrey GU10 4LE
☎/fax 01420-23049
e kmpmmsc@aol.com
W www.cookeryschool.net

Murray's non-residential courses are for up to nine students at a time. The two courses below are of real interest to gap-year students. It has contacts with ski companies and yachting agencies.

Types of Course: Certificate Course and Chalet Chef Course.

Timing & Length of Course: The Certificate Course lasts four weeks and runs seven times a year; the Chalet Chef Course lasts one week and runs twice a year in October.

Costs/Pay: The Certificate Course costs from £1500, the Chalet Chef Course from £395; accommodation is extra.

Eligibility: The minimum age is 18.

Shaker UK

4th floor, Exchange House, 494

Midsummer Blvd, Central Milton Keynes
MK9 2EA
☎ 01908-306010
fax 01908-255700
e gapyear@shakerbartending.co.uk
W www.shakerbartending.co.uk

Shaker offers practical courses for a durable and transferable skill in bartending and cocktail-making (mixology).

Types of Course: International Cocktail Bartenders' Course.

Timing & Length of Course: The course is for five days and runs monthly.

Costs/Pay: The course costs from £464, tuition only.

Destinations: London & Edinburgh.

Eligibility: The minimum age is 16.

Tante Marie School of Cookery

Woodham House, Carlton Rd, Woking, Surrey GU21 4HF
☎ 01483-726957
fax 01483-724173
e info@tantemarie.co.uk
W www.tantemarie.co.uk

Founded in 1954, courses range from diploma standard to short courses for amateurs. Gap-year students usually do the two courses listed below.

Types of Course: Cordon Bleu Certificate Course and Essential Skills Course.

Timing & Length of Course: The Certificate Course runs for three months, three times a year; the Essential Skills lasts one month and runs five times a year.

Costs/Pay: The Certificate Course costs from £4050, the Essential Skills from £1700; accommodation is excluded.

Eligibility: The minimum age is 16.

COOKERY ABROAD

Apicius Cooking School

Via Guelfa, 85 50129 Florence, Italy
☎ 00 39 055-2658135
fax 00 39 055-2656689
e info@apicius.it
W www.apicius.it

As well as offering professional one- and

three-year courses, this school has many different weekly and monthly courses plus a Culinary Programme for amateurs where you can study five out of 15 possible subjects, from Italian vegetarian cooking to an introduction to Italian wines.

Types of Course: The Culinary Programme for Amateurs.

Timing & Length of Course: The course runs for 15 weeks and starts in January and September each year.

Destination: Florence, Italy.

Costs/Pay: The tuition-only course costs from £3404, plus there's a lab fee of £50. Weekly and monthly courses are cheaper at under £625.

Ballymaloe Cookery School

Shanagarry, Co.Cork, Republic of Ireland
☎ 00 353 21-4646 785
fax 00 353 21-4646 909
e info@cookingisfun.ie
w www.cookingisfun.ie

Set in the countryside, close to the sea, this well-known Irish school runs short courses ranging from one day to one week, plus there are longer courses.

Types of Course: Certificate Course and Introduction Course.

Timing & Length of Course: The Certificate Course is 12 weeks starting in January and September each year; the Introduction Course lasts one week and runs once each July.

Costs/Pay: The Certificate Course costs from £4480, the Introduction Course from £445, tuition only.

Eligibility: The minimum age is 16.

How to Apply: Online applications are preferred.

Flying Fish

25 Union Rd, Cowes, Isle of Wight PO31 7TW
☎ 01983-280641
fax 01983-281821
e mail@flyingfishonline.com
w www.flyingfishonline.com

Flying Fish is a training provider for watersports staff (see Watersports, Sailing & Crewing later in this Contacts section). A new course started in 2003 where students are trained to cook on yachts. The cookery element of the course lasts six weeks and involves cooking both on dry land and at sea.

Types of Course: Galley Chef Training Course.

Timing & Length of Course: The course is for 10 weeks and runs two to three times a year.

Destinations: UK (three weeks) & Australia (seven weeks).

Costs/Pay: The course costs from £6970, including accommodation and flights.

Eligibility: The minimum age is 18.

Indus Tours & Travel Ltd

MWB Business Exchange, 2 Gayton Rd, Harrow, Middx HA1 2XU
☎ 020-8901 7320
fax 020-8901 7321
e holidays@industours.co.uk
w www.industours.co.uk

Indus primarily offers culinary tours with hands-on cooking along with talks, visits to markets etc, but can also fix up cookery courses for students in cookery schools, or with private chefs.

Timing & Length of Course: Courses are from one week upwards and can be arranged at any time.

Destinations: India, Nepal, Sri Lanka & Malaysia.

Costs/Pay: Courses cost from £30 a week for five lessons, excluding flights and accommodation.

Eligibility: The minimum age is 18.

How to Apply: Call the office to talk about your precise needs.

Laskarina Holidays

St Mary's Gate, Wirksworth, Derbyshire DE4 4DQ
☎ 01629-822203
fax 01629-822205
e info@laskarina.co.uk
w www.laskarina.co.uk

Laskarina is a specialist holiday company offering courses in the Greek Islands, incluuding a cookery course with the owner of the well-known Mythos restaurant on the island of Symi.

Types of Course: Cooking with Stavros.
Timing & Length of Course: The course lasts five days and runs in May or October.
Destination: The island of Symi, Greece.
Costs/Pay: Tuition costs from £195, excluding accommodation, flights and transfers.

Le Baou d'Infer Cookery School

63 Campden St, London W8 7EL
☎/fax 020-7727 0997
e alex@lebaou.com
w www.lebaou.com

On offer here are week-long cooking courses on a working vineyard 20 minutes by car from St Tropez. There's a swimming pool and a lively social life in the evenings.

Timing & Length of Course: The five-day courses run weekly from mid-May to the end of July and during the month of September.
Costs/Pay: The course costs from £1245, including full-board accommodation and transfers but not flights.
Eligibility: The minimum age is 18.

Mexican Home Cooking School

Apdo. 64, Tlaxcala 90000, Mexico
☎ 00 52 246-46 809 78
fax 00 52 246-46 809 78
e info@mexicanhomecooking.com
w www.mexicanhomecooking.com

On offer here is a hands-on cookery course with small classes of only four people. The mornings are spent in the kitchen and the afternoons are free for exploring.

Types of Course: Mexican Home Cookery.
Timing & Length of Course: The course is for five days and runs year round, depending on bookings.
Costs/Pay: The course, six nights full-board accommodation plus beer and wine costs from £625. There is a 10% discount for Lonely Planet readers.

How to Apply: There's usually a two-month waiting list so book early.

Tasting Places

Unit 108, Buspace Studios, Conlan St, London W10 5AP
☎ 020-7460 0077
fax 020-7460 0029
e ss@tastingplaces.com
w www.tastingplaces.com

Tasting Places offers cookery holidays in three main countries. It can also fix up bespoke courses for students anywhere in the world, at any time.

Timing & Length of Course: Holidays are for one week in spring or autumn.
Destinations: Thailand, Greece & Italy.
Costs/Pay: Tuition, full board and lodging costs from £895; flights cost extra.

THE ARTS

Writing

The Arvon Foundation (National Administration Office)

2nd Floor, 42a Buckingham Palace Rd, London SW1W ORE
☎ 020-7931 7611
fax 020-7963 0961
e london@arvonfoundation.org
w www.arvonfoundation.org

Although these are all UK-based courses, this registered charity has some of the best writing courses you'll find. Courses cover writing for many genres, including poetry, fiction, stage drama and writing for TV and radio.

Types of Course: Over 30 different courses, from Travel Writing to Song Writing.
Timing & Length of Course: All courses are for 4½ days and run weekly between April and December.
Destinations: Totleigh Barton (Devon), Lumb Bank (West Yorkshire), Moniack Mhor (Inverness-shire) & The Hurst (Shropshire).
Costs/Pay: Courses cost from £395, including tuition, accommodation and food – some

grants are available for those who cannot afford the fees.

Eligibility: The minimum age is 16.

How to Apply: Book through the centre that is running the course. All telephone details are online or in the brochure that you'll get from the national administration office.

Freie Universität Berlin, International Summer University

Abteilung Aubenangelegenheiten, Kaiserwerther Strasse 16-18, D-14195 Berlin, Germany

☎ 00 49 30-83873 445

fax 00 49 30-83873 442

e fusummer@fu-berlin.de

W www.fu-berlin.de/summeruniversity

Founded in 1948, the university runs an extensive summer-school programme, with several courses conducted in English.

Types of course: Creative Writing: Travel Memoir.

Timing & Length of Course: The course runs for two days a week from mid-July to mid-August.

Destination: Berlin.

Costs/Pay: Tuition costs from £416 and there's a £50 application fee. Accommodation can be arranged for early bookers.

Eligibility: Applicants must have completed at least one year of study at a university or college.

Skyros

92 Prince of Wales Rd, London NW5 3NE

☎ 020-7267 4424/7284 3065

fax 020-7284 3063

e enquiries@skyros.com

W www.skyros.com

Skyros is a specialist holistic holiday company offering courses that engage the mind, body and spirit. A variety of writing courses run nearly all year round, often with well-known writers such as Steven Berkoff or Mavis Cheek. Skyros also runs courses on writing for theatre.

Types of Course: Anything from The Short Story to Theatre & Screenplay Writing.

Timing & Length of Course: Courses last from two weeks. A writing course runs at least every two weeks.

Destinations: Two centres on the island of Skyros, Greece; one centre on the island of Ko Samet, Thailand.

Costs/Pay: Two weeks tuition and half-board accommodation in Greece costs from £450; flights cost extra. Under-25s get a 30% discount on the list price.

Eligibility: The minimum age is 15.

Art & Craft

Art Workshops in Guatemala

4758 Lyndale Ave South, Minneapolis, Minnesota 55409-2304, USA

☎ 00 1 612-825 0747

fax 00 1 612-825 6637

e info@artguat.org

W www.artguat.org

This is an Art School in Antigua set up and run by Liza Fourre, an American lady.

Types of Course: Backstrap Weaving, Beading, Textiles, Carpet Making, Ceramics with a Mayan Touch, Hand Paper-making.

Timing & Length of Course: All courses are for eight days and usually run once a year from February to April, in July and from the end of October to the beginning of November.

Destination: Guatemala.

Costs/Pay: Tuition, lodging, breakfast and transfer cost from £875; flights are extra.

Eligibility: The minimum age is 18.

Centro D'Arte Dedalo

Loc. Greppolungo 43-44, 55041 Camaiore (LU), Italy

☎/fax 00 39 0584 984 258

e info@dedaloarte.org

W www.artcoursestuscany.com or

W www.dedaloarte.org

In a farmhouse near Pienza, southern Tuscany, this international association of artists runs residential art courses in all media. All courses are taught in English and Italian.

Types of Course: Lots of courses are available covering bronze casting, sculpture, clay, mixed-media painting and fresco work.

Timing & Length of Course: Courses are for two weeks but you can stay for longer or shorter periods; they run from June to October.

Destination: Tuscany, Italy.

Costs/Pay: Courses cost from £740 for two weeks, including half-board and lodging.

Eligibility: The minimum age is 16; you need to find out which courses are for beginners.

Scuola Orafa Ambrosiana

Via Tadino 30, 20124, Milan, Italy
☎/fax 00 39 02-29405005
e info@scuolaorafaambrosiana.com
w www.scuolaorafaambrosiana.com

This is a famous goldsmith's school in the centre of Milan where students can learn the art of jewellery-making. Each master only teaches up to three students at a time. Many courses are taught in English and beginners are welcome.

Types of Course: There are nine different courses from a Hobby Course to a Gemstone Workshop through Enamel and Wax Casting classes.

Timing & Length of Course: Courses last from 22 to 115 hours and start daily except in August.

Destination: Milan.

Costs/Pay: Tuition only costs from £190 to £990.

Eligibility: The minimum age is 15.

The Verrocchio Arts Centre

119, Lynton Rd, Harrow, Mddx HA2 9NJ
☎/fax 020-8869 1035
e maureen.ruck@ukgateway.net
w www.verrocchio.co.uk

Located between Siena and Florence, this residential art school offers a range of fine-art courses with visiting tutors. All classes are taught in English.

Types of Course: There are 20 courses in painting and sculpture.

Timing & Length of Course: The two-week courses run fortnightly from mid-May to the end of September.

Destination: Tuscany, Italy.

Costs/Pay: Tuition and half-board accommodation costs from £780; flights are extra.

Fashion

Istituto di Moda Burgo

Piazza San Babila 5, 20122 Milan, Italy
☎ 00 39 02-3655 7600
fax 00 39 02-3655 7605
e imb@imb.it
w www.imb.it

This school of fashion and design has summer courses, shorter special courses for beginners and special courses for students with a degree in fashion. Lessons take place in Italian and English. You can preview the school on its website, thanks to the web cast.

Types of Course: Special courses include: Theatre Costume, Menswear, Womenswear, Childrenswear, Underwear, Wedding Dresses, Beachwear, Pattern Grading, Jewellery, Textile Design, Shoes, Accessories and Pattern Making. There are summer courses in Fashion Design and Pattern Making.

Timing & Length of Course: Short special courses are from 50 to 80 hours and normal ones are between 300 and 450 hours. Summer courses range from 54 to 104 hours.

Destinations: Milan.

Costs/Pay: Short special courses start at £312 and normal ones cost from £1375, tuition only. Summer courses cost from £562 and longer ones from £937. There is also an enrolment fee of £156.

Eligibility: The minimum age is 14. For some of the courses you need prior industry experience or a degree in fashion.

History of Art & Architecture

Art History Abroad

26 Delaune St, London SE17 3UU
☎/fax 020-7582 8082
e info@arthistoryabroad.com
w www.arthistoryabroad.com

Art History Abroad runs gap-year art-history trips to Italy with up to 20 different tutors, rather like a modern-day Grand Tour.

Types of Course: Art History.

Timing & Length of Course: Six-week trips run once in spring and once in autumn.

Destinations: Rome, Florence, Naples & Venice.

Costs/Pay: The course costs from £4500, including tuition, flights, B&B accommodation, transport, museum entrance fees, basic Italian lessons, reading list and notes.

Eligibility: The minimum age is 18.

The British Institute of Florence

Palazzo Strozzino, Piazza Strozzi 2, I-50123 Florence, Italy

☎ 00 39 055-2677 8200
fax 00 39 055-2677 8222
e info@britishinstitute.it
w www.britishinstitute.it

Established in 1917 to promote the cultures and language of Great Britain and Italy, the institute runs many courses throughout the year, plus August summer courses in the Tuscan hill town of Massa Marittima. The institute also runs Italian language courses.

Types of Course: Art History, Italian Opera, Film, Tuscan Cooking, Painting and Architecture.

Timing & Length of Course: Courses are from two days to one year; most run monthly.

Destinations: Florence & Massa Marittima.

Costs/Pay: Tuition only costs from £95 for one week and from £300 for four weeks. Help can be given to find accommodation.

Eligibility: The minimum age is 18.

John Hall Pre-University Course

12 Gainsborough Rd, Ipswich, Suffolk IP4 2UR

☎ 01473-251223
fax 01473-288009
e info@johnhallpre-university.com
w www.johnhallpre-university.com

Established in 1965, this company offers a course for gap-year students covering European civilisation, art history, architecture, music, literature, cinema, photography and life-drawing classes, with optional Italian language courses. Thirty different lecturers are used during the course.

Types of Course: The Pre-University Course.

Timing & Length of Course: The course is from seven to nine weeks and starts at the end of January each year.

Destinations: One week is spent in London and six weeks in Venice, with an optional week in Florence and five days in Rome on top of that.

Costs/Pay: Seven weeks cost from £5800, including flights, half-board accommodation, lectures, visits, classes, etc.

Eligibility: The minimum age is 18.

University of Sydney

Continuing Education, Locked Bag 20, Glebe, NSW 2037, Australia

☎ 00 61 2-9351 2907
fax 00 61 2-9351 5022
e info@cce.usyd.edu.au
w www.cce.usyd.edu.au

Continuing Education is a not-for-profit centre of the University of Sydney. It runs 1200 part-time short courses a year on a whole variety of subjects, some specialising in Aboriginal art and culture like the one following.

Types of Course: Australian Aboriginal Art.

Timing & Length of Course: There are four terms: summer, autumn, mid-year and spring (remember that summer in Australia means January to February) and two courses per term.

Destination: Sydney.

Costs/Pay: Tuition only costs from £45.

Eligibility: The minimum age is 16.

How to Apply: Enrol online.

Film

The Film School

PO Box 27-044, Marion Square, Wellington, New Zealand

☎ 00 64 4-380 1250
fax 00 64 4-939 2951

e info@filmschool.org.nz
w www.filmschool.org.nz
This new school is rapidly gaining an excellent worldwide reputation – New Zealand is also a cheap place to study. There's one course designed to fast-track students for a working career in the screen-production industry, initially in a crew position.
Types of Course: A certificate course in Introduction to Film and Television Production.
Timing & Length of Course: The course is for 40 weeks and there are two intakes a year in February and July.
Destination: New Zealand.
Costs/Pay: The course costs from £5981, tuition only.
Eligibility: The minimum age is 18 and you'll have to apply for a student visa.

Freie Universität Berlin, International Summer University

See Writing earlier in this Contacts section for contact details.
Types of Course: German Cinema Classics (taught in English).
Timing & Length of Course: The course runs for two days a week from mid-July to mid-August.
Destination: Berlin, Germany.
Costs/Pay: Tuition costs from £416 and there's a £50 application fee. Accommodation can be arranged for early bookers.
Eligibility: You must have completed at least one year of study at a university or college.

New York Film Academy

King's College, The Strand, London WC2R 2LS
☎ 020-7848 1523
fax 020-7848 1443
e filmuk@nyfa.com
w www.nyfa.com
This academy runs both long and short courses on Filmmaking and Acting for Film. These are very hands-on, practical courses.

Additional courses on Screen-writing, Digital Editing and Digital Filmmaking might be available by the time this book is published.
Types of Course: Filmmaking.
Timing & Length of Course: Courses are from four weeks to one year. Short courses start every month and the yearlong course starts four times a year.
Destinations: New York & Los Angeles, and other worldwide locations during the summer.
Costs/Pay: Four weeks' tuition (including equipment) costs from £2188, one year from £14,000. On top of this is the cost for film stock and processing.
Eligibility: The minimum age is 18.
How to Apply: Contact the London office or apply online. You'll need to get a student visa from the US embassy.

Photography

La Maison Rose

Rue Gerard Roques, 81630 Salvagnac, France
☎/fax 00 33 563 40 59 22
e fchallis@photohols.com
w www.photohols.com
Located in the south of France, there's even a swimming pool here for use between Golden Hours (early morning and late afternoon). Courses are taught in English.
Types of Course: The Landscape in Colour, Wild Orchids Special, The Landscape in Black & White, Freestyle.
Timing & Length of Course: All courses are one-week long and run during the months of May, July, September and October. They start weekly; some start on a Saturday, some on a Wednesday.
Destinations: The area around Salvagnac, France.
Costs/Pay: Courses cost from £350 for tuition, half-board accommodation, transfers from Toulouse airport and travel to all photographic locations.
How to Apply: Please use the online booking system. If you need to send a fax ring first so phone can be switched over.

PS Travel Group

The Royal Photographic Society, The
Octagon, Milsom St, Bath BA1 1DN
☎ 01225-462841
fax 01225-448688
e chairman@rpstravel.org
w www.rpstravel.org

This is an offshoot of the Royal Photographic
Society (RPS) that organises photographic
trips and workshops abroad a couple of times
a year. The trips are not strictly courses;
their aim is for you to take as many photos
as possible in beautiful areas of the world
and learn from other members and non-
members of the RPS.

Types of Course: Overseas photographic
trips.

Timing & Length of Course: There are
usually two-week trips twice a year.

Destinations: In 2003 it was the Galápagos
Islands. Other possible destinations for 2004
onwards include: Jordan, Mexico, Scottish
Outer Islands, Iceland & Greenland.

Costs/Pay: The Galápagos trip cost from
£2380 all inclusive.

Eligibility: The minimum age is 18.

How to Apply: Email the chairman for a
booking form.

Music

Agoro Ciltad

PO Box 711, Cape Coast, Ghana,
West Africa
☎ 00 233 42-32654
e agoro@agoro.org or
e agorociltad@yahoo.com
w www.agoro.org

Ghanaian drumming and dance, African
music and culture courses have been available here since 1993. Accommodation is
arranged at the self-catering Agoro Guest
House.

Types of Course: There are four different
Rhythm and Drums courses, from beginners
upwards.

Timing & Length of Course: Courses last
three, eight or 10 weeks and run one after
the other year round.

Destination: Cape Coast in the Central
Region of Ghana.

Costs/Pay: The three-week course costs
from £406, including full board and lodging. The other courses start from £750 for
tuition, accommodation and five welcome
meals.

Eligibility: The minimum age is 18.

David Hill

Calle del Pino, 17-11408, Jerez de la
Frontera, Cadiz, Spain
☎ 00 34 956-34 09 74
e bebitajoon@hotmail.com
w www.geocities.com/jerezflamenco

David is an English-born flamenco guitar
teacher based full-time in Jerez. Classes at
all levels are taught in English. David can
also put you in touch with flamenco dance
academies that will be open at the time you
want to visit.

Types of Course: All forms of flamenco
guitar.

Timing & Length of Course: You can have
one lesson or more year round. If you're a
beginner, 50 hours of tuition is advised to
cover the basic forms.

Destination: Jerez de la Frontera.

Costs/Pay: Lessons cost from £15 per
hour. There's a special rate for more than
30 hours of tuition.

Drama

Year Out Drama Company

Stratford-upon-Avon College,
The Willows North, Alcester Rd,
Stratford-upon-Avon CV37 9QR
☎ 01789-266245
fax 01789-267524
e yearoutdrama@Stratford.ac.uk
w www.yearoutdrama.com

There are 24 places available each year at
this college. It runs an intensive, broad-based
drama course for gap-year students of all
abilities. Subjects studied include acting,
directing, script-writing, design, movement,
music and costumes.

Types of Course: The Year Out Drama Course.

Timing & Length of Course: The course runs for one year from September.

Destination: Stratford-upon-Avon.

Costs/Pay: The course costs from £3900, including all tuition, production costs and numerous theatre visits. You will be housed in halls of residence at your own cost.

Eligibility: The minimum age is 18.

How to Apply: Application forms are processed year round but it's best to give at least four months' notice. Successful candidates will then have an interview.

HIGH SCHOOLS/COLLEGES IN THE US, CANADA OR EUROPE

Academic Associates International
46 High St, Ewell Village, Surrey
KT17 1RW
☎ 020-8786 7711
fax 020-8786 7755
e enquiry@aaiuk.org
w www.aaiuk.org
Cultural exchange programmes arranged in America and Europe.

Types of Course: You attend a high school in America and a language/local school in Europe, eg, in France you might attend the Sorbonne.

Timing & Length of Course: Courses are from 12 weeks to nine months and start at the beginning or middle of the year.

Destinations: The USA, France, Germany, Italy & Spain.

Costs/Pay: Twelve weeks in Europe costs from £2875. Nine months in the USA starts from £3790. Accommodation is included.

Eligibility: Applicants must be aged between 16 and 21.

Accommodation: The package includes accommodation either with a host family or in student residences.

How to Apply: Obtain an interview application form from the office. Interviews are held monthly in London and Edinburgh.

Challenge Educational Services
See Language Agencies earlier in this section

for contact details. This company also provides cross-cultural exchange programmes where you get to spend an academic year in an American high school.

Types of Course: You attend six to eight 45-minute classes per day and can choose your own subjects.

Timing & Length of Course: programmes are for either five or 10 months and start in January or August.

Destination: The USA.

Costs/Pay: Ten months cost from £3495, including accommodation and £500 towards your flight.

Eligibility: Applicants must be aged between 15 and 18 (the maximum age is 18 and six months at enrolment).

Accommodation: Accommodation is with host families.

English-Speaking Union
Dartmouth House, 37 Charles St, London
W1J 5ED
☎ 020-7529 1550
fax 020-7495 6108
e esu@esu.org
w www.esu.org
A number of programmes, scholarships and opportunities are offered worldwide by this registered charity that promotes international understanding through the use of English.

Types of Course: Secondary School Exchange Programme at a boarding school in the US or Canada.

Timing & Length of Course: Programmes are for two or three academic terms: September to July or January to July.

Destinations: Canada & the USA.

Costs/Pay: There are around 30 scholarships available each year that are worth about £18,750 each and cover full-board accommodation and tuition. All other expenses such as flights, uniform and books have to be met by the student (around £2500).

Eligibility: The minimum age is 19 years and six months at the time school starts.

How to Apply: Apply to the education officer by letter and an application form will be sent to you. There is then a selection and interview process. Application closing dates are mid-January and early September.

HEALTH & EXERCISE

Annaharvey Farm Equestrian Centre
Tullamore, Co. Offaly, Ireland
☎ 00 353 506-43544
fax 00 353 506-43766
e info@annaharveyfarm.ie
w www.annaharveyfarm.ie
In the middle of Ireland, four miles from Tullamore, this equestrian centre has indoor and outdoor arenas plus its own accommodation so you can stay for a weekend, a week or longer.
Types of Course: Show Jumping, Cross-Country and Dressage.
Timing & Length of Course: Lessons last one hour. You can book as many you want, whenever you want.
Destination: Ireland.
Costs/Pay: Lessons cost from £14 per hour. B&B at the centre costs £20 and full board is £40.

Càlédöñiâ Languages Abroad
See Language Agencies earlier in this section for contact details. This company also offers a number of holidays with dance instruction combined with a language element. It can also fix up salsa lessons in Cuba any time of the year.
Types of Course: Salsa & Spanish Language in Cuba, Flamenco & Spanish Language in Spain.
Timing & Length of Course: Both courses run for between two and four weeks. The Cuba trip departs in February, July and November; the Spanish trip departs in February, April, June, September and October.
Destinations: Santiago de Cuba & Vejer de la Frontera.
Costs/Pay: A two-week course in Cuba costs from £695, including half-board accommodation, three evenings out to local clubs, two cultural activities and a day trip; flights are extra. A two-week Spanish trip

costs from £335, tuition only – everything else is extra.
Eligibility: The minimum age is 17.

Circus Oz
40 Bay St, Port Melbourne, Victoria 3207, Australia
☎ 00 61 3-9646 8899
fax 00 61 3-9646 9334
e admin@circusoz.com.au
w www.circusoz.com.au
This celebrated Australian circus has been going since 1978 and offers a series of workshops and courses for beginners or professionals.
Types of Course: From Tumbling to Clowning, Hula Hoops to Flying Trapeze.
Timing & Length of Course: Courses run four times a year and vary considerably in length, so it's best to ask at the time you're applying.
Destination: Melbourne, Australia.
Costs/Pay: Tuition costs from £30.
How to Apply: Download the application form from the website.

Karuna Yoga School
79 Clarendon Rd, Southampton SO16 4GD
☎/fax 02380-773 987
e paul.riddy@virgin.net
w www.karuna-yoga.co.uk
The yoga school has a purpose-built house in Romania and has offered yoga lessons there for years. The Spanish trip was new in 2003 and might expand.
Types of Course: Yoga & Walking (four to five hours of yoga a day).
Timing & Length of Course: Trips last one week and depart in May and September to Romania and in June to Spain.
Destinations: Romania & Spain.
Costs/Pay: Trips cost from £250 for tuition and full-board accommodation. Flights are extra.

The Peligoni Club
PO Box 88, Chichester,
W Sussex PO20 7DP

☎ 01243-511499
fax 01243-513132
e fairlie@peliclub.fsnet.co.uk
w www.peligoni.com
The Peligoni is a watersports club, which offers holidays for those interested in learning about a variety of mental and physical exercise.
Types of Course: Reiki, Pilates, Yoga, Movement, Meditation.
Timing & Length of Course: Holidays are for one or two weeks in June and September.
Destination: The Island of Zakynthos, Greece.
Costs/Pay: One week costs from £500, including full-board accommodation; flights cost extra.
Eligibility: The minimum age is 18.

Skyros

See The Arts section earlier for contact details. Skyros also runs loads of 'alternative' lifestyle and curative courses.
Types of Course: Many types of Yoga, Reiki, Massage, Meditation, Aromatherapy, Reflexology, Tai Chi and a combination of several similar disciplines.
Timing & Length of Course: Two-week courses run at least every fortnight.
Destinations: There are two centres on the island of Skyros, Greece, and one on the island of Ko Samet, Thailand.
Costs/Pay: Two weeks cost from £450, including half-board accommodation but not flights. Under-25s get a 30% discount on the list price.
Eligibility: The minimum age is 15.

Susan French Belly Dancing Holidays

42 Sefton St, Putney, London SW15 1LZ
☎ 020-8789 4968
e susandeniz@hotmail.com
w www.bellydancingholidays.co.uk
Susan has been belly dancing since 1992 and teaching since 1997. She holds classes in Fulham, London. Two or three times a year she takes groups abroad to teach.
Types of Course: Belly-dancing.

Timing & Length of Course: Trips abroad are for one to two weeks and depart in May and October for Turkey. A trip to Dubai may be slotted in from 2003.
Destinations: Turkey & Dubai.
Costs/Pay: A one-week trip costs from £524, including tuition, half-board accommodation, flights, transfers and a show.

Tai Chi Chuan Center

Naisuan House, Room 201, 3/7 Doi Saket Kao (Rattanakosin), Soi 1, T.Watgate, A.Mung, Chiang Mai 50000, Thailand
☎ 00 66 017067406 (mobile)
e keithtaichi@yahoo.com/
keithtaichi@hotmail.com
w www.taichithailand.com
There are morning, mid-day and evening practical sessions held here, combined with discussion on topics such as Tai Chi Philosophy and theory, the I-Ching and the Tao Te Ching.
Types of Course: Intensive-training programme on The Essential Postures of Tai Chi Chuan.
Timing & Length of Course: This is a 10-day course (60 hours) with year-round classes starting on the 1st and 16th of every month.
Destination: Chiang Mai, Thailand.
Costs/Pay: The programme costs from £123, including lodging.

DIVING

Camel Dive Club & Hotel

Sharm El Sheikh, South Sinai, Egypt
☎ 00 20 69-600700
fax 00 20 69-600601
e info@cameldive.com
w www.cameldive.com
This is a PADI-registered dive school with multi-lingual instructors. Many courses are offered from beginner to dive master.
Types of Course: PADI Open Water Diver Course for beginners.
Timing & Length of Course: This course lasts for four to five days and runs every couple of days.

Destination: The Red Sea, Egypt.

Costs/Pay: Tuition and equipment costs from £200.

Eligibility: The minimum age is 10. You must be reasonably fit and healthy, and be able to swim and feel relaxed in water.

Dive Centre Manly

10 Belgrave St, Manly, NSW 2095, Australia

☎ 00 61 2-9977 4355

fax 00 61 2-9977 3664

e dcm@divesydney.com.au

w www.divesydney.com

This is a PADI 5-star IDC (Instructor Development Courses) centre offering courses for beginners through to instructor/divemaster training programmes and shark dive courses. There's also a school in Bondi.

Types of Course: PADI Open Water Diver Course for beginners.

Timing & Length of Course: The course takes place over four to five days and starts every Monday.

Destinations: Qualifying dives take place at Shelly Beach, Little Manly, Fairy Bower & Fairlight in Australia.

Costs/Pay: Tuition and all equipment costs from £123. A diving medical costs an extra £18.

Eligibility: The minimum age is 12. You must be able to swim for 200 metres and tread water for at least 10 minutes.

London Scuba Diving School

Rabys Barn, New Chapel Rd, Lingfield, Surrey RH7 6LE

☎ 07000 27 28 22

fax 07000 34 83 85

e team@londonscuba.com

w www.londonscuba.com

Based in London, this PADI-registered dive school offers many courses including the Open Water Diver Course with two days pool and theory in London followed by one week in the Red Sea doing qualifying dives.

Types of Course: PADI Open Water Diver Course for beginners.

Timing & Length of Course: The course runs for 11 days and there are nine start dates a year.

Destinations: London & Red Sea.

Costs/Pay: The course costs from between £600 and £850, including flights, transfers and B&B.

Eligibility: The minimum age is 18. You must be able to both swim and tread water for 10 minutes. There's also a medical form to complete.

WATERSPORTS, SAILING & CREWING

Acorn Adventure

Acorn House, 22 Worcester St, Stourbridge, W Midlands DY8 1AN

☎ 01384-378827

fax 01384-378866

e inquiries@acornadventure.co.uk

w www.acornadventure.co.uk

Acorn has 10 centres in Europe offering training in all watersports, plus National Governing Body instructor qualifications and all levels within the dinghy scheme.

Types of Course: There are 14 watersports and dinghy sailing courses leading to nationally recognised certification.

Timing & Length of Course: Courses are for one day to one week from April to September and start daily.

Destinations: France, Italy, Spain & the UK.

Costs/Pay: Courses cost from £50 to £400, including board and lodging but excluding flights.

Eligibility: The minimum age is 16 or 18, depending on the course.

Flying Fish

25 Union Rd, Cowes, Isle of Wight

☎ 01983-280641

fax 01983-281821

e mail@flyingfishonline.com

w www.flyingfishonline.com

Flying Fish is a training provider for watersports staff and arranges employment for sailors, divers, surfers, kitesurfers and windsurfers. Much of the training takes place abroad.

Types of Course: There are 50 different courses leading to professional qualifications as a watersport instructor or yacht skipper; some courses are for beginners, others require previous experience.

Timing & Length of Course: Most courses start eight times a year and last from two weeks to three months, depending on the course. Everything is linked to their recruitment service.

Destinations: Vassiliki in Greece & Sydney in Australia.

Costs/Pay: Courses cost from £1290 to £10,350, including flights and accommodation.

Eligibility: The minimum age is 18.

Jubilee Sailing Trust

Hazel Rd, Woolston, Southampton, Hants SO19 7GB
☎ 023-8044 9108
fax 023-8044 9145
e youth@jst.org.uk
w www.jst.org.uk

Jubilee is a registered charity for able-bodied and disabled young people to crew a tall ship together. You can take part in the Youth Leadership @ Sea scheme. This could lead to sailing as bosun's mate or watch leader on future voyages, either free of charge or at discounted rates.

Types of Course: Youth Leadership @ Sea and informal sail training.

Timing & Length of Course: Courses are from five days to four weeks; a ship sets sail each week.

Destinations: The Mediterranean, Canary Islands and Caribbean in winter, and around the UK and wherever the Tall Ships Race is held in summer.

Costs/Pay: Courses cost from £195 for five days (you get a £300 discount for doing the Youth Leadership scheme), from £1600 for four weeks.

Eligibility: The minimum age is 16.

Lymington Cruising School

24 Waterloo Rd, Lymington, Hants SO41 9DB
☎ 01590-677478
fax 01590-689210
e lymingtoncruisin@aol.com
w www.lymingtoncruising.co.uk

This Royal Yachting Association (RYA) training centre on the River Lym offers the whole range of RYA national cruising scheme courses, both shore-based and practical.

Types of Course: Competent Crew Practical Course.

Timing & Length of Course: The course is for five days and runs weekly between March and October.

Destinations: From Lymington to The Solent and Poole.

Costs/Pay: Courses cost from £480 for five days, including board and lodging.

Eligibility: The minimum age is 16.

Neilson Active Holidays

Locks View, Brighton Marina, Brighton, E Sussex BN2 5HA
☎ 0870 909 9099
fax 0870 909 9089
e sales@neilson.com
w www.neilson.com

Neilson is a holiday company offering RYA-recognised courses in windsurfing, yachting and dinghy sailing, plus PADI diving courses.

Types of Course: RYA Levels One to Four for windsurfing, Levels One to Three for dinghy sailing, Levels One and Two for keel boats.

Timing & Length of Course: Courses are from one to two weeks, or longer if required.

Destinations: Greece, Croatia, the Caribbean, Egypt, Spain & Turkey.

Costs/Pay: One week costs from £619, including flights, half-board accommodation and tuition.

Eligibility: The minimum age is 18.

Sail Training Association

2a The Hard, Portsmouth, Hants PO1 3PT
☎ 023-9283 2055
fax 023-9281 5769
e Tallships@sta.org.uk
w www.sta.org.uk

Various sailing courses run while at sea are offered by this registered charity running voyages on tall ships. You can move from being voyage crew to becoming volunteer crew and to sailing around the world for long periods of time for a nominal fee.

Types of Course: Competent Crew Practical Course, Duke of Edinburgh gold award scheme (residential section), STA Recommendation Award.

Timing & Length of Course: Courses last from 10 to 30 days.

Destinations: Europe & the Caribbean.

Costs/Pay: Courses cost from £800 for 10 days, including board, lodging and a berth. Some funding is available for people aged between 16 and 25 if needed.

Eligibility: You must be aged between 16 and 26, although there are some adult voyages that young people can join too.

How to Apply: Ring the office. If you're looking for funding there's an interview process.

Solent School of Yachting

Unit 11, Universal Marina, Crableck Lane, Sarisbury Green, Southampton, Hants SO31 7ZN
☎ 01489-577383
fax 01489-572054
e info@solentsail.org
w www.solentsail.org

A RYA-recognised sailing school on the River Hamble offering courses from Competent Crew through to Ocean Master.

Types of Course: Competent Crew Practical Course.

Timing & Length of Course: The course runs for five days or three weekends and starts weekly.

Destinations: From the River Hamble up to the Isle of Wight, Beaulieu and Portsmouth/Gosport.

Costs/Pay: Courses costs from £418 for five days, including board and lodging but excluding mooring fees (maximum £20 a week).

Eligibility: Applicants must be aged over 16 and able to swim.

Sunsail

The Port House, Port Solent, Portsmouth, Hampshire PO6 4TH
☎ 023-9222 2222
fax 023-9221 9827
e sales@sunsail.com
w www.sunsail.com

Sunsail is a holiday company that specialises in watersport activities and yacht charter. A number of sailing courses run for beginners to advanced students.

Types of Course: Yacht Sailing Course.

Timing & Length of Course: Courses are from two to five days, throughout the year on demand.

Destinations: Thailand, Malaysia, Australia & America.

Costs/Pay: Courses cost from £340 for five days half-board, living aboard, and tuition.

Eligibility: The minimum age is 18.

Wildwind Holidays

2a Star St, Ware, Herts SG12 7AA
☎ 01920-484516
fax 01920-484704
e wildwind@dial.pipex.com
w www.wildwind.co.uk

Wildwind is a holiday company specialising in high-performance catamaran and dinghy sailing courses. It is a recognised RYA teaching establishment offering courses up to Level Five.

Types of Course: Fourteen courses from Level One to Five.

Timing & Length of Course: Courses last from two days to two weeks and run from May to October.

Destination: Vassiliki, Greece.

Costs/Pay: Courses cost from £399, including flights and accommodation.

Eligibility: The minimum age is 18.

SKIING & SNOWBOARDING INSTRUCTOR COURSES

Basecamp Group

Howick, Balls Cross, Petworth, W Sussex GU28 9JY
☎/fax 01403-820899

e contact@basecampgroup.com
w www.basecampgroup.com

Basecamp offers the BASI trainee and instructor courses for skiing or snowboarding, and also provides racing, bumps, freeride and freestyle training. The programme also includes first aid, avalanche/mountain awareness and French classes.

Types of Course: Gap Snowsports programme.

Timing & Length of Course: The programme runs for 11 weeks and starts in January.

Destination: Meribel, France.

Costs/Pay: From £5695, including tuition, accommodation and transfers but excluding flights.

Eligibility: The minimum age is 17.

British Association of Snow Sport Instructors (BASI)

Glenmore, Aviemore, Inverness-shire PH22 1QU

☎ 01479-861717
fax 01479-861 718
e gap@basi.org.uk
w www.basi.org.uk

BASI is the training and grading agency for all snowsport instructors in the UK on snow (ie, real snow, not artificial slopes). BASI hopes to have a dedicated gap-year adviser by the time this book is published.

Types of Course: Ski or Snowboard Instructor qualification.

Timing & Length of Course: 10-week courses start in January.

Destinations: Andorra, Italy, Switzerland & the USA.

Costs/Pay: Courses cost from £4000, including accommodation, half-board, training fees but excluding flights.

Eligibility: The minimum age is 17.

The International Academy

St Hilary Court, Copthorne Way, Culverhouse Cross, Cardiff CF5 6ES

☎ 02920-672500
fax 02920-672510
e info@international-academy.com
w www.international-academy.com

The academy provides professional instructor training courses mainly in skiing and snowboarding. The national governing body of the country in which you train awards qualifications.

Types of Course: Snowboard Instructor and Skiing Instructor courses.

Timing & Length of Course: Courses are from four weeks to 12 weeks in January, March and July.

Destinations: The USA, Canada, New Zealand, Europe & South America.

Costs/Pay: Courses cost from £4500 for four weeks, including flights, accommodation, food, tuition and examination fees.

Eligibility: The minimum age is 16. Applicants need to have some snow experience but all levels can be catered for.

Peak Leaders

Mansfield, Strathmiglo, Fife KY14 7QE, Scotland

☎/fax 01337-860 079
e info@peakleaders.co.uk
w www.peakleaders.co.uk

Peak Leaders offers gap-year and time-out programmes in skiing and snowboarding courses, including mountain safety, avalanche awareness, first aid and leadership skills.

Types of Course: Snowboarding Instructor Certificate, Ski and Snowboard Leadership.

Timing & Length of Course: Courses run for nine weeks and start in January and July.

Destinations: Canada & Argentina.

Costs/Pay: Courses cost from £5450, including accommodation and flights.

Eligibility: The minimum age is 17.

Ski Le Gap

220 Wheeler St, Mont-Tremblant, Québec J8E 1V3, Canada

☎ 0800 328 0345
fax 00 1 819-425 7074
e info@skilegap.com
w www.skilegap.com

Catering particularly to British gap-year students, the school runs two courses – the Mini Gap and the Main Gap. Ski Le Gap can also help you to get work visas and jobs after the courses.

Types of Course: CSIA (Canadian Ski Instructor's Association) Ski and CASI (Canadian Association of Snowboard Instructors) Snowboard instructor courses.

Timing & Length of Course: Mini Gap is a four-week course starting late November and the Main Gap course is for three months starting in January.

Destination: Mont Tremblant resort, Québec.

Costs/Pay: Courses cost from £2600 for four weeks, including half-board accommodation but excluding flights. The Main Gap is from £6000, including half-board accommodation, flights, French lessons, first-aid course, city trips and an outdoor experience weekend.

Eligibility: The minimum age is 18. Intermediate level is needed for the four-week course but beginners can do the three-month one.

GAP YEAR, WILDERNESS & JUNGLE SURVIVAL

Bear Creek Outdoor Centre

RR#3 Campbell's Bay, Québec J0X 1K0, Canada

☎ 00 1 819-453 2127 (summer),
☎ 00 1 613-622 0553 (winter)
fax 00 1 819-453 2128 (summer),
fax 00 1 613-622 0554 (winter)
e info@bearcreekoutdoor.com
w www.bearcreekoutdoor.com

Bear Creek is an outdoor centre in the Ottawa Valley, at the foothills of the Laurentian Mountains. Solar energy and gravity provide all electricity and running water. Courses are run in Outdoor Adventure Leadership, with a bent towards watersports. There are over 10 different certificates you can gain during the course.

Types of Course: Gap Year Programme.

Timing & Length of Course: Courses last for 10 weeks from mid-June.

Destination: Canada.

Costs/Pay: Courses cost from £3700, including certification, full board and lodging, and all in-country transportation. Flights are extra.

Eligibility: The minimum age is 18. You must consider yourself in good health and be able to swim.

Frontier

50–52 Rivington St, London EC2A 3QP
☎ 020-7613 2422
fax 020-7613 2992
e info@frontier.ac.uk
w www.frontier.ac.uk

Frontier is an international conservation organisation that runs environmental-research expeditions for self-funding volunteers. The training you'll receive in the field can qualify you for two BTEC (Business Training and Education Council) awards.

Types of Course: BTEC Advanced Diploma in Tropical Habitat. Conservation and/or BTEC Certificate in Expedition Management (biodiversity research).

Timing & Length of Course: Expeditions run for 28 days, 10 weeks and 20 weeks; they depart four times a year.

Destinations: Tanzania, Vietnam, Madagascar & Nicaragua.

Costs/Pay: Expeditions cost from £1850 for 28 days, £2150 for 10 weeks and £3400 for 20 weeks, including full board, lodging and all in-country costs; flights and the cost of BTEC assessment (£200) are extra.

Eligibility: The minimum age is 17.

How to Apply: Contact Laura Perry for an application form; there will then be an interview and full briefing process if selected.

Global Vision International (GVI)

Amwell Farm House, Nomansland,
Wheathampstead, St Albans AL4 8EJ
☎ 01582-831300
fax 01582-834002
e info@gvi.co.uk
w www.gvi.co.uk

Global Vision runs expeditions and community projects in conjunction with registered charities worldwide. It also runs one course that covers ecology, botany, taxonomy, tracking, identification, weapons handling and bush driving. This is the first part of the FGASA (Field Guide's Association of South Africa) programme.

Types of Course: Safari Field Guide Course.

Timing & Length of Course: The course last four weeks and runs monthly except December.

Destination: Karongwe Game Reserve, South Africa.

Costs/Pay: The course costs from £835, including full board and lodging, transfers and project equipment but excluding flights.

Eligibility: The minimum age is 18 and applicants must have a driving licence.

Newbury College

Monks Lane, Newbury, Berks RG14 7TD
☎ 01635-845255
fax 01635-845313
e student-services@newbury-college.ac.uk
W www.newbury-college.ac.uk

Year 2003 sees a new course for gap-year students on how to teach rock-climbing, kayaking, open canoeing, rafting, mountain-biking and orienteering. The course is totally geared towards you getting a job either abroad or at home afterwards.

Types of Course: Introductory Outdoor Pursuits Instructor Training – Gap Year.

Timing & Length of Course: Courses run from September to early May each year.

Destinations: Newbury and away-day destinations.

Costs/Pay: Tuition costs from £600; weekends away cost extra.

Eligibility: The minimum age is 18. Enthusiasm and an interest in outdoor pursuits are vital.

Peak Leaders

See Skiing and Snowboarding Instructor Courses earlier in this section for contact details. This company also runs a jungle course covering expedition planning and leadership, diving, sailing and then a proper expedition to remote islands.

Types of Course: Jungle Leadership.

Timing & Length of Course: The course lasts for six weeks and starts mid-September.

Destination: Indonesia.

Costs/Pay: The course costs from £2950, all inclusive.

Eligibility: The minimum age is 17.

Plas y Brenin

Capel Curig, Conwy LL24 0ET
☎ 01690-720214
fax 01690-720394
e info@pyb.co.uk
W www.pyb.co.uk

Plas y Brenin is a national mountaineering centre based in Snowdonia. A former hotel, the accommodation is excellent for residential courses.

Types of Course: Summer & Winter Mountain Leadership Certificate.

Timing & Length of Course: You must complete the summer award before registering for the winter one. The summer course runs from January to November and takes six days, followed by 20 logged mountain days. The winter course runs from January to March and takes six days, followed by another 20 logged mountain days. Courses run twice a month.

Destinations: The summer course takes place in North Wales, the winter course in Scotland.

Costs/Pay: The summer course costs from £375, the assessment from £375 and the first-aid course from £150. The winter training costs from £395 and the assessment from £370. Both courses are residential and include all meals, accommodation and equipment.

Eligibility: The minimum age is 20 and you need to have completed 20 logged mountain days before starting either of the courses.

Ridgefellows Outdoor Training Ltd

21 Belle Meade Close, Chichester,
W Sussex PO20 6YD
☎/fax 01202-479497

e ridgefellows@aol.com
w www.ridgefellows.com
Ridgefellows provides beginner and advanced courses in all aspects of wilderness survival for groups or individuals. Although all training except for Jungle Skills takes place in the UK, they are good courses to do before going off on your gap-year abroad.
Types of Course: Lone Female Traveller Safety, Basic & Advanced Wilderness Survival Skills, Navigation & Orienteering, Jungle Survival Skills.
Timing & Length of Course: Courses last from two to 10 days and run once a month from March to October; some courses also run over winter.
Destinations: Dorset, Wales & Scotland. Jungle training takes place in Peru, Ecuador or Belize.
Costs/Pay: Courses cost from £100 for the two-day Lone Female Traveller Safety course, including full board and lodging, with a 10% discount for NUS cardholders.
Eligibility: The minimum age is 17.

Wilderness Expertise
The Octagon, Wellington College, Crowthorne, Berks RG45 7PU
☎ 01344-774430
fax 01344-774480
e info@wilderness-expertise.co.uk
w www.wilderness-expertise.co.uk
Specialising in the personal development of students, Wilderness Expertise runs a Uni Survival Guide, Leadership and Key Skills training plus courses specifically geared towards the gap-year student intending to go overseas.
Types of Course: Year-Off Traveller's Survival Guide and six levels of the Rescue, Emergency, Care First Aid course (REC), from beginner to trainer.
Timing & Length of Course: Each REC level takes place over one to five days, and courses run over 20 times a year. The Year-Off Traveller's Guide is tailor-made to the student but usually lasts two to five days and runs about six times a year.
Destination: The UK.

Costs/Pay: REC courses range from £110 to £600, tuition only. The Year-Off course costs from about £25 a day, tuition only.

MISCELLANEOUS

Leconfield Jackaroo and Jillaroo School
Kootingal, NSW 2352, Australia
☎/fax 00 61 2-6769 4230
e jillaroojackaro@austarnet.com.au
w www.leconfieldjackaroo.com
This school is a good 40-minute drive from the nearest shop, and students are taught from beginner level in groups of 20 on the working property. Beginner horseriders are welcome.
Types of Course: Jackaroo and jillaroo courses.
Timing & Length of Course: Courses last 11 days and run about twice a month.
Destination: NSW, Australia.
Costs/Pay: Courses cost from £265, including full board and lodging.
Eligibility: Minimum age is 16.

Peter Kirk Memorial Scholarships
c/o Mrs Angela Pearson, 17 St Paul's Rise, Addingham, Ilkley LS29 0QD
e mail@kirkfund.org.uk
w www.kirkfund.org.uk
Each year around 10 scholarships of up to £1000 are available to students who wish to live and study abroad (usually in Europe) and undertake a project that increases their understanding of modern Europe.
Types of Course: The project is up to you but examples of recent ones include: The Traditional Music of Corsica & Sardinia and Work Experience Opportunities in Paris.
Timing & Length of Course: Study lasts two to three months and takes place once a year.
Destinations: At least one country needs to be in Europe.
Costs/Pay: Students have to meet all costs in excess of the scholarship amount.
Eligibility: Applicants must be British and aged between 18 and 24.

How to Apply: You cannot ring or fax the office; email for an application form. You'll have to give a project outline, a budget and an itinerary. The deadline for applications is mid-February each year. There is then an interview and selection process.

The Royal Victorian Aero Club

First Avenue, Moorabbin Airport, Mentone, Victoria 3194, Australia
☎ 00 61 3-9580 0088
fax 00 61 3-9587 5085
e flying@rvac.com.au
W www.rvac.com.au or
W www.flighttraining.com.au
An accredited flight-training organisation approved under the Australian Federal Government requirements, this school offers a number of flying courses.
Types of Course: Private Pilot Licence (Aeroplanes).
Timing & Length of Course: Courses last 12 weeks (53 hours of flying and theory) and run monthly.
Destination: Melbourne.
Costs/Pay: Courses cost from £4500, tuition only.
Eligibility: The minimum age is 18. You'll have to pass a medical and you'll need a student visa, which the club can help you with.

How to Apply: Overseas students are encouraged to fill out the application form online.

Wallace School of Transport

Unit 5a, Pop-in Building, South Way, Wembley, Middx HA9 0HF
☎ 0845 602 9498
fax 020-8903 1376
e info@wallaceschool.co.uk
W www.wallaceschool.co.uk
Wallace is one of only seven DSA (Driving Standards Agency) Accredited Training Centres in the UK. An associate company is Drivers on Demand, an employment agency, meaning you can start earning money with your new qualifications immediately.
Types of Course: All groups of Large Goods Vehicle (LGV) and Passenger Carrying Vehicle (PCV) licences.
Timing & Length of Course: An intensive course takes around five to eight days, depending on your experience and aptitude. You can start any day of the week by arrangement.
Destination: Sunny Wembley, London.
Costs/Pay: It costs from £600 per licence. There's an Assessment Lesson costing £30 for training advice and a course quotation.
Eligibility: The minimum age is 18 and you'll need a full UK car licence.

Gapper Itineraries

Here are some examples of what some gappers have been up to recently. It's always exciting to hear where others have been and what they have done. If inspiration strikes after reading these examples (or after reading the whole book, for that matter), then have a go at plotting your own gap year with the Gap Planners later in this chapter.

NAME: Ros Walford
AGE: 25
FAVOURITE COUNTRY: Nepal
MY GAP YEAR: I took my gap year as a break from working and travelled solo through Nepal, Thailand and Vietnam, which was the adventure of a lifetime. I trekked the Annapurnas in Nepal, dodged tuk-tuks in Thailand, motorbiked to the Chinese border in Vietnam, snorkelled with sharks in Australia, skydived over Fox Glacier in New Zealand, camped under palm trees in Tahiti and sipped mescal on the beach in Mexico. I started my trip with three months in Asia and then toured Australia's west coast (which has the best beaches in the world) before working for five months in Sydney in a multitude of temporary jobs. A friend and myself bought a cheap car in New Zealand and toured the west coast, and then I continued via Tahiti to Mexico.
TOP GAP-YEAR TIP: Earplugs are essential for a good night's sleep when staying in those noisy hostels. Also, my best buy before I left was antibacterial hand wash – especially useful in Asia.

NAME: Richard Satchell
AGE: 22
FAVOURITE COUNTRY: Too tough but three favourites are Ghana, New Zealand and Cambodia.
MY GAP YEAR: During my final year at uni I applied for various jobs but always knew I wanted a year off. With the security of a job offer, which I deferred for a year, I was ready to set off on my travels. First up was a trip with a RTW ticket and a friend from uni. We travelled from coast to coast across the States, through the North and South islands of New Zealand, and up the east coast of Oz. From there we flew to Indonesia and Singapore, then travelled through Malaysia, Thailand, Laos, Cambodia and Vietnam, finally flying home from Bangkok. After Christmas, I went off to California for a 12-week ski instructor course – it was awesome! My gap year ended with four months as a volunteer, teaching maths in a secondary school in Ghana, West Africa, before the harsh realities of real life finally began!
TOP GAP-YEAR TIP: There's much more to a gap year than going to Australia and sitting on a beach – think BIG and go for it!

NAME: Finola Collins
AGE: 24
FAVOURITE COUNTRY: Belize
MY GAP YEAR: On finishing school I had no idea what I wanted to do other than travel. Not having travelled solo before, I was a bit nervous about heading off into the sunset with my backpack. So, I worked for a few months in the UK to save some money to join the Tall Ships as a member of crew. I then spent the following months sailing around the Canary Islands doing everything from scrubbing decks to sailing and navigation. It was hard work but a fantastic lifestyle!
TOP GAP-YEAR TIP: There'll be good times as well as hard times when you'll ask yourself 'Why am I doing this?' But, looking back, those hard times will be some of the best times of your life, and you'll gain a lot of satisfaction from having gone through them and survived.

NAME: Tom Hall
AGE: 26
FAVOURITE COUNTRY: Chile
MY GAP YEAR: When university finished I was unable to decide what I wanted to do next. After a few months temping in London I hit the road and learnt Spanish in Chile, fulfilling a lifelong ambition to see Patagonia and Easter Island. Next came New Zealand, where I got involved in volunteering and spent far too much money trying to drown in fast-flowing rivers and hurtle to my death off tall structures. I then travelled through Australia by train, which is a great way to see some unforgettable outback scenery. The trip didn't answer the questions about what I wanted to do with my life but it remains the source of some of my happiest memories.
TOP GAP-YEAR TIP: Relax and enjoy it. Live for the moment – you don't know when you'll be back.

NAME: Gennaro Serra
AGE: 20
FAVOURITE COUNTRY: Australia
MY GAP YEAR: I bought an Inter-Rail ticket after school to travel around Europe for a month with a couple of mates. I then flew to Sydney, Australia, to do a watersports instructor course. I travelled up the east coast of Oz for a month, teaching windsurfing on the way. I then flew back to the UK for a few days and then to Uruguay for a few weeks. Now I'm applying to start teaching windsurfing around the Med.
TOP GAP-YEAR TIP: Travel by yourself as much as you can. I found I learnt so much more by myself rather than going with friends.

NAME: Imogen Franks
AGE: 25
FAVOURITE COUNTRY: Tanzania
MY GAP YEAR: I graduated in June and worked in an off-licence all summer to raise money for the trip. In September I flew to Kenya with a team of people and we all worked in a deaf school teaching rudimentary English and helping to care for the pupils. After a break climbing Mt Kenya, another girl and I went to work at a monkey sanctuary, organising educational workshops for the local school children. We finished off by travelling through Tanzania, including an unforgettable few weeks on the beautiful island of Zanzibar. I'm still friends with many of the people I met in East Africa.
TOP GAP-YEAR TIP: If you're going with a group of people you don't know, try not to judge those books by their covers.

NAME: Angeline Hamilton
AGE: 25
FAVOURITE COUNTRY: Australia
MY GAP YEAR: I quit my job in London and flew to Bali where I spent two weeks travelling, then landed in Australia and stayed in Sydney for three months working for a big corporation. I then flew to New Zealand and spent seven weeks travelling, then returned to Australia where I worked for the same company in Melbourne for a further three months (they liked me!) before flying to Perth and spending a leisurely four months travelling all the way back to Sydney by various methods of transport – stopping to fruit pick or work in hostels along the way. I abandoned plans to go to Thailand on my return to Sydney when I was hit by Olympic Games fever. I spent my last six weeks partying rather than travelling – no regrets.
TOP GAP-YEAR TIP: Be spontaneous. It's your trip, do what you want and don't be afraid to veer from any plans or itineraries you have made.

NAME: Christian Walsh
AGE: 26
FAVOURITE COUNTRY: Morocco
MY GAP YEAR: I arranged a job working at Waterstone's in Paris, opposite the Louvre. A tiny maid's flat overlooking the Paris rooftops completed the dream, until I realised my glamorous lifestyle far outstripped my measly wage. I spent that summer in Sri Lanka, a guest of my girlfriend's generous family. It remains one of my favourite countries and inspired me to follow a career in travel writing.
TOP GAP-YEAR TIP: Expect the best of people, not the worst. The world is 99% friendly, in spite of what the press/government might say.

NAME: Lisa Oliver
AGE: 26
FAVOURITE COUNTRY: Morocco
MY GAP YEAR: I worked in advertising sales until January when I'd saved up enough money for a flight to Australia. I didn't have enough money to travel for the whole year so I started temping as soon as I arrived in Sydney, using this as a base but taking holidays when I could, including a fantastic month spent living in a dive school in Byron Bay. In early May I planned to travel around the west coast of Australia but three days before I was due to leave I took up the opportunity to crew on a racing yacht up the east coast to Cairns. I then bought a car (which was older than me!) and drove with some friends through the red centre of Australia, down to Adelaide, around to Victoria for a spot of skiing, then back to Sydney. I then worked in Sydney again until I'd saved enough to go to New Zealand, Bali, Singapore, Malaysia and Thailand on my way home.
TOP GAP-YEAR TIP: Keep a duplicate copy online of all the contact details of the people you meet on the way. I didn't, and lost my address book on a bus in New Zealand. Also, don't pack any clothes that you don't mind losing.

NAME: Katrina Browning
AGE: 27
FAVOURITE COUNTRY: Morocco (I met my husband there!)
MY GAP YEAR: I worked in the local department store before heading off to join a summer camp in New Hampshire through Camp Counselors USA. After the camp, some fellow counsellors and I travelled up and down the east coast of the US, from Niagara Falls to Key West. Arriving back in England I looked through *The Lady* and found an au-pair job with a Belgian family around the corner from the Palace of Versailles in France. I had most days free and was able to attend an advanced French class at the Alliance Française. After travelling south to Morocco and east to the former Soviet Union I landed a job as a housekeeper in Zurich. With leads from other travellers I looked after children in Belgium, and fried fish in a Kerry (Ireland) chippie. Living with a family helped to keep costs down and with the money I had saved I flew to Caracas and travelled down through Brazil, Argentina, west to Chile and north to Quito in Peru. I learnt Spanish there for six weeks but eventually the money ran out and it was time to go back to England.
TOP GAP-YEAR TIP: Put your money into a credit-card account so that you're in credit. That way you can usually get money at more places than just through ATMs and you won't be paying cash-advance fees because you are spending your own money in the account – not the bank's!

NAME: Emily Crane & Frances Yates
AGE: 19 & 18
FAVOURITE COUNTRY: Thailand
OUR GAP YEAR: We wanted to see a bit of the world before settling into university. Deciding on India, Thailand, Singapore, Australia, New Zealand, Rarotonga (and the Cook Islands) and North America (Los Angeles) as our ports of call, we spent the next seven months raising the capital to fund our trip. We made no solid plans for any of our destinations but just went. Admittedly this was due to lack of organisation but as it transpired, our plan, or lack thereof, worked out perfectly, giving us the freedom to go and do as we pleased. For instance, while visiting Ko Phang Nga in southern Thailand we decided to stay on longer. Our friends, however, were forced to move on as a result of having booked, and paid for internal flights and hostels at their next destinations.

TOP GAP-YEAR TIP: Work out your budget before setting off on your trip. If something goes a little over your daily allowance don't write it off, as it would be a shame to miss out on a once-in-a-lifetime experience for the sake of a few pounds. However, do be mindful of your spending and don't spend all your money in the first few destinations leaving yourself with only £126 and four countries left to see!

NAME: Robert Reid
AGE: 27
FAVOURITE COUNTRY: Mexico (the India of the Western Hemisphere)
MY GAP YEAR: Bored with a New York City publishing job, I applied online for a teaching-English job in Vietnam and got it. I worked for a year in Saigon and did a few hours a day editing at an English-language paper. I returned home afterwards on a RTW ticket, hitting Thailand, India, Nepal, Italy and France.

TOP GAP-YEAR TIP: If you stay in one place long term expect highs and lows. If you're in a developing country, it's OK to pamper yourself by going to a five-star hotel for a buffet on occasion. Also, there's a strong inclination – particularly if you're teaching English and focusing on 'language' at work – to hang out with native English speakers at the end of the day. Make sure you don't limit your trip to expats only – you're going to get less out of it if you do. Note that many English-language papers in non-English-speaking lands are very keen to get original stories and will pay a little money for them. If you are keen to write, drop by an office and ask about it. Don't limit story ideas to 'my life in Manila!' but look for things-to-do type stories (weekend trips, attractions loved by locals, local lores) that will appeal to short-term visitors AND expats.

NAME: Fiona Christie
AGE: 26
FAVOURITE COUNTRY: Cuba
MY GAP YEAR: I spent the summer working for my mum at her nursery school and followed that with four months in a bookshop doing all the overtime I could. I then did voluntary work in Australia for three months and Fiji for two, with a bit of travelling in Australia and New Zealand in between.
TOP GAP-YEAR TIP: Don't be afraid to travel on your own. Even though it's very scary when you set off, you'll soon realise how independent you can be and it feels great.

NAME: Verity Hardie
AGE: 26
FAVOURITE COUNTRY: New Zealand
MY GAP YEAR: After finishing a science degree in 2000 and not feeling very enthusiastic about working in a laboratory I decided to take a year off. My favourite pastime is horse riding, so I decided it was a good way to start off my travels. I was offered a job training young showjumping horses in Calgary, Canada. The horses, facilities and people were great and the farm was only a few miles from a ski field which had night-skiing. This was a great bonus as most day-light hours were spent in the saddle. I learnt loads in my year away and gained some of my best memories yet.
TOP GAP-YEAR TIP: Appreciate different cultures and immerse yourself in them even if it's not always easy!

NAME: Ed Pickard
AGE: 26
FAVOURITE COUNTRY: Iceland
MY GAP YEAR: One day in late September 2001 I decided to take a year out from working and skip the dreary winter. Eight days later I had landed myself a job as a ski technician and was on a bus heading for Val d'Isère in the French Alps. My work hours were a few in the morning, a few in the evening and about 22 hours on a Saturday. The rest of the time I just skied. Seven months later I'd had the best winter ever and was en route to the best summer: deckhand on a 217ft tall ship leaving Alicante, Spain, and following the coastline to the Atlantic, across to the Canary Islands and then about turn. The rope burns blistered well but I never saw the same beach twice and I lost count of the number of flying fish jumping.
TOP GAP-YEAR TIP: Don't expect to get any sleep and don't expect to save any cash. Work hard, play hard would definitely by the most apt phrase.

Gap Planners

Here are three blank Gap Planners that will help you map out your next year or so. You'll probably change your mind time and time again, and want to try out several itineraries, which is why we've printed three of them here.

July
....
....

August
....
....

September
....
....

October
....
....

November
....
....

December
....
....

January
....
....

February
....
....

March
....
....

April
....
....

May
....
....

June
....
....

July
....
....

August
....
....

September
....
....

Planner 2

July

August

September

October

November

December

January

February

....
....
....

March

....
....
....
....

April

....
....
....
....

May

....
....
....
....

June

....
....
....
....

July

....
....
....
....

August

....
....
....
....

September

....
....
....

Planner 3

July
....
....

August
....
....

September
....
....

October
....
....

November
....
....

December
....
....

January
....
....

February
....
....

March
....
....

April
....
....

May
....
....

June
....
....

July
....
....

August
....
....

September
....
....

Appendix I – Airlines

For many trips, the airline you fly with is of little consequence. Most travellers choose their airline on the simple basis of cost but there are a few reasons to be a little more choosy. On many long-haul flights interesting stopovers are permitted and these secondary travel destinations depend on which airline you fly with; go to Australia with ANA and you can explore Japan, go with Emirates and you could stop in the United Arab Emirates and Indian Sub-continent. With some airlines it's expensive and a hassle to change dates and routes, with others it's cheap and a breeze. And some of the below are simply just more enjoyable to travel with than others:

Aer Lingus (☎ 0845 084444; W www.aer lingus.ie) has cheap flights to Europe and North America from London.

Aeroflot (☎ 020-7491 1764; W www .aeroflot.org), Russia's national carrier, flies to North and South America as well as numerous destinations in Africa and Asia.

Aeromexico (☎ 020-7801 6234; W www.aeromexico.com) has pretty good American connections and the odd cheap flight into Mexico from Europe.

Air Canada (☎ 0870 524 7226; W www .aircanada.ca) mainly services routes out to Canada and North America but also has some connections to Australia, South America and Asia.

Air China (☎ 020-7630 0919; W www.air-china.co.uk) has nonstop flights to Beijing and flights to Europe, America, Asia, the Middle East and Australia.

Air France (☎ 0845 082 0162; W www .airfrance.com/uk) has some of the best connections to West and Central Africa, plus a truly global network via Paris.

Air New Zealand (☎ 0800 028 4149; W www.airnz.com) often has good fares to Southeast Asia via stop-offs in New Zealand, North America and the South Pacific.

Air Nippon (☎ 020-7224 8866; W www .ananet.or.jp) services loads of routes to Southeast Asia, Europe and North, South and Central America.

Air Portugal (TAP; ☎ 020-7932 3601; W www.tap-airportugal.pt) offers routes to Europe, former Portuguese colonies in Africa and South America, plus some Eastern European and US destinations.

Alitalia (☎ 0870 000 0123; W www.al italia.it) has loads of cheap fares to long-haul destinations across the globe. Flights go via Rome.

All Nippon Airways (ANA; ☎ 020-7224 8866; W www.fly-ana.com) is great for services into Northeast Asia via Japan, where the airline has a vast network.

American Airlines (☎ 020-7365 0777; W www.aa.com) is a powerful US carrier with global coverage. It commonly offers cheap deals into South and Central America.

Austrian Airlines (☎ 020-7434 7350; W www.aua.com) punches above its weight on European, Middle Eastern and Asia routes (including Kathmandu) plus Australia and eastern USA. Its hub is Vienna.

British Airways (☎ 0845 773 3377; W www.ba.com) has good global connections and fills any gaps with airline alliances. Very cheap online European fares at the time of writing.

bmi (☎ 0870 607 0555; **W** www.flybmi
.com) services North American destinations,
but cheap fares to European airports are
the main focus (also see its no-frills sub-
sidy **W** www.bmibaby.com).

Cathay Pacific Airways (☎ 020-7747
8888; **W** www.cathaypacific.com) flies to
Australia and New Zealand via Southeast
Asia and the Indian Subcontinent. It also
has flights to the USA, Europe, South
Africa and the Middle East. It code shares
with American Airlines.

Continental Airlines (☎ 0800 776 464;
W www.continental.com) has formed
various alliances to extend its reach. It
flies to Europe, Southeast Asia, the South
Pacific, and North and South America.

Czech Airlines (☎ 0870 444 3747;
W www.csa.cz/en/) has a large European
network and visits a few destinations in
North America and elsewhere.

Delta Airlines (☎ 0800 414 767; **W** www
.delta.com) is big in America (North and
South) but also has connections to the
Middle East, Africa, Asia and Europe.

EgyptAir (☎ 020-7734 2343; **W** www
.egyptair.com) is just about global but has
good connections to the Middle East.

El Al (☎ 020-7957 4270; **W** www.elal.co
.il) services several destinations in the
USA, plus Mumbai, Southeast Asia and
Africa.

Emirates (☎ 020-7590 1444; **W** www
.emirates.com/uk) flies throughout the
Middle East, Asia, Africa, Australasia and
Europe, with a hub in Dubai, and allows in-
line stopovers. It is allied with Sri Lankan
Airlines.

Ethiopian Airlines (☎ 020-8987 7000;
W www.flyethiopian.com) is probably
the second-best African airline (don't let
passengers applauding when your plane

lands put you off) with transcontinental
routes (east to west) and some in North
America and Asia.

Finnair (☎ 0870 241 44 11; **W** www.finn
air.com) has great Baltic and Scandinavian
connections, plus routes into Northeast
and Southeast Asia, including a service to
Shanghai.

flybe (British European; ☎ 0870 567 6676;
W www.flybe.com) flies from regional
airports around the UK to many European destinations. Low one-way fares are
available online if you book well in
advance.

Garuda Indonesia (☎ 020-7467 8600;
W www.garuda-indonesia.com), the Happy
Shopper of the skies, offers a few Euro-
pean destinations via the Middle East and
Southeast Asia. Cheap flights are available
to Australia.

Gulf Air (☎ 0870 777 1717; **W** www.gulf
air.com) services worldwide destinations
including the USA, Middle East, Africa,
Southeast Asia and Australia. Cheap deals
to the Indian Subcontinent and Asia are
common.

Iberia (☎ 0845 601 2854; **W** www.iberia
.com), Spain's national airline, is good for
destinations in Europe and South America.
It also has flights to Africa, North America
and Asia.

Japan Airlines (JAL; ☎ 0845 774 7700;
W www.jal.co.jp) heads into Europe, the
USA, Asia and the South Pacific from Japan.

Kenya Airways (☎ 01784-888222; **W** www
.kenya-airways.com) has a pretty large
African network and flies to destinations
in the Middle East and India.

KLM (☎ 0870 507 4074; **W** www.klm.com)
offered some of the best deals into and
out of different cities in East and southern Africa at the time of writing. Flights

go via Amsterdam and are code shared with Northwest Airlines.

Korean Air (☎ 0800 0656 2001; W www .koreanair.com) has flights from Seoul to North America, Europe, the Pacific and Southeast Asia.

Kuwait Airways (☎ 020-7412 0006; W www.kuwait-airways.com) offers some great deals to the Middle East, Indian Subcontinent and Asia.

LanChile (☎ 01293-596607; W www.lan chile.com) is good for flights to South America but it also covers North America, the Caribbean, the Pacific and Europe.

LanPeru (☎ 01293-596607; W www.lan peru.com) has a limited but useful network within South and North America.

Lufthansa (☎ 0845 773 7747; W www .lufthansa.com) is another good airline with links (albeit recently cut back) across Africa and offers some uncommon destinations such as Addis Ababa (Ethiopia) and Windhoek (Namibia) via Frankfurt.

Malaysia Airlines (☎ 0870 607 9090; W www.malaysiaairlineseurope.com) has a global network with numerous flights into Asia and Australasia.

Mexicana Airlines (☎ 020-8492 0000; W www.mexicana.com) has great connections around Central and South America.

Northwest Airlines (☎ 0870 507 4074; W www.nwa.com) concentrates on North America but has global reach and alliances with numerous international airlines including KLM and Air China.

Olympic Airways (☎ 0870 606 0460; W www.olympic-airways.gr) is based in Greece and flies within Europe and to the USA, the Middle East, Russia and Africa.

Pakistan International Airways (☎ 020-8741 8066; W www.piac.com.pk) offers numerous destinations in Southeast Asia and the Middle East, as well as flights to Libya and the USA.

Point-Afrique (☎ 00 33 820 000 154; W www.point-afrique.com) is a French-based operation with cheap charter flights into Saharan West Africa from Paris and Marseille (winter only).

Qantas Airways (☎ 020-8600 4307; W www.qantas.com.au) is a global player and flies into numerous destinations in Australia, New Zealand, Oceania and Southeast Asia.

Qatar Airways (☎ 020-7896 3636; W www .qatarairways.com) operates flights to a host of North African, Middle Eastern and Asian destinations and often offers cheap ways into Southeast Asia.

Royal Brunei (☎ 020-7584 6360; W www .bruneiair.com) links London to a number of Middle Eastern, Southeast Asian and Australasian destinations (including Darwin) via Brunei.

Royal Jordanian (☎ 020-7878 6333; W www.rja.com.jo) offers (often cheap) flights to the Middle East and Indian Subcontinent via Amman.

Scandinavian Airlines (SAS; ☎ 0870 6072 7727; W www.sas.se) has a broad network in Scandinavia and the Baltic and services numerous destinations from Southeast Asia to the US.

SilkAir (W www.silkair.com) is the regional wing of Singapore Airlines and services a great list of Asian destinations from Singapore.

Singapore Airlines (☎ 0870 608 8886; W www.singaporeair.com) is a king among airlines offering a great network and good, flexible ways into Australasia and Southeast Asia.

SN Brussels Airlines (☎ 0870 735 2345; W www.brusselsairlines.com) emerged from the wreckage of Sabena and now serves a few niche routes in West and Central Africa via Brussels.

South African Airways (SAA; ☎ 0870 747 1111; W www.flysaa.com) is the biggest and best African airline, with a wide African network and routes across the globe from Johannesburg.

SriLankan Airlines (☎ 020-8538 2000; W www.srilankan.lk) has a network linking the Indian Subcontinent, Asia and Europe from its hub in Colombo, Sri Lanka.

Swiss (☎ 0845 601 0956; W www.swiss .com) is not the biggest airline but offers some good deals to destinations across the world.

Turkish Airlines (☎ 020-7766 9333; W www.turkishairlines.com) offers some good flights around Europe, the Middle East and Asia.

Thai Airways International (☎ 020-7491 7953; W www.thaiair.com) is particularly strong on Asian destinations and also flies to Australia, the USA and Europe.

United Airlines (☎ 0845 8444 777; W www.ual.com) is massive and comes up trumps on fares to North, Central and South America. It also flies to Southeast Asia, the Indian Subcontinent, Australia and New Zealand.

Varig (☎ 020-8321 7170; W www.varig .com.br/english/), Brazil's national airline, has great contacts to Europe, South Africa, and North and Central America.

Virgin Atlantic Airways (☎ 01293-450150; W www.fly.virgin.com) has its majority of routes into North America and the Caribbean. It also flies to West and South Africa, India and Southeast Asia.

No-Frills Airlines

Bmibaby (W www.bmibaby.com)

Easyjet (W www.easyjet.com)

Jet2 (W www.jet2.com)

MyTravelLite (W www.mytravellite.com)

Ryanair (W www.ryanair.com)

Virgin Express (W www.virgin-express .com)

AIRLINE ALLIANCES

There are a number of major airline alliances that are worth remembering when booking your ticket. All of them offer round-the-world (RTW) tickets and by checking out the following airlines' routes you'll get an idea of the depth of possibilities available on RTW tickets:

Oneworld (W www.oneworld.com) – Aer Lingus, American Airlines, British Airways, Cathay Pacific, Finnair, Iberia, LanChile and Qantas.

SkyTeam (W www.skyteam.com) – Aero-mexico, Air France, Czech Airlines, Delta Airlines, Korean Air and Alitalia.

Star Alliance (W www.star-alliance.com) – Air Canada, Air New Zealand, All Nippon Airways, Austrian Airlines, bmi, Lufthansa, Mexicana Airlines, SAS, Singapore Airlines, Thai Airways International, United Airlines and Varig.

Appendix II – Global Tour Companies

The companies listed below operate overland truck trips and specialist small-group tours to destinations across the globe. Most trips only last a matter of weeks, some are four-month overland odysseys, but all of them can be a great way to start/finish your travels. Most of the tours offered can be joined 'on the ground' should you want to organise your own way to their starting point.

Arctic Experience (☎ 01737-214214; e sales@arctic-experience.co.uk; W www.arctic-experience.co.uk; 29 Nork Way, Banstead, Surrey SM7 1PB) runs arctic experiences ranging from hardcore activity trips (dog-sledging, cross-country skiing) to gentle cruises and sightseeing tours.

Contiki (☎ 020-8290 6777, fax 020-8225 4246; e reservations@contiki-tours.ch; W www.contiki.com; Wells House, 15 Elmfield Rd, Bromley, Kent BR1 1LS) is a huge company popular with young, party-minded tourists for their good-value, multi-country bus tours of Europe. It offers loads of trips (not all by bus) in Australia, New Zealand, the USA and Canada.

Dragoman (☎ 01728-861133, fax 01728-861127; e info@dragoman.co.uk; W www.dragoman.co.uk; Camp Green, Kenton Rd, Debenham, Suffolk IP14 6LA) runs overland trips (some by truck) of varying lengths across Africa, the Americas, the Middle East and Asia. It also has a Kathmandu to Cape Town trip.

Encounter (☎ 01728-862222, fax 01728-861127; e info@encounteroverland.com; W www.encounteroverland.com; Camp Green, Kenton Rd, Debenham, Suffolk IP14 6LA) runs overland trips (some by truck) across South America, Africa, the Middle East, Central Asia and India.

Exodus (☎ 020-8675 5550, fax 020-8673 0779; e info@exodus.co.uk; W www.exodus.co.uk; 9 Weir Rd, London SW12 0LT) is a truly global tour company that offers specialist activity trips as well as sightseeing and overland tours. It has a great reputation.

Explore Worldwide (☎ 01252-760000, fax 01252-760001; e res@exploreworldwide.com; W www.exploreworldwide.com; 1 Frederick St, Aldershot GU11 1LQ) is another major global player with tours to the four corners of the earth. There's less emphasis on specialist activities than with Exodus, but it too has a good reputation.

Footloose Adventure Travel (☎ 01943-604030, fax 01943-604070; e info@footlooseadventure.co.uk; W www.footlooseadventure.co.uk; 3 Springs Pavement, Ilkley, W Yorks LS29 8HD) offers tours in selected destinations around the globe. Some specialist activities are offered.

Footprint Adventures (☎ 01522-804929, fax 01522-804928; e sales@footprint-adventures.co.uk; W www.footprint-adventures.co.uk; 5 Malham Drive, Lincoln LN6 0DX) offers a range of adventure tours to select destinations across the globe, with an emphasis on trekking, wildlife, bird-watching and camping trips.

Guerba (☎ 01373-858956, fax 01373-858351; e info@guerba.co.uk; W www.guerba.com; Wessex House, 40 Station Rd, Westbury BA13 3JN) is another well-respected tour company that runs everything from overland truck tours to trekking trips. It's very well respected for its Africa packages.

High Places (☎ 0114-275 7500, fax 0114-275 3870; e treks@highplaces.co.uk; W www.highplaces.co.uk; Globe Centre, Penistone Rd, Sheffield S6 3AE), a well-established specialist trekking company, runs tours to destinations ranging from Greenland to New Zealand.

Himalayan Kingdoms (☎ 01453-844 400, fax 01453-844422; e info@himalayan kingdoms.com; W www.himalayanking doms.com; Old Crown House, 18 Market St, Wotton-under-Edge, Glos GL12 7AE) runs some fantastic treks, not only in the Himalayas but also Europe and Central, Northern and Southeast Asia.

Hinterland Travel (☎ 01883-743584, fax 01883-743912; e hinterland@tinyworld.co .uk; 12 The Enterdent, Godston, Surrey RH9 8EG) offers overland journeys through the region to Kathmandu, and tours of Iraq and Afghanistan (war/chaos permitting).

Imaginative Traveller Ltd (☎ 020-8742 3049, fax 020-8742 3045; e info@imagina tive-traveller.com; W www.imaginative-traveller.com; 14 Barley Mow Passage, Chiswick, London W4 4PH) offers tonnes of worldwide tours for all budgets. Some trips include trekking and sailing.

Intrepid Travel (☎ 020 8960 6333, fax 8960 5444; e uk@intrepidtravel.com; W www.intrepidtravel.com; Buspace Studios, Conlan St, London W10 5AP) is an Asia specialist with other adventurous tours and special-interest trips in Russia, Japan and Egypt. It also runs 'Oxfam Journeys' that take a look at the work of NGOs in Asia.

KE Adventure Travel (☎ 017687-73966, fax 017687-74693; e keadventure@enter prise.net; W www.keadventure.com; 32 Lake Rd, Keswick, Cumbria CAI2 5DQ) is

an adventurous trekking and mountain-biking specialist with great treks in the Americas, Northeast and Central Asia, the Indian Subcontinent, Europe and Africa.

Kumuka (☎ 0800 068 8855, fax 020-7937 6664; e enquiries@kumuka.com; W www .kumuka.co.uk; 40 Earls Court Rd, London W8 6EJ) offers adventurous overland truck tours and small group trips (sometimes on public transport) on most of the world's continents.

The Moorings (☎ 01227-776677; W www.moorings.com; Bradstowe House, Middle Wall, Whitstable, Kent CT5 1BF) is a huge yacht-charter company with bases in the Seychelles, Tonga, Tahiti, Australia, New Zealand, Baja California (Mexico), the Mediterranean and the Caribbean.

Naturetrek (☎ 01962-733051, fax 01962-736426; e info@naturetrek.co.uk; W www .naturetrek.co.uk; Cheriton Mill, Cheriton, Alresford, Hants S024 0NG) runs tours worldwide and also offers treks guided by naturalists focusing on botany, bird life and natural history.

Nautor's Swan Charters (☎ 023-8045 4880, fax 023-8045 5547; e enquiries@ swanyachts.co.uk; W www.nautorgroup .com; Port Hamble Marina, Satchell Lane, Hamble, Southampton SO31 4QD) is a major yacht-charter operation with bases in Norway, Sweden, England, New England (USA) and the Caribbean.

Oasis Overland (☎ 01963-363400, fax 01963-363200; e info@oasisoverland .co.uk; W www.oasisoverland.com; The Marsh, Henstridge, Somerset BA8 0TF) runs overland truck tours in Africa, the Middle East and South America.

OTT Expeditions (Alpine Mountaineering; ☎ 0114-258 8508, fax 0114-255 1603; e andy@ottexpd.demon.co.uk; W www .ottexpeditions.co.uk; Unit 5b, Southwest

Centre, Troutbeck Rd, Sheffield S7 2QA) is a hardcore mountaineering/high-altitude trekking outfit offering select trips across the world.

Regent Holidays Ltd (☎ 0117-921 1711, fax 0117-925 4866; e regent@regent-holidays.co.uk; W www.regent-holidays .co.uk; 15 John St, Bristol BSl 2HR) runs weekend city breaks and longer tours to Eastern Europe, Russia (including the Trans-Siberian Railway), Greenland, Iceland and Central Asia.

Sherpa Expeditions (☎ 020-8577 2717, fax 020-8572 9788; e sales@sherpa-walking-holidays.co.uk; W www.sherpa-walking-holidays.co.uk; 131a Heston Rd, Hounslow TW5 0RF) offers treks and self-guided walking in Europe, Africa, Russia, Turkey, South America and the Himalayas.

Silk Steps (☎ 01454-888850; e info@silksteps.co.uk; W www.silksteps.co.uk; Tyndale House, 7 High St, Chipping Sodbury, Bristol BS37 6BA) runs tailor-made trips across Asia plus Uzbekistan, Turkmenistan and Ethiopia.

Steppes East (☎ 01285-810267, fax 01285-810693; e sales@steppeseast.co .uk; W www.steppeseast.co.uk; Castle Eaton, Cricklade, Swindon, Wilts SN6 6JU) offers a variety of tours to North Africa, Asia, the Indian Subcontinent, Russia and Central Asia.

Sunsail (☎ 0870 777 0313, fax 023-9221 9827; e sales@sunsail.com; W www.sun sail.com/uk/; The Port House, Port Solent, Portsmouth, Hants PO6 4TH) is one of the world's largest yacht-charter operations, with bases in the Seychelles, Thailand, Malaysia, Tonga, Tahiti, Australia, New Zealand, Canada, and the Mediterranean, Caribbean, Atlantic coast of the USA, England and Scotland.

Top Deck Travel (☎ 020-7244 8000, fax 020-7835 1820; e res@topdecktravel.co .uk; W www.topdecktravel.co.uk; 125 Earls Court Rd, London SW5 9RH) runs cheap, multi-country coach trips around Europe that are close to being an 18-30 on wheels. It also runs skiing holidays and the odd trip in Egypt.

Travel For The Arts (☎ 020-7483 4466, fax 020-7586 0639; W www.travelforthearts .co.uk; 117 Regent's Park Rd, London NWl 8UR) organises luxury culture-based tours to Russia (particularly St Petersburg) and other European destinations for people with a specific interest in opera and ballet.

Travelbag Adventures (☎ 01420-541 007, fax 01420-541002; e info@travelbag @adventures.co.uk; W www.travelbag-adventures.co.uk; 15 Turk St, Alton, Hants GU34 lAG) covers tours to destinations worldwide plus the odd weekend break.

WildWings (☎ 0117-965 8333, fax 0117-937 5681; e wildinfo@wildwings.co.uk; W www.wildwings.co.uk; 577–579 Fish-ponds Rd, Fishponds, Bristol BS16 3AF) not only offers a huge range of bird-watching trips but wildlife-related experiences, expeditions and conservation programmes of all kinds and budgets. Somewhat bizarrely, it also offers space flights.

World Expeditions (☎ 020-8870 2600; W www.worldexpeditions.com.au; 3 North-fields Prospect, Putney Bridge Rd, London SW18 1PE) covers the world with standard and 'hardcore' options. It also does cruises to Antarctica and the Arctic.

Appendix III – Destinations Websites

AFRICA

W **www.bbc.co.uk**, W **www.newafrica .com** and W **www.allafrica.com** – great starting points for African news and background.

W **garamond.stanford.edu/depts/ssrg/ africa/** – an enormous academic resource.

W **afrika.no** – literally thousands of links.

W **www.africacentre.org.uk** – Africa Centre.

W **www.soas.ac.uk** – School of Oriental and African Studies.

W **www.fespaco.bf** – Fespaco or Pan-African Film Festival.

W **www.unaids.org** – UN AIDS/HIV information.

AUSTRALASIA

W **www.southpacific.org/air.html** – useful and factual travel information.

W **www.pacificislands.com** – more useful and factual travel information.

W **www.sidsnet.org/pacific/sprep** – information on the South Pacific Environment Program.

W **www.aboriginalaustralia.com** – covers culture, art and tourism.

W **www.australiaonline.com.au** – an offbeat site packed with information.

W **www.csu.edu.au/education/autralia .html** – a mine of useful information with links to government organisations.

W **www.bushwise.co.nz** – women-specific information about accommodation and activities.

W **www.doc.govt.nz** – Department of Conservation site with practical information.

W **www.kiwinewz.com** – up to date and packed with information about Queenstown and the Southern Lakes.

W **www.greyhound.com.au** – Greyhound Pioneer coaches in Australia.

W **www.mccaffertys.com.au** – McCafferty's coaches in Australia.

W **www.ozexperience.com** – Oz Experience hop-on hop-off buses.

W **www.waywardbus.com.au** – The Wayward Bus hop-on hop-off buses.

W **www.intercitycoach.co.nz** – InterCity Kiwi bus company.

W **www.kiwiex.co.nz** – Kiwi Experience hop-on hop-off buses.

EUROPE

W **www.viaferrata.org** – Via Ferrata site offering climbing and mountaineering information.

W **www.raileurope.co.uk** – Rail Europe, offering Inter-Rail passes etc.

W **www.gobycoach.com** – European coach travel.

W **www.busabout.com** and W **www .straytravel.com** – offers hop-on hop-off tours across Europe.

INDIAN SUBCONTINENT

W **travelbangla.com** – Bangladeshi tourism overview.

W **www.bhutan.org** – general information on Bhutan.

W **www.khoj.com** – good portal for things Indian.

W **www.info-nepal.com** – great Nepalese travel site.

W **www.bena.com/sherpa1/** – Nepalese trekking site.

W **www.south-asia.com** – good Nepalese portal.

W **www.pakistanlink.com** – US-based Pakistan news service.

W **www.lanka.net** – broad portal into all things Sri Lankan.

W **www.lacnet.org** – academic Sri Lankan links galore.

MEXICO, CENTRAL & SOUTH AMERICA

W **larutamayaonline.com** – concentrates on Guatemala and Central America.

W **www.centralamerica.com** – reasonably detailed site with lots of links.

W **www.lanic.utexas.edu/** – great link to some fantastic academic resources, mostly in Spanish.

W **www.saexplorers.org** – travel-club site with bulletin board and volunteer information.

W **www.southamericadaily.com** – a good place for a low-down on the region's news.

W **www.gosouthamerica.about.com** – multifaceted portal to Latin America.

W **www.latinworld.com** – gateway to loads of information, some in Spanish.

W **www.360graus.com.br** and W **www.guiaverde.com.br** – cover activities in Brazil.

W **www.lastfrontiers.co.uk/airpass.htm** – single-country and multi-country air passes in Central and South America.

MIDDLE EAST

W **www.arabia.com** – Middle East portal.

W **www.albawaba.com** – another Middle East portal.

W **www.birzeit.edu** – handy for an insight into the Palestinian Territories.

W **www.royalasiaticsociety.org** – the Royal Asiatic Society.

W **www.soultospirit.com/calendar/holiday_by_religion.asp** – lists the dates of many religious festivals.

NORTH AMERICA

W **www.roadsideamerica.com** – the 'online guide to offbeat attractions'.

W **www.historic66.com/index.html** – slightly anal Belgian site about the 'Mother Road'.

W **www.uq.edu.au/~zzdonsi/us_tips.html** – helpful Aussie hints on travelling in the USA.

W **www.travel.org/na.html** – huge travel directory for North America.

W **www.canoe.ca** – Canadian news and culture portal.

W **www.caribseek.com** and W **www.caribbean-on-line.com** – general portals into all things Caribbean.

W **www.greyhound.com** – Greyhound buses in North America.

W **www.greentortoise.com** – The Green Tortoise group-orientated tours.

W **www.moosenetwork.com** – Moose Travel site; runs a hop-on hop-off bus service in Canada.

W **www.allostop.com** – Canadian and French lift-sharing organisation Allô Stop.

NORTHEAST ASIA

W **tour2korea.com** – stacks of Korean travel information and links.

W **www.japantravelinfo.com** – portal of the Japan National Tourist Board.

W **www.hkta.org** – Hong Kong's Tourist Association website.

W **www.cnta.com/lyen** – the portal of the China National Tourism Administration.

W **www.cybertaiwan.com** – a funky and functional Taiwanese site.

W **www.ChinaPage.com** – covers Chinese art, poetry and language.

W **www.tibet.org** – examines Tibet's sad occupation and repression.

W **www.outdoorjapan.com** – a light overview of the outdoor possibilities in Japan.

W **www.silk-road.com** – an insight into culture along the Silk Road.

W **www.chinaski.com** – China Ski Corporation.

RUSSIA, CENTRAL ASIA & THE FORMER SOVIET UNION

W **www.eurasianet.org** – a good news source and portal for Central Asia.

W **cesww.fas.harvard.edu** – a good academic resource for Central Asia.

W **www.departments.bucknell.edu/russian** – an academic resource.

W **www.russia-travel.com** – good tourist-orientated site.

W **www.russianculture.ru** – a background on Russian culture and museums.

W **www.wps.ru** – good links to press and web media.

W **www.brama.com** and **W** **www.ua zone.net/Ukraine.html** – Ukrainian information.

W **www.belarusguide.com** – a good start for Belarus.

SOUTHEAST ASIA

W **www.cambodia.org** – a great site with a comprehensive list of links.

W **Indonesia.elga.net.id** – a great introduction to Indonesia.

W **www.visit-mekong.com** – a general site on Laos and Cambodia.

W **www.vientianetimes.com** – not the official government mouthpiece it first appears.

W **www.filipinolinks.com** – an impressive set of links relating to the Philippines.

W **www.thaiindex.com** – includes general information and loads of links.

W **www.vietnamadventures.com** – details more than just adventure travel.

W **www.thingsasian.com** – good portal to the whole of the region.

W **www.amnesty.org** – Amnesty International site, an international human-rights organisation.

Appendix IV – Other Websites

African Medical & Research Foundation W www.amref.org – an NGO whose mission is to improve the health of disadvantaged people in Africa.

Agency Central W www.agencycentral .co.uk – provides links to recruitment agencies and job sites.

Airline Network W www.airline-network .co.uk – an independent travel company.

Altitude Sickness W www.princeton .edu/~oa/altitude.html – Outdoor Action guide to high altitude.

American Diabetes Association W www .diabetes.org

American Express W www.american express.com

Around the World Traveler W www .atwtraveler.com/frei-faq.htm – includes RTW freighter travel.

BBC Health W www.bbc.co.uk/health/travel

BBC World Service W www.bbc.co.uk/ worldservice

Berghaus W www.berghaus.com – specialist outdoor retailer.

Blacks W www.blacks.co.uk – specialist outdoor retailer.

British Airways Travel Clinic W www .britishairways.com/travel/healthclinintro/ public/en_us

British Diabetic Association W www .diabetes.org.uk

British Red Cross W www.redcross.org .uk – part of the International Red Cross and Red Crescent Movement.

Card Protection Plan W www.cpp.co.uk

Career Development Loan W www.life longlearning.co.uk/cdl – offers deferred repayment loans.

CDC (US Centers for Disease Control & Prevention) W www.cdc.gov/travel/index.htm

Charities Direct W www.charitiesdirect.com

Cheapflights W www.cheapflights.co.uk

Climate Care W www.co2.org – how to reduce your impact on global warming.

Columbus Direct W www.columbusdirect .com – a travel insurance company.

Country Calling Codes W www.country callingcodes.com

Department of Health W www.doh.gov .uk/traveladvice

Department of Immigration & Multicultural & Indigenous Affairs in Australia (DIMIA) W www.immi.gov.au

Diabetic Resource W www.diabetic resource.com

eBay W www.ebay.co.uk – one of the world's largest online marketplaces.

ebookers W www.ebookers.com – one of Europe's largest online travel agencies.

Endsleigh W www.endsleigh.co.uk – offers gap-year travel insurance.

euro26 W www.euro26.org – a youth card for under-26s offering great discounts across Europe.

Eurolines W www.eurolines.com – express coach network.

Expedia W www.expedia.co.uk

Fairydown W www.fairydown.co.uk – offers a range of outdoor clothing and equipment.

Ferry Booker W www.ferrybooker.com

Flight Centre W www.flightcentre.com

Gapyear.com W www.gapyear.com

Gear Zone W www.gearzone.co.uk – outdoor equipment and clothing shop.

Globetrotters W www.globetrotters .co.uk – a club for independent travellers and travel enthusiasts.

Guardian W www.guardian.co.uk

Hostelling International W www.iyhf .org

Hostelling International (Northern Ireland) W www.hini.org.uk

Hotmail W www.hotmail.com

Interhike W www.interhike.com – specialises in camping and hiking in Europe.

International Association of Air Travel Couriers (IAATC) W www.aircourier.co.uk

International Diabetes Federation W www.idf.org

International Herald Tribune W www .iht.com

International Society of Travel Medicine W www.istm.org

International Student Travel Confederation (ISTC) W www.isic.org/index.htm

Internet Café Guide W www.netcafeguide .com – a list of internet cafés worldwide.

Interrail W www.interrail.com – Inter-Rail pass information.

Jobs 1 W www.jobs1.co.uk – lists employment agencies and work-related job sites, plus there's a job search engine.

Jobs Abroad Bulletin W www.payaway .co.uk – information on working holidays and jobs abroad for young people.

Karrimor W www.karrimor.co.uk – specialises in products for mountaineers and expeditions.

Lariam or not to Lariam W www.geocities .com/TheTropics/6913/lariam.htm – an article about the anti-malarial drug Lariam.

Lastminute.com W www.lastminute.com – travel and leisure website.

London Hospital for Tropical Diseases W www.uclh.org/services/htd/index.shtml

Lonely Planet Travel Ticker W www .lonelyplanet.com/travel_ticker/travel_ advisories.htm – Lonely Planet's travel advisory.

Lowe Alpine W www.lowealpine.com – an international outdoor company.

Malaria Foundation W www.malaria.org

Marie Stopes W www.mariestopes.org .uk – provider of sexual and reproductive health information.

Maris Freighter Travel W www.freighter-cruises.com – its online office.

MASTA (Medical Advisory Services for Travellers) W www.masta.org

MasterCard W www.mastercard.com/atm

Mefloquine W www.indiana.edu/~pri mate/lariam.html – an article on the anti-malarial drug Mefloquine.

New York Times W www.nytimes.com

Newsweek W www.newsweek.com – a weekly magazine covering world events.

Nomad Travel W www.nomadtravel.co .uk – offers a wide range of travel-related products and a travel health service.

North South W www.northsouthtravel .co.uk – through the NST Development Trust, this travel agency's profits are channelled to projects in Africa, Asia and Latin America.

Opodo W www.opodo.co.uk – for flights, hotels, travel insurance and car rental.

Outdoor Gear W www.outdoorgear.co.uk

PADI W www.padi.com – provides details of PADI scuba-diving courses.

Post Office W www.postoffice.co.uk – offers a range of online travel services.

Quest Travel W www.questtravel.com – a long-haul travel specialist.

Responsible Travel W www.responsible travel.com – offers holidays that maximise the benefits to local communities.

Russia Experience W www.trans-siberia .com/ – information about Russia's Trans-Siberian Railway.

St John Ambulance W www.sja.org.uk – first-aid, transport and care charity.

STA Travel W www.sta-travel.co.uk – specialises in travel for students and young people.

Strand Voyages W www.strandtravel.co .uk – specialises in voyages on passenger-carrying cargo vessels.

Student Flights W www.studentflights.co .uk – a university-based travel agent that specialises in travel for young people.

Thames Consular Services W www .thamesconsular.com – a leading independent passport and visa agency.

Thomas Cook W www.thomascook.co.uk

Thorn Tree (Lonely Planet) W thorntree .lonelyplanet.com – a travel forum where people can exchange advice, stories and opinions.

Time W www.time.com – news magazine.

TNT W www.tntmagazine.com/uk/ – magazine providing travel and lifestyle information.

Tour du Monde des Musiques W www .2001-odyssee.net – how four French ex-students raised money by recording world music.

Tourist Office Worldwide Directory W www.towd.com

Trailfinders W www.trailfinder.com – one of the UK's largest independent travel companies.

Trains Across Canada W www.train-canada.net

Travel Health Information Service W www.travelhealth.com

Travel Health Online W www.triprep.com

Travel with Care W www.travelwithcare .co.uk

Travellers Medical and Vaccination Centre W www.tmvc.com.au/info.html

Travelocity W www.travelocity.com – US travel agency.

UCAS W www.ucas.com

UK Foreign & Commonwealth Office W www.fco.gov.uk – provides details of all embassies and consulates in the UK.

UK Passport Agency, The Home Office W www.ukpa.gov.uk

Universal Currency Converter W www .xe.com/ucc

US Embassy W www.usembassy.org.uk

USA Today W www.usatoday.com – US newspaper.

Visa W www.visa.com/globalgateway – Visa card site.

Voice of America W www.voa.gov – world news broadcaster.

Wanderlust W www.wanderlust.co.uk – travel magazine.

Warrior W www.warrior.com – specialist in laptop and mobile equipment.

Western Union W www.westernunion .com – offers a money transfer service.

WHO (World Health Organization) W www.who.int/en/

World Tourism Organisation W www .world-tourism.org

Yahoo! W www.yahoo.co.uk

YHA of England & Wales W www.yha .org.uk

YHA Ireland (An Óige) W www.ireland yha.org

YHA of Scotland W www.syha.org.uk

YHA W www.yhaadventure.com – the YHA's online store.

Youth Information W www.youthinfor mation.com

Index

Contacts

THANKS

FROM THE AUTHORS

Charlotte Hindle

I would like to thank Michelle Hawkins, John Coppock of Itchy Feet (Bath & London), Claire Harrison, Paul Goldstein of Exodus, Gary Ashdown of Guerba, David Else, David Green, Laetitia Northmore-Ball, Angeline Hamilton, my fellow authors and Fiona Christie. I would also like to thank my husband, Simon, for proofreading and valuable advice.

Joe Bindloss

Firstly, my thanks to all the helpful human resources managers who took the time to explain their graduate programmes. Thanks also to Charlotte Hindle for being tirelessly flexible and answering my daily emails. Finally, thanks to the readers who wrote in with their tales of gapping round the world.

Matt Fletcher

I'd like to thank Charlotte, Simon, Blob, Ag, Bando (and Rick, though he'll never know), Bev and Clare for all their help, but top honours go to the excellent staff at STA Travel (especially Daniel Heatly and David Scannell) and the numerous LP authors without whose work my sections wouldn't have been possible.

Abigail Hole

Many thanks to Charlotte Hindle, Laetitia Northmore-Ball, Arabella Perry, Fiona Christie, William Sutcliffe, Tom Hall, Kelda Hole, Ginnie Quiney, John Hole, Sumeet Desai, Sophie Gorell Barnes, Carrie Hindmarsh and especially to all the gappers who were so articulate about their experiences and willing to help.

Joshua White

I would like to thank all those who gave me the time to share their knowledge and experience, especially those individuals who discussed their gap-year stories: Stephen Bell, Diane Clasby, Rebecca Crossland, Hannah Durden, Chris O'Rourke, Camille Shah, Stephanie Stasiuk, Beth Tash, Ruth Unstead-Joss and Cate Vinton. Some individuals who work in the field of gap years were also particularly supportive such as Richard Oliver of the Year Out Group, John Locke of Teaching & Projects Abroad, Catherine Raynor of VSO and both Emily Wrigglesworth and Laura Hisgrove representing the Millennium Volunteer programme.

FROM LONELY PLANET

This book has been a labour of love for all the people involved in its creation and it's been a labour gainfully undertaken by all. Thanks go first to the tireless commissioning editor and project manager, Laetitia Northmore-Ball, who nursed and nurtured this book like a baby. Annika Roojun designed the cover and inside pages, and consulted on all other design aspects of the book; her help was invaluable. Angela Watts laid out the whole book and huge thanks go to her for that considerable task. Emma Sangster was coordinating editor on the title and her thorough approach and dedication were greatly appreciated. Emma was ably assisted by Arabella Perry who did a tremendous job as assistant editor. The world map was created by Ed Pickard and Wayne Murphy and the way they've squeezed all the routes onto it is impressive! Adriana Mammarella and John Shippick were huge helps at the end, so thanks to them. Thanks go to Fiona Christie for stepping into the breach with some excellent research for the book and thanks to Jason and Cathy from Nomad Travel for reading through and verifying the Health chapter.

Lonely Planet

THIS BOOK

This first edition has been lovingly crafted by our five Lonely Planet authors, who are after all professional gappers.

Please write to us at go@lonelyplanet.co.uk if you have any feedback on this book. Use it to plan your gap year and take it on your travels – armed with all of this thoroughly researched information, you can't fail to have an interesting and memorable year off. Lonely Planet has several other products that will help you once you have planned your gap year. For information on these, see below.

THE LONELY PLANET STORY

The story begins with a classic travel adventure: Tony and Maureen Wheeler's 1972 journey across Europe and Asia to Australia. There was no useful information about the overland trail then, so Tony and Maureen published the first Lonely Planet guidebook to meet a growing need.

From a kitchen table, Lonely Planet has grown to become the largest independent travel publisher in the world, with offices in Melbourne (Australia), Oakland (USA), London (UK) and Paris (France).

Today Lonely Planet guidebooks cover the globe. There is an ever-growing list of books and information in a variety of media. Some things haven't changed. The main aim is still to make it possible for adventurous travellers to get out there – to explore and better understand the world.

At Lonely Planet we believe travellers can make a positive contribution to the countries they visit – if they respect their host communities and spend their money wisely. Since 1986 a percentage of the income from each book has been donated to aid projects and human rights campaigns, and, more recently, to wildlife conservation.

OTHER LONELY PLANET PRODUCTS

travel guidebooks in-depth coverage with background and recommendations

shoestring guides big trips on small budgets

best of guides highlight the best a city has to offer

outdoor guides walking, cycling, diving & watching wildlife series

phrasebooks don't just stand there, say something!

healthy travel practical advice for staying well on the road

travel literature travel stories for armchair explorers

pictorial lavishly illustrated pictorial books

www.lonelyplanet.com all your travel needs online